WITHDRAWN

FASHION DESIGN 741-2003 DEPT.

J.J. PIZZUTO'S
Fabric Science

NINTH EDITION

fb

J.J. PIZZUTO'S
Fabric Science

NINTH EDITION

Allen C. Cohen

Fashion Institute of Technology
New York, NY

Ingrid Johnson

Fashion Institute of Technology
New York, NY

FAIRCHILD BOOKS
New York

Executive Editor:	Olga T. Kontzias
Assistant Acquisitions Editor:	Amanda Breccia
Senior Development Editor:	Jennifer Crane
Associate Art Director:	Erin Fitzsimmons
Production Director:	Ginger Hillman
Senior Production Editor:	Elizabeth Marotta
Cover Design:	Erin Fitzsimmons
Text Design:	Tronvig Kuypers
Photo Research:	Sarah Silberg

Library of Congress Catalog Card Number: 2009924853

ISBN: 978-1-56367-855-4
GST R 133004424

Printed in the United States of America
TP08

Contents

Extended Contents

Preface

The ninth edition of *Fabric Science* is part of a complete information package. This includes an updated and revised textbook, an accompanying *Swatch Kit* containing 114 market fabrics, an Instructor's Guide (for both the text and *Swatch Kit*), and a PowerPoint Presentation that could be used as a teaching aid.

Concept

Whereas the textile industry continually changes, the fundamental concept of *Fabric Science* remains the study of textiles. This book builds on 40 years of tradition to provide the most up-to-date and comprehensive resource for students and professionals in the textile, fashion, and related industries.

This edition reflects the latest changes in technology, innovation, and the global market that affect advances in the field, as well as containing information about how today's fabrics behave and why. The vocabulary of textiles appears throughout the book so that readers can quickly become fluent in the language of the industry.

Fabric Science is designed for anyone who desires to possess a thorough knowledge of textiles: their design, structure, and application. Students who are choosing a career that will require textile knowledge will acquire a broad and detailed understanding, and professionals who are already engaged in textile-related occupations will find this an invaluable reference for staying current in their fields.

Format

The format of the textbook follows a logical flow of textiles from fibers through finished fabrics. Each chapter begins with objectives and key terms that emphasize the industry-oriented nature of the book. The chapter then provides a thorough analysis of a textile topic, and cross-referencing allows the reader to follow a particular topic across chapters. Study questions at the end of each chapter encourage direct application to the material covered. The CD-ROM enclosed with this text contains assignments that enable students to reinforce what was learned in each chapter.

Informative and descriptive headings allow the reader to focus easily on the subject matter under discussion. The range of information is exceptionally wide, including fiber types and fabric makeup, determination of fabric quality, care of textile products, laws that regulate textiles, and the global marketplace of the textile, fashion, and related businesses. Uses of textiles covered includes apparel, interior furnishings, and industrial products.

The most obvious change to the format of the ninth edition is the introduction of color and easy-to-use hardcover binding, which gives the text an exciting new look. Photographs are enhanced with more detail, and tables are clear and easy to read. Illustrations have also been added and updated.

Major Content Changes

In this ninth edition we set forth the major changes and developments in the textile industry. Many of these advances are a result of the ever-rapid technological transformations in the industry—never before, in fact, has innovation been such a driving force. Technology has also contributed to the true globalization of the textile industry through wireless communication, rapid-air transport, and an active fashion and entertainment media that transmits style trends world-wide, further fueling demand. This means that the product cycle has never been shorter. Production sources throughout the world have expanded, too: Manufacturers not only want to export to the United States, but also need to keep pace with their own domestic markets whose economies are building momentum in response to the global boom. *Fabric Science* addresses these changes and provides insight into the future direction of the industry.

Topics such as new fiber innovations, high-performance fabrics, nanotechnology, color evaluation, and global sourcing options are discussed and put in context with traditional subject matter. A new section on industrial fabrics focuses on textiles used for construction, transportation, medicine, and safety. An entirely new chapter on the environment has been added to present the latest information on eco-friendly textiles, "green" products, and the role of the textile industry in becoming environmentally responsible.

In keeping with the global aspect of textiles, this edition updates textile industry terms and phrases, and provides a list of fiber names in seven languages. Also discussed are topics that have an impact on international textile practices and procedures, such as customs regulations, quality assurance, import quotas, and other concerns related to both domestic and overseas manufacturing. In Chapter 14 we provide tables and procedures for converting to and from metric measurements, and an analysis of textiles performance testing—particularly useful for those readers of *Fabric Science* who do not have access to a textile laboratory.

Finally, the shifting of textile production to overseas sources has had another notable result: new career opportunities. People with the multifaceted skills required for the design, production, marketing, and merchandising of textiles and textile products are in demand world-wide—and it is often difficult to define the difference between apparel manufacturing and retailing in today's market. These changes in industry-related jobs are discussed here as well.

Fabric Science Swatch Kit and the Instructor's Guide

The study of textiles is significantly enhanced through the utilization of the accompanying *Fabric Science Swatch Kit*, which features 114 sample fabrics produced in the industry. New and unique fabrics are included, as well as traditional ones. Each fabric is selected to illustrate one or more features, such as weave, dye method, or fiber content—and they offer a visual demonstration of the basic principles covered in the textbook. This combination provides a comprehensive approach to the study of textiles.

An item that has helped to make *Fabric Science* the outstanding success it has been is the Instructor's Guide for this edition. This is a valuable aid because it includes answers to all the questions, comments about the assignments, suggestions for course planning, and additional teaching materials. It also includes information about each of the swatches in the *Swatch Kit*.

The *Swatch Kit* includes a key, mounting boards, and a pick glass for the swatches. It also contains 32 special assignments, as well as helpful information about how the *Swatch Kit* can be used to supplement the study of textiles. The instructor's guide for the *Swatch Kit* provides specific information about each of the swatches in the *Swatch Set*. Special assignments, questions (with answers), and instructional comments are included to assist the instructor. An instructor's set of duplicate swatches (7″ × 12″) is available as an additional teaching aid.

The final part of this unique information package is the PowerPoint Presentation. It represents a view of the face and back of each swatch. The captions provide the additional information to the viewer. The teaching aids in this new edition are extremely helpful.

Acknowledgments

Fabric Science continues to reflect the ever-changing textile industry, and the body of knowledge contained in it is of such magnitude that a true team effort was required to pull it all together.

This ninth edition could not have been written without the guidance and aid the authors received from their friends and colleagues in many segments of the textile industry and at the Fashion Institute of Technology. We are indeed grateful to all who have helped, but special acknowledgments are due to the following companies and organizations: AATCC, Cotton Incorporated, DOW XLA™, Nano-tex, Sferra Bros., and Stoll America.

We would also like to thank the faculty in the Textile Development and Marketing Department of the Fashion Institute of Technology: Wayne Barker, Anna Bartosz, Robert Beaulieu, Sean Cormier, Ann Denton, Juliana Fetter, George Ganiaris, Joseph Garofalo, Patrice George, Salvatore Giardina, Marian Grealish, Theodore Hoffman, Kay James, Georgia Kalivas, Jules Lavner, Melanie Santoriello, Jeffrey Silberman, Richard Silvia, George Tay, and Joel Zucker.

In addition, we thank Kathryn Malik, who provided expert technical analysis of the fabrics contained in the *Swatch Kit* accompanying this textbook. This enabled our selection of fabrics to be greatly enhanced. Victoria Bukowski designed and created the expanded computer illustrations, one of the highlights of the ninth edition. Thank you, Tori, for your outstanding work and endless hours. A special note of gratitude for manuscript preparation is given to Gisela Zabriskie. Once again, her unique abilities and patience were invaluable.

We are especially appreciative of the help and guidance received from the professional staff of Fairchild Books. We commend and thank Olga Kontzias for her supervision in keeping to the schedules that resulted in the timely publication of this edition. We appreciate the efforts of Elizabeth Marotta, and also recognize Erin Fitzsimmons and Sarah Silberg for the excellent art.

J.J. PIZZUTO'S

Fabric Science

NINTH EDITION

CHAPTER ONE
The Textile Industry

Objectives

▶ To understand the textile industry as the primary material source for the apparel, interior furnishings, and industrial products industries.

▶ To know the various segments of the textile industry.

▶ To be able to follow the channels of distribution of textile products.

▶ To be aware of the careers requiring a professional knowledge of textiles.

Key Terms Related to Textiles

apparel	industrial products	private label
converter	interior furnishings	put-up
dyeing	jobber	recycling
environment	market planning	remnants
fabric	mill	retail
Fair Trade	overrun	sewn products
fiber	overseas agent	shorts
finished goods	over-the-counter	sourcing
greige	pound goods	vertically integrated mill
importer	printing	yarn

The basic needs of people are food, clothing, and shelter. The textile industry is intertwined with all three of these essential sectors of our lives. Fabrics are used in the food industry to provide plant covers, absorbent liners in prepackaged meats, and reusable cloth bags. The use of fabrics in clothing is well known for its warmth, protection, and aesthetic properties. Fabrics also provide for shelter in the form of tents, building materials, and awnings. Most people don't realize how much further intertwined with our lives textiles really are. In fact, textiles touch nearly every facet of life, from the carpeting we walk on, to the bandages we use for injuries, to the conveyer belt used to move items in a factory, to the textiles used in space vehicles orbiting the earth.

Textiles were also important in ancient times. Prehistoric man wove fishing nets, the ancient Egyptians wrapped their rulers in hand-woven linens at the time of their burials, and the Chinese wove beautiful silk fabrics over 3,500 years ago. Thus, textiles are one of the oldest products used by mankind.

The textile industry played a significant part in the initial growth of the United States. The manufacture of textiles was the first craft to be successfully mechanized in this country. The interstate commerce in cotton that began in the late 1700s, from the areas of cultivation in the South to the textile mills of New England, helped to bind the states of the new nation together. As an indication of the importance of the textile industry in the pre-Civil War period, of the 106 manufacturing concerns in the United States in 1832 with assets over 100,000 dollars, 88 were textile companies.

Textiles are often the raw materials used by other industries, primarily the apparel, interior furnishings, and industrial products industries. These industries in turn manufacture dresses, draperies, truck covers, and countless other products for sale to department stores, mail-order companies, and retailers. Although the textile industry is separate from these other businesses, there is nevertheless strong continuing dialogue and exchange of design ideas, marketing strategies, and quality/cost levels not only between the textile industry and its direct customers (apparel, interior furnishings, and industrial products industries), but also often including the retailer. For example, design ideas are often exchanged and collaborated on among a mail order retailer, an apparel manufacturer, and a textile manufacturer.

Figure 1.1 shows the flow and movement of how textiles reach the final retail consumer. Beginning with raw materials, the product passes through various manufacturing and distribution segments before culminating at the retail consumer level.

International Trade

International trade in textiles and apparel is not a new situation. The silk trade from China through the Middle East to Italy by way of camel caravans was a major international trade route of centuries ago. The first ships that arrived in the Americas included textiles as items for trading with the natives living there. One reason the South lost the Civil War was because of the significant loss of revenue from the interrupted cotton trade with Great Britain.

In the mid-twentieth century, the vast majority of textile and apparel products in the United States and the developed nations were produced within the United States. Now many of these products have changed from domestic to international to multinational sources. The international nature of this industry has resulted in new centers of production challenging the old ones. The traditional labor-intensive aspect of production and the low cost of entry have ensured that textiles and apparel are established as one of the first forms of industrial activity for any emerging country in search of employment and economic growth.

After World War II, international trade agreements encouraged textile and clothing imports from many small, underdeveloped nations to stimulate their industrial development. But in the last 25 years, the textile and apparel industries in some of these countries have become so strong that they pose a serious threat to the established industries of Western Europe and North America. Over 150 nations now send their textile and apparel goods to the United States, controlling more than 65 percent of the domestic clothing market combined. Imports of these products have grown so rapidly that many domestic plants have closed and many American workers have lost their jobs to foreign exporters.

As the international marketplace for textile products continues to change and evolve so does the textile industry. Many factors contribute to the industry's state of flux. Technology, the economy, the world political environment, and local issues are all factors. Cheap labor, for example, may be less important when technology is utilized for production. Currency fluctuation, production delays, high transportation costs (charges), striking workers at ports, customs holdups, and political unrest may encourage those who source fabrics to look domestically.

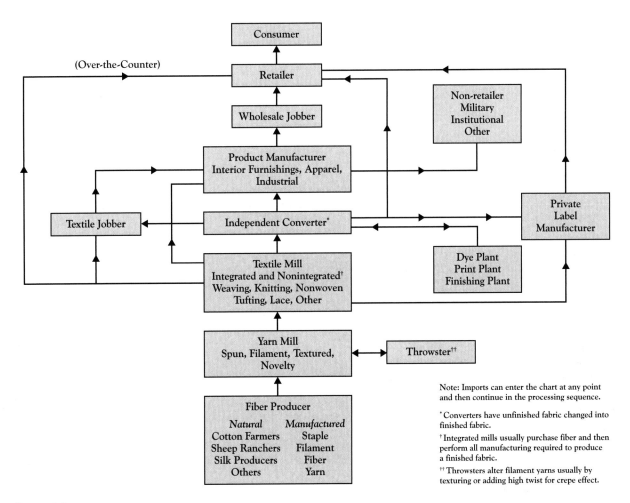

FIGURE 1.1
How textiles reach the consumer.

Note: Imports can enter the chart at any point and then continue in the processing sequence.

* Converters have unfinished fabric changed into finished fabric.

† Integrated mills usually purchase fiber and then perform all manufacturing required to produce a finished fabric.

†† Throwsters alter filament yarns usually by texturing or adding high twist for crepe effect.

General Fields of Textile Products

The textile industry is segmented into three large groupings: **Apparel,** the textiles used in clothing; **interior furnishings** (also called home fashions), the textiles used in furniture, bath, kitchen and bed; and **industrial,** the textiles used in such items as luggage, flags, boat sails, bandages, dust filters, and so on. The market is divided into approximately 35 percent apparel, 35 percent interior furnishings, and 30 percent industrial and miscellaneous consumer-type products. See Table 1.1 for a more detailed listing of the items included in each grouping.

The Major Textile Production Segments

The textile industry uses many different raw materials and many steps in the process of manufacturing a finished textile material. Each segment in the pipeline is not only involved with production, but also with buying the product of a previous producer. Thus, the entire process from fiber to consumer (or other ultimate buyer) involves the coordinated activities of many firms and many individuals within each firm. The following sections describe the major production segments, each of which is discussed in much more detail later in this book.

TABLE 1.1	Fabric End-Use Groupings				
Apparel		**Interior Furnishings**	**Industrial**		

Sportswear
  Tops—blouses, shirts
  Bottoms—pants,
    shorts, skirts
*Swimwear and
beach wear*
Dresses
  Casual
  Evening wear
  Bridal wear
Intimate apparel
  Undergarments
  Sleepwear
  Robes
  Loungewear
Maternity wear
Knit wear
Active wear
Outerwear
  Sweaters
  Jackets
  Rainwear
  Coats
	*Sport coats and
	  suits*
	Accessories
	  Scarves
	  Handkerchiefs
	  Belts
	  Gloves
	  Handbags
	  Backpacks
	  Ties
	  Hosiery
	  Hats
	  Umbrellas
	Athletic uniforms
	Footwear
	  Sneakers
	  Soft shoes
		Furniture
		  Upholstery
		  Slipcovers
		Hangings
		  Draperies
		  Curtains
		Domestics
		  Sheets
		  Pillowcases
		  Bedspreads
		  Blankets
		  Comforters
		  Duvets
		  Mattress covers
		Linens
		  Tablecloths
		  Placemats
		  Napkins
		  Towels
		Floor coverings
		  Carpets (indoor/
		    outdoor)
		  Rugs
		  Padding
		Miscellaneous
		  Lamp shades
		  Decorative pillows
		  Aprons
			Recreation
			  Backpacks
			  Luggage
			  Fishnets
			  Hiking and
			    mountain
			    climbing gear
			  Ropes
			  Rafts
			Outdoor products
			  Furniture
			  Awnings
			  Tents
			  Boat sails
			  Artificial turf
			  Domes over
			    sports arenas
			  Flags
			Medical
			  Artificial blood
			    vessels
			  Bandages
			  Casts
			  Disposable sheets,
			    surgical gowns, etc.
			  Hygiene
			  Sutures
			  Tape
				Manufacturing plants
				  Conveyor belting
				  Printers' blankets
				  Tapes
				  Filters
				  Polishing cloths
				Civil engineering
				  Soil-erosion fabrics
				  Road construction
				    reinforcing lining
				  Reservoir lining
				  Drainage screens
				Protective gear
				  Chemical-resistant
				    gloves
				  Heat-resistant suits
				  Bullet-resistant vests
				  Biological-protective
				    clothing
				  Space suits
				  Hazardous waste-
				    protective gear
				*Transportation
				  (automobiles,
				  airplanes, etc.)*
				  Flooring
				  Tires
				  Interior walls,
				    ceilings, bulkheads
				  Belts
				  Brake linings	

Prices of the various fabric components (e.g., fibers and yarns) as well as fabric treatments (e.g., dyeing and finishing) have not been included. There are too many variables, including price fluctuations, mill efficiencies, production sources (imports), and government subsidies, to present an accurate cost.

Fibers

Fibers are the smallest part of the fabric. They are fine, hairlike substances, categorized as either natural or manufactured. Cotton, which grows on a plant, and wool, which is shorn from a sheep, are two examples of natural fibers. Manufactured fibers are created from chemicals and include acrylic, nylon, and polyester.

Yarns

Most textile materials contain **yarns,** which are continuous threadlike strands composed of fibers that have been twisted together. (Felt is an example of a material made directly from fibers but containing no yarns.) There are various types of yarn, from flat and dull to slubby and lustrous. Each one could be made from different fibers.

Fabrics

Most **fabrics** are made from yarns and are either woven or knitted. The companies that make fabric are called mills; Springs Global and Milliken & Company are two of the largest U.S. mills. The range of fabric types and weights is tremendous, fulfilling a variety of consumer demands.

Dyeing and Printing

Color is usually applied to the woven or knitted fabric by either **dyeing** or **printing.** Dyeing is the process for imparting a solid color to textiles (blue, green, red, etc.). Printing is the process of imparting designs to textiles (dots, florals, stripes, etc.). The purpose is to make the fabric more appealing. These operations are performed in dye plants or print plants, and the companies are called dye houses or print houses.

Finishing

Most fabrics need additional treatments called finishes before they can be used. For example, special chemicals are used to make a fabric water-repellent and suitable for a raincoat. A special brushing machine is required to make the fuzzy surface on flannel fabrics. The processes are done in finishing plants whose facilities are most often part of dye plants or print plants.

After finished fabric has been produced, it is usually used by other manufacturers to make such items as blouses, draperies, tents, or automobile tires. A particular fabric might be used for several different articles, such as a dress, a shirt, and curtains. Frequently, the same fabric that is shipped to the apparel or interior furnishings manufacturer is also sold to a retail store for direct sale to home sewers.

Textile Put-Up

Put-up is the term used to indicate the way fabric is packaged when it is sold. Most fabrics sold to garment and other manufacturers are in a rolled put-up, where the fabric is wound around a cardboard tube. A full roll or piece of woven fabric traditionally contains from 60 to 100 yards. Knit fabrics are usually shipped in 35- to 50-pound rolls, in either open-width or tubular form.

With the mechanization and automation of larger apparel and interior furnishings manufacturers, larger rolls of fabrics can now be handled. Thus wider widths—up to 100 inches—are becoming more commonplace. And in place of the traditional 60- to 100-yard pieces, 1,000 yard pieces are becoming the norm. The wider and larger rolls result in higher efficiency for the manufacturer using the fabric.

Some fabrics are doubled and rolled; such fabrics are folded in half lengthwise and then wound around a flat piece of cardboard. Cloth sold to retail stores is usually in this put-up, in less than 30-yard lengths. Some fabrics, such as velvet and other plush fabrics, are usually not rolled because the resulting pressure would flatten the surface; these fabrics are placed on a frame so that the surface does not come into contact with any other part of the cloth.

Pieces of fabric shorter than 40 yards in length are called **shorts.** These pieces are usually sold in either 20- to 40-yard pieces (called 20s to 40s), 10- to 20-yard pieces (called 10s to 20s), or 5- to 10-yard pieces (called 5s to 10s). Jobbers normally are the buyers of these short pieces of fabric.

Remnants are usually 1- to 10-yard pieces of cloth. **Pound goods** are usually very short pieces of fabric (often containing pieces of less than one yard in length); they are sold by the pound and not by the yard. Fabric that cannot be sold in any other manner is sold this way. These goods are bought at the buyer's risk and receive the lowest price. End uses include stuffing for furniture and clothes for dolls.

Primary Sources of Fabrics

Whether foreign or domestic, a primary source of fabric is a company that makes or creates the material. The firms in this category are mills and converters. Some of the mills produce woven fabrics exclusively, others make only knit fabrics, and some large mills manufacture both.

In the primary fabric market, most sales are based on contracts, with shipments to be made months later. The converters and mills work closely with their customers' designers and merchandisers to create designs and working samples. New designs created by the mills are also presented at trade shows and exhibits held in many cities throughout the world. Sales of fabric either in inventory or nearly ready for sale (called spot or nearby goods) also occur, but on a much smaller scale. Usually, mills and converters do not take very small orders; this is the function of the jobber. (See p. 8)

Mills

A **mill** is a company that owns textile machinery and makes fabric. Most U.S. textile mills today are located in the southeastern portion of the United States, with a large percentage in North Carolina, South Carolina, and Georgia. Foreign mills are located throughout the world, especially England, France, Italy, Japan, South Korea, India, Thailand, and China.

Large textile mills are **vertically integrated,** meaning that they not only make the fabric, but also produce their own yarn and perform the finishing processes required after the fabric has been created. (However, they do not make their own fibers.) Some mills also manufacture and distribute apparel. Major integrated U.S. textile mills (and headquarters) include Milliken & Company (Spartanburg, SC), Springs Global (Fort Mill, SC), and Culp, Inc. (Highpoint, NC).

The mills sell their finished fabrics to various customers. Converters, discussed in the next section, are important buyers. Apparel and interior furnishings manufacturers and private label manufacturers use fabrics in making their products. **Jobbers,** who help dispose of excess or surplus merchandise for the mill, are another customer. Large retail stores, which in turn sell to the home sewer, also buy from mills.

Converters

The **converter** is an individual or organization that buys **greige** goods (that is, unfinished fabric), usually from mills, has the fabric dyed or printed and finished by other companies, and then sells the finished fabric.[1] All aspects of the fabric, including construction, design, color, and finish, are determined by the converter. The converters are much smaller than the large textile mills.

The numbers of converters and converter-jobbers are gradually decreasing and being replaced by vertically integrated mills. Furthermore, increasing volumes of both fabrics and completed sewn products produced outside the United States and imported have eliminated much of the necessity for this type of production and distribution.

Converters sell their finished fabrics to the same customers as the mills (apparel and interior furnishings manufacturers, jobbers, and retail stores), but occasionally one converter will buy from another. If, for example, a converter is unable to buy sufficient fabric from the mills to cover a very large order, the converter will buy additional fabric elsewhere, perhaps from another converter.

Importers

Textile importing companies are of two types. The direct **importer** buys fabric or manufactured textile products (e.g., clothing, soft luggage, other **sewn products**) from a foreign mill or other supplier and brings it into the United States. It is then sold to an American apparel manufacturer or other customer, such as a retailer. The other type, the import mill, is a foreign company that owns textile machinery and makes the fabric (or yarn) that is then exported to the United States, and operates similarly to an American mill in selling its fabrics and obtaining orders.

Secondary Sources of Fabrics

A secondary source of fabric is a company that buys cloth and then sells it, but such a company is not involved in making or creating the material. Therefore, any seller of fabric other than mills and converters is considered a secondary source. Jobbers and retail stores are the major secondary sources, although an apparel or interior furnishings manufacturer that has overbought and wishes to sell the excess fabric is also a secondary source. Textile brokers are also involved in the secondary market. Their function is to match a textile buyer and a textile seller; usually, the textile broker facilitates the exchange of goods for money and does not obtain ownership of the merchandise during the transaction.

Jobbers

A jobber buys from mills, converters, and garment manufacturers, as well as other users. Jobbers are valuable customers of the mills and converters because they often buy mill or converter fabrics that would otherwise be difficult to sell, including discontinued styles, colors, and mill overruns. (An **overrun** occurs when a mill produces more dyed, printed, or finished fabric than the order specifies. An overrun occurs for various reasons, including allowances for damaged yardage and short pieces unacceptable to the customer.) The jobber also occasionally buys fabric from users who have excess cloth, which usually results from lower-than-anticipated sales.

Jobbers periodically buy large quantities of a fabric they expect to become greatly in demand in the near future. Thus, they also can be a source of hard-to-get items.

Jobbers can often offer low prices and interesting fabrics, but they cannot offer continuity of a fabric. When a company wants to reorder a specified fabric and color from a jobber, the jobber quite likely does not have the fabric in stock any longer and cannot obtain more.

Some textile jobbers conduct business only in current and regular textile lines rather than in discontinued styles and goods that mills have found difficult to sell. These jobbers purchase relatively large quantities from mills and converters and sell to either small or specialized

---

1. Greige (pronounced gray) goods are unfinished fabric directly from a weaving loom (or knitting machine) that must be converted to a finished, salable condition by dyeing or printing and finishing for crease resistance, water repellancy, or other possible effects.

end-user companies. For example, small entrepreneurial companies, producing perhaps several hundred garments of one style for exclusive boutique sale or perhaps a thousand specialized decorative pillows, would purchase their fabric from these textile jobbers. Also, custom makers of shirts and blouses or coats and suits (custom tailors), as well as furniture reupholsterers and custom furniture makers traditionally purchase fabrics from jobbers that carry regular and current style lines.

The large regional jobbers are located in major textile centers, such as New York City, Atlanta, Boston, Philadelphia, Chicago, Dallas, and Los Angeles. The small ones service smaller regions, and usually smaller accounts.

Retail Stores

Home sewers purchase fabrics sold in **retail** stores; this type of sale is called an **over-the-counter** sale. Retail stores usually have a large variety of fabrics, with a small inventory of each one. Although the consumer usually purchases only several yards each time, the volume sold in a large store or chain is appreciable. Home sewing is still big business.

Overseas Agents

An **overseas agent** (sometimes called an intermediary) is a person or company that represents an exporter or importer in the countries overseas where it conducts business. Having an agent in the country where business is being conducted is almost a requisite to conducting overseas business. Agents serve their clients in many ways; they have knowledge and access to local business contacts, buying sources, and customers. Additionally, they understand local customs and regulations, and serve a myriad of tasks including translation and advising their clients in proper courtesies and dress when overseas. It would be difficult to conduct overseas textile business, either export or import, without capable agent representation.

The Domestic and Import Textile Industries

Textile companies, as primary or secondary source organizations, conduct business as either domestic or import companies. Import companies produce or buy textiles and/or finished products (apparel, interior furnishings, or industrial products) from all over the world for import and sale in their own countries. Domestic companies produce or buy textiles in their own countries for sale within or export outside their own countries. Domestic textile companies usually sell only piece goods or yarn

and not completed products, as is frequently the case for the import companies.[2]

The textile industry of the United States is both a major import industry and a domestic industry. More than half of all apparel consumed in the United States is made from textiles produced outside the country and then imported by the United States, while less than half are produced by the domestic industry within the United States. Also, approximately 12 percent of the domestic industry product is exported to countries outside the United States.

The import industry and the domestic industry have distinct differences with respect to market and management. Most companies operate as either import or domestic enterprises. A few operate in both areas. Each is explained in the following sections.

The Domestic Textile Industry

The U.S. textile industry is composed mainly of companies that develop, produce, and/or distribute fabrics or textile materials. This includes yarn mills; fabric mills; companies that process fabrics, such as dyeing, printing, and finishing companies; and companies that sell fabrics. In addition, companies that develop and style fabrics, such as converters are included as part of the textile industry. Nonproduction segments include trade associations, textile-testing companies, and trade publications. (See Table 1.2 for an overview of the U.S. textile industry.)

The textile industry is complex, large, and diversified. Compared to many other industries, it is labor intensive (although the trend is toward greater automation), and highly competitive. The fiber that is purchased to make textiles is either grown or produced in various states in the continental United States. Textile companies convert this fiber into yarn, fabric, or finished material. The industry employs more than 400,000 people and generates sales of more than $60 billion per year. About 70 percent of textile employment is located in the southeastern part of the United States.

Since the late 1980s, the U.S. domestic textile industry has been in a state of change created by the shift from what was once nearly an entirely domestic industry to the present large import industry. The competitive condition created by the growth of imports over the past 25 years has forced the closure of many textile producers. The surviving producers are those that have invested heavily to modernize and make production more efficient, make

---

2. Exceptions are certain knitted products (hosiery, sweaters, T-shirts) that are produced as completed garments by domestic producers (see Chapter 6).

TABLE 1.2 An Overview of the U.S. Textile Industry*	
Sales:	More than $60 billion
Companies:	Large, medium, and small
Employees:	About 400,000
Products:	Diversified (various fibers, yarns, weaves, colors, designs, and finishes used)
End user:	Diversified (apparel, interior furnishing, and industrial)
Types of positions:	Diversified (production, design, sales, quality assurance, purchasing, technical writing, and others)
Companies employing textile specialists:	Wide range (fiber producer, textile mill, textile product manufacturer, retail store, publication, museum, government agency, and others)
International trade:	More than 150 countries trade with the United States in textiles and textile products

*Does not include apparel or other end-use product industries.

specialty niche-market fabrics, and develop export sales programs.

Textile Exports

U.S. producers of most products, including textiles, previously found ready markets for their outputs to the large U.S. consumer-oriented, relatively rich, population. That changed as textile imports grew to become a major source of apparel for American consumers. The U.S. textile industry response to meeting this competition was to become more efficient, competitive, and for the first time, export oriented. Major expansion in aggressive export selling and overseas market research by domestic textile companies to accommodate the tastes, styles, and cultures of foreign customers now occurs continuously. Textile exports are small compared to imports, but are growing. Additionally, U.S. textile producers are making direct investments in joint ventures with foreign textile producers and/or building wholly owned overseas production facilities.

The Textile Import Industry

Have you ever shopped for clothing and observed on labels where this blouse, that dress, this skirt, or those pants came from? Made in China, South Korea, India, Mexico, Costa Rica, Colombia, Vietnam, Indonesia and so on are typical labels. Made in the United States from imported fabrics is another common label. As indicated earlier, less than half of the apparel that Americans wear and the fabrics that go into their manufacture are made in the United States. The rest is produced elsewhere and imported by the United States.

Reasons for Imports

The manufacture of textiles, and especially sewn products, involves labor-intensive production. Most imported textile products are produced in low-wage, developing countries. These countries' low labor costs and low selling prices are their competitive edges and create high demand in the United States. Even when weighed against the cost of transportation and the problems of lengthened delivery schedules (e.g., long lead time), difficulties in communication, occasional inferior-quality shipments, and dealing with myriad governmental regulations and red tape, both U.S. and foreign, the cost advantage of imports is often sizable. Not all textile imports, however, are based only on their price advantage. Some fabrics, such as woolens from England or Scotland (Harris Tweed, for example) or silk fabric from Japan, and certain finished apparel from France and Italy, are examples of imports that are either superior to domestic products or are products that the United States does not make.

Buying and Selling Fabric

Fabrics are purchased either according to written specifications or from a sample. If fabrics are bought according to written specifications, then the seller, either foreign or domestic, must ship the fabric exactly as specified. Items such as yarns per inch, width, weight, thickness, breaking strength, and degree of colorfastness are examples

FIGURE 1.2
Buyers of fabric need to keep careful notes and fabric samples for new and potential purchases.

of specifications. Fabric buyers (Figure 1.2) need to keep careful records of these specifications for the materials they are purchasing.

[If fabrics are purchased from a sample, the seller is required to deliver a fabric almost identical to the sample because the sample is a representation of what the buyer will later receive. A comparison check between the sample and the delivered fabric is made to ensure that what was specified is what has been made.]

Fabric quality varies from mill to mill as well as from country to country. Fabric buyers must be aware of this. An importer can include a phrase in the sales confirmation which states that the fabric will be "first quality, country of origin." This phrase does not have the same meaning from one country to another or from one importer to another.

Some less-developed countries do not have a first-quality standard that is published by the industry or the government. Nevertheless, some governments stamp fabric with a "chop mark" (i.e., identification mark) indicating that the fabric has been inspected and approved. Thus, the buyer should be familiar with the fabric quality of the mill and/or country when purchasing.

Most fabrics and sewn products bought as United States imports are purchased by specification and require laboratory testing and customer approval before shipping. When fabrics are bought from sample, or where laboratory testing is not possible, the import customer usually requires a seller to submit a piece of fabric (a minimum of 60 yards), and then a case (a minimum of 600 yards), for approval before authorizing release of the main lot of production fabric. A sample of several yards is never sufficient to allow an adequate evaluation of the overall quality of a fabric.

When fabrics are purchased as a **finished goods** package (see p. 7), they must first be approved by the buyer before proceeding to the sewn product manufacture stage. Many of the countries that are major exporters to the United States possess certified textile laboratories that are often branches of U.S. textile testing companies. Standardized textile laboratory tests (see Chapter 14) and reports are transmitted by fax or e-mail to the U.S. importing customer, and decision making for acceptance or rejection of the import fabric is not unduly delayed despite the distances between countries.

Fabric is sold either as greige or as finished fabric. Most mills and converters make a wide range of fabric types and designs. Because no mill or converter can carry a fabric line that will satisfy all fabric users, most try to supply a specific segment of the industry (for example, junior dresses, men's trousers, or industrial uses).

Fabrics presented for sale are usually shown to the end-product (apparel, furniture, etc.) manufacturer's designer or to an appropriate executive involved with the end-use item. A first sample order is placed by the buyer based on aesthetic and color appeal, but also on such factors as fabric weight, yarn density (yarns per inch), and fiber content for several yards or enough

FIGURE 1.3
Computer-aided design systems are used extensively in designing and presenting textile lines.

fabric to make a sample sewn product item. If the interest remains, the manufacturer often orders enough additional sample yardage to make other sample articles that the company salespeople can show to their customers (e.g., retail stores). If the reaction is favorable, the manufacturer then places an order for the fabric. A reorder may occur if the item made of the fabric is selling well. Once the fabric is accepted, the actual purchasing and follow-up are usually performed by the piece goods buyer.

Frequently fashion designers or other end-product designers work closely and collaboratively with textile mill designers to create specific fabrics to meet their needs. This method is especially efficient when computer-aided design (CAD) systems are used, as shown in Figure 1.3. A fashion designer and mill designer can actually be many miles apart, even in different countries, and collaborate on ideas by showing each other computer images (transmitted by phone or satellite) of fabric and apparel designs. When the designers agree on computer images, the designs are made into sample cuts of fabric and sewn into sample products, and finally, active orders are placed.

Sometimes the customer wants a design or fabric to belong exclusively to his or her company. If the yardage is great enough, the mill or converter may agree to sell the particular design or fabric only to that company, but normally the exclusivity is limited to a segment of the industry (e.g., men's shirts), and the supplier's salespeople are free to sell the design or fabric to companies making other end uses (e.g., men's pajamas).

The knitting industry and the woven-goods industry differ in makeup, which results in differences in fabric distribution. Chapter 6 gives more detailed information about the knitting industry.

Private Labels

Very large quantities of textiles are sold directly to department stores, mail-order houses, or discount chains for manufacture by the retailer or a contractor into private-label clothing or other articles. A **private label** is a retail brand in which apparel or other sewn products are manufactured specifically for a retailer and sold exclusively by that retailer. Several well-known private label brands are Sears Arizona® jeans, Federated Department Stores' (Macy's) Charter Club®, and Wal-Mart's Hannah Montana® lines of clothing. Designing of the fabric and finished product is usually done by the retail designers and technical staffs employed by the retailer.[3] In effect, the retailer is the manufacturer.

Private-label programs are an important part of the textile/fashion industries. Unique design not seen by every other store in the mall or city and better value than national brands are the main reasons for this growth.

A substantial portion of private-label textile sales to retailers involves imported goods that use both fabrics and sewing services from sources outside the United States. In fact, import **sourcing** in private-label programs is so widely used that most major retailers (e.g., JCPenney, Federated Department Stores, Sears, Wal-Mart) maintain full staffs and offices in foreign production centers.

Market and Production Planning

Each segment of the textile industry must plan well ahead of the next selling season. Unless schedules are maintained and deadlines met by the fiber producers, fabric mills, and other textile companies, it may not be possible to ship products when the buyers are ready to buy. Because so many operations must be performed before finished fabric is made, a delay in any phase of the operation will extend the fiber-to-fabric time period.

---

3. The design and technical staffs and facilities of many large retailers engaged in private-label production are the most extensive in the industry; they are complete and have more current state-of-the-art design and work rooms than all but the very largest apparel manufacturers.

Market planning in textiles almost always involves long-range planning. (See Figure 1.4.) The design of woven fabrics for apparel actually begins about a year and a half to two years before those designs will appear on retail racks. Fabric designing for a new season takes about six months. New fabrics are shown at fabric shows and exhibitions, about one year before the retail selling season begins (Figure 1.5). Apparel manufacturers immediately begin designing their lines with these new fabrics and present their new designs at openings, trade shows, and press events about six months later. The remaining six months of the cycle involve the apparel manufacturers in selling, producing, and delivering goods to retail stores.

Seasons

The two main retail selling seasons for apparel are fall and spring. The former starts around August 1 and the latter begins around February 1. The other seasons are summer and holiday. Interior furnishings such as bed sheets and comforters have two retail selling seasons, which coincide with the apparel seasons. Furniture fabrics and floor coverings have one annual retail-selling season, which begins in September. Industrial fabrics are not seasonal items.

The Environment

Various environmental problems relate to the textile industry, as they do to other industries. These include air and water pollution, disposal of waste products, health of workers in mills, and possible water pollution from home laundering.

FIGURE 1.4
Views of the Los Angeles International Textile Show in Los Angeles, California.

FIGURE 1.5
Textile designers and apparel designers seek out textile information, new trends, and fabric design ideas at textile shows and exhibits.

The textile industry, aware of these problems, takes steps to reduce the effects of pollution. Water used in production is treated (i.e., cleaned and filtered) before being discharged, toxic waste materials are disposed of in registered waste dumps, and air emissions (e.g., fumes, ash) are filtered to eliminate as much pollution as possible. Some chemicals are reused and some materials are recycled to reduce the quantity of waste produced. Noise levels and the quality of air in textile mills are monitored to reduce hazards to textile workers.

Recycling is a large component of the environmental movement to reduce ecological damage. (See Figure 1.6.) As landfill costs rise and available landfill space decreases, the pressure to increase recycling of non-hazardous waste continues to mount. Recycling must be an integrated effort between consumers, retailers, manufacturers, recyclers and the government. Within the textile industry recycled products include fibers, yarns, fabric, garments, and used chemicals. The waste of one company can become the raw material of another.

A much fuller discussion of the topic of eco-friendly products can be found in Chapter 15.

FIGURE 1.6
PET bottles are an example of an environmentally friendly product.

Fair Trade

The term **Fair Trade** is used to indicate that a product was produced without labor exploitation, by using environmentally sustainable practices, and that the producers received fair prices for their product. This term is used especially with regard to small businesses (farms, artisans, etc.) in developing countries who sell to companies in developed countries. Traditionally, the latter takes advantage of the former.

There are two major international groups to which most Fair Trade organizations worldwide belong. Their memberships include organizations representing the Fair Trade chain, from production to sales. The first is the Fair Trade Labeling Organization (FLO) International, based in Bonn, Germany. In addition to promoting Fair Trade products internationally, it also develops and reviews Fair Trade standards. Products which meet FLO standards are able to show the Fair Trade Organization Mark.

The second is the International Federation for Alternative Trade (IFAT). It helps to develop the market for Fair Trade products, is a Fair Trade monitor, and also is an advocate for Fair Trade. It uses the FLO mark to identify registered Fair Trade organizations. IFAT is headquartered in Amsterdam, the Netherlands.

TransFair USA is a member of FLO and is the only third-party certifier of Fair Trade products in the United States. It audits transactions between American companies offering Fair Trade products and the international suppliers from whom they source. Licensed U.S. companies can display a Fair Trade CertifiedTM label. Transfair USA is headquartered in Oakland, CA.

The Fair Trade Federation (FTF) is an American association of members committed to Fair Trade. Headquartered in Washington, DC, it has organized conferences where there is public exhibition of Fair Trade goods, business services offered, and seminars held.

The Fairtrade Foundation is the British member of FLO International. It issues a Fairtrade Mark to indicate Fair Trade certification for products sold in the United Kingdom (UK). The British department store chain Marks and Spencer is a major participant in this program, including cotton apparel.

Fair Trade is becoming increasingly popular because of the social responsibility movement (i.e., obligation to a group for their well-being). It has increased public awareness of irresponsible social behavior by business firms, including labor exploitation and environmental violations. Each year IFAT sponsors a World Fair Trade Day (global) and Transfair USA sponsors a National Fair Trade Month (U.S.).

At the present time certified Fair Trade products include mostly agricultural products, such as coffee, fruit, sugar, and flowers. Cotton apparel has been certified in Europe, etc., (e.g., Marks & Spencer in the U.K.) but not yet in the United States. Nevertheless, it is important to recognize the beginning of a movement that will definitely affect the textile industry.

Trade Shows

There are many foreign textile and textile products shows. These include Interstoff (fabric exposition), SEHM—The Salon International de l'Habillement Masculin (men's and boys' fashions), Techtextil (technical textiles), Heimtextil (home textiles), and ITMA—International Exposition of Textile Machinery. Major domestic shows include ATME—American Textile Machinery Exhibition, IFFE—International Fashion Fabric Exposition, and Magic International (men's apparel). There is also a sizable number of more localized textile and textile products trade shows organized in countries around the world.

Textile Careers

The textile industry is one of the largest and most diversified segments of business. As indicated earlier in this chapter, nearly every country in the world is involved with textiles.

The industry requires a wide range of talented people, and jobs call for a wide variety of job skills. Unfortunately, many careers in textiles do not have the visibility of designer jobs, so many people do not know they exist. Although the textile industry is a part of the fashion industry and relies heavily on designs and creative talents, it also relies on other areas such as technology, merchandising, and management—to build success (see Table 1.3).

Many careers require textile knowledge. These are career areas for men and women equally, and many require both domestic and international travel. Because a large amount of merchandise is produced overseas, companies are continuously needing representatives to develop products as well as to determine value and quality.

Some students may be concerned with the large number of textiles and related products being imported. Actually, the growing volume of imports and exports, foreign textiles corporations with offices and facilities in the United States, and the growth in retailer private-label programs have increased the need for trained textile-knowledgeable persons. Although the domestic textile manufacturing sector has shrunk, significant management, technical, and marketing adjustments have been

TABLE 1.3 Textile Careers	
Examples of Companies and Organizations Employing Textile-Knowledgeable Personnel	**Textile Positions and Specialties**
Fiber companies (Solutia, Inc.)	Administrative assistant (technical)
Textile producers (Springs Global)	Consultant
Textile converters	Converter
Apparel and interior furnishing manufacturers (Liz Claiborne, Thomasville Furniture Industries)	Coordinator-production/sales/design
Retailers (Gap, R.H. Macy's)	Education
Direct merchandisers (L.L. Bean)	Environmental protection
Quality assurance testing companies (Intertek Testing)	Forecasting—color, trends, etc.
Publications (HFN, W.W.D.)	Museum curator/conservator
Colleges and secondary schools	Production
Museums	Public relations/advertising
Military	Quality assurance testing
Legal firms	Reporter/writer
Importers and exporters	Sales, domestic, and/or import/export
Government agencies (U.S. Customs Service, Consumer Product Safety Commission)	Sourcing specialist
International consulting firms	Specifications writer
	Textile designer/colorist
	Textile purchasing agent
	Textile research and development

made (e.g., modernization) so that it is an efficient, modern industry. Also, the need for textile-knowledgeable persons in the import sector to provide liaison and technical and management support to foreign producers remains high.

The textile industry combines art, structured engineering, technical styling, marketing, and business to produce the correct aesthetics, performance properties, and value. It is an exciting industry that can be very lucrative and personally satisfying.

Speaking of Textiles

Phrases relating to textiles and textile products are contained in everyday language. This is not surprising since the textile industry is part of everyday life. The following are various examples, grouped by category:

Fiber Related:

- It was smooth as silk.
- He pulled the wool over my eyes.
- He has no moral fiber.
- He cottoned to her.

Yarn/Thread Related:

- He was spinning a yarn.
- I was hanging by a thread.
- He is threadbare.
- He was threading his way through a crowd.

- He had me in stitches.
- This is the common thread.
- A stitch in time saves nine.

Construction Related:

- It was built into the fabric of society.
- We were weaving through traffic.
- He was knitting up his brow.
- My nerves are frayed.
- It has become unraveled.

Product Related:

- He tossed his hat into the ring.
- He is throwing in the towel.
- He received a golden parachute upon leaving.
- They roped me into it.
- He was sailing along without a care.
- He gave the wall a coat of paint.
- He was a wolf in sheep's clothing.
- Every cloud has a silver lining.
- You can't make a silk purse out of a sow's ear.
- He was sacked.
- It fit me like a glove.
- He had a pocket full of miracles.

1. List five job titles that require textile knowledge. For each, state a brief description of the duties and the name of a company that would have such a position. (Library research required.)

2. Over the past two decades there has been a decrease in the quantity of apparel fabrics made in the United States. Why?

3. A curtain manufacturer wants to purchase 10,000 yards of a printed chintz fabric. Explain whether any of the following resources can be used:

   a. Textile mill
   b. Textile converter
   c. Jobber
   d. Retail fabric store

4. How can a knowledge of textiles be of value to: (a) the textile product manufacturer, (b) the retail store, and (c) the customer?

5. Name five product categories in addition to apparel and interior furnishings, in which textile materials are used. Indicate in what way they are utilized.

6. State several reasons why (a) a company would import textiles/textile products and (b) possible problems that could result.

7. Private labels result in the retailer becoming a manufacturer. Explain.

8. List some of the differences buyers from the United States encounter in buying textiles made overseas compared to textiles made in the United States.

9. What are the differences between buying textiles by specification and buying by sample?

10. Explain how it is possible for production to increase while employment decreases.

11. The textile industry faces various environmental problems. State several.

12. Explain how the production of an apparel article (e.g., pants) can be considered a globalized effect, interconnecting people around the world.

13. Measures of fairness with regard to Fair Trade practices include (a) human rights, (b) business relationships, and (c) the environment. State an example for each which should be examined when determining the degree of product Fair Trade.

CHAPTER TWO

Fiber Characteristics

Objectives

▶ To become familiar with and understand the terminology used to express and communicate the properties of textile fibers.

▶ To understand how these properties will affect the usage of textile fabrics and finished products.

▶ To know the sources of textile fibers, both natural and manufactured.

Use fabrics in the Fiber section of the Fabric Science Swatch Kit *for this chapter.*

Key Terms Related to Textiles

abrasion resistance	flammable fibers	specific gravity
absorbency	flexibility	spinnerette
cover	hand	staple fibers
crimp	hydrophilic	static electricity
dry spinning	hydrophobic	strength
elasticity	luster	thermoplastic
epitropic fibers	manufactured fibers	tow
filament fibers	melt spinning	wet spinning
flameproof fibers	natural fiber	wicking
flame-resistant fibers	pilling	
flammability	resiliency	

The process of developing textile products for the home, fashion apparel, and high-tech industries begins with a thorough understanding of fibers and their properties. This essential groundwork helps produce fabrics with end-use characteristics consistent with the consumer's expectations. Thus fibers are the building blocks for the end product and crucial to its success in the marketplace.

A fiber is an individual, fine, hairlike structure. Fibers have a comparatively high ratio of length to width, thus ensuring the flexibility required for manufacturing and end use. Differences among the textile fibers result from their different chemical compositions, the arrangement of their molecules, and their external features (e.g., shape).

Fibers usually are grouped and twisted together into continuous strands called yarns. The yarns are then used to make various textile materials (e.g., woven fabrics, knitted fabrics, lace).

Fibers can also be used directly to make a fabric without first being made into yarns. Felt and nonwoven materials (e.g., interfacing) are two examples of fabrics made directly from fibers.

Fiber Sources

Fibers are classified into those found in nature, called **natural fibers,** or those that are manufactured through the use of science and technology. **Manufactured fibers** are designed to resolve particular problems and answer specific needs. Even today, with the numerous advances made by technology, we have not yet been able to create the perfect fiber. Every fiber, both natural and manufactured, has identifiable characteristics that can be viewed as assets or drawbacks depending on the intended end use of the fiber.

Natural Fibers

Natural fibers are obtained from plants or animals. Plant fibers may come from stems (e.g., flax, hemp, jute, ramie), leaves (e.g., sisal, abaca), or seeds (e.g, cotton, kapok) of plants. Animal fibers (e.g., wool, cashmere, mohair, vicuña) protect people against the cold the same as they do animals. Silk is considered an animal fiber, although it comes from the cocoon of a silkworm rather than a mammal's fur.

Manufactured Fibers

Manufactured, or man-made, fibers are made from chemical solutions that are forced through tiny holes, similar to water passing through a shower head. The device used to form the filaments is called a **spinnerette.** It can be as small as a thimble or as large as a plate, with tiny holes on the top or flat surface area. The fine liquid streams of solution that are forced through the holes are hardened into continuous strands called filament fibers. This action is copied from nature. The silkworm extrudes streams of silk liquid, which harden into filaments on contact with the air. (See Figure 2.1.)

The number of holes in the spinnerette, as well as their shape and their size, varies according to the filament fiber and yarn desired. A small spinnerette has as few as 10 holes, and a large one can have more than 10,000. Spinnerettes are made of different metals, such as platinum and stainless steel. The shape of the hole can be varied to produce a round, a triangular, a "T," or some other shape of fiber, similar to varied shapes offered by a pasta machine. The size of the holes varies to make filaments finer than silk or heavier than fishing line.

Different techniques are used to harden the liquid streams and produce the filament fibers. The technique used depends on the chemical composition of the solution. The more commonly used methods are **dry spinning, wet spinning,** and **melt spinning:**

▶ **The dry spinning method:** The fiber solution, mixed with a solvent, is forced through the spinnerette into warm air. The warm air helps evaporate the solvent, and the liquid stream then hardens. Acetate and modacrylic fibers are made in this manner.

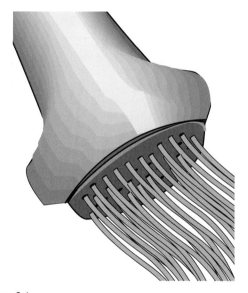

FIGURE 2.1
A spinnerette producing filament fibers. The holes can be made in different shapes to form the cross-sectional shape of each fiber.

- **The wet spinning method:** The solution is forced through the spinnerette and then into a liquid solution in which the fiber solution streams harden into continuous filaments. Acrylic fibers as well as viscose rayon fibers are made with this method.

- **The melt spinning method:** A solid material is melted to form a liquid solution that is forced through the spinnerette and into cool air, where the liquid fiber streams harden into continuous filaments. Glass, nylon, polyester, and olefin fibers are made in this way.

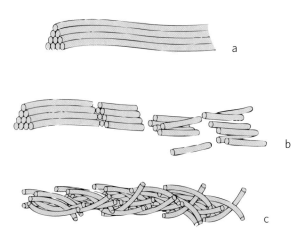

FIGURE 2.2
(a) Filament (b) filament being cut (c) and staple fibers.

Fiber Structure

A fiber's structure contributes to the performance characteristics of a fabric and the products made from it. Some fiber properties contribute favorably, whereas others do not, depending on the end-use application. The properties are determined by a fiber's physical attributes, chemical composition, and molecular formation.

Physical Attributes

Physical properties include the fiber's length, shape, surface, longitudinal configuration, and diameter. Fiber length can be measured by the naked eye, but determining the other attributes may require the use of a microscope.

Fiber Length

Fibers vary from less than one inch to miles in length. Fibers whose lengths are measured in inches are called **staple fibers.** Fibers of longer length are called **filament fibers.**

Silk is the only natural fiber that is found in filament form. It is usually about 1,600 yards (1,463 m) long, although it can be cut and used in lengths as short as several inches. All the other natural fibers vary in length, from about ½ inch to 36 inches (1.27 cm to 91.44 cm). Cotton is usually ½ to 2½ inches (1.27 to 6.35 cm), flax is usually 2 to 36 inches (5.08 to 91.44 cm), and wool is usually 1 to 18 inches (2.54 to 45.72 cm). Some fibers, such as natural rubber and metallic fiber, are made into filament form, but are not found naturally in that condition.

All manufactured fibers are produced originally as filament fibers. Sometimes they remain as such, but often they are made into shorter-length staple fibers from 1½ to 6½ inches (3.81 to 16.51 cm). The process frequently involves crimping the filament fibers and then heat-setting (see p. 22) to maintain the crimp configuration.

Thousands of the filaments are sometimes grouped to form a thick rope called **tow** and are then cut or broken into the required lengths before being twisted into yarns. (See Figure 2.2a–c.)

Some manufactured fibers, such as spandex, are always used as filament fibers. Other manufactured fibers, such as acrylic for apparel, are almost always made into staple fibers.

When making filaments that are later to be cut into short pieces, large spinnerettes with many holes are used in order to obtain high production. Small spinnerettes are used when making filaments for filament yarns because the number of holes in the spinnerette must equal the number of filament fibers that the particular filament yarn will contain. This is a basic reason why staple fibers are less expensive per pound than comparable filament fibers.

Fiber Shape

When viewed with the naked eye, all fibers look very similar. When viewed under a microscope, however, fibers' varying configurations are visible. The microscopic cross-sectional shape of the fiber and the surface construction determine the bulk, texture, luster, and hand of the fiber. (See p. 26 for a discussion of hand.) This in turn affects the performance properties and thus the end-use applications of the fabric.

As shown in Figure 2.3, a fiber's cross-sectional shape influences the way light is reflected from the surface. A flat-surfaced fiber has more luster than a round one. A round fiber reflects light in one general direction, causing a shiny surface. A multilobal-shaped fiber tends to scatter the light, causing a diffuse glow with sparkles (glitter). The sparkles are caused by bright spots from

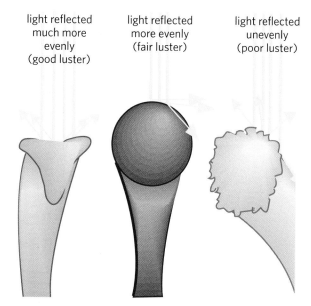

light reflected much more evenly (good luster)

light reflected more evenly (fair luster)

light reflected unevenly (poor luster)

FIGURE 2.3
Light reflection from surfaces of different cross-sectional fiber shapes.

the light reflected from the tips of the rounded lobes. An irregular cross-section scatters light in many directions, resulting in a dullish appearance with few highlights. Scattered light tends to mask soiling, particularly in carpeting. It also lowers perceived color strength (saturation).

Round fibers, such as wool, result in bulkier fabrics because they do not pack as much as flat fibers, such as cotton. Round-shaped, rodlike fibers, such as nylon, offer a smoother, more slippery hand than wool, which has a round shape but a scaly surface. Figure 2.4 shows cross-sectional shapes of various fibers.

Fiber Surfaces

The surfaces of fibers vary. For example, they can be smooth, rough, slightly grooved, deeply channeled, or wrinkled. Wool fiber is scaly, cotton is smooth, and rayon is serrated. The fiber surface affects such properties as hand, luster, and wicking. (See Chapter 3.) Figure 2.5 shows photomicrographs of various fibers.

Fiber Longitudinal Configuration

Lengthwise, fibers have varying configurations. They may be straight, twisted, coiled, or crimped. Cotton fiber, for example, is naturally twisted, whereas nylon fiber is fairly straight. Various performance properties—such as resiliency, elasticity, and abrasion resistance—are affected by fiber longitudinal configuration.

Crimp refers to the bends and twists along the length of a fiber. Greater crimp increases resiliency, bulk, warmth, elongation, absorbency, and skin comfort. However, hand becomes harsher and luster is reduced as crimp increases. Crimp allows the fiber to stand off the skin so fabric will not cling to the wearer's skin and to produce a cold sensation when worn. Crimp also helps make the fiber able to withstand being bent back on itself many times without breaking.

Crimp is inherent in wool fibers. Although it is not inherent in manufactured fibers, crimp can be added to the fiber by heat setting the fibers in a crimped configuration. This is called tow. Crimp can also be added after the yarn has been produced by a process called texturing (see p. 71). Crimp can also be seen when a yarn is removed from a woven or knitted fabric due to the interlacing or interlooping configuration of the fabric.

Fiber Diameter

Fiber diameter refers to the thickness of the fiber. Thicker fibers result in greater stiffness, which improves

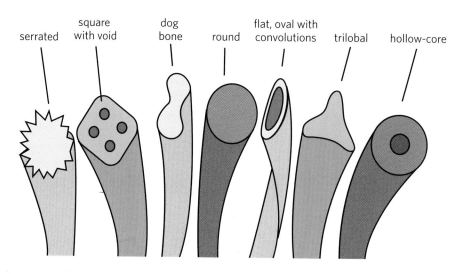

serrated · square with void · dog bone · round · flat, oval with convolutions · trilobal · hollow-core

FIGURE 2.4
Various fiber cross-sectional and longitudinal shapes.

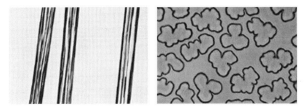

Acetate. Longitudinal view (left); notice striations. Cross-sectional view (right); notice lobular shape.

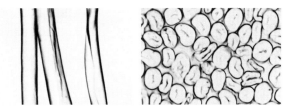

Cotton (mercerized). Longitudinal view (left). Cross-sectional view (right).

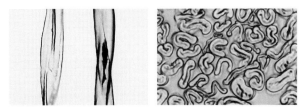

Cotton (not mercerized). Longitudinal view (left); notice fiber twisting. Cross-sectional view (right); notice kidney-bean shape.

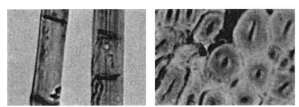

Flax. Longitudinal view (left); notice bamboo pole shape. Cross-sectional view (right).

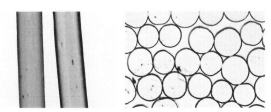

Nylon (bright). Longitudinal view (left). Cross-sectional view (right).

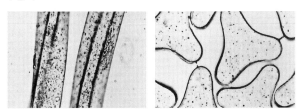

Nylon (high modification ratio). Longitudinal view (left). Cross-sectional view (right).

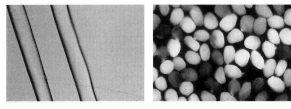

Permanently crimped lyocell. Longitudinal view (left). Cross-sectional view (right).

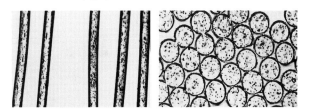

Polyester (regular melt spun). Longitudinal view (left). Cross-sectional view (right).

Silk. Longitudinal view (left). Cross-sectional view (right).

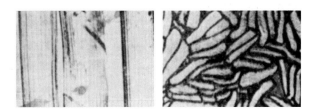

Silk (tussah). Longitudinal view (left). Cross-sectional view (right).

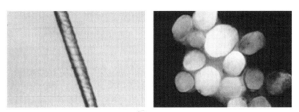

Wool. Longitudinal view (left); notice scaly surface. Cross-sectional view (right); notice round shape.

FIGURE 2.5
Photomicrographs of various textile fibers (magnification between 250× and 500×).

wrinkle resistance but can also result in an undesirable roughness. Large-diameter fibers result in bulkier fabrics because they do not pack as well as thin fibers. Fine-diameter fibers can result in fabric that is sheer, lightweight, and generally more drapable and softer to the touch than fabric of thicker fibers.

The size of the diameter of natural fibers varies depending on fiber type. Natural fibers grow irregularly and do not have uniformity along the length. Manufactured fibers are uniform along the length and are available in a range of fiber diameter controlled by the producer.

Chemical Composition and Molecular Formation

Fibers are classified into various groups by their chemical composition. Fibers with similar chemical makeup are placed in the same category. Cotton and flax are placed in the same category—cellulosic fiber—because both are natural cellulose. Cotton, wool, and polyester, however, are each in a different category—cellulosic, protein, and synthetic, respectively.

Although fibers in the same category have similar properties, they can also have different properties. For example, polyester and acrylic synthetic fibers are both resilient (wrinkle resistant), but polyester fiber is much stronger than acrylic fiber. Furthermore, although each group of fibers has different properties from fibers in another group, there may be some similar properties. For example, although cotton and acetate fibers are in different groups (cellulose and synthetic), each is **hydrophilic** (i.e., absorbs water easily).

A fiber's chemical composition relates to its reaction to various items, such as bleaches, sunlight, moths, mildew, flame, and perspiration. It also determines whether the fiber is **thermoplastic** (able to be melted), which dyes can be used to color it, and its reaction to chemical finishes.

The arrangement of the molecules within a fiber affects its strength, abrasion resistance, and resiliency. With natural fibers, little modification is possible, but with manufactured fibers, modifications are possible within limits determined by the chemical structure. This has allowed the development of numerous variations of manufactured fibers through the application of textile science and technology.

Fiber Performance Properties

A textile fiber is of commercial importance only when it possesses certain desirable physical, chemical, and molecular properties. In addition, it must be readily available (including the raw material, if it is a manufactured fiber), economical, and capable of being made into a yarn, fabric, or product and sold to a consumer.

All fibers possess certain basic characteristics. By knowing these properties, a determination can be made as to whether a fiber is suitable for use in a specific fabric. For example, if a soft, absorbent fabric is desired for men's undershirts, cotton would be excellent, but nylon would be undesirable. However, for a ski-jacket shell, where great strength and wear resistance are required, nylon fiber would be a good choice, whereas cotton would not.

Through textile science and technology, we can determine the optimum fundamental properties required of a fabric that will serve specific uses and then design the structure to achieve these ends. This is referred to as reverse engineering. Not only are the properties of the fibers considered, but so are those of the other components—yarns, fabric construction, coloration, and finish—that govern how the textile material will ultimately perform. If a property of any component is altered, then a property of the fabric will change. Although the identification of various properties in this section relates to fibers, it must be remembered that other components also interrelate. One such example is flexibility. Even though a fiber itself may bend easily, fabric made from it may be quite stiff when the fiber is spun into coarse, high-twist yarns, woven with a fabric construction in which the yarns are tightly pushed together, and finished with a chemical coating.

Fiber performance properties determine the behavior characteristics of fibers and thus their suitability in specific use conditions. Standardized tests and laboratory procedures are used to measure and compare fiber properties, which can be categorized in four groupings—aesthetics, durability, comfort, and safety—as indicated in Table 2.1.

Each property is briefly discussed in the following sections. The properties are alphabetized for ease of location.

Abrasion Resistance

Abrasion resistance is the ability to resist wear from rubbing that contributes to fabric durability. Garments made from fibers that possess both high breaking strength and abrasion resistance can be worn often and for a long period of time before signs of physical wear appear.

Nylon is used extensively in action outerwear, such as ski jackets and soccer shorts, because it is very strong and resists abrasion extremely well. Acetate is often used for linings in coats and jackets because of its excellent

TABLE 2.1	Categories of Fiber Performance Properties		
Aesthetics	Durability	Comfort	Safety
Properties relating to visual and tactile effects	*Properties relating to resistance to signs of wear*	*Properties relating to physical comfort*	*Properties relating to danger or risk of injury*
Flexibility	Abrasion resistance	Absorbency	Flammability
Hand	Chemical effects	Cover	
Luster	Environmental conditions	Elasticity	
Pilling	Strength	Wicking	
Resiliency			
Specific gravity			
Static electricity			
Thermoplasticity			

drapability and low cost. However, because of acetate's poor resistance to abrasion, the lining of a jacket can fray or develop a hole long before the outer fabric shows substantial signs of wear.

Absorbency

Absorbency is the ability to take in moisture. It is usually expressed as a percentage of moisture regain, which is the amount of water a bone-dry fiber absorbs from the air under standard conditions of 70°F (21°C and 65 percent relative humidity.

Fibers able to absorb water easily are called hydrophilic fibers. All the natural animal and vegetable fibers are hydrophilic, as are three of the manufactured fibers, rayon, lyocell, and acetate. Fibers that have difficulty absorbing water and are only able to absorb small amounts are called **hydrophobic fibers.** All the manufactured fibers besides rayon, lyocell, and acetate are hydrophobic. Glass absorbs no water at all.

Fiber absorbency affects many conditions of use, including the following:

▶ **Skin comfort.** Little absorption or wicking (see p. 28); and thus movement of perspiration can result in a clammy feeling.

▶ **Static build-up.** Problems such as clinging clothing and sparks occur with hydrophobic fibers because there is little moisture content to help dissipate the built-up charge on the fiber surface. Dirt is also drawn to the fiber and clings to it because of static build-up.

▶ **Dimensional stability in water.** Hydrophobic fibers shrink less when washed than hydrophilic fibers. Little fiber swelling, which is one reason for fabric shrinkage, occurs.

▶ **Stain removal.** It is easier to remove stains from hydrophilic fibers because water and detergent are absorbed into the fiber.

▶ **Water repellency.** A more durable repellency finish usually occurs with hydrophilic fibers because the chemicals used to achieve the repellency react better with these fibers.

▶ **Wrinkle recovery.** Hydrophobic fibers usually possess better wrinkle recovery, particularly when laundered, because they do not absorb moisture, swell, and then dry in a wrinkled configuration.

Chemical Effects

Fibers usually come into contact with chemicals either during textile processing (e.g., dyeing, finishing) or during home/professional care or cleaning (e.g., contact with soaps, bleach, and dry-cleaning solvent). The type of chemical, its strength, and time of exposure determine the effect on the fiber. Understanding the effects of chemicals on the various fibers is important because it relates directly to the care required in cleaning.

Fibers react to chemicals in different ways. For example, cotton fibers have relatively low resistance to acids but excellent resistance to alkalies. In addition, cotton fabric loses appreciable strength when finished with resin chemicals (see p. 194), which are used to create permanent press.

Cover

Cover is the ability to occupy an area. A thick fiber or one with crimp or curl gives fabric better cover than a thin, straight fiber. The fabric is warm and looks and feels substantial, but requires fewer fibers to be made.

Wool is a widely used fiber for cold weather garments because its crimp gives excellent cover, resulting in a large amount of air being trapped in the fabric. These "dead air" spaces provide insulation against the cold. The effectiveness with which fibers cover an area depends on cross-sectional shape, longitudinal configuration, and weight.

Elasticity

Elasticity is the ability to increase in length when under tension (elongation) and then return to the original length when released (recovery). Stretch and recovery when tension is placed on the fiber or fabric makes for a more comfortable garment and causes less seam stress. It also tends to increase the breaking strength of the fabric. Complete recovery helps prevent bagginess from occurring at elbows or knees, and it prevents the garment from becoming loose fitting.

Fibers that can elongate at least 100 percent are called elastomeric fibers. Spandex, elasterell-p, lastol, and rubber are fibers in this category. After being stretched, these elastic fibers return forcibly to approximately their original dimensions.

Environmental Conditions

The effects of environmental conditions on fibers vary. How fibers react and, ultimately, how fabrics react to certain exposure or storage is important. The following are some examples:

▸ Wool garments need to be mothproofed when stored because they are susceptible to damage by these wool-eating insects.

▸ Nylon and silk show strength losses from extended exposure to sunlight. Therefore, they are normally not used for window treatments.

▸ Cotton has poor resistance to mildew and should not be allowed to remain wet for long periods of time.

Flammability

Flammability is the ability to ignite or burn. This characteristic is important because people's lives are surrounded with various textile products. We know that the burning of apparel or interior furnishings can cause serious injury and/or result in significant material loss for the consumer.

Fibers are usually classified as being flammable, flame resistant, or flameproof:

▸ **Flammable fibers** are relatively easy to ignite and sustain combustion.

▸ **Flame-resistant fibers** have a relatively high ignition temperature and slow rate of burning. They may also be self-extinguishing.

▸ **Flameproof fibers** will not burn.

Flammable fibers can be made flame resistant through finishing or by making a manufactured fiber variant. For example, regular polyester is flammable, but polyester which is treated is flame resistant.

Flexibility

Flexibility is the capability of a fiber to bend easily and repeatedly without breaking. A flexible fiber such as acetate can be made into a highly drapable fabric and garment. A rigid fiber such as glass, which is not used in apparel but can be found in draperies, usually makes a fabric that is relatively stiff. Usually the thinner the fiber, the better its drapability. Flexibility also influences the hand of a material.

Although a highly drapable fabric is often desired, there are also times when a more rigid fabric is wanted. For example, in a swing coat (a coat that hangs from the shoulders and flares out), a more rigid fabric is needed to produce the desired shape.

Hand

Hand is the way a fiber, yarn, or fabric feels when handled. The hand of the fiber is affected by its shape, surface, and configuration. Fiber shapes vary and include round, flat, and multilobal. Fiber surfaces also vary having attributes such as smooth, serrated, or scaly. Fiber configuration is either crimped or straight. Type of yarn, fabric construction, and finishing processes used also affect the hand of a fabric, as discussed in later chapters. Terms such as soft, crisp, dry, silky, stiff, boardy, or harsh are used to describe the hand of a textile material.

Luster

Luster refers to the light reflected from a surface. Various characteristics of a fiber affect the amount of luster. Increased light reflection occurs from a smoother surface, less crimp, flatter cross-sectional shape, and longer fiber length. The drawing process used in producing manufactured fibers increases the amount of luster by making the surface smoother. The addition of delusterant agents breaks up the reflected light so less luster occurs. Thus, by controlling the amount of delusterants added, we can make manufactured fibers bright, semi-dull, or dull.

Fabric luster is also affected by the yarn type, weave, and finish used. The desired amount of luster depends on fashion trends and customer desires.

Pilling

Pilling is the formation of groups of short or broken fibers on the surface of a fabric that are tangled together in the shape of a tiny ball called a pill. They are formed when the ends of a fiber break from the fabric surface, usually from wear. Pilling is not a desirable property because it makes fabrics look worn and unsightly and feel less comfortable, such as when formed on sheets. The pills usually form in areas that are rubbed, such as collars, along the underside of sleeves and at the edges of cuffs.

Hydrophobic fibers tend to pill much more than hydrophilic fibers because hydrophobic fibers have greater electrical static attraction (see p. 27) for each other and do not fall off the fabric surface. Pills are hardly ever seen on the collar of a 100 percent cotton shirt, but are quite common after a period of wear on a similar shirt made of 100 percent polyester. Wool, although hydrophilic, pills because of its scaly surface. The fibers snag each other, tangle, and form a pill. Strong fibers tend to hold pills to the fabric surface. On weak fibers, which are prone to breaking, pills fall off easily and pilling is not noticeable.

Resiliency

Resiliency is the capability of a material to spring back to shape after being creased, twisted, or distorted. It is closely connected with wrinkle recovery. A fabric that has good resiliency does not wrinkle easily and, therefore, tends to retain its good appearance.

Thicker fibers possess greater resiliency because there is more mass to absorb the strain. Also, fiber shape affects fiber resiliency; round fibers usually possess greater resiliency than flat fibers.

Fiber properties are also a factor. Polyester has outstanding resiliency; cotton has poor resiliency. Thus it is not surprising to find that the two fibers are often blended in items such as men's shirts, women's blouses, and sheets.

A resilient fiber creates a problem if a sharp crease is desired in a garment. It is easy to make a sharp crease on a cotton or rayon fabric, but not on a dry-wool material. The wool fibers resist being bent or creased and so eventually straighten out.

Specific Gravity

Specific gravity is the ratio of the mass of the fiber to an equal volume of water at 4°C. A lightweight fiber enables a fabric to be warm without being heavy. A fabric can be made thick and lofty and still remain relatively lightweight. Acrylic fiber is an excellent example. It is much lighter weight than wool, but it has wool-like properties and so is used extensively to make lightweight-yet-warm blankets, scarves, heavy socks, and other winter-wear items.

Static Electricity

Static electricity is a frictional electric charge caused by the rubbing together of two dissimilar materials. The effects, such as clothes clinging to the wearer or lint being attracted to the fabric, occur when the electric charge is retained and builds up on the surface. A spark or shock occurs when the surface comes in contact with a good conductor and there is a rapid discharge. The effects are eliminated if the static charge can be removed as quickly as it forms on the fiber surface.

Moisture contained in fibers acts as a conductor to remove the charge and prevent the previously mentioned effects from occurring. Hydrophobic fibers, because they contain very little moisture, are prone to static electricity. Static can also occur with natural fibers, but only if they are very dry, in which case they act as if they are hydrophobic. Glass is the hydrophobic fiber exception; no static charge can build up on its surface because of its chemical composition.

Fabrics containing **epitropic fibers** (fibers that conduct electricity) have no static problems. The carbon or metal content enables these fibers to remove static buildup. Filament fibers, such as Ultron® nylon made by Solutia Inc., are used in carpets because static problems frequently exist with carpeting. Epitropic fibers eliminate shocks, fabric cling, and dust attraction. Because of the danger of static electricity in certain work environments, carpets made of fibers containing a low-static propensity are especially important in hospitals, in work areas near computers, and near areas of possible exposure to flammable or explosive liquids or gases (see p. 59).

Strength

Strength is a fiber's ability to withstand stress. Fiber strength, the force needed to break the fiber, is known as tenacity and expressed in grams per denier or grams per fiber weight (see p. 77).

Some fibers, such as glass, nylon, and polyester, are very strong, whereas others, such as acetate and acrylic, are weak. Like abrasion resistance, strength contributes greatly to fabric durability. Performance fabrics, as they are called, are used in outerwear, uniforms, tires, parachutes, and other end-use applications where strength is critical.

Thermoplasticity

The ability of fibers to withstand heat exposure is an important factor affecting their suitability for many end uses. It is an important consideration because fibers are heated in many fabric-forming processes, such as dyeing, singeing, and heat setting. In addition, heat is often used in the care and renovation of apparel and interior furnishings.

Some heat effects are temporary and evident only during exposure. For example, in dyeing, the properties of a fiber may be changed during the heat-exposure period but return to normal after cooling. Other heat effects evident after exposure may be durable or permanent because a change in the molecular arrangement causes a degradation of the fiber itself. Thus heat-setting may change the molecular arrangement, causing the fabric to be more stable (little shrinkage) and more wrinkle resistant, without significant degradation. However, prolonged exposure to high temperatures may cause degradation, such as loss of strength, fiber shrinkage, and discoloration. Many consumers have experienced this when ironing at too high a temperature, causing a severe degradation of the fabric and even the loss of the garment.

A thermoplastic fiber softens when heat is applied and may melt to a liquid state when higher heat is applied. Many manufactured fibers are thermoplastic. Permanent creases and pleats can be made on fabrics containing thermoplastic fibers by applying enough heat to create a crease or pleat but not enough to melt the fiber; when the heat is removed, the crease or pleat is permanently set. When heated (softened), thermoplastic fibers can be molded or pressed to shape, and when cooled, the molding or shaping remains as set. (Care must be exercised when ironing garments made from manufactured fibers so that they do not begin to soften or melt. When they do, the fabric begins sticking to the iron.) The creases are permanent, until a higher temperature is applied to negate the heat-setting effect. Shape can also be imparted to garments by this process, giving thermoplastic fabrics good dimensional stability.

Fiber thermoplasticity is an important property that makes many textile innovations possible. Examples are textured yarns (see p. 71), permanent embossing (see p. 189), durable press (see p. 193), and others. Shaped hat bodies and bra cups are also examples of applications of thermoplastic fibers.

Wicking

Wicking is the ability of a fiber to transfer moisture from one section to another. Usually the moisture is along the fiber surface, but it may also pass through the fiber when a liquid is absorbed by the fiber. The wicking propensity of a fiber usually is based on the chemical and physical composition of the outer surface. A smooth surface reduces wicking action.

Some fibers, such as cotton, are hydrophilic and also possess good wicking action. Others, such as olefin,

FIGURE 2.6
COOLMAX® fabric from INVISTA™ uses four-channeled fibers that transport perspiration away from the skin to the fabric's surface for quick evaporation. COOLMAX® is an INVISTA™ certification mark for fabrics.

are hydrophobic but possess good wicking action when microdenier in size (i.e., very thin filament fibers). This property is especially desirable in work out clothes and running clothes. (See Figure 2.6.) Body perspiration is transported by wicking action along the fiber surface to the outer surface of the cloth and evaporated into the atmosphere, thus providing improved comfort.

Identification of Textile Fibers

Because it is often not possible to distinguish one fiber from another merely by touch or sight, textile fibers may be identified using different techniques. Different tests, each of which has advantages and disadvantages, may be performed. Some are easy, quick, and relatively inexpensive, but do not allow clear distinctions to be made between fibers with the same characteristics. For example, a burning test will not differentiate between flax and cotton because both have the same burning properties. Others enable positive identification, but require much more time and a more sophisticated testing apparatus (e.g., chemical analysis).

Determining Fiber Identification

Burning Test

The burning test is a simple method for identifying fibers. All that is needed is a flame and knowledge of the burning properties. Relatively little skill or training is required, and it is a quick test because it lasts only as long as the material burns.

The burning test can be used to identify fibers by groups, such as the cellulose group (forms an ash) or the synthetic (melts) group. It can also be used to identify specific fibers, such as nylon or wool, because of the distinctive odor of the fumes, color of the smoke, and type of residue.

The burning test does have certain limitations. The burning behavior of the fiber may be affected by the finish applied to the fiber. For example, a flame-retardant finish on a cotton fabric greatly reduces the degree of flammability, whereas napping or brushing of the same fabric increases the rate of burning. Also, the presence of some finishes masks the odor of the fumes.

The use of blends frequently complicates the identification of fibers by burning. Two or three different kinds of fiber burning together in one yarn may be difficult to distinguish. However, with practice, many common blends, such as polyester and wool, can be identified by this method.

Some fibers burn almost identically because they have the same chemical composition. Cotton, flax, lyocell, and viscose rayon are examples, and other methods are required to differentiate these four from one another.

Test Procedure

In the burning test, the following items are considered:

▸ Melting and/or burning characteristics

▸ Odor of the fumes

▸ Appearance, shape, feel, and color of the residue or remains after burning (see Table 2.2)

The burning test is made on a small bundle of yarns twisted together, or on a fringe of the fabric, exposing only one set of the yarns for burning. Often the yarns in one direction of a fabric are not made of the same kind of fiber as the yarns in the other direction. For this reason, warp and filling yarns should be burned separately.

A bundle of at least five or six yarns, twisted together and forming a grouping about $1/8$ inch in diameter, is held at one end, and the free end of the bundle is placed in the flame of a match or candle, as shown in Figure 2.7. (It is better to use a candle when a number of tests are to be made than to use matches.) A sheet of aluminum foil about 1 foot squared, placed on the table or bench, with the candle in the center of the foil, forms a good fireproof surface on which to work; if a small sample burns out of control, it can be dropped on the foil without damage.

The use of two coins or a pair of tweezers to hold the yarns to be tested is important to avoid burns. Some fibers are slow to ignite, but then burn quickly. Others form a hot bead that may stick to a finger, producing a painful burn. Care also must be exercised so that one's hair does not get close to the flame.

The first part of the burning test should determine whether the fiber melts. This is done by bringing the fiber bundle close to, but not into, the flame. Fibers that melt shrivel up and harden. If only the tip of the yarn is heated, it forms a tiny, solid, hard bead. Even though silk and wool do not melt, they form a hollow, irregular bead at the end of the burned yarn. This should not be considered melting. Some fibers that melt also drip, so additional care must be exercised to avoid burns from drips.

The burning characteristics should be checked next. Such properties as the fabric being self-extinguishing once the flame is removed, or the smoke being very dark or black, should be recorded because they help with fiber identification. The rate of burning cannot usually be used to identify the fiber because this is also affected by other factors such as size of yarns, amount of yarn twist, fabric construction, and finish on the fabric. In general, though, manufactured fibers burn faster than natural ones.

As they are brought close to the flame, some fibers (fabrics) tend to physically move away. It appears that they are shrinking from the flame, similarly to two

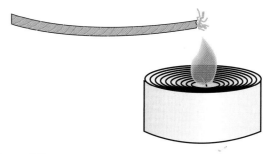

FIGURE 2.7
The burning test for fiber identification.

TABLE 2.2 Burning Characteristics of Textile Fibers

Fibers	Burns or Melts	Shrinks from Flame	Odor	Residue	Other Properties
Cellulosic fibers					
Cotton	Burns only	No	Burning paper, leaves, or wood	Fine, feathery, gray ash	Afterglow
Flax, hemp, jute, ramie	All burning characteristics same as for cotton				
Protein fibers					
Wool, mohair, cashmere, alpaca	Burns only	Yes	Very strong odor of burning hair or chicken feathers	Black, hollow, irregular bead that crushes easily to a gritty, black powder	Self-extinguishing
Silk	All burning characteristics same as for wool, except odor is not as strong and may smell more like charred or burning meat (no sulphur content as in wool)				
Manufactured fibers					
Acetate	Burns and melts	Yes	Combination of burning paper and vinegar	Dark, hard, solid bead	—
Acrylic	Burns and melts	Yes	Broiled fish or acrid	Hard, irregular, black bead	Flame gives off black smoke; sputters when burning
Glass	Melts only*	Very slowly	No odor	Hard, whitish bead	Flame-resistant fiber; heat from match will not cause fiber to melt
Lyocell	All burning characteristics same as for cotton (fiber is mostly cellulosic)				
Modacrylic	Burns and melts	Yes	Chemical	Hard, black irregular bead	Self-extinguishing
Nylon	Burns and melts	Yes	Celery	Hard, cream-colored bead; if fibers are overheated, bead becomes dark	Flaming usually caused by finish present; drops of melted fiber may fall from heated portion of sample
Olefin (Lastol)	Burns and melts	Yes	Chemical or paraffinlike	Hard, tan bead	Flame gives off black smoke
PLA	Burns and melts	Yes	Acrid	Hard grey bead	Self-extinguishing
Polyester (Elasterell-p)	Burns and melts	Yes	Sweet chemical	Hard cream-colored bead; if fibers are overheated bead becomes dark	Drops of melted fiber may fall from heated portion of sample; flame gives off black smoke
Rayon	All burning characteristics same as for cotton (fiber is mostly cellulosic)				
Saran	Burns and melts	Yes	Chemical	Hard, black, irregular bead that becomes dark	Self-extinguishing, gives off black smoke
Spandex	Burns and melts	No	Chemical	Soft, black ash	—
Vinal	Burns and melts	Yes	Paraffinlike chemical	Hard, tan bead	—
Vinyon	Burns and melts	Yes	Acrid	Hard, black irregular bead	—

*Occurs at high temperatures; not attainable with a match or candle flame.

magnets repelling one another when the same poles are brought together.

The odor in the smoke or fumes gives clues to fiber content. Once the burning or smoldering has ceased, there is no odor.

The residue from the burning test is of various shapes, colors, and hardnesses for different fibers. Sometimes there seems to be no residue; in such a case, it has dropped off. This occasionally occurs with cotton, where the residue is a light ash.

Other Fiber Identification Tests

The burning test is not the only means of identifying fiber content. The tests described in the next section offer additional ways to determine fiber content and are sometimes used to verify a specific result.

Acetone Test

Acetate fibers become soluble in acetone. If several drops of acetone are dropped on the acetate fabric (or yarns) and the acetone is rubbed into the fabric, the area dissolves. The rubbing must be done quickly after moistening because acetone is volatile and dries very quickly. Acetone is also flammable and, therefore, must be kept away from flames.

The percentage of two fibers present in a blend or mixture of acetate fabric can be calculated by weighing a swatch of the fabric before and after an acetone treatment. Saturating the fabric with acetone for a few minutes dissolves the acetate fibers and leaves the other fiber unaffected (assuming that the other fiber is not soluble in acetone).

The acetone test can be used by garment buyers and product developers to verify the fiber content of a product in relation to the specifications that were called for when developing the product.

Chlorine Bleach Test

If a yarn of silk or wool is wetted with liquid chlorine bleach, it will first turn yellow and then slowly disintegrate from the action of the chemical. Liquid household bleaches, such as Clorox®, are usually chlorine bleaches.

For this test, the yarns should be untwisted and separated into individual fibers to provide maximum fiber exposure to the bleach.

Dry and Wet Strength Test

The strength of many fibers is affected by the amount of water they contain; a few fibers get a little stronger when wet; some remain about the same in strength; and others get weaker.

The dry and wet strength test can be made by breaking the yarns when they are dry and then again when they are wet, and comparing the amount of force required. Only the middle of the yarn, not the entire length, needs to be saturated with water. If the yarn is one that becomes weaker when wet, it will break in the middle because this section would be the weakest. One technique for wetting the yarn is to hold the ends of the yarn and then wet the middle of the yarn with saliva by passing it over the tongue. An alternate method is to use drops of water.

This test can also be done by tearing a piece of the cloth when it is dry and then when it is wet and comparing the difference in strength.

The dry and wet strength test can be used to distinguish spun viscose rayon from cotton and flax, after the burning test shows one of these three to be present. If the yarn or fabric is much weaker when wet, it is rayon because cotton and flax are stronger when wet. If the yarn is not noticeably weaker, then it is either cotton, flax, or high wet modulus rayon, and must be differentiated in another way (e.g., microscopic examination).

The strength of a fabric when wet is important when considering the care and maintenance of the fabric. An automatic washing machine can put tremendous stress on a wet fabric in the washing process and even greater stress during the spin cycle. Strength when wet must be taken into account when determining the appropriateness of a fabric for a particular end use and the care or maintenance of that item by the consumer.

Chemical Solubility Test

Fiber identification can be made when it is determined which chemical will dissolve the specimen. The fiber, yarn, or fabric specimen should be tested using the solvents in the sequence indicated in Table 2.3. More fibers become eliminated as the sequence continues. The specimen is stirred in the liquid and the results are noted. Extreme care should be taken because most of the liquids are hazardous. Gloves, aprons, goggles, and laboratory-exhaust hoods should be used during these tests.

TABLE 2.3 Chemical Solubility Test for Textile Fibers	
Solvents[a]	Fiber that Will Dissolve[b] (Regular Type)
1. Acetic acid, 100% concentration, 20°C temperature, 5 minutes.	Acetate.
2. Acetone, 100% concentration, 20°C temperature, 5 minutes.	Vinyon (also acetate).
3. Hydrochloric acid, 20% concentration, 20°C temperature, 10 minutes.	Nylon and vinal. Nylon dissolves in meta-cresol 100% concentration, 139°C temperature, 5 minutes, whereas vinal does not.
4. Sodium hypochlorite, 5.25% concentration, 20°C temperature, 20 minutes.	Silk and wool. Differentiate visually.
5. Meta-xylene, 100% concentration, 139°C temperature, 5 minutes.	Olefin and saran (also vinyon). Saran dissolves in 1,4 dioxane, 100% concentration, 101°C temperature, 5 minutes, whereas olefin does not.
6. Dimethyl formamide, 100% concentration, 90°C temperature, 10 minutes.	Spandex, acrylic, and modacrylic (also acetate and saran). Spandex is elastomeric; others are not. Modacrylic dissolves in cyclohexane, 100% concentration, 156°C temperature, 5 minutes, whereas acrylic does not.
7. Sulphuric acid, 70% concentration, 38°C temperature, 20 minutes.	Cotton, flax, and rayon (also acetate, Nylon, silk, and vinal). Rayon dissolves in 38% concentration hydrochloric acid, 24°C temperature, 5 minutes. Although cotton and flax do not, they can be distinguished by observing their longitudinal appearance with a microscope.
8. Meta-cresol, 100% concentration, 139°C temperature, 5 minutes.	Polyester (also acetate, nylon, and vinyon).

a. Solvents to be used in the sequence shown.
b. The fibers in parentheses will also be dissolved by the indicated solvent, but they have already been eliminated as an unknown by a preceding solvent solubility test.

Study Questions

1. State the fiber property that most affects the indicated condition:

   a. Pilling propensity
   b. Producing permanent pleats
   c. Improving insulation
   d. Resistance to wear from rubbing
   e. Static buildup
   f. Determination of hand
   g. Excessive wrinkling
   h. Good drapability
   i. Preventing clammy feeling on a hot day
   j. Resisting pulling force
   k. Degree of luster

2. What changes in the spinnerette would have to be made for the following to occur:

   a. To produce thicker filament fiber
   b. To increase the number of filaments being produced
   c. To change the cross-sectional shape of the fiber being produced

3. What differences in appearance and hand would you expect between two identical fibers, one with round-shaped fibers and the other with triangular-shaped fibers?

4. Why can cotton be produced only in staple form but manufactured fiber such as polyester can be produced in both filament and staple form?

5. What is crimp and how does it affect the properties of a textile?

6. How does fiber absorbency affect the properties of a textile?

7. What is pilling? Why is it more apparent on some fibers than on others?

8. Which fiber would be more suitable for athletic wear: one that wicks or one that absorbs moisture? Why?

9. State two everyday occurrences where static buildup is common.

10. What is covering power? Why is it an important consideration in the production of blankets containing manufactured fibers?

CHAPTER THREE
Natural and Manufactured Fibers

Objectives

▸ To know the classifications of textile fibers.

▸ To correlate fibers with their properties for end-use requirements.

▸ To recognize various trademarks, logos, and names used to market textile fibers.

▸ To recognize the importance of fibers to the industrial products industries.

Use fabrics in the Fiber section of the Fabric Science Swatch Kit for this chapter.

Key Terms Related to Textiles

acetate	elasterell-p	melamine	ramie
acrylic	felting	metallic	rayon
alpaca	flax	microfiber	rubber
angora	fluorocarbon	micron	saran
anidex	glass	modacrylic	silk
antistatic	HWM rayon	mohair	sisal
aramid	hemp	multicomponent	spandex
azlon	heterogeneous fibers	nanotechnology	sulfar
bamboo	jute	novoloid	trademark
bast fibers	lastrile	nylon	triacetate
bicomponent	lastol	nytril	vicuña
camel hair	leaf fibers	olefin	vinal
carbon	llama	PBI	vinyon
cashgora	lyocell	PLA	wool
cashmere	matrix	polyester	yak
cotton	matrix-fibril	qiviut	

The properties and characteristics of textile fibers form the foundation for apparel, home, or industrial applications. A fiber is viable when it possesses the desired chemical and physical attributes for a specific end use. In addition, the fiber must be able to be produced in commercial quantities and available at prices consistent with market demands.

This chapter discusses the various major natural and manufactured fibers. The focus is on their properties and characteristics because fibers are the major building blocks of any material. Using the proper fibers helps produce the appropriate fabric for a specific end use.

FIGURE 3.1
A cotton boll.

Natural Fibers

Natural fibers have been used throughout the world for thousands of years. Early civilization relied on crude coverings and simple clothing made from natural fibers collected in the wild. Cotton, wool, silk, and flax are the most commonly used natural fibers found in the apparel and home textiles markets (Table 3.1). They are discussed in more detail than the other natural fibers included in this chapter. The United Nations General Assembly declared 2009 the International Year of Natural Fibers.

Cotton

Of all the natural fibers, cotton is the most important. Approximately 125 million bales are produced annually, by far the largest amount of all natural fibers. It is produced in 90 countries around the globe with about 80 percent coming from small farms. Cotton production affects social, economic, and environmental conditions around the world. It is an economic catalyst for developing countries as well as a mainstay of industrial nations. Fluctuation of cotton production and use is closely monitored because oversupply and undersupply affect the price and economic conditions of the entire pipeline from farmer to the consumer.

Cotton is a seed fiber—that is, it is attached to the seed of the cotton plant—and has been used for over 7,000 years (see Figure 3.1). It is the most widely used fiber in the world. The leading producers of cotton include the United States, China, India, Turkey, Pakistan, and Uzbekistan. The most used cotton species in the United States is American Upland cotton. The other major species raised in the United States is American Pima cotton, which is a high-quality cotton because it has an extra-long staple length, over 1⅜ inches (approximately 3.49 cm). Sea Island cotton, perhaps the best-quality cotton in the world, was once grown in the United States, but now grows only in a small quantity in the West Indies. Egyptian cotton is another species of high-quality, long-staple cotton.

Cotton is classified not only by its species, but also by its fiber length, color, and cleanliness (leaf and stem content), all of which contribute to the cost of the fiber. The fiber length is the most important because the longer the staple length, the better the fiber properties. Additionally, color and cleanliness can be addressed in processing. The more expensive extra-long staple Pima cotton has greater strength, more luster, and a silkier hand than

Fiber	Durability		Comfort	Appearance	
	Abrasion Resistance	*Strength*	*Absorbency*	*Resiliency*	*Pilling Resistance*
Cotton	Good	Good	Good	Poor	Good
Flax	Fair	Excellent	Excellent	Poor	Good
Silk	Fair	Good	Excellent	Fair	Good
Wool	Fair–good*	Poor	Excellent	Good	Fair

TABLE 3.1 **Comparison Chart of the Most Commonly Used Natural Fibers**

*Fair for finer apparel wool; good for coarser carpet wool.

Upland cotton. Cotton is grown predominately in Texas, Mississippi, and California. Farmers often plant genetically modified crops which offer a greater yield per acre with less dependence on pesticides.

Interestingly, cotton became a major fiber in the United States only after the Industrial Revolution began in this country (in the late 1700s). Cotton, with its short fiber length, was not suited to the hand carding and spinning being performed before that time. Wool, flax, and hemp, whose fibers are longer, were the main fibers the colonists used to make their clothing and other textile products.

Because it is a plant fiber, cotton is composed mainly of cellulose. It is a medium-weight fiber of natural cream or tan color with a length between ½ and 2½ inches (1.27 and 6.35 cm). Most cotton used is about 1 to 1½ inches (2.54 to 3.18 cm) long. Under a microscope, cotton looks like a flat twisted tube.

Cotton Incorporated® is the promotion organization for United States Upland Growers. Supima® is the organization of the American Pima Cotton Growers.

Properties
Favorable   The fiber has good strength and abrasion resistance. It is hydrophilic (8½ percent moisture regain), absorbs moisture quickly, and dries quickly. Quick drying gives a cooling effect, which makes cotton a comfortable fiber to wear in hot weather. (See Figure 3.2.) It has a 10 percent increase in strength when wet, which makes it completely launderable. It is dry cleanable and has no static or pilling problems. It has fair drape and a soft hand, and it is inexpensive.

Figure 3.2
This cotton shirt is made up of natural fibers.

Unfavorable   Cotton has little luster and has poor elasticity and resiliency. It is attacked by mildew and silverfish. It is highly resistant to alkalies but is weakened by resin chemicals used in finishing. It is also compromised when exposed to acids which can be used to create a 'worn' look or holes in jeans. Cotton fabrics form lint because the short fibers are able to come out of the fabric easily.

End Uses
The end uses of cotton include a wide range of products in the apparel, interior furnishings, and industrial areas. Examples include blouses, jeans, jackets, towels, sheets, trousers, T-shirts, belts, and sneakers. It takes about 24 ounces of cotton fiber to make an average pair of jeans and about 8 ounces to make a T-shirt.

Flax

Flax comes from the stem or stalk of the flax plant and is harvested by pulling the entire plant from the ground. When the fiber is processed into fabric, it is called linen. It is generally considered to be the oldest textile fiber, having been used in the Stone Age. The largest producer is France, with most of the other leading producers—including Germany, Belgium, and Russia—located in Europe. Northern Ireland, Italy, and Belgium are leading exporters of linen cloth.

Flax is raised for both its fiber and seed. The seeds contain linseed oil, used primarily in paints and varnishes. The long fibers are used to make fabric, and short fibers are used for twine, rope, and rug backings (see Figure 3.3).

Because it is a plant fiber, flax is composed mainly of cellulose. It is a medium-weight fiber of naturally light tan color with a fiber length between 2 and 36 inches (5.08 to 91.44 cm). The average is from 6 to 20 inches (15.24 to 50.8 cm). The fiber, when viewed under a microscope, is shaped like bamboo.

Properties
Favorable   The fiber has excellent strength. It is the strongest of the plant fibers. Flax is also 10 percent stronger when wet. Its hand is good and the fiber has good luster. It is more hydrophilic than cotton (12 percent moisture regain), absorbs moisture quickly, and also dries quickly. These properties make it a good fiber for hot-weather wear because quick drying has a cooling effect. Flax is completely washable and dry cleanable. Sometimes, however, dry cleaning is mandated due to finishes applied to the fabric or the construction of the product. It has the highest safe-ironing temperature (450°F ≈ 232°C), and it has no static or pilling problems. Linen fabrics are lint free because they contain no very short fibers.

FIGURE 3.3
A field of flax plants.

Unfavorable Flax has only fair resistance to abrasion, making it less durable than cotton. It has poor drape, elasticity, and resiliency, and it is vulnerable to mildew and silverfish.

End Uses

The principal end uses of flax include dresses, suits, sports jackets, luxury tablecloths, napkins, and wallpaper.

Silk

Silk is said to have been discovered in 2640 B.C. by a Chinese princess. It is a continuous strand of two filaments cemented together, which forms the cocoon of the silkworm. The silkworm secretes silk by forcing two fine streams of a thick liquid out tiny openings in its head. On contact with air, the fine streams of liquid harden into filaments. The worm winds the silk around itself, forming a complete covering (cocoon) for protection while changing from a worm into a moth. As much as 1,600 yards (1,463 meters) of fiber are used to make the cocoon.

Silkworms are usually cultivated and are raised under controlled conditions of environment and nutrition; this is called sericulture. The food for sericulture silkworms consists solely of mulberry leaves. These worms produce the finest, silkiest fibers (see Figure 3.4). To keep the silk in one continuous length, the worms in the cocoons are subjected to heat before they are ready to leave. Some moths, however, are allowed to mature and break out of their cocoons to produce the eggs for the next crop of silk. Sericulture is a very labor-intensive enterprise.

The other type of silk commercially practical for textile manufacture is a wild, uncultivated type called tussah silk. The worms that produce this silk feed on the leaves of other trees, such as oak and cherry. The brown fiber produced is flat, very nonuniform, and much thicker and less lustrous than the triangular, thin, cultivated silk fiber. Tussah silk is used for heavier, rough-textured fabrics.

At times, two silk worms nest together and form one cocoon made of a double strand. The fibers are not separated, and the resulting yarn has a varying thick and thin appearance. This type of silk is called duoppioni or dupion silk.

Spun silk yarn can be made of short fibers taken from pierced cocoons, from the first and last part of the cocoon, which is of poorer quality, from waste silk that accumulates around the machines during the various operations, or from a combination of these sources. Staple silk fibers are made from waste silk.

China is the leading silk producer in the world. Other producers include India, Japan, Thailand, and Brazil.

Silk is composed mainly of protein because it is an animal fiber. It is a medium-weight fiber of naturally white color. The fiber may look gray or yellow because that is the color of sericin, which is the gummy substance that makes cocoons hard. Silk that has not had the sericin removed is called raw silk. Silk is the only natural filament fiber. When viewed under a microscope, silk has a rounded, triangular shape with an uneven diameter.

Properties

Favorable The fiber has excellent drape and a luxurious hand. It is the thinnest of the natural fibers. It is lustrous and hydrophilic (11 percent moisture regain). Silk has very little problem with static, and no pilling occurs. Silk fabric can be washed or dry cleaned, although sometimes the dye or finish used necessitates dry cleaning only.

Unfavorable Silk has only fair resiliency and abrasion resistance. Its strength is good; it loses about 15 percent strength when wet, but recovers when dried. The fiber has poor resistance to prolonged exposure to sunlight and can be attacked by moths. It is also expensive and turns yellow if washed with chlorine bleach. It is weakened and made harsher by alkalies such as those found in strong soaps. Silk also degrades over time by exposure to atmospheric oxygen, which makes it especially difficult to preserve, even in climate-controlled museum settings.

End Uses

The principal end uses of silk include dresses, ties, scarves, blouses, and other apparel. Silk is also used in home furnishings, particularly decorative pillows, and can be found in washable sheets for the luxury market. It takes approximately 110 silk cocoons to make a tie and over 600 cocoons to make a blouse.

Wool

Wool is the fiber that forms the covering of sheep. It is also a fiber with history, known to have been used by people at the end of the Stone Age. Approximately 40 different breeds of sheep produce about 200 types of wool fiber of varying grades. Examples of well-known breeds of sheep raised in the United States are Merino and Debouillet (fine-wool grade), Southdown and Columbia (medium-wool grade), and Romney and Lincoln (coarse-wool grade). Grading is the process of judging a whole fleece for fiber fineness and length. Sorting is the process of breaking up an individual fleece into its different qualities. The best-quality wool comes from the back, sides, and shoulder; the poorest comes from the lower legs.

The grades of wool vary widely, depending on the breed and health of the sheep and the climate. The thinner the fiber diameter, the better the properties of the wool. Merino wool is considered the best grade of wool. It has the most crimp, best drape, most strength, best resiliency, best elasticity, softest hand, and most scales on its surface.

Shorn wool is called fleece wool or clipped wool. Lamb's wool is wool taken from a sheep younger than one year (first clip); it is desirable because it is fine in diameter, which can make a very soft product.

Leading producers of apparel-class wool include Australia, New Zealand, South Africa, and China (see Figures 3.5). Leading producers of carpet-class wool include, China, Argentina, and Turkey.

Wool is mainly composed of protein (similar to human hair) because it is an animal fiber. It is a medium-weight fiber of a natural cream, brown, or black color, it has much natural crimp, and it has a fiber length between 1 and 18 inches (2.54 to 45.72 centimeters). When viewed under a microscope, its shape is round and it has a scaly surface.

Properties

Favorable The fiber has good resiliency. Wrinkles come out if the garment is hung in a moist atmosphere. Its hand is fair to excellent, depending on the quality of the wool fiber. Wool has good drape and elasticity and

FIGURE 3.4
Silk cocoons on fabric made of silk.

WOOLMARK   WOOLMARK
                BLEND

is hydrophobic. Wool has very little problem with static, but its abrasion resistance is good only if it is coarse.

Wool makes warm fabrics for two reasons. First, it absorbs moisture vapor slowly. Second, wool fabrics have an excellent insulation property because the fibers have a natural crimp, which prevents them from packing together and so forms dead air spaces (trapped air). The trapped air is the insulating barrier. Wool's crimpy fibers allow bulky fabrics to be made and also give strength; the high crimp allows it to be pulled with great force without breaking.

Unfavorable It has fair to good abrasion resistance, depending on its thickness—fair for the finer wool used for apparel, and good for the coarser wool used for carpets. It loses strength when wet. It has poor luster.

Though recent innovations promote its easy care, traditionally wool garments must be dry cleaned. **Felting** occurs in the presence of heat, moisture, and agitation, which cause the fiber surface scales to interlock with one another; this leads to a tangled mass on the fabric surface that cannot be combed or brushed out. With these scales snagging adjacent wool fibers, the fibers cannot return to their original positions in the fabric. Wool fiber surface scales can be either chemically removed or covered with a resin to create a washable fabric in which no felting and only a little shrinkage occur. There are certain applications in which felting is desirable for specific end uses such as hats and banners.

Wool is vulnerable to moths, but can be moth-proofed. Wool has problems with pilling, it turns yellow if washed with chlorine bleach. It is also weakened and made harsher by alkalies, such as those found in strong soaps. However, wool is highly resistant to acids. Wool is

an expensive fiber due to the limited quantities available and the cost associated with production.

End Uses
The principal end uses of wool include overcoats, suits, sweaters, carpets, luxury upholstery, and felt fabric.

Other Natural Fibers

Specialty Hair Fibers
Specialty hair fibers are rare animal fibers that possess special qualities of hand, fineness, or luster. They are usually stronger, finer, and more expensive, but lower in abrasion resistance, than most wool fibers.

Angora comes from the Angora rabbit raised in France, Chile, China, and the United States. The fiber is very slippery due to its shape and is often blended with other fibers. It is used in yarns for the hand knitting market.

Alpaca comes from the alpaca of South America. It is durable, silky, and very lustrous. Alpaca is frequently used in sweaters, ponchos, and craft items.

Camel hair comes from two-hump camels of Mongolia, Tibet, and other areas of Asia. It is a weak fiber with a wool-like texture. Its scales are not as defined as wool, so it does not felt rapidly. Camel hair is mainly used for overcoats.

Cashgora is produced in Australia and New Zealand. The fiber comes from the breeding of cashmere and angora goats. It has characteristics similar to both cashmere and angora and is used for less expensive overcoats and suits.

Cashmere comes from the inner coat hair of an Asian Cashmere goat. It is extremely fine and is noted for its outstanding softness. Pashmina is Persian for cashmere. China is the world's leading exporter of cashmere fiber. The hair from three goats is typically needed to produce one cashmere sweater. Principal end uses include scarves, sweaters, suits, and coats for the luxury market.

Llama comes from the llama of South America. It is weaker than camel hair and alpaca, but still fairly strong. Uses include sweaters and blankets.

Mohair comes from the Angora goat, found mainly in Turkey, South Africa, and the southwestern United States. It is the strongest of the specialty animal fibers, with very good abrasion resistance. It is the most resilient natural textile fiber. It possesses little crimp and its scales are flat, resulting in a slippery, smooth hand and high luster. The fiber can be dyed bright colors and is often used in fashionable specialty clothing, luxury throws, bouclé yarns (see p. 75) and velvet fabric for furniture sold in the contract market.

Qiviut (pronounced key-vee-ute) is the under belly hair from the musk ox found in Alaska and Canada. This fiber is straight, smooth, and has hardly any scales, which make it resist shrinking and felting. It is odorless and has no lanolin. Qiviut is second to vicuña in cost and is used in overcoats.

Vicuña comes from the vicuña of South America. It is the finest and softest of all wool and specialty fibers but is also quite weak. The fiber has very fine scales with a smooth hand and high luster. It is three times warmer than wool, has almost no lanolin and is hypoallergenic. Vicuña is the rarest and most costly of the specialty fibers because attempts to domesticate the animals have not been successful. Additionally the fibers grow very slowly so shearing occurs every 3–4 years. It takes the wool of six vicuña to make a sweater. The export of vicuña in fiber form and fabric form is controlled by the Peruvian government. Because vicuña is so rare, the cost of vicuña is ten times the cost of cashmere.

Yak fiber comes from Mongolia and is a fiber traditionally used by Tibetan nomads. The fiber from the undercoat is compared to cashmere at substantially discounted prices. Shokay is a company who is promoting these fibers.

Bast Fibers

Bast fibers are those that grow in the stem section of the plant and thus are cellulosic in content. Flax is the most important of these fiber types, with hemp, jute, and ramie also having commercial importance.

Hemp is a yellowish-brown fiber from the hemp plant that grows easily and quickly in many parts of the world. Leading producers of hemp for textile applications are China, Romania, and Australia. It is a fast growing fiber requiring little or no pesticides. Land planted with hemp can yield 2½ times the production of cotton and 6 times the production of flax. This fiber resembles linen but is coarser and harsher. It is strong and lightweight and has very little elongation. Hemp was used in canvas for the early sailing ships and was later used to make the first

Levi's® jeans. Today its principal end uses are twine, rope, and cordage. Hemp has gained popularity as a specialty fiber for the apparel market as an environmental friendly "green" textile.

Jute is a yellowish-brown fiber that grows mainly in Bangladesh, India, and Pakistan. It is coarse and harsh, with good resistance to microorganisms and insects. The fiber has moderate dry strength but low wet strength. It has low elongation, which helps it retain its shape when made into items such as sacks. Jute is shorter than most bast fibers and is inexpensive to produce. It also has fair abrasion resistance. Its main end uses include burlap fabric for bagging, fabric for interior furnishings, carpet backing, and cordage.

Ramie is a white fiber that is also known as China grass. Although China is the major producer, ramie is also grown in other countries, such as the Philippines and Brazil. It is a fine, absorbent, and quick-drying fiber. It is the most resistant to mildew and rotting of all plant fibers, and it is the strongest. Ramie is slightly stiff and has high natural luster and low elongation. It is similar to flax, and its end uses include apparel for the mass market, some interior furnishings, ropes, and industrial threads.

Leaf Fibers

Leaf fibers are taken from the leaf section of a plant such as yucca, banana, pineapple and other plants with similar leaf structure. Sisal is most important of these fibers.

Sisal is a fiber taken from the yucca or cactus plants which grow in warm climates. The fiber is rough, coarse, and woody. It is primarily used for cordage for its strength, durability, and resistance to degradation from saltwater. It is also used in a natural or bleached state to produce mats, or rugs. Due to its unique structure it is also used for wall coverings.

Micron System

The International System of Units (SI) uses metric units for indicating measurements. The micron system is used to measure the diameter of fibers. A **micron** is equal to $1/1,000$ of a millimeter or $1/1,000,000$ of a meter or $1/25,400$. The symbol μm is used to indicate microns. The following table (Table 3.2) indicates the general average diameter range of specific animal and plant fibers.

TABLE 3.2	Diameters of Various Fibers		
Fiber	Diameter	Fiber	Diameter
Vicuña	8–13 μm	Yak	12–24 μm
Merino wool*	10–18 μm	Camel	17–23 μm
Silk	11–12 μm	Wool	17–40 μm
Angora rabbit	12–13 μm	Alpaca	19–29 μm
Flax	12–16 μm	Llama	20–30 μm
Cashmere**	12–17 μm	Mohair	23–40 μm
Cotton	12–20 μm	Human hair	40–80 μm

*Merino wool fibers in the 10.5 to 18.5 μm range are typically found in fine men's suiting. In the 1950s as the need for higher end men's suiting grew, the fabric was made of 18.5 μm wool to spin a 1/74 worsted yarn (see p. 77). The yarn was called a Super 70's and suits were marketed with this designation. Eventually the designation was changed to Super 100's made from that same size wool fiber. Today the coarser, 18.5 μm is used to make fabrics advertised as Super 100's. Generally a Super 120's has wool measuring 17.5 μm, Super 140's is made of 16.5 μm, Super 160's is made of 14.5 μm, Super 180's is made of 12.5 μm, and Super 200's made of 10.5 μm. The fabrics made from these ultra-fine fibers are not only extremely costly but prone to wrinkling and require expert tailoring. Some industry experts feel the "Super" reference has become overused and can misrepresent the true quality of the fabric.

**Although the fineness of cashmere can be measured in microns, the quality of cashmere fibers generally starts with the place of origin. It ranges from low quality, Iranian, to ultra fine, Inner Mongolian. The quality determines the price, which can be substantial. For this reason cashmere can be found in luxury retailers to lower priced specialty stores.

𝓜anufactured 𝓕ibers

The era of manufactured fibers began in the early 1900s with the commercial production of rayon fiber. It was helped along by the introduction of acetate, the second manufactured fiber, in 1924. Both fibers contain mostly cellulose because the technology was insufficient to produce a fully synthetic fiber entirely from chemicals.

The delay in the development of manufactured fibers was largely due to the inability to look into the structure of a fiber to see how it was constructed. Without this knowledge, scientists did not know how to go about making a manufactured fiber. With the advent of X-ray technology in the 1920s and 1930s, the obstacle was removed. The discovery was then made that the basic building blocks, or molecules, that make up a fiber are long and narrow (or fibrous) themselves. By 1938, nylon was ready to be presented to the marketplace (by E. I. DuPont™ de Nemours & Company). The development of the manufactured fibers industry is an amazing success story resulting in many consumer-recognizable advancements in textiles, such as spandex, microfibers, and products such as Gore-Tex®, and Teflon®.

The most significant advancements in the textile industry for apparel and home furnishing applications come from innovations within the textile fibers sector. Many of these advancements have been developed after careful analysis and the exploration of potential needs within the marketplace. These advancements are as innovative and provocative as the initial conception and introduction of the first commercial manufactured fiber from wood pulp over a hundred years ago or as simple as Teflon® moving from a protective covering for pots to a protective covering for pants.

Generic Names

The generic names and definitions in this section are from the Rules and Regulations of the Textile Fiber Products Identification Act (TFPIA). All manufactured fibers used for consumer articles of apparel or textile articles customarily used by the consumer in home furnishings application have been placed into the generic categories listed in this federal act. The Federal Trade Commission establishes the generic names and definitions for manufactured fibers (see Table 3.3).

To receive a new generic classification, a fiber producer must spell out how the physical properties and chemical composition radically differ from other classified fibers. The commercial use must be explained as well as its importance to the public marketplace.

TABLE 3.3 The FTC Recognizes the Following Generic Names and Generic Fiber Subclasses of Manufactured Fibers	
Acetate	Olefin
Triacetate	Lastol
Acrylic	PBI
Anidex	PLA
Aramid	Polyester
Azlon	Elasterell-p
Elastoester	Rayon
Fluoropolymer	Lyocell
Glass	Rubber
Metallic	Lastrile
Melamine	Saran
Modacrylic	Spandex/Elastane
Novoloid	Sulfar
Nylon	Vinal
Nytril	Vinyon

To meet the criteria for granting application for a new generic fiber subclass name, a fiber must have the same general chemical composition as an established category and have distinctive properties, which lead to the distinctive features that set it apart from the original recognized classification (Table 3.4). Thus, subclass designations are used when a textile fiber technically falls within a generic classification but is commercially distinguishable due to significant enhancements or differences. For example, a fiber which is a polyester but has stretch characteristics similar to spandex.

Marketing of Manufactured Fibers

Manufactured fibers are marketed as commodity fibers, as trademark fibers, as controlled trademark fibers, or under a certification mark. Each is briefly explained in the following sections.

Commodity Fibers

Fibers marketed as commodities are used without identification of source and are sold to any buyer in the open market. A shirt labeled 100 percent polyester has been made with commodity polyester fibers. This is the cheapest way to purchase manufactured fibers.

Fiber Trademarks

Manufactured fibers are often identified by trademarks. The fiber producer spends promotion money to establish a trademark and expects manufacturers, wholesalers, and retailers down the line to take advantage of it. The fiber producer receives a slightly higher price from mills than if the fiber were sold without a trademark.

A fiber **trademark** is a word or words used by a fiber supplier or producer to distinguish its fibers from fibers of the same generic class produced or sold by others. It is intended to attract the attention of potential customers, both industrial (e.g., textile mills) and consumer. Trademarks appear on product labels and promotional material.

A person or company first using the trademark in commerce usually constitutes ownership of the mark. The letters ™ accompany the mark initially. If the user elects to apply for registered ownership of the trademark with the United States Patent and Trademark Office and the application is approved, the symbol ® is used instead of the ™ to indicate registered ownership.

Companies usually promote their trademarks widely to ensure benefits by its use. The use of the mark is carefully monitored, and unauthorized use of the trademark is illegal. Such well-known registered fiber trademarks include Dacron® (polyester, INVISTA™), Anso® (nylon, Honeywell Nylon, Inc.), and Modal® (rayon, Lenzing Fibers). See specific fibers for additional trademark names.

Recently, there has been a shift in ownership for fiber trademark names. Well-known producers such as DuPont™ have strategically moved closer to the chemical business and entrusted much of their brand recognition to INVISTA™ Inc. Additionally, chemical companies are creating partnerships with commodity producers such as Cargill Inc. to develop new markets. It is expected that these changes and alliances will continue to create new companies and opportunities for the global textile industry.

Controlled Trademarks

The controlled-trademark approach enables the fiber maker to rigidly control the selling and subsequent use of the fiber. Relationships are established with specific textile mills and fabric users that will use the fiber properly. A quality control program of the fiber producer

Fiber	Durability		Comfort	Appearance	
	Abrasion Resistance	Strength	Absorbency	Resiliency	Pilling Resistance
Cellulosic					
Acetate	Poor	Poor	Fair	Good	Good
Viscose rayon	Fair	Fair	Excellent	Poor	Good
Lyocell	Fair	Excellent	Excellent	Fair	Good
Non-Cellulosic					
Acrylic	Fair	Fair	Poor	Good	Fair
Nylon	Excellent	Excellent	Poor	Excellent	Poor
Olefin	Excellent	Excellent	Very poor	Excellent	Good
Polyester	Excellent	Excellent	Poor	Excellent	Very poor

TABLE 3.4 Comparison Chart of the Most Commonly Used Manufactured Fibers

ensures that only products that have satisfactorily passed various tests related to the end use are allowed to use the fiber brand name. Unfortunately, consumers are usually unable to distinguish between a controlled trademark fiber and an uncontrolled trademark fiber.

Certification Marks

Various fiber producers, such as INVISTA™ (formerly E. I. DuPont™ de Nemours & Company), also have certification programs. The following is an explanation from INVISTA™ promotional material:

> Certification marks are marks licensed by INVISTA™ for use by manufacturers of products in which a INVISTA™ fiber or other material is used and which meet specified performance quality standards. It is important to distinguish between trademarks and certification marks. Trademarks appear on products made by INVISTA™. Certification marks, on the other hand, may not be used on products made by INVISTA™, for, under U.S. trademark law, a mark may not be a trademark and a certification mark at the same time.

Thus INVISTA™ uses two types of marks: the trademark that identifies its fibers, such as Dacron® polyester, and the certification mark that identifies a product not made by INVISTA™ but that contains its fibers. An example of the latter is Thermolite® which is used for thermal underwear made of a special INVISTA™ fiber (see Figure 3.6) and that meets specified performance quality standards. (It is a hollow polyester fiber that provides thermal insulation, wicking of perspiration away from the body, and softness.) Both marks are registered to INVISTA™ and, therefore, cannot be used by other companies.

Descriptions of Principal Manufactured Fibers

The following sections present the properties and characteristics of each principal generic category of manufactured fibers. The generic names and definitions in this section are from the Rules and Regulations of the TFPIA.

Acetate

The first commercial production of **acetate** fiber in the United States was in 1924 by the Celanese Corporation. In 1952 the Federal Trade Commission made acetate a generic category, separating it from the rayon fiber family.

Acetate is a manufactured fiber in which the fiber-forming substance is cellulose acetate. It has a round shape with striations on the surface.

Properties

Favorable Acetate is a medium-weight fiber with excellent drape and a luxurious hand. It has fair resiliency and fair absorbency (6½ percent moisture regain). It has no pilling problem and very little static problem, and it is inexpensive.

Unfavorable Acetate has poor strength; it becomes about 30 percent weaker when wet, but recovers original strength when dried. It has poor abrasion resistance and poor elasticity. It should be dry cleaned or carefully laundered. Washing by machine should be avoided because the wet strength of acetate is very low, and the garment may be damaged. Hot water and dryers cause significant loss of strength at about 195°F ≈ 90°C. Thus casual creases may become permanent or excessive shrinkage may occur from the heat. Acetate is also subject to gas fading from pollutant gases in the air that tend to easily fade or change the color of fabric. (See p. 297.) This can be a problem particularly for deep blue and navy lining material, which can change to purple and then red from exposure.

End Uses

The principal end uses for this fiber include lining fabric, lingerie, graduation gowns, ribbons, backing fabric for bonded materials, and cigarette-filter material.

Producers and Trademarks

Celanese: Celanese®

Eastman Chemical Co.: Estron®, Chromspun® (solution dyed)

Acrylic

The first commercial production of **acrylic** fiber in the United States was in 1950 by E. I. DuPont™ de Nemours & Company. The fiber soon began to replace wool, initially in sweaters and blankets and then later in other items. Consumers responded well to acrylic because it was less expensive than wool and washable.

Acrylic is a manufactured fiber in which the fiber-forming substance is any long-chain synthetic polymer composed of at least 85 percent by weight of acrylonitrile units. Acrylic has a round shape with a smooth surface.

Properties

Favorable Acrylic is a lightweight fiber with good drape. It creates fabrics that are warm yet lightweight. It

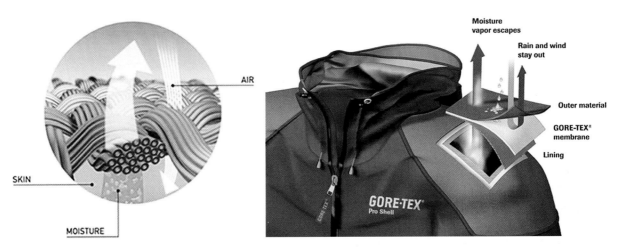

FIGURE 3.6
Thermolite® is an INVISTA™ certification mark for thermal wear fabric of hollow-core polyester fiber meeting its quality standards and results in a more thermally efficient Thermolite® fabric (© INVISTA™); Gore-tex® garments combine fashion and practicality.

has good resiliency and elasticity and has excellent resistance to sunlight and weathering. It may be washed or dry cleaned.

Unfavorable Acrylic has only fair strength; it becomes about 20 percent weaker when wet, but recovers when dry. It is a hydrophobic fiber (1½ percent moisture regain), and static and pilling are frequent problems. Its abrasion resistance is fair.

End Uses
The principal end uses for this fiber include sweaters, blankets, carpeting, children's garments, and outdoor products, such as awnings, market umbrellas, and tents.

Producers and Trademarks
GmbH Co.: Dralon®

Mitsubishi Rayon Textile Co.: Silpalon®

Lyocell
The Federal Trade Commission approved the **lyocell** generic fiber name as a subclass under Rayon in 1996. The fiber was developed by Courtaulds Fibers Ltd. (Great Britain) and took ten years and $100 million to produce.

Lyocell is a manufactured fiber composed of solvent-spun cellulose. The self-contained solvent-spun process used to produce this fiber creates less water and air pollution. The fiber has a round cross-section with a smooth surface.

The process used to produce lyocell has less negative impact on the environment than the process used to produce rayon because a different spinning technique is used. Difficulties relating to environmental standards for air and water pollution have become a concern for most producers in the textile industry.

Properties

Favorable   Lyocell is stronger than all other cellulosic fibers and has less shrinkage. It is launderable with an 11.5 percent moisture regain and is stronger when wet. It is noted for creating fabrics with great luster, soft hand, and good drape.

Unfavorable   Fabric wear and tear may cause the fibers to splinter on the surface. This may result in fuzziness and pilling over the life of the product. Color changes can occur, as well as changes in hand from splintering. It can be washed or dry cleaned, but laundry agitation can accelerate surface change. It is also vulnerable to mildew and some insects.

End Uses

End uses for this fiber include dress slacks, blouses, pajamas, shirts, and dresses.

Producers and Trademarks

Lenzing Fibers: Tencel®

Nylon

The first commercial production of **nylon** fiber in the United States was in 1939 by the E. I. DuPont™ de Nemours & Company. It is the second-most-used manufactured fiber in the United States, behind polyester. The two major types of nylon today are nylon 6, 6 and nylon 6.

Nylon is a manufactured fiber in which the fiber-forming substance is a long-chain synthetic polyamide in which fewer than 85 percent of the amide linkages are attached directly to two aromatic rings. The fiber has a rodlike shape with a smooth surface.

Properties

Favorable   Nylon is a lightweight fiber with excellent strength and abrasion resistance. It is about 10 percent weaker when wet. It has very good elasticity, good resiliency, and good drape. It can be washed or dry cleaned.

Unfavorable   Nylon is a hydrophobic fiber (4½ percent moisture regain). Static and pilling are problems. It has poor resistance to prolonged and continuous exposure to sunlight, thus usually making this fiber unsatisfactory for use in draperies or outdoor furniture (unless modified to improve its resistance).

End Uses

The end uses include a wide range of products in the apparel, interior furnishings, and industrial areas (for example, lingerie, swimwear, exercise wear, hosiery, jackets, bedspreads, carpets, upholstery, tents, fish nets, sleeping bags, rope, parachutes, and luggage). (See Figure 3.7.)

Producers and Trademarks

The following is only a partial list of nylon producers and trademarks:

Honeywell Nylon, Inc.: Anso®, Caprolan®

INVISTA™: Antron® (trilobal), Supplex®, TACTEL®

Nylstar, Inc.: Meryl®

Olefin

The first commercial production of an **olefin** fiber in the United States in a textile-grade multifilament form was in 1961. It was a polypropylene type. A polyethylene-type olefin fiber followed and today both are commercially produced.

Olefin is a manufactured fiber in which the fiber-forming substance is any long-chain synthetic polymer composed at least 85 percent by weight of

FIGURE 3.7
One of the wide range of textile products made of nylon is luggage, such as these T-Tech hydro bags.

ethylene, propylene, or other olefin units, except amorphous (noncrystalline) polyolefins that qualify as a rubber fiber. The fiber has a rodlike shape with a smooth surface.

Properties

Favorable Olefin is a very lightweight fiber. It has very good strength and abrasion resistance. This fiber also has excellent sunlight resistance and weatherability. Olefin is almost completely hydrophobic (less than 0.1 percent moisture regain). Spills and staining liquids can be readily wiped up, making for favorable use of this fiber in indoor/outdoor carpeting, bathroom and kitchen floor covering, and upholstery. Olefin can be washed and dry cleaned. Although this fiber is hydrophobic, it possesses excellent wicking action when very thin. It also has excellent resiliency.

Unfavorable The almost completely hydrophobic nature of this fiber makes it unfavorable for most clothing. Blended with other fibers, its hydrophobic nature and excellent wicking action make olefin a practical component of fabrics used for running clothes and other high-performance applications. Static occurs and pilling is a problem at times. Ironing, machine laundering, and machine drying must be done at low temperatures (about 150°F ≈ 65°C) because the fiber has a very low softening point.

End Uses

Important end uses are running and cycling clothing along with apparel for diving and surfing because of its excellent wicking action. Significant uses are nonwovens (see p. 140) and carpet face yarns. The fiber is also used in upholstery, auditorium seating, industrial fabrics (e.g., filter cloth, bagging, cordage), and geotextiles.

Producers and Trademarks

The following is only a partial list of olefin producers and trademarks:

American Fibers and Yarns Co.: Essera® (polypropylene)

Hercules, Inc.: Herculon® (polypropylene)

Honeywell, Inc.: Spectra® (polyethylene)

Lastol

Lastol is an olefin fiber with a cross-linked polymer network. The first production of a lastol fiber was in 2000 by The Dow Chemical Co. The Federal Trade Commission approved lastol as a subclass for olefin in January 2003.

Properties

Favorable Lastol is lightweight with excellent resistance to chemicals. It is extremely resistant to acids, alkalies, enzymes, and oxidizing agents. It is highly resistant to ultraviolet light and high temperatures during processing. Lastol has stretch and recovery properties.

Unfavorable Lastol has less elongation than spandex. It is not suitable for high compression end uses as required in support hose.

End Uses

The principle end use is in applications that require stretch, such as denim, swimwear, intimate apparel, and active wear.

Producers and Trademarks

Dow Chemical Co.: DOW XLA™ Fiber

PLA

PLA is a new generic fiber classification approved by the Federal Trade Commission in February 2002. It is a manufactured fiber in which the fiber forming substance is composed of at least 85 percent by weight of lactic acid ester units derived from naturally occurring sugars. The polylactic acid, or polylactate, comes from sugars found in corn or sugar beets. Cargill Inc. applied for this new classification for their NatureWorks™ fiber. Cargill Inc. developed a way to capture the carbon that plants use during photosynthesis. The carbon and natural sugars found in the plants are used to make a polymer called polylacide (PLA). Cargill Inc. believes a fiber based on annually renewable agricultural crops offers environmental soundness missing in the marketplace.

Properties

PLA has excellent resiliency, outstanding crimp retention, and good wicking ability. It offers good thermal insulation, breathability, high UV protection, and has excellent hand and drape. It is made from a renewable resource which is biodegradable.

End Uses

It is found in the marketplace in pillows, comforters, and mattress pads, and is suitable for performance active wear and fashion apparel, outdoor furniture, wipes, and disposables.

Producers and Trademarks

Cargill Inc.: NatureWorks LLC™: Ingeo™
DuPont™: Sorona®

Polyester

The first commercial production of **polyester** fiber in the United States was in 1953 by E. I. DuPont™ de Nemours & Company. It is the most used manufactured fiber in the United States.

Polyester is a manufactured fiber in which the fiber-forming substance is any long-chain synthetic polymer composed of at least 85 percent by weight of an ester of a substituted aromatic carboxylic acid, including, but not limited to, substituted terephthalate units and parasubstituted hydroxy-benzoate units. The fiber has a rodlike shape with a smooth surface.

Properties

Favorable   Polyester is a medium-weight fiber with very good strength and abrasion resistance. It can be washed and dry cleaned. The fiber has excellent resiliency and is the best wash-and-wear fiber. It also possesses good elasticity.

Unfavorable   Polyester is almost completely hydrophobic (0.4 percent moisture regain). It is difficult to get water and detergent into the fiber to remove stains. Visa® finish helps release soil from polyester fibers (see p. 197). Static and pilling are also major problems. In addition, polyester is oleophilic (absorbs oil easily).

End Uses

The end uses include a wide range of products in the apparel, interior furnishings, and industrial areas. Suits, skirts, career apparel, performance fabrics, curtains, carpeting, sails, tire cord, fiberfill used to stuff pillows, and comforter threads are some examples of its uses (see Figure 3.8).

Producers and Trademarks

The following is only a partial list of polyester producers and trademarks:

Foss Manufacturing Co., LLC: Eco-fi™ (Formerly EcoSpun®)

INVISTA™: Dacron®, COOLMAX®, ESP®, Polargard®

Unifi: Repreve® (post-consumer polyester)

Wellman, Inc.: Fortrel®

Elasterell-p

The Federal Trade Commission approved a new subclass of polyester called **elasterell-p** in November 2002. This fiber consists of two substantially different forms of polyester that offers significant stretch and recovery. It is a bicomponent fiber (see p. 58). Given the unique structure and characteristics of this fiber, the existing generic name (polyester) would not be suitable. It exhibits low shrinkage, excellent shape retention, and is chlorine resistant. It is utilized in products that require low to moderate stretch such as stretch denim, shirt fabric, and socks. INVISTA™ will market this as a new class of fiber under the Lycra® umbrella to offer brand recognition from a variety of sources.

Producers and Trademarks

INVISTA™: Lycra®

Rayon

The first commercial production of **rayon** fiber in the United States was in 1910 by the American Viscose Company. It was the first manufactured fiber. Because it is largely cellulose in content, it greatly resembles cotton in its chemical properties.

By using different chemicals and manufacturing techniques, two basic types of rayon were developed: viscose rayon and cuprammonium rayon. Cuprammonium rayon, called "cupro", and viscose rayon have nearly identical

FIGURE 3.8
Recycled polyester skiwear at Pyua.

physical and chemical properties. Cupro, however, can be produced in much finer (thinner) filaments than viscose, which may then translate to finer, sheerer and/or to softer, more drapable fabrics than can be achieved with viscose. Fabrics of cupro are most frequently used in higher-priced lines (cupro is more expensive than viscose) for coat linings and sheer, lightweight dresses.

Rayon is a manufactured fiber composed of regenerated cellulose, as well as manufactured fibers composed of regenerated cellulose in which substituents have replaced not more than 15 percent of the hydrogens of the hydroxyl groups. Because it is a cellulosic fiber, it shares many of the same properties as other cellulosic fibers, such as cotton and flax. The fiber has a serrated, round shape.

Properties

Favorable Viscose rayon is a medium-weight fiber with fair to good strength and abrasion resistance. It is hydrophilic (11 percent moisture regain). The fiber is washable under proper care conditions and is dry cleanable. There are no static or pilling problems, and it is also inexpensive.

Unfavorable Viscose rayon loses 30 to 50 percent of its strength when wet, thus requiring great caution in laundering. It recovers strength when dry. (The modified type of rayon, HWM rayon [see the next section], does not require this caution.) Rayon has very poor elasticity and resiliency. It also shrinks appreciably from washing and is attacked by mildew and silverfish.

End Uses

The end uses for viscose rayon include a wide range of products in the apparel, interior furnishings, and industrial areas (for example, dresses, shirts, lingerie, jackets, draperies, medical products, nonwoven fabrics, hygiene products).

Producers and Trademarks

Acordis Fibers Ltd.: Galaxy® Rayon

Bemberg SpA.: Bemberg™

Lenzing Fibers: Lenzing Viscose®

HWM Rayon

A variation of rayon is classified as **HWM (high wet modulus) rayon,** or high-performance rayon. HWM rayon was developed in 1951 in Japan and is also referred to as polynosic rayon. This type of rayon is completely launderable. Although it loses strength when wet, its wet strength is significantly higher than that of regular viscose rayon. In addition, this type of rayon can be shrink-resistant when treated by compressive shrinkage methods (see p. 195). It can also be mercerized (see p. 190). The hand of HWM rayons is similar to that of high-quality cotton.

Producers and Trademarks

Lenzing Fibers: Lenzing Modal®

Spandex

The first commercial production of **spandex** fiber in the United States was in 1959 by E. I. DuPont™ de Nemours & Company. It is an elastomeric manufactured fiber (able to stretch at least 100 percent and snap back like natural rubber). Spandex is used in filament form exclusively because elastomeric properties are available only in filament form. Elastane is the generic fiber name used outside the United States and Canada.

Spandex is a manufactured fiber in which the fiber-forming substance is a long-chain synthetic polymer composed of at least 85 percent of a segmented polyurethane. The fiber is extruded as a monofilament or in many very fine filaments that immediately fuse together to form a monofilament.

Properties

Favorable Spandex is a lightweight fiber with excellent stretch and recovery properties (over 500 percent elongation) and good durability. It can be washed or dry cleaned, although chlorine bleach causes yellowing of the fiber. There are no pilling or static problems.

Unfavorable Spandex has poor strength, but this is not critical because it has so much stretch. It is a hydrophobic fiber (1 percent moisture regain). White spandex becomes yellowed from prolonged exposure to air. This is not a problem, however, in covered yarns or in dyed spandex, in which the yellowing effect is masked. Ironing should be done quickly, with a low-temperature setting. Spandex is an expensive fiber; however, as little as 1 percent is needed in fabric to achieve desirable stretch.

End Uses

The principal end uses include denim, undergarment, support products, ski pants, swimwear (Figure 3.9), athletic apparel, and other articles where stretch is required.

Producers and Trademarks

INVISTA™: Lycra®, XFIT Lycra®

RadiciSpandex Corp.: Glospan®

Asahi Kasei Fibers: Dorlastan®

Hyosung Corp.: Creora®

FIGURE 3.9
The additional spandex in this swimsuit offers a competitive edge to the wearer.

Properties of Major Textile Fibers

Textile fibers are categorized into three broad types: natural, manufactured cellulosic, and manufactured noncellulosic. Each exhibits different properties and is used in a variety of applications depending on the desired properties requried of the finished goods. Table 3.5 highlights the fibers and specific properties.

Microfibers

Microfibers, also called microdenier fibers, are manufactured fibers that are much finer (thinner) than normal fibers. The fibers that may be produced as microfibers are acrylic, nylon, polyester, lyocell, and rayon.

The microfiber was invented in Japan in the early 1980s. The first such fiber was made of polyester. It was next produced in Europe by Hoechst A.G. of Germany in 1986, and finally in the United States by DuPont™ in 1990. In 1991, DuPont™ and BASF began producing a nylon microfiber, and American Cyanamid Corporation began to make an acrylic microfiber in the United States. Courtaulds Fibers and BASF were first to produce a rayon microfiber in the United States.

There are two major processes used to produce microdenier fibers. The first is to extrude very fine filaments from the spinnerette and then further reduce the fiber size by drawing the yarn. The second method is to produce filament fibers of two different polymers. After the fabric is made, the fibers are made to split apart into much finer filaments through a finishing process (see Figure 3.10).

Properties

The physical and chemical properties of a fiber in microdenier form are not different from those of the same fiber in normal thickness. However, many important characteristics are improved in microfiber form. The hand becomes softer, the drape becomes more fluid, and the wicking effect is greatly improved. Also, fabrics made with microfibers produce more vivid color contrasts in the print design (when printed) because there are more fibers per unit of surface area.

Microfibers can be used in blends, with wool, cotton, or other manufactured fibers. Using microfibers alone or as a large percentage in a blend creates a silklike fabric. When used in smaller percentages in a blend, microfiber provides a softer hand and better drape. Blends with wool are very effective because the result is a wool fabric that

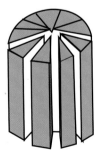

FIGURE 3.10
A filament fiber composed of two incompatible polymers is extruded from the spinnerette and then separated into microfibers.

TABLE 3.5 Properties of Major Textile Fibers

Properties	Natural				Manufactured Cellulosic			Manufactured Noncellulosic					
	Cotton	Flax	Wool	Silk	Acetate	Lyocell	Viscose Rayon	Acrylic	Glass	Nylon	Olefin	Polyester	Spandex
Abrasion resistance	Good	Fair	Fair	Fair	Poor	Fair	Fair	Fair	Poor	Excel.	Excel.	Good	Good
Absorbency (% M.R.)	8.5%	12%	13.5%	11%	6.5%	11.5%	11%	1.5%	0%	2.8–4.8%	0.01–0.1%	0.4%	1%
Flexibility	Fair	Poor	Good	Excel.	Excel.	Fair	Good	Good	Poor	Good	Fair (when thin)	Fair	Good
Elasticity @ 70 F., 65% R.H.													
% elongation at break	3–10	3	20–40	20	25–45	13–15	15–30	35–45	3–4	16–75	30–100	19–55	400–700
% recovery	75	65	99	90	48–65	—	95	92	100	82–100	96	81	99
from % strain	2	2	2	3	4	—	2	3	3	3	5	3	50
Environment													
Mildew resistance	Poor	Fair	Good	Good	Excel.	Fair	Fair	Excel.	Excel.	Excel.	Excel.	Excel.	Excel.
Renovation (wash or dry clean)	W or DC	W or DC	DC	W or DC	DC	W or DC	W or DC	W or DC	W-hand	W or DC	W or DC	W or DC	W or DC
Safe iron limit (°F°)	400	450	300	300	325	400	350	300	—	350	250	325	300
Sunlight resistance	Fair	Good	Good	Poor	Good	Good	Fair	Excel.	Excel.	Poor	Good	Good	Fair
Hand	Good	Fair	Fair-Excel.	Excel.	Excel.	Excel.	Good	Good	Poor	Fair	Fair	Fair	Poor
Pilling resistance	Good	Good	Fair	Good	Good	Good	Good	Fair	Excel.	Poor	Good	Very poor	Excel.
Resiliency	Poor	Poor	Good	Fair	Fair	Good	Poor	Good	Excel.	Good	Excel.	Excel.	Excel.
Specific gravity	1.54	1.52	1.32	1.30	1.32	1.56	1.48–1.54	1.14–1.19	2.54	1.14	.91	1.38	1.21
Static resistance	Good	Good	Fair	Fair	Fair	Good	Good	Poor	Excel.	Poor	Good	Very poor	Excel.
Strength dry (grams/denier)	3.0–5.0	3.5–6.0	0.8–2.0	2.4–5.0	1.2–1.5	4.5–5.0	1.2–3.0	2.0–3.5	9.5	2.5–7.3	2.5–5.5	3.0–6.0	.07–1.1
Strength loss when wet (approx. %)	+10%	+10%	20%	15%	30%	11%	30–50%[b]	20%	0	10	0	0	0
Thermoplastic	No	No	No	No	Yes	No	No	Yes	Yes	Yes	Yes	Yes	Yes

a. Compensated by high fiber stretch.

b. HWM (high wet modulus) rayon has much higher wet strength than viscose rayon.

feels and looks like a better-quality, more expensive wool fabric (softer, better drape, and increased durability).

Although microfibers can be used to make many fabric types such as velvet, chiffon, brocade, and gabardine, there are various drawbacks in using these fibers. Microfibers are much more costly than the regular generic manufactured fibers. The weaving costs of fabrics with microfibers are higher (slower weaving speeds), as are the dyeing costs (much more dye is required to produce a color due to the increase of surface area).

The impact of microfibers in the marketplace is across the board. From luxury applications to mass markets, microfibers can be found in almost every application in which manufactured fibers are utilized.

End Uses

Microfibers have a significant presence in a broad range of end uses, including blouses, slacks, tailored suits, lingerie, dresses, raincoats, upholstery, sheeting, running clothes, undergarments, nonwovens, and industrial products.

Producers and Trademarks

The following is only a partial list of microfiber producers and trademarks:

Acetate:
  Celanese: MicroSafe®

Nylon:
  INVISTA™: Supplex® Micro
  Honeywell Nylon Inc.: Silky Touch®

Polyester:
  Wellman, Inc.: Fortrel MicroSpun®
  KoSa: Microtherm®

Rayon:
  Lenzing: Micro Modal®

Nanotechnology

Microfibers come from the first generation of technology in the 1980s that produced extremely fine filaments. Microfibers are filaments that measure less than 1 denier per filament. The term denier becomes impracticable when referring to a fiber finer than 1 denier. When fiber diameter is less than 1 denier it is measured in microns. A 1-denier fiber has the diameter of approximately 10 microns. The term nanometer is used when the fiber is finer than 0.5 of a micron. A nanometer is one billionth of a meter or 10^{-9}. A single grain of sand is about 100,000 nanometers. Thus, microtechnology has led to **nanotechnology.** (See Figure 3.11.)

Nanotechnology is the ability to manipulate individual atoms to significantly enhance products. The ability to utilize polymer chemistry and molecular engineering on a nano scale has made a huge impact on the textile industry. Many advanced performance characteristics are used in fabrics created for major manufacturers and sold at Eddie Bauer, Lands' End, Gap, Old Navy, Brooks Brothers, and Lee Jeans. Since these enhancements are done in nano size the fabric preserves its original hand and comfort. NANO-TEX™, Inc. is a company that

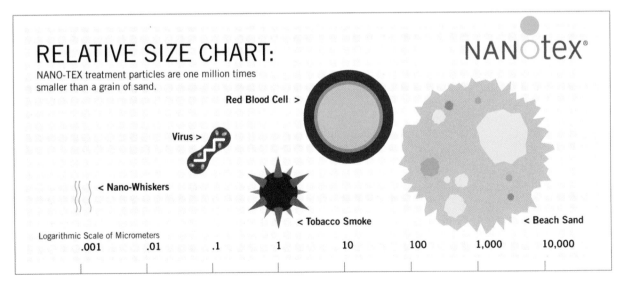

FIGURE 3.11
NANO-TEX Inc. treatment particles are one million times smaller than a grain of sand.

licensees its innovation to textile makers and manufacturers. NANO-TEX™, Inc. has developed technologies which improve fabric performance. These improvements include the following enhancements:

▶ provides water and oil repellency and wrinkle resistance to fabrics of cotton fibers

▶ provides advanced moisture control for greater comfort for fabrics of manufactured fibers

▶ provides water and oil repellency for fabrics of a range of fibers types

▶ provides antimicrobial property

▶ provides filtration applications (chemical, biological and radioactive)

Nanoparticles (molecular size or smaller) can be embedded in liquid polymers used to make manufactured fibers. Nanoparticles can be applied to the fiber surface in finishing, providing various beneficial properties. Nanoparticles are used as fillers to improve strength, dimensional stability, flame retardancy, ultraviolet protection, and process ability. They can provide antimicrobial properties, odor control, and insect repellency. The particles are permanently attached.

Most nano-fibers are produced by an electro-spinning process. The liquid polymer is charged with a current, then extruded through the spinnerette, and finally collected. By changing the process of extrusion, nanofibers can be made with different diameters. Very fine nanofibers are referred to as nanowhiskers.

Islands-in-the-sea is a special type of fiber. Two different polymers are combined, producing fibrils (islands) in a matrix (sea) fiber. When the polymer of the matrix is dissolved, a very thin fiber remains. Micro- and nano-fibers can be produced in this manner.

Nano Innovation

Many new applications of technology have been identified and some are being developed in laboratories. The following list of applications has potential market relevance:

▶ fabric that can purify toxic gas

▶ fabric that can change color when exposed to toxic gas or allergens

▶ dye embedded in the fiber on a nanoscale which can change color

▶ fibers that use the heat of the sun to generate energy to cool or heat the wearer

▶ fabric with communication capabilities

▶ fabric that can monitor the wearer's heath and transmit it

Secondary Manufactured Fibers for Consumer Use

This section presents the properties and characteristics of generic categories of the secondary manufactured fibers for consumer use. These fibers are more specialized than the principal manufactured fibers and are used in apparel or products for the home. The generic names and definitions in this section are from the Rules and Regulations of the TFPIA.

Bamboo

Bamboo is a regenerated fiber from bamboo pulp, made in a process similar to rayon. This fiber provides a soft hand with great luster. It has a 13 percent moisture regain, very good wicking, and elasticity (almost 20 percent). Bamboo colors easily with less dye needed. It is antimicrobial, blocks ultraviolet rays, and naturally neutralizes odors. Bamboo has a problem with abrasion resistance and is often blended with cotton, polyester, and Micro Modal® HWM rayon. The bamboo plant is known for quick growth, estimated to be a third faster than any other plant. It requires no pesticides and absorbs carbon dioxide at five times the rate of most trees. Almost all bamboo comes from China. It is used for towels, robes, mats, socks, underwear, T-shirts, and baby garments.

Glass

The first commercial production of **glass** fiber in the United States was in 1936 by the Owens-Corning Fiberglas Corporation.

Glass is a manufactured fiber in which the fiber-forming substance is glass. The fiber has a round, rodlike shape with a very smooth surface.

Properties
Favorable   Glass has excellent strength. It is a stiff fiber and requires no ironing. It suffers no effect from exposure to sunlight, even over extended periods, which makes glass an excellent fiber for curtains and drapes. Also, glass does not burn, but it melts at 1500°F ≈ 815°C.

Unfavorable   Glass is a heavy fiber with poor drapability. Its abrasion resistance is extremely poor, which makes it unusable for clothing or other items that involve significant movement of fibers or fabric. Additionally, the glass fragments would cause skin abrasion on a person who came in direct contact with it. Therefore, it is not used for clothing or carpet. It has very poor elasticity and also has a poor hand. Glass is completely hydrophobic, not absorbing any moisture. It should not be laundered in a washing machine because its poor flexing property causes the fiber to crack or break.

End Uses

The principal end uses of this fiber include draperies, electrical and thermal insulation, tires, and optical fiber for communication, electronic, and medical equipment.

Producers and Trademarks

The following is only a partial list of glass producers and trademarks:

Owens-Corning Fiberglas®

PPG Industries, Inc.: PPG™

Metallic

The earliest **metallic** fibers were strips of real gold and silver. These can be seen in ancient saris, carpets, and tapestries. Later, less expensive metals such as steel, copper, and aluminum were used. The first commercial production of metallic fiber in the United States was in 1946.

Metallic fibers are now commonly made by laminating, using a roll of aluminum foil and two rolls of transparent plastic film, which are joined together with the aluminum foil sandwiched between the two sheets of plastic. An adhesive binds the three layers together. Sometimes, instead of two sheets of plastic, a resin coating is used to protect both sides of the aluminum foil or metallized plastic film. Color can be added (e.g., gold, silver, blue) by applying pigments on the foil or in the adhesive or lacquer coating. The roll is then cut into narrow strips to form a length of metallic yarn equal to the length of the roll.

Metallic is a manufactured fiber composed of metal, plastic-coated metal, metal-coated plastic, or a core completely covered by metal. The width of the metallic yarn can be measured in millimeters and the thickness in microns. Metallic film can be made of an iridescent plastic that has been dyed with fluorescent dyes to create new looks and markets.

Properties

Metallic fibers are used primarily for decorative effects, although when placed in carpeting (as little as 2 percent) the functional effect is to lessen the accumulation of static. These fibers (not completely metal) do not tarnish or cut adjacent yarns. They can be ironed at low temperatures and can also be washed and dry cleaned. Metallic fibers increase fabric stiffness.

End Uses

Metallic fibers are used in a wide variety of items, including draperies, tablecloths, dresses (Figure 3.12), sweaters, swimwear, shoes, accessories, ribbons, and carpet.

FIGURE 3.12
A dress with metallic fibers.

Producers and Trademarks

The following is only a partial list of metallic fiber producers and trademarks:

Lurex Co. Ltd.: Lurex®

Meadowbrook Inventions: Angelina®

Modacrylic

The first commercial production of **modacrylic** fiber was in 1949 by the Union Carbide Corporation in the United States. The word modacrylic comes from the term *modified acrylic.*

Modacrylic is a manufactured fiber in which the fiber-forming substance is any long-chain synthetic polymer composed of fewer than 85 percent but at least 35 percent by weight of acrylonitrile units. The fiber has a circular shape with a smooth surface.

Properties

Favorable Modacrylic is a medium-weight fiber with fair strength and abrasion resistance but good elasticity and resiliency. It has good drape and is highly resistant to sunlight. It may be washed or dry cleaned. This fiber has excellent resistance to chemicals and flame. It has fair resistance to pilling and little static problem.

Unfavorable   Modacrylic is hydrophobic (0.4 to 3 percent moisture regain). It can be ironed, but only at a low temperature (about 225°F (107°C or less).

End Uses
The principal end uses include fake-fur fabrics, wigs, children's sleepwear, fleece fabric for stuffed animals, upholstery, and drapery and industrial fabrics. (See Figure 3.13).

Producers and Trademarks
Kaneka Corp.: Kanecaron®

Triacetate

The first commercial production of **triacetate** fiber in the United States was in 1954 by the Hoechst Celanese Corporation. It is a subclass of acetate.

Production of this fiber was discontinued in the United States in 1986 because of its limited market and high cost relative to other manufactured fibers. It is still being produced in Europe.

Triacetate is a manufactured fiber in which the fiber-forming substance is cellulose acetate, not less than 92 percent of the hydroxyl groups being acetylated. The fiber has a lobular, round shape with a smooth surface.

Properties
Favorable   Triacetate is a medium-weight fiber with a luxurious hand and excellent drape. It has good resiliency and excellent pleat and crease retention when heat-set. The fiber may be washed and dry cleaned. There is no pilling problem and only occasionally a static problem.

Unfavorable   Like acetate, triacetate also has poor strength, becoming about 30 percent weaker when wet but regaining its original strength when dry. It is hydrophobic (3½ percent moisture regain). It also has poor abrasion resistance and poor elasticity.

End Uses
The principal use for this fiber is various forms of apparel in which good pleat or crease retention is needed (e.g., pleated dresses and skirts) as well as in knitted sleepwear and robes.

Secondary Manufactured Fibers for Industrial Applications

This section presents the properties and characteristics of generic categories of the secondary manufactured fibers for industrial applications. These fibers are not typically recognized by the consumer but may have significant industrial applications in various markets. Others are referenced to complete the generic fiber classification recognized by the TFPIA.

Anidex

The first commercial production of **anidex** fiber in the United States was in 1970 by the Rohm & Haas Company.

Anidex is a manufactured fiber in which the fiber-forming substance is any long-chain synthetic polymer composed of at least 50 percent by weight of one or more esters of a monohydric alcohol and acrylic acid. Commercial manufacture of this fiber was discontinued.

Aramid

The **aramid** generic fiber name became effective January 1974. The first commercial production of this fiber was by E. I. DuPont™ de Nemours & Company.

Aramid is a manufactured fiber. The fiber-forming substance is a long-chain synthetic polyamide in which

FIGURE 3.13
These slippers are lined with modacrylic fibers.

at least 85 percent of the amide linkages are attached directly to two aromatic rings.

Properties

The unique properties of aramid fibers include high levels of tensile strength, abrasion resistance, stretch resistance, toughness, and heat resistance. Aramid does not melt; it chars and degrades above 700°F ≈ 371°C. It has a 5½ percent moisture regain.

End Uses

The end uses for this fiber include heat-protective clothing, cables, tires, combat helmets, and ballistic protective vests. Its use in protective clothing for racecar drivers, as well as pit crews, military pilots, combat vehicle crews, and others.

Producers and Trademarks

DuPont™: Kevlar® and Nomex®

Azlon

Azlon is a manufactured fiber composed of regenerated, naturally occurring proteins found in nature, such as peanuts, corn and soybeans. SOYSILK® is a trademark name of an Azlon fiber made from soybeans. It is marketed as part of a new class of green textiles with many applications, including batting and the stuffing of pillows.

Lastrile

Lastrile is a manufactured fiber in which the fiber-forming substance is a copolymer of acrylonitrile and a diene (such as butadiene) composed of not more than 50 percent but at least 10 percent by weight of acrylonitrile units. It is a subclass of rubber.

Lastrile fibers have never been commercially produced.

Melamine

Melamine is a manufactured fiber of a synthetic polymer composed of 50 percent or more cross-linked melamine polymer. This fiber is not thermoplastic, but instead stays in the same configuration once set. This is known as thermosetting, which means once the fiber is set, it cannot be changed. Melamine has very high heat resistance and does not degrade from exposure to chemicals.

End Uses

End uses include airplane seating, fire blocks, protective clothing, and heat resistant gloves.

Producers and Trademarks

BASF Corp.: Basofil®

Novoloid

The novoloid generic fiber name became effective February 1974. Although this fiber is no longer being produced in the United States, it is being imported and used.

Novoloid is a manufactured fiber containing at least 85 percent by weight of a cross-linked novolac.

Properties

Its most unique properties are excellent flame and chemical resistance.

End Uses

End uses for this fiber include protective apparel for fire fighters, liners in aircraft seats, and fire-protection curtains.

Producers and Trademarks

American Kynol, Inc. (distributor): Kynol™

Nytril

Nytril is a manufactured fiber containing at least 85 percent of a long-chain polymer of vinylidene dinitrile in which the vinylidene dinitrile content is no less than every other unit in the polymer chain.

Production of this fiber has been discontinued in the United States.

PBI

The PBI generic fiber name became effective in June 1986. The first commercial production of this fiber was by Hoechst Celanese Corporation.

PBI is a manufactured fiber in which the fiber-forming substance is a long-chain aromatic polymer having recurring imidazole groups as an integral part of the polymer chain.

Properties

Its most unique property is its excellent flame resistance. This fiber does not burn or melt, and it has low shrinkage and low smoke emission when exposed to flame. Even when charred, PBI fiber remains relatively supple and intact. Its moisture regain is high, about 15 percent.

End Uses

End uses for which this fiber are suitable include heat-resistant apparel (e.g., for fire fighters and industrial workers), racecar-driver apparel, rescue gear, hazmat suits, and space suits.

Producers and Trademarks

Celanese Advanced Materials, Inc.: PBI Gold®

Rubber

The first commercial production of synthetic **rubber** fiber was in 1930 by the U.S. Rubber Company, now Uniroyal, Inc. Lastex™ was a major trade name for the fiber.

Rubber is a manufactured fiber in which the fiber-forming substance comprises natural or synthetic rubber. The manufacturing process consists of extending the natural rubber latex into a coagulating bath to form filaments. The material is cross-linked to obtain fibers that exhibit high stretch.

Properties

Very little rubber fiber is used today, having been mostly replaced by spandex fiber for products requiring stretch properties because the latter has superior elastic properties (i.e., greater stretch, higher recovery force, greater resistance to aging). Rubber has low resistance to perspiration but is much less expensive than spandex.

End Uses

End uses of this fiber include elastic bands and tapes.

Saran

The first commercial production of **saran** fiber was in 1941 by the Firestone Plastics Company (now Firestone Fibers and Textiles Company) in the United States.

Saran is a manufactured fiber in which the fiber-forming substance is any long-chain synthetic polymer composed of at least 80 percent by weight of vinylidene chloride units.

Properties

Saran has good strength and abrasion resistance. It is highly resilient as well as very resistant to the effects of sunlight and weather. It is easily washed and, if it burns, is self-extinguishing. The fiber is stiff and has a very low safe-ironing temperature. It is a heavy fiber with a poor hand (slippery) and 0 percent moisture regain. Saran is used in monofilament form.

End Uses

End uses for saran include upholstery in transportation vehicles (e.g., cars, trains), outdoor garden furniture, filters, and doll hair.

Producers and Trademarks

Dow Chemical Co.: Saranex™

Sulfar

The **sulfar** generic fiber name became effective in June 1986. The first commercial production of this fiber was by Phillips Fibers Corporation.

Sulfar is a manufactured fiber in which the fiber-forming substance is a long-chain synthetic polysulfide in which at least 85 percent of the sulfide linkages are attached directly to two aromatic rings.

Properties

This fiber is highly resistant to acids and alkalies and has excellent resistance to heat.

End Uses

End uses for sulfar include hot gas filtration (e.g., coal-fired industrial boilers), electrical insulation, paper-makers' felt, and rubber reinforcement.

Vinal

Vinal is a manufactured fiber in which the fiber-forming substance is any long-chain synthetic polymer composed of at least 50 percent by weight of vinyl alcohol units and in which the total of the vinyl alcohol units and any one or more of the various acetate units is at least 85 percent by weight of the fiber.

Vinyon

The first commercial production of **vinyon** fiber in the United States was in 1939 by the American Viscose Company. Production of this fiber was discontinued in the United States in 1990. It is still being produced in Japan, however.

Vinyon is a manufactured fiber in which the fiber-forming substance is any long-chain synthetic polymer composed of at least 85 percent by weight of vinyl chloride units.

Properties

Vinyon fibers have a high resistance to chemicals, which makes them very desirable for certain industrial uses. Their low softening temperature also makes them useful as bonding agents for nonwoven fabrics. The fiber is hydrophobic (0.5 percent moisture regain).

End Uses

End uses for vinyon include industrial uses, bonding agent for nonwoven fabrics, and fishing nets.

Other Generic Fiber Categories

Other generic fiber categories are industrial fibers which have unique end uses. Examples include carbon, fluoro-carbon, and heterogeneous fibers.

Carbon Fibers

Carbon fibers are manufactured by pyrolosis of organic precursor fibers (e.g., rayon, polyacrylonitrile, or pitch) in an inert atmosphere at 1000°–3000°C. The result is a fiber from which all the elements except carbon have been removed. Carbon fibers are black in color, are stiff, possess high strength, and are lightweight. Their main application is in plastics reinforcement in industrial uses. Carbon fiber reinforced with plastic provides high strength and is lightweight and therefore is ideal for use in bridge components, aircraft structures, sporting goods (e.g., golf club handles), and brake discs.

Carbonized fiber is also very thermal protective and has been used in the heat shields of space shuttle wings.

Fluorocarbon Fibers

Fluorocarbon fibers are formed from long-chain carbon molecules in which all available bonds are saturated with fluorine. These fibers are exceptionally resistant to heat and chemicals, are completely hydrophobic (0 percent moisture regain), and possess very good resistance to abrasion, sunlight, aging, and mildew. Their main application is industrial uses, such as protective clothing, hot-gas filters, and chemical and heat-resistant threads. Producers and trade names of this fiber include W. L. Gore & Associates, Inc. (Gore-Tex®) and INVISTA™ (Teflon®). The material formed into fibers can also be formed into sheets or applied as a coating to other substances. Thus Gore-Tex® fabrics have a thin membrane covering for water resistance and Teflon® is used as a coating for cooking items as well as rainwear.

Heterogeneous Fibers

So far only homogeneous fibers (i.e., fibers composed mainly of a single chemical substance) have been discussed. Another fiber category is the **heterogeneous fibers** (see Figure 3.14a–c). These fibers are prepared from two or more chemically or physically distinct components. Each component, if separately extruded into a fiber, would be classified as one of the generic fibers of the TFPIA. Fiber properties that are not obtainable with the normal generic fiber types previously described in this chapter can be achieved with these special fibers. These additional categories are bicomponent or multicomponent fiber and matrix or matrix-fibril fiber.

Bicomponent or Multicomponent Fiber

Bicomponent or **multicomponent** fiber is a manufactured fiber that is a combination or mixture of two or more chemically and/or physically different components combined at or prior to the time of extrusion. Each component, although possessing some different properties, if separately extruded into a fiber, could be classified in the same generic category of textile fiber. Thus, if the fiber is composed of two different types of nylon, the industry might label this fiber 100 percent bicomponent nylon, although, according to the TFPIA, 100 percent nylon is all that is necessary.

The fiber could also be composed of two different generic categories. This fiber would be referred to as a bicomponent bigeneric fiber. The label for such a fiber might read as follows:

100 percent bicomponent bigeneric fiber

(60 percent polyester, 40 percent nylon)

The most commonly used bicomponent fiber type is side-by-side, where each fiber component is formed along the lengthwise axis. The different polymers are fed separately to the spinnerette opening, but exit through the hole together, side-by-side. Because the two sections of the fibers are composed of slightly different chemicals, a cross-sectional microscopic view of the fiber shows two different areas, with a line of separation easily observed.

The other large usage for bicomponent fibers is the sheath/core type. This type is produced by having one polymer (sheath) surround the other polymer (core) as both are being extruded from the spinnerette opening.

Wool can be considered a natural bicomponent fiber because it contains two types of cells. One is nearer the outside and the other is further inside. Because they have somewhat different chemical compositions, they react differently to changes in temperature and humidity. This response to environmental conditions helps give wool its crimped, curled structure.

Various effects are obtainable in bicomponent or multicomponent fibers, three of which are the following:

1. Self-crimping effect: Self-crimping occurs when one component shrinks more than the other in processing or fabric finishing and so pulls the yarn into a helical, crimped shape. Bulk, cover, and elasticity are better in this case than in mechanically induced crimp.

2. Cross-dyeing effect: If each of the two parts of the bicomponent fiber reacts to a different dye, then a two-color fabric can be created because each fiber part can be a different color. This can be accomplished with a single-dye bath containing one dye for one fiber type and a second dye for the other fiber type. Each type is dyed with only one of the dyes and is not affected by the other. Carpet yarn can be dyed in this manner to create heather effects.

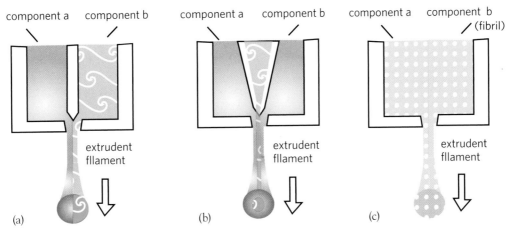

FIGURE 3.14
Three ways to form an extruded heterogeneous fiber: (a) side-by-side type (b) sheath-core type and (c) matrix-fibril type.

3. Heat-bonding application: KoSa produces a fiber (Celbond®) with a sheath-core structure. The core is polyester for toughness and resiliency. The sheath, which is one-third to one-half of the fiber, is a special low-melting polymer. After exposure to heat, it is designed to form a solid bond with adjacent fibers. The fiber is used as the binding fiber when producing such materials as nonwoven fabric (see p. 140) and high-loft batting. Binder fibers are normally from 10 to 40 percent of the material, depending on the required characteristics.

When the sheath and core are made from different polyester polymers (Type K54), the fiber is a polyester bicomponent fiber. When the sheath and core are made from different generic fiber polymers (e.g., polyester core and polyethylene olefin sheath), as with Type K56, the fiber is a bicomponent bigeneric fiber.

Antistatic Fibers
The antistatic fibers now being produced contain a section of carbon. Because the quantity of carbon is small, these fibers are identified by the generic name of the major fiber component and not as a bicomponent fiber. An example is BASF's Resistat® nylon, which has carbon chemically saturated into the entire outer skin of the nylon fiber. Its uses include the aforementioned as well as antistatic conveyor belts, gloves, and conductive brushes.

Matrix or Matrix-Fibril Fiber
Matrix or **matrix-fibril** fiber is a manufactured fiber composed of two or more chemically distinct components in a matrix-fibril configuration. Each component, if separately extruded into a fiber, would be classified in a different generic category of textile fiber.

A matrix-fibril fiber form is one in which very fine short filaments (the fibril) are embedded in the rest of the fiber (the matrix). The fibril and matrix are made of different generic substances.

The process is similar to that of mixing oil and water and then freezing the solution. The drops of oil are embedded in the resulting ice. If the drops of oil elongated upon freezing, then the resulting configuration would resemble the matrix-fibril fiber. Although the fiber-forming process does not use a freezing technique to obtain solidification, the example is a simple way of expressing the formation of the fiber with its two physical components, one embedded in the other. UltraSuede® is an example of a bicomponent fiber made of polystyrene and polyurethane used in a matrix configuration.

Fiber Innovation

Innovation and technology are the controlling forces that can accelerate the growth or retard the decline of a product. They have played an important role in the growth of the manufactured fiber industry. Textile chemists initially modified the shape of the manufactured fibers. Then, chemical changes were made to the fiber to meet specific industry and consumer needs. Today, fiber innovation enhanced by technology has cut across the entire fiber-to-fabric pipeline. From this a wide range of products have exploded onto the marketplace. Many are marketed as high-performance products that have been engineered to address a specific need for the consumer. They may be crafted by a high-performance fiber, yarn, fabric, finish, or a combination. They are designed to manage moisture, regulate heat, inhibit the growth of bacteria, or other identified requirements. The following are examples of such products.

- Acrylic fibers combined with PCM (phase-change materials) to help maintain body temperature. The product absorbs and stores excess body heat and then leases it when needed.

- Merino wool blended with either Thermolite® or COOLMAX® (both by INVISTA™) to make a lightweight, warm fabric than can be machine washed.

- Dow Chemical Co. markets Dow XLA CP™, which is the first chlorine proof stretch fiber that is also resistant to ultraviolet light. It is used to make competitive swimwear, among other applications.

- Cocona® is made from polyester fibers that are embedded with carbon made from coconut shells. The carbon creates tiny channels that allow moisture to disperse very quickly and generate rapid moisture evaporation. Cocona® is used in applications that require enhanced moisture management plus odor control and can be found in products from Champion® among others.

- RadiciSpandex Corp. has developed a black spandex used to prevent 'grin-through' when a fabric is stretched.

- Meadowbrook Inventions has created an ultra soft, very fine metallic fiber called Angelina®. It is used

in staple form only and blended with cotton, rayon, and cashmere for used in couture apparel.

- Unifi Inc. is marketing a polyester called Repreve® made from 100 percent recycled post-consumer material. The company has stated that every pound of Repreve® fiber is equivalent to ½ gallon of gas conserved. Repreve® can be found in products from Perry Ellis, Geoffrey Beene, Patagonia, and others.

- TYR Sport Inc.® created a fabric designed for applications in competitive swimming. It is made of two lightweight fabrics of 70 percent nylon and 30 percent spandex with stretch in both directions. One fabric is coated with Teflon® for water repellency and the other with polyurethane for buoyancy. The suit is downsized to further compress the wearer and reduce drag in the water.

Successful and continual innovation requires a company to have not only a large research and development staff, but also sizable financing. Few are able to afford the expense associated with innovation and technology. Strategic alliances and partnerships have been the answer. Companies have reshaped their focus and established new joint ventures to continue creating innovation in fibers, yarns, fabric, and finishing. Tables 3.6 and 3.7 provide lists of fiber names in other languages and international abbreviations. These are important for global communication within the textile industry.

TABLE 3.6	Fiber Names in Other Languages						
English	Chinese	French	German	Italian	Japanese	Korean	Spanish
Acetate	cu suan xian wei su	acétate	acetat	acetato	sakusan	acetate	acetate
Acrylic	bing xi suan	acrylique	acryl	acriico	akuriru	acrylic	acrilico
Cotton	mian	coton	baumwolle	cotone	momen	myun	algodón
Linen	ya ma	lin	leinen	lino	asa	ma	lino
Nylon	nilong	nylon	nylon	nylon	nairon	nylon	nilón
Olefin	shi la	olefins	olefinpreise	olefine	ourehin	olefin	olefina
Polyester	di lun	polyester	polyester	poliestere	polyester	polyester	poliestero
Ramie	zhu ma xian wei	ramié	ramie	ramié	ramil	mo shi	rame
Rayon*	ren zao si	rayonne	reyon	rayon	reyon	rayon	rayon
Silk	sichou	soie	seide	seta	kina	kyun	seda
Spandex**	an lun	élasthanne	elasthan	elastan	supandekkusu	supon	elastano
Wool	yangmao	laine	wolle	lana	keito	mo	lana

* viscose

** elastane

TABLE 3.7	International Abbreviations for Designating Fibers in Yarns		
AC	Acetate	SE	Silk
CLY	Lyocell	SI	Sisal
CO	Cotton	ST	Tussah Silk
EL or EA	Elastane	TA	Triacetate
GL or GF	Glass Fiber	VI	Viscose/Rayon
HA or CA	Hemp	WA	Angora
JU	Jute	WG	Vicuña
LI	Linen/Flax	WK	Camelhair
MD	Modal	WL	Lama
MA or MAC	Modacrylic	WM	Mohair
ME	Metallic	WO	Wool
PA	Polyamide, Nylon	WP	Alpaca
PL or PES	Polyester	WS	Cashmere
PP	Polypropylene	WY	Yak
RA	Ramie		

Study Questions

1. List differences and similarities between the following natural fiber types and their manufactured fiber substitutes:

   a. Cotton and HWM rayon
   b. Wool and acrylic
   c. Silk and acetate

2. Why are some fabrics made from two different fiber types and others made completely from one fiber type?

3. Compare a fabric made with polyester filament microfiber with a similar fabric made of filament silk fibers.

4. Differentiate between a generic fiber name and a fiber trademark.

5. You have determined that your line of fitted blouses would benefit from stretch and have three different generically classified fibers to choose from. What are they and what advantage might each one offer?

6. You have purchased pillows, comforters, and mattress pads made of PLA for your store. What unique aspects of PLA will you highlight to market these products to your customers?

7. Why are microdenier fibers so popular for lingerie?

8. Nylon is used for each of these end uses. What fiber property modification would be beneficial for each?

   a. Carpet
   b. Rope
   c. Fiberfill for quilt
   d. Pajamas
   e. Drapery

9. Because wool fibers readily form pills, why is pilling less of an aesthetic problem on a fuzzy-surface fabric verses a flat-surface fabric?

10. A cross-country skier must choose between a 100 percent wool jacket and a 100 percent polyester fleece jacket of similar construction. Which jacket would you advise as a better choice? Why?

CHAPTER FOUR

Yarns and Sewing Threads

Objectives

▸ To understand that the type of yarn used has an important effect on the properties of fabric.

▸ To know the distinctions between the various yarn types as well as their properties and end-use applications.

▸ To understand the systems for determining yarn sizes.

▸ To be able to know the types, uses, and optimum applications of sewing threads.

Use fabrics in the Yarns section of the Fabric Science Swatch Kit *for this chapter.*

Key Terms Related to Textiles

air-jet	filament yarn	mixture	stretch-textured
bare elastic yarn	gear crimping	monofilaments	tex system
blended yarn	hard twist	multifilaments	textured yarn
bulk-textured	high-bulk or hi-bulk	novelty yarn	thread size
carded	yarn	open-ended spun	tow linen
chenille yarn	knife-edge	ply	turns-per-inch or TPI
combed	knit-deknit	ring spinning	turns-per-meter or TPM
core-spun yarn	lea	ring-spun	turbo-bulk yarn
cotton count system	line linen	run	woolen
covered elastic yarn	metallic yarn	set-textured	worsted
crepe-filament	metric yarn count	sewing thread	worsted count system
crepe twist	microdenier	single	yarn count
denier	microfibers	soft twist	yarn number or size
false twist	microfilament	spun yarn	yarn numbering system

The formation of yarns is the next major step in the development of textile products.

The simple process of making yarn predates recorded history. Cave dwellers used hair fiber from animals that were twisted into coarse yarn for ropes and nets. Eventually they refined their techniques to make yarn capable of being intertwined to produce crude fabrics.

While seemingly unimportant, this invention, along with the inventions of fire and the wheel, is considered a major milestone of the world's civilization. The ability to create a yarn, and to subsequently interlace the yarn (weaving) freed primitive humans to leave their caves in an expanded search for food, and eventually to migrate to other regions.

The invention of spinning was so profound and yet so simple that the principle of making yarn, by twisting fiber while simultaneously pulling or drawing it out, has remained unchanged throughout the ages and continues to this day.

Yarns are by definition groups of fibers twisted together to form a continuous strand. All textile fabrics, except for a few, such as felt (p. 145) and nonwoven fabrics (p. 140), are produced from yarns. The yarns are interlaced (woven), interlooped (knitted), or combined in other ways to form a textile fabric. There are many types of yarns, some lustrous, some dull, some smooth, some rough, some thinner than human hair, some thick and bulky. Two fabrics each made from the same fiber (e.g., polyester) and each woven in the same weave (e.g., plain weave; p. 91) may be substantially different from one another in appearance, durability, and cleanability due to the yarn differences in each of the fabrics.

Spun and Filament Yarns

Yarns are classified into two main categories: spun and filament.

Spun yarns are composed of relatively short lengths of fiber twisted or spun so that they hold together. The short lengths of fiber (measured in inches) are called staple fibers. Staple fibers are made into yarn by mechanical processes that first make the fibers more or less parallel, and then alternately pull and twist them. High twist is necessary to press the fibers together to give strength to the resulting yarn. It is important that staple fibers possess sufficient surface friction to adhere to each other.

Filament yarns are composed of continuous strands of fiber that may be miles (kilometers) long. These yarns are produced directly from a spinnerette (see p. 20) or from a silk cocoon (see p. 39). Because filament yarns, unlike spun yarns, contain fibers of infinite length, they do not need to be highly twisted. Most filament yarns are of low twist (enough to hold the fibers together) to provide a smooth, lustrous surface. However, filament yarns may be tightly twisted, thus producing special effects such as crepe. (See Figure 4.1.)

Identifying Spun and Filament Yarns

Spun yarns may be identified by untwisting the yarn so that all fibers are parallel and by then pulling slightly, so the yarn simply comes apart without breaking. When a filament yarn is untwisted and pulled, the fibers remain parallel and the yarn does not come apart.

Spun yarns composed of longer fibers are stronger, more uniform, and more lustrous than similar spun yarns made from shorter fibers. Long-staple cotton, for example, is cotton fiber of longer-than-average length and commands premium prices on cotton commodity markets.

Filament yarns are composed only of manufactured fibers or silk. Spun yarns, however, may consist of both natural and manufactured fibers. In the latter instance, the long strands of fiber extruded from a spinnerette are chopped into short fiber lengths (staple) and later processed into spun yarns (see p. 21). These yarns are called spun nylon, spun polyester, or spun whatever the generic fiber composition.

Manufactured yarns are made and marketed by chemical fiber producers. Spun yarns are made by yarn-spinning mills that are either engaged exclusively in the

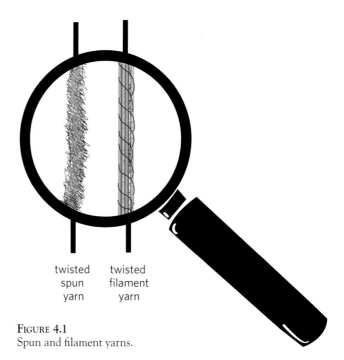

twisted spun yarn   twisted filament yarn

FIGURE 4.1
Spun and filament yarns.

yarn-spinning business or are a branch or department of a weaving mill or vertically integrated textile producing company.

Monofilament, Multifilament, and Microfilament Yarns

Filament yarns may be composed of one single filament or of many filaments, and are known as **monofilaments** or **multifilaments,** respectively. (See Figure 4.2.) Both have the same fundamental properties, governed by the fiber composition of the yarn. An important physical difference is that a monofilament yarn of a given diameter is stiffer and less flexible than a multifilament yarn of the same diameter. And given two multifilament yarns of equal diameter (or equal denier, see p. 77), the yarn composed of fewer, but coarser, filaments is stiffer and less flexible than the yarn consisting of a higher number of finer filaments. Supple, soft fabrics, such as lining fabrics, are typically made from yarns composed of a large number of fine filaments. The large number gives the appropriate string of coverage and the fine filament offers greater flexibility.

Technological developments in manufactured fiber processes have made possible the generation of fibers such as nylon, polyester, lyocell and others to be produced in diameters finer than silk (**microfilament**) (see Figure 4.3). These fine fibers are called **microfibers,** and are also known as **microdenier.** The name also applies to the yarns made from them (see p. 77 for an explanation of denier). Microfibers are used as multifilament yarns in flat or textured (see p. 71) configuration or are processed as staple fibers and then spun into yarn. Fabrics made from microfiber filament yarn are extremely soft and drapable and can be almost indistinguishable from silk. Spun yarns from microfibers can be blended

FIGURE 4.2
A very fine filament dress.

with cotton, wool, or other fibers to produce yarns that possess much greater softness and flexibility, thus creating a more drapable or fluid fabric.

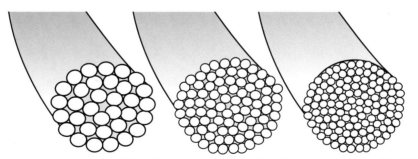

standard yarn 2.0 dpf   microdenier yarn 1.0 dpf   microdenier yarn 0.5 dpf

FIGURE 4.3
Assume the three yarns are the same size, e.g. 80 d. The yarn on the left at 2 dpf would have 40 filaments. The yarn in the center at 1 dpf would have 80 filaments. The yarn on the right at .5 dpf would have 160 filaments. Thus, although the three yarns are of the same size, as the fibers get thinner (lower denier per filament) there is a higher filament count in the yarn.

Comparison of Spun and Filament Yarn Properties

There are a variety of properties used to compare and contrast spun and filament yarns. The three most important are yarn uniformity, yarn smoothness and luster, and yarn strength.

In general, filament yarns are more uniform in diameter than spun yarns, although these differences are not visible to the naked eye. In filament yarns, the same number of filaments are present at every point along the yarn. A multifilament yarn composed of 40 filaments has 40 filaments along its entire length. This is not the case with spun yarns, where, for example, at one point there may be 40 fibers, at another, 43, and at still another, 37.

Filament yarns are generally smoother and more lustrous than spun yarns. Satin, a familiar filament-yarn fabric, is smooth and lustrous, whereas sheeting, a typical spun-yarn fabric, is less smooth and somewhat duller with a slight surface fuzz that is characteristic of spun yarns. A filament yarn viewed against light shows uniform diameter and no fuzziness. Because each filament is as long as the yarn itself, there are no fiber ends protruding from the yarn surface as in spun yarns. This uniformity and smoothness in filament yarns is the main reason for their greater luster and smoother surface.

The smooth surface of the filament yarns can sometimes be disadvantageous, causing yarns to slip and slide easily within a fabric. Excess stress on a seam, for example, may cause slipping of yarns and opening of a seam without the actual breakage of thread. This is more likely to occur in fabrics of low construction, fabrics with a low number of yarns per square inch (see p. 89) or where improper seam allowance is taken in sewing. The test described on page 290 should be used to determine the suitability of a filament yarn fabric for yarn and seam slippage.

When a spun yarn is broken, some fibers break and others just slide away from each other. When a filament yarn is broken, every filament in the yarn breaks. Thus, filament yarns are stronger than spun yarns of the same diameter and fiber type because it requires more force to break yarn if all the fibers break than if only some fibers break while others slip apart.

More twist in a spun yarn increases its strength by increasing the pressure exerted on the fibers. This results in reduced fiber slippage when force is exerted on the yarn. Up to a certain point, the more twist in a yarn, the stronger it is. After that point, the extra twist begins to cause the fibers to cut into each other and the yarn strength decreases. This happens because the fiber direction and thus the yarn's strength is no longer in a spiral direction but has been forced into more of a horizontal steplike direction.

Uses of Spun and Filament Yarns

Some fabrics are made only of spun yarns, some of only filament yarns, and others of a combination of spun and filament yarns. Each type of yarn is best for certain uses. Spun yarns may provide warmth, softness, and lightness of weight and are, for example, ideal in fabrics for T-shirts, sweaters, and blankets. Filament yarns are better for items where smoothness and luster are desired because the yarns are finer, more uniform in diameter, and lustrous. Filament yarn fabrics can offer a smooth, uniform surface. They are used in linings because their smoothness makes it easier to slide into and out of garments. They are also used for the outer shell of ski jackets, in a tightly packed construction, to resist the penetration of wind.

Yarn Twist

Yarns are made by twisting together parallel or nearly parallel fibers. The amount of twist in a yarn is designated as the **turns-per-inch** (2.54 centimeters), or **TPI**, of the yarns. The TPI in a yarn has an important bearing on the appearance and durability of the yarn and the fabric that will be made from it.

Spun yarns with relatively low twist (from 2 to 12 TPI) are frequently called **soft-twist** yarns because the yarn is softer, fluffier, and more flexible. They are not as strong as spun yarns with high twist. Knitting yarns are usually soft twist.

Spun yarns with relatively high TPI (20 to 30 TPI) are called **hard-twist** yarns. The higher twist causes them to be smoother, firmer, and kinkier than spun yarns with low twist. They are also stronger.

Filament yarns usually have very low twist (½ to 1 TPI). Twist in filament yarns does not increase strength but merely serves to keep the filaments in the yarn together. Some filament yarns are purposely made with high twist to produce a pebbly, harsh surface effect. These yarns are called **crepe-filament** yarns and the twist is referred to as **crepe twist**. (See Figure 4.4.)

Twist Direction

In addition to the amount of twist in a yarn, the direction of the twist is also designated. As shown in Figure 4.5, there are two types of yarn twist: S and Z. In an S-twist yarn, the spirals run upward to the left, corresponding to the direction of the diagonal part of the letter S. In a

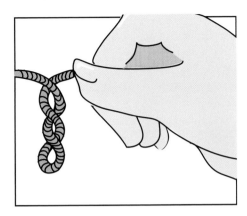

FIGURE 4.4
A crepe yarn kinks when slackened because of the high twist.

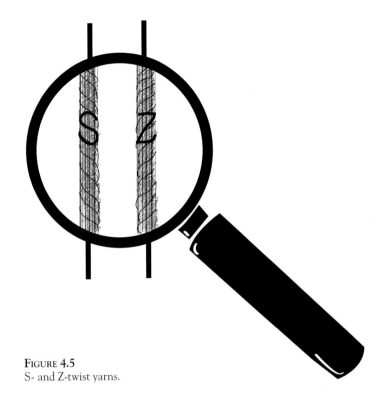

FIGURE 4.5
S- and Z-twist yarns.

Z-twist yarn, the spirals run upward to the right, similar to the diagonal part of the letter Z. Yarn-twist direction is not an element of quality because it does not affect properties such as strength and abrasion resistance. S- and Z-twist are important to the fabric designer and stylist because the direction of the twist affects the surface appearance of fabrics. Crepe fabrics are sometimes made by combining S- and Z-twist yarns to produce the balanced, pebbly effect on the fabric surface.

Yarns for the towel business typically are made of cotton, twisted in a Z direction with a high TPI. This results in a final product that is relatively hard. Twistless cotton or Zero Twist cotton has been used in the luxury towel industry to market terrycloth that is noticeably softer. Zero Twist is accomplished by plying a PVA (polyvinyl alcohol) yarn around the cotton yarn in the opposite direction (S direction) thus untwisting the cotton yarn. The PVA holds the cotton yarn together as it makes the pile in the terrycloth as it is woven (see p. 99). After the fabric is formed, the PVA is removed in the finishing process. The resultant towel offers consumers a very soft hand with excellent absorption.

Carded and Combed Cotton Yarns

Carded and **combed** refer to the methods used to make cotton and cotton-blend spun yarns as well as to the designation of fabrics made from such yarns. A broadcloth fabric used as shirting fabric, for example, may be carded broadcloth or combed broadcloth, depending on the yarn used.

All staple fibers have to be carded to help clean and disentangle them. For less costly fabrics, the fiber is carded and formed into a thick rope of loose fiber called sliver. The sliver is made into yarn by drawing and spinning.

For finer fabrics, the carded cotton in the form of sliver goes to the combing unit, which further cleans the fibers and puts them in parallel position. Combing also removes short fibers. The comb delivers a loose sliver of parallel, long fibers called combed sliver, which is used to make the spun yarns, known as combed yarns.

A combed yarn thus has longer fibers, fibers in more parallel position, fibers of more uniform length, fewer speck and dirt impurities, and more uniformity of diameter than a yarn that is not combed. Fabrics of combed yarn look better, feel smoother, and are stronger and more expensive than comparable fabrics of carded yarn. Fine, lightweight yarns need to be combed because long fibers are required for proper strength. They may be found in fine shirting and luxury sheeting.

For some fabrics, combed yarns are not only unnecessary, but also less desirable than carded yarns. A napped fabric, such as cotton flannel, should be made from shorter fibers to create a fuzzier surface. (See p. 190.) Denim and terry cloth are two fabrics typically made exclusively of carded yarns. This gives denim the natural, rugged look consumers recognize. The fuzzy, soft bulkiness of carding helps terry cloth remove moisture.

Tow and Line Linen Yarns

Linen yarns are classified into two types called **tow** and **line.** Tow linen yarn is composed of short fibers and is irregular and rather coarse in texture. Tow linen is used for coarser types of linen fabrics found in sports jackets and trousers. Line linen is composed of long fibers averaging about 15 inches (38.1 centimeters) in length. Line linen yarns are smooth and fine and are used for fabrics such as fine table linens and tissue-weight blouses.

Woolen and Worsted Yarns

There are two types of wool or wool-blend fabrics: **woolens,** made of carded yarns, and **worsteds,** made of combed yarns.[1] A woolen yarn is fuzzier, has a more uneven diameter, is bulkier, and has a wider range of fiber length (including short fibers) than a worsted yarn. Worsted yarn is smooth with little fuzz, has an even diameter, and is more tightly twisted and firmer than woolen yarn. (See Figure 4.6.)

Fabrics made from worsted yarn are not necessarily better than fabrics made from woolen yarn. Each kind of yarn is suitable for a specific type of fabric. Tweed is an example of a woolen fabric; gabardine is an example of a worsted fabric. There are expensive woolens as well as expensive worsteds.

The following are additional facts about woolen and worsted yarns:

▶ Fabrics of woolen yarn are more important in heavy winter coatings, ski sweaters, and blankets because woolens generally provide better insulation than worsteds. The fuzziness and soft bulkiness of woolen yarns provide the dead air spaces needed for better insulation.

▶ Because worsted yarns are more tightly twisted than woolen yarns, fabrics of worsted yarn are usually firmer and denser than fabrics of woolen yarn. The more tightly twisted yarns help worsted to hold its pressed creases and generally to better keep its shape between cleanings than fabrics made of woolen yarn.

---

1. Wool fibers are first carded and then combed as part of the worsted yarn-manufacturing process. Combed sliver of wool is called top.

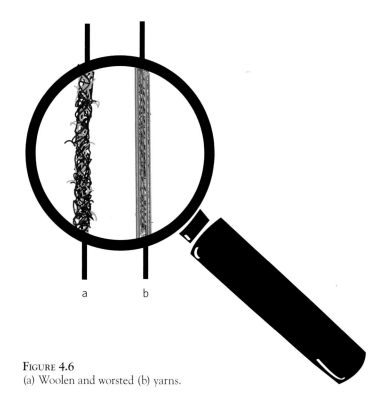

FIGURE 4.6
(a) Woolen and worsted (b) yarns.

▶ Fabrics made from worsted yarn usually show the yarns and weave clearly and sharply on the face of the fabric. Fabrics made from woolen yarns, on the other hand, may have a napped surface or look like the surface of felt.

Worsted fabrics, such as gabardine and serge used in trousers and suiting, tend to develop a shine with wear. Because the yarns are very smooth and tightly twisted, pressure on the fabric (e.g., from sitting) and rubbing tend to flatten the yarns and produce the luster. A popular suiting fabric known as unfinished worsted is given a light napping and fulling finish, which tends to cover up the yarns (see p. 190). Thus the appearance of the yarns and the weave are more subdued and the shine problem is eliminated or greatly reduced. (Unfinished worsted is a misnomer because the fabric is, in fact, given extra finishing treatments.)

Single and Ply Yarns

Yarns are also categorized as **single** or **ply.** When a ply yarn is untwisted, it separates into two or more finer yarns. As shown in Figure 4.7, when a single spun yarn is untwisted, it comes apart. Ply yarn, therefore, may be defined as two or more single yarns twisted together to form one new yarn. Two-ply yarns are two singles twisted together, three-ply are three singles twisted together, and so forth. Most ply yarns used in clothing are two-ply. Little is gained by using yarns of higher ply. If a yarn is not ply, it is referred to as single, never single-ply.

Advertisements of two-ply worsted suiting and of 2 × 2 broadcloth shirts aim to indicate quality. 2 × 2 broadcloth shirts have two-ply yarns in both warp and filling. In a 2 × 1 broadcloth, the warp is two-ply and the filling is single.

In a ply yarn, two or more finer yarns are usually twisted to produce the same thickness as a single yarn, but with many additional benefits. In spun yarns, each fiber can wind more times around a thinner yarn and so hold more firmly. In plying the finer-spun yarns, more twist is added, holding the fibers more firmly in place and making the yarn stronger. Spun yarns are not perfectly even in diameter. By twisting together two or more yarns, the thin, weaker spots are reinforced. Thus, plying improves spun yarns because the fibers cannot slip as easily, the yarns are stronger, the yarn diameter is more uniform, and there is a reduced tendency to pill.

Most single yarns have a Z twist. When plied with another single yarn, an S twist is used. Open end yarns (see p. 69) always have a Z twist. Ring spun (see p. 69) and air-jet (see p. 70) usually have a Z twist, but the system can produce S twist if modified.

In filament yarn, the diameter is uniform and the filaments cannot slip when the yarn is pulled. Twist is not needed to hold the filaments in place. For these reasons, plying does not improve filament yarns as it does spun yarns. However, plying of filament yarns can be done to produce unique effects on novelty yarns and metallic yarns (see p. 76).

Ply yarns require better-quality fiber, more labor, and special machinery. Because of this expense, ply yarns are more costly than singles. Thus, most fabrics are made of single yarns.

Yarn Spinning

Staple fibers are spun into yarns by a variety of methods. The most widely used is **ring spinning** where fibers are carded to bring them to a more parallel position and bundled into a loosely formed rope about one inch in diameter, known as sliver. Multiple slivers are grouped together and then drawn or pulled slightly to decrease into a smaller diameter, known as roving. Further drawing and more twist are needed to form the desired yarn size with the required turns per inch. The final yarn is then wound onto a cone or package. (See Figure 4.8.)

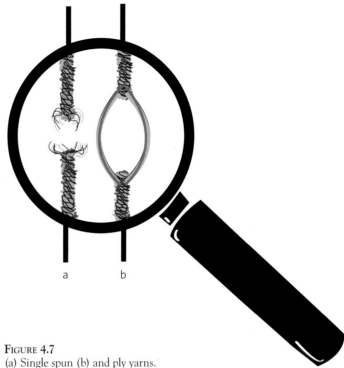

FIGURE 4.7
(a) Single spun (b) and ply yarns.

Ring spinning can produce anything from uniform yarns to the more complex, novelty yarns. It can produce yarns in a wide range of sizes and excels in the finer counts (see p. 77). Ring spinning produces yarns with the softest hand available and are noted for making fabrics that feel soft. However, low production rates and additional steps make this a more costly process. Products made from ring spun yarns are advertised to promote their quality and are found in t-shirts, hosiery, sheets, towels, and even denim, all for the luxury market.

Open-end (OE) spinning is a method of producing spun yarns. It is different from conventionally spun yarn, frequently called **ring-spun yarn,** in that only one process from carded sliver to spun yarn is required. Substantially higher rates of production, coupled with savings in space and power requirements, are realized in OE spinning. Carded sliver is fed to the open-end spinning unit, which separates the fibers, twists them together to form the completed spun yarn, and then winds the yarn onto spools or cones. Yarns made by this process are sometimes called roto-spun yarns or turbine-spun yarns.

Some advantages of OE spun yarns are better regularity and uniformity; improved abrasion resistance, especially in high-twist types; improved distribution of fibers in blends; and improved absorption, resulting in brighter shades and print-pattern definition. Two

FIGURE 4.8
Yarn spinning at the Jiayi textile factory in China.

important shortcomings are that yarn strength averages 20 percent lower than conventionally spun yarns, and manufacture is limited to coarse and medium-size yarns.

These yarns are more uniform, somewhat weaker, and less expensive than ring-spun yarns. Their rate of production is 10 times faster than ring spun yarns. It has a limited range for yarn sizes and is best when under Ne 20 (see p. 77). Almost all yarn produced for denim is spun with this method. End yarns are used in fabrics such as interlock, fleece, and almost all yarns used in denim for mass markets.

Air-jet spinning, also known as Vortex spinning, uses compressed air to aide in the spinning process. In this system, one end of a fiber is pushed toward the center of the yarn and the other end to the outside to wind around other fibers. This process is very fast with production twice that of open-end production and 20 times faster than ring spinning. The fibers are more securely locked into the yarn, do not slide as easily as other methods, and exhibit less fuzz or hairiness along their length. However, they have less uniformity, are limited to coarse yarn sizes, and have a lower yarn strength then ring-spun yarns. Fabrics made from this yarn will exhibit fewer pills and do not show wear easily. The largest end use is for sheeting or print cloth made of cotton and polyester blended yarns (see p. 70). It is also ideal for active wear, uniforms, and sweatshirts.

Yarn Pilling

As described on page 27, certain fibers are more likely to pill than others. The yarn construction bears importantly on whether pills will occur. Provided that the fiber is prone to pilling, pills will develop more readily on spun yarns than on filament yarns because fiber ends are already on the surface. Filament yarn fabrics form pills only when the filaments break (e.g., from wear). Short-staple, fiber-spun yarns pill more readily than long-staple spun yarns because there are more fiber ends on the surface. Soft-twist yarns pill more than hard-twist yarns because it is easier for the fiber ends to move and protrude on the surface.

Blends and Mixtures

A **blended yarn** is made of two or more fiber types. Both spun yarns and filament yarns may be blended, but spun yarns are the type most widely used.

Blending is usually done to combine the desirable properties of different fibers. Wool, for example, is blended with staple polyester because wool has excellent drape and polyester helps to retain shape and reduce the cost of the fabric. Polyester is stronger than wool but thinner, so a blend of the two can be lightweight.

It is difficult to obtain perfectly uniform blending of fibers in a spun yarn because of differences in specific gravity, length, diameter, surface shape and texture, the moisture regain property. There is also some variation along the length of blended yarn and in composition from inside to outside. Longer fibers tend to travel toward the center and shorter fibers toward the outside of yarns. When the blending occurs in a uniform manner, it is referred to as an "intimate blend".

A common blended yarn is cotton and polyester, which is used extensively to make fabrics for shirts and sheets. Each fiber type in the blend adds not only its favorable properties, but also its unfavorable qualities. Thus, a shirt or dress fabric composed of 50 percent polyester and 50 percent cotton is less comfortable in hot humid weather than a 100 percent cotton fabric because of the low moisture absorption of the polyester.

Not all blended yarns are perfect intimate blends. In some instances, depending on manufacturing procedures, the fibers may be dispersed in a nonuniform manner, such as a side-by-side or sheath-and-core configuration (see Figure 4.9).

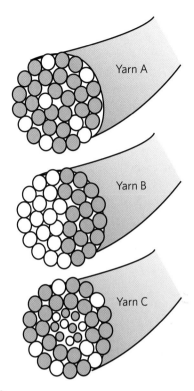

FIGURE 4.9
Blended yarns are not always perfectly blended. Yarn A, blended at the opening stage, is a true intimate blend, which is most desirable. Yarn B, blended at the roving stage, is nonuniform and is less desirable. Yarn C is a blend consisting of long and short fibers. The long fibers tend to move to the center. Outside fibers contribute to hand, abrasion resistance, and pilling; inside fibers contribute to strength and flexibility.

A **mixture** is fabric composed of two or more different types of yarn. Filament and spun yarns combined in a fabric is an example of a mixture. A fabric with acetate warp and rayon filling is another example. Fabric mixtures are used to achieve certain design and color effects, as in cross-dyeing (see p. 162). They also are used to lower the cost of certain fabrics by combining less-expensive yarns with the more costly. They can be used to add strength to a weak yarn, such as adding nylon to a metallic yarn. A mixture is sometimes referred to as a combination fabric.

Special Types of Yarns

Textured Yarns

The appearance and touch of multifilament yarn can be altered from smooth, lustrous, and flat to crimped, dull, and soft (somewhat like the appearance of spun yarn). This modification yields entirely new yarn properties, which in turn provide entirely new fabric properties. The filament yarns are modified before they are woven or knitted. Because the modified yarn takes on an entirely new surface or texture, it is called **textured yarn.**

The ability of filament yarns to be modified to give them new shape, crimp, and bulk derives from the thermoplastic nature of the fibers from which they are produced (see p. 27). The various methods for making textured yarn involve shaping the yarn to some desired configuration of crimp or bulk by setting the yarn, heating it to near its melting point, and then cooling the material. (The exception to this is the air-jet method, described on p. 70.)

Favorable Properties
The following are favorable properties of textured yarns.

▶ Possess high stretch and/or bulk

▶ Provide greater cover (opacity) than regular filament yarns

▶ Afford greater breathability and absorption than regular filament yarns

▶ Afford greater insulation than regular filament yarns

▶ Provide softer and drier hand than regular filament

▶ Provide spunlike yarn characteristics

▶ Are more wrinkle resistant than spun yarns or regular filament yarns

Unfavorable Properties
The following are unfavorable properties of textured yarns.

▶ They have a tendency to snag on broken fingernails, chair seats, and similar objects. Because it is a long filament rather than a short-spun fiber that snags, the likelihood of damaging the fabric is high. Textured yarns should, therefore, be avoided in such garments as children's playwear, where hard, rough use is anticipated.

▶ Possible growth problem

▶ Poor abrasion resistance

▶ Easy soil penetration

Types of Textured Yarn

There are several methods of producing textured yarns. They are classified into three main categories: stretch-textured, bulk-textured, and set-textured type. (See Figure 4.10.)

Stretch-Textured Stretch-textured yarn is made primarily from nylon and used extensively in leotards, stretch ski pants, stretch hosiery, and similar items. These yarns can be stretched from 30 to 50 percent of their relaxed length.

Stretch-textured yarns are produced by several methods. The **false-twist method** is the most widely used technique for producing textured yarns in finer deniers. Yarns are twisted, heat-set, and untwisted in one operation.

Stretch-textured yarns are also produced by the **knife-edge method.** This process consists of passing the filaments over a heated roll and then pulling them over a sharp edge at an acute angle. When relaxed, the filaments take the form of coiled springs, but the spiral direction reverses itself at random, which helps produce a balanced yarn.

Gear crimping is a third method for producing stretch-textured yarns. This method consists of passing the filament yarn through a series of heated rollers or sets of heated gears that deform the filaments. Variations in crimp can be obtained by controlling the number of crimps per inch as well as the depth of gear deformation.

Bulk-Textured The most important property of **bulk-textured yarns** is their high bulk with low or minimal stretch. A method for producing bulk-textured yarn is the stuffer-box method, which produces an increase in bulk from 200 to 300 percent and can be found in yarns used for carpets. In this process, the filaments are compressed into the confined space of a heated chamber and heat-set with a wavy, random crimp. The resultant yarn is relatively bulky, possesses some degree of stretch, and is torque-free. Torque-free means the yarn will stay flat and motionless as opposed to a yarn that has a tendency to curl around itself.

The air-jet method is a second way to produce bulk-textured yarns. In this method, a jet of high-velocity air is directed at a multifilament yarn, which separates the fibers, forcing some filaments to form loops and turns. The result is a bulkier, less lustrous yarn. Many yarn style varieties are possible by varying the yarn types and air-jet volume. No heat is involved, so the yarns need not be thermoplastic.

The **knit-deknit** method is a way of producing a bulky yarn that has more stretch than yarn produced using the stuffer-box or air-jet methods. The filaments are knit into a narrow-diameter tubular form. The fabric is rolled up, heat-set, and then unraveled.

Set-Textured Textured yarns in the **set-textured** category undergo an additional heat-setting step in the texturizing process to set the yarn and eliminate or greatly minimize stretch. This is accomplished in some instances by winding previously textured stretch yarns onto spools under moderate tension, and then heat-setting the yarn a second time. The yarn then becomes set in the bulked condition with either minimal or no stretch. Textured yarns of this type, made of filament polyester fiber, can be used in many fabrics including gabardine, interlock, and crepe de chine.

Stretch Yarns

Yarns that have the capability of stretching are increasingly being used in textile materials. Aside from being the traditional materials used in foundation garments and swimwear, fabrics made from yarns that stretch are being used in apparel to provide increased comfort when sitting, bending, stooping, or engaged in active sports or work activities.

Stretch fabrics are generally classified into two categories: power stretch and comfort stretch. (See Figure 4.11.) Power-stretch materials are fabrics in which holding power is required, as in foundation garments, swimwear, surgical support garments, and suspenders. The yarns used for power-stretch fabrics have high elasticity and high recovery force. Comfort-stretch fabrics are designed to yield with body movement. These fabrics have low recovery force and, in most instances, the yarns from which they are made and the fabrics themselves look the same as non-stretch materials.

Stretch yarns and the fabrics made from them require not only that they stretch to the extent required, but also that they return to their original dimensions on release of the stresses that cause the stretch. Fabrics that do not readily recover are inadequate for the particular end use.

A pair of pants that stretches at the knee from sitting, and that remains baggy at the knee for a long period of time after standing, may be less desirable than a pair of pants made from rigid fabric that does not stretch in the first place.

Unrecovered stretch in textile fabrics is called growth. Growth has not been completely eliminated in

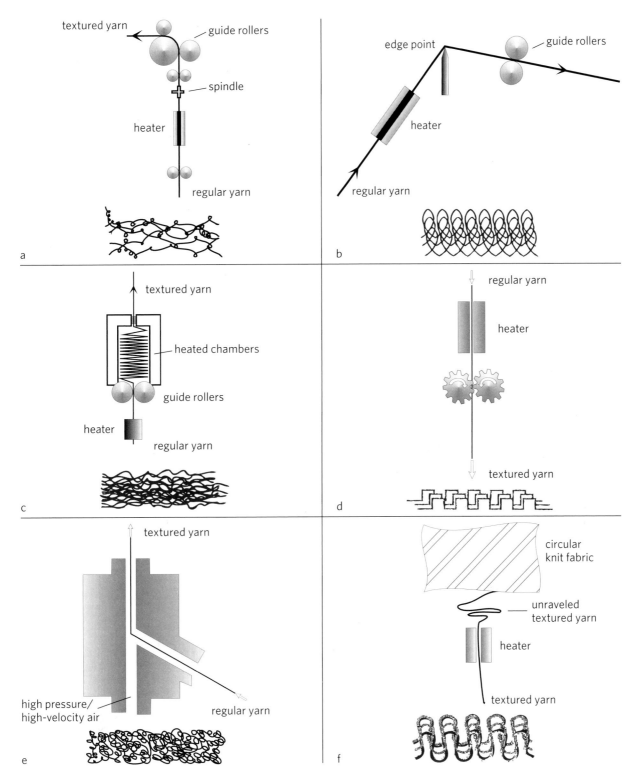

FIGURE 4.10
Methods of producing textured yarn: (a) false twist (b) knife-edge (c) stuffer box (d) gear crimping (e) high-pressure/high velocity air-jet and (f) knit-deknit.

FIGURE 4.11
Power stretch fabrics are often used for activewear.

Types of Stretch Yarns

The following common types of stretch yarns are compared in Table 4.1:

Bare Elastic Yarns **Bare elastic yarns** are usually composed of monofilament spandex fiber. Bare elastic yarns are used in power-stretch fabrics. In general, they provide softer and more gentle shape control (moderate recovery force) than covered yarns.

Covered Elastic Yarns **Covered elastic yarns** are monofilaments that are wrapped or covered with a spun or filament yarn to hide the elastomeric yarn. Covered yarns tend to be thick and heavy and are used in power-stretch fabrics. In general, they provide firmer and more powerful shape control (high recovery force) than bare elastic yarns.

Core-spun Yarns **Core-spun yarns** have a central filament core of spandex with staple fiber that has been spun around the core. The core in the center does not appear on the yarn surface, so the hand, texture, and appearance are identical to what the spun yarn would be without the core center. Core-spun elastic yarns are used in comfort stretch fabrics because they possess very low recovery force. These yarns can be spun very fine and thus provide elasticity without the bulk usually associated with other types of stretch yarns. Stretch chino, a popular cotton sportswear fabric used for tennis shorts and other active sportswear, is made from core-spun cotton yarns. Core-spun stretch yarns are the most expensive of all stretch yarns.

Textured Yarns **Textured yarns** are the most widely used of the comfort stretch yarns. The "ease" or "give" these yarns contribute to the fabric is a quality many consumers find attractive.

most stretch fabrics, but can be kept to very low, tolerable minimums in properly constructed fabrics. In general, tightly constructed fabrics recover more quickly than loosely constructed fabrics. Also, fabrics made from high-denier stretch textured yarns recover more quickly than fabrics from fine-denier stretch textured yarns. A method for determining fabric growth is given on page 293.

TABLE 4.1	COMPARISON OF STRETCH YARNS			
Yarn Type	Stretch Fiber Component	Stretch Type	Recovery Power	Uses and Features
Textured yarns	Nylon or polyester	Comfort	Low	Blouses, sportswear, stretch pants, hosiery, polyester men's socks. Polyester has a tendency to pill.
Bare elastic	Spandex	Power	Moderate	Lightweight foundations, swimwear, athletic wear—gym clothing, bike shorts.
Covered elastic	Spandex or rubber	Power	High	Heavy foundations, elastic bandages, surgical stockings, athletic supporters. Rubber has higher power and recovery than spandex, but poor shelf life—it begins to decay in one year.
Core spun	Spandex	Comfort	Very low to low	Active sportswear, stretch denim.

High-Bulk Yarns

High-bulk, also called **hi-bulk** or **turbo-bulk,** yarns are acrylic spun yarns that are specially processed to yield lofty, bulky, and soft yarns without stretch.

These yarns are produced by a unique process that involves spinning yarn by blending acrylic fibers of high and low potential shrinkage. When the finished yarn is treated with boiling water or steam, the high-shrinkage fibers contract and move to the center of the yarn, forcing the low-shrinkage fibers to buckle, which forms a yarn that is greater in diameter than the original and has more loft and bulk. Some high-bulk yarns are bulked (boiled or steamed) in yarn form, and others are bulked in garment form (e.g., knitted sweaters).

Fabrics made of high-bulk acrylic yarns feel soft and luxurious, and frequently have the hand and appearance of high-quality worsted. They have the disadvantage of tending to pill easily, and they should be checked carefully for conformity to current flammability regulations.

Novelty Yarns

Novelty yarns, sometimes also called fancy yarns, are yarns that are not of uniform thickness throughout their length, but have deliberate irregularities on their surfaces (Figure 4.12). These irregularities may be knots, bumps, curls, or similar effects.

The naming of novelty yarns is confusing, however. Because there is no established terminology for novelty yarns, their names are often used interchangeably. Novelty yarns, or fabrics containing novelty yarns, should never be purchased on the basis of yarn name alone, but only when accompanied by samples. Typical novelty yarns are slub, thick and thin, spiral, flock, and bouclé. (See Figure 4.13.)

Novelty yarns give fabrics made from them interesting and decorative surface effects. Using novelty yarns is one means by which textile designers can create cloth with raised or nubby surface textures as distinguished from the usual flat surface of most textile materials.

Fabrics made from most novelty yarns are not durable and are especially susceptible to wear from abrasion or rubbing. The parts of the yarn exposed beyond the surface of the substrate are particularly vulnerable to rubbing action. Novelty yarn fabrics should be avoided in applications where durability and long wear must take precedence over fabric beauty and interesting surface effects.

Chenille Yarns

Chenille yarns are yarns that have a soft pile protruding from their surface. Their appearance resembles pipe

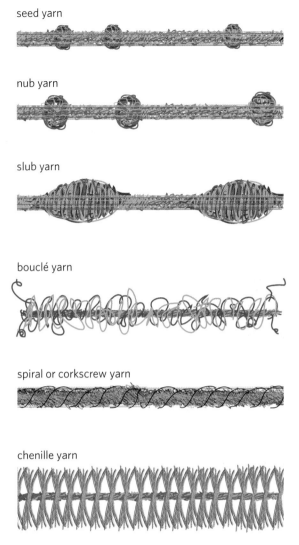

seed yarn

nub yarn

slub yarn

bouclé yarn

spiral or corkscrew yarn

chenille yarn

FIGURE 4.12
Popular types of novelty yarns.

cleaners without the wire. Unlike pipe cleaners, however, chenille yarns are soft, supple, and very flexible.

Chenille yarns are made in an unusual manner. The yarn is made by slitting narrow lengths from $\frac{1}{8}$ inch to $\frac{1}{4}$ inch (3.18 millimeters to 6.35 millimeters) of a fabric that has first been woven especially for this purpose. This fabric is a leno-effect weave (see p. 97) and has a filling of soft, twisted yarns. After the fabric is woven, it is cut lengthwise into narrow strips, each strip becoming a chenille yarn. The crisscrossing leno warp prevents the soft filling from falling out. (See Figure 4.14.)

Chenille yarns may be made from any fiber, but most commonly they are made of cotton, wool, rayon, or nylon. Chenille yarns are used in woven fabric to produce soft pilelike effects on bedspreads and other decorative fabrics. Chenille yarns have rather low resistance to abrasion, and their use should be avoided in products that will be subjected to even minimal fabric rubbing.

Metallic Yarns

A strip of metallic fiber (see p. 54) is also a **metallic yarn.** Such yarn is flat and ribbonlike rather than round or elliptical in cross-section, as are other yarns. Strips of metallic yarns are usually from $1/32$ inch (0.80 millimeter) to $1/128$ inch (0.20 millimeter) wide. These yarns can be supported by loosely twisting one or more fine-filament yarns around them (e.g., two 15-denier nylon yarns). This increases its strength and abrasion resistance.

Metallic yarns are mostly used for decorative rather than functional purposes; a wide range of colors and effects is available. Metallic yarns tend to be expensive. Lurex Co., Ltd. is a major metallic yarn manufacturer.

Yarn Numbering Systems

Yarns are bought and sold by the pound. Knitting mills, for example, purchase their yarn requirements in pounds rather than in yards. Even home knitters purchase yarns in packages sold by ounce or gram weight.

Yarn numbering systems are used to express a relationship between a unit length and weight of yarns—either meters per gram or yards per pound. The relationship between unit length and weight also reflects the diameter or thickness of a yarn. This is because a yarn of low weight per unit of length would be finer (thinner) than a yarn with a higher weight per equal unit of length. However, the diameter of the yarn may vary for any given yarn number because of differences in the specific gravity of the fibers from which yarns are made,

FIGURE 4.13
A garment made of bouclé yarns.

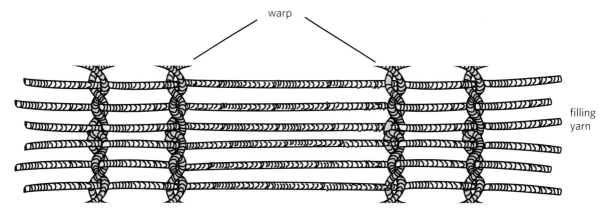

FIGURE 4.14
Making chenille yarn: Filling yarns are cut between each section of warp leno.

and because some yarns are highly twisted whereas others have low twist.

The terms **yarn numbers** and **yarn sizes** are used interchangeably. Despite the words "yarn size," bear in mind that the size (or number) expresses a relationship between a unit of length and weight, and only a close, but not exact, relationship to diameter or thickness.

There are two main numbering systems in use: the denier system, which is used for all filament yarns, and the yarn-count system, which is used for all spun yarns. A third system known as the tex system was developed to bring all yarn numbering systems into a single system for all types of yarns.

The Denier System

The **denier** system is the simpler of the two numbering systems. In this system, heavier and usually thicker filament yarns are designated by higher denier numbers. Very fine yarns, of 10 denier, for example, are used in sheer hosiery. The heavy, coarse yarns used in carpeting are around 2,000 denier. The denier system is called a direct system because higher denier numbers designate heavier (thicker) yarn. A 100-denier nylon filament has twice the weight of an equal length of 50-denier nylon filament. Thus the system is based on weight in grams per 9,000 meters.

A 1-denier yarn is a yarn in which 9,000 meters, if weighed, would equal 1 gram. A 2-denier yarn would weigh 2 grams per 9,000 meters, and so forth. Thus the yarn has twice the thickness per unit length.

Filament yarns are sold by indicating the number of filaments the yarn contains, and the twist as well as the denier size. For example, a 300-10-$\frac{1}{2}$ Z filament yarn indicates a yarn of 300 denier in size, containing 10 filaments with $\frac{1}{2}$ TPI of Z twist. Each filament fiber in this yarn would be 30 denier. A 400-40-$\frac{1}{2}$ Z would be thicker than the 300-10-$\frac{1}{2}$ Z, but have finer filaments because each filament fiber would be a 10-denier fiber and thus finer.

The Yarn Count System

In the **yarn count** system, the yarn count number is inversely proportional to weight. This system, therefore, is indirect. A 50-count spun yarn has twice the weight (thickness) of a 100-count spun yarn. The weight of the yarn is indirectly proportional to the yarn-count number. Cotton yarn, for example, which is used for sheer voile fabrics, may be as fine as 100 count, whereas thicker yarns used in many poplin fabrics may be a 30 count. Heavy cotton duck fabric used for truck tarps may be made of 5-count yarn.

How Spun Yarn Count Is Expressed

The method of expressing yarn size of spun yarns differs by the fiber content. Yarns spun on the **cotton count system,** for cotton and cotton blends, are designated as **c.c.** for cotton count. They may also be specified as **Ne** for Number English and cc could be replace with **Nec.** Cotton and cotton-blend yarns are expressed by two numbers: The first is the yarn size and the second indicates the yarn ply. For example, 50/1 means a size-50 single yarn. (In oral communication, it is called a "fifty single" or "fifties yarn".) A 70/1 is a size-70 single yarn or 70 s; 60/2 yarn is called a 60 two-ply or 60 s two.

Worsted, worsted blends, and acrylic fibers are spun on the **worsted count system** and are designated by **w.c.** or **New.** These yarns are indicated in the reverse order from the cotton count system. For example, 1/50 (referred to as one 50 or singles 50) is a singles yarn of 50-count size. A 2/40 yarn is two size-40 yarns plied together. This yarn is called a two-40 s yarn.

Woolen and woolen blends yarns are designated by the term **run,** or **Nar** such as 4-run yarn. They are rarely plied and are single yarns unless otherwise indicated.

Linen yarns are expressed by the term **lea,** or **Nel,** which are used for flax, jute, hemp, and ramie fibers. They are almost never plied because the fiber length is so long that plying does not improve the yarn measurably. Thus, they are considered single yarns unless otherwise indicated. Yarns as fine as 400-lea are used to make fine lace.

Spun yarns can also be expressed in the metric system. The yarn size is indicated using the term metric. For example, a 50-count metric yarn would be designated as a 50's metric. The **metric yarn-count** system expresses the number of kilometers of yarn per kilogram of weight. The system is used for all spun yarns and is an indirect count method. It may be indicated by **Nm.**

Several classifications are used for determining yarn counts. These classifications are called yarn-count standards and are different for each fiber-spinning system. The yarn-count standard represents the number of yards in one pound of a number 1 count of that specific yarn. The following standards are in general use:

Cotton and cotton blends	840
Spun silk and all spun 100 percent manufactured fiber yarns except acrylic	840
Worsted, worsted blends, and acrylic	560
Woolen and woolen blends (run)	1,600
Linen (lea)	300
All spun yarns (metric)	496.055

TABLE 4.2   YARN NUMBER CONVERSIONS

	Denier	Worsted	Cotton	Woolen (Run)	Linen (Lea)	Tex	Metric
Fine yarns range	50*	160	106	56	298	5.6	180
	75	106	72	37	198	8.3	120
	100	80	53	28	149	11.1	90
Medium yarns range	150	53	35	19	99	16.6	60
	200	40	27	14	74	22.2	45
	300	27	18	9.3	50	33.4	30
	400	20	13	7.0	37	44.4	22.5
Coarse yarns range	500	16	11	5.6	30	55.5	18
	700	11.4	7.6	4.0	21	77.7	12.9
	1000	8.0	5.3	2.8	15	111	9
	1500	5.3	3.5	1.9	10	166	6
	2000	4.0	2.7	1.4	7	222	4.5

* Much finer filament yarns, as low as 10 denier, are commonly used.

A number-1-count cotton has 840 yards in one pound (768 meters per 453.6 grams) of the yarn, and a number-1-count worsted has 560 yards in one pound (512 meters per 453.6 grams) of the yarn. Both are called number-1 yarns, yet each is of different weight per unit of length. Thus a 20 cotton count would be finer than a 20 worsted count because the former has 16,800 yards per pound (15,362 meters per 453.6 grams) and the latter has 11,200 yards per pound (10,214 meters per 453.6 grams).

Table 4.2 provides typical yarn number and denier comparisons. When using this table, remember that a 200-denier filament yarn is of equal weight per unit of length (and approximate thickness) to a 40-count worsted yarn, a 27-count cotton yarn, a 14-count woolen (run) yarn, a 74-count linen (lea) yarn, and a 45-count metric.

There are many other variations of yarn numbers used outside the United States.

Ply Yarn Counts and Singles Equivalent

Spun yarns that are plied are expressed as, for example, 40/2 (cotton type). This means that two yarns of 40/1 each have been twisted together. The thickness of the resulting ply yarn is about twice that of the original 40/1 yarn, or about the same thickness as 20/1 yarn because this is an inverse proportion system. The singles equivalent of a 50/2 is 25 count, and of a 45/3 is 15 count.

Filament yarns are rarely plied because they gain little by being plied. When they are, the usual method of expressing such a yarn would be, for example, two-ply 40 denier. The singles equivalent of such a yarn would be 80 denier.

Ply yarns and single-yarn equivalents are illustrated in Figure 4.15.

The Tex System

The **tex system** is intended to replace all the existing count and denier systems with a single system for designating all yarn sizes. The International Organization for Standardization (ISO) has adopted this system and it is utilized in the sewing thread business. The tex system is a direct numbering system in which higher tex numbers correspond to increasingly heavier (thicker) yarns. The tex standard uses grams per 1,000 meters. Thus, a 10 d yarn used for pantyhose would be equivalent to a 1.1 tex yarn.

Sewing Threads

Sewing threads are special kinds of yarns that are engineered and designed to pass through a sewing machine rapidly, to form a stitch efficiently, and to function while in a sewn product without breaking or becoming distorted for at least the useful life of the product. How adequately a specific thread performs these tasks depends on proper thread selection for the specified fabric and seam type used. American & Efird, Inc., is a major thread manufacturer.

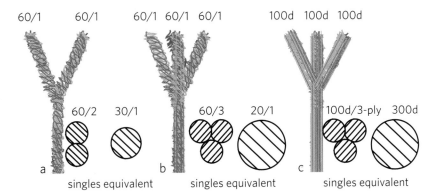

FIGURE 4.15
Ply yarn and singles equivalents:
(a) spun yarn (b) spun yarn and
(c) filament yarn

Fibers Used for Threads

The fibers used for sewing threads are primarily cotton, nylon, polyester, and rayon. Cotton-covered polyester is the most widely used because of its relatively low cost and high versatility. The properties and characteristics of each of the fibers prevail when they are used as threads, and these properties should be considered in thread selection for specific end uses. Rayon, for example, is usually used for thread intended primarily for embroidery or decorative stitch work rather than for seaming to hold parts together.

Types of Threads

Threads may be spun, filament, or core-spun type. Each has distinctive properties and therefore certain advantages in specific seams. A comparison of these thread types is shown in Table 4.3.

All sewing threads, whether spun, filament, or core spun, are ply yarns. Sewing threads are more highly twisted and firmer than regular yarns and are often treated with special finishes or lubricants to improve sewability.

Thread Finishes

Threads are produced with various finishes, such as mercerized, soft, glacé, and bonded. In addition, special finishes, which include flame-resistant and heat-resistant types (for high-speed sewing), are also produced. Table 4.4 indicates the properties and use characteristics of thread finishes.

Thread Sizes

Sizes (weight per unit length) of thread are marketed and expressed with their Tex number designation (see p. 78). An older system of specifying **thread size,** the ticket number system, based on denier and yarn-count systems, is still in use but is gradually being replaced in the thread industry. Table 4.5 indicates typical Tex numbers in thread applications for various sewn products.

TABLE 4.3 COMPARISON OF SEWING THREAD TYPES		
Spun	**Filament**	**Core Spun**
Lower strength than filament.	Higher strength than spun; permits use of finer thread without sacrifice of seam strength.	Combines the best features of filament and spun threads.
Versatile and adaptable to a wide variety of machine adjustment conditions.	Produces neatest seams, but careful machine adjustments necessary.	Especially useful in seaming durable-press garments.*
Less likely than filament thread to cause seam pucker.	Greater possibility of seam pucker than with spun thread.	Same seam puckering tendency as spun thread.
Least costly.	Less costly than core spun, but more costly than spun thread; textured filament threads would be good for knits because they have additional stretchability.	Most costly.

* Residual resins present in permanent press garments are absorbed by the thread, causing strength loss and abrasion-resistance loss in the cotton cover of the thread. The polyester core is unaffected by the resin, thus providing continuing seam integrity.

TABLE 4.4	THREAD FINISHES AND THEIR USES	
Type	Description	Sewing Properties and Uses
Soft	Natural cotton thread without finishes that appears somewhat fuzzy. Small amount of lubricant sometimes added to improve sewability.	Excellent sewability, lowest cost.
Mercerized	Treated cotton thread that is stronger, more lustrous, more stable (less stretch) than soft cotton thread. The finish reduces the thread loop strength.	Increased tensile strength, lustrous appearance, and brighter shades provide for better seams than soft threads. More costly than soft thread and used in premium products.
Glacé	Highly polished cotton thread that is difficult to unravel. The polish and finish are usually obtained with waxes and starches.	Strongest cotton thread. Rarely used in apparel. Used in the manufacture of shoes, luggage, canvas goods, and similar applications.
Bonded	The term applies only to threads of manufactured fibers, both filament and spun. Waxes and resins produce high polish, eliminate fuzz (on spuns), bond together filaments and plied yarn, and impart a smooth protective coating.	Increased strength and sewability compared to same thread unbonded. Apparel usage largely in heavyweight and coated-fabric sewing. Mainly used for manufacture of shoes, luggage, tents, and other heavy-duty applications.

TABLE 4.5	SEWING APPLICATIONS BY THREAD SIZE		
Fine Tex (18 Through 30)	Medium Tex (30 Through 60)	Heavy Tex (60 Through 105)	Extra Heavy Tex (105 Through 135)
Blouses	Aprons	Footwear	Decorative stitching or when a bold design look is desired
Dresses	Athletic wear	Overcoats	
Lingerie	Caps	Parkas	Luggage
Sleepwear	Coats	Protective clothing	Golf bags
Swimwear	Draperies	Work wear	
Other light articles	Foundation garments		
	Jeans		
	Pants		
	Rainwear		
	Shorts		
	Windbreakers		

Important Factors in Thread Selection

Selecting the correct thread for assembly of finished goods is of critical importance. The type of thread used will determine the ease of manufacture, durability of the product, and satisfaction of the consumer.

Thread size should be as fine as possible, consistent with the strength requirements of the seam. Finer threads tend to become buried below the surface of the fabric and are, therefore, subjected to less abrasion than seams with heavier thread, which are on top of the fabric. Finer threads also require smaller needles, producing less fabric distortion than heavier needles.

The breaking strength of a seam (see p. 287) should be less than that of the fabric sewn. Many authorities agree that the seam should be about 60 percent of the fabric strength. This is to ensure that if excessive stress is placed on a seam, the seam, rather than the fabric, breaks. Seams are easily repairable; fabric is not.

If a garment is to be washed in hot water, then its thread should have excellent resistance to color change from this medium. Also, the thread should not shrink as a result of the cleaning method.

Important Thread Factors That Govern Seam Appearance

When woven-filament yarn fabrics and/or fabrics that have been finished with resins are sewn, there is sometimes a tendency for seams to pucker and ripple rather than to lie flat and smooth. The tendency is greater in lightweight fabrics than in heavyweight materials. Some of the causes of puckering are excessive tension on sewing thread during the sewing process, displacement or movement of fabric yarn in the sewing operation, and thread shrinkage that is greater than fabric shrinkage.

Puckering of seams can frequently be reduced or eliminated through awareness of the following factors:

▶ **Thread size.** Heavyweight thread should be used for heavyweight fabrics, lightweight thread for lightweight fabrics and extra fine thread for sheer fabrics or fabrics made of microdenier yarns.

▶ **Direction of seam.** Seams made parallel to the warp pucker most seriously, those on the filling pucker considerably less, and seams on the bias hardly pucker at all. Sometimes turning a pattern slightly off-grain results in a pucker-free seam.

▶ **Thread tension.** Fabrics susceptible to puckering should be sewn with the lightest thread tension possible.

▶ **Stitches per inch.** Seams with a large number of stitches per inch are more likely to pucker because more yarn displacement is occurring. Stitches per inch, therefore, should be kept at a minimum. If possible, they should be kept within a range of 8–12 stitches per inch.

▶ **Sewing machine adjustments.** The bottom fabric and top fabric of a sewn seam should feed into the machine at the same rate if smooth seams are expected. In some instances, use of a fine-tooth sewing machine feed dog aids in uniform feeding. Sewing machine operator skills also play a major role in uniform feeding of seam components.

Study Questions

1. Explain why combed yarns are more costly than carded yarns of the same fiber content and size.

2. What are novelty yarns? Comment on the use of novelty yarns for fabrics to be used for children's play wear.

3. Is it easier to make spun yarn from staple fibers or filament yarn from filament fibers? Explain your answer.

4. What is meant by the term "growth" with regard to fabrics made from stretch yarn?

5. What differences in performance would you expect in a jacket made from woolen yarns as compared to one made from worsted yarns?

6. Rank the following five yarns from the lightest (thinnest) to the heaviest (thickest):

   a. 40/2 cotton
   b. 2/40 worsted
   c. 70-denier nylon filament
   d. 13-run-woolen
   e. 50-lea flax

7. Explain how a sewn seam made from fine thread might actually be more serviceable than one made from heavier and stronger thread of the same fiber and type.

8. Why are ply yarns more likely to be found in better, higher-priced garments than in moderate to lower-cost items? Explain your answer.

9. You are launching a line of junior dresses made of micro polyester. What advantages might yarns of this fiber have over dresses with yarns of silk?

CHAPTER FIVE

Woven Fabrics

Objectives

▸ To convey how woven fabrics are produced.

▸ To explain why woven fabrics look and perform the way they do.

▸ To recognize various weaves and know their identifying characteristics.

▸ To define the terminology used regarding woven fabrics.

▸ To identify various well-known woven fabrics.

 Use fabrics in the Woven Fabrics section of the Fabric Science Swatch Kit *for this chapter.*

Key Terms Related to Textiles

air-jet loom	cut-pile weave fabric	jacquard head	plain weave	twill weave
back	dobby head	jacquard loom	projectile loom	uncut-pile weave
balanced twill	dobby pattern	jacquard pattern	rapier loom	fabric
basket weave	double cloth	jet loom	reed	warp
bias	end	left-hand twill	ribbed	warp beam
bottom	face	leno weave	right-hand twill	warp-face satin
broken-twill weave	filling	loom	sateen fabric	warp pile
chevron	filling-face satin	multiphase loom	satin weave	water-jet loom
clip-spot pattern	filling-pile fabric	napped fabric	selvage	weave
cloth roll	float	off grain	shed	woven fabric
color-and-weave	harness	on grain	shuttle	woven pile fabric
effect	heddle	pick	shuttleless loom	yarns per inch
crepe-back satin	herringbone	pile fabric	top	(cloth count)

Over 4,000 years ago, man created fabric through the use of a crude wood-framed loom. Typically this weaving device held yarns in an upright position as they were interlaced with one another by hand. Primeval man used this to make fabric to clothe and protect. As civilization began to develop, some woven fabric was used to indicate standing within the community. Eventually, royalty and religious figures used ornately woven fabric to indicate their stature. Looms were also used to depict stories in woven fabric, some of which are now highly valued (e.g., tapestry). Centuries later, as looms became more sophisticated and yarns smoother and finer, looms were used to create some of the world's most intricate woven fabrics.

Woven fabrics are made by interlacing two sets of yarns at right angles to each other. The length-wise yarns are known as **warp** yarns, or **ends,** and the width-wise yarns are known as **filling** yarns, or **picks.** The length-wise edges of the fabric are the selvages. The selvage is usually easily distinguishable from the rest of the material. (See p. 87.)

Grain indicates a direction parallel to either the warp or filling yarns. The term **on grain** is used if a fabric has been cut parallel to either the warp or filling yarns.

A direction not parallel to either of these yarns is called **off grain,** or **bias.** Fabric cut off grain results in a skewed portion of the textile product (e.g., pants leg or drapery). Woven fabrics elongates most in a direction that is 45° to both sets of yarns. The reason for this is that there is maximum yarn bending and shifting from the pulling force being exerted. Pulling that is on grain results in only a slight yarn extension, with the least amount usually in the warp direction.

Woven fabrics also have their best drape in a bias direction. This is the result of the bending and shifting of the yarns from the fabric weight. Some garments are cut on the bias (i.e., the bias direction is vertical in the garment) to obtain maximum drapability, as shown in Figure 5.1. A problem that can occur, however, is the garment may grow (i.e., increase in length) and become uneven in length when worn.

Bias bindings are narrow strips of fabric cut in the bias direction used to finish the edges of seams in sewn products. This binding elongates to conform to the shape of curved seams, thus eliminating the puckering or small wrinkles that would occur if the binding were cut on grain.

a

b

FIGURE 5.1
An example of (a) the body of a summer dress and (b) the waistband of a skirt cut on the bias.

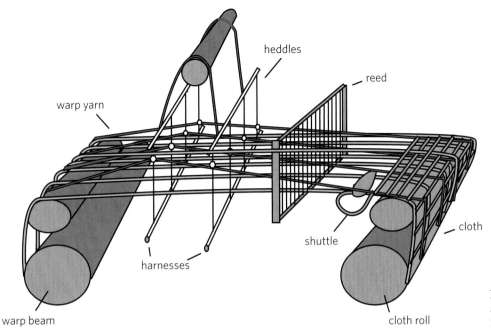

FIGURE 5.2
A simplified sketch of a two-harness loom.

The Loom

Woven fabric is produced on a **loom** (see Figure 5.2). The following is a simplified explanation of the process utilized to produce woven fabric:

▸ The **warp beam,** located at the back of the loom is a large roller on which all the warp yarns to be used for the fabric are wound parallel to each other.

▸ The warp yarns pass through the **harnesses,** which look like picture frames holding many thin vertical wires called **heddles,** each with a hole in the middle. Each warp yarn is threaded through the hole of a heddle and thus is controlled by that harness.

▸ When a harness or group of harnesses is raised with others left in the down position, a V-like opening is formed. This is called the **shed.**

▸ A filling yarn is inserted in the shed and travels across the width of the loom, passing over some warp yarns and under other warp yarns. (See Figure 5.3.)

▸ The **reed** is a comb-like device that pushes the filling yarn in the shed into the body of the cloth.

▸ The sequence in which harnesses are raised or lowered determines the **weave** of the fabric.

▸ The woven fabric produced by the repetition of the above steps is slowly wound onto the **cloth roll** located in the front of the loom.

Types of Looms

Production looms can be categorized several ways, such as by method of raising ends to form the shed (e.g., dobby device, or jacquard attachment—see p. 100), by number of sheds (one to make a single fabric or two to make a double fabric), or by method of inserting the filling yarn. The most significant advances in weaving are in the methods of inserting the filling yarn (see Figure 5.4).

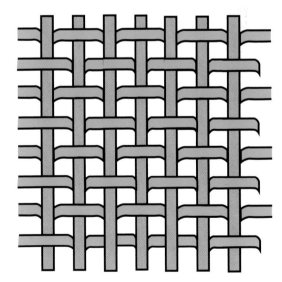

FIGURE 5.3
The interlacing of warp yarns and filling yarns.

Production Looms

For early looms, the insertion of the filling yarn was done by hand, with the weaver passing the filling yarn over and under different warp yarns. Later, harnesses were added to looms which allowed groups of yarns to be lifted. Also with the use of a shuttle the weaver could insert the filling yarn at a greater rate. A **shuttle** is a wooden device with a bobbin placed inside with filling yarn wound around it. As the shuttle is projected across the loom, the filling yarn unwinds from the bobbin, leaving a trail of yarn behind. Adding power to shuttle looms mechanized the weaving process and significantly increased the rate of production yet again.

Most looms used for production are **shuttleless** looms. These looms employ various other devices to bring the filling yarn through the shed. With shuttleless looms the yarn comes directly from cones placed at the side of the loom. Once the filling yarn is brought across the loom, the yarn is cut, often leaving a fringe at the edges of the fabric. Except for the means of transporting the yarn across the shed, the steps in the weaving process are the same. The main devices used to insert the filling yarn across the shed are referred to as projectile, rapier, jet, or multiphase.

The speed of a loom, and thus the loom's productivity, is designated by the number of picks per minute (ppm) a loom can insert for a specified width. The maximum number of meters per minute (m/min.) indicates the maximum length of filling yarn that can be inserted in a minute. These measurements are critical since they control productivity or the length of time required to weave a particular length of fabric and therefore affect the cost of a fabric.

Shuttleless looms available in today's marketplace operate at speeds that produce fabric at a high rate of productivity. They are designed to function using different fiber contents, yarn counts, structures, and modifications. They must be energy efficient, quiet, and compact in space usage. They are equipped with state of the art electronics, including internet-ready touch screen terminals. Although the use of shuttle looms is very limited, they have been used to produce authentic denim for vintage looking garments.

Projectile Loom   A **projectile loom** uses a projectile to insert the filling yarns. A projectile is a small, light gripper device (about the size of a pocketknife) that is propelled across the loom, pulling the filling yarn behind it. It can utilize a range of filling yarns and produce fabrics at a variety of widths. The range of widths usually falls within 190 centimeters (75 inches) to 540 centimeters (213 inches). It is used to produce denim and sheeting.

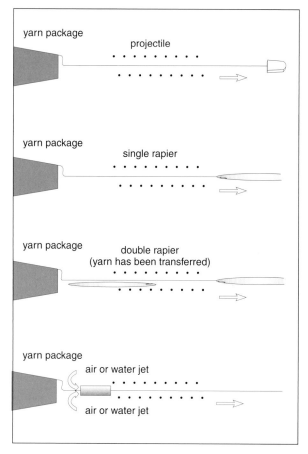

Figure 5.4
Inserting the filling yarn for shuttleless looms.

This loom also can produce fabric up to 18 feet (5.49 meters) wide and is used for the production of carpet.

Since the projectile loom drags the filling yarn across the width of the loom, a strain is placed on the filling yarn. Thus this method is not suited for weaving with weak or fragile filling yarns. This loom is ideal for fabrics to be made of medium weight to coarse or bulky yarns, as well as yarns made of hard fibers, such as jute, and fabrics to be made of metal threads.

With a production of only 400 ppm and limited versatility, projectile looms are being replaced by air-jet and rapier looms.

Rapier Loom   The **rapier loom** uses a rapier rod or steel tape to pull the filling yarn across the loom or a double rapier where the filling yarn is transferred at the midway point from one rapier to the other. This loom is noted for a large range of patterns produced. Because the rapier rod is not in free flight as is a projectile, less strain is placed on the filling yarn. Thus fine or delicate yarns can be used.

Rapier looms are used to produce high-quality wool and silk fabrics along with fine to coarse spun yarns and delicate filament yarns. It is also utilized to produce technical textiles, such as fabrics made of glass or high-strength fibers such as Kevlar® for air bags used in automobiles. It has a weft insertion rate (meters/minute) of filling yarn inserted from 900 meters (980 yards) to 1,300 meters (1,422 yards) per minute for fabric ranging in width from 140 centimeters (55 inches) to 280 centimeters (110 inches).

Jet Loom **Jet looms** take the filling yarn across the loom by using a high-speed jet of either air or water. The force of the air or water carries the yarn from one side to the other. Jet looms are faster than projectile or rapier looms (higher picks per minute). They cannot, however, produce as great a variety of fabrics (no heavy and bulky yarns), nor can they produce as wide a fabric (jets have less yarn-carrying power than projectiles and rapiers). Jet looms also do less damage to the warp because there is no abrasion of this yarn by the jets of air or water. This is in contrast to the projectile or rapier, which rides across the warp yarns left in the down position of the shed.

With **air-jet looms**, the initial propulsion force is provided by a main nozzle. Relay nozzles along the shed produce additional booster jets to help carry the yarns across the loom.

Air-jet looms are used for spun or filament yarn fabrics such as those found in men's outerwear, sheeting, and denim. It has a speed of 800 ppm and up. Widths vary from 190 centimeters (75 inches) to 540 centimeters (213 inches).

With **water-jet looms**, there is only a main nozzle to provide the propulsion of the filling yarn. These looms require large amounts of clean water without minerals in it to produce efficiently.

Because wet fabric cannot be stored in a roll, water-jet looms are equipped with efficient drying units. These units use vacuum suction and heat to remove the water from the fabric. Water-jet looms are best suited for weaving filament yarns made of hydrophobic fibers, such as nylon, although they can handle some blends, such as polyester/cotton. These looms cannot be used with yarns made of fibers that lose strength when wet (e.g., rayon).

Multiphase Loom **Multiphase looms** offer enormous output for light to medium weight fabrics. This is accomplished with the use of multiple sheds operating separately across the loom instead of only one shed. Thus, filling yarns can be inserted one after another, similar to a wave, as they travel across the width of the loom. This system is not as versatile as other looms, but it can produce fabric at a rate of 2,800 ppm with a weft insertion

rate of 5,500 meters/minute (6,015 yards/minute). It is used for the staple fabrics of basic weaves, such as plain, rib, or simple twills.

Loom Production

The filling yarns are inserted at a constant rate (e.g., 650 picks per minute). The rate at which the warp yarns pass through the loom determines the picks per inch, which affects the tightness or looseness of the fabric. For example, if the warp yarns move at the rate of 5 inches per minute and the speed of the loom is 650 picks per minute, the picks per inch (ppi) of the resulting fabric is 130 ppi (650 ÷ 5 = 130). Loom production (yards produced per hour) is low and more costly when making fabrics with high picks per inch.

The ends per inch of the fabric is calculated by the number of warp yarns on the warp beam. For example, if 9,000 warp yarns are wound on a warp beam to make a fabric 60 inches wide, the fabric has 150 ends per inch (9,000 ÷ 60 = 150). If the desired fabric has 160 ends per inch and is 60 inches wide, then the new warp beam must have 9,600 ends (160 × 60 = 9600).

Fabric Features

Several features are found in all woven fabrics:

▶ Selvage

▶ Warp and filling yarns

▶ Face and back

▶ Top and bottom

▶ Yarns per inch

Knowledge of these fabric characteristics is needed to understand fabric structure and suitability in particular uses.

The Selvage

The **selvage** is a lengthwise edge of a fabric. It is usually between ¼ and ½ inch (.64 cm and 1.27 cm) wide and exists on both edges of the cloth. The term selvage is derived from the descriptive term self-edge (see Figure 5.5a–d).

The main purpose of the selvage is to ensure that the edge of the fabric will not tear when the cloth is undergoing the stresses and strains of the finishing process. (See Chapter 10.) Sheets and bath towels are two products in which the selvage is left intact as a finished edge of the fabric.

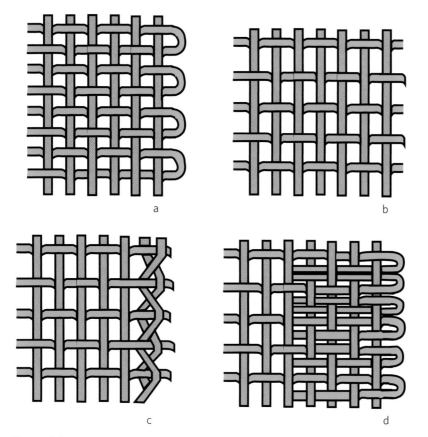

FIGURE 5.5
Various types of selvages: (a) Selvage as produced by the shuttle loom. Selvages made on a shuttleless loom such as (b) fringe (c) leno and (d) tucked-in selvage.

Various techniques are used to make the selvage area stronger than the body of the cloth, including using heavier warp yarns; more warp yarns per inch; plied warp yarns; greater twist, if spun warp yarns; and different weave. Because the selvage is usually constructed differently than the body, it is fairly easy to identify.

If the selvage warp yarns are different from the body warp yarns, their shrinkage characteristics may be different. If the selvage warp yarns have greater shrinkage during the finishing process, a tight selvage occurs, resulting in the puckering of an area within several inches of the fabric edge. This is a problem when the material is unrolled on the cutting table and the cloth does not lie flat.

Identifying Warp Yarns and Filling Yarns

One way to better understand the characteristics of woven fabric is to know the differences between the warp yarns and the filling yarns. Because fabric swatches are mounted with the warp yarns vertically, it must be determined which set of yarns is the warp so the mountings are correct. More importantly, garments are usually cut with the warp yarns running lengthwise, so the

drapability of the fabric must be checked by the designer to ensure that it meets the garment requirements. In all cases, distinguishing warp from filling is necessary. Finally, a textile expert making a complete analysis of a cloth must be able to identify both the warp and filling yarns in order to report such information as size, amount of twist, and fiber content.

The following are some of the ways warp yarns can be distinguished from filling yarns:

Selvage The warp yarns are always parallel to the selvage.

Yarn sizes Usually the warp yarns are thinner, so they abrade less as they pass through the loom and rub against the various parts (e.g., heddles, reed). A fabric that contains both filament yarns and spun yarns usually has the filament yarns as the warp set.

Twist For the most part, spun warp yarns have more twist than spun filling yarns. Because they usually are thinner, more twist is necessary to enable them to have sufficient strength to withstand the tensions exerted on the yarns in weaving and in finishing.

Yarns per inch Usually there are more warp yarns per inch than filling yarns per inch, making the fabric stronger in the lengthwise direction. This is necessary because most of the tension exerted on the fabric in the finishing processes is in the lengthwise direction. Sometimes, however, the ends and picks per inch are equal (e.g., 80 square-print cloth) or occasionally the picks per inch is greater (e.g., soft filled sheeting).

Ply yarns As discussed in Chapter 4, a plied yarn is stronger than a single yarn of the same size. Thus, the warp yarns are occasionally plied to give added strength, and the filling yarns usually remain single.

Stiffness In 100 percent spun-yarn fabrics, the warp yarns are generally stiffer than the filling yarns because they usually have more twist. In 100 percent filament-yarn fabrics, the filling yarns are usually stiffer because they generally are thicker. A stiffer set of yarns usually results in less fabric drapability in that direction.

Stretchability Usually there is more elongation in the width-wise direction. In most cases there are more ends per inch, so the picks usually have more crimp as they interlace (go under and over the warp yarns more frequently) to a greater degree.

Stripes Most woven stripes appear in the lengthwise direction. Warp-wise woven stripes only require the appropriate color yarns to be properly grouped when the warp is made on the warp beam. When fabric is cut with the stripe in the length direction, the garment gives the wearer the illusion of more height and a leaner look. Checks and plaids are created by making stripes in both the warp direction and the filling direction.

Face and Back

Fabric developers generally address issues such as quality or durability, with the yarns on the face of the fabric. Thus, fabrics have a technical **face** side and a technical **back** side. The face side has the better appearance and usually forms the outside of the garment (or other textile product). Sometimes fashion dictates the use of the back of a fabric as the outside of the garment for the particular effect desired. Fabric developers generally address quality or durability issues with the yarns on the face of the fabric.

There are various reasons that the face and back of cloth appear different. The two sides of a fabric may be different because of the weave or finish. Any fabric in which the warp yarns or the filling yarns appear more on one side than on the other shows a difference between the face and back. Fabrics with a plain weave (see p. 91) or leno weave (see p. 97) are reversible, but fabrics with a satin weave are not (see p. 95). In a satin fabric, the warp yarns predominate on the face and the filling yarns on the back so that the two sides differ greatly in appearance. Usually the shinier, smoother side is the face. An exception is antique satin in which slub filling yarns create the slightly irregular effect on the surface.

Some finishes, such as napping or brushing, affect only one surface of the cloth, whereas others, such as mercerizing, penetrate the entire fabric. Napping gives a fabric an obvious face side as, for example, in a flannel material. Mercerizing, however, produces the same change on both sides, as in a broadcloth fabric; thus a reversible fabric results. In printed fabrics, the color is usually placed only on one side. Therefore, unless the fabric is very sheer, the printed side is obvious and is considered the face. Some sheer printed fabrics may appear to be reversible because the print design seems to be the same on both sides.

Caution: A garment should not be made with some parts cut from one side of the fabric and other parts cut from the other side. Even though both sides of the fabric may initially appear alike, there is often a slight difference in luster or color that does not become obvious until the garment is made and worn. This difference may become significant after cleanings and wear.

Top and Bottom

Besides having a face and a back, some fabrics have a **top** and a **bottom** on the face side. Where there is a difference, it is usually caused by the weave or the finish. In pile fabrics such as velveteen and corduroy, the pile is not perfectly erect, but lies at an angle. The color may vary from dark to light as the fabric is turned 180° on a flat surface because of the difference in the angle of light reflection. Sometimes these fabrics are used in garments where the pile lies upward in order to obtain a richer or darker color. With fabrics having an obvious top and bottom, the garment must be made with all its parts in the same top-down or bottom-down direction.

A fabric with a woven or printed figure in an obviously upright position (e.g., horse, tree) can be cut in only one direction because in every piece forming the garment, the figure must be in the upright position. Printed fabrics that can only be used in one direction are called directional prints.

Most fabrics, however, when resting on a flat surface with the face side up and the warp yarns vertical, have the same appearance as when the fabric is turned so that the edge that was at the top is at the bottom. Thus, it usually does not make any difference in appearance with these fabrics if a garment is made with its parts placed from top-to-bottom or if its parts are turned 180° and placed bottom-to-top. In fact, most mass-produced apparel is cut this way to interlock patterns efficiently. Nevertheless, this could be undesirable because there may be a slight difference in color or luster that is not noticeable in a smaller piece of fabric but is obvious in the full garment.

Yarns Per Inch: A Measure of Fabric Quality

The **yarns per inch** in a fabric is given by two numbers with an × between them. For example, 80 × 74 (pronounced "eighty-by-seventy-four") means 80 yarns per inch in the warp and 74 yarns per inch in the filling. The first number is for warp yarns per inch and the second is for filling yarns per inch. A fabric with the same number of yarns per inch in both directions is said to be square. An 80-square print cloth has 80 ends and 80 picks per inch. The yarns per inch in the warp and in the filling is known as the fabric count.

Yarns per inch is a measure of fabric quality. Two broadcloths may differ in price because one has more yarns per inch. A higher number of yarns per inch gives the fabric more strength, more weight, better hand, reduced possibility of yarns shifting out of place (yarn distortion; see p. 290), and better abrasion resistance. Increasing the yarns per inch also increases the cost of the fabric.

The type numbers given for sheeting are based on the number of yarns per square inch. The sum of the yarns per inch in the warp and the yarns per inch in the filling is referred to as the type number. For example, if sheeting has 100 ends and 100 picks per inch, the type number is 200 (100 plus 100). It is also referred to as 200-count. For other fabrics, the value is given as 100 × 100, and not as a sum.

Historically, manufacturers of sheets with a cloth count of 100 × 100 made of single yarns would indicate a 200 thread count on the package. Recently some manufacturers of sheets have counted ply yarns as two separate yarns when indicating the thread count. Thus the same sheet made of 2 ply yarns might indicate a 400 thread count. This confusion triggered a concern for the industry as well as the retailers and resulted in a class action suit and settlement. Thread count has long been recognized by consumers as a tool to determine quality (see Figure 5.6). A contradiction in cloth count causes doubt and confusion for consumers.

To learn how to determine the yarns per inch of a woven fabric, see page 275.

Determining the Weave of a Fabric

Woven fabric is analyzed to determine the weave. It is done by determining the order in which the yarns interlace. Fabric is usually analyzed on the face side, but sometimes the weave may be more clearly seen on the back. To determine the weave of the fabric, every interlacing is examined to determine whether the warp yarn or the filling yarn is on the surface. The weave may be illustrated on graph paper indicating the location of the warp yarn on the surface. If the warp yarn is on the surface of the fabric, it is indicated by marking in one box on the graph paper; if the warp yarn is on the back of the fabric, the box is left empty. Refer to page 280 for further information.

The vertical and horizontal rows of squares are the same size. A weave diagram only shows the order in which the yarns interlace (see Figure 5.7a–c). The weave diagram does not show the relative number of yarns per inch between warp and filling, nor does it indicate the yarn size and type. Thus sheeting fabric, voile, overcoat fabric, and lining could all have the same weave diagram but entirely different appearances and end-use applications.

Weave Floats

Warp yarns and filling yarns in a fabric interlace with each other. When one yarn does not interlace with the next adjacent yarn, but passes over two or more adjacent yarns, it is said to **float**. If a warp yarn passes over two or more adjacent filling yarns, a warp float results. When the filling yarn passes over warp yarns, a filling float occurs.

Floats tend to make the fabric surface flat and increase the amount of luster. They also enable yarns to slide under each other in the fabric and are, therefore, used when fabrics of many yarns per inch are to be made. (See p. 96.)

When the float is relatively long, a snagging problem frequently results. The yarn can easily catch and break on broken fingernails or other rough surfaces. Floats also

FIGURE 5.6
Percale sheets by Martha Stewart Collection™ for Macy's.

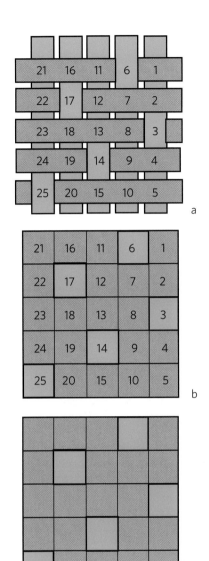

FIGURE 5.7
The interlacing yarns of a (a) satin weave; the numbered squares that correspond to the (b) interlacings of the weave; and (c) the weave on graph paper.

weaken the fabric because they reduce the frequency with which yarns pass from one side of the fabric to the other (from the face to the back or from the back to the

face). This affect can be offset by increasing the yarns per inch of the fabric.

Basic Fabric Weaves

There are three basic weaves: plain weave, twill weave, and satin weave. All other weaves are a variation or a combination of these weaves.

The type of weave used in a fabric depends on the desired appearance and performance (see Table 5.1). Such factors as luster, strength, pattern, color effect, and, most importantly, cost, are considered before the fabric weave is chosen.

Plain Weave

Plain weave is the simplest and the most used weave. It is found in a wide range of fabrics, from the sheerest to the heaviest. Fabrics with a plain weave are reversible unless one side is made the face by a finishing or printing process.

More fabrics are made with plain weave than any other weave. These include such well-known fabrics as gauze and chiffon (sheer), gingham, chambray (shirting/blouse weight), taffeta and chintz (medium weight), and burlap and canvas (heavier weight).

In plain weave, each warp yarn passes alternately over one and then under one filling yarn, for the whole length of the fabric. Two adjacent warp yarns interlace exactly opposite. One warp yarn goes under the same filling yarn that the next warp yarn goes over. The third and fourth warp yarns weave the same as the first and second, respectively (see Figure 5.8a and b).

As shown in Figure 5.8 each filling yarn passes alternately over one and then under one warp yarn, for the full width of the fabric. Two succeeding filling yarns weave exactly opposite. When one filling yarn passes over a warp yarn, the next filling yarn passes under the same warp yarn. The third and fourth filling yarns weave the same as the first and second. The plain weave, therefore, makes one complete cycle on two ends and two picks. By definition, we say the repeat of this weave is on two ends and two picks. More complex weaves have larger repeats.

TABLE 5.1	Comparison of Basic Weave Properties				
Weave	Luster	Snag Resistance	Surface Effect	Tearing Strength	Wrinkle Resistance
Plain	Poor	Good	Flat, uninteresting	Low	Poor
Twill	Fair	Good	Twill lines	Medium	Fair
Satin	Good (especially with filament yarns)	Poor if long floats	Smooth	High	Good

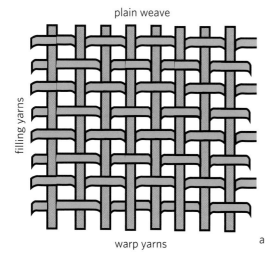

plain weave

filling yarns

warp yarns

a

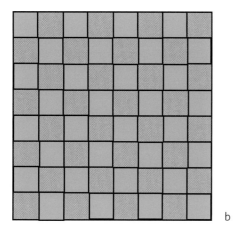

b

FIGURE 5.8
(a) Plain weave and (b) plain weave on graph paper.

Plain-weave fabrics require only two harnesses to weave the body of the fabric (excluding the selvage) because the weave repeats every two ends. One harness controls half the warp yarns (1, 3, 5, etc.), and the second harness controls the other warp yarns (2, 4, 6, etc.). When one harness is raised, the other is lowered, and then the sequence is reversed for the next pick.

Plain-weave fabrics have firm constructions. They tend to wear well and ravel less than comparable fabrics of other weaves. Because the surface is plain, it offers a good background for printed and decorative designs.

Plain-weave fabrics tend to wrinkle more than fabrics of other weaves. Frequent interlacing does not allow the yarns to move in the fabric to relieve stress from the bent fibers. A high number of interlacings also results in less bias stretch. Plain weaves usually have little surface

interest unless colored yarns are used to make designs (for example, a plaid) or special yarns or finishes are used to produce texture.

The tearing strength of a plain weave is lower than that of any other weave. Because this weave has no floats, when tearing a plain-weave fabric, the yarns break one at a time. When tearing other woven fabrics, however, the yarns shift and bunch together from the tearing force being exerted. The fabric tearing strength of such fabrics is higher because several yarns must be torn simultaneously instead of only one at a time.

Ribbed Plain Weave

A fabric with a plain weave may have a **ribbed** surface. The rib is produced because the filling yarns are thicker than the warp yarns. The rib can be very pronounced, as in a bengaline or ottoman fabric; easily visible, as in a faille or poplin fabric; or less noticeable, as in a broadcloth or taffeta. The rib, however, can always be detected by running a fingernail up and down the fabric.

Although rib effects are popular, they can have problems. The filling yarns that form the ribs may have been made bulky by having little twist and/or short staple fibers. Because wear occurs mainly on the top of the ribs, if the heavy filling yarns are not well protected by the set of thinner warp yarns, the fabric will not wear well because the heavy yarns will abrade quickly.

Ribbed fabrics with thin warp yarns and fine ribs possess better drape and a smoother surface, and fabrics with large ribs possess an uneven surface and more body. Sometimes, the ribbed fabrics are also called unbalanced fabrics because the sizes of the warp and filling yarns, as well as the number of ends and picks per inch within the fabric, are greatly different from one another.

Basket Weave

A major plain-weave variation is the **basket weave.** Basket weaves are made by having groups of two or more warp yarns interlacing as one yarn with groups of two or more filling yarns that also interlace as one yarn. The groups of yarns interlace in plain-weave sequence. Fabrics with basket weaves are reversible unless the finish or print makes one side the face. Two well-known fabrics made with basket weave are monk's cloth and hopsacking.

The two-by-two (2 × 2) basket weave is the most common. In this weave, the warp yarns in pairs interlace in plain-weave sequence with the filling yarns in pairs. (See Figure 5.9a and b.) The weave repeats on four ends and four picks and requires two harnesses to make.

Basket weave is a decorative weave. Most basket-weave fabrics are made with relatively few yarns per inch

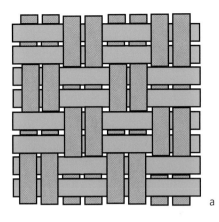

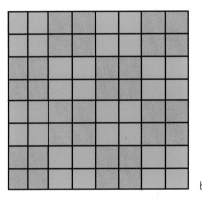

FIGURE 5.9
(a) A 2 × 2 basket weave and (b) a 2 × 2 basket weave on graph paper.

and frequently with low-twist yarns to increase the weave effect. Thus, these types of fabric tend not to be durable and easily shrink when washed. They are frequently difficult to sew because the yarns can move easily; this also causes the fabric to lose its shape.

Twill Weave

Twill weaves (Figure 5.10) produce diagonal lines on the cloth. In a **right-hand twill,** the diagonals run upward to the right; in a **left-hand twill,** the lines run upward to the left. The direction of the twill on the back of the cloth is opposite to the twill line on the face. Some well-known twill weave fabrics are denim, gabardine, serge, and chino.

There are many twill weaves. The simplest is a $\frac{2}{1}$ twill (referred to as two up, one down) or a $\frac{1}{2}$ twill (one up, two down), which repeat on three ends and three picks. (Only three harnesses are required for body

FIGURE 5.10
Denim twill weave.

of the cloth.) Most twills are made on fewer than six harnesses.

In a $\frac{3}{1}$ twill (three up, one down), each warp yarn passes over three filling yarns and then under one filling yarn. The warp is on the face three times more than the filling, forming a warp-face twill. In a $\frac{1}{3}$ twill (one up, three down), the warp passes over one filling yarn and then under three filling yarns, to produce a filling-face twill. A $\frac{2}{2}$ twill has both warp and filling showing to the same extent on the face, and it is known as a balanced twill. A balanced fabric would have about the same size and number of warp and filling yarns per inch. Most twills are either warp face or balanced. (See Figure 5.11a–c.) This produces a more obvious twill line and also a more abrasion-resistant surface.

In a twill weave, every warp yarn interlaces in the same order, which may be $\frac{2}{1}$, $\frac{2}{3}$, $\frac{3}{2}$, or any other sequence. However, each succeeding warp yarn starts the sequence of one or more filling yarns higher or one or more filling yarns lower. If each succeeding warp yarn to the right has the corresponding interlacing one filling yarn higher, the weave is a 45° right-hand twill (see Figure 5.12a and b). If each succeeding warp yarn to the right has a corresponding interlacing one filling yarn lower, the weave is a 45° left-hand twill. The step can also be more than one. If the corresponding interlacing on the succeeding warp yarn is two filling yarns higher or lower, a 63° twill weave is produced. Stepping up or down three filling yarns produces a 70° twill, up or down four produces a 75° twill. Most twills are 45° twills but the difference in yarn size of the warp (finer) and the filling (coarser) may cause the perception of a 63° twill (i.e., steeper twill line).

A twill weave with a diagonal line greater than 45° is also referred to as a steep twill. If the diagonal line is less than 45°, it is sometimes referred to as a reclined twill. Figure 5.13 shows the different twill angles.

Important Features

Twill lines can be made more prominent by using plied yarns, high-twist yarns, twill weaves with longer floats, high yarns per inch, and yarn twist opposite to the twill-line direction. Fabrics with these prominent lines (e.g., gabardine) may become flattened by wear and pressure, and thus become shiny.

Twills are widely used for work clothes (e.g., denim), suiting fabrics (e.g., serge), and dress fabrics (e.g., surah). Twill weaves have fewer interlacings than plain weave, which permits more yarns per inch in the fabric and makes twills more compact, stronger, heavier, and more durable than plain- and basket-weave fabrics. In twill, the floats are short, so yarn snagging is not a problem.

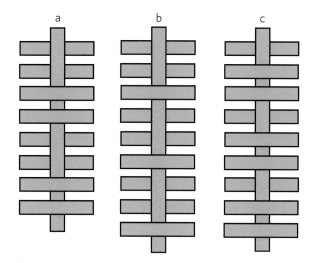

FIGURE 5.11
(a) Balanced twill $\frac{2}{2}$ (b) warp-face twill $\frac{2}{1}$ and (c) filling-face twill $\frac{1}{2}$.

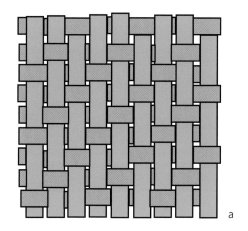

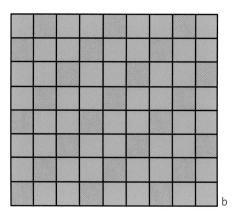

FIGURE 5.12
(a) 45° right-hand twill weave and (b) 45° right-hand twill on graph paper.

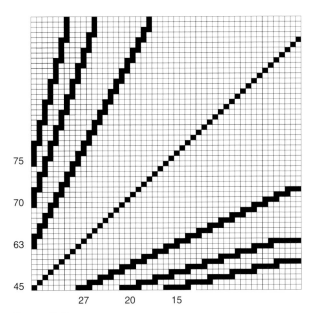

FIGURE 5.13
Degree of twill angle.

Broken-Twill Weave

Although the twill lines usually run in one direction, sometimes a fabric combines right- and left-hand twills. This weave is called a **broken-twill weave.** It is made from a regular twill weave in which the twill runs in one direction (e.g., right) for a desired number of yarns, and then the direction of the twill is reversed (e.g., left) for a desired number of yarns. The pattern then repeats.

A well-known broken-twill design is **chevron.** This design produces stripes in a zig-zag effect. Usually yarns in two different colors are used to accentuate these designs. **Herringbone** is considered a broken twill by many. It is so called because the vertical stripes of both right- and left-hand twill resemble the backbone of a herring fish. (See Figure 5.14.)

Satin Weave

In a true **satin weave,** there is only one interlacing for each warp yarn, and only one interlacing for each filling yarn in each repeat of the weave. Also, no two interlacings ever touch or are adjacent. This means the satin weave fabrics have relatively long floats.

One set of yarns forms most of the face; the other set forms most of the back. In a **warp-face satin,** the face is predominantly warp yarns. A **filling-face satin** has filling yarns predominant on the face. Thus there are no balanced satins comparable to the balanced twills. (See Figure 5.15a–d.)

Satin weaves are designated by the number of harnesses they require in weaving. A satin may be named a five-harness satin, or a five-shaft satin. Five is the lowest possible and also most common number of harnesses for making satin. Some seven-harness and eight-harness satins are also produced, but beyond eight is not economical.

For a five-harness satin there are only five interlacings in one repeat of the weave. The number of interlacings is the same as the number of harnesses used to produce the weave. The length of the floats in satin is one fewer than the number of harnesses used. The number of harnesses used is also the size of the repeat in the warp and in the filling directions.

Satin is also the name of a fabric of satin weave. Satin fabric is made from filament yarns, with the warp yarns predominant on the face. Satin fabrics are smooth and lustrous for a number of reasons: lustrous filament yarns are used; the weave has few interlacings, and thus, long floats; and the face yarns are very fine and closely packed. Since the greatest luster is in the lengthwise direction (the direction of the floats of satin), garments using this fabric are made so this direction is vertical in the garment to maximize the luster.

Sateen fabric is a durable cotton fabric usually with a filling-face satin weave. It is not as lustrous as satin fabric because spun yarns are used in it. Because it is also heavier, and is made with thicker yarns, it is not as drapable as satin fabric.

In **crepe-back satin,** the warp yarns are fine and have little or no twist, and the filling yarns are highly twisted. The face of the fabric is almost entirely warp yarns, and the back is almost entirely filling yarns. Because of the

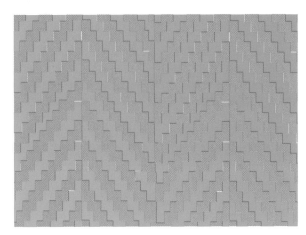

FIGURE 5.14
Herringbone weave shown on graph paper.

FIGURE 5.15
(a) Five-shaft warp-face satin weave
(b) five-shaft filling-face satin weave
(c) five-shaft warp-face satin weave on graph paper and (d) five-shaft filling face satin weave on graph paper.

a

b

c

d

high twist, the filling gives the back a crepe, or pebbly, appearance and leaves the face fairly smooth.

Satin weaves produce a very even surface because of the many warp or filling floats. (Satins have the minimum number of interlacings, which are widely distributed.)

Although the long floats of the yarns provide luster to the satin-weave fabrics, they are also responsible for the poor wearing quality of many of these cloths. The floats cause the yarns to be greatly exposed to abrasive forces. Also, with filament yarns common in these fabrics, the floats catch on rough surfaces and the filaments break. Thus, satin-weave fabrics are most common in end uses that are not subject to hard wear, such as evening dresses, fine lingerie, and draperies.

Under certain conditions, however, good abrasion resistance and strength can occur in satin-weave fabrics. The long floats found in this weave enable the yarns to slide under one another, thus allowing more yarns per inch than if woven with shorter floats or none at all. If the fabric is made with a very large number of yarns per inch, an extremely durable fabric results because the

fiber is very dense. With yarns tightly packed, and using spun yarns, snagging is not a serious problem. Examples of several of these fabrics, which also have satisfactory drapability, are the sateen materials used for military combat uniforms frequently used for camouflage.

Which Weave Makes the Strongest Fabric?

Weaves with long floats produce the strongest fabric because these fabrics can be made with the greatest number of yarns per inch. Figure 5.16a shows the yarns at the edge of fabric with a weave that has no floats. Figure 5.16b shows the yarns at the edge of a fabric with a weave that does have floats. In Figure 5.16a the filling yarn is interlacing with six yarns, whereas in Figure 5.16b the filling is interlacing with eight yarns. Thus, satin-weave fabric is the strongest because it can be made with the most yarns per inch since it has the fewest interlacings.

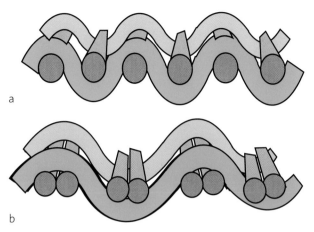

a

b

FIGURE 5.16
Weave influence on maximum yarns per inch of a fabric.
Notice that illustration b has fewer interlacings and therefore
more yarns per inch.

Special Fabric Weaves

Various special fabric weaves besides the basic weaves
are also used. Three of the most common special weaves
are leno weave, pile weave, and weaves that make a
double cloth.

Leno Weave

In the simplest **leno weave,** the warp yarns twist back
and forth in pairs around each pick, firmly holding the
filling yarn in the figure-eight loops formed. Because the
filling yarns are firmly held in place, they cannot shift in
the warp direction (see Figure 5.17). However, the warp
yarns can shift in the filling direction. Adhesive may be
used in finishing leno fabrics to cement the yarn in place
to further reduce slippage.

In counting yarns per inch in leno weave, the two
warp yarns that twist to form a loop for the filling count
as two separate yarns. They do not form a ply yarn. These
yarns twisting identify this as a leno fabric.

Leno weave is especially useful for reducing yarn
slippage in fabrics that require yarns spaced far apart. It
has greater firmness and strength than plain weave of
the same low cloth count. The construction is used in
mosquito netting, sheer curtains (e.g., marquisette), and
some summer apparel fabrics in open and see-through
constructions. It is used for industrial purposes and as
packaging for fruits and vegetables. It is also used to
make chenile yarns (see p. 75).

Pile Weaves

Woven-pile fabrics are material with a raised hairlike or
furlike surface. Two well-known fabrics with such a surface are velvet and terry cloth. The surface is produced
with an extra set of yarns (warp or filling) known as pile
yarns. Thus, pile fabrics have the regular warp yarns and
filling yarns (called ground yarns) that are common to
all wovens, plus an additional set of yarns to create the
pile surface.

There are two basic types of pile-weave fabrics:
the **warp-pile fabrics,** which have an extra set of warp
yarns, and the **filling-pile fabrics,** which have an extra
set of filling yarns. When the pile yarns are cut, the
resulting fabric is referred to as a **cut-pile weave fabric.**
These yarns are cut between interlacings to form many
cut ends, which point up on the surface of the cloth and
form the pile. If the pile yarns are not cut, an **uncut-pile
weave fabric** is produced. (See Figure 5.18.)

Velvet is an example of a cut warp-pile weave fabric, and terry cloth is an example of an uncut warp-pile
weave fabric. Filling-pile weave fabrics, such as corduroy
and velveteen, are always cut. (See Figure 5.19.)

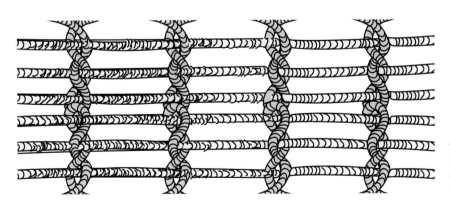

FIGURE 5.17
Leno weave. Notice how each pair
of warp yarns twists to hold the
filling yarns.

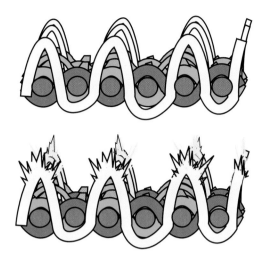

FIGURE 5.18
Filling pile weave fabric: ground filling (purple and dark blue), ground warp (brown), and pile filling (light blue).

A **napped fabric** is different from a **pile fabric.** Nap is a fibrous surface produced by brushing up fibers on the cloth during a textile finishing process. (See p. 190.) Extra yarns are not used to produce the surface effect.

When warp yarns are removed from corduroy or velveteen fabrics, they are covered with short lengths of fibers. The same occurs with filling yarns removed from velvet. The pieces of pile yarns that were cut cling to the yarns that were removed.

Cut-Pile Fabrics

Cut-pile fabrics are cut on the face after the fabric is completely woven. Two methods are used for making cut-warp pile fabrics. In one method, a **double cloth** is woven (see p. 100) with pile yarns interlacing between and connecting the two fabrics. The completed double cloth is cut into two fabrics by cutting the interlacing warp yarns. These cut yarns form the pile for each of the resulting fabrics. In the second method, after a number of filling yarns have been inserted, a special rod with a blade at one end is interlaced instead of a filling yarn. The harnesses operate so that only pile warp yarns pass over the rod. After several more filling yarns have been woven beyond the rod, the rod is removed and the knife at the end of the rod cuts all warp yarns that pass over the rod. The cut yarns stand up to form the pile. The weaving continues with the insertion of the rod after weaving a few additional filling yarns and the removal of the rod after weaving a few more filling yarns.

With filling cut-pile fabrics, there is no raising of yarns by wires. The pile-filling yarns are woven to float over a group of warp yarns. The pile yarns are then cut

FIGURE 5.19
This corduroy jacket is an example of a filling-pile weave fabric.

at the center of the float. The ends of the cut yarns produce the cut-pile effect. The floats in corduroy fabric are placed in lengthwise rows, and the floats in velveteen are randomly spaced. Thus, when corduroy fabric is cut, the characteristic wale or hill-and-valley effect is produced. The thickness of the wales can be varied, from narrow (used for apparel) to very wide (used for furniture fabric). When velveteen fabric is cut, an overall cut-pile surface is produced. Decorative patterns and effects can be created by cutting floats selectively.

Cut-pile weave fabrics are made with different heights of pile. For example, velvet has a low pile height, velour has a higher pile, and plush has still higher pile.

The face of cut-pile fabrics has an up-and-down direction (top and bottom) because of the position of the pile. A garment made with the pile fabric facing downward offers a smoother surface for light and so appears more lustrous. If the pile is up, the color is richer because more of the interior of the fabric (and color) is visible. However, the fabric is less durable because the pile fibers are more exposed to rubbing forces.

In cutting fabric for a garment, the pile of all pieces in the garment must lie in the same direction to produce a uniform effect. Velvet, a cut-pile warp fabric is especially sensitive to crushing and must be stored so that the pile is not flattened.[1] Also, special care must be exercised in cleaning and refinishing velvet apparel.

Pile construction affects the fabric wearability. The short lengths of cut-pile yarn may have a V shape or a W shape. The W-shape pile is more firmly held in place because it interlaces with three yarns, and the V-shape interlaces with only one yarn. Thus, the W-shape pile yarn is held more securely, preventing a bald spot from developing.

The W-shape pile, however, is not as dense as the V-shape pile because the latter has two pile ends for each interlacing, and the W-shape pile has two pile ends for every three interlacings. (See Figure 5.20.) To obtain the same pile density for a W-shape pile as for a V-shape pile, more yarns per inch would have to be used. A denser pile can better resist crushing, gives better cover, and stands more erect, but also is more costly.

At times combinations of V-shape and W-shape pile are used in the same fabric. The V-shape adds depth to the pile and the W-shape adds stability. This alternative is often utilized in the construction of wide wale corduroy.

Different ground weaves are used for cut-pile fabrics. Usually the body of corduroy and velveteen fabrics are made with either a plain weave or a twill weave. Because the twill weave can result in a stronger fabric (more yarns per inch are possible; see p. 94), the twill-back pile fabrics are usually more durable than those with plain weave ground.

Uncut-Pile Fabrics

Terry cloth is an example of a fabric with an uncut-pile weave (see Figure 5.21). The fabric consists of ground warp and filling yarns plus an extra set of warp yarns for the pile, in the form of loops on the surface of the cloth. The loops are formed by having the extra warp yarns (pile yarns) raised by a wire inserted across the loom. The wire is then removed until the next set of loops is to be formed.

The warp direction of terry is readily determined because the extra yarn that forms the pile is length-wise. The weave varies so that there may be one pile end for one ground end, two pile ends for two ground ends, or some other simple arrangement.

---

1. Yard goods of velvet are shipped and stored on special bolts that keep the layers separate to avoid crushing.

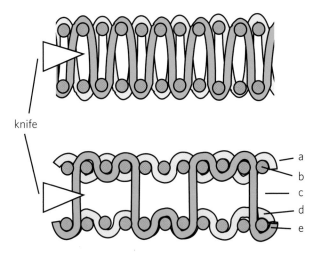

FIGURE 5.20
Double cloth pile weaving. Knife cuts pile warp yarns to make two velvet fabrics: V pile formation (top) and W pile formation (bottom) with (a) ground filling (top); (b) ground warp (top); (c) pile warp; (d) ground filling (light blue) (bottom); and (e) ground warp (bottom).

FIGURE 5.21
Terry cloth is an example of pile fabrics, often used for robes.

Two warp beams are used for weaving terry. On one beam, the warp yarn is tight, and on the other, the yarn is quite loose. The extra length in the loose warp yarn forms the loops in the fabric. A pile warp yarn may be almost four times longer than a ground warp yarn from the same cloth.

Frieze fabric, a thick pile fabric with patterns made from its loop surface, used for upholstery, is an example of an uncut-pile weave fabric.

As in cut-pile weave fabrics, a strong ground fabric with a large number of yarns per inch and a dense pile makes a durable uncut-pile material. High loops and thick, low-twist pile yarns make a more absorbent, but less durable, fabric. Towels rented at the beach frequently are scratchy and have poor absorption, but are usually very durable because of the high-twist pile yarns.

Sometimes the pile loops are cut in a terry cloth for decorative effect. This is then considered a cut-pile fabric.

Double Cloth and Variations

A double cloth is actually two fabrics held together by a separate set of yarns. Each fabric is made using one set of warp yarns and one set of filling yarns (a total of two warp and two filling sets), with a third set of warp yarns moving back and forth between the two layers of fabrics to hold them together. All yarns are woven simultaneously to produce the double cloth.

Some double cloths are specifically designed to be cut into two separate fabrics, such as velvet. Here, both of the resulting fabrics have a cut-pile surface. Other fabrics are structured to remain as one fabric, such as some tapestries.

A double-cloth fabric used to make coats may be made with a solid color face and plaid back. Blankets are sometimes made in this manner. Some fabrics resemble a double-cloth construction but are made with one set each of warp and filling. The three-dimensional effect is the result of the weave forcing some of the yarns to be raised. An example of this fabric type is piqué.

Woven Designs

If a fabric containing a woven design is carefully examined (using a pick glass), it is clear that the design was created by long and short floats as well as the placement of interlacings. So-called white-on-white shirtings and brocades are examples of this type of fabric. Depending on their design and how they are produced, they are known as dobby patterns, jacquard patterns, clip-spot patterns, or color and weave effects.

Dobby Pattern

A **dobby pattern** is a design that contains simple geometric forms or motifs. It is made on a loom with a special harness control mechanism called a **dobby head.** The loom, referred to as a dobby loom, uses computer-controlled mechanisms to determine which harnesses are raised or lowered. Since up to 32 harnesses can be controlled this way, complex and expensive weaves can be produced. If more complex designs are desired, a jacquard loom must be used.

Jacquard Pattern

A **jacquard pattern** is a design that contains very detailed, intricate motifs (see Figure 5.22). Because these designs exceed the capacity of harness looms, a special loom must be used. This loom usually has no harnesses, and the ends are controlled by a **jacquard head** located at the top of the loom. The loom is referred to as a **jacquard loom** because the control device was perfected in 1805 by Joseph-Marie Charles Jacquard.

The jacquard head uses a computer tape to control the warp yarns, in the same way that a punched paper roller controls the keys in a player piano. The position of the holes in the tape determines the sequence in which the warp yarns are moved. Hooks and needles are used to raise and lower the warp yarns by controlling a cord attached to each heddle. Because there are no harnesses, any combination of yarns can be raised or lowered to produce the design.

FIGURE 5.22
The design in this fabric is created by a jacquard loom.

The jacquard loom operates more slowly than do the other, simpler looms, so the fabrics produced on this loom are more expensive. Damask, tapestry, and brocade are several fabrics commonly made with jacquard designs.

Clip-Spot Pattern

Woven designs can also be obtained by using extra warp yarns or filling yarns. In a **clip-spot pattern,** the extra yarns interlace in the fabric to make a simple design and then float until the yarns again interlace to repeat the pattern. The long floats between the patterns are often cut away and discarded. The ends of the cut yarns are easily seen on the back of the fabric.

Dotted Swiss fabric has extra filling yarn, and clip-spot shirting fabric contains extra warp yarn to make the design.

The durability of the design (i.e., how well the extra yarns remain in the fabric) depends on the number of interlacings in the design and the closeness of the yarns in the fabric. The additional yarns do not substantially affect the strength of the fabric.

Color-and-Weave Effect

A **color-and-weave effect** is a pattern produced in a fabric by using a certain weave and a certain arrangement of differently colored yarns in both the warp and the filling. A houndstooth pattern is a common example of a color-and-weave effect design (Figure 5.23). The houndstooth pattern shown in the chapter opening pages is made from a two-up, two-down, 45°, left-hand twill. In this example, both warp and filling have black and white yarns arranged four of one color, followed by four of the second color.

Wherever a warp yarn and a filling yarn interlace, a small spot of the color of the yarn passing over is seen on the face of the cloth. The sum of the colors of all the yarns interlacing on the face produces various stripes, checks, and plaids.

Computer Technology

One of the most dynamic changes in the fabric-formation process has been the application of computer technology. From a design and production perspective, computers have enabled the industry to produce a variety of woven fabric more quickly and effectively than ever before. They have allowed the woven-fabrics industry the opportunity to offer value-added merchandise with a shortened production cycle. This quick turnaround has fueled new opportunities in the use of woven fabrics in broad applications for both the apparel and interior furnishings industries.

The initial design can be made in minutes with the colored pattern shown on the computer screen. Any modifications and/or alternatives can be produced with the same ease. The images of the color monitors are very realistic, as are the designs that are reproduced by color printers. These computer-generated designs are sent directly to buyers anywhere in the world and when approved can be electronically transmitted to computer-operated loom systems at the textile mill.

The use of the computer allows the textile designer to work directly with the consumer (e.g., dress designer). Any changes in color or pattern can quickly be accomplished. The print hard copy that is finally approved usually has a remarkable similarity to the fabric to be made. The designer can choose the type of yarn (e.g., tightness of twist and thickness) as well as the surface (e.g., smooth or brushed, slightly blurred look).

Equipment is now available that can scan a woven fabric and analyze the warp and filling yarns, colors, the cloth count, and the particular weave. This can be done to actual fabric samples that are as complex as multifaceted dobby patterns found in upholstery and men's suiting.

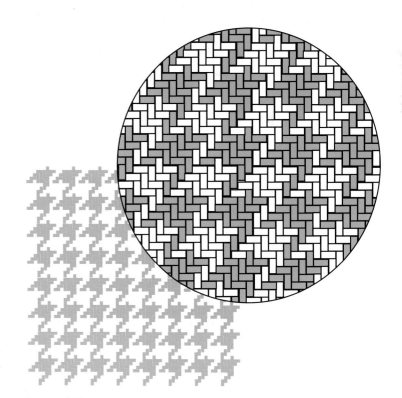

FIGURE **5.23**
Houndstooth plaid.

The fabrics can be shown as a three-dimensional object. Thus the effects of changing in yarns, fabric construction (ypi), and finish can be viewed. Also both sides of the material can be seen.

The garment designer can also use a computer system to draw the garment on the screen. When the garment is completed and approved, any pattern of fabric stored in the computer can be displayed on the garment. The garment can also be displayed on a model, with the computer simulating draping, shadowing, and light-pattern changes to create a realistic three-dimensional form. A printout can be produced for distribution to customers, sales personnel, or management.

Technological advances have provided the opportunity for full integration of design and production of woven fabric. Technology has given the textile industry the catalyst to enhance the designer's creativity, to suggest production alternatives when needed, and to establish accurate information regarding quick delivery of goods to a global marketplace.

Factors Affecting the Cost of Woven Fabrics

The selling price of a fabric is based on the cost to produce it as well as the demand for the cloth. Fabric is bought and sold both in unfinished and finished states. The following are some of the factors that affect the cost of producing woven fabrics:

Fiber content: The cost of fibers is based on quality as well as generic type. Pima cotton is more expensive than upland cotton because it is a better-quality fiber. Polyester is more expensive than acetate because of the higher cost of manufacturing. Antron® nylon costs more than the regular type of nylon for the same reason.

Yarn type: The cost of yarns is based on fiber content and the type of yarn. Novelty yarns are more expensive to produce than the regular type. High-twist spun yarns cost more than low-twist spun yarns of the same yarn size because the former take longer to produce. Thinner spun yarns are usually more expensive than thicker yarns for the same reason. Worsted yarn is more expensive than woolen yarn because additional production steps are required. Lighter-weight filament polyester yarn (lower denier) is more expensive than heavier

polyester yarn composed of the same number of filament fibers because smaller spinnerette holes are used to make the lighter fibers, causing lower production rate. Ply yarn is more costly than an equivalent size single yarn because both thinner yarns and a plying process are required.

Construction: The weave used is an important fabric cost factor. A jacquard design costs more than a plain, twill, or satin weave because of additional preliminary and loom set-up costs, the lower production of the jacquard loom, and the relatively few jacquard looms one operator can tend.

The fabric yarns per inch must also be considered. A fabric with greater warp yarns or filling yarns per inch costs more than one with fewer yarns because it has greater yarn content. The more picks per inch in the fabric, the fewer yards of fabric per hour are produced. Increasing or decreasing the ends per inch usually has no effect on the production rate of the loom.

The number of yarns per inch and the type of yarns used in a fabric affect the weight of the fabric. Therefore, fabric weight directly affects the cost of woven cloth. In fact, some textiles are bought and sold primarily on the basis of their weight. This is more fully discussed in Chapter 14.

Other costs include those for dyeing or printing and finishing. These areas are discussed in subsequent chapters. Basic fabric types, such as broadcloth and print cloth in their various constructions, are widely sold and traded in the textile market.

New Developments

Three major concerns for the manufacturers of products are: the cost of raw materials, capital costs, and the costs of energy. Because of these concerns all industries continues to evaluate and reshape their operations and equipment. The following list presents opportunities in the weaving industry:

► Enhanced mill flexibility

► Quicker response to demand shifts

► Development of niche (special) products

► Joint ventures

► Increased productivity

► Improved ability to use new fibers, yarns, and finishes

Classic Woven Fabrics

This section contains a brief description of many of the classic woven fabrics (Figure 5.24). Identifying features are emphasized and a general indication of their use is also included to help the reader obtain a better mental image of the cloth. It should be noted that the following glossary of classic woven fabric names can only give the reader an approximate mental picture of the fabrics listed. As a reinforcement, it is strongly recommended that, wherever possible, the actual fabric be examined, many of which are in the *Fabric Science Swatch Kit*.

Fabrics are referred to as classic or traditional fabrics when they have been in use for many years and are continually made in virtually the same manner by textile mills.

FIGURE 5.24
The skirt of this dress is an example of a well-known classic woven fabric—tulle. The particular fiber content, yarn type, and fabric construction yields very fine, slightly stiff, net-like fabric.

Although originally these fabrics were either 100 percent cotton, flax, silk, or wool, now they frequently are made with yarns blended with manufactured fibers. Excessive cost or disappearing end use are two main reasons some classic fabrics have ceased to be made.

The origins of woven-fabric names are varied. Batiste, for example, was named for its French creator, Jean Batiste, a linen weaver. Denim was named after the French city in which it first appeared (fabric "de Nimes" or "from Nimes"). Corduroy was derived from the French cord du roi, meaning "King's cord." Taffeta is the modern name for the old Persian fabric name taftah. Challis originated from the Native American word shallee, meaning soft. Cheesecloth was named after its original use—to wrap cheese.

It should be noted that these classic woven fabric names are given primarily on the basis of the appearance and approximate weight of the fabrics (see Table 5.2). For example, poplin fabrics, although they vary somewhat, all have fine horizontal ribs and are constructed similarly with regard to yarn sizes, yarns per inch, and fabric weight.

A great number of fabrics in use today do not possess classic names. They are referred to either by style numbers (e.g., Style No. 473) or by names given to them by the mill, converter, or store (e.g., "Sea Breeze" for a sheer curtain fabric or "Iron Wear" for a very durable work-clothes fabric). Sometimes fabrics are referred to by names that describe their end use, such as "shirting fabric" or "dress fabric." Most of these fabrics are developed for a particular market and then fall out of fashion within one or two seasons. Thus, the student of textiles should not despair if he or she does not recognize various fabrics in the marketplace because there is an excellent possibility that they are of the nonclassic type.

The following is a list of definitions for classic fabrics and a description of each fabric's characteristics and use.

Antique satin: Satin fabric with slub filling yarns prominent on the dull side (back). See *satin*. Usually used for draperies, with the back as the exposed side.

Antique taffeta: Heavy, crisp taffeta with slub filling yarns. See *taffeta*.

Barkcloth: Medium-weight fabric with a rough surface that resembles the bark of a tree. Used for furniture slipcovers and draperies.

Batiste: Lightweight, plain-weave, soft fabric. Made primarily of cotton (blend) but can be of wool (blend). If made of wool, it is lighter than challis. Used for dresses.

TABLE 5.2   Woven Fabrics by Common Characteristics

Sheer	Light		Heavy	Ribbed
Buckram	Batiste		Burlap	Bengaline
Cheesecloth	Calico		Canvas	Broadcloth
Chiffon	Chambric		Crash	Faille
Crinoline	Chambray		Cretonne	Gorsgrain
Dotted Swiss	Gingham		Duck	Ottoman
Gauze	Lawn		Muslin[a]	Poplin
Marquisette	Madras		Osnaberg	Repp
Ninon	Nainsook		Sailcloth	Taffeta
Scrim	Organdy		Ticking[b]	
Tulle	Organza			
	Oxford (rib weave)			
	Percale			
	Toile de Jouy			
	Voile			

Twill	Woven Design	Brushed	Cord	Novelty Yarn
Cavalry twill	Brocade	Challis	Bedford cord	Antique satin
Cheviot	Brocatelle	Flannel	Dimity	Antique taffeta
Chino	Damask	Flannelette		Butcher fabric
Denim	Frieze	Melton		Honan
Drill	Huck			Pongee
Gabardine	Matelassé			Shantung
Jean	Piqué			
Serge	Tapestry			
Tweed				
Whipcord				

Pile	Puckered		Lustrous	Miscellaneous
Corduroy	Crepe (types)		Charmeuse	Monk's cloth
Terry cloth	Plissé		Chintz	Sharkskin
Velvet	Seersucker		Foulard	
Velveteen			Habutai	
			Peau de soie	
			Sateen	
			Satin	
			Surah	

[a]Also is made in lighter weight.
[b]Sometimes with woven design.

Bedford cord: Heavy, cotton-type fabric with prominent lengthwise raised cords on the face. Used for trousers and upholstery.

Bengaline: Medium-weight, lustrous fabric with prominent crosswise ribs. Ribs are covered with filament warp yarns. Lighter, with thinner ribs, than an ottoman, but heavier, with more prominent ribs, than a faille. Used for cummerbunds and lapels of tuxedos, coats, and upholstery.

Broadcloth: Lightweight, plain-weave, tightly woven, thin-yarn fabric with slight crosswise rib. Made of cotton (blend) or wool (blend). If cotton type, it has a lustrous surface and resembles a lightweight poplin.

Used for shirts. If a wool type, it is slightly heavier and was a one-way brushed surface. Used for dresses.

Brocade: Heavy, luxurious fabric with supplementary warp yarns or filling yarns, forming a slightly raised jacquard design. Used for apparel and decorative fabrics.

Brocatelle: Heavy, luxurious fabric, similar to a brocade but with the jacquard design puffed up or blistered, making it very noticeable. Also has a heavy widthwise rib. Used for draperies and furniture.

Buckram: Lightweight, plain-weave, open construction, stiff, cottonlike fabric. Has slightly more yarns per inch and stiffer than crinoline. Used for apparel interfacing and interlining, and bookbindings.

Burlap: Heavy, plain-weave fabric with open construction and coarse, irregular yarns usually made of jute fiber. Used for sacks, upholstery, and wall coverings.

Butcher cloth: Medium-weight, plain-weave fabric with slightly irregular coarse yarns. Sometimes made from flax and called butcher linen. Most frequently made from polyester blend (e.g., polyester/cotton). Used for apparel.

Calico: Lightweight, plain-weave, cotton-type fabric, usually with bright, small print design on contrasting background. Used for blouses and dresses.

Cambric: Lightweight, closely woven, plain-weave, cotton-type fabric with slight luster. Used for undersides of chairs and children's dresses.

Canvas: Heavy, plain-weave, cotton-type, durable fabric. Used for tents, awnings, and industrial purposes.

Casement cloth: Any open-constructed fabric used for draperies.

Cavalry twill: Medium-weight, durable, worsted-type fabric with prominent, fancy twill lines. Used for slacks.

Challis: Lightweight, plain-weave, slightly brushed, supple, woolen, or cotton-type fabric, usually with a printed design. Used for dresses, scarves, and infants' wear.

Chambray: Lightweight, plain-weave, cotton-type fabric usually with colored warp and white filling yarns. Square construction (about 80 × 76) and used for shirts.

Charmeuse: Lightweight, satin-weave, silklike fabric with soft hand and very shiny face. Used for dresses and pajamas.

Cheesecloth: Very lightweight, plain-weave, soft, cotton-type fabric, with very open construction. Used for polishing cloths and dress costumes.

Cheviot: Medium/heavy, rough, twill-weave fabric with fuzzy surface and uneven yarns. Similar to tweed, but more casual in appearance (suitable for rough use). Used for suiting and coats.

Chiffon: Lightweight, sheer, plain-weave, silklike fabric. Filament yarns are highly twisted. Used for dresses.

Chino: Medium-weight, closely woven, twill-weave, cotton-type fabric with a slight shine. Used for uniforms and pants.

Chintz: Light- to medium-weight, plain-weave, closely woven, fine, cotton-type fabric with a glazed (polished) finish. Usually printed in bright colors. Used for draperies, upholstery, and dresses.

Corduroy: Medium-weight cotton fabric with lengthwise wales produced by cutting the pile filling yarns. Used for slacks and jackets.

Covert: Lightweight overcoating fabric, usually made with two shades of the same color (e.g., dark brown and medium brown). A rugged fabric with a twill weave. Either woolen or worsted-type, and used for coats, uniforms, and hunting clothing.

Crash: Medium-weight, plain-weave, coarse, cotton-type fabric with uneven yarns. Often made from flax and used for linen towels, curtains, women's jackets, and bookbindings.

Crepe: Fabric with a pebbly or crinkled surface. Obtained by using crepe (high-twist) yarns, chemicals, or weave. Used for apparel or home furnishings. Varieties include crepe-back satin, crepe de chine, and georgette.

Crepe de chine: Light- to medium-weight, fine crepe fabric with crepe filament yarns. See *crepe.*

Crepe-back satin: Satin fabric with crepe surface on the dull side (back). See *satin.*

Cretonne: Light- to medium-weight, plain-weave, closely woven cotton-type fabric similar to an unglazed (unpolished) chintz, but not as fine quality. Usually printed with large designs. Used for draperies and slipcovers.

Crinoline: Lightweight, plain-weave, stiff, cotton-type fabric with very open construction. Stiffer and slightly more closely woven than cheesecloth. Used for supporting hoopskirts or hem edges and interlining.

Damask: Heavy, bright, fine-yarn fabric with a reverse jacquard design on both sides. Flatter than brocade. Used for draperies and tablecloths.

Denim: Medium-weight, twill-weave, cotton-type fabric. Warp is colored and filling is white or gray. Traditional color is indigo blue, which usually begins to fade after only a few washings. Used for slacks and work clothes.

Dimity: Lightweight, sheer, cotton-type fabric with lengthwise cords formed by grouping several warp yarns together (rib weave). Plain-weave sections occur between the cords. Used for curtains and dresses.

Donegal tweed: Plain-weave tweed with colorful nub or slub yarns. See *tweed*.

Dotted Swiss: Lightweight, sheer, fine-yarn fabric with small dotted areas that have been either woven (clip-spot design) or flocked (glued) to achieve the dot effect. Used for dresses and curtains.

Drill: Medium-weight, durable, cotton-type fabric with twill weave. Similar to denim. Called khaki when dyed that particular color. Used for pockets, work clothes, and sneakers.

Duck: Medium- or heavyweight, plain-weave, durable, cotton-type fabric. Slightly lighter than canvas, but heavier than sailcloth. Used for apparel and industrial purposes.

Duchess satin: Heavy, rich-looking satin fabric. Used for wedding dresses. See *satin*.

Faille: Medium-weight, semilustrous fabric with very noticeable crosswise ribs. Used for evening dresses.

Faille taffeta: Taffeta with very visible crosswise ribs. See *taffeta*.

Flannel: Light- to medium-weight, soft cotton, or woolen-type fabric, usually brushed on both sides. Used for shirts and pajamas.

Flannelette: Light- to medium-weight soft cotton-type fabric, usually brushed only on one side. Lighter weight than flannel. Used for shirts and pajamas.

Foulard: A lightweight, filament-yarn, twill-weave fabric with a soft hand. Frequently printed with small overall design (foulard print). Similar to surah. Used for scarves, ties, and dresses.

Frieze: Heavy, thick, rough-surface pile fabric with patterns made from its raised, small loop surface. The loops are sometimes sheared to give a cut-pile effect. Ribbed effect on face. Used for upholstery.

Gabardine: Medium-weight, fine-yarn, durable, twill-weave fabric with slight twill lines. Cotton or worsted types. Used for slacks and suits.

Gauze: Very light, sheer, open-construction, plain-weave, cotton-type fabric. Used for dresses, curtains, and bandages.

Georgette: Light, sheer fabric with crepe surface. Usually has the same yarns in warp and filling. See *crepe*.

Gingham: Lightweight, plain-weave, cotton-type fabric, usually with a plaid or check pattern (gingham plaid or gingham check). Used for shirts, dresses, and curtains.

Grosgrain: Heavy, closely woven lustrous fabric with pronounced crosswise ribs. Used for ribbons (narrow-width fabric), graduation gowns, and vestments in churches.

Grospoint: Heavy, thick, rough-surface pile fabric with loop surface. Has larger loops than frieze. Used for upholstery.

Habutai: Lightweight, plain-weave, spun-yarn, soft, silklike fabric.

Harris tweed: Trademark for tweed fabrics from islands of the Outer Hebrides off the northern coast of Scotland. Used primarily for sport jackets.

Honan: Lightweight, plain-weave, silklike fabric with slightly uneven (thick and thin) yarns in both warp and filling. Used for blouses and dresses.

Hopsacking: Heavier-weight, coarse, irregular yarns made with basket weave. Resembles burlap fabric. Used to store hops, but now also used for apparel and wall hangings (when printed).

Huck: Medium-weight, flat, coarse, cotton-type fabric, usually with dobby design. The spun filling yarns have low twist to add to absorbency. Used for towels.

Irish tweed: Tweed fabric from Ireland, usually with white warp and colored filling. See *tweed*.

Jean: Medium-weight, fine-yarn, cotton-type, durable fabric with slight twill lines. Lighter and finer than drill fabric. Used for slacks and skirting. The term jean now usually refers to slacks.

Lamé: A flat, lightweight fabric woven with metallic yarns that create a shiny surface. Used for dresses, blouses, and eveningwear.

Lawn: Lightweight, fine, plain-weave, cotton-type fabric, slightly stiff. A little less sheer than voile. Used for blouses and dresses.

Madras: Lightweight, usually plain-weave, carded, spun-yarn fabric, frequently made with a plaid design. Made so that colors bleed when fabric is washed (bleeding Madras), resulting in ever-changing shades. Imported from Madras, India. Used for shirts and dresses.

Marquisette: Lightweight, sheer, open-construction fabric with leno weave. Similar to mosquito netting. Used for curtains.

Matelassé: Medium- or heavyweight, luxurious, jacquard weave, double-cloth fabric with a blistered or quilted surface. Used for draperies, upholstery, and evening dresses.

Melton: Heavyweight, closely woven woolen fabric, completely fulled (i.e., felted) with nap. Used for coats and uniforms.

Moiré taffeta: Taffeta with moiré or watermark design. See *taffeta.*

Monk's cloth: Heavyweight, soft, coarse, cottonlike fabric with pronounced basket weave design. Used for slipcovers and draperies.

Muslin: Light- to medium-weight, plain-weave, stiff, unfinished cotton fabric with speckled effect from the "trash" content (i.e., foreign matter such as twigs and leaves not thoroughly removed during processing to cut costs). Used for designer sample garments and interfacing. When finished, the fabric is soft and used for sheets, furniture coverings, and dresses.

Nainsook: Lightweight, plain-weave, cottonlike fabric, either crisp or soft. Slightly heavier than lawn. Used for blouses and infants' wear.

Ninon: Lightweight, plain-weave, sheer, open-construction fabric with high-twist filament yarns that give the fabric a crisp hand. Heavier than chiffon. Warp yarns grouped in twos. Used for curtains and evening wear.

Organdy: Lightweight, plain-weave, cotton-type open-construction fabric with fine-spun yarns and a stiff finish. Used for blouses and curtains.

Organza: Similar to organdy, except made of silk or manufactured filament fiber. Used for dresses and trimmings.

Osnaberg: Medium- to heavyweight, coarse, durable, plain-weave, cotton-type fabric that is unfinished. Used for industrial purposes.

Ottoman: Heavy, lustrous fabric with large horizontal ribs covered by the warp yarns. Similar to bengaline but heavier. Used for upholstery, draperies, and evening dresses.

Oxford: Lightweight, soft, cottonlike fabric with small 2×1 basket weave (rib weave) repeats. Fine warp and coarse filling yarns, with smooth surface. Used for shirts.

Panne velvet: Velvet fabric in which the surface pile is flattened in one direction. See *velvet.*

Paper taffeta: Lightweight taffeta with a crisp finish. See *taffeta.*

Peau de soie: Heavy, twill-weave, satin-effect, luxurious, soft, silklike fabric. Used for evening gowns.

Percale: Lightweight, plain-weave, fine-yarn, combed cotton-type fabric. Used for sheets (up to 200 yarns per square inch), dresses, and blouses.

Piqué: Medium-weight, crisp, cotton-type fabric with raised dobby design. Some patterns used are cords, waffle, and bird's eye. Used for women's and children's wear, collars and cuffs, and infants' bonnets.

Plissé: Lightweight, plain-weave, puckered-striped, cotton-type fabric. Slightly resembles seersucker. Used for dresses and summer pajamas.

Pongee: Lightweight, plain-weave, silklike fabric with slight-slub filling yarns. Used for blouses and dresses.

Poplin: Medium-weight, cotton-type fabric with fine horizontal ribs. Usually a solid color. Used for golf jackets and raincoats.

Repp: Medium-weight, spun-yarn, coarse fabric with distinct horizontal ribs. Similar to poplin, but with more obvious ribs. Used for neckties, upholstery, and sportswear.

Sailcloth: Medium- to heavyweight, plain-weave, durable, cotton-type fabric. Slightly lighter than duck. Used for jackets, shorts, and boat sails.

Sateen: Medium-weight, cotton-type fabric with satin weave and semi-lustrous surface. Used for slacks, work uniforms, and shoe uppers.

Satin: Medium-weight fabric of filament yarns. Satin weave has fine, closely woven warp yarns. Highly lustrous, smooth face and dull, rougher back. Used for fancy dresses. Varieties include antique satin, crepe-back satin, dutchess satin, and slipper satin.

Scrim: Very lightweight, sheer, open-construction, plain-weave, cotton-type fabric. Similar to slightly stiff cheesecloth. Used for curtains and as support for nonwoven fabrics.

Seersucker: Lightweight, cotton-type, color-striped fabric. Also with permanent, length-wise, alternating, puckered-striped and flat-striped sections. Used for dresses and sport jackets.

Serge: Heavy, worsted-type, durable, solid-colored, smooth-surface fabric with twill weave. Yarns that have a higher-than-normal twist and are closely woven result in fabric becoming shiny after wear. Used for suits.

Shantung: Medium-weight, plain-weave, silklike fabric with pronounced-slub filling yarns. Heavier and more textured surface than pongee. Used for dresses.

Sharkskin: Medium-weight, semilustrous hard-finish, twill-weave, worsted or synthetic-type fabric. The surface resembles the skin of a shark. Used for suits and skirts.

Surah: Lightweight, silklike, lustrous, fine fabric with twill weave. Frequently printed. Used for dresses and blouses.

Taffeta: Medium-weight, plain-weave, lustrous fabric, made with filament yarns. Slight crosswise ribs. Fabric has great rustle when rubbed. Used for dresses, blouses, and women's suits. Varieties include antique taffeta, faille taffeta, moiré taffeta, paper taffeta, and tissue taffeta.

Tapestry: Heavy, spun-yarn, ribbed fabric with colored jacquard design resulting from different-colored groupings of filling yarns (visible as stripes on fabric back). Made with two sets of warp yarns and two sets of filling yarns. Used for wall hangings, upholstery, and handbags. With hand-woven tapestry, the filling yarns used to produce the design only interlace within the perimeter of the design being cut. The yarns are left hanging fringelike on the back. With machine-made woven tapestry, these filling yarns weave from selvage to selvage.

Terry cloth: Medium-weight, soft, cotton-type fabric with low-twist yarns forming surface loops. Used for towels and beach robes.

Ticking: Heavy, strong, closely woven, cotton-type fabric, usually made with stripes or woven design. Used for mattress and pillow coverings, upholstery, and work clothes.

Tissue faille: Lightweight faille. See *faille.*

Tissue taffeta: Lightweight, transparent taffeta. See *taffeta.*

Toile de Jouy: Light- to medium-weight, plain weave, fine, cotton-type fabric, usually with one color-printed scenic design. Used for interior furnishings and clothing.

Tulle: Very fine, slightly stiff, silky, netlike fabric. Used for wedding veils, party gowns, and trimmings.

Tweed: Medium- to heavyweight, woolen, rough-twill-weave fabric with a fuzzy surface and colored nub or slub yarns. Used for suits and coats. Varieties include Donegal tweed, Harris tweed, Irish tweed, and Scottish tweed.

Velvet: Medium-weight, manufactured or silk-filament yarn fabric with cut-pile surface that stands erect. Used for dresses, suits, and interior furnishings. (See Figure 5.25.)

Velveteen: Medium-weight, cotton-type fabric with cut-pile surface that lies flat. Used for dresses and robes.

Voile: Lightweight, sheer, crisp, plain-weave, high-twist spun-yarn, cotton-type fabric with very, very fine yarns. Used for curtains and blouses.

Whipcord: Heavy, strong cotton or worsted-type fabric with prominent, round, diagonal twill lines. Similar to heavy gabardine with a more prominent twill line. Used for riding clothes and uniforms.

FIGURE 5.25
This velvet jacket is an example of a cut warp-pile weave fabric.

1. Why do woven fabrics stretch more on the bias, or diagonal, direction?

2. State three reasons fabrics with the same weave can have different appearances.

3. State two major indicators of quality in a velvet fabric.

4. Which of these two fabrics would be the more costly to produce, assuming that they are identical in all other aspects (e.g., fiber content)? Explain.

   Fabric A: 120 × 80
   Fabric B: 110 × 90

5. You are in a store and see two sheets for sale. Each is labeled "200 percale." What differences in construction could there be between these two fabrics, even though both have the same identification?

6. State three reasons one side of a woven fabric can be different from the other side.

7. Other than by dyeing or printing, indicate three ways by which a fabric woven with the plain weave may be given added surface interest.

8. A woven fabric with jacquard design contains long floats. What possible problems would result from this construction if the fabric is used for apparel?

9. Which of the following fabrics is lightest, assuming that each fabric is made with size 40/1 yarns? Why?

   a. 100 × 70
   b. 90 × 90
   c. 110 × 70
   d 100 × 80

10. Compare a high-count fabric (many yarns per inch) with a similar low-count fabric, considering the following characteristics:

    a. Abrasion resistance
    b. Cover
    c. Drape
    d. Flame resistance
    e. Seam slippage
    f. Shrinkage potential
    g. Stability
    h. Strength
    i. Wind resistance

CHAPTER SIX
Knitted Fabrics

Objectives

▶ To understand why knitted fabrics look and perform the way they do.

▶ To recognize various knit structures and their identifying characteristics.

▶ To explain how knitted fabrics are produced.

▶ To be knowledgeable of the important differences between knitted and woven fabrics and to be able to indicate optimum choice of which to use for specific end uses.

▶ To define the terminology used regarding knitted fabrics.

 Use fabrics in the Knitted Fabrics section of the Fabric Science Swatch Kit *for this chapter.*

Key Terms Related to Textiles

CAD	high-pile knit	laid-in yarns	rib knit
circular machine	inlay yarns	milanese	simplex
commission knitter	intarsia	miss stitch	sliver knit
courses	interlocking gaiting	needle bed	tricot
cut	interlock knit	patterning	tuck stitch
double knit	interlooping	pile knit	underlap
flat knitting machine	jacquard	plating	wales
flatbed machine	jersey knit	purl knit	warp knit
full fashioning	knit stitch	purl stitch	weft-insertion knits
gaiting	knitted terry	raschel	weft knit
gauge	knitted velour	rib gaiting	weft knitting
			yarn guide bar

The knitting industry, like the weaving industry, is diverse, creative, and global. While knitting might not be as old a method of producing material as weaving, it is a major type of material in the marketplace. Knitted fabrics are used in a wide range of products, including apparel, blankets, carpets, upholstery, and bedding. Knit fabrics frequently are used in applications where stretchability, drapability, crease resistance, and wrinkle recovery are needed attributes. Technological advances in such areas as computerized design and production as well as advances in fiber technology and yarn manufacture have made possible the development of continuing streams of new designs and new fabrics with wide consumer acceptance. The scope of machine knitting has certainly expanded from its original purpose of making stockings.

The first knitting machine was developed in England by Reverend William Lee in 1589. It was basically unchanged for almost 200 years, until the Industrial Revolution. It was a flatbed warp knitting machine (see p. 114). The first circular knitting machine (see p. 114) was developed in France in 1798 by Marc Decroix. It was a weft knitting machine (see p. 120). Knitting now ranks with weaving as one of the most used methods of making fabric. Figure 6.1 shows an area in a knitting mill.

This chapter offers a basic understanding of the characteristics, types, and uses of knit fabrics, and provides a brief discussion of knitting machines. To understand the characteristics, properties, uses, limitations, and manufacturing structure of the various types of knits, it is necessary to have some knowledge of the machinery used to produce them.

The Knitting Industry

The knitting industry is a unique and distinct part of the textile industry. In general, textile mills that manufacture knit fabrics do not manufacture woven fabrics.

Within the framework of the knitting industry, there are several branches. The hosiery industry, for example, differs in markets, styling, fabric type produced, and many other respects from the industry that produces knitted fabrics for sweaters. They are separate and distinct operations with separate and distinct problems, methods of manufacture, and products produced.

The distinctive branches of the knitting industry exist because of the highly specialized machinery and technical skills required to produce the various types of knits. For example, machinery used to make sweater bodies cannot be used to make hosiery, even though both are knitted products. Thus the organization of the knitting industry tends to follow the lines of the specialized machinery used in specific kinds of production.

The knitting industry's two main branches are (1) the knitted yard-goods industry, which produces full-width fabric sold to sewn-products manufacturers, sewing center retail shops, and others and (2) the knitted end-products industry, which produces completed consumer products such as hosiery, sweaters, T-shirts, and sweat shirts. American Apparel Company, the largest T-shirt manufacturer in the United States, is a vertically integrated manufacturer and a retailer.

Several factors are common throughout the knitting industry. First, practically all knit producers purchase yarn rather than spin or texturize their own (although

FIGURE 6.1
Production in a knitting mill.

many larger knitters do their own yarn texturing). In the weaving industry, on the other hand, producers usually spin and prepare their own yarn. Second, all knitters are either direct knitters or **commission knitters.** Direct knitters purchase yarn, knit products in their own plants, and sell their merchandise under their own names or trademarks. Commission knitters produce products for a second party, who furnishes the yarn to the commission knitter and receives the completed knit fabric or product. Commission knitters are paid only for what they produce. They never hold title (ownership) to the yarns or products worked with nor assume any of the risks of marketing and distribution or share in their profits.

Commission knitters, sometimes called contract knitters, perform work for the accounts of converters (see p. 8), distributors of knit apparel products, and directly for retailers in private label programs (see p. 12). Many of these companies are small, often with limited financial resources.

Growth in the production and use of knitted apparel has been helped by new technology being used. There has been an increase in the capability for knitting mills to produce finished knit garments directly from yarn.

General Knitting Fabric Terms

Knitted fabrics may be described as structures produced by the **interlooping** of yarns. In actual construction of the fabric, loops are formed, and then new loops are drawn through those previously formed. The continuing addition of new loops creates the knitted fabric. A knitted loop is usually referred to as a stitch when it is pulled through another loop. Stitches are produced with knitting needles. Because of the loops, the yarns have great crimp, which is what imparts the stretch in knits.

Wales

Columns of stitches in a knitted fabric are called **wales.** Wales run lengthwise through the entire fabric, and in that sense they are similar to the warp in a woven fabric.

The number of *wales per inch* is dependent on the density of needles, (the needles per inch) and the size of the loop. This in turn depends on the closeness of the needles and their thickness. The use of thinner needles can result in higher wales per inch because there can be more needles per inch. The knitting needles are held in position by **needle beds,** pieces of metal into which slots or grooves have been cut.

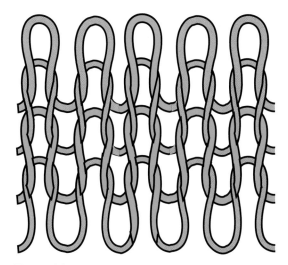

FIGURE 6.2
Yarn formation and stitches in a weft knit fabric. Note the wales (vertical stitches) and courses (horizontal stitches).

Courses

Rows of stitches are called **courses.** Courses run widthwise, from side to side of the cloth, and in that sense are similar to the filling in a woven fabric. Figure 6.2 illustrates the wales and courses configuration in a weft knit fabric.

The number *courses per inch* of fabric is dependent on the height of the stitch loop. This in turn depends either on the distance the needle pulls the yarn when the loop is made (weft knitting) or the amount of yarn fed and wrapped around the needle (warp knitting). When small loops are formed, the fabric has a large number of courses per unit length. The reverse is also true: When large loops are formed, the fabric has a small number of courses per unit length.

Wales and courses per inch contribute to the fabric weight, hand, insulation, shape retention, drapability, and cost.

In the metric system, the suggested unit length is 100 mm for wale and course density instead of 1 inch as in the English system. Thus a knitted fabric with 24 wales per inch could also be expressed as having 94 wales per 100 millimeters. (One inch equals 25.4 millimeters.)

Face and Back

Like woven fabrics, knit fabrics have a technical face side and a technical back. The technical face of knits with no pattern or design is usually the side in which there are more **knit stitches** (see p. 106). The general ways that are used with woven fabrics to differentiate face and back (see p. 89) usually apply to knits (e.g., finish, pattern, and fancy yarns).

Machine Nomenclature

The knitting machine allows production of a complete row of loops at one time instead of only one loop at a time, as in hand knitting. Each machine may hold from several hundred to several thousand knitting needles. The needles are substantially different from hand-knitting needles. The formation of the stitch is also somewhat different in that only one needle is required to make a stitch rather than two, as with hand knitting.

Each wale of the fabric in machine knitting is produced by its own needle. This means, for example, that if there are 600 wales across the width of a 40-inch fabric (assuming 15 wales per inch), then 600 needles must be used to produce the fabric.

Circular and Flat Machines

Knitting machines are divided into two main categories: circular knit and flat knit. With **circular knitting** machines, the knitting needles are in a circular configuration and the fabric produced is tubular in form (Figure 6.3). The diameter of the machine varies from about

2½ inches (6 centimeters) to over 30 inches (76 centimeters), depending on what product the machine was designed to produce. For example, a hosiery machine has a smaller diameter than a sweater machine. Also, with different machine diameters, garments such as T-shirts can be knit in different sizes (e.g., large, medium, small). Circular knits can be cut open along their entire length and become, in effect, flat fabrics (see Figure 6.4).

A **flat knitting machine** has the knitting needles in a straight line, thus producing fabrics in an open width, or flat, similarly to how woven fabric comes off a loom (see Figure 6.5). Flat knitting machines range from about 12 inches (30 centimeters) to over 200 inches (500 centimeters), depending on end use. For example, a machine used to make trim is narrower than one used to make open-width fabric for cut-and-sew articles. Although often a flat knitting machine produces fabric more slowly than a circular machine, it can produce items that a circular machine cannot. Examples include shaped articles, such as full-fashion sweaters (see p. 125), cable patterns (see Figure 6.6), and certain trim.

There are now complete garment flatbed systems. The machine can produce a complete and seamless garment that lowers manufacturing costs by eliminating the cutting and sewing operation as well as saving on yarn waste. Also, now there is knitting machine technology that offers designers the ability to knit combinations

FIGURE 6.3
A circular knitting machine with electronic controls. A weft knit fabric with jacquard design is being produced.

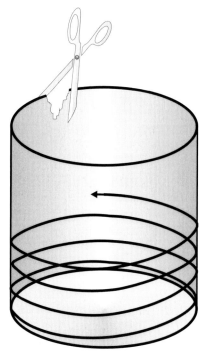

FIGURE 6.4
A diagram of a circular knit. Note that the fabric is actually knitted in a circular spiral.

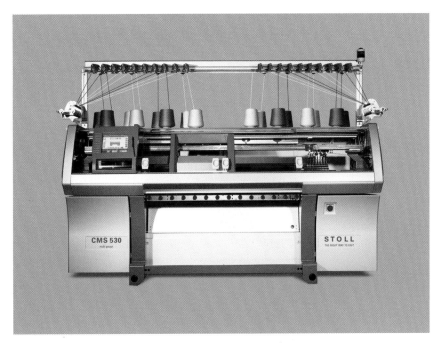

FIGURE 6.6
Cable pattern produced on a flat knitting machine.

of patterns and stitches that were not possible before. Whereas whole garment technology has been available for the past decade, today's styles and concepts are much greater than the first ones offered, in terms of fit, appearance, and comfort.

Knitting Needles

The three main types of needles used in industrial knitting are latch needles, spring beard needles, and compound needles (see Figure 6.7). The latch needle is used primarily in weft knitting, and the other two are used in warp knitting. The compound needle enables higher rates of production. The manner in which the knitting stitch is produced is illustrated in Figures 6.8–6.10.

A coarse (large and thick) needle usually knits with a coarse yarn (large hook), whereas a fine (small and thin) needle usually knits with a fine yarn (small hook).

Needles in the knitting machine are usually oriented either vertically, horizontally, or at a 45° angle. They are held in position by needle beds, pieces of metal into which slots or grooves have been cut. The beds can be rectangular (flat or straight knitting machine) or circular (circular knitting machine).

Cut and Gauge

In knitting machines, needles are put into slots that hold them in position. (Selected slots sometimes may be left empty—without needles—to make certain types of fabrics.) The number of slots or grooves per inch (or per centimeters) in any given knitting machine is fixed, different machines having different numbers of slots. The number of slots per inch is called the **cut** of the machine. The higher the cut, the more closely knit a fabric can be made; with more needle density, a higher wales-per-inch

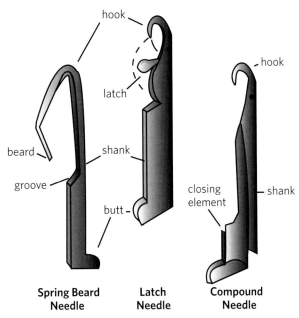

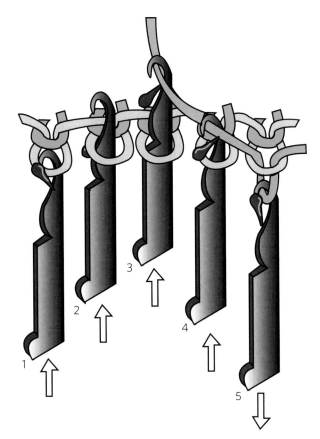

FIGURE 6.7
The three main types of knitting needles used in industrial knitted fabric manufacture: spring beard needle (left), latch needle (middle), and compound needle (right).

FIGURE 6.8
Latch needle forming knitted stitches. From left to right (in a five-step sequence):

1–3. The needle rises and, as it does, the previous loop opens the latch and slides down onto the needle shank.
 4. As the needle begins to descend, a new yarn is fed onto the needle hook. As the needle continues to descend, the previous loop slides onto it and causes the latch to close.
 5. The needle continues downward and the old loop slides off the needle completely. (This is called the knock-over.) In so doing, it becomes interlooped with a new loop, which has just been formed in the needle hook, thus creating the knitted fabric structure.

fabric can be produced. The term cut is used regarding weft knit machines only.

Typically, a heavy sweater made with thick yarns might be made on a 6-cut machine and a T-shirt made of fine yarns, a 28-cut machine. Fine hosiery may be made on a 80-cut machine.

When a knitting machine is purchased, the machine manufacturer must be informed as to what cut machine is desired (based on knitted product to be made). It is difficult and expensive for the cut to be changed later because entire needle beds must be replaced and internal mechanisms must sometimes also be changed. Thus the cut of knitting machines is generally not changed after the machine has been made.

Gauge is a term used in both weft- and warp-knitted fabrics. It also refers to the needles per measured length (e.g., per inch) in the knitting machine. Like the term cut, gauge also reflects the fineness and coarseness (closeness or openness) of knitted cloth. The higher the gauge number of the machine, the finer the fabric. One can become easily confused when using the term gauge, however, because it refers to different unit lengths in different types of knitted fabric. In full-fashioned knits (see p. 125), gauge refers to the number of needles in 1.5 inches (3.81 cm). In circular-knit hosiery, it refers to the number of needles in 1.0 inches (2.54 cm). In warp-knitted tricot (see p. 129), the term also refers to 1.0 inches (2.54 cm), but in warp-knitted raschel (see p. 130), the gauge is the number of needles in either 2.0 inches (5.08 cm) or one inch.

Gauge is also used to refer to fabric wales per inch as well as slots per inch in the machine needle bed. Thus it is important to be sure to know how the terms cut and gauge are being used, and to ask if unsure.

One should be mindful of the fact that the terms cut and gauge refer to machinery measurements. The number of wales per inch in a fabric may not exactly correspond to the cut or appropriate gauge designation. The wales per inch of fabric will usually differ from the cut or

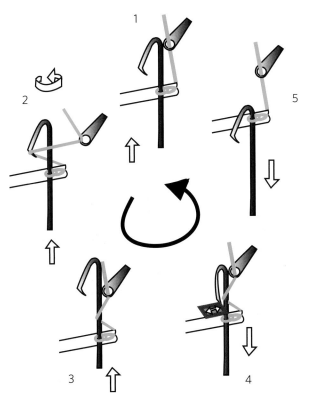

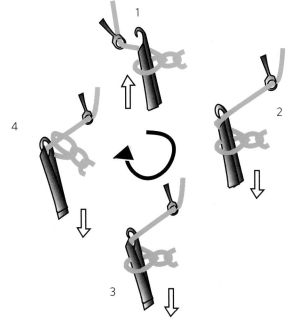

FIGURE 6.9

Spring beard needle forming knitted stitches. Counter-clockwise (in a five-step sequence):

1. As the needle moves upward, the previously formed loop slips down to the needle shank.
2. A new yarn is fed onto the needle through the action of the yarn guide.
3. The needle continues to rise and the new yarn slides onto the needle shank.
4. The needle begins its descent and the new yarn slides under the beard. When the new yarn is under the beard, a presser bar comes forward and closes the beard. As the needle continues downward, the old loop slides onto the closed beard. The presser bar then moves back to allow the old loop to slide freely.
5. The needle continues downward, and the old loop slides off the needle completely. (This is called the knock-over.) In so doing, it becomes interlooped with a new loop that has just been formed in the needle hook, thus creating the knit fabric structure.

FIGURE 6.10

The steps for forming a knitted stitch with the compound needle, used in warp knitting:

1. As the needle moves upward, the previously formed loop slides down the shank.
2. The new yarn is wrapped around the needle through the action of the yarn guide. The needle begins to move downward and the closing element begins to cover the hook.
3. The needle continues to move downward and the closing element completely covers the hook.
4. The needle continues to descend and the old loop slides off the needle completely. (This is called the knock-over.) The new yarn is pulled through the previously made loop, forming a new loop and thus creating a knit stitch.

gauge designation because the fabric (a) may have been stretched or shrunken; (b) may have been influenced by tensions on yarns during the knitting process; (c) may have been influenced by the size of yarns used for knitting; and (d) may have been influenced by the stitch-setting adjustments of the knitting machine. Nevertheless, it is standard procedure among people dealing in knitted fabric to refer to cut or gauge. One hears, for example, expressions such as "12-cut jersey" or "18-cut

rib knit." What is referred to is a specific knit fabric type (jersey or rib knit) made on that cut machine. Page 134 contains information on the ways in which varying the wales and courses per inch affects fabric properties.

Types of Knitting Stitches

There are four principal stitches utilized in knit fabrics: the knit, purl, miss, and tuck. These four stitches, or combinations of them appearing in the same fabric, form the basis of all knitted fabrics.

Knit Stitch

The knit stitch is the basic knitting stitch. It is also called the plain stitch. The looping configurations of the stitch are illustrated in Figure 6.11a.

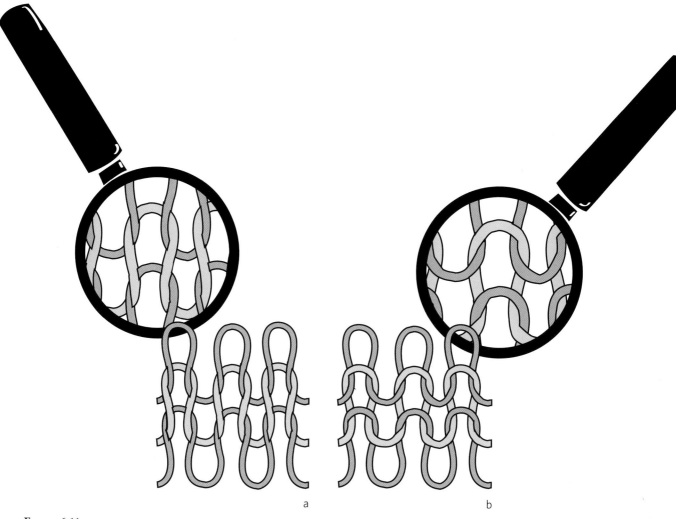

FIGURE 6.11
(a) Knit stitch and (b) purl stitch. Note that the purl stitch is the same as the underside (or back) of the knit stitch.

Purl Stitch

The **purl stitch** is the reverse of the knit stitch and, in fact, is sometimes called the reverse knit stitch. The back of the jersey knit fabric is a purl stitch configuration, as illustrated in Figure 6.11b.

Miss Stitch

A **miss stitch** is created when one or more knitting needles are deactivated and do not move into position to accept a yarn. The yarn merely passes by and no stitch is formed. Figure 6.12 illustrates a miss stitch with two needles deactivated. Because the unknit yarn passes or floats on the back of the fabric, it is sometimes called a float stitch. Another name for this stitch is the welt stitch. A miss stitch can be recognized by

the floating unknit yarn on the back of the fabric. It is used to create color and figure designs in knitted fabric since it permits the selective positioning of yarns in a fabric. The miss stitch also has a tendency to increase fabric weight, and reduce both stretch, and width.

Tuck Stitch

A **tuck stitch** is formed when a knitting needle holds its old loop and then receives a new yarn. Two loops then collect in the needle hook. The action may be repeated several more times, but the yarns eventually have to be cast off the needle and knitted. Figure 6.13 illustrates a tuck stitch. The resultant stitch is elongated. Tuck stitches appear on the back of a fabric and may be recognized as an inverted V, sometimes elongated for two or

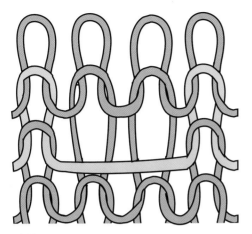

FIGURE 6.12
Miss stitch. Note the floating unknit yarn in this diagram on the fabric back and the stitch elongation in the wale.

of machinery for producing fabric and each produces different types of fabrics. Examples of weft-knit fabrics are those used in sweaters and hosiery; an example of warp knit fabric is the material used in lingerie. Hand knitting is a weft knitting procedure. In weft knits, yarn traverses from side to side (or around), interacting with the needles to form new fabric stitches. In warp knits, a set of yarns traverses lengthwise, interacting with the needles to form new fabric stitches. The terms weft and warp are derived from woven terms, but unlike woven fabrics, knits are made from one set of yarns interlooping, as distinct from woven fabrics, which have two sets of yarns interlacing. (See Figure 6.14a and b.)

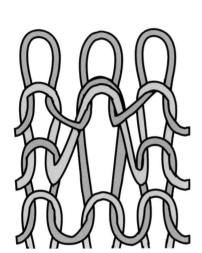

FIGURE 6.13
Tuck stitch. Note the elongated stitch in the wale in this diagram of the fabric back. The tuck stitch appears in a fabric as an inverted V.

more courses, depending on how many times the stitch was tucked. The tuck stitch is used in knitted fabrics to create design effects in color, raised surface texture, or a hole or eyelet effect. The tuck stitch also has a tendency to increase fabric weight, width (wales are pushed apart), and thickness (yarn from the tuck stitch lies on top of the preceding stitch).

Knit Fabric Classifications

There are two main classifications of knitted fabrics: **weft knits** and **warp knits.** Each uses different kinds

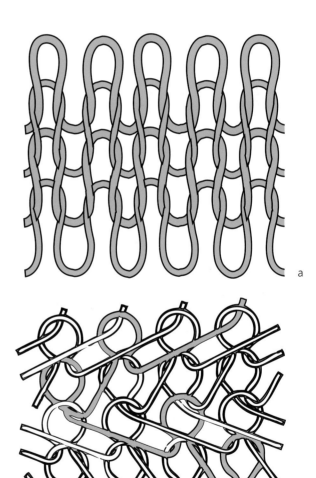

FIGURE 6.14
Yarn formation and stitches in the two main classifications of knitted fabrics: (a) weft knit and (b) warp knit. Note the way yarns interloop with each other in the weft knit as compared to the warp knit.

Knit Fabric Names

Classic knit fabrics are named primarily on the basis of their construction, not on the basis of appearance and weight, as with classic woven fabrics. For example, if a weft-knit fabric is made with all knit stitches on one side and all purl stitches on the other, it is referred to as a plain jersey-knit fabric. Thus a 4-ounces-per-square-yard material with thin-spun yarn and close construction, and a 10-ounces-per-square-yard material with heavy novelty yarns and an open construction are both called jersey knit, providing each is made entirely of knit stitches. A style number or marketing name could also be used instead of the classic name, as previously indicated with woven fabric names.

Weft Knitting

Weft knitting, as its name implies, is a type of knitting in which yarns run horizontally, from side to side, across the width of the fabric. The yarns are oriented horizontally, as in the filling of woven fabrics (see Figure 6.14a). The fabric is formed by manipulating the knitting needles to make loops in horizontal courses built one on top of another. All loops in a course are made by one yarn. In its simplest form, a weft knit can be made from one yarn. Weft knits are made on both flat and circular knitting machines.

In weft knitting the needles slide back and forth in a slot. Cams cause the needles to move by having the needle butt move through a cam track. The needle is moved up to pick up yarn and form a new loop. The previously formed loop is cast off when the needle is moved down (see Figures 6.8 and 6.15). Cones are the source of yarns on a weft-knitting machine.

Some weft-knit fabrics are made by knitting machines with one set of needles (e.g., jersey). Others need to be made by knitting machines with two sets of needles (front set and back set). The positioning of these needles in relation to one another is called **gaiting.** With **rib gaiting,** the two sets of needles alternate with each other. With **interlocking gaiting,** the two sets of needles are positioned opposite each other. By changing the needle positions, the type of fabric being produced is changed (e.g., rib fabric or interlock fabric).

Basic Weft-Knit Fabrics

The basic types of fabrics in weft knitting are **jersey knit, rib knit,** and **purl knit.** Each of these fabric types is unique in appearance and function. All textile fabrics of weft-knit construction are made from these basic types. A comparison of these three fabrics is shown in Table 6.1.

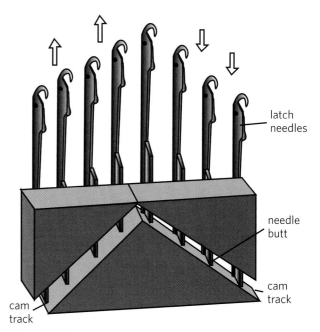

FIGURE 6.15
Needles in weft knitting are raised and lowered by the use of cams. The needle butts move through the cam tracks, sliding up and then down to achieve the desired knitting effect.

Jersey-Knit Fabrics   Jersey fabric is also known as single knit. Fabrics of this type have all loops drawn to one side of the fabric (all knit stitches) and are most easily recognized by the fact that the face is smooth and the back has a textured and mottled appearance, giving the fabric a definite face and back. Figure 6.16 illustrates the knit configuration of a plain jersey fabric, the most utilized jersey construction.

The knitting machines that produce jersey-knit fabrics have one set of needles in one needle bed and are called jersey machines, plain-knit machines, or single-knit machines. All needles in one bed can pull loops in only one direction. As a consequence, jersey-knit materials are unbalanced and have a tendency to curl at the edges. This condition can frequently be corrected in fabric finishing. If not corrected, this problem can be quite troublesome in cutting and sewing operations.

Jersey-knit fabrics stretch more in the width directions. These fabrics are produced on flat as well as circular machines.

A wide variety of knitted fabrics are made with the jersey-knit construction, ranging from sheer, lightweight hosiery to thick, bulky sweaters. Most full-fashioned sweaters (see p. 125) are fundamentally jersey-knit fabric types. Additional fabrics that use jersey-knit construction are men's underwear, T-shirts, pantyhose, knit terry, knit velour, and many more. One shortcoming of

TABLE 6.1	COMPARISON OF JERSEY, RIB, AND PURL FABRICS	
Jersey	**Rib**	**Purl**
Fabric Recognition:	*Fabric Recognition:*	*Fabric Recognition:*
Knit stitches on face, purl stitches on back	Wales predominate on face and back; knit stitches only in same wale, purl stiches only in same wale	Courses predominate on face and back; knit and purl stitches in same wale
Definite face and back	May be reversible	May be reversible
Stretches approximately equally in length and width	Greater stretch in width	Greater stretch in length
Highest machine productivity	Next highest machine productivity	Lowest machine productivity
Uses:	*Uses:*	*Uses:*
Hosiery and pantyhose	Collars and cuffs	Infants' wear
T-shirts	Socks	Fancy sweaters
Sweaters	Double-knit jackets	Fancy garment parts
Knit terry robes	Interlock dresses	
Knit velour jogging suits		
Full-fashion garments		

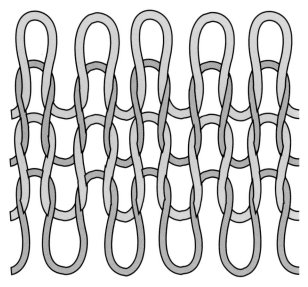

FIGURE 6.16
Jersey-knit fabric. Note that the fabric face has all knit stitches (all loops drawn to the fabric face).

jersey-knit fabrics is that if one yarn breaks, it causes an unraveling of adjoining stitches in the wale, called a run. Lightweight filament-yarn jerseys are especially susceptible to runs due partially to the very smooth surface of filament yarn.

Rib-Knit Fabrics Rib-knit fabrics have knit stiches on both sides and there is no knit and purl stitch in the same wale.

Rib-knit fabrics are produced with knitting machines that are somewhat different from those used for jersey knits. Because rib knits have stitches drawn to both sides of the fabric, the machines used to make them, called rib-knit machines, require two sets of needles usually positioned at right angles to each other; each set of needles is capable of producing stitches. The fabric is formed between the two needle-holding beds. The machinery required to produce rib-knit fabric is substantially more complex and operates at slower speeds than knitting machines used for jersey fabrics. Rib knits are produced on flat as well as circular machines.

Rib-knit fabrics can have a very distinct lengthwise rib effect on both sides of the fabric: They have ridges of knit stitch wales. If two wales of knit stitches and two wales of purl stitches appear alternately on both sides of the fabric, it is called a 2 × 2 rib. If one wale of knit stitches and one wale of purl stitches appear alternately on both sides of fabric, it is a 1 × 1 rib. A 3 × 1 rib has three wales of knit stitches and one wale of purl stitches on the technical face and one wale of knit stitches and three wales of purl stitches on the other side. Many combinations of rib arrangements are possible. Figure 6.17 illustrates a 2 × 2 rib fabric.

To identify rib-knit fabrics, especially when they are closely knitted, it may be necessary to stretch the fabric in the width direction. The appearance of alternating columns of knit stitches and purl stitches in the length (wales) direction is evidence of a rib knit. The raised stitches are wales of knit stitches, and the recessed stitches are the wales of purl stitches.

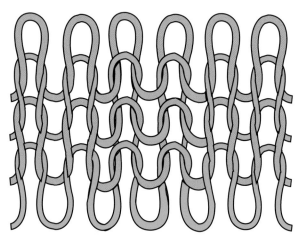

FIGURE 6.17
2 × 2 rib knit fabric. Note the alternate wales of two knit
stitches, two purl stitches, two knit stitches, and so on.

Rib-knit fabrics generally lie flat and do not curl at
the edges as do jersey knits. Also, rib knits have greater
elasticity in their width than their length. For this reason, they are often used for sweater waistbands, knit
cuffs, knit hats, men's hosiery, and similar applications.
(See Figure 6.18.)

Purl-Knit Fabrics   In purl-knit fabrics, each wale contains both knit stitches and purl stitches. This differs
from the rib fabric described previously, in which the
wales contain either knit or purl stitches. A simple purl
fabric looks somewhat like the back of a jersey knit on
both sides of the fabric. The simplest purl fabric is known
as 1 × 1 purl, in which one course has all knit stitches and
the next course has all purl stitches. The cycle repeats on
the third course. A 2 × 2 purl knit fabric is made with two
courses of knit stitches followed by two courses of purl
stitches. Figure 6.19 illustrates a 1 × 1 purl knit fabric.

Purl-knit fabrics are made on knitting machines
called purl-knit machines or links-and-links machines.
Fabrics of this type, therefore, are sometimes called
links-and-links fabrics.

To identify a purl-knit fabric, it is frequently necessary to stretch the fabric in its length direction. The
appearance of alternating rows of knit stitches and purl
stitches in the horizontal (course) direction is evidence
of a purl knit. The raised stitches are courses of purl
stitches, and the recessed rows are the courses of knit
stitches. Thus a three-dimensional effect can be created
without the use of miss or tuck stitches.

Purl knits are produced on flat or circular machines.
Because stitches are sometimes drawn to the front and
sometimes to the back, two sets of needles are required

FIGURE 6.18
A rib knit at the neck, cuff, and bottom shows easy stretch
and body conforming shape. The cable knit adds texture to
the sweater.

to produce these fabrics. In purl machines, however,
rather than two distinct, separate sets of needles, one set
of double-headed latch needles is used. The two needle
beds are in alignment with each other. The double-
headed needles move from one needle bed to the other,
from side to side of the knitted fabric as it is produced,
alternately making stitches on one fabric side and then
the other. Figure 6.20 illustrates the knitting action of a
purl knit machine.

Generally purl-knit fabrics tend to lie flat and do not
curl as do jersey knits. Most purl knit fabrics are used for
outerwear (e.g., sweaters).

The purl-knit machines used to produce purl-
knit fabrics are the most versatile industrial knitting
machines. These machines can produce plain and rib as
well as purl fabrics. By selective programming of needle
motion, fabrics of all three types, sometimes with unique
design effects, are possible. Purl-knit machines are widely
used in the sweater industry.

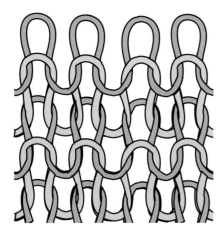

Figure 6.19
1 × 1 purl knit fabric. Note that each succeeding course alternates as one purl, one knit, one purl, and so on.

Although extremely versatile, the purl knit machines have the lowest rate of production of all knitting machines. Therefore, the cost per pound of fabric produced is highest for purl knit fabrics. Knitting machines for jersey knits have the highest productivity but the lowest versatility. Productivity for rib-knit machines falls between those for jersey and purl machines.

Specialized Weft-Knit Fabrics

Many unique and versatile fabrics can be created in weft knitting. Fabrics that look like terry cloth toweling, a smooth velour, or even a simulated fur are examples of this group of specialized knit fabrics.

Interlock Knits Interlock-knit fabrics are a variation of rib knits made on the interlock machine. In rib knits, columns of adjacent wales appear both on the face and back of the cloth. The back of any given wale of knit stitches on the rib fabric shows as a wale of purl stitches. On interlock knits, however, columns of wales are directly behind each other. Thus, the back of any given knit stitch on the interlock fabric reveals another knit stitch directly behind it.

To determine whether a fabric is an interlock or a rib, hold the top of the fabric, spread it apart widthwise, and view the fabric wales carefully at the top edge of the cloth. If the knit stitches are one behind the other, the fabric is interlock. (See Figure 6.21.) If the wales of knit stitch alternate, the fabric is rib (refer to Figure 6.17).

Compared to similar 1 × 1 rib knits, interlock knits are smoother, more stable, better insulators, and more expensive. Interlock fabrics are popular for blouses, dresses, and dressy T-shirts. Their dimensional stability and the fact that they do not tend to easily stretch out of

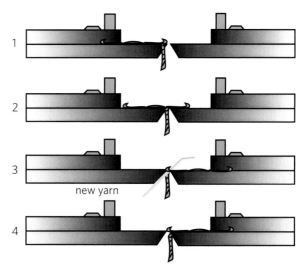

Figure 6.20
The motions of a purl knit machine. The double-headed latch needle action produces purl fabrics, as illustrated in the following steps:

1. The needle at the left needle bed holds the stitch previously formed.
2. The movement of the needle has caused the stitch to pass over the open latch. It is now over the body of the needle.
3. The needle is continuing its movement and receives the new yarn.
4. A new stitch is formed on the right needle bed. The needle now reverses direction.

shape contribute to these popular uses. Interlock fabrics offer a smooth surface for printing by both screen and heat-transfer methods. (See pp. 171, 174.)

Double Knits Double-knit fabrics are classified as a specialty type of rib-knit fabric since they utilize miss and/or tuck stitches. They are produced on rib machines or interlock machines. These fabrics have close stitches, which provide good stability and shape retention. They also have a patterned or design effect. Simple types of double knits are nearly similar on both sides, and they appear much like regular rib-knit fabrics, with distinct knit stitches on both sides of the fabric. This reason, as well as the fact that they are usually thicker and heavier than jersey, probably gave rise to the name double knit.[1] They are not, as might be suspected from their name, twice-knitted fabrics or two adhered fabrics. Complex double knits most often have different appearances on the face and the back of the cloth.

---

1. Double knits are generally heavier and thicker than jersey knit, but some jersey fabrics are very heavy and bulky, and some double knits are relatively lightweight.

FIGURE 6.21
A stitch formation diagram of an interlock knit. Note that knit stitches are directly in back of each other.

High-Pile Knits   Not many people think of imitation furs (or faux furs, as they are sometimes called) as knitted fabrics. They are, however, a type of jersey knit made by a unique procedure that involves feeding staple fiber in the form of sliver (a loose ropelike strand of fibers) into the knit material while the yarns are passing through the knitting needles as the fabric is being made. The fiber is caught in the knit structure and is thus held within and between the plain stitches. These fabrics are also known as **pile knits** or **sliver knits.**

After knitting, a variety of finishing treatments are given to produce the desired furlike effect. The finishing treatment and the specific fiber used for the pile govern the appearance and hand of the material. Animal fur simulations, such as leopard skin and tiger skin, are often printed directly on these fabrics by screen-print methods. (See p. 171.) The prints often produce highly realistic copies of natural furs. Knitting and fiber technology in this field have become so advanced that sometimes it is difficult to be sure by ordinary sight and touch whether a fur is fake or real. One must examine the fabric back to see whether it is knitted, indicating fake fur, or whether it has an animal-skin back, indicating real fur.

The usual precautions for all pile fabrics should be practiced with fake furs. Garments made from these fabrics should not be crowded into a closet in such a way that the pile is distorted. If it does become distorted, the pile should be brushed in the direction of the nap as soon as possible. Brushing with moistened (but not

FIGURE 6.22
A coat made from high-pile knit. This fake fur garment is luxurious and warm.

wet) bristles on a soft- to medium-bristled brush usually restores distorted pile.

In addition to their popular use in imitation fur coats, high-pile knits are widely used as coat lining, in children's snow suits, as car and airline blankets, as pillow and couch covers, as scatter rugs, as footwear linings, in hats and hat lining, for stuffed animals, and even as powder puffs in the cosmetics industry (see Figure 6.22).

Knitted Terry   **Knitted terry** fabrics are jersey-knit materials that are knitted with two yarns feeding simultaneously into the same knitting needles. When the fabric is knitted, one yarn appears on the face and the other on the back. The method is known as **plating.** One of the yarns is called a loop yarn, the other a ground yarn. The loop yarns are pulled out by special devices and become the loop pile of the knitted terry fabric. The ground yarns form the basic construction of the knitted fabric.

Knitted terry fabrics are softer, more flexible, and usually more absorbent than woven terry fabrics. However, they do not hold their shape as well, nor are they as durable as woven terry fabrics. Knitted terry fabrics are used in robes, beach wear, and similar applications.

Knitted Velour   **Knitted velour** fabrics are made in the same way as knitted terry. After the fabric is knitted, the loop pile is cut by a process called shearing (see p. 191), and then it is brushed. Knitted velours have a soft, downy, suedelike texture, somewhat resembling velveteen. They are, however, softer and more flexible than velveteen. Knitted velour is used in dresses, jogging suits, and similar applications.

Full-Fashioned Knits   **Full fashioning** is a method of shaping a knitted fabric during the knitting process. Full fashioning is popular in sweater manufacture, where the shape and contour of the shoulder and bust actually can be knitted to body contour shape. Sleeves are later sewn in as part of a separate operation to complete the sweater.

Full fashioning is done on flatbed full-fashioned knitting machines, which are capable of producing the shaped garment by increasing or decreasing the number of total wales at the shaped area. Fabric is widened by increasing the number of needles in action or narrowed by decreasing the number of needles in action. Where narrowing occurs, a fashion mark results from stitches being transferred to adjacent needles. The marks appear as distorted stitches (see Figure 6.23).

The alternative to full-fashion knitting of sweater blanks (i.e., the body of the sweater with a rib bottom) is to knit the sweater blank in a rectangular form and then cut to obtain the desired shape (thus creating a cut-and-sew garment). This results in fabric waste, which can be costly with expensive fabric.

Other Weft-Knit Fabrics

There are other weft-knit fabrics produced for the marketplace, which are more complicated than the basic fabrics mentioned in this chapter. Each is made with a different stitch sequence, and so each has a different appearance. Examples include Lacoste®, Ponte de Roma, Swiss pique, Milano rib, and Cardigan fabrics.

Design in Weft-Knit Fabrics

The great popularity of knitted fabrics largely results from their fashion versatility. The ability of designers and product developers to provide imaginative color effects

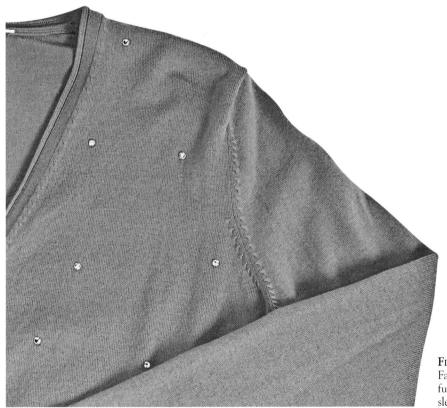

FIGURE 6.23
Fashion marks are evident on this full-fashioned sweater where the sleeve joins the body.

as well as interesting and novel surface effects in a wide variety of weft-knit fabrics is important in the continuing consumer demand for knitted fabric apparel.

Design in knitted fabric may be done by printing methods described in Chapter 9, or by various techniques that occur as part of the knitting process, such as the arrangement of yarns by color or the construction of the fabric.

Design by Color Arrangement of Yarns   Horizontal color stripes in weft-knit fabrics is the simplest designer technique, requiring merely the proper selection and sequence of the yarns to be fed to the knitting machine (see Figure 6.24). No mechanical adjustments or alteration of stitch types is necessary. Using this method, a wide variety of colors and combinations are possible without seriously affecting knitting productivity or costs. Producing vertical stripes in weft-knit fabrics requires a more complicated machine setup (increased cost and reduced productivity) and so is usually not done. There is, however, a limitation on the size of the repeat pattern of the horizontal color stripes. This limitation varies with different knitting machines. Color-stripe design effects can be achieved in jersey, rib, and purl fabric types. (See Figure 6.25.)

Design by Construction of Fabric   Design effects can be achieved by mechanically or electromechanically controlling how knitting needles behave when a yarn passes by them during the knitting process. Either a plain stitch, purl stitch, miss stitch, or tuck stitch is formed.

The miss stitch and the tuck stitch are widely used for creating design effects because their use permits the selective positioning of knitting yarns in a fabric so that designs in color effects, surface effects, open texture, and lace effects can be created. There are various other methods used in creating design of knit fabric, but these more complicated techniques are not discussed in this chapter.

The machine needle action is controlled to create the plain, miss, and tuck variations and is governed by the **patterning** mechanisms in the knitting machine. There are several major types of patterning mechanisms, and many variations within these types, depending on the design and manufacture of the various knitting machines. The designer of knit fabrics must understand the capabilities and limitations of the machines that are used to produce the proposed fabric.

The most sophisticated and versatile of the various patterning mechanisms is the **jacquard** system. In jacquard knits, each needle can be individually controlled for each course and, therefore, complicated patterns can be knitted. In addition, selection of yarn color from among those mounted on the machine feeds can also be

programmed. The result is an unlimited design scope. The intricate and large-sized repeat noted on such items as ski sweaters is made on knitting machines with jacquard controls.

Intarsia is a knitted structure characterized by areas of solid colors within the fabric. There are no miss-stitches, as in jacquard structures, to produce the pattern. The back of the fabric has the same color definition as the face. The majority of Intarsia fabrics are jersey structure, since it is easier to make this structure when only one needle bed is in action. They are produced on flat machines, usually with special yarn carriers.

Use of Electronic and Computer-Controlled Design Systems   The most modern systems for creating design in knitted fabrics consist of electronic and computer-controlled adaptations of the methods previously described. Computer-controlled weft-knitting machines have had a profound impact on the knitting industry. They permit the designer to conceive of a new design and to produce

FIGURE 6.24
Most weft knit fabrics have stripes in the width direction.

FIGURE 6.25
Knitted fabrics and hosiery can
be either thick or sheer and have
horizontal or vertical stripes.

samples of the fabric within a few minutes. The designer
can make an assessment of what has been created, alter
or improve it, and obtain new knitted samples within several more minutes. The computer-aided design (**CAD**)
and production systems reduce from several weeks to several hours the time required to conceive, make samples
of, and approve or reject new creations in knitted fabric.

CAD systems for knitting were developed in about
1980. It has become a very important tool to the sweater
designer. The growth in popularity and variety of styles
in sweaters, for both high fashion as well as mass markets, has been attributed in part to CAD developments
(Figure 6.26).

Seamless Knitting

A seam is a line along which two or more fabrics are
joined, usually by sewing, adhesive, stapling, or fusion.
The seam usually is near the edge of the fabric pieces.

Seamless knitting was commercialized in the mid-
1990s as the knitting technology became commercially
available. One yarn can be used to complete an entire
garment, without cut-and-sew assembly. Most models are
integrated with CAD systems for design development.

Today both circular and flat-knitting machines can
produce whole panels or entire garments, thus eliminating the need for seams. These seamless garments appear
in sportswear, intimate apparel, sleepwear, and swimwear. Seamless hosiery is probably the most well-known
such garment. (Originally, there was a seam on the back
of all stockings.)

FIGURE 6.26
A designer is using a computer-aided design (CAD) system to
create a knit pattern. The color screen permits the designer to
choose and control the particular colors desired.

Seamless knitting can produce interesting styles as well as enhanced comfort and fit. Manufacturing costs are reduced with the elimination of the cutting and sewing processes as well as reduced yarn waste. Seams can create bulkiness in a garment and form holes in the material. Also stress is often concentrated at seam locations, sometimes resulting in premature product failure (e.g., seam slippage, see p. 290; and seam strength).

Seamless is also a popular buzzword as indicated in the terms seamless transition, seamless program, and seamless marketing strategy.

Warp Knitting

Warp-knit fabrics and the machinery used to produce them are substantially different from weft-knit fabrics and their machinery. A comparison of weft-knit and warp-knit fabrics is shown in Table 6.2.

In warp knitting, as its name implies, yarns run vertically in the length of the fabric, as in the warp of woven fabrics. The source of yarn on a warp-knitting machine is a warp beam containing a very large number of parallel yarns, similar to a warp beam on a loom. In warp-knit fabrics, the yarns run the length of the fabric. The yarns form a vertical loop in one course and then move diagonally to another wale to make a loop in the following course. The yarns zigzag from side to side along the length of the fabric. Each loop in a course is made by a different yarn. In the diagram in Figure 6.14b, the side-to-side diagonal movement of the yarn is two wales one way, and then continues in the same direction for one more wale in the next course, followed by a reversal of the same sequence. Warp-knitting machines are usually flat machines since the circular machines are more complicated for making warp-knit fabrics and would result in higher costs. Figure 6.27a and b shows the basic weft-knit and warp-knit loops.

All the needles of the machine are mounted on a long needle bar equal to the width of the machine. When the needle bar is activated, all the needles act in unison. (They do not move up and down individually, as in weft

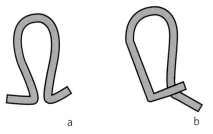

FIGURE 6.27
Differences in weft knitting and warp knitting are visible in the basic (a) weft knit loop and (b) warp knit loop.

knitting.) Thus if all these needles of the machine are mounted on one needle bar, and if the fabric being made is 168 inches wide with 28 needles per inch, there are 4,704 knitting needles with 4,704 warp yarns knitting (i.e., $28 \times 168 = 4{,}704$) producing 4,704 stitches on one course at the same time.

Each yarn is threaded through a yarn guide (a thin plate with a hole through which the yarn passes). All the yarn guides are mounted on a **yarn guide bar.** Movement of the guide bar moves all the yarns mounted on it. The yarn guide bar moves laterally from left to right for several wales, and then back again. In this lateral left-to-right-and-back-again movement, it guides the yarn to a new needle and wraps the yarn around it for its next stitch. Moving warp yarns from one knitting needle to another in this manner ties in all the vertical plain stitches in a warp-knit fabric. When you look at the back of a warp-knit fabric and see the nearly horizontal zigzag floats of yarn, you are in effect seeing the result of the sideways-and-back-again motion of the guide bar. In a simple tricot fabric, the guide bar moves two wales to the right, and then back two to the left. Figure 6.28 shows a warp knitting machine.

It is possible to have more than one guide bar, with some warp yarns going through one guide bar, and others through another. The guide bars can be programmed to operate independently. The greater their number, the greater the design capability of the machine. Thus a

TABLE 6.2	COMPARISON OF WEFT KNITS AND WARP KNITS	
Property	**Weft Knits**	**Warp Knits**
Stretch	In length and width (more in width)	Limited stretch (some in width, less in length.)
Run/Ravel	May run or ravel	Do not run or ravel easily
Machine changeover	Rapid to new designs	Slower and more costly to new designs
Production	May be flat or circular	Flat only
	Yardage, shaped garments, garment parts, and finished edges	Produces yardage only

FIGURE 6.28
Tricot warp knitting machine with weft insertion capability. Note the warp beams at the top of the machine.

4-bar warp knitting machine is not able to produce the complex patterns a 20-bar machine could make.

The movement and patterning of the guide bar are computer controlled through CAD systems, allowing rapid changeover of fabrics for new designs. A designer sitting at the CAD console may create images of new fabrics onscreen. Older warp-knitting systems require tedious and costly mechanical adjustment for changeover to new designs. These older machines usually run standard fabrics where new designs are rarely made.

Warp-Knit Fabrics

Practically all warp-knitted fabrics can be identified and distinguished from weft-knitted materials by careful examination of the face and back of the fabric, usually with the aid of a pick glass. The face of the fabric has rather clearly defined knit stitches generally running vertically (in the lengthwise direction), but slightly angled from side to side. The back of the fabric has slightly angled, horizontal floats. These floats, called **underlaps,** are formed from the sideways movement of the warp yarns as the fabric is made. The recognition of laps in a knitted fabric is the most important distinguishing feature identifying warp knits. (See Figure 6.29.)

Warp-knit fabrics are classified into two main categories, tricot (pronounced "tre-ko") and raschel, and several minor categories, including simplex and milanese.

Tricot Fabrics Tricot fabrics represent the largest portion of yardage produced in the warp-knit category. The name tricot is taken from the French word tricoter, meaning "to knit." The tricot knitting machine is a flat machine made in various widths, some producing fabric over 200 inches wide (5 meters). These machines are characterized as fine-gauge machines ranging from 14 to 36 gauge (needles per inch), with the most popular being 28 gauge for intimate apparel and 22 to 26 for outerwear.

Tricot machines are commonly equipped with from two to four yarn guide bars. Tricot fabrics are often described by the number of yarn guide bars used to make the fabric, such as two-bar fabrics or three-bar fabrics. The number of yarn guide bars gives the fabric its complexity of design. Most lingerie tricot is two-bar fabric. Dress wear tricot and men's wear tricot are often three-bar or four-bar fabrics. Fabrics of one-bar tricot are rarely made because this material is usually unstable. A tricot knitting machine operating rapidly, at 1,000 cycles per minute, can produce 1,000 courses each minute. Modern tricot knitting produces fabric at rates of speed considerably higher than woven cloths or any other type of knitted cloth.[2]

Tricot fabrics are produced in a wide range of fabric-weight types, surface textures, and designs and are used in an equally wide range of products. Typical uses for these fabrics, in addition to the popular types used for lingerie, include fabric types for loungewear, waitresses' and medical uniforms, and backing for bonded fabrics (see p. 145), blouses and dresses, men's shirting, slacks, and automobile upholstery fabric.

Tricot jersey: This fabric is the most-used tricot construction. It is made on machines usually employing two guide bars but only one needle bar. Tricot-jersey fabrics can be identified by the face having all knit stitches appearing in vertical columns and the crosswise underlaps on the back (see Figure 6.29b). These fabrics are stable (i.e., little stretch), are run resistant, and tend not to ravel. Lingerie is the major end use.

Satin tricot: This fabric is a variation of the plain jersey tricot. It is made with long underlaps up to six wales wide on the back of the fabric, providing an exceptionally smooth, satinlike hand to the fabric. Satin tricot has excellent widthwise stability.

Brushed tricot: This fabric, sometimes called napped tricot, is tricot with long underlaps that has been given a mechanical napping finish. (See p. 190.) The fabric is widely used for robes and sleepwear. As with all

---

2. Although tricot-machine speed is faster and the rate of production higher than any other method, it does not automatically follow that costs of production are lower for two reasons: tricot requires more uniform and, therefore, higher-cost yarns and preparation of carefully controlled precision warp beams is required. Because weft knits can use less-costly yarns and are fed to the knitting machine directly from cones or spools, their prices are competitive with that of warp knits.

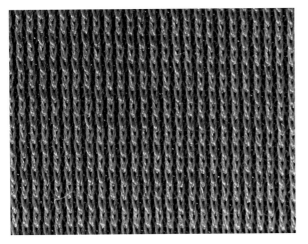

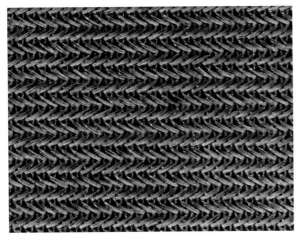

b

FIGURE 6.29
Enlarged view of (a) the face and (b) back of a tricot warp knit fabric. The yarns zigzag down the length of the fabric back.

napped or pile fabrics, these materials should be cut in one direction in a garment.

Although tricot knitting machines have a small number of yarn guide bars, they can make a variety of fabrics. With the use of heavier yarns, fabrics for upholstery (automotive and furniture) can be made. Omitting some yarns at intermittent places can result in a mesh effect or open effect in tricot fabrics for novelty lingerie or curtains. (Raschel fabrics, discussed in the next section, have greater capabilities for this effect.) Laid-in yarns (see p. 131) can provide unique design and physical properties.

Raschel Fabrics Raschel fabrics, like tricot fabrics, are warp-knit fabrics, and, therefore, share many of their characteristics. The principle of knitting in tricot knits is identical to the principle of knitting in raschel knits.

The significant differences between tricot and raschel are that raschel knitting machinery utilizes latch or compound needles rather than spring beard needles and has anywhere from 4 to more than 50 yarn guide bars. The large number of yarn guide bars in raschel knitting provides the potential for great variation in raschel-knit fabric. Sometimes more than one needle bar is used. Figure 6.30 shows a raschel knitting machine.

Raschel knitting systems can produce fabrics ranging from fine lacelike material to heavy blankets and even carpets. Each of these, of course, is done on different gauges of raschel machines. Raschel knitting systems are capable of producing fabrics with interesting surface effects, almost to the point of being three-dimensional. A widely used type of thermal underwear with a distinct waffle surface effect is a raschel knit. (See Figure 6.31.)

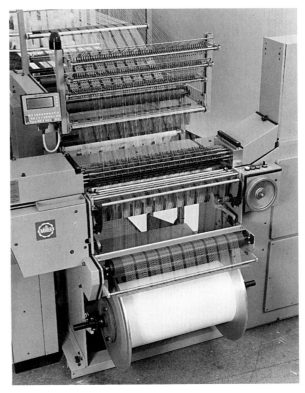

FIGURE 6.30
Raschel warp knitting machine with weft insertion making lace-like patterned narrow fabrics. The yarn guide bars are electronically controlled for more innovative patterns.

FIGURE 6.31
Raschel knits are popular in thermal underwear and other fabrics with raised surfaces.

Power-net fabrics used in foundation garments and swimwear are other examples of raschel knitting. In these materials, spandex yarns are used as run-in yarns.

A knit tulle is a thin, netlike fabric with hexagonal-shaped openings. It is used for veils, tutus, and evening wear.

Distinguishing Between Tricot and Raschel Fabrics
Tricot-knit fabrics and raschel-knit fabrics, as previously indicated, are both warp-knit materials produced on the same knitting principle. Distinguishing whether a particular fabric was produced on a raschel machine or a tricot machine can frequently be determined by the following guidelines: (a) fabrics having heavy yarns, intricate designs, complex "open spacing" (as in lace), and surface effect patterns are usually raschel constructions; (b) fabrics with fine yarns, without design or with simple geometric design, are usually tricot fabrics. Many warp-knit fabrics can be easily classified as tricot or raschel by applying these guidelines. Very often, however, fabrics fall somewhere between the two criteria, and it is not possible to distinguish between them without detailed and complex analysis of the fabric.

Minor Warp Knits Two minor warp-knit categories include simplex and milanese. Fabrics in these categories are made in very limited quantities.

Simplex fabrics are characterized by having both sides looking like the face of a tricot fabric. Knit stitches appear on both sides of the fabric, and the resulting fabric is thicker and firmer than a comparable tricot fabric, but still has a fine gauge. End uses include handbags and gloves.

Milanese fabrics are characterized by having a fine rib on the face and a diagonal patterning effect on the back. They are made with two sets of yarn. One yarn forms the fabric face and the other the fabric back. Each yarn moves across the width of the fabric while knitting. One set of yarns knits from left to right while the other set knits from right to left. End uses include gloves and some types of lingerie and dresses.

Laid-in Yarn Fabrics

Sometimes extra yarns are added to knit fabrics during the knitting process: these are called **laid-in yarns.** Laid-in yarns are not knitted in, but are caught in the knit stitches. They are merely laid in and can be done with both warp- and weft-knit fabrics. The process permits the use of novelty yarns that might not have the strength to be used as knitting yarns. Also, heavier yarn than usual can be used as laid-in yarn for increased cover, stability, and warmth. In addition, a

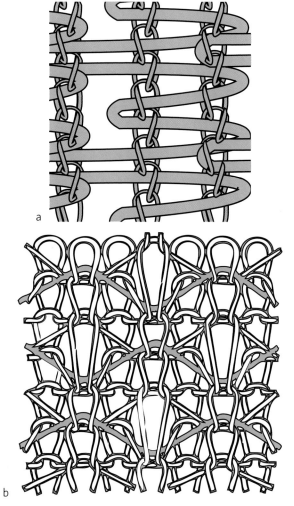

Narrow Knitted Fabrics

Some knit fabrics are made using only a relatively few needles. The result is narrow fabrics. They can be produced on both weft and warp machines. About one-third of the narrow knit fabrics are elastic. Knit elastic fabrics are used in hosiery, underwear, slacks, and trim for various apparel.

Important Differences Between Knitted and Woven Fabrics

There are various important differences between knitted and woven fabrics, including those described here:

▶ **Movement, mobility, and elasticity.** Knitted fabrics tend to mold and fit easily to body shapes and to move easily with body movement (Figures 6.33 and

FIGURE 6.32
Knit fabric with laid-in yarns: (a) warp knit and (b) weft knit.

loosely twisted yarn that will adapt well to brushing can be added. (When later brushed to form a napped fabric (see p. 190), the fabric strength will not be affected.) Knit-elastic fabrics such as power net and stretch twist are produced with bare yarns or covered yarns of spandex (see p. 74) added as the extra laid-in yarns. (See Figure 6.32a and b.)

When the extra yarns run lengthwise in a warp-knit fabric and come from a separate warp beam, they are called **inlay yarns.** In addition to inlay yarns, methods have also been adopted for inserting yarns crosswise into warp-knit fabric. Fabrics made by this method are called **weft-insertion knits.** Fabrics can also be made containing both inlay yarns and weft-insertion yarns.

FIGURE 6.33
A very drapable dress has been made by using a lightweight knitted material.

FIGURE 6.34
Knitted fabric provides fit and ease of movement.

6.34). Woven fabrics are usually rigid (unless made with stretch yarns), do not mold to body shape, and tend to resist body movement. Warp knits tend to be more rigid than weft knits, but not quite as rigid as woven fabrics. Because of these qualities, hosiery is always made from knit constructions, never from woven fabric.

▶ **Recovery from wrinkling.** Knitted fabrics recover from wrinkling more readily than woven fabrics. Knitted fabrics, however, take a less-sharp crease than wovens. The wrinkle-recovery property of knits is what makes them so suitable for traveling.

▶ **Insulation and warmth.** Bulky knit fabrics provide excellent insulation in still air, but because of the open structure of knitted fabric, they provide poor insulation in wind. Tightly woven fabrics provide a high degree of wind resistance. Thus, sweaters are good clothing insulators indoors, but when worn outdoors in wind conditions, they need to be covered by a tightly woven wind-resistant jacket or parka.

▶ **Problems.** Knit fabrics, particularly loosely knitted constructions, tend to stretch out of shape and/or snag on sharp articles (e.g., a broken fingernail) more than woven fabrics. Knit-fabric garments should not be hung on hangers for long periods, but should be folded and stored.

Knit fabrics tend to stretch out when being spread or laid out for cutting during the garment-manufacturing process. Many garment cutters allow knit fabrics to relax in an unstretched condition overnight before cutting the fabric. Under-sized garments (smaller than specifications) could result from not following this practice.

The Effect of Fabric Construction (Wales and Courses per Inch) on Knitted Fabric Properties

If two fabrics are otherwise equal (yarns and knit type), but of differing wales and courses per inch, then their fabric properties differ in the following ways:

1. The fabric with more wales per inch is more stable and rigid in the width direction.

2. The fabric with more courses per inch is more stable and rigid in the length direction.

3. The fabric with both more wales and more courses per inch, in addition to being more stable in both length and width, possesses better ability to recover from stretching than one with fewer wales and courses per inch. (See Figure 6.35a and b.)

4. The fabric with both fewer wales and fewer courses per inch stretches more easily (is less rigid) and molds to body shapes and figures more readily, but has poorer recovery properties than one with higher wales and courses per inch.

5. The fabric with more wales per inch tends to shrink less in the width direction.

6. The fabric with more courses per inch tends to shrink less in the length direction.

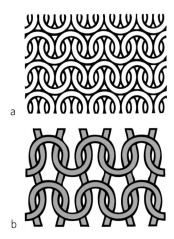

FIGURE 6.35
A (a) tighter knit structure is more stable, but a (b) loose structure tends to stretch out of shape more easily.

Defects in Knit Fabrics

Following are descriptions of some of the more frequently occurring imperfections found in knitted fabrics. These fabric imperfections are usually caused by some knitting machine malfunction, but they also may be caused by imperfect yarns or improper fabric finishing:

Barré: Streaks or bands in the fabric, caused by differences in yarn size, tension on yarns or fabric, color, luster, or shrinkage, from one section of the cloth to the adjacent area. The bands are horizontal and are found only in weft-knit fabrics.

Birdseye or tucking defect: Unintentional tucking caused by a bent latch on the latch needle or by the needle not being raised to the proper height for the old loop then to be cast off.

Boardy: Very harsh or stiff hand, caused by stitches being too tight or yarn being too large.

Bowing: Design or line effect that curves across the fabric, a distortion caused by the take-up mechanism of the knitting machine, or through malfunctions in a machine later used in processing knitted fabric.

Broken filaments: Filament-yarn fabrics in which some filaments of the yarn have broken or split. The resultant fabric may have a mottled or somewhat fuzzy appearance, depending on the amount of filament breakage.

Cockled fabric: Fabric puckers and does not lie flat; caused by uneven stitches or uneven yarn size.

Drop stitch: An unknitted stitch, caused by a stitch being too loose or the yarn carrier being set improperly.

Float: Unwanted miss stitch(es) caused by needle(s) not raised to receive a new yarn.

Needle line: Lengthwise marks or lines in the fabric resulting from a wale that is tighter or looser than the others. This may be caused by a needle being tight in the machine slot.

Press-off: A large hole in fabric, caused by a yarn breaking at a particular feed so knitting cannot occur.

Run or ladder: A series of dropped stitches in a wale.

Skewing: Design or line effect that is straight across in the fabric, but not perpendicular to the fabric edges.

Sleazy: A flimsy or underconstructed knit fabric, one lacking in body.

Stop mark: A horizontal fabric streak resulting when the knitting machine is stopped. It is caused by a tension difference in the yarns.

Classic Knit Fabrics

Classic knit fabrics are named primarily on the basis of their construction, not on the basis of appearance and weight as is the case with most woven fabrics. For example, if a weft knit is made entirely of knit stitches, it is referred to as jersey knit. Thus, both a lightweight, closely constructed filament yarn fabric and a heavyweight, open constructed novelty yarn fabric can be called a jersey fabric providing each is made with knit stitches. See the following descriptions:

Argyle: Diamond-shaped design of different colors, where the diamond areas are formed with their own complete stitches rather than by miss stitches. (See Figure 6.36.)

Bird's eye: A salt and pepper color effect on the back of a double-knit fabric.

Cable-stitch fabric: Fabric having the appearance of a plaited rope or cable running in the wale direction. Basic fabric structure is a rib knit and is widely used in sweaters.

Cardigan fabric: A modified form of rib knit produced by selective tuck stitches to produce a thicker

FIGURE **6.36**
Complete stitches are visible in the diamond-shaped areas of these argyle sweaters.

FIGURE **6.37**
This Intarsia Missoni dress shows colored designs knitted into a solid color fabric.

fabric. Cardigan stitches are either full cardigan or half cardigan and appear the same on both sides.

Double knit: A specialty type of rib-knit fabric. Usually close stitched with a pattern or design effect.

Flat knit: Any fabric produced on a flatbed knitting machine.

French terry: A weft-knit fabric made with a weft-insertion yarn. The technical back is used as the face. It has a fleecelike hand.

Full fashioned: Knitwear that is shaped during the knit manufacturing process as seen on the shoulder areas of a full-fashioned sweater.

Intarsia: A decorative, colored design knitted into a solid color fabric. The design areas are formed with colored yarns using their own complete stitches rather than with miss-stitches or other techniques. (See Figure 6.37.) Intarsia fabrics do not have a bird's eye backing. Argyle is a form of intarsia.

Interlock: A variation of a rib-knit fabric in which wales of knit stitches are directly behind each other

on the face and back of the fabric. They tend to be firmer than regular ribs.

Jacquard knit: A knit fabric with designs in color and/or texture that is produced by attachments on the knitting machine that regulate the action of the knitting needles.

Jersey: Describes any knitted fabric where all the stitches on one side of the fabric are knit stitches while the stitches on the reverse side are either purl stitches or combination of purl, tuck, and/or miss stitches; also known as single knits.

Knitted velour: Fabric where knitted loops have been sheared to create a velvetlike surface.

Lacoste®: A fine-cut jersey fabric that contains a specific pattern of knit and tuck stitches.

Ottoman rib: A double-knit fabric having pronounced ribs or rolls across the width of the fabric. This is achieved by knitting more courses per unit length on one side than the other.

Pile knit: A special type of jersey-knit fabric made by feeding staple fiber in the form of sliver onto the knitting needles while the fabric is being knitted. The fiber is caught in the knit structure to produce fabric like fake fur.

Pointelle: A rib fabric utilizing transfer stitches to create selective openings in a fabric.

Ponte di Roma: A double-knit fabric type usually produced in one color rather than a color pattern. It is very elastic and has a slight horizontal stripe character.

Poor boy: Describes an entire category of fabric rather than one specific cloth. The general designation for rib-knit fabrics (often 2 × 2 ribs) used in sweaters, sports pullovers, and T-shirts.

Power net: A warp-knit fabric produced on a raschel machine having elastic yarns laid in the fabric.

Purl fabric: Any knitted fabric with knit stitches and purl stitches in the same wale.

Raschel: Describes a class of warp-knit fabrics which range from lacelike to carpets.

Rib fabric: A knitted fabric where wales of knit stitches alternate with wales of purl stitches. Rib fabrics have good elasticity in the width direction.

Shaker: A term given to a sweater made from 1 × 1 rib stitch of heavy yarn.

Tricot: Describes a class of fabrics of the warp-knit type usually made from filament or textured filament yarns. These fabrics are relatively stable and do not stretch as much as most weft knits.

Tulle: A warp-knit fabric made by skipping needles so a hexagonal net is created.

Study Questions

1. Name five different weft-knit fabrics.

2. State three reasons why knits are popular in the fashion market.

3. How does fabric construction (wales and courses per inch) affect the stretching and ability-to-recover properties of a knit fabric?

4. Describe some differences you would expect between two weft-knit T-shirts if both are identical, except that one is made from a jersey fabric and the other is made from a 2 × 2 rib fabric.

5. Why do many knit fabrics provide excellent insulation and warmth in still air, but tend to be poor insulators under windy conditions?

6. How can a tricot fabric and a jersey fabric be distinguished from one another?

7a. Distinguish between the expressions cut and wales per inch.

b. Why does a high-cut machine produce a fine fabric and not a coarse fabric?

8. Explain how modern computer-aided design (CAD) systems for developing knit fabrics help retailers to respond more rapidly to changing consumer fashion needs.

9. Explain why most weft-knit fabrics with stripes have these stripes in the width direction, whereas woven fabrics are almost always striped in the length direction.

10. State various ways in which different patterns and surface textures can be achieved in knitted fabrics.

11. Why should most garments made from weft-knitted fabric constructions be folded and stored on shelves or in drawers rather than hung on hangers in a closet?

12a. Why will a knit sweater keep you warmer than a comparable woven jacket in a no-wind atmosphere?

b. What happens if there is a strong wind?

CHAPTER SEVEN
Other Types of Textiles

Objectives

▸ To explain how textile materials can be constructed by methods other than weaving and knitting.

▸ To be able to recognize the identifying characteristics of these materials.

▸ To know the end uses of these materials by being able to relate their performance properties.

 Use fabrics in the Other Types of Textiles section of the Fabric Science Swatch Kit *for this chapter.*

Key Terms Related to Textiles

batting	fiber fill	needle-punched
bonded	foam	nonwoven
carded-web	foam-flame bonding	quilted
disposable	foam-laminate	Schiffli machine
down	fusible	spunbonded
drylaid	hot-melt	spunlaced
durable	hybrid	spunlaid
embroidery	lace	stitch bonding
eyelet	laminated	tufted
felt	melt-blown	wet-adhesive bonding
		wetlaid

While weaving and knitting are two major methods of producing textile materials, they are not alone. There are a number of other methods for producing textile materials, and although each of these represents a smaller percentage of total textile production, their total annual consumption amounts to many millions of yards.

These other types of textiles are often used as small, but critical, components of a total garment or other textile application. Such elements as lace trim, felt-appliqué trim, and garment interlinings are examples of these. The fact that failure or poor performance of these small components could render a whole article useless is one reason for the importance of understanding the properties and characteristics of the types of textiles.

These other types of textiles include nonwovens, felt, bonded and laminated materials, quilted material, stitch bonding, lace, embroidery, and tufted fabrics. A much greater number of pages are devoted to nonwovens since the structure is becoming increasingly important as a textile material.

Nonwoven Fabrics

Nonwoven fabrics are generally defined as a textile structure produced by bonding or interlocking of fibers, or both, accomplished by mechanical, chemical, thermal or solvent means and combinations thereof. A web of fibers is the result.

It is a confusing term since the name seems to include all fabrics "not woven" (e.g., knitting). Paper could seemingly qualify as a nonwoven material, but the fiber length usually is very short and so has too low a fiber length-to-diameter ratio. The distance between fibers is also usually too small. Felt is not considered a nonwoven since the density is usually too high (i.e., too heavy). With new constructions (based on new technology), it is becoming more difficult to define what is a nonwoven.

Nonwovens are becoming increasingly important as a material. With new technologies, a wide variety of nonwoven materials for a very diverse group of end uses have been developed, using many different new materials (see Table 7.1 and Figures 7.1 and 7.2).

Background

The first nonwovens were introduced in 1942 (drylaid technology for making the web). In the mid-1950s Chicopee Mills marketed Handi-Wipes®, one of the earliest identifiable nonwoven consumer products. At this time Pellon Corporation became an important United States producer of nonwovens, specializing in inner linings and interfacing for the apparel trade. In the 1960s additional technologies were introduced which expanded the variety of nonwovens being made. The rest of the century saw increasing growth of nonwovens worldwide, with the development of composite materials made by combining different types of nonwovens and/or nonwovens with other materials, such as fibers and foams. The beginning of the 21st century shows a combination of hybrid structures, new developments and widespread acceptance of nonwovens.

Major suppliers include Freudenberg Group, DuPont™ Nonwovens, Kimberly-Clark Corporation, Polymer Group, Inc. (PGI), Fiberweb plc, and Johns Manville.

The basic materials to produce nonwoven fabrics are fibers (primarily olefin, polyester, and rayon), specialty chemicals, such as bonding agents to provide strength, and auxiliary agents, which can be used, for example, to control flexibility, enhance surface texture, or alter moisture-transport capability. The performance profile

TABLE 7.1	End Uses of Nonwoven Fabrics
Industry	**End Use**
Agriculture	Seed strip, greenhouse cover, and others
Apparel	Interfacing, bra padding, gloves, shoe lining, protective, and others
Automotive	Battery separator, carpet backing, insulation batting, and others
Civil engineering	Road bed, silt fence, landfill underliner, drainage liner, and others
Construction	Roofing and tile underlay, insulation batting, and others
Household	Wipes, glove liner, vacuum-cleaner bag, laundry softener/antistatic sheet, dust cloth, tea bag, placemat, ironing-board pad, garment bags, and others
Industrial	Filter, abrasive, tape, cable insulation, lab coat, coated fabrics, and others
Interior furnishing	Quilt, bedspread, mattress cover, tablecloth, upholstery backing, window shade, carpet backing, and others
Health care	Surgical gown, bandage, dental bib, bedding underpad, chair headrest, slippers, shoe covers, privacy curtain, and others
Personal care	Diaper, sanitary napkin, cosmetic applicator, wipes, and others
Miscellaneous	Pennant, mailing envelope, kite, book cover, and others

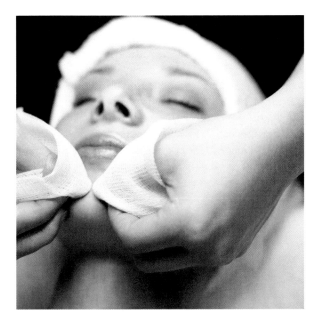

FIGURE 7.1
The cosmetic industry uses many nonwoven products.

FIGURE 7.2
An example of industrial end uses for nonwoven products.

of a nonwoven (i.e., strength, softness, absorbency, and filtering ability) depends upon the fiber solution, arrangement of the fibers in the web, and how the component fibers are held together.

While all nonwovens do not need to be finished, some finishes that are used include embossing, flame retarding, and making a surface more hydrophilic or hydrophobic. The production rates of nonwoven machinery far exceed those of modern weaving and knitting and are approaching those of high-speed papermaking. The weight range of nonwoven materials is very wide, from about 15 grams/meter to over 1000 grams/meter, whereas the density can be as low as 40 kilograms/centimeter^3 or as high as 300 kilograms/centimeter^3. A primary advantage of nonwoven is their versatility and low cost.

Durable and Disposable Nonwoven Fabrics

There are two general categories of nonwovens:

Durable materials are not intended to be thrown away after a single or limited number of applications. Examples include apparel interlinings, carpet backings, subsoil covers for road beds, and tiles on a space shuttle. Some items, such as reuseable cleaning cloth, might be considered semi-durable.

Disposable materials are manufactured with the intention of being thrown away after a single or limited number of uses. They are important when the convenience of throwing away the item is more important than additional costs or when cost of the item is less than the cleaning or sterilization expense would be for durable products. Disposables have a benefit that there are no contaminants that may remain from previous use (reusable). Examples include, headrests, filters, surgical gowns, coveralls, and absorbent hygiene products (e.g., diapers).

Manufacturing Nonwovens

Fibers are the basic units of the nonwoven structure. They are arranged into webs and consolidated (bonded). The distance between the fibers is much greater than the fiber diameter and the weight of the web is usually low. The result is usually a thin, porous web material. The most frequently used fibers are polyester, rayon, and polypropylene.

Three major manufacturing methods are used to produce nonwoven materials: drylaid, wetlaid, and spunlaid. Each differs in fiber, usage, range of properties, and financial requirements.

With the **drylaid** system, the material structure is found by having the fibers manipulated while in a dry state. This is the most-used system worldwide. Its methods include *carded* and *airlaid*. With the **wetlaid** system, the material structure is formed by having the fibers manipulated while in a wet state. This is the least used system. With the **spunlaid** system, the material structure is formed by blowing thermoplastic fibers onto a collection surface as the fibers are being extruded. The webs can be bonded by a mechanical (entanglement), chemical (adhesive), or thermal (fusing) process.

Materials are also referred to by the method in which they are bonded as well as how the web was formed. The following are well-known nonwoven materials.

Carded-Web Nonwovens
Carded-web nonwovens were the first nonwovens, produced in the early 1940s. The largest volume of nonwovens is made using this method. They can be made from any staple fiber, and are produced by forming a web of fibers and then bonding the fibers. The web is formed by using mechanical means, such as a carding machine (carded-drylaid), air-blowing fibers (airlaid-drylaid), or liquid to manipulate the fibers (wetlaid). Bonding of fibers may be accomplished with an adhesive, or through heat fusion if the fibers from which the nonwoven is being made are of the thermoplastic fiber type. Carded-web nonwovens may be unidirectional, cross-laid, or random web, indicating the orientation of the fibers in a specific fabric.

Carded-web nonwovens are used extensively in disposable items, such as cooks' hats, hospital and hair-salon protective gowns, disposable bed sheets, towels, tablecloths, draperies, and female hygiene products.

Spunlaced Nonwovens
Spunlaced nonwovens are formed by the entanglement of staple fibers, using needlelike, high-pressure water jets on the web (wetlaid). The fibers knot or curl around each other, causing mechanical binding (hydroentangling). Since no binders are used, softness, drape, and bulk result. End uses of the material include robes, mattress pads, backing of quilted tablecloths, mops, and wipes.

Spunbonded Nonwovens
Spunbonded nonwovens are made from the continuous extrusion of filaments into a web (spunlaid). They consist of randomly oriented filament fibers subsequently consolidated by thermal bonding, mechanical entanglement, adhesive bonding, or etched filament surfaces to interlock the fibers. This method produces the second largest amount of nonwovens.

Spunbonded products are fairly opaque, possess high strength-to-weight ratios, high tear strength, somewhat isotropic properties due to random lay-down of the fibers, good fray and crease resistance, and have high in-plane shear resistance.

Spunbonded nonwovens are made in a wide variety of weights, degrees of softness, and drapability. They are used in an equally wide variety of end uses, including geotextiles, padded mailing envelopes, clothing interliners, backing for wallpaper and vinyl films, carpet backing, shoe linings, hygiene products, and protective apparel. In general, they possess all the physical and chemical properties of the fiber from which they are made. Moreover, most spunbonded fabrics can be sewn with a minimum of pucker.

Spunbonded products include Tyvek® (DuPont™), Reemay® (Fiberweb plc), Accord® (Kimberly-Clark), and Typar® (DuPont™ Nonwovens).

An interesting end use for spunbounded materials is for housewrap. Wrapping the outside of a house covers the cracks and gaps that are normal parts of a building and so prevents bulk water and air from penetrating these cavities. The material is made with millions of small pores which allow the building to breathe (transmission of moisture vapor) so there is no mildew or mold buildup. There is also a saving on heating and cooling costs. Finishing the outside of the building covers the wrapping material. Tyvek® Home Wrap (DuPont™) is a well-known brand.

Melt-Blown Nonwovens
Melt-blown nonwovens are produced in a process similar to spunbonded nonwovens in that fiber extrusion is used (spunlaid). However, upon passage through the spinnerette, the molten polymer is accelerated by high-velocity hot-air jets that reduce the filaments to microdenier size. The individual filament fibers break into staple fibers and are propelled to a collection surface. Because the fibers are in a tacky state upon collection, cohesive web structures result. Some of the potential shortcomings include low fiber strength and low abrasion resistance. End uses of this material include insulation of outdoor garments and boots (Thinsulate™ by the 3M Corporation), filtration, battery separators and industrial wipes.

Needle-Punched Nonwovens
Needle-punched nonwovens are sometimes called mechanical felt or needle-punched felt, which they somewhat resemble. Unlike felt (which is primarily made from wool), needle-punched nonwovens can be made from any staple fiber.

Needle-punched nonwovens (drylaid) are made by a method that involves the entanglement of fibers to hold them together. The process for making this material consists of passing a continuous web of fibers through a needle-punch machine. The essential parts of the machine are a multitude of barbed needles or hooks (the

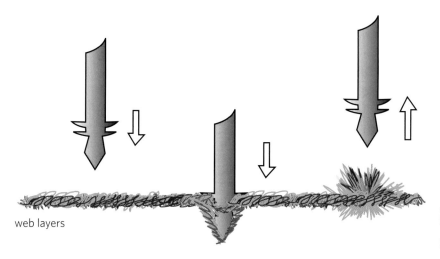

web layers

FIGURE 7.3
The process for making needle-punched nonwovens.

barb somewhat resembles a fishhook barb) mounted on a grid that vibrates up and down. As the web of fibers passes the vibrating grid, the needles pierce the web and entangle the fibers as they withdraw. When this occurs continuously, the fibers form an entangled mass of material. If the fibers are thermoplastic, they can be heat-fused to increase the tensile strength of the nonwoven. (See Figure 7.3.)

Needle punching is a relatively inexpensive method for producing fabric. The well-known type of flat, feltlike indoor/outdoor carpeting made from olefin fibers is the most popular needle-punched fabric. Other applications include blankets and apparel insulation. Needle-punched carpeting is now being used in automobiles as floor covering as well as for other end uses, such as acoustical insulation.

Fusible Nonwovens

An additional category of nonwovens is **fusible** nonwovens, which are either made from thermoplastic fibers or are thermoplastic films. They are used more widely in clothing than any of the other varieties, yet most consumers are unaware of them. The fusible nonwovens are used primarily as interlining for clothing and have two major functions: to provide shape to cut parts of garments and to hold garment parts, such as skirt hem or shirt facing, together. These fabrics provide shape because they are rigid. Garment parts are held together by sandwiching the nonwoven material between the cloth pieces. On application of heat at the proper temperature, the nonwoven material softens and attaches itself to the parts of the garment with which it is in contact. Upon cooling, the nonwoven material is firmly attached to the garment parts.

Of the two major functions, providing shape to cut parts of the garment is probably the more important. The development of these fabrics in the late 1960s replaced the need for the highly skilled tailor to stitch on the underliner portions of tailored clothing (especially in men's suits) that gave the garment fronts their shaping.

Fusibles are smooth and stable in cleaning processes. The material Pellon® fusible (Pellon Consumer Products Group, LLC) is of this type.

Hybrid Products

Combining technologies to make **hybrid** nonwoven products increases versatility and extends nonwovens' marketplace reach. Each production technique used, such as spunlaid, drylaid, or wetlaid, has limitations which are reflected on the final product. For example, if absorbent, soft, bulky material is needed, the spunlaid method cannot be used. Combining or laminating two or three different nonwovens into a single nonwoven sheet can result in obtaining all of the required properties or characteristics.

Key factors in the recent growth of nonwovens are the range of types of nonwovens that are available, the versatility of these fabrics, and their ability to be combined with a wide range of other materials to produce hybrid materials. An early composite structure was a scrim-reinforced laminate for disposable patient examining gowns. Using thermal (radiant heat), chemical (adhesive), or mechanical (needle-punching) methods, hybrid combinations can be produced, including the following:

▶ nonwovens with other nonwovens—spunbond/melt-blown/spunbond (SMS) products (3-layer) for protective clothing (breathable, but liquid repellent);

- nonwovens with film—drylaid nonwoven/cellophane for (2-layer) battery separators;

- nonwovens with foam—needle-punched nonwoven/polyurethane foam/vinyl coating (3-layer) for automotive landau tops;

- nonwovens with an extrusion coating—needle-punched nonwoven/vinyl coating (2-layer) for upholstery fabric; and

- needle-punched nonwovens with meltblown nonwovens—filtration applications.

Multilayer nonwoven composite materials are also being made in various weights and thicknesses. They are designed to integrate blends of various fibrous webs to offer a variety of properties, such as strength, thermal resistance, anti-microbial, and water repellency. End uses include apparel, shelters, and equipment related.

Nonwoven Wipes

A brief examination of the consumer nonwoven-wipes market offers an opportunity to understand the growth of a product through good marketing and use of technology. This is one of the fastest growing nonwoven sectors and its rapid growth is expected to continue.

The wipes market first expanded nonwovens' role in consumer markets with the launch of two home-care products—disinfectant wipes (antibacterial) and disposable floor-cleaning products (combined bottle of cleaner, rags, and paper towels into one disposable product). In the skin- and facial-care area, wipes were later produced that combined exfoliator, cleansing, conditioning, and moisturizing in one disposable product. Dual-texture laminates were offered, one side smooth for wiping and moisturizing, and the other side textured for cleaning and exfoliating. Facial wipes now also contain sunscreen as well as moisturizer and cleaner. In the home care area, both wet and dry floor wipes as well as dusting cloths were made with a polypropylene scrim cloth incorporated into the nonwoven web to provide greater strength and durability. Some of these factors which contributed to the strong consumer demand were convenience, as well as a desire for improved skin health, superior hygiene, and cleanliness.

Wipes are either wet, dry, or coated. The fibers used include rayon, polyester, and polypropylene as well as wood pulp. The vast majority of wipes available are either spunlaced or airlaid. Spunlace offers excellent softness (no binders or chemical additives), bicomponent composition to balance absorbency with other characteristics, and good machine direction strength. Airlaids, by nature, have a rougher surface and therefore tend to have better wiping characteristics. However, they suffer from poor tensile properties in both the machine and cross directions. Both spunlace and airlaid processes are very cost effective for manufacturing disposable products. Spunlace products include Mr. Clean®, Pledge® and Clorox® disinfecting wipes.

Categories of wipes include baby wipes, disinfectant wipes (antibacterial hand wipes), moist towelettes, medicated wipes, electrostatic wipes (for dusting), floor-cleaning wipes, and general purpose wipes. Industrial wipes include shop wipes (grease), specialty wipes (polishing), instrument and lens cleaners, heavy-duty removal (paint, corrosion), and sanitizing cleaners.

In 2000, Proctor & Gamble Company introduced Swiffer® dry electrostatic floor cleaning cloths, creating a whole new major category. This product was followed by Swiffer Wet (wet version), Swiffer Sweepervac (paired with a vacuum), Swiffer Duster (fluffy dusting cloth), Swiffer Wet Jet (pulls dirt deep inside a thick pad), and Swiffer Carpet Flick (disposable adhesive cartridge). This product is an example of finding a new consumer market and successfully providing products to satisfy the buyers (consumers) in that sector.

Trade Shows and Associations

Various nonwoven conferences and expositions are held periodically worldwide, in which exhibitors show new products and technologies. These include ANEX Expo and Conference (American Nonwovens Exhibition and Conference), INDEX (International Nonwovens Exhibition), and SINCE (Shanghai International Nonwoven Conference and Exhibition).

The Association of the Nonwoven Fabrics Industry (INDA) is the organization which represents the nonwovens industry. It is dynamic, disseminating information to its members and directing its efforts towards improving the nonwoven industry.

The Environment

Nonwoven producers are becoming more interested in making eco products. Fiberweb PLC has launched Eco-Fibers®, a line of nonwovens made from at least 50 percent renewable materials. It also features Ingeo™ fibers in its product. (Nature-based fiber derived from agricultural sustainable resources—NatureWorks™ polymer.) It is ideal for coverstock and backsheet applications in the baby diaper, feminine care, and adult incontinence markets. It is also used in wipes and garden covering material to control weeds (50 percent Ingeo™ fiber).

Biodegradable wipes are emerging (called flushable). Also, printed wipes are beginning to be produced without using conventional inks (more eco friendly).

Felt

Felt is probably the oldest known textile. Primitive man discovered that fur coverings entangled and formed a solid mass when moisture, body heat, and agitation acted on the furs.

Wool and related animal fibers, such as camel and goat hair, have a unique property. Their scalelike surface serrations become interlocked and entangled when subjected to heat, moisture, and agitation. This property is what makes felt fabric. Felt is made directly from fibers treated in machines designed to accomplish the felting action.

The fiber content of felt ranges from 50 percent to 100 percent wool, with the other fibers usually being rayon or cotton. Felt with higher wool content can be blocked and shaped more effectively than lower-wool-content types. Although blending with cotton or rayon reduces the cost of felt, it also reduces the strength because the blending fibers have smooth surfaces and cannot interlock with other fibers.

The manufacture of felt begins with the fiber being blended in a mixing or picking machine. They are then carded where the fibers are arranged into a thin web. The webs are removed from the carding machine and assembled in layers until the desired thickness is attained. The batt, or layers of fibers, is moistened and passed through a hardening machine, where mechanical motion is provided, either with moveable heated rollers pressing and agitating the batt into a material or with a heavy heated plate vibrating horizontally as it presses the batt and forms the material. Then the material is usually sent to a fulling mill where it is further agitated and appreciably shrunk (as much as 50 percent) in both length and width. This is similar to the fulling process done to woven woolen fabrics. When the felting process is completed, the material is *finished* to make it more consumer-usable. Additional processing would include flameproofing, calendering (pressing), tentering (stretching the fabric to shape while it dries), or water repellency. The density, hardness, and thickness are closely controlled from $1/32$ of an inch to over 3 inches in thickness and from less than 3 ounces to over 60 pounds per square yard.

Felt does not fray or ravel because it has no yarns. It can be blocked to shape in all directions because it has no grain. This is the reason for its popular use in hats. The material is an excellent shock-absorbing and sound-absorbing substance. Unfortunately, most felt has poor drapability, rather low tensile strength, a tendency not to return to shape if unduly stretched, and a propensity to form tears and holes that cannot be mended. Other uses include pennants, billiard-table covers, padding, and crafts.

Felt should not be considered a nonwoven material since it is primarily the interlocking of the fiber surface serrations that holds the fibers together and not adhesive, fusion, or mechanical binding (e.g., by use of hooks).

Bonded and Laminated Materials

Bonded and laminated materials are both layered structures with different constructions. They are used for apparel, shoes, upholstery, geotextiles, drapes, tents, luggage, and other end uses.

Bonded material is a layered fabric structure in which a face (or shell) fabric is joined to a backing fabric with an adhesive that does not significantly add to the thickness of the combined fabrics. The backing fabric is often tricot, while the face fabric can be almost any conceivable type of cloth.

Laminated material is a layered fabric structure in which a face (or outer) fabric is joined to a continuous sheet material, such as polyurethane foam or a nonwoven. The identity of the continuous sheet material is retained after the process is completed. Often this structure is joined on the back with a (backing) fabric such as tricot, creating a sandwich effect (sandwich laminate).

Bonded Fabrics

There is nearly an infinite variety of textile materials that can be utilized as the face fabric of bonded cloth. Primarily, however, bonded fabrics are made from lightweight face fabrics that, because of their construction, are low cost and that alone are unsuitable as apparel fabric. When bonded to a tricot backing, they take on the weight, stability, and hand of a heavier fabric that is now usable for the particular end use. The tricot backing cloth is also of relatively low cost, and the bonding process is rapid and economical. Bonded fabrics, therefore, are important in the textile market as they provide the consumer with relatively low-cost fabrics having the appearance, surface, touch, stability and, when bonded properly, the hand and durability of higher-cost materials.

There are two basic methods of producing bonded fabrics: the wet-adhesive process and the foam-flame bonding process. In the **wet-adhesive** process adhesives are applied to the fabric, and then the fabric is passed between two series of hot rollers to activate and set the adhesive (see Figure 7.4). **Foam-flame bonding** uses an extremely thin layer of polyurethane foam that is heated to make it tacky and adhesive. The tacky foam is then sandwiched between the face and back fabric. Heating of the foam is done over gas jets, hence the term foam-flame bonding. In this method, the foam is melted and practically disappears, although often the process is engineered so that a layer of about a $1/100$ inch remains between the face and back and gives body to the cloth.

Of the two methods, the foam-flame method is more widely used. Wet-adhesive bonding is more highly favored if the face fabric is one of open or netlike construction because there is a likelihood that traces of foam will be seen on the face if foam-flame bonding is used.

Quality control in production and the proper selection and balance of components is very important for the ultimate performance and durability of bonded fabrics. A bonded fabric is not one, but three products combined in one (face, adhesive, backing). The three must be combined under carefully controlled conditions or they will delaminate (separate). Different rates of shrinkage of the face and back fabrics cause puckering of the fabric when it is dry cleaned or laundered. In addition, the incorrect adhesive or improper application of adhesive results in the separation of the face and back components.

A material can be treated with a nanocoating and then bonded to another fabric with desirable properties of its own, like warmth and elasticity. For example, a fabric that was treated on one side with a wicking function that takes away sweat from the body can be bonded to a fabric now coated on the face to be highly resistant to liquids which cause stains. The fabric now has two functional features—comfort and protection.

Laminated Fabrics

Laminated fabric using foam as the middle layer is referred to as foam-laminated fabrics. **Foam-laminated** fabrics are similar to foam-flame bonded materials, except that a thicker layer of foam is used in them. The foam remains as the laminate when the process is completed. Foam laminate can be produced with up to $1/2$ inch foam layers, although they are usually in the range of $1/8$, to $3/16$ inch (see Figure 7.5).

Foam-laminated fabrics are primarily intended for clothing insulation. They are relatively lightweight in proportion to their thickness; their cellular structure entraps dead air. They may be laminated directly to an outer fabric, or the foam laminate may be used as a garment interlining. Laminating directly to an outer fabric is a more economical method of producing garments because it eliminates the need for sewing in a separate

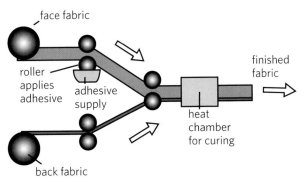

FIGURE 7.4
The process for making adhesive-bonded materials.

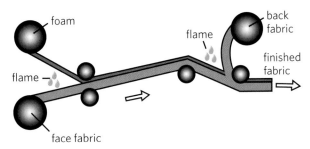

FIGURE 7.5
The process for making foam-laminated material.

lining. However, the foam laminates lack drapability, and most garments produced in this manner appear stiff and boardy. When the foam laminate is used as an interliner, the garment outer shell retains all of its drapability, so a coat, for example, does not take on an unsightly appearance.

An additional method for laminating is called the **hot-melt** method. It uses either a web (nonwoven) or lightweight fabric, made of thermoplastic material (e.g., nylon or polyester) as the adhesive. A sandwich is formed with the adhesive material in the middle, between the outer fabric and the lining fabric. Heat and pressure are applied and the thermoplastic material melts and becomes sticky, thus holding the two fabrics together. This one-step process can be used to combine other materials, such as films, papers, foams, metals, glass, and plastics.

Newly developed laminates have as the middle layer a thin microporous film that allows the material to breathe (it transmits water vapors from the body of the outside air—for thermal comfort) but also be waterproof (for protection). The result is a desirable outerwear material.

Quilted Material

A **quilted** material consists of an insulating filler secured between two layers of fabrics. The filler material is usually fiberfill, batting, or foam. The three layers are held together either by sewing or bonding to prevent the filler material from shifting. A pattern on the surface fabric is produced since the bonding areas are scattered and occupy a very small total surface area so not to sacrifice the bulk desired (for insulation).

Most quilted materials are made by sewing (using quilting machines that produce sewn seams). Well-made quilted material should be made with durable thread, lock-type stitches, small stitches (to reduce snagging and abrasion), a pattern that will keep the filling material in place but not appreciably reduce the loft (insulation) of the material, and a durable outer fabric.

Bonding may also be done with heat or adhesives. Thermal bonding requires that all of the components be at least 50 percent thermoplastic (fiber) content. The heat applied causes the components to fuse together and form a seam. Machines using ultrasonic vibrations to cause the heat required are being used, as well as the traditional heated rollers. Adhesives can also be applied in a pattern or design to hold the layers together. Sewn stitching, however, is the technique that is most used, since the other techniques result in the attached areas tending to separate and open more easily.

The insulation component of quilts may consist of polyester fiberfill or batting, polyurethane foam, or down. Polyester **fiberfill** is the most widely used product and provides excellent resilience combined with light weight in thick layers (better insulation). Polyester fiberfill is relatively low in cost. Polyester **batting** is used when relatively thin layers of insulation are required (as in a summer quilt). This product is low in cost, has good resilience, and is lightweight. **Foam**, when used, results in a stiffer material which does not drape well. **Down** insulation is a luxury product, highest in cost than all quilt and comforter combinations. It is the lightest in weight per unit volume and is the least resilient. To prevent the very fine down fibers from coming through the top or bottom layers, products insulated with down require very tightly woven top and bottom layers with a calendered finish (see p. 188). Alternatively, a separate inner lining that is tightly woven and calendered may be used.

Seams used in quilted materials for insulation purposes provide a source of heat loss. They bring face and back fabrics closer together, thus reducing the thickness of the quilting and lessening the amount of insulation provided.

Quilted materials have been used in apparel (ski jackets and robes) (see Figure 7.6), household articles (quilts and mattress pads), and camping equipment (sleeping bags).

Stitch Bonding

Stitch bonding is a mechanical bonding system in which needles and threads (or yarns) are used to sew or stitch yarns or fibers (webs) together into a fabric. The resulting fabrics are produced at very high speeds. These fabrics were first produced in the United States in the late 1960s by the Malimo Company, which has been acquired by the Karl Mayer Textile Machine Company (Karl Mayer Textilmaschinenfabrik GmbH).

The materials were initially made by literally sewing fibers or groups of yarns together. Today, a technique called *knit-through* is used, in which the material is made with a warp-knitting machine. There are three different types of fabric produced in this manner. They are Malimo®, Maliwatt®, and Malipol®, all trade names for the Karl Mayer Company.

Malimo® fabrics are usually made with two groups of yarns—one lengthwise and the other widthwise. They are positioned one on top of the other, as laid-in yarns, and then warp knit together with (stitching) yarn. When the stitching yarns are fine and the base yarns are thick, the

FIGURE 7.6
Vests of quilted material.

fabric resembles a woven structure. The stitching yarns tend to disappear into the surface. When the stitching yarns are dominant, the fabric surface tends to resemble a knit structure. Often, only one set of base yarns is used to make the fabrics. Uses for this material include tablecloths, dishcloths, draperies, apparel, and industrial applications.

Maliwatt® fabrics are made by knitting yarns (warp knit) through a fiberweb structure (matting). Uses for this fabric include blankets, linings, window-treatments, insulating material, and geotextiles.

Another technique creates a pile fabric by stitching yarns into a fabric base. The fabric produced is called Malipol® and can appear as a terrycloth or plush material. It can be used as a coat-lining fabric, imitation fur, or pile fabric for toys.

Lace Fabrics

Lace is a fabric that consists of a decorative design created with threads or yarns on a netlike, open background. Lace making is the most complicated of all textile-making processes. Lace is made by various techniques, such as intertwining, knotting, and looping of threads or yarns.

Laces may be of full fabric width, used in making dresses and evening wear, or they may be of narrow widths, sometimes with scalloped edges, when used as trim. The material can be delicate or heavy. Through the efforts of modern textile technology, lace materials are available for a variety of prices. Many laces are now machine washable.

Lace-making techniques are also used in hand-crafts to produce less delicate lace material, such as macramé, netting, or crochet materials.

Some laces are handmade, although the quantity is small because of the very high cost. These come mostly from France, Belgium, Italy, and Ireland. Handmade lace, sometimes referred to as real lace to differentiate it from machine-made lace, is made by a variety of methods. Depending on the kind of lace being made, bobbins, pins, needles, hooks, or shuttles may be used. Handmade lace includes needlepoint, bobbin, darned, crocheted, and knotted lace.

Machine-made laces were first produced in the early 1800s and are frequently named for the type of machine used to produce them. Thus, the Leavers machine, which produces the finest and most intricate of machine-made laces, produces Leavers lace. Thin, small bobbins (yarn holders) move between lengthwise yarns and twist yarn around them to produce the pattern. The Nottingham machine produces a heavier, rougher-textured lace, referred to as Nottingham lace. Most lace today is machine made.

FIGURE 7.7
A lace dress by Prada.

Two other fabrics are marketed as lace, but are not made on a lace-making machine. The first, raschel lace, is an intricate knitted fabric, made on a raschel-knitting machine. (See p. 130.) It is the most widely used lace material produced, and can be made inexpensively or as a high-cost couture material. The second of these fabrics, Schiffli lace, is produced by the Schiffli machine and uses an embroidery technique. (See p. 149.)

Because lace has an open construction (netlike), it can easily snag. Also, many laces are fragile and so they can tear or break easily. Thus, cleaning should be done carefully with minimum rubbing and pulling.

Laces may also be identified by a specific style, type, or weight range, as well as the town in which the lace was originally made. Some of the styles and names were given to these laces hundreds of years ago, before the invention of lace-making machines, when all laces were handmade. Some of the most popular names of lace are included in the following list:

Alençon lace: A delicate lace usually made with fine, solid flower designs and outlined by heavy threads. One edge may be scalloped.

All-over lace: Any lace at least 36 inches wide, with the pattern repeated over the entire surface. There are no scallops on either side. Used for dresses and gowns. (See Figure 7.7.)

Artificial lace: Simple design lace not produced by lace machines but by chemical methods, usually burn-out prints. (See p. 181.)

Chantilly: A delicate lace, somewhat similar to Alençon, except that the designs are most often fine floral or vine motifs. Chantilly is a popular lace for bridal veils. It was first made in the French city of Chantilly. (See Figure 7.8.)

Edging: A narrow lace with one edge straight and the other scalloped.

Flouncing: A fashion trimming lace 18 to 36 inches wide, with one main edge scalloped. The opposite edge is straight or scalloped.

Galloon: A narrow lace with both edges scalloped. It may be sewn onto a garment for trim or, in narrow widths (usually about 1 inch), may have shoulder straps inserted through its center.

Insertion: Trimming lace in the form of a strip with two straight edges.

Leavers lace: Lace made on the Leavers lace machine. This lace is a fine lace, usually used for apparel.

Nottingham lace: Lace made on the Nottingham lace machine. Nottingham laces have large designs and are usually of rougher texture than most apparel laces. These laces are widely used for tablecloths. The original use was for curtains.

Reembroidered lace: Lace on which the pattern is outlined, usually with heavy thread or cord, after the lace is made.

Ribbon-hole lace: Narrow lace with slots through which ribbon can be threaded.

Embroidery

Embroidery is the art of creating and producing raised designs or motifs on woven fabrics, paper, or plastic and, in rare instances, on knitted fabrics. The designs are produced with needles and threads, sometimes using a variety of colors to produce specific designs. Hand embroidery is a widely practiced pastime. Embroidery threads are not necessarily placed vertically or horizontally, but may be at an angle. Embroidery designs are usually very durable.

Different stitches are used to outline and fill in the design, depending upon the desired pattern. The use of different fibers and yarns can provide a variety of effects. The closeness and amount of stitching, as well as the background fabric used, varies greatly. **Eyelet** is an embroidery fabric with small, round holes cut in the fabric. Stitching occurs completely around the holes to give a finished appearance. (See Figure 7.9.)

Practically all the embroidery sold in the United States is machine-made on a machine known as a **Schiffli machine**, and this embroidery is known as Schiffli embroidery.

A Schiffli embroidery machine is an extremely complex apparatus. A hand embroiderer works with a single needle. In the Schiffli machine, the number of needles is usually about 1,000, and all may be working at the same time. The selection of thread and needles that governs the design is programmed in a manner similar to

FIGURE 7.8
A chantilly lace dress by Armani.

FIGURE 7.9
Lace eyelet used as trim on gown and robe.

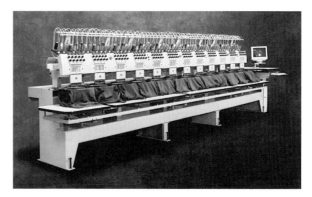

FIGURE 7.10
The multiple high-speed machine heads on this embroidery machine are controlled by a computer and are capable of intricate designs. Pattern changes can be made rapidly.

that of the jacquard system in weaving. With the use of a computer, changes (e.g., stitch type and pattern) can be accomplished quickly. A Schiffli machine may weigh 40,000 pounds. It is capable of producing embroideries from narrow webs of several inches up to widths of 15 yards. (See Figure 7.10.)

Schiffli embroidery designs are often done on lightweight fabrics, such as batiste and lawn, to produce delicate embroideries. Heavier embroideries on such items as military-uniform chevrons and emblems are also the product of the Schiffli industry. When delicate Schiffli embroidery is done on net fabrics, the product is known as Schiffli lace.

Some embroidery is made on a multihead embroidery machine. Several small machines attached to each other are operated by the same computer system simultaneously. They are very versatile as they can create small size designs and emblems that are later sewn on to jackets, hats, and other articles. Embroidered logos on a shirt were probably made on a multihead machine.

Apparel and footwear are the two categories seized most often by enforcement agencies as being counterfeit. The embroidered trademarks and logos are applied in the United States to blank goods which were manufactured overseas. With 18-head machines being available, thousands of items per day can be embroidered and then illegally sold as an original.

Tufted Fabrics

Tufted fabrics are another type of pile fabric, but they are unlike the pile fabrics produced by weaving (see p. 97) or by knitting (see p. 124). Machine tufting is performed by inserting extra yarns into an already woven fabric of a relatively open weave. With machine-made tufted fabrics, the insertion is done using a row of adjacent needles as wide as the material to be made. Each needle is fed a yarn from a spool. The needles all come down together, going through the ground fabric as a sewing machine needle goes through material. A hook or looper moves to hold the loop as the needle is withdrawn. (See Figure 7.11.) A row of loops has now been produced. The fabric moves forward from a predetermined distance and the needles move downward again to make another row of loops. (The machine is stationary.) Thus the yarns run lengthwise in the fabric. To produce a cut-pile material, a knife attached to the hook cuts the loop and forms a tuft as the needles are retracted. In order to obtain certain design effects, a piece of cut yarn (tuft) can also be inserted instead of a section of continuous yarn.

Tufted fabrics are made only in heavier weights. By far the largest proportion of production is for carpeting. Practically all carpets produced in the United States are made by the tufting process. (See Chapter 13 for a discussion of tufted carpet types and properties.) A relatively

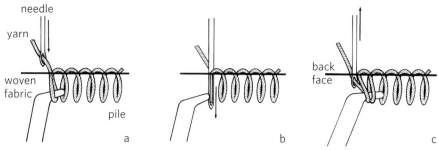

FIGURE 7.11
Steps used for loop tufting:

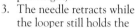

1. Needle begins its descent.
2. After the needle reaches the proper penetration, the looper moves to hold the yarn (the needle movement determines the pile height).
3. The needle retracts while the looper still holds the yarn. The backing material is advanced for the next needle penetration. The loops could be cut to produce a cut-pile surface by the addition of a knife attached to the looper.

small amount of upholstery, blankets, bedspreads, and fake furs are also produced by this method.

Machines for tufting are capable of producing a tufted material up to 18 feet wide. The tufting machine may have more than 1,200 needles operating simultaneously. Tufting is done at a very rapid rate; an entire room-size carpet may be produced in less than an hour of operation.

Study Questions

1. How do fusible nonwoven fabrics contribute to lower costs and higher production rates in apparel manufacturing?

2. The desired properties of nonwoven materials will dictate the optimum fiber to use. For each of the following examples, state two fibers which would be suitable.

   a. High resilience and hydrophobic
   b. High tensile strength
   c. High absorbency
   d. High abrasion resistance

3. If you were designing women's two-piece suits (jacket and skirt), name five parts of the suit where you would specify the use of nonwoven fabrics.

4. List three different uses for nonwoven household cleaning wipes.

5. Distinguish between nonwoven fabric and felt fabric, indicating the fibers used to produce each, the method of making each, and several end uses of each.

6. Much felt today is made of a wool/rayon blend as well as 100 percent wool. Compare the two materials.

7. Bonded and laminated fabrics, when improperly produced, can result in unsatisfactory performance. List three problems than can confront customers who utilize poorly constructed bonded or laminated fabrics.

8. Why is the backing fabric of a bonded/laminated material usually a knit fabric?

9. Compare a bonded material to a foam-laminated material that is made with the same face and back fabrics, considering the following properties:

   a. Drape
   b. Insulation
   c. Resiliency

10a. What is the primary problem with bonded fabrics?

   b. Is there any difference in performance between wet-adhesive bonding and foam-flame bonding? Explain.

11. Why would a quilted lining increase the insulation capability of a coat?

12. Distinguish between Nottingham lace and Leavers lace.

13. Distinguish between lace and embroidery.

14. Explain how a tufted carpet can be as durable as a woven carpet of the same weight.

15. The economic advantages of machine tufting may be overridden by the selection of more expensive fibers, yarns, and finishes as well as the use of high pile construction density. Explain

CHAPTER EIGHT
Textile Dyeing

Objectives

▶ To understand how fashion colors are developed, standardized, and communicated by electronic and manual systems.

▶ To understand the differences between dyes and pigments and their effects on textile coloration.

▶ To understand the phenomenon of dye penetration and its effects on textile performance.

▶ To know the effects of different dye classes on various textile fibers as well as on colorfastness.

▶ To understand the dyeing process and the reasons for using various stages of dyeing.

Use fabric in the Dyed Fabrics Section of the Fabric Science Swatch Kit for this chapter.

Key Terms Related to Textiles

affinity
beam dyeing
colorfastness
color management
  system
color-matching booth
color-matching
  systems
computer-management
  systems
continuous dye system

crocking
cross-dyeing
curing
depth of shade
dope dyeing
dye classes
dye lot
dyes
dyeing
garment dyeing
jet dyeing

jig dyeing
lab dip
Macbeth Lamps
metamerism
package dyeing
pad dyeing
piece dyeing
pigment
poor penetration
skein dyeing
solution dyeing

spectrophotometer
standard
stock dyeing
substrate
tone-on-tone effects
top
top dyeing
union dyeing
yarn dyeing

Color is an important marketing factor with textile products. It is the color of the dyed (or printed) fabric that first attracts and then draws consumers to particular items for sale. It is often the color of a product that sells the product. (See Figure 8.1.)

Natural dyes and pigments were used exclusively until the discovery of synthetic colorants. The sources included insects, plants and minerals. In 1856, William Henry Perkin discovered the first synthetic dye (mauve). Today almost all industrial dyeing uses synthetic dyes since they produce a greater color range, improved colorfastness, better shade consistency, and more reliable resources. Natural dyes are used today mainly for craft and hobby items, although some such as indigo (blue) have commercial value.

Adding color to textiles, thus making fabrics marketable as fashion components, is a sophisticated and complex area where art and creativity meet with science and technology. (See Figure 8.2.) Although the chemistry of dyes and dyeing are extremely complex, the development of electronic and computer science applied to **color management systems** as made possible the color shade consistency for large scale dyeing production. Matching shades and the approval of colors may now be executed by phone and fax, without the necessity of seeing visual samples that must be sent by mail or courier. Details covering electronic and computer usage are included in this chapter as are explanations of the traditional processes of textile dyeing.

Although color is recognized as the most important element in textile sales and merchandising, it is also a source of problems that consumers and the textile industry encounter in the production and use of fabrics. Shade variation in production lots, fading, bleeding, color staining, and color streaking are typical examples. Understanding the dyes and dyeing processes discussed in this chapter can aid in reducing or eliminating many of these problems.

Whereas this chapter focuses on how color is added to textiles, the topic of understanding color and "why we see what we see" is discussed in Chapter 14.

FIGURE 8.1
Color makes this dress sell.

FIGURE 8.2
A multicolored Herve Leger design.

Dyes and Pigments

There are two main ways of imparting color to textiles. The first and by far the most widely used method is with the use of dyes (sometimes called conventional or aqueous dyeing). The process involves the use of chemical dyes called dyestuffs and the treatment of the textile material in aqueous (water) solutions. The second method is by the use of **pigments.** Pigments are microscopic-sized, insoluble colored particles made to adhere to a fabric. Dyes and pigments each impart separate characteristics or properties to a textile product. Each is discussed in further detail in this chapter.

Color is also imparted to textiles by a third process that is actually part of manufactured fiber production, and normally associated with fiber manufacturing rather than textile manufacturing. This type of coloring involves adding microsized, colored pigment to manufactured fiber while the fiber is in liquid or solution form and before extrusion from a spinnerette. The resultant fiber or yarn is aptly called solution dyed (sometimes called dope dyed). Solution-dyed fibers are not widely used and represent a small but unique role in textiles. They are more fully described on page 164.

Conventional, or Aqueous, Dyeing

Conventional, or aqueous, dyeing is usually simply called **dyeing**. As previously indicated, coloration by dyeing involves the use of dyestuffs that are capable of reacting and combining with the textile fiber molecule, usually when in a water solution, and usually with other auxiliary chemicals to enhance the process.

Initially the fabric is cleaned (scoured) to remove warp starches (aids in the weaving process), oils, and dirt. This procedure insures better acceptance of dyes and chemical additives. Fewer problems result, such as color spots or uneven coloration.

In the dyeing process, the water, dye, chemicals, and textile material are brought together for a period ranging from several minutes to several hours, depending on the dyes being used and the fibers being dyed. Most dyeing occurs at temperatures near the boiling point, but can vary from dye baths cooled with ice to temperatures above the boiling point and requiring special pressurized equipment. During the process, the material being dyed, or the dye bath, must be agitated so that the dye molecules combine with the material uniformly, thereby producing even color. Figure 8.3 demonstrates the sequence of dye combining with fiber.

At the completion of the dyeing cycle, the goods must be thoroughly scoured with soaps or detergents, and then rinsed thoroughly to remove excess dye that has not reacted with the fiber. This is an important part of the dyeing procedure. Failure to remove the excess and unreacted dye results in poor initial washfastness (that is, at the first laundering by the consumer) and excessive rubbing off of color, called **crocking,** even after extensive wear (see p. 298).

The darkness or lightness of color in dyeing, known as the **depth of shade,** is dependent on the quantity of dye used as a ratio with the fiber, yarn, fabric, or garment weight being dyed, known as **substrate.** Deep navy may require as much as 8 percent of the fiber weight in dye, which is usually expressed as 8% OWF (on weight of fiber) or 8% OWG (on weight of goods). Dyers and colorists may speak of such a shade as an 8 percent dyeing. A light pastel baby blue may require as little as 0.25 percent of the fiber weight in dye. Dyeing costs for dark shades are higher than those for light shades because of the additional dye required and because the materials have to be treated for a longer period of time in order for the larger quantity of dye to combine with the fiber.

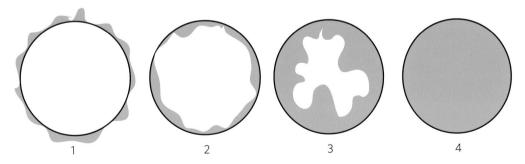

FIGURE 8.3
A cross-section of a fiber during the dyeing process. Note the dye molecules first (1) adhere to the fiber, then (2) penetrate, and now begin to (3) migrate in the fiber, until the (4) fiber is completely dyed.

Classes of Dyes

Dyestuffs are highly complex organic substances that combine both chemically and physically with an equally complex textile fiber molecule.

Thousands of different dyestuffs are used for textiles. None is capable of combining with all textile fibers. Textile fibers are also chemical substances. Some dyes, for example, combine with protein (as in wool) and not with cellulose (as in cotton). When a particular dye is capable of combining with a fiber and can impart color to it, the dye has **affinity** for that fiber.

To make order out of what otherwise would be chaos in classifying which dye reacts with which fiber, all of the thousands of dyes are grouped into **dye classes,** which are shown in Table 8.1. Most dyes in each class possess similar (but by no means equal) colorfastness characteristics and are applied with similar techniques at similar temperatures.

Color Formulations and Matching Shades

The development and choice of a specific color for a particular material is the domain of the textile designer or colorist. It is then the task of the textile dyer and chemist to match the designer's color with the proper dyes or pigments that also meet the colorfastness requirements for the end use of the material. The role of the designer is in the world of artistry and creativity. The dyer's role is in the world of science and technology.

Matching of color shades by the dyer requires the skillful blending and formulation of different color dyes within the chosen dye class or pigments as well as an understanding of the behavior of fibers and of the numerous chemicals needed to carry out the process. Color-match formulas are first developed in a small laboratory. More recently computers may also be used to develop color formulas.

Once the dyer has formulated a color match, a sample swatch of the finished dyeing known as a **lab dip** is made. Several lab dips, each with a formula adjustment, may be needed to exactly duplicate the desired colors. This becomes the **standard** to which all future orders of the same colors must conform. In actual practice, however, each new batch, or **dye lot,** is slightly different in shade from all other lots before or after. These variations from lot to lot are caused by slight differences in chemical concentrations or in molecular fiber structure, or even slight differences in the water used for dyeing. Variations in shade may even occur within the same lot. Variations may also occur from slight differences in the greige goods being processed as well as with the actual dyeing procedure.

Human eyes are extremely sensitive to color variations. The variables that occur, although small and in some instances even unmeasurable, cause shade variations visible to the eye. (See Figure 8.4.)

Manufacturers of apparel and other sewn products normally exercise caution to ensure that fabrics from different lots do not come together in the same garment. Many quality-minded producers carry this a step further and produce all parts of a garment from the same bolt of fabric, thus avoiding problems that may result from intralot variability.

Computer Shade Matching and Computer-Controlled Dyeing

The traditional trial-and-error practice of color dye formulas is the most widely used practice. The simplicity and low-tech approach of this methodology makes it the foremost of trade practices. The development of computer-driven color matching and shade matching systems described in this section, also known as **computer-management systems,** by contrast are high-tech approaches which require higher skills to achieve proficiency. Nevertheless, the newer computer-driven color formula development and shade-matching and **color-matching systems** are coming into increasingly widespread use. Color-management systems, when operational, are more accurate and efficient than the trial-and-error methods. These computer-management systems also have an important advantage of time saving. Approvals can be executed via electronic mail in a matter of days rather than in weeks or even months using trial-and-error methods.

Color-management systems all require rather sophisticated computer systems in order to be functional. Several software companies market their products and service the textile industry for textile dyeing. One of these is Gretag-Macbeth Corporation.

Color-management systems are now extensively used for producing and maintaining high standards of color matching and lot-to-lot shade consistency. These systems enable dyers to rapidly produce the original color formulations and are also capable of monitoring the dyeing cycle for samples and later large-scale production.

TABLE 8.1   Major Dye Classes and Their Fastness Properties

Dye Class	Fibers	Important Characteristics
Acid dyes	Protein fibers, nylon, spandex, special type acid-dyeable acrylic.	Bright colors. Most are not fast to washing. Vary from poor to good in fastness to light and perspiration. Excellent fastness to dry-cleaning. Widely used on silk.
Premetalized acid dyes	Same as above.	Less bright than acid dyes, but better fastness to laundering, perspiration, and light.
Chrome dyes (also called mordant dyes)	Same as above.	Dull colors, but excellent fastness to light, laundering, and perspiration. Widely used on wool floor coverings.
Cationic dyes (also called basic dyes)	Acrylic, modacrylic, cationic-dyeable polyester, and cationic-dyeable nylon. Also cellulosic and protein fibers.	Bright shades with excellent fastness to light, laundering, perspiration, and crocking on manufactured fibers. Very poor fastness to washing and light on cellulosic and protein fibers.
Direct dyes (also called substantive dyes)	Cellulosics.	Poor fastness to washing. Fastness to light varies, but some are excellent and used in drapery and upholstery. Fastness to perspiration and dry-cleaning good to excellent.
Direct developed dyes	Same as above.	Same as above, except fastness to laundering is good to excellent.
Disperse dyes	Acetate, acrylic, modacrylic, nylon, polyester, and olefin.	Wash fastness varies with fiber. Poor on acetate, excellent on polyester. Fastness to perspiration, crocking, and dry-cleaning good to excellent. Light fastness fair to good. Gas fading* on acetate, especially blues and violets.
Naphthol dyes (also called azoic; insoluble azo, ice, or ingrain dye)	Cellulosics.	Bright shades. Mostly deep reds, yellows, oranges. Vary from poor to excellent fastness to light. Fastness to laundering and perspiration good to excellent. Dark shades may have poor fastness to crocking.
Reactive dyes	Mostly cellulosics. Also to a lesser degree used on protein fibers and nylon.	Bright shades. Generally good to excellent fastness to light, laundering, perspiration, and crocking. Poor fastness to chlorine. Difficult dye with which to attain close shade matching.
Sulfur dyes	Cellulosics.	Dull shades. Predominantly navy, black, and brown. Excellent fastness to light, laundering, and perspiration. Poor fastness to chlorine. Some sulfur dyes cause tendering (weakening) of fabric if stored for great lengths of time.
Vat dyes	Cellulosics.	Mostly excellent fastness to light, laundering, and perspiration. Exceedingly fast to chlorine and other oxidizing bleaches. May crock if improperly applied.
Pigments	All fibers.	Not a dye. Mechanically bound to fiber by resins. Heavy shades tend to stiffen fabric. Mostly excellent fastness to light. Light to medium shades have fair to good fastness to hand laundering. Medium to heavy shades have poor fastness to crocking.

*Gas fading is the loss or change of color that results from exposure to nitrous oxide, which is a gas pollutant in the atmosphere. Fading may occur after several weeks or months, depending on the amount of nitrous oxide present. This fading occurs more rapidly in highly industrialized areas than in rural areas. Gas-fading inhibitor chemicals are sometimes used in conjunction with dyeing and finishing processes, but they offer only temporary relief.

FIGURE 8.4
Weatherproof color range.

A typical color-management system consists of a **spectrophotometer**[1] (which is capable of analyzing the color of an input sample) and a digital computer (in whose memory are stored the color characteristics, in computer language, of the dyer's dyestuff inventory). The computer software enables the system to take the spectrophotometer reading of the sample, scan the computer memory, mathematically mix the dyes to reproduce the original sample shade, and output dye-color selections and percentages of each to be used for reproducing the color of the original sample. The computer can be commanded to give a formula that produces the lowest-cost dyeing, or alternatively that provides any given colorfastness requirement (best lightfastness, for example). The final choice is made by examining the degree of color match, performance, and price for the end use product. (See Figure 8.5.)

The computer output does not deliver a visual color rendition, but rather a digital (numeric) or graphic output of color values. Buyer and seller can then communicate this output instantaneously anywhere in the world, undertake approval or corrections by electronic mail,

and move toward production and delivery in a matter of hours or days instead of the weeks or months needed to approve visual samples by using the trial-and-error method.

Metamerism

Sometimes in dyed fabrics the color has been formulated to match an already existing color. (For example, sleeve cuffs dyed to match the color of a body-shell fabric for a ski jacket.) When the two colors match each other under one light condition—for example, daylight—but look different from each other in a different light—such as indoor light illumination—the condition is known as **metamerism.** The term color flare is used to indicate a fabric that has changed color because of the change of light source.

Metamerism may be caused when the dye components for the shade being matched are chemically different from the components that were used for the original. It is highly unlikely that metamerism would occur from dye lot to dye lot of the same color if all the dyeings were performed by the same dyer. Metamerism is a possible problem whenever two or more fabric types, each dyed by different dyers, come together to be used as matched items.

---

1. A spectophotometer is an instrument that measures the percent of light reflected at each wavelength in the visible spectrum by a colored surface.

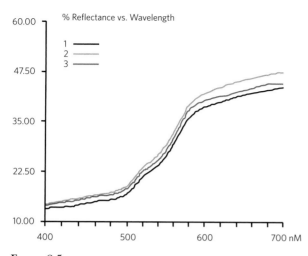

FIGURE 8.5
The dye formula and the sample are displayed in graphic form on the screen. The same dye formula or the sample to be matched can also be displayed in numeric (digital) form, and, if desired, printed on a computer-driven printer. It is possible to communicate and transmit these readings to any place instantaneously without sending an actual sampling of the color.

It is especially important that the phenomenon of metamerism be understood and considered in apparel, such as coordinated sportswear. It is equally critical in items such as a ski jacket constructed of a nylon shell, polyester lining, acrylic cuffs, and cotton zipper tape, where each component must be the same shade under all conditions of sunlight and artificial light.

A box-type device known as a **color-matching booth** is widely used to test for metamerism. This standardized source of illumination can simulate natural daylight as well as produce incandescent, fluorescent, and ultraviolet light. Color-matching booths are sometimes called **Macbeth Lamps,** which is the name of the original device.

When Dyeing Is Done

Dyeing can be done during any stage in the manufacture of a textile product. Textiles may be dyed as fiber, as yarn, as fabric, or as garments, depending on the type of fabric or garment being produced. Descriptions of the various stages and the reasons for their use are given in the following sections. Dyeing will occur in the most efficient stage, which will meet the requirements of the intended end uses. Table 8.2 describes the special features, including the advantages and disadvantages, of each stage of dyeing.

Stock Dyeing

Stock dyeing refers to the dyeing of fibers, or stock, before it is spun into yarn. It is done by putting loose, unspun fibers into large vats containing the dye bath, which is then heated to proper temperature. From 500 to 3,000 pounds (227 to 1,363 kilograms) of fiber are dyed at one time, and the average is about 1,000 pounds (454 kilograms). (See Figure 8.6.)

TABLE 8.2 Comparison of Dyeing in Various Stages			
Stage of Dyeing	**Features and Advantages**	**Limitations and Disadvantages**	**Typical Dyed Fabrics**
Stock and top	Fabrics have soft, heatherlike coloration. Easiest dye penetration.	Most costly dyeing method. Dyeing long before season begins carries risk of fashion changing. High percentage of fiber loss from dyeing and later yarn spinning.	Cheviot covert melton tweed
Yarn	Used for fabrics with stripes, checks, plaids, and other multi-colored patterns.	Second most costly dyeing method. Dyeing before season begins carries risk of fashion changing, but less than for stock dye.	Chambray gingham brocade jacquard knits
Piece	Least costly stage for dyeing of fabrics. Adaptable to all fabrics—woven and knitted. Dyeing is close to fashion season; minimal color risk.	Limited to solid colors (except for cross-dye).	Batiste broadcloth challis corduroy satin
Garment	Choice of colors closest to fashion season. Elimination of material (yarn and fabric) waste from prior processing.	Limited to garments of simple construction.	Hosiery pantyhose sweaters T-shirts

FIGURE 8.6
A stock dyeing machine.

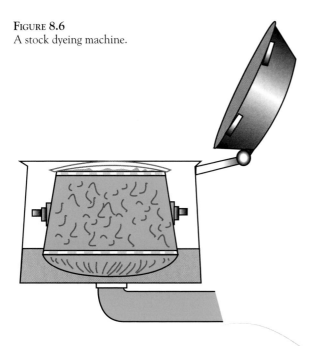

Stock dyeing is used mostly for woolen materials when heatherlike color effects are desired. Wool fiber dyed black, for example, might be blended and spun with undyed (white) wool fiber to produce a soft heatherlike shade of gray yarn.

Tweed fabrics with a heatherlike color effect such as Harris tweed are examples of stock-dyed material. Other examples include heatherlike colors in covert and woolen cheviot.

Top Dyeing

Top dyeing is also the dyeing of fiber before it is spun into yarn and serves the same purpose as stock dyeing—that is, to produce soft, heatherlike color effects. The term **top** refers to fibers of wool from which shorter fibers have been removed. Top is thus the select long fibers that are used to spin worsted yarn. The top in the form of sliver is dyed and then blended with other colors of dyed top to produce desired blended heather shades. Stock dyeing is not used for worsteds because the process for making sliver of top removes short fibers. It would be a waste of money if all the fibers, both short and long, were dyed before being made into sliver and then some of them were removed prior to the making of top. Some typical top-dye fabrics include gabardine, worsted cheviot, and serge.

Yarn Dyeing

Yarn dyeing, as its name implies, is the dyeing of yarns before they have been woven or knitted into fabrics. The main reason for the dyeing of yarn is for the ultimate production of multicolored designs such as plaids, stripes, and checks. Some typical yarn-dyed fabrics are multicolored gingham, madras, brocade, and multicolored weft knits. Yarn dyeing is also used in special cases for solid-color fabrics. Yarns may be dyed in different forms: skeins, packages, or beams.

Skein Dyeing

Skein dyeing consists of immersing large, loosely wound hanks (skeins) of yarn into dye vats that are especially designed for this purpose. Soft, lofty yarns, such as hand-knitting yarns, are usually skein dyed. Skein dyeing is the most costly yarn-dye method.

Package Dyeing

In **package dyeing,** yarn is wound on a small perforated spool or tube called a package. Many spools fit into the dyeing machine in which the flow of the dye bath alternates from the center to the outside, and then from the outside to the center of the package (see Figure 8.7). Package-dyed yarns do not retain the softness and loftiness that skein-dyed yarns do. They are, however, satisfactory and are very widely used for most types of yarn found in knitted and woven fabrics.

Beam Dyeing

Beam dyeing is a much larger version of package dyeing. An entire warp beam is wound onto a perforated cylinder, which is then placed in the beam-dyeing machine, where the flow of the dye bath alternates as in package dyeing. Beam dyeing is more economical than

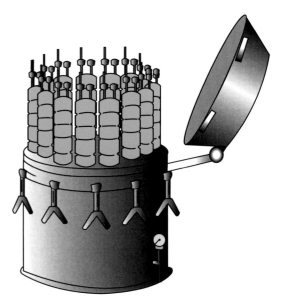

FIGURE 8.7
A package dyeing machine.

skein or package dyeing, but is only used in manufacture of woven fabrics where an entire warp beam is dyed. Knitted fabrics, which are mostly produced from cones of yarn are not adaptable to beam dyeing.

Piece Dyeing

The dyeing of cloth after it has been woven or knitted is known as **piece dyeing.** It is the most common method of dyeing used. The various methods used for this type of dyeing include jet dyeing, jig dyeing, pad dyeing, and beam dyeing. Each of the methods and their operations are described in the following sections.

When heavy or densely woven fabrics, or tightly twisted yarn fabrics, are piece dyed, sometimes the dye does not penetrate into the center of the yarn material. The condition, known simply as **poor penetration,** leaves the fibers in the center of the yarns, or at fabric interlacing, lightly colored or undyed. It can be recognized by taking some yarns out of the fabric, untwisting them, and observing the nonuniform color of fibers in the untwisted yarn. There is no problem with such materials when they are relatively new. After a brief period of wear, however, fabrics such as uniform clothing, children's wear, upholstery fabrics, and other fabrics subjected to hard use take on a faded appearance at points of wear, and white, undyed fibers shift toward the fabric surface. For this reason, many high-quality, heavyweight, and densely woven fabrics, especially furniture covering, are yarn dyed even though they are of a solid shade. The latter method, though more costly, eliminates the problem of poor dye penetration.

Jet Dyeing

In the **jet-dyeing** process, the fabric being dyed is circulated in a rope form through a closed-system dyeing machine on a jet flow of the dye bath (see Figure 8.8). The fabric is moved by the fast moving dye bath. Since no pressure and little tension occurs with the material, even delicate fabrics can be dyed using this process. Most jet-dyeing machines can be pressurized and are capable of achieving dyeing temperatures exceeding the boiling point of water.

Jig Dyeing

The **jig-dyeing** process involves treating fabric in open width. Fabric is not immersed in a dye bath, but rather is passed through a stationary dye bath. Upon completion of the first pass, the fabric reverses and is passed again through the dye bath. To produce darker colors the fabric must pass through the dye bath more times than when a lighter shade is desired.

Jig dyeing places a tension on the fabric while it is being passed from roll to roll, which causes flattening and degradation in the hand of the material (see Figure 8.9).

Jig dyeing is more economical than jet dyeing since runs of several thousand yards are possible. Most lining fabrics and many other lightweight cloths, such as taffeta and surah, are usually jig dyed, but the fabric must not be so light in weight or of such construction that it would become damaged from the tensions exerted by the jig machine. Knitted fabrics and stretch woven fabrics cannot be jig dyed because the tensions exerted by the jig would stretch them out of shape.

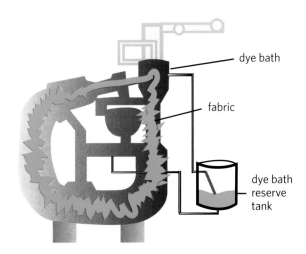

FIGURE 8.8
The side view of a jet dyeing machine.

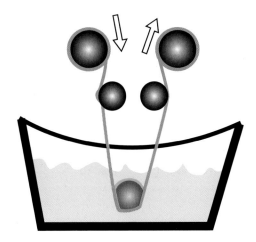

FIGURE 8.9
A jig dyeing machine (dye jig). Fabric unwinds from one reel, passes through the dye bath, and is rewound onto another reel. Numerous passes—reel-to-reel—through the dye baths are required to complete the dyeing process.

Fabrics that are jig dyed sometimes become dyed with a slight shade variation from the center to the selvage of the fabric, or from end to end of a fabric piece. The shading is often caused by uneven tensions on the fabric while it is on the jig. Jig-dyed fabrics must be carefully examined for this type of defect.

Pad Dyeing

Pad dyeing is accomplished with a machine called a dye pad. Its appearance somewhat resembles a giant clothes wringer. Fabric in open width first passes through the dye bath, and then through the rollers, where the dye solution is squeezed into the fabric.

Pad dyeing, like jig dyeing, places tension on the fabric while it is passing through the pad, which causes flattening and degradation in the hand of the material. (See Figure 8.10.)

Most pad dyeing is done as part of a **continuous dye system** or continuous dye range, where large quantities of fabric are continuously run through a pad, into heat or steam chambers (to set the dye); and then into washers, rinsers, and dryers. Finally, they emerge as completely dyed fabric.

Beam Dyeing

Beam dyeing for piece dyeing is practically identical to beam dyeing used for yarns. Fabric is wound on to a perforated cylinder where the dye bath is forced through the fabric layers. The fabric remains stationary. The process is used to dye fabrics of lightweight, open constructions because the dye bath cannot circulate through a beam of densely constructed fabric. Tricot is a fabric type that is frequently dyed in beam dyers. Beam dyeing is a

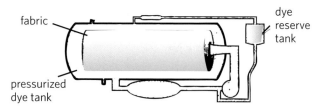

FIGURE 8.11
The side view of a beam dyeing machine.

rapid and economical method for dyeing lightweight, open fabrics. Moreover, beam-dyed fabric is not subject to the stresses and tensions common to the jig and pad methods. As much as 10,000 yards (9,144 meters) or 4,000 pounds (1,818 kilograms) of fabric can be wound on the beam and placed into one dye bath. (See Figure 8.11.)

Garment Dyeing

Garment dyeing is the dyeing of completed garments. The types of apparel that can be dyed are mostly non-tailored and simpler forms, such as sweaters, sweatshirts, T-shirts, hosiery, and pantyhose. The effect on sizing, threads, zippers, trim, and snaps must be considered. Tailored items, such as suits or dresses, cannot be dyed as garments because the difference in shrinkage of the various components and linings distort and misshape the article.

Garment dyeing is done by placing a suitable number of garments (usually about 24 sweaters or the equivalent, depending on weight) into a large nylon net bag. The garments are loosely packed. From 10 to 50 of the bags are placed in large tubs containing the dye bath and are kept agitated by a motor-driven paddle in the dye tub. The machine is appropriately called a paddle dyer.

Special Dyeing Effects

Piece dyeing, as described previously, primarily produces a solid color throughout the goods being dyed. It is possible, however, to create effects such as multicolors or multishades by any yarn-dye or piece-dye method. (See Table 8.3.) Each of these is described in the following sections.

Cross-Dyeing

Cross-dyeing is a type of dyeing in which a yarn, a fabric, or even a garment made with two or more generic fiber types having different dye affinities is dyed in a single bath containing two different classes of dyes. Each class of dye colors only one type of fiber. Two different colors can be dyed in one dye bath or either type of fiber may be dyed, leaving the other white.

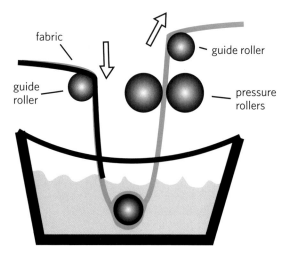

FIGURE 8.10
A pad dyeing machine, or padder, is used to apply dyes, pigments, or finishes to fabrics.

If different fibers are blended in the same yarn, a stock-dyed effect is obtained. If yarns of one kind of fiber and yarns of another fiber are used in the warp direction, vertical stripes form. A plaid can be produced by weaving yarns of different kinds of fiber in both warp and filling directions and then dyeing the fabric in a single bath with a mixture of two kinds of dyes. Whereas certain fiber combinations allow for a one-bath process (e.g., acetate/rayon), other fiber combinations may require a two-step dyeing process to produce two colors.

Cross-dyeing is a more economical and quicker way to produce the same effects obtained by other dyeing methods. For example, a sweater composed of acrylic and cotton-blend yarns that was knitted and fabricated in an undyed state could be garment dyed to yield a heather stock-dyed effect. Otherwise, the more expensive stock-dyeing method would be required to obtain this effect.

Cross-dyeing effects can also be achieved with one generic fiber type. This can be done because some of the manufactured fibers are modified during their production to permit them to combine with other dye classes not compatible with the unmodified form of the same fiber. It is possible, for example, to achieve multicolor effects on a fabric of 100 percent polyester by the piece-dyeing or garment-dyeing methods instead of the more expensive yarn-dyeing method. The classes of dyes capable of combining with the various fibers (both regular and modified) are given in Table 8.1. Cross-dyeing effects can also be achieved within the same textile filaments when bicomponent fibers are selectively used (see page 58).

Union Dyeing

Union dyeing is the same as cross-dyeing except that instead of multicolor effects, one solid color is produced. The dyer accomplishes this by using two or more classes of dye, each of the same color. For example, a fabric composed of rayon and acetate can be dyed a solid green color by using a direct dye for the rayon and a disperse dye of the same color for the acetate (see Table 8.1). A frequently seen example of union dyeing is in solid-color bed sheets made of a blend of polyester and cotton. Each fiber is dyed by a different dye class, both of the same color. The use of Rit®, and other packaged household dyes, which are mixtures of several classes of dyes of the same color, results in union dyeing.

Tone-On-Tone Effects

Tone-on-tone effects are also possible by using one dye bath. They are light and dark shades of the same color on a fabric containing only one generic fiber—for example, deep red and light red colors on the same piece-dyed polyester fabric. This effect can be produced by combining two different types of polyester in the same fabric. Both types are capable of combining with the same dye class, but one fiber has a stronger affinity for dye than the other. The fiber with the stronger affinity combines with a greater quantity of dye, becoming deeper in shade, and the second fiber remains a lighter shade of the same color.

Tone-on-tone effects can only be achieved with specific varieties of nylon, polyester, and acrylic fibers. These special properties are imparted during the manufacture of the fiber, and the fibers are marketed to textile producers as deep-dye types. In addition, nylon is produced in both deep-dye and ultra-deep-dye varieties, thus providing the possibility for three-tone effects of the same color.

The tone-on-tone effect is widely used in the carpet industry for producing tweed-effect designs on piece-dyed carpeting.

Pigment Coloring

Pigments are completely different substances for coloring textiles. Pigments, unlike dyes, are insoluble in water and do not unite or combine in any way with the textile fiber. Pigment particles are microscopic colored chips that may be held on the surface of a fiber by resin-binding agents.

Pigments, like dyes, can be applied to formed fibers, yarns, and fabrics as solid color or as prints. Solid-color pigments are applied by the pad method described on page 161. Because the pigment particles do not dissolve in water and do not easily penetrate the fabric, they must be forcibly squeezed into the cloth so that the inside fibers are colored.

Pigment color is usually mixed with a resin binder and applied as a resin/pigment mixture. In order for the pigment to adhere to the fabric, the resin must be heated in a process known as **curing.** This step, done after the pigment/resin mixture is applied to the fabric, involves heating the material to temperatures between 300°F and 400°F (150°C and 200°C) for from 30 seconds to several minutes.

Pigments can be applied rapidly and economically, and in general, pigment-treated fabrics are less costly than aqueous-dyed fabrics. They come in a wide variety of available colors, and they result in excellent color shade matching from lot to lot.

Because pigments do not combine or react with the textile fibers (as dyes do), they may be used with any fiber or combination of fibers. Many pigment colors have excellent colorfastness to light and are used extensively for draperies and curtains.

Fabrics colored with pigments show loss of color and fading with each succeeding cleaning (laundering or dry-cleaning) because the resins holding the pigment become separated from the fabric. The effect is most serious on heavy shades. Most colors show a distinct faded-out appearance by about the 15th or 20th cleaning.

The resins used in conjunction with pigments can cause stiffening of the fabric to which they are applied. This effect is minimal in light colors, but can be great in dark shades if softeners are not used in finishing (see p. 194).

Color loss by crocking is encountered in pigment-colored fabrics. Again, the effect is minimal in light colors, but can be serious in dark shades.

Solution Dyeing

Solution dyeing, also called **dope dyeing,** is unlike either of the two categories (dye and pigment) described earlier in this chapter. Solution dyeing is part of the process of manufacturing fibers. In this method, the coloring agent is added to the liquid spinning solution of manufactured fiber before it is extruded from a spinnerette. The liquid spinning solution is sometimes called fiber dope, hence the term dope dyeing. The color becomes part of the fiber itself and is permanent.

Solution dyeing is required when it is difficult to dye using aqueous-dyeing procedures because of heat sensitivity (e.g., modacrylic) or the hydrophobic nature (e.g., olefin) of the fiber.

Solution-dyed colors are practically fade-proof under all common conditions of use. Their colorfastness to light is particularly outstanding. Fabrics made from solution-dyed yarns are thus well suited for draperies, automotive fabrics, and other applications where great sunlight exposure is anticipated.

Unfortunately, solution-dyed materials are available in only a limited range of colors because the systems for the production of manufactured fibers require high and continuous outputs from the machinery used. The required time to clean up and change colors makes frequent color changes economically unfeasible. As a consequence, only a limited range of standard and popular colors is produced by this method. Fiber producers sometimes accept orders for special colors, but only for very large production orders.

Solution-dyed yarns are not widely used in apparel fabrics because the range of available colors is too limited to satisfy the great variety of colors desired for the fashion markets.

Solution-dyed materials are used where permanence of color over a long period is required. Applications include automotive seating and carpeting, household and outdoor carpeting, and some upholstery and drapery fabrics. Almost perfect color reproduction consistency from dye lot to dye lot can be achieved with solution dyeing.

Solution-dyed fabrics of acetate do not gas fade (see p. 297), and are especially desirable in this fiber because this problem is eliminated.

Colorfastness

Colorfastness refers to the property of a dyed or printed textile to resist color loss or fading resulting from laundering, dry cleaning, sunlight, bleach, perspiration, environmental gases, swimming pool chlorine, and various other conditions of use.

Particular dyes may be colorfast to one condition—for example, laundering—and not colorfast to another condition—for example, perspiration. A matte-jersey fabric intended for use in dresses that will be dry cleaned only may be unsuitable for swimwear. It is therefore important for fabric buyers and converters to specify the conditions of use of fabrics being ordered.

Colorfastness to the various conditions of use is governed by the particular dye class, the individual dyes within each class, and the fiber to which the dye is being applied. Laboratory methods to determine colorfastness and colorfastness ratings for particular fabric uses are discussed in Chapter 14.

Imperfections of Dyed Fabrics

The following is a list and descriptions of the most frequently occurring imperfections that may result from dyeing processes. These imperfections may be due to faulty or improper dyeing procedures, faulty or improper preparation of the fabric prior to dyeing, or imperfections in the material itself:

Barré: A horizontal band of off-shaded yarns extending across the fabric. Caused by differences in size (diameter) or in tension of yarns.

Color crocking: Color in a dyed fabric that rubs off rather easily onto other fabric surfaces. May be caused by inadequate scouring (soaping) at the completion of the dyeing cycle.

Color bleeding: Loss of color from a dyed fabric when immersed in a liquid. The liquid subsequently

FIGURE 8.12
An example of end-to-end shading.

becomes colored, often coloring other fabrics in the liquid (e.g., washing process).

Off shade: The color of the dyed fabric does not match the standard color or referenced sample.

Shade bar: A shade change in a fabric that appears as a horizontal selvage-to-selvage change. Caused by a filling change (new filling bobbin) or loom stop and subsequent start-up.

Stained cross-dye: In cross-dyed fabric, usually of one color and white, the dye of the colored portion stains the white portion. It is sometimes called unclear cross-dye. In solid-color fabric, the term refers to specks of foreign fiber that have been caught in the material and do not become dyed.

Stained, streaked, or colorspots: A discolored area on the cloth. Caused by foreign matter such as dirt, grease, oil, or residues of sizing on the fabric being dyed. May also be caused by improper wetting out.[2]

Tender spots: Places in the fabric that have been excessively weakened, usually by exposure to processing chemicals. When the entire fabric is weakened, it is referred to as tender goods. Also occurs in printing and finishing procedures.

Uneven shade (shading): Differences in the shade of a fabric from edge to edge or one end of a fabric to the other. Called selvage-to-selvage (or selvage-to-center) shading or end-to-end, respectively. (See Figure 8.12.)

---

2. Wetting out is the practice of thoroughly wetting the textile material with water before entering it into the dye bath. The wet material then absorbs the dye-bath solutions uniformly, which is necessary for uniform dyeing.

New Developments

Advances in technology and computer application in dyeing (and printing) processing continue to grow. Reduced amount of seconds, improved color control, faster changeover of machines, as well as more efficient use of colorants, chemicals, and water is the result.

Dyes with new properties have been developed. Higher utilization rates result in less colorants being used. Also dyes which change color or hue when ultraviolet light shines on them are being utilized. These photochromatic or photosensitive dyes return to their original color when the UV light (e.g., sunlight) is removed.

Heat-sensitive dyes result in color change of garments when exposed to body heat. A fabric coating contains very small liquid crystals that change color when there is a temperature change has been developed.

Dyeable polypropylene fiber, using conventional disperse dyes, has been developed. This makes the fiber more attractive for apparel. Previously this fiber had to be solution-dyed, which made the introduction of new colors difficult. Large dye lots were required; extended time periods resulted until final colored fabrics could be made available (no greige goods were available for piece dyeing), and costs were higher than for other dyeing methods. Rapid response to market demand was not possible and a wide range of colors could not be offered without greatly increasing inventory expense. Also dyes could be used in printing on the fabric rather than only pigments. (Softer hand and better colorfastness results.) The fiber characteristic is the result of incorporating an additive within the polypropylene fiber. It is being marketed under the trademark Cool Visions™.

The Environment

Dyeing is one focus of environmental concern. The common assumption is that natural dyes must be more environmentally friendly than synthetic dyes. Ironically, "natural" does not automatically mean "environmentally friendly." The environmental impact of natural dyes can be worse than that of their synthetic equivalents.

Additional chemicals are required to fix natural dye into or onto the fiber (e.g., mordant). Some are not environmentally friendly. Often more dye is required than synthetic dye when dyeing material. Substantial amounts of land and machinery are required to produce large quantities of plants to produce sufficient quantities of natural dye (not practical). A wide range of bright colors cannot typically be achieved at the present time. The best compromise for commercial use is to use low-impact

TABLE 8.3	Classical Woven Fabrics with Colored Effects Created by Dyeing of Yarns
Buffalo Check	large box pattern usually created using colored yarns
Chambray	color created with colored warp yarns and white filling yarns
Denim	color created with colored warp yarns and white or gray filling yarns
Gingham Check	small box pattern usually created using groups of two colored warp yarns and the same two-colored filling yarns
Glen Plaid	cross-barred pattern usually using groups of different colored yarns in both warp and filling
Houndstooth Suiting	houndstooth pattern using two groups of colored yarns in warp and filling
Iridescent Taffeta	color created with different colored filament warp and filling yarns
Irish Tweed	color usually created with white warp and colored filling
Madras	cross-barred pattern (plaid) usually using groups of different color yarns in warp and filling
Seersucker	colored lengthwise stripes of white and color using groups of white and colored yarns
Tapestry	colored jacquard design resulting from different colored groupings of yarns
Ticking	usually warp stripes using black or blue warp yarns and white filling yarns

synthetic fiber-reactive dyes, where the dyeing process uses a smaller amount of auxiliary chemical, requires less water and uses less energy to heat the water.

A dyeing process in which solvents are used instead of water has been developed. The result is water saving, and dyeing can then be performed in areas requiring water conservation.

The use of ultrasonic energy (sound) in the dyeing process has been studied. Ultrasonic sound refers to sound above the human hearing range. Benefits would include energy savings, reduced processing time, little adverse environmental input, lower processing costs, and an improved dye fixation rate. A major difficulty for using ultrasound technology in dyeing is that it is difficult to produce uniformity in large dyeing machines due to the high intensities required. Thus, a more promising area would be applications where dyeing takes place in smaller, compact units (i.e., small amounts of dye solution).

Study Questions

1. State three reasons why mostly synthetic dyes instead of natural dyes are used commercially.

2. List several factors that will determine the selection of dyestuffs to be used for a particular dyeing.

3a. State three ways in which pigments differ from conventional dyes.

b. Indicate how each of the differences stated above affects the properties of the colored fabric.

4. How has the use of computers for color shade matching in textile dyeing affected global trading in the textile and apparel markets?

5a. Explain why the phenomenon known as metamerism is not likely to occur on two different dye lots of the same color, each dyed by the same dyer.

b. Why is it especially important that retail fashion buyers who buy coordinate outfits (skirt with matching sweater, for example) be cautious of metamerism?

6a. How might a stock-dyed effect be achieved in piece dyeing of a 50 percent cotton/50 percent polyester-blend fabric?

b. What are the advantages of such a dyeing method?

7. Why are some types of solid-color fabrics yarn dyed instead of being more economically piece dyed?

8. Garment dyeing is the most economical form of dyeing. It also has a lesser element of fashion risk than other methods because dyeing occurs at a time closest to the point of sale to the ultimate consumer. This being the case, why are all garments not garment dyed?

9. Explain why apparel manufacturers usually exercise great care to ensure that all common components of the same sewn garment (back, front, sleeves, etc.) are from the same dye lot.

10. If classes of dyes are fiber-specific, how can over-the-counter home dyeing kits (those sold in supermarkets and drug chain stores) be used successfully on a broad range of fiber types?

11. Identify the type of coloring agent (pigment or dye and class of dye) and method of application (fiber, yarn, fabric form) that would provide the most satisfactory results for children's play clothes. Justify your answer.

12. State four factors that influence the colorfastness of a fabric.

CHAPTER NINE

Textile Printing

Objectives

▸ To understand the principles of applying printed design to fabrics.

▸ To know the different methods of printing and the uses and limitations of each.

▸ To know the various types of prints attainable by the different printing methods.

▸ To be knowledgeable of colorfastness similarities and differences between dyed and printed fabrics.

▸ To know the terminology used regarding textile printing.

Use fabrics in the Printed Fabrics section of the Fabric Science Swatch Kit *for this chapter.*

Key Terms Related to Textiles

aging
automatic-screen printing
blotch print
burn-out prints
curing
digital printing
direct print
discharge prints
disperse dyes

dry prints
duplex prints
electrostatic charge
electrostatic flocking
engineered prints
fall on
flatbed
flock printing
flocking

halftone
hand-screen printing
heat-transfer printing
ink-jet printing
mechanical flocking
overprint
print paste
print register/off register
registration

resist printing
roller printing
rotary-screen printing
screen printing
strike off
thermal-transfer printing
warp prints
wet-on-dry
wet-on-wet
wet prints

Printing is defined as dyeing in a localized, patterned area. Early examples of applying color in the form of a print date back to 3000 B.C. The development of blocks and stencils offered consistency to this early form of decoration. Printing with blocks requires the background to be cut away from a flat surface, originally made of wood. Color or dyes are applied to the remaining raised area thus providing a design when stamped or pressed onto fabric. In stencil printing the background is left intact and the design is cut away. Color is pushed through the cut out areas to form a pattern.

Both techniques allowed the production of large printed areas but could not effectively create intricate designs. Engraved blocks were followed by engraved plates that permitted the formation of fine lines and greater detail. Stencils were replaced with silk fiber to create an open fabric mesh secured in a wooden frame. This made possible detailed prints for paper and fabric and was known as a silk screen. Engraved blocks and silk

FIGURE 9.2
Print designs are typically executed by textile designers using computer-aided design (CAD) systems.

FIGURE 9.1
Print designs are sometimes executed by hand by textile designers. This is the design studio of a textile converter.

screens helped make fabric with distinctive designs more accessible in the marketplace as printed fabric became more commonplace.

Textile printing uses the same dyes or pigments applied to produce dyed fabric. The same principles of specific dye classes having select fiber affinities and the general fastness characteristics apply equally to printing and dyeing.

The designs for printed fabrics are an important element of the printed fabrics industry. A continuous supply of new designs are required for this highly fashion-oriented segment of the textile industry. (See Figure 9.1.) These designs are shown in Figure 9.2 being produced by computer-aided design (CAD) method.

Dyes or pigments used in dyeing are usually in a water-bath solution. When the same dyes or pigments are used for printing, they must be thickened with gums or starches to prevent the wicking or flowing of the print design. The thickened solution, about the consistency of heavy buttermilk, is called the **print paste**. Some dyes cannot be used in printing pastes for reasons such as insufficient solubility and low color yield.

Textile printers are the specialized branch of the textile industry that produces printed textiles. They may be commission printers or divisions of large integrated textile corporations. Commission printers, like commission knitters (see p. 112), perform the printing function on fabrics that they do not own. Also, they have no part in the design or color selections of the fabric entrusted to them for printing. Design and color selection are usually the function of the designer organization or owner of greige goods (e.g., textile converter, import agent, private label producer).

Methods of Printing

There are several major methods for printing textiles: the screen-print method, the roller-print method, heat-transfer printing, and digital printing. Other printing methods rarely used in commercial production of textiles are block, batik, ikat, and resist printing.

Screen Printing

Screen printing involves the preparation of a printing screen made from fine-mesh screen fabric of nylon, polyester, or metal tightly mounted on a frame or rolled into a cylinder.[1] The screen fabric is coated with an opaque, nonporous film. The pattern areas of the opaque film are removed, leaving the fine-mesh screen that will be the printed pattern. Most commercial screen fabric is coated with a film that is photosensitive, and the removal of the pattern portion occurs through a photochemical process.

Printing is done by placing the screen on top of the fabric to be printed. Print paste is forced through the mesh areas of the screen by a squeegee (an implement similar to that used for sweeping water from an auto windshield).

Each color in a print design requires its own screen and separate application of color. A three-color print, for example, requires three screens and three applications of color to the fabric. Also, each color of the design must be precisely located on the screen so that it becomes properly placed and avoids, for example, the green stem of a flower being located in the middle of a red rose petal. Print

registration is the industry term to indicate when all of the colors of the print have been supplied to the fabric.

There are three systems for making screen prints and each basically uses the same principle. The first, **hand-screen printing**, originally used by ancient cultures, is still used today. The second system, known as **automatic-screen printing**, is also referred to as flatbed printing. This type is essentially an automated version of the first. The third system, known as **rotary-screen printing**, is the most widely used method of printing. Here the screens are reoriented from a flat configuration of the hand and the automatic screen processes to a cylinder or rotary configuration.

Hand-Screen Printing

Hand-screen printing is done commercially on long tables (up to 60 yards or 54.9 meters in length). The roll of fabric to be printed is spread smoothly onto the table, whose surface has first been coated with a light tack adhesive. The screens are made of material stretched over a frame. The print operators then move the screen frames by hand successively along the whole table, printing one frame at a time, until the entire fabric is printed. Each frame contains one color of the print. The rate of production ranges from 50 to 90 yards (45.7 to 82.3 meters) per hour by this method.

A substantial amount of commercial hand-screen printing is also done on cut garment parts. In printing cut garments, an apparel manufacturer arranges by contract with screen printers specializing in this service. Customized or unique patterns are printed on garment parts before the pieces are sewn together. Items such as printed beach towels and novelty printed aprons, draperies, and shower curtains are also printed by hand-screen methods because it is possible to make large screen frames for large design repeats.

Hand-screen printing is also used for printing limited-quantity, high-fashion couture as well as for printing small-quantity runs to market-test a design. The hand-screen print method is illustrated in Figure 9.3.

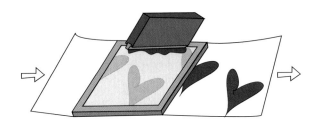

FIGURE 9.3
Hand-screen printing.

---

1. At one time, the screens used for this process were made from fine silk yarns, and the process was called silk-screen printing. The process is still often referred to by that name, although screens of silk are no longer used.

Printing T-Shirts

A special niche in the hand-screen printing industry is the printing of T-shirts, either assembled or cut garment parts (e.g. front). (See Figure 9.4.) The colorant most used is plastisol ink. It coats the yarns and fabrics and does not penetrate the fibers as do aqueous dyes. It can be used to print on most surfaces and it is stretchable and durable. It can be printed thin for general apparel or thick for athletic uniforms. Plastisol ink prints cannot be ironed or dry-cleaned, however, garments can be turned inside out for ironing and T-shirts usually are washed and not dry-cleaned. These printed materials also must be able to withstand a required curing temperature of about 300°F (≈150°C).

Today, the T-shirt industry is a multibillion dollar business. This garment, which was initially an undergarment, has progressed to an everyday piece of clothing, frequently with customized print designs. The screen-print T-shirt industry is characterized by many small shops, some of which are "mom and pop" shops. They do both custom and stock designs and have a reputation for rapid turnaround.

Automatic-Screen Printing

In **automatic-screen printing** (or **flatbed** printing), the fabric being printed is moved to the screens on a wide rubberized belt. Like hand-screen printing, automatic-screen printing is an intermittent rather than a continuous process. (See Figure 9.5.) The screens are usually nylon mesh stretched over a metal frame. In this instance, the fabric moves to the screen, and then stops for the screen squeegee action (which is done automatically). After the squeegee action, the fabric moves again to the next screen frame. The rate of production is about 500 yards (457 meters) per hour. Automatic-screen printing is used for whole rolls of fabric only. Cut garment parts cannot ordinarily be printed by this method.

Rotary-Screen Printing

Rotary printing is continuous since the screens are cylinders. The fabric being printed is moved on a wide rubber belt under the rotary-screen cylinders that are in continuous motion. (See Figures 9.6 and 9.7.) The screens are metal mesh in a cylindrical form. Rotary-screen printing is the fastest method of screen printing, with production of more than 120 yards (100 meters) per hour. Seamless, perforated metal (mesh) screens are used. The largest

FIGURE 9.4
Printed T-shirt by Alexander McQueen.

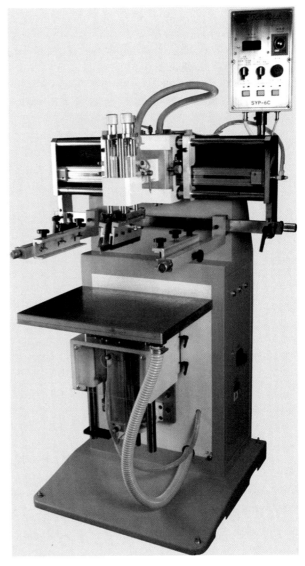

FIGURE 9.5
An automatic flatbed screen printing machine for T-shirts.

FIGURE 9.6
Rotary-screen printing.

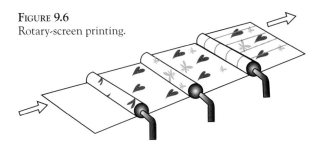

FIGURE 9.7
A rotary-screen printing machine.

rotary screens have a circumference greater than 40 inches (101.6 cm), and the maximum repeat size of patterns is, therefore, greater than 40 inches. Rotary-screen printing machines of more than 24 colors have been produced. As mentioned, rotary-screen printing is the most widely used method of printing textiles.

Rotary-screen printing can print fine particles through the screen mesh to achieve special effects with gold, silver, pearls, glitter, or the like. It is also used to apply coating and laminates. Finishes such as waterproofing, flame retardant, and stain repellent are applied in this manner.

Roller Printing

Roller printing is a high-speed process, capable of producing more than 6,000 yards (5,486 meters), of printed fabric per hour. In roller printing, the design is put on fabric by copper engraved rollers (or cylinders). Copper rollers can be engraved with very fine, delicate details with very close tolerances, and thus enable the printing of very fine, delicate designs. Fine and closely detailed paisley prints are an example of the type of fabric designs that can be printed by roller printing. The roller engravings exactly match the designer's creative sketch. A separate engraved cylinder is required for each color in the print.[2]

Roller printing is uneconomical unless very large yardage of each color run is produced. High cost and long lead time for roller preparation and machine setup make using this method impractical in most situations. However, roller printing is used for staple designs that are made in large quantities for many seasons. Figure 9.8 illustrates a schematic side view of a roller-printing machine.

Setting the Color in Screen and Roller Printing

Once the color is registered on the cloth, further treatment is needed to set the color. When a dye is used as the

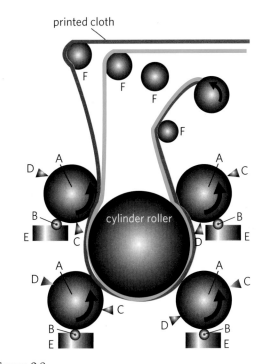

FIGURE 9.8
A schematic side view of a roller-printing machine.

A. Engraved copper roller　　D. Lint doctor
B. Color furnisher　　　　　　E. Color box
C. Doctor blade　　　　　　　F. Guide roller

printing colorant, it must be made to combine with the fiber. This is accomplished by exposing the printed fabric to steam at temperatures near or sometimes exceeding the boiling point of water (pressure steaming); this step is called **aging**. Following the aging process, the fabric

2. In the textile industry, the expressions five-screen print, six-screen print, etc., are often used to express five or six colors in a particular print.

is passed through soap baths to remove the thickeners and other substances used in formulating the print paste. Finally, the fabric undergoes several rinses and drying. Large quantities of water and heat energy are consumed in the printing process.

If pigments rather than dyes are used in the printing, the fabric is subjected to dry heat up to 400°F (≈210°C) for several minutes to set the resin that holds the pigment. This step is known as **curing.** No further treatment is required. Considerable financial water and energy savings are attained in printing with pigments rather than with dyes.

The textile industry frequently refers to fabrics that have been printed with dyes as **wet prints** and to those that have been printed with pigments as **dry prints.** This is because wet prints require steam, and later washing and rinsing, as part of their processing. Dry prints, on the other hand, are simply subjected to the dry heat of curing as part of the coloration process, without the wet washing treatment.

Heat-Transfer Printing

Heat-transfer printing is sometimes called **thermal-transfer printing**. The principle of heat-transfer printing is somewhat similar to that of familiar decal transfers. In this method, the design is first printed on paper with printing inks containing dyes of the disperse dye class. The printed paper (called transfer paper) is then stored until ready for use by the textile printer.[3] (See Figure 9.9.)

When fabric is to be printed, it is passed through a heat-transfer printing machine, which brings the printed transfer paper and the unprinted fabric together face-to-face, and passes them through the machine at about 400°F (≈210°C). Under this high temperature, the dye on the printed paper sublimates and is transferred onto the fabric,[4] completing the printing. No further treatment

is needed. The process is relatively simple and does not require the expertise necessary for producing roller- or rotary-screen prints. (See Figure 9.10.)

Disperse dyes are the only dyes that can be sublimated, and the only ones that respond in a way that permits heat-transfer printing. The process is therefore limited to fabrics that are composed of fibers having affinity to this class of dyestuff. This includes acetate, acrylics, polyamides (nylon), and polyesters. Blended fabrics with a high percentage of these fibers and a low percentage of cotton can also be printed this way. Fabrics made of 50/50 cotton and polyester must be first treated with a resin.

In heat-transfer printing, the textile printer purchases printed paper from one of the several sources of these highly specialized papers. The transfer paper is printed in accordance with the designer's or customer's art. (Stock patterns are also available from the paper printers.)

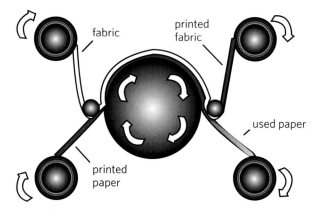

FIGURE 9.9
A schematic drawing of the heat-transfer printing method.

FIGURE 9.10
In a heat-transfer print, the fabric to be printed moves over guide rolls at the top, and then down into the machine. The pattern paper, pattern side up, is fed along with the fabric into the heat chamber of the machine. A new roll of pattern paper is always in position so that the printing operation can continue without interruption.

---

3. Iron-on (or press-on) prints used as emblems and decorations on garments (or other uses of textile fibers) are usually vinyl plastic or pigments mixed either into a paraffin wax or a thermoplastic base. The heat of the iron melts the substance, which then becomes bound to the fabric when cooled. These iron-on emblems stiffen the fabric in the area of print. When subjected to machine laundering and tumble drying, they gradually lose color and become considerably lighter and faded. They are, however, not adversely affected by dry-cleaning.

4. A substance that is capable of passing directly from the solid state to the gaseous state, without an intervening liquid phase, is called a sublimating substance. Dry ice is a familiar product that sublimates. Water, however, does not ordinarily sublimate. When changing from ice to steam, water passes through the liquid phase. Dyes of the disperse dye class are the only dyes that sublimate. Upon application of heat in the heat transfer process, the dye becomes a gas and is then absorbed by the fabric being printed.

Heat-transfer printing can be used for printing garment parts (logos, emblems, etc.), in which case specially designed heat-transfer presses are used. A heat-transfer print emerges from the printing process as a completed printed fabric. Thus, utilization of large and costly dryers, steamers, washers, and tenter frames is eliminated.

Paper can be inspected so that off-register and other defects can be eliminated before printing. Seconds quality in heat-transfer printed fabric is therefore rare. The rate of production for continuous heat transfer printing is about 250 yards (228.6 meters) per hour.

Advancements in the Print Industry

Printed textiles account for less than 15 percent of the total textile market. They are more sensitive to changes in fashion than dyed fabrics and are often utilized in niche markets. For the print industry, changes throughout each fashion season can mean as many as six to eight new lines produced each year. This is very challenging for conventional printing methods, which cannot turn around quickly and are better suited for long runs of the same pattern. This is because the production of screens or rollers is costly and time consuming. Thus the traditional print industry must run printing machines at high speeds to mass produce printed fabric.

The printing industry has been confronted by changes in market conditions and advancements in technology. Fashion changes and directives are occurring faster than ever before. Manufacturers want low minimum stock requirements with easy reorders and quick turnaround times. In order to meet the market demands the printing industry is looking to new methods for printing textiles.

Digital Printing

Although **digital** or **ink-jet printing** has been used for office printing on paper for many years, it is only more recently being used for textiles. Microdrops of color liquid ink are applied through tiny nozzles into the fabric surface.

Jets in the print heads are controlled by valves which open and close independently. Streams of ink droplets are ejected at a high velocity. The pressure from the valve is sufficient to ensure that inks penetrate into the surface of the fabric. A vacuum attachment under the fabric allows for greater penetration. The inks are suitable for application for home furnishings, outdoor fabrics, and apparel. The color (applied from refillable cartridges), quantity, and location of the drops are controlled by a computer.

All colors are printed at the same time by separate tiny nozzles. Color technology results in four process colors being used—cyan, magenta, yellow, and black inks. The colors can overlap and so are able to give a full range of visual effects, with half tones. The droplets are so fine, often 720 dpi—drops per inch or per 2.54 centimeters—that color is created or "mixed" right on the fabric similar to color produced for magazine photographs or pixels on a computer screen. The inks used enable the printer to print on most textile fibers.

Designers who create patterns on a CAD system can use digital printing to modify repeat size, create different color ways, and print immediately. With this system, designers can engineer the print for the shape of the product as opposed to the dimensions of the screen. Additionally with designs or patterns made digitally, fabric waste can be minimized. Also, digital printers can produce extremely complex photographic imagery that cannot be done with rotary screens.

Digital printing is used primarily for sampling, just-in-time delivery, and large, custom orders (mass customization). It is utilized to test market designs and color combinations directly to the consumer before committing to longer production runs. When used for sampling the turnaround time can drop from six to eight weeks to one to two days. Since screens, separation of each color in the pattern, and extended drying times are not a factor, labor and material costs are reduced significantly (see Figure 9.11).

Ink-jet printing is now a slow process because of technical limitations. It is, however, very economical for small production yardage or to make samples before investing

FIGURE 9.11
This on-demand digital textile printer provides greater design variety and lower production costs.

in screens for large production runs. This method is also very desirable to produce customized printed apparel or furnishings. The production rate of digital ink printing is extremely slow, (approximately 120 meters per hour) compared to rotary-screen printing (approximately 120 meters per minute). The fabric for ink-jet printing must be pretreated and it works best with reactive, disperse, and acid dyes as well as pigments. It may require extensive post-printing processing to set the color. There is also less color penetrating than with screens so there can be a problem with materials like velvet or carpeting.

DuPont™ offers the same colorants in its Artistri™ digital ink-jet printer as those used in screen printing. New ink-jet inks have sufficiently high fastness to be used by automotive manufacturers. Greater color range and intensity of these inks are being developed.

Digital technology is the fastest growing method of printing textiles. Whereas it only accounts for about one percent of the global market, its share will probably rise appreciatively in the future.

The Environment

Digital printing is more eco-friendly than the other major methods for a variety of reasons. There is less energy and water used. Inks are water-based rather than solvent-based. Industry estimates are that less than 40 percent of screen-print designs produced into finished fabric actually make money for the producer. Patterns or designs created in a digital format can easily be recolored and resized directly on the computer. Currently, digital production is cost effective when printing less than 500 yards.

Color Features of Printed Fabrics

Several color features of printed fabrics should be examined: how long the color will last (colorfastness), color effects by application of one color on top of another (wet-on-dry and wet-on-wet), and duplication of color (color matching). Each of these features is discussed in the following sections.

Colorfastness

The printing of fabrics is a surface treatment of the material. Except in lightweight fabrics, the printed colors rarely penetrate deeply into the fabric structure. Laundering or dry-cleaning, accompanied by tumble drying or the abrasion resulting from use, tends to wear off the surface fibers and the lighter colored or uncolored fibers emerge on the fabric surface, making the material appear faded.

Fabrics such as shirtings, most utility clothing, and children's wear materials retain their color much longer if they are yarn dyed or piece dyed rather than printed. For materials such as those for draperies or evening dresses, for example, it would not be important whether they are printed or dyed because they are not normally subjected to excessive wear or cleanings.

Sometimes printed designs are made to duplicate woven-yarn-dyed stripes or plaids because the printed designs are less costly. For the reasons stated previously, the color will not last as long in the printed fabric. Alert buyers and others dealing with fabrics routinely check whether the design is woven or printed.

Lengthwise stripes cannot be printed by hand screen or flatbed automatic screen because the lengthwise stripes cannot be perfectly matched for each screen change.

Wet-on-Dry and Wet-on-Wet Effects

Wet-on-dry is the printing of a second color on top of a previously printed color when the first color is moderately or fully dry. The second color covers the first, and only the second color appears. Wet-on-dry is usually used only on hand-screen prints.

Wet-on-wet is the printing of a second color over a first color that is still wet. The second color is applied immediately after the first, while the fabric is still on the imprint stage of printing. When the second color goes over the first, the two become mixed and a third color is produced. The third color is referred to as **fall on.** Print designers can thus create a three-color print with two screens or rollers.

Halftone

A **halftone** is the gradual shading from light to dark in the same color of a pattern. Thus, the appearance of a two-color pattern can be created with one color. Halftones are produced in roller printing by gradually increasing or decreasing the depth of the copper engraving of the roller. In rotary-screen prints, halftones are produced by increasing or decreasing the density of screen perforations in the pattern. Hand-screen, automatic-flat-screen, and heat-transfer prints cannot produce halftones because the technology to vary the density of screens has not been developed.

Strike-Off and Color Matching in Printed Fabrics

The problems of color matching, laboratory formulations, and metamerism in dyed fabrics are discussed in Chapter 8. The same problems and procedures apply equally to printed fabrics.

In printed fabrics, the first several sample yards are printed for approval by the textile designer or customer prior to full-scale production. This is called a **strike off.** In many instances, it is impossible for a printer to color match all the shades that the design contains, and it is not unusual under these circumstances for several strike offs to be run before a print is approved for production.

The time required for the production of first sample screens and strike off may take as long as six to eight weeks and often creates problems in the high-fashion, rapidly changing printed fabrics business. New technologies being utilized can reduce this time drastically to merely a few hours to produce a strike-off design on fabric starting with a paper original art sketch.

Which Method of Printing is Best?

So which of the several methods of commercial printing is the best? There is no one best method. Each of the methods used is the most advantageous for particular kinds of designs and quantities to be printed. Some methods may be entirely improper for certain designs and quantities.

Table 9.1 indicates under which general conditions each printing method would be most suitable.

Basic Types of Prints

In the first section of this chapter, the various methods (i.e., screen, roller, heat transfer) are discussed. Each of the methods, however, is capable of printing one or more print types, each with its own unique properties. These types are direct prints, discharge prints, and resist prints.

Direct Prints

A **direct print**, also called an application print, is one in which the design is printed directly onto a white cloth or over a previously dyed fabric. The latter is called an **overprint**[5] and, of course, the printed design must be considerably darker than the dyed background. The most common print types are direct prints.

You can recognize a direct print if the background is white, or has large portions of white and the printed design is a lighter shade on the back of the fabric than on the face. (This may not be evident on lightweight fabrics because of the strike-through of the print paste.)

The fabric is an overprint if the background color is the same shade on the face and back (piece dyed), and the print design is substantially darker than the background.

Discharge Prints

Discharge prints are produced through a two-step process. In the first step, the fabric is piece-dyed a solid color. In the second step, the fabric design is printed onto the fabric.

The print paste for the second step contains a powerful bleaching agent that destroys the color of the background dye. Thus a white polka dot on a blue background can be produced by this method. It is called a white discharge. A color discharge can be produced when the bleach agent and a dye that does not react with the bleach are mixed in the same print paste (vat dyes are in this category). Thus a yellow polka dot can be printed on a blue background when an appropriate yellow dye (vat dye) is mixed with the color-removing bleach.

Because the background color had been originally pieced dyed, the color is richer and has greater depth than if the background had been printed as in blotch prints (see p. 180).

Discharge prints can be made with roller and screen methods, but not by heat-transfer printing. They are not widely used because their production is very costly compared to that of direct prints and because very careful and precise control of reducing chemicals are required. Where used, they are marketed in better and higher-priced lines. Sometimes, use of the reducing chemical in the process results in weakening or destruction of fabrics in the printed pattern.[6]

You can recognize a discharge print if the background color is the same shade on the face and back of the fabric (piece dyed), and the print design area is white or a different color or shade than the background; and careful examination of the back of the print design reveals traces of the original background color. (This occurs because the color-destroying chemical does not penetrate completely through to the back of the fabric.)

Resist Prints

Resist printing involves a two-step procedure: (1) printing a pattern design on a white fabric with a chemical or waxlike resinous substance that prevents or resists the penetration of dyes; and (2) piece dyeing the fabric. The result is a dyed background with a white patterned area. Notice that the results are the same as those of discharge prints. The methods of achieving the result is, however, the reverse of that for discharge printing.

Resist printing is not a popular method. It is used where background colors in a fabric cannot be discharged.

---

5. Overprints are often done to mask defects in dyeing or to make otherwise poor selling colors marketable. The types of prints are almost always pigment prints. Low fastness to washing and crocking are common problems.

6. This tendered, or weakened, pattern area, when it occurs, is not always immediately apparent. Sometimes small tears or holes begin to appear after the second or third laundering or dry cleaning.

Printing Method	Important Features and Advantages	Limitations and Disadvantages
Hand screen	• Method for low yardage; samples; exclusive, limited-quantity designs • Large repeat sizes (up to 120 in. ≈ 3.5 m.) possible • Wet-on-dry print effects possible • Better color definition than roller print due to heavier lay-on of color • Acceptable for all woven and knitted constructions • Rapid preparation of screens and rapid pattern changeover possible • Possible to print cut garment parts and small items (towels, scarves, etc.)	• Halftone designs not possible • Fine-line paisley prints not possible • Slow production; uneconomical for large production yardage
Automatic screen (flatbed)	• Large repeat size (up to 120 in. ≈ 3.5 m.) possible • Better color definition than roller print; equal to hand screen • Adaptable to all woven and knitted constructions • Rapid changeover of designs possible • Best machine registration	• Screen preparation and special mountings more costly than for hand screen • Not adaptable to low yardage • Halftone designs not possible • Lengthwise stripes not possible
Rotary screen	• Over 40-inch repeat size possible; larger than roller printing, but smaller than flat-screen methods • Lengthwise stripe effect possible • Fall on designs possible • Adaptable to all woven and knitted constructions • Cleaner and brighter colors than on roller prints • Excellent color definitions, but less than with flat-screen methods • Rapid changeover of designs possible • Efficient for long runs and moderately small (1,000 yards ≈ 914.4 m.) runs	• Fine-line paisley prints not possible • Halftone designs not as effective as roller printing • Screens do not last as long as rollers
Roller	• Requires long production runs of same pattern (10,000 yards ≈ 9,144 m.) • Can produce halftones and fall-on effects • Can print woven fabrics • Knitted fabrics require special handling	• Except for special machines, size of pattern repeat limited to 16-inch (≈40.6 cm) maximum for apparel patterns, and 22 inches (≈55.9 cm) for interior furnishings • Not economical for short runs • Long production delays in pattern changeovers • Engraving is expensive
Heat transfer	• Produces bright, sharp, clear fine-line designs • Can print cut garment parts and small items • Adaptable to long and short yardage runs • Rapid pattern changeover possible • Simple, low-investment installation possible • Steamers, washers, dryers, etc. not required (no posttreatments) • Fewest second-quality pieces of all print processes • Heat setting (see p. 196) also accomplished	• Lead time for paper preparation can cause problems in high-fashion markets • Limited to fabrics having minimum 50% manufactured fibers. Cellulosic and protein (100%) fibers cannot be printed • Overprint only on pastels or else will not completely cover the original color
Digital	• Photographic detail • Repeat can be endless • Quick color change • Size range easily modified • Unique, one-of-a-kind runs • Little fabric waste	• Limited production due to slow speed • Expensive inks • Substrate must be specifically prepared • Cannot handle specialty inks like metallic or glitter

Most resist printing is performed as craft or hand print-ing (such as batik)[7] rather than on a production basis. It is usually not possible to distinguish by ordinary visual examination between discharge prints and resist prints because both types of prints produce the same results.

Pigment Prints

Textile prints that are produced with pigments rather than with dyes are so widely used that they have come to be regarded as a separate print-type category. Pigment prints are direct prints made with pigments. The process is frequently called **dry printing**, as distinguished from **wet printing** (or dye printing).

Pigment prints can be distinguished from dye prints by comparing the differences in fabric stiffness between a design-printed portion and a nonprinted portion of the same fabric. The pigment print area is slightly stiffer and perhaps a bit thicker than the nonprint area. If the fabric were printed with dyes, there would be no discernible difference in stiffness between the printed and non-printed portions.

Deep shades of pigments are likely to be stiffer and less flexible than light shades or pastels. When check-ing a fabric for the presence of pigment printing, be sure

---

7. These artistic designs are made by artists and craftspeople who first make their designs on fabric with wax, and then dye the fabric using selective dyes that do not require heat. Repeated waxing, removal, rewaxing, and dyeing ultimately create the batik design, which may have a dozen or more colors.

to check all colors because the same fabric may contain both dyes and pigments. White pigments are also used in prints; this factor should not be overlooked.

Pigment prints are the least costly type of print to pro-duce because they are relatively simple to apply and require the least amount of processing because the usual steaming and washing are not required. Pigments produce bright, rich colors, and may be applied to all textile fibers. They have good to excellent fastness to light and dry-cleaning, and are, therefore, widely used for drapery and curtain fab-rics as well as for apparel fabrics that will be dry-cleaned. Also, they offer excellent lot-to-lot shade matching and excellent cover of ground color on overprint designs.

Pigment prints lose color gradually and become more faded with each succeeding laundering or dry-cleaning. This is caused by the gradual loss of the resin binders from the tumbling and agitation of the clean-ing process. These prints usually show a distinctly faded appearance after 20 to 30 cleanings, but colorfastness is enhanced with the application of resins and silicone softening treatments in final finishing (see p. 191). Dark shades fade more readily than light or pastel shades.

Pigments cause stiffening in the printed design por-tion of the fabric. This condition is barely noticeable in light shades, but may be noticeable in deep colors. Pig-ments are not particularly fast to crocking, especially in dark shades. Dark shades of pigment colors should espe-cially be avoided in applications such as upholstery fab-rics. Table 9.2 summarizes and compares wet, dry, and heat-transfer prints.

TABLE 9.2 Comparison of Wet (Dye) Prints, Dry (Pigment) Prints, and Heat-Transfer Prints			
	Wet (Dye) Prints	Dry (Pigment) Prints	Heat-Transfer Prints
Fibers applied	All fibers: Fiber/dye affinity required	All pigments can be applied to all fibers	Polyester, nylon, and acetate
Nature of application	Chemical action	Physical action	Sublimation action
Application method	Roller or screen	Roller or screen	Transfer paper
Effect on fabric hand	None	Slight to heavy stiffening and thickening in printed portion depending on depth of shade	Some stiffening on acetate
Colorfastness to sunlight	Varies depending on dye	Good to excellent	Good to excellent
Colorfastness to crocking	Varies depending on dye	Fair in light shades, poor in deep shades	Excellent
Colorfastness to laundering	Varies depending on dye	Fair in light shades, poor in deep shades	Excellent on polyester, fair to good on nylon, fair to poor on acetate
Cost of printing	Highest	Lowest	Second highest

Special Types of Prints

The basic types of prints (described in the preceding section) represent the various ways in which color as designed patterns is applied to textiles. Special types of prints, described in this section, are a second grouping and are classified as such because special effects are achieved or because they are not in widespread use, often due to high processing costs.

Blotch Prints

A **blotch print** is one in which the background color has been created by printing rather than piece dyeing. It is a special variety of direct print. The ground and pattern design colors are printed onto a white cloth, usually in one printing operation. Sometimes blotch prints are designed to imitate more costly discharge or resist-print effects. Each can easily be identified from the back of the fabric. The blotch print background color is lighter on the fabric back. The discharge or resist-color background is the same on the face and back because the fabric has previously been piece dyed.

One of the problems with blotch prints is that sometimes the large background color areas of the print are not covered with the full depth of color. When this occurs, critical examination of the blotch area reveals small bits of faded or shaded areas. The overall appearance might be almost a washed-out look, rather than that of full, rich color cover. This condition does not occur on quality blotch prints produced under controlled conditions. The condition is less likely to occur on screen-print blotch printing, where print paste is laid onto the fabric rather than pushed into the fabric, as with roller prints. Pigment-printed blotch fabrics often have an objectionable stiff, or boardy, hand.

Flock Prints

Flock printing is a type of printing in which tiny particles of fiber called fiber flock, (ranging from about $1/10$ to $1/4$ inch or 2.5 to 6.4 mm), are made to adhere to a fabric surface in conformance to a particular design. The process consists of first printing the design onto a fabric with an adhesive rather than a dye or a pigment, and then exposing the fiber flock to the fabric. The flock is held to the fabric surface only in those portions where the adhesive was first applied.

There are two methods of adhering the flock to the adhesive-treated fabric surface: mechanical flocking and electrostatic flocking. Each yields its own distinct touch to the flock surface. In **mechanical flocking**, the fiber flock is sifted onto the fabric while the fabric is passing in open width through a flocking chamber. Mechanical beaters cause the fabric to vibrate. The flock becomes embedded in a randomized manner. In **electrostatic flocking**, the flock particles are given an **electrostatic charge**, which results in nearly all the fibers being oriented in an upright position when they adhere to the fabric. Electrostatic flocking is slower and more costly than mechanical flocking, but results in a more uniform and denser flock. (See Figures 9.12 and 9.13.)

The fibers used for flocking include practically all the manufactured fibers. Rayon and nylon are the two most popular. In most instances, the flock fiber is dyed prior to its application to the fabric.

The ability of flocked fabrics to withstand dry-cleaning and/or laundering procedures depends on the characteristics of the adhesive. Many high-quality adhesives available to textile processors provide excellent fastness to laundering, dry-cleaning, or both. Because not all adhesives are fast to all cleaning methods, it is important to verify that any particular flocked fabric is compatible with the cleaning method to which it will be subjected.

Flocking

In addition to flock printing or print designs in flock, **flocking** is also done overall to cover the entire fabric surface. Depending on the fiber used and the flocking process, flock appearance can range from suede to velvet and even plush. These kinds of fabrics are used for shoes and clothing, imitation plush, nonslip patch fabrics on boat decks and swimming areas, handbags and belts,

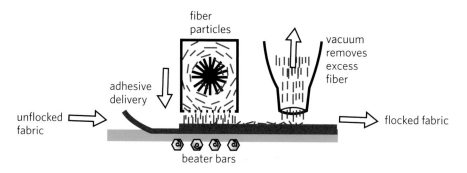

FIGURE 9.12
A schematic drawing of the mechanical flocking process.

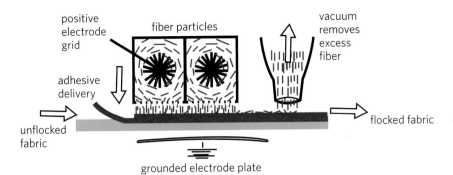

positive
electrode
grid

fiber particles

vacuum
removes
excess
fiber

adhesive
delivery

unflocked
fabric

flocked fabric

grounded electrode plate

FIGURE 9.13
A schematic drawing of the
electrostatic flocking process.
Note the grounded electrode plate.

bedspreads, furniture, automotive seating, and a wide variety of other uses. The fiber and the adhesive must be suitable for the desired end use.

An important factor in overall-flocked fabrics is the effect of adhesives on the vapor (air) permeability of the fabric. Some adhesives that otherwise are entirely satisfactory may also be completely or almost completely nonbreathable. (This is caused by the film of cement laid on the entire fabric surface to hold the flock.) These fabrics can become highly uncomfortable for certain end uses such as shoes, vests, skirts, and coats. To judge the relative permeability of fabrics, hold up a sample large enough to cover your mouth, and exhale into the fabric. If the fabric is breathable, you will be able to exhale through the fabric with moderate effort.

Warp Prints

Warp prints involve printing the warp yarns of a fabric before they are placed on the loom for weaving. Then the fabric is woven with a solid-color filling, usually white, but sometimes one that contrasts with the warp print used. The result is a soft, shadowed, somewhat blurred design on the fabric. Producing warp prints requires careful, meticulous labor. These prints are therefore found almost exclusively on high-quality and rather costly fabrics. The one exception is with fibers that can be heat-transfer printed (see p. 174). Developments involving the heat-transfer printing of warp yarns have resulted in significantly reduced costs of warp prints.

Warp prints may be identified by unraveling both warp and picks from a fabric. The colors of the design are on the warp yarns only. The picks are white or a solid color. Warp-print imitations are also made, but these can easily be distinguished because the color of the design are seen on both warp and filling.

Burn-Out Prints

Burn-out prints involve printing with a chemical substance that destroys the fiber in the pattern-design print area.[8] Thus, a hole in the fabric results where the chemical made contact with the fabric. Simulated eyelet embroideries are made with a 2- or 3-roller print, where one roller contains the fiber-destroying chemical and the other roller(s) prints a pattern simulating embroidery stitching.

These fabrics are used in low-cost summer blouses and in cotton lingerie trim. The edges of the holes in burn-out prints are subject to premature fraying. These fabrics, therefore, are not very resistant to prolonged wear.

Another type of burn-out print involves fabrics that are made from blended yarns, core-spun yarns, or fabric mixtures of two or more types of fibers. The burn-out print chemical destroys one fiber (the cellulosic) and leaves the others undamaged. Many unusual and interesting fabrics are created with this method of printing. Such a fabric might be a rayon/polyester blend where each yarn is a 50/50 blend of polyester and rayon. When the burn-out printing is done the rayon portion disappears (burn out) leaving the polyester unchanged. The result is a gauzelike print portion of polyester and the unprinted portion of original polyester/rayon blend.

Duplex Prints

Duplex prints are fabrics in which both sides of the fabric are printed. Interesting effects can be achieved with reversible fabrics. The look is similar to gift wrap on which both sides have been printed with coordinating designs. The end uses are limited but include reversible sheeting, table covers, and unlined or reversible jackets and vests.

Engineered Prints

Engineered prints are prints that have two or more distinct designs, each located in separate areas of the fabric, and each design is to become a specific part of the garment. For example, a clothing designer wants to create

---

8. Sulfuric acid, mixed into a colorless print paste, is the usual chemical used. This acid, in the strength used for burn-out prints, destroys cellulosic fibers but leaves all others unaffected.

TEXTILE PRINTING

a blouse whose front and back are blue-and-white polka dot, and whose sleeves are the same blue and white colors, but in a stripe design. In this instance, the clothing designer works with the textile designer to engineer a print in which both the polka dot elements and stripe elements are on the same bolt of cloth. The placement within the print and yardage of each of the design elements must be carefully worked out so that optimum fabric utilization, without inordinate waste, is achieved.

Another type of engineered print consists of printing on already-cut garment parts such as a pocket or garment collar. Many unique and distinctive apparel designs are thus created. The garment parts are printed by hand-screen or heat-transfer processing.

Imperfections on Printed Fabric

The following is a list and descriptions of the most frequently occurring imperfections that may result from printing processes. These imperfections may result from faulty or improper printing procedures, faulty or improper preparation of the fabric prior to printing, or imperfections in the material being printed. Because the printing of textiles is in many respects similar to the dyeing of textiles, many of the imperfections found in dyed fabrics are also found in printed fabrics. Therefore, also refer to the section titled "Imperfections of Dyed Fabric" on page 164.

Color drag: Color of the print smears or smudges from rubbing against an object before it becomes dry.

Color splatter: Instead of being placed on the fabric, the print paste is thrown or splattered onto the fabric surface, causing color spots or splatters on the printed fabric.

Fuzzy pattern: The edges of patterns are not sharp, clear lines, but are instead rather fuzzy lines. Most frequently caused by improper singeing (see p. 187) or improperly thickened print paste.

Off-register: Printing rolls or screens improperly aligned so pattern parts do not meet properly. This imperfection is also called out-of-fit or out-of-register.

Stop mark: Color streaks across the fabric as a result of the printing machine being stopped and restarted during the printing process.

Tender spots: In printed fabrics, one or more colors of the print may cause weakened areas where they were printed, which is usually due to excessive use of injurious chemicals in the print paste. May also be found in the discharged area of discharge prints.

Study Questions

1. Describe how you distinguish between a printed plaid and a woven plaid on a lightweight fabric in which the print paste would have penetrated through to the back of fabric if printed.

2. You are a department store fabric buyer for the store's private label lines of apparel and interior furnishings. A new print line is being developed. You are seeking the services of commission printers and want to be sure they have the proper printing machinery for your needs. For each of the following fabric printing needs, indicate the type of printing machinery you would require and state the reason for each selection:

   a. Cotton sateen. Shower curtain fabric. One pattern of repeat is 72 inches vertical (warpwise) height. Long design life; several seasons.

   b. Polyester/cotton batiste. Blouse fabric. Striped print with vertical (warpwise) stripes. Design is seasonal; one season.

   c. Rayon challis. Dress fabric. Small repeat. Design has very fine lines and print details. Staple design; many seasons.

   d. Cotton flannel. Children's sleep wear. Small repeat in children's motif (animals or cartoon figures). Staple design; many seasons.

   e. Polyester interlock knit. Ladies' sportswear tops. Bright bold design motif. High yardage expectations but seasonal; one season.

   f. Cotton poplin. Men's novelty shirt. Large patterned geometric. Risky design; fad item.

   g. Acetate and rayon faille. Tablecloth fabric. Large 20 × 20-inch repeat of floral design. High yardage expectations; many seasons.

3. Explain how you can distinguish between a blotch print and a discharge print.

4. A fabric is made in an engineered print, with two different designs on a single bolt of cloth. When the fabric is cut, one design will become the front, and the other the back of a blouse. Why has the print been made in the manner stated instead of printing each design on separate bolts of cloth?

5. What advantages does the digital printing process offer to the fabric development process?

6. What is the most important factor relating to the ability of flock prints to be laundered or dry-cleaned?

7. What is a strike off? What is its purpose in a printing process?

8. What is the difference between a wet and a dry print?

9. If a dye used to print a textile is chemically locked into the fabric, why may the printed design fade over time?

CHAPTER TEN
Textile Finishing

Objectives

▶ To understand how textile finishing alters and adapts fabrics for their intended end uses.

▶ To understand the differences between aesthetic and functional finishes.

▶ To be familiar with specific textile finishing processes and their effects on fabrics.

▶ To be knowledgeable concerning the adverse effects and compromises involved in many textile finishes.

Use fabrics in the Textile Finishes section of the Fabric Science Swatch Kit *for this chapter.*

Key Terms Related to Textiles

acid stiffening
acid washing
aesthetic finishes
antimicrobial finishes
antistatic finishes
bleaching
boil-off
calendering
carbonizing
cellulase
chlorination of wool
ciré calendering
compressive shrinkage
crease-resistant finishes (CRF)
curing
desizing
durable finish
durable press

durable water repellents
embossed calendering
fabric softening
fabric stiffening
finishing
flame-resistant finishes
fluorocarbon
foam-chemical finishing
fragrance
fulling
functional finishes
glazed calendering
hot-head pressers
mercerization
moiré
mothproof finishes
nanotechnology
napping

no iron
nondurable repellents
oleophilic
optical brighteners
permanent finish
plissé
postcuring
precuring
pretreatment processes
progressive shrinkage
relaxation shrinkage
repellant finishes
residual finishes
resin add-on
resins
Schreiner calendering
scour or scouring
seersucker

semidurable finish
shearing
shrinkage control
simple calendering
singeing
softener finishes
soil-release finishes
solvent scouring
sponging
stiffening finishes
stone washing
sueding
temporary finish
textile wet processing
ultraviolet
waterproof
water repellents
wrinkle resistance

A marketable textile fabric is not completed after fabric formation, dyeing, or printing. Fabrics usually still need to undergo an additional processing known as **finishing**, which is the final processing before the fabric is cut into apparel or made into articles such as towels, curtains, or draperies. Finishing is what makes fabrics more suitable for their intended end use. Final inspection to ascertain fabric quality is performed at the completion of finishing. There are many types of finishes; some make fabrics softer, some stiffer, some water repellent, some shrink resistant. Some fabrics may have two or more finishing treatments.

Finishes have such a profound effect on fabrics that the same greige goods can be finished to produce several types of fabrics. Muslin, chintz, and plissé (imitation seersucker) can all be made from the same construction of cotton-print cloth greige goods.

Not all finishes produce entirely positive results on treated fabrics; sometimes tradeoffs have to be made. Making fabric crease resistant, for example, also causes stiffening of some types of cloth. Certain finishes are so temporary that they completely lose their effectiveness after one laundering. Therefore, understanding textile finishes and the properties they impart, the fibers and fabrics to which they may be applied, and their limitations and shortcomings are important to an overall understanding of textiles.

Most finishing processing is performed in the same plants as dyeing or printing. Most dyers and printers are also finishers, with finishing being considered a separate but integrated department of the dyeing or printing organization.

Computers have become commonly used in the finishing process (as well as in the dyeing and printing processes). Their use results in a more efficient operation. Better controls means corrections are quickly made (e.g., chemicals, quantities, temperature, and fabric tension). Computers also result in improved recycling processes. Combining finishing processes is also a trend. The result is reduced use of chemicals, water and energy, as well as a shortening of processing time.

Classification of Finishes

Textile finishes and finishing are classified in several ways, the most common classifications being aesthetic finishes, which modify the appearance and/or hand or drape of fabrics, and functional finishes, which improve the performance properties of fabrics. The textile finishes discussed in this chapter are presented in these two categories.

Finishes are also categorized as chemical finishes and mechanical finishes. These are sometimes called wet finishing and dry finishing, respectively. Chemical finishes are usually applied to fabric by padding (see p. 161), followed by curing or drying. Mechanical finishes usually involve specific physical treatment to a fabric surface to cause a change in fabric appearance.

Finishes are also categorized by their degree of permanence. These finishes are called permanent, durable, semidurable, and temporary:

Permanent finishes usually involve a chemical change in fiber structure and do not change or alter throughout the life of a fabric.

Durable finishes usually last throughout the life of the article, but effectiveness becomes diminished after each cleaning, and near the end of the normal-use life of the article, the finish is nearly removed.

Semidurable finishes last through several launderings or dry cleanings and many are renewable in home laundering or dry cleaning.

Temporary finishes are removed or substantially diminished the first time an article is laundered or dry cleaned.

Pretreatment Processes

Pretreatment processes consist of cleaning operations to rid the fabric of all soil and additives that have accumulated during the weaving or knitting process. These processes are usually the first treatments a fabric undergoes after leaving the loom or knitting machine, and are required before any dyeing, printing, or finishing can be accomplished. In the strict definition of finishing, pretreatment processes do not qualify as textile finishes because they are performed prior to dyeing or printing. However, many authorities consider these processes as basic finishes; therefore, they are included in this chapter.

Greige goods contain warp starches or other sizing (to add stiffness and strength to warp yarns during weaving), as well as oils, waxes, and other lubricants, plus floor dirt or other soils picked up during processing. Complete removal of all these impurities is necessary before any dyeing, printing, or finishing can be done. The processes for cleaning are varied depending on the fiber, the impurities present, and the fabric construction. In cotton, cotton-blend, silk, and manufactured-fiber fabrics, the processes are generally known as the **boil-off**. In woolens and worsteds, it is called a **scour** or **scouring**. Boil-off or scouring is similar to ordinary laundering. Fabrics are treated with soaps or detergents, rinsed, and then dried. If warp starches are present, the fabric is treated with an additional process known as **desizing**. Enzyme solutions are used to dissolve the starch.

Many knit fabrics contain oils that were used for lubricating and softening yarns and to reduce static during knitting. These are removed in a process called **solvent scouring**. This is actually dry cleaning, and is efficient and effective for knit fabrics. The solvents used can be recycled and therefore do not impose a burden on local sewage and waste systems.

Woolen and worsted fabrics may undergo an additional pretreatment process known as **carbonizing.** This process removes leaf particles and bits of grass and other cellulosic impurities that become embedded in the wool while sheep are grazing. The treatment consists of steeping the wool fabric in sulfuric acid, which destroys the cellulose but leaves the wool unharmed.

Another pretreatment process is an operation called **singeing,** which involves burning off projecting fibers or filament splinters from the surface of a fabric. Improper singeing or elimination of this operation results in unclear print patterns, mottled fabric surface, or premature pilling of fabrics.

Pretreatment processes may also include **bleaching.** Fabrics to be dyed in light to medium shades, as well as most prints, are first bleached. Bleaches are required to obtain pure whites because natural fibers are rarely pure white in their natural state; they are usually slightly yellowish or grayish. Bleaches are chemical agents that react with the color compounds in the fiber and render them colorless. Our eyes see the fabric as pure white. (Bleaches are also important in the home care of clothing and are discussed on p. 207.)

Most bleached fabrics are also additionally whitened with **optical brighteners** if the fabric is to remain white or dyed to pastel shades.[1] These substances have the capability of absorbing ultraviolet light and emitting visible blue fluorescent light. The result is a whitening and brightening effect. They have poor fastness to light and washing. Because almost all household soaps and detergents contain optical brightener additives, the whitening effect is renewed with each laundering.

Sometimes a fluorescent brightener is added to the spinning solution of a manufactured fiber to brighten it optically. Bleach may not be effective on some fibers.

The effectiveness of optical brighteners is dependent on an ultraviolet source of light. Natural sunlight is

such a source. Fluorescent lighting is also, but to a small degree. Ultraviolet lamps (also called blacklight lamps) are another source. Incandescent lighting (regular household bulbs) contains no ultraviolet, so optical brighteners have no effect on fabrics used under this lighting.

Resins

Resins are the chemical group applied as wet finishes and used in many of the finishes described later in this chapter. For example, they are the principal chemical ingredient in many crease-resistant finishes and also for durable press (see p. 193), and are used primarily on cellulosic and cellulosic-blend fabrics.

There are several types of resins, but most belong to the urea formaldehyde or related groups of organic compounds. These formaldehyde components have been suspected of being carcinogenic (cancer-causing) materials. Another group of resins, used less extensively due to their relatively high cost and limited effectiveness, are the dimethyl urea glyoxal compounds. The latter are nonformaldehyde producing. Resins are colorless and are applied to fabrics in liquid form (usually on a padder, as described on p. 161), then dried, and finally treated at high temperature, causing the resin to react chemically with the cellulosic component of the fabric. This heat treatment is called **curing** and requires from 30 seconds to 2 minutes at temperatures of 300°F to 350°F (145°C to 165°C), depending on fabric type and the amount of resin used. Resins are classified as durable (rather than permanent). Curing can be performed at lower temperatures, but this requires longer exposure time.

Resins have a profound effect on and cause changes in the hand, drapability, and physical characteristics of textiles. Although many benefits are achieved through these changes, there are also some shortcomings. Resins modify fabrics in the following ways:

▶ They add stiffness to fabrics and are thus used as stiffening agents or to create a firm hand.

▶ They stabilize fabrics in the same shape or configuration as when the resin was cured. Fabrics cured in a smooth, nonwrinkled condition will return to that shape after being wrinkled in wear, and fabrics cured with creases in garments will retain these creases.

▶ Yarns in fabric are stabilized and resist shrinkage in laundering.

▶ Fabrics become less moisture absorbent and thus dry more rapidly. They are also less comfortable in warm, humid weather.

1. These substances are also called ultraviolet brighteners, UV brighteners, fluorescent brighteners, optical whiteners, and white dyes.

- Resins combine chemically with cellulosic fibers (cotton, rayon, etc.) to cause significant reductions in abrasion resistance, breaking strength, and tear strength. This reduction can be as high as 50 percent.

- Most resins produce an offensive fishlike or formaldehyde odor in fabric. This odor eventually disappears on exposure to air and/or laundering. Ethylene glycol and similar compounds added to the resin bath have been found to be very effective in eliminating or reducing this odor.

- Resins have an affinity for oily soils, creating a soiling problem. Soil-release finishes (see p. 197) help alleviate this problem.

The degree of these changes is dependent on the amount of resin applied (called the **resin add-on**). Add-on may range from less than 2 percent for certain crease-resistant finishes to 10 percent for some durable-press applications.

Aesthetic Finishes

Aesthetic finishes change the appearance, drapability, and hand (feel) of fabrics. For convenience, each aesthetic finish is listed and discussed alphabetically and not necessarily in order of importance. Table 10.1 provides a summary of textile finishes.

Calendering

Calendering is a process of pressing or ironing a fabric at high speed and under high pressure. It is not a single type of finish. There are various types of calender machinery,

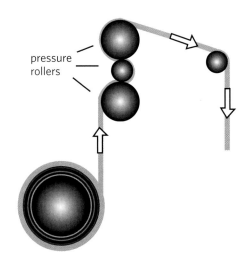

FIGURE 10.1
A calendar finishing machine.

each producing different types of pressed surface. All calender finishes are classified as mechanical finishing.

A calender machine, as shown in Figure 10.1, is fundamentally a mechanical device consisting of two or more large, rotating cylindrical rollers stacked on top of each other, generally about 70 inches wide (178 cm) and usually heated. The cylindrical rollers are in contact with each other under great pressure. Fabric being calendered passes around and between these cylinders and is pressed under great pressure. The specific type of calender-finished fabric varies with the nature of the cylinder surface, the speed of the cylinders, and the nature of the fabric being finished.

Simple Calendering
Simple calendering is a high-speed, high-pressure pressing of fabric (at approximately 100 yards/minute). The high pressure tends to flatten the yarns and makes the fabric softer and smoother, and it enhances the fabric's luster. The finish is used for woven flat fabrics of plain or simple twill weaves such as broadcloth, taffeta, chambray, chino, and sheeting.

Excessive pressure in this process produces excellent-looking lustrous fabric that may be seriously weakened because the yarns have been excessively flattened. Experienced buyers and quality control persons are usually cautious of fabrics tendered (see p. 202) by overcalendering.

Simple calendering is a temporary finish. The yarns in the fabric usually return to their natural round configuration on the first laundering or steaming. Figure 10.2 illustrates the before and after conditions of a fabric finished with simple calendering.

TABLE 10.1 Summary of Textile Finishes	
Aesthetic—Improved/Altered Appearance	Functional—Improved/Altered Performance
Calendering	Antimicrobial
Fragrance	Antistatic
Fulling	Crease resistant
Mercerization	Durable press
Napping and sueding	Flame resistant
Plissé	Mothproofed
Shearing	Shrinkage control
Softening	Soil release
Stiffening	Water and stain repellent
	Waterproof

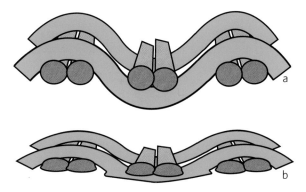

FIGURE 10.2
Yarn configuration in a fabric (a) before calendering and
(b) after calendering. The changed shape from round to flat
gives the fabric a smoother hand and more lustrous appearance.

FIGURE 10.3
Embossing rolls. The machine is initially run without fabric so
the pattern of the metal roll will be impressed in the soft roll.

Glazed Calendering

Polished cotton and chintz are two typical fabrics finished by using glazed calendering. **Glazed calendering** is the calendering finish to produce the high sheen of polished cotton and chintz. The calender machine used for these fabrics is a friction calender, sometimes called a chasing calender. One cylinder of the highly polished steel cylinder rotates at speeds much higher than the fabric passing through it, thus polishing the fabric.

Fabrics are first treated with starches or resins before calendering to help fill up the spaces between the yarns to yield the glazed appearance. Starches that are low in cost are semidurable; they are not suitable for laundering. Resins are usually durable for the life of a garment or product.

Ciré

Ciré calendaring is a type of glazed alendaring wherein the friction roller rotates at speeds much greater than with ordinary friction alendaring. The resultant fabric becomes highly lustrous and takes on a wet look. Fabrics of cotton, rayon, polyester, nylon, and blends of these may be given a ciré finish. The fabrics are treated with waxes or resins prior to friction alendaring, to achieve the highly polished effect. When thermoplastic fiber filament-yarn fabrics are ciré finished, the fabric becomes moderately water repellent due to the flattening and partial fusing of fibers. The fabric also develops a highly polished surface.

Ciré is not the name of a fabric, but fabrics with this finish are popularly called ciré fabric or ciré cloth.

Embossed Calendering

Embossed calendering produces a three-dimensional design on the fabric. This is done on a special embossing calender in which the roller cylinder is engraved with the

embossing design. The pattern is thus pushed or shaped into the cloth when the fabric passes between the rollers. (See Figure 10.3.)

Some embossed fabrics are made to imitate more costly woven jacquard or dobby designs. You can distinguish embossed fabrics by careful examination with a pick glass. Embossed fabrics reveal a regular, consistent weave (plain or twill weave) and jacquard or dobby fabrics have yarn floats in the design area.

Embossed patterns of fabrics treated with resins and cured after embossing are durable. Embossing of fabrics of thermoplastic fibers is permanent because the heated metal roll heat-sets the design.

Moiré Calendering

A **moiré** finish produces a wood-grain design on the face side of the fabric.

There are two methods for producing moiré. The first uses an engraved cylinder roller on the calender, which flattens one part of the fabric more than another, causing the different light reflectance that we see as moiré. The second method utilizes smooth calender rollers. In this method, two fabrics, each face to face, are fed through the calender. Ribbed fabrics, such as taffeta or faille, are necessary for this process. The high pressure on the calender rolls causes the ribs to squeeze into each other in certain areas, thus flattening parts of the fabric and creating the light reflectance pattern we see as moiré. In the first method, definite repeat pattern moiré is produced. The second method produces a completely random, nonrepetitive moiré.

Moiré finishes may be temporary, durable, or permanent. A cotton or rayon moiré finish is temporary, unless the fabric has first been resin treated and then cured after calendering to make a durable finish. Moiré finishes on thermoplastic fiber fabrics are permanent if a heated roller is used (heat sets the pattern).

Schreiner Calendering

Schreiner calendering produces a low, soft-key luster on the fabric surface as distinct from the high glaze of the glazing calender or the luster shine of the simple calender. The finish is widely used on nylon tricot, cotton and cotton-polyester sateen, and damask table linens.

To produce this effect, one of the steel cylinders of the calender is embossed with very fine diagonal lines, about 250 lines per inch. These embossings are barely visible to the naked eye.

In addition to the soft luster, Schreiner calendering also produces a softer hand and improved fabric cover.

Schreiner calendering may be a permanent, durable, or temporary finish. The finish is permanent if the fiber content of the fabric being finished is thermoplastic (heat-set with heated roller). It is a durable finish if the fabric is resin treated (but not cured) prior to calendering, and it is temporary if the fiber is nonthermoplastic and has not been previously treated.

Fragrances

New technology now provides textiles with an aromatherapeutic effect. Various **fragrances** are available as well as an odor eliminator that neutralizes unpleasant odors, such as perspiration and smoke.

FIGURE 10.4
Prada-owned British footwear brand Church's designs weekend bag made from boiled wool in contrasting colors.

The fragrances are enclosed in microcapsules and applied during finishing processes. The microcapsules rupture on movement or as a result of rubbing with the skin. The fragrance is gradually released.

The same technique can be utilized for other benefits to the wearer. A skin moisturizer, vitamins, or repellents (e.g., insect) could be contained in a microcapsule and thus bring added value.

Fulling

Fulling is a permanent finish used on wool fabrics. The process is a carefully controlled scouring or laundering process to induce progressive felting shrinkage in wool fabrics. The resultant fulled fabric is smoother, more compact, and has yarns more tightly embedded than an unfulled fabric. Woolens are frequently heavily fulled. Some woolen cloths, such as melton (used in coats), are so heavily fulled that careful examination is required to distinguish them from true felt. The presence of yarns is the distinguishing factor. Fabrics of worsted are usually very lightly fulled. (See Figure 10.4.)

Mercerization

Mercerization is one of the most important chemical finishes for cotton. This finish imparts luster to the cotton, increases its strength by nearly 25 percent, and improves dye affinity, producing brighter shades than are possible with unmercerized cotton. It also enhances fabric hand and drapability. The finish consists of treating the material while under tension with cold, concentrated sodium hydroxide solution (lye). Fabrics and yarns can be mercerized, but fibers cannot. Mercerization is a permanent finish, and it is one of the few finishes applied prior to dyeing.

Napping and Sueding

Napping is a mechanical finish in which woven or knitted fabrics are passed against rotating, bristled, wire-covered brushes. This action results in fibers being raised from the fabric face. The overall effect is a fabric with raised fiber surface. Examples of napped fabrics are flannelette, canton flannel, rayon flannel, and brushed rayon. Woolen and worsted napped fabrics include kersey, melton, and wool fleece.[2]

Napped fabrics have a softer hand and provide better insulation than the same materials unnapped because they can entrap more air, hence their wide use in blankets,

---

2. Fine woolens are napped with brushes whose surfaces are embedded with vegetable burrs known as teasels, rather than the convenient bristled wire. This process is known as teaseling.

sleepwear, and winter clothing. However, the insulating value of cotton and rayon napped fabrics is not long lasting. The low resilience of these fibers causes premature flattening of the fiber nap. The nap can be partially restored by frequent brushing.

One difficulty with napped fabrics is that the napped-fiber ends are subject to pilling and/or rather rapid wear at sleeve ends, coat fronts, buttonholes, elbows, and other abrasion points. Wearing out of the nap at these points can occur in less than one season's wear in a garment that is worn every day. Napped-fabric garments are not recommended for garments in which hard wear is anticipated.

Fabrics must be especially constructed for napping. The filling yarns used are made with soft (low) twist, as these are the yarns that are napped. Most napped fabrics are brushed in one warpwise direction after napping and take on a definite top and bottom configuration. They must, therefore, be examined carefully before being cut into garments.

Sueding, a finish similar to napping, is a mechanical finish that produces a soft, suedelike surface on the fabric. Instead of the rotating, bristled, wire-covered brushes used in napping, the rotating cylinders used for sueding consist of a sandpaperlike material.

Many napped fabrics are also sheared, a process that makes the napped surface more uniform.

Plissé

Plissé is the name of a finish as well as the name of a fabric produced with this finish. It is a permanent finish, produced on cotton by the action of sodium hydroxide. The sodium hydroxide is printed on the fabric as a paste. The fabric shrinks only where the sodium hydroxide is applied, producing a puckered effect.

Plissé fabrics usually do not require ironing. If they must be ironed, caution should be exercised not to pull the fabric while pressing because the plissé effect can be severely flattened. An inexpensive plissé can also be made by embossing, but the effect does not last as long as in plissé made with the use of a chemical. When the sodium hydroxide is applied as lengthwise stripes, the fabric puckers and takes on the appearance of seersucker.

Seersucker is a fabric with a lengthwise-striped puckered effect, but it is produced by alternate stripes of loose and tight warp yarns. Plissé is a cheaper imitation of seersucker. It does not have the depth or degree of pucker that is common to seersucker. You can distinguish seersucker from plissé by stretching the fabric in the warp direction. Plissé puckers stretch out flat; seersucker puckers do not.

Shearing

Shearing is a process used to cut off surface fibers on fabrics. It makes uniform the surface of napped fabrics and pile fabrics to provide uniform pile height. A fabric shear, the high-speed machine that performs this operation, has cutting action similar to that of a lawn mower. The blades are stationary and the fabric moves to the cutting blades.

Softening

Cotton batiste, nylon taffeta, and polyester-cotton blend broadcloth (the latter two have been heat-set finished) are examples of fabrics having **softener finishes**.

Some fabrics need to be softened to give a more pleasant hand and to provide better drapability. Finishes to make fabrics softer are used for this purpose. Prior to being finished by a softening process, the fabrics may have been harsh and stiff because of their construction (i.e., tightly twisted yarns, dense woven plain weave) or possibly due to some prior finishing process (i.e., heat-setting to render the fabric shrink-resistant, resin treated to make the fabric durable press).

Fabric softening may be accomplished by either mechanical or chemical finishing procedures. Simple calendering softens hand, but is only a temporary finish. Chemical finishes for softening involve treatment of fabric with various chemicals. The most effective and most widely used are silicone compounds, which are durable. This finish is applied by pad method and dried. Other chemical finishes, less costly than silicone, and semidurable, are various types of emulsified oils and waxes, and cationic detergents. The latter are also used in softeners for home and commercial laundering (see p. 210).

Stiffening

Typical fabrics that have **stiffening finishes** are buckram, crinoline, lawn, and voile.

Some fabrics need to be made stiffer and more crisp than they would otherwise be in order to properly fulfill an intended end use. **Fabric stiffening** may be done with several chemical finishes, all applied by pad and either dried or cured. Starch of various types is widely used as a stiffening finish. In addition to making fabric stiffer, the starch also adds body and weight to the fabric, and sometimes misleads consumers into believing they are purchasing better fabrics when, in fact, the fabrics may be poorly made. Starch finishes are temporary and need to be restored by home or commercial laundering (see p. 210) to maintain their stiff hand. Resins are widely used as stiffening agents. Use of resins on cellulosic fibers, however, causes tendering when heavy add-ons of the resins are used.

Fine-yarn, sheer cotton fabrics can be finished to be both stiff and transparent. The process, called **acid stiffening,** involves the rapid immersion of fabric in sulfuric acid, followed by immediate neutralization in sodium hydroxide. The finish is permanent. Organdy is an example of fabric produced by the acid-stiffening process.

Stone Washing, Acid Washing, and Cellulase

Stone washing, acid washing, and cellulase are garment finishing processes primarily used for denim and similar items to make them appear worn and partially faded. **Stone washing** transforms new unworn garments into used-looking, faded garments. These items are softer and more comfortable to wear, and they have a more casual appearance than traditional stiff and boardy new denim.

The process is a mass-production laundering procedure. (Production ranges from 50 to 3,000 garments per hour, depending on machine type and size.) Pumice stones, which are lightweight and porous, are added to the laundry mix to provide the abrasion for the worn look, hence the term stone wash.

Acid washing is a bleaching process that consists of soaking or dampening the pumice with an oxidizing bleach (sodium hypochlorite). The term acid wash is a misnomer because no acid is used. The same process is also called frosting and ice washing. Each new season brings new names to market for the same bleaching process, but with different degrees of intensity.

Cellulase is an enzyme that is sometimes added to pumice stones and/or bleach, or used separately. The cellulase attacks and weakens cellulosic fiber, first on the fiber surface. Because dyes used in denim are mostly on the surface, the effect is a lightening of color, which gives a worn look. Cellulase also destroys fiber fuzz on fabric which reduces the chance of pilling. Denim is a very strong fabric to begin with, so carefully controlled cellulase treatment has only minimal effect on durability.

Garment finishing for denim and similar apparel has grown over the past decade from small, almost cottage-industry, to a major industry with exacting test procedures and standards for quality assurance. This work is not performed by traditional textile finishers, but by companies that specialize in this work, most of which were originally industrial laundering facilities. (See Figure 10.5 a–c.)

Functional Finishes

Functional finishes are finishes that improve the performance properties of fabrics. They usually relate to comfort,

safety, or health. For convenience, each category of functional finishes is listed and discussed alphabetically and not necessarily in order of importance.

Antimicrobial Finishes

Textiles are an excellent material for the growth of microorganisms since the basic ingredients of nutrients, moisture, oxygen, and the appropriate temperature are often present. Wool (protein), cotton (cellulose), soil, and some finishes can be a source of nutrients for microorganisms.

Antimicrobial finishes, also known as antibacterial and antiseptic finishes, involve chemical agents that inhibit the growth of bacteria and fungi. The result is a reduction or even prevention of odor-causing germs as well as the elimination of fungi, such as mold and mildew, that feed on cellulosic fibers, producing stains, odors, and weakened fabric.

The finish is important for items in contact with the skin, such as underwear and diapers, shoe linings, socks, bed linens, and surgical packs. These finishes are low in cost, easily applied, and durable to laundering and dry cleaning.

The use of protective antimicrobial textiles can also provide protection to medical and healthcare facilities against the potential transmission of diseases. It has been found that infectious diseases have been transmitted from surface contacts to textile products such as furniture, bedding, privacy curtains, surgeon gowns, and nurses' clothing.

Antistatic Finishes

Antistatic finishes involve chemical substances applied as wet finishes for the purpose of reducing or eliminating static. These chemicals absorb small amounts of moisture from the atmosphere, thus reducing the dryness of the fabric that causes the static condition (see p. 27).

Antistatic finishes are semidurable, and they wash out or wear out in several launderings or dry cleanings. They can, however, be renewed at home with commercial sprays made for the purpose. Fabric softeners used in home laundering also reduce static. Permanent antistatic effects are obtainable with manufactured fibers that have been especially modified for this purpose. Other methods used for static control are using fiber coating, metal-conductive latex fabric backing, and 100 percent metallic yarns.

Antistatic fabrics are used in carpeting, apparel (noncling), operating room gowns, drapes, clean-air suits, and barriers around electronic equipment. Medical antistatic apparel must be able to be sterilized during laundering and still retain its antistatic properties.

a

b

Crease-Resistant Finishes

Crease-resistant finishes, popularly known as **CRF**, are applied to fabrics for the purpose of reducing annoying and unsightly wrinkling in apparel such as blouses, shirts, pants, and dresses. CRF are most often applied to fabrics made from cotton, rayon, and flax (fibers with low resilience), which are especially susceptible to wrinkling. Resin-pad treatment and curing (see p. 187) is the usual method by which CRF is achieved.

CRF are low-resin add-on applications (about one-fifth of that usually used in durable press) whose purpose is to reduce wrinkling during wear. Ironing and pressing are still required after laundering, but somewhat less than for an untreated article. CRF fabrics are only slightly stiffer and have only slightly less resistance to abrasion and compared to nontreated fabrics.

Durable Press

Durable press and **wrinkle resistance** are not specific textile finishes but rather descriptive terms for garments or other sewn products (e.g., bed sheets, table linens) that maintain a pressed appearance through many launderings and wearings and do not require ironing. Permanent press is often used as a synonymous term.

The object of durable press is to provide fabrics and sewn products with the ability to resist or shed wrinkles formed during wearing and washing as well as to retain or resist the removal of creases or pleats (which, in effect, are sharp wrinkles) intentionally put into the fabric.

There are two basic systems by which these objectives may be attained. The first is by heat-setting of thermoplastic fibers (see p. 27). The second is by resin treatment and curing in fabrics of cellulosic-polyester

c

FIGURE 10.5
Finishing techniques in use at the Von Dutch factory in Los Angeles.

blends and of 100 percent cellulosic fibers. The durable press finish can be performed either to fabric or to the completed garment (product). The chemical used can be applied either to the fabric or later to the product.

These finishing treatments stabilize the fibers in the fabric in the particular configuration it had when it was heat-set or cured. If a fabric is heat-set or cured with no wrinkles but with pleats, it tends to shed the wrinkles formed from wearing and laundering and retain the pleats put into it during processing. When washing durable press articles, they should be removed promptly when dry. The heat and weight of the other items in the dryer may cause wrinkles to form. (See Figure 10.6.)

Performance parameters for wrinkle-resistant fabrics include smoothness rating, shrinkage control, crease retention, finish durability, strength retention, shade retention, and compatibility with other finishing agents.

Resin Treatment and Curing

Resin treatment and curing of fabrics referred to previously are done by one of two processes: precuring or postcuring.

Precuring

Precuring is the most frequently used resin treatment process and involves treating and curing the fabric at the textile finishing plant. The fabric is sold to an apparel producer in a completely finished state. The fabric is set in a flat position and used for items that do not require extensive shaping (e.g., blouses, shirts, dresses, bed sheets, curtains, draperies).

Almost all precured fabrics are blends of cellulosic fibers and polyester. The polyester component is unaffected by the resin-induced strength- and abrasion-resistance loss of the cellulosic component.

Precured fabrics may sometimes be used for shaped garments (such as pants with a center crease). When this is done, items are pressed with high-temperature pressing equipment called **hot-head pressers**. This equipment reaches temperatures that heat-set the polyester component of the fabric. The results, although satisfactory, are less effective than those resulting from the postcuring method.

Postcuring

The second method, **postcuring**, involves curing the resin on an already sewn and completed garment. Actually, there are two types of postcured processes. In the first the textile finishing plant applies and dries the resin, but does not cure it. The fabric is sold to an apparel producer in an uncured but sensitized state. It is sewn into garments and then pressed (at relatively low temperature) to impart pants and/or sleeve creases, pleats, and other shaping. The entire garment is then cured as an individual item of clothing. Postcured, durable-press garments retain their wrinkle-free and crease-retentive properties better than the precured type. They may be expected to retain these properties through 40 to 50 launderings.

The fabrics and garments produced by this type of postcuring are almost always blends of cellulosic fiber and polyester. The polyester compensates for the abrasion-resistance and strength loss the cellulose undergoes due to the resin application.

The second type of postcuring process is performed on 100-percent-cotton fabrics. Apparel products made by this process are usually described as **wrinkle-free, wrinkle-resistant, no iron**, or simply **WR**. The fabrics used, methods of application, and results obtained are different from those of the durable-press method described above. To reduce the resin-induced loss of abrasion resistance and tensile strength of cellulose, specially constructed fabrics and unique finishing treatments are required. The fabric used is of long-staple cotton, tightly twisted yarn, and tightly constructed (thus stronger and more abrasion-resistant than average fabric). The resin finish consists of the following modified postcuring process:

1. The completely sewn but untreated garments are first immersed in or sprayed with a resin solution, and then semidried and pressed at warm temperatures while still damp.

2. Curing of the garments follows quickly after pressing in specially constructed conveyor ovens.

This method minimizes deterioration of cellulose because relatively low add-on of resin is required. The resultant product has a medium-soft hand often enhanced with silicone softeners as compared to the firm hand and somewhat stiffer cotton-polyester postcured garments. The wrinkle-free/no-iron condition is retained for about 12 to 15 launderings, rather than the 40 to 50 launderings to be expected with the cotton-polyester durable press method. Despite the lowered performance and higher costs (premium grades of cotton fibers and tighter construction of fabric), the wrinkle-resistant types are preferred by many consumers because of the greater comfort and softness provided by the 100-percent cotton product.

Most 100-percent cotton, wrinkle-resistant fabrics are used for casual wear and sportswear such as pants and shorts. The process is also used for men's dress shirts, skirts, blouses, and sleepwear.

Flame-Resistant Finishes

Most textiles burn if ignited. Serious injury and even death have resulted from clothing articles that have caught fire. Carelessly lighting a cigarette, having a draped, flowing sleeve caught in a cooking stove flame, and being in a burning building can result in clothing catching fire.

A 1967 Amendment to the Flammable Fabric Act of 1953 prohibits the use of fabrics that burn very rapidly and are considered dangerous (see Chapter 17). This law separates (and makes illegal) the dangerously flammable fabrics from those that may be normally burnable. There are no federal laws covering the flammability of the normally burnable fabrics except for special federal regulations pertaining to children's sleepwear, carpets and rugs, mattresses, and mattress pads. Upholstery fabric flammability is also regulated by a voluntary industry standard.

Fabrics may be flame resistant if made from fibers that resist burning. This includes wool and similar hair-protein fibers as well as manufactured fibers that have been modified to impart flame-retardant properties during fiber manufacture. If flame-resistant properties are not used, flame-resistant finishes must be applied to achieve this property.

Flame-resistant finishes[3] are applied as wet finishes and, depending on the chemical used, are either dried or cured on the fabric. Many chemical flame-retardant products are used by finishers. None are universally suitable for all fabrics. Fiber content, end use, method of cleaning, and desired hand and drapability are factors that a finisher needs to consider in selecting proper flame retardants.

Unfortunately, use of these finishes results in fabrics with one or more of the following shortcomings: stiffening and loss of fabric drapability, significant strength loss in fabric, loss of finish in laundering (nondurable), and ineffectiveness when laundered in household bleach, with soaps (as distinguished from detergents), or with water softeners.

Mothproof Finishes

Moth larvae and carpet beetles are known to attack animal-fiber fabrics. When these fibers are in blends, the blend fiber as well as the animal fiber may be attacked.

There are several ways to provide mothproof finishes. Some are merely temporary sprays or finishes that may be applied by the consumer. Far more effective is a chemical finish that is permanent, easy to apply, and relatively low in cost, but that must be added at the time of dyeing. This chemical, usually added to the dye bath while the wool or other animal fiber is being dyed, simply makes the wool indigestible to the larvae or carpet beetle, resulting in permanent mothproofing.

Shrinkage-Control Finishes

Some knowledge of the causes of shrinkage is required to appreciate the methods and effectiveness of the various finishes used in shrinkage control.

Fabric design and construction affect the amount of shrinkage that occurs. An openly constructed fabric (low number of yarns per inch) shrinks more than a comparable compact fabric (high number of yarns per inch) because in the first fabric the fibers (and yarns) are able to move more easily. For the same reason, fabrics containing low-twist yarns tend to shrink more than fabrics with tightly twisted yarns.

It is important to know a fabric's shrinkage potential because it helps determine how a garment should be designed and constructed. All the garment components, including fabric, decorations, linings, and thread should be compatible shrinkagewise or else puckering and garment distortion can result. Table 10.2 lists various shrinkage-control treatments and their features.

Frequently, even after fabrics have been properly preshrunk in finishing, a small amount of shrinkage potential remains. This shrinkage is called residual shrinkage.

There are two major kinds of fabric shrinkage: relaxation shrinkage and progressive shrinkage.

Relaxation Shrinkage

Relaxation shrinkage occurs because the fibers and yarns are under considerable tension when fabrics are made. For example, fibers have been drawn and twisted to spin the yarn, warp yarns have been tightly stretched on a loom, and knitted stitches elongate when they are off wound from a knitting machine. Later, when the fabric becomes wet or steamed in a tensionless condition, the stresses and strains become relaxed, the fabric draws up on itself and, as the name implies, relaxation occurs. Relaxation shrinkage can also occur when a fabric is exposed to high heat (molecular shifting occurs, releasing stresses within the fibers). Relaxation shrinkage occurs only once—the first time the fabric is laundered or dry cleaned.

---

3. It should be noted that the terms flame-resistant, flame-retardant, fire-resistant, and fire-retardant are all used interchangeably in the text. This has been done because these terms are used interchangeably in the textile industry. The terms mean that the textile material (i.e., fiber, yarn, fabric, or finish) possesses the property of difficulty of ignition, and, if ignited, a slow rate of burning or self-extinguishment.

TABLE 10.2 Shrinkage Control Methods	
Method, Name, and Use	Special Features and Comments
Compressive shrinkage	
For woven fabrics of cotton, high wet modulus rayon, linen, and tubular-knit cotton fabrics	A relaxation shrinkage method. Consists of mechanically compressing the fabric lengthwise by overfeeding onto a large roller covered by damp blankets. Sanforized® is a well-known trademark for fabrics treated by this method, but many fabrics treated by the method carry no trademark. Special adaptations of compressive shrinkage are used for cotton-knit underwear fabrics.
Heat-set	
For fabrics made from thermoplastic fibers (e.g., nylon, polyester, acrylic)	A relaxation shrinkage method. Based on the principle that thermoplastic materials will become stabilized in the configuration in which they happen to be when heated to their softening temperature. Woven and knitted fabrics thus become stabilized by being heated.[a]
Sponging	
For fabrics made from wool (woolens and worsteds)	A relaxation shrinkage method. Consists of thoroughly wetting the fabric (with water or steam) and allowing the material to dry slowly in a relaxed, tensionless state. London shrunk, cold-water shrunk, and open-steam sponged are the names of three methods of sponging. It is important to note that this process does not make wool washable or shrinkproof because it does not control progressive shrinkage.[b] It merely permits wool to be steam pressed or caught in rain without severe shrinking.
Resin treatment	
For rayon and cotton fabrics	A relaxation shrinkage method. Impregnating rayon or cotton with resins and then curing stabilizes the fabric and thus reduces its tendency to distort. The resins also provide crease resistance. Increasing the resin content improves shrink and crease resistance but also causes fabric stiffness. Resin-treated rayons may be machine washable, but on gentle cycle only. Hand laundering is preferable.
Chlorination	
For wool fabrics	A progressive shrinkage method. Chlorine treatment attacks the wool surface scales, thus reducing the ability of the wool to felt. A low-cost method, but it has serious disadvantages: loss of strength and rough, harsh hand. As a consequence, chlorination is rarely used.
Special application resins	
For wool fabrics	A progressive shrinkage method. Applications of resins for wool shrinkage control have been practiced for some time, using many different formulas, none of which has proved successful. Reasons include: some only last several launderings, and most do only a marginal job in control of shrinkage. The certification mark Superwash® indicates a standard of machine-washability performance for wool fabrics.

a. Permanent pleats can also be produced with these fabrics by heat-setting. The material is first mechanically pleated and then heat-set (e.g., at about 375°F for nylon).

b. Many textile mills sell wool fabrics in an unsponged state. Sponging is then undertaken by the apparel manufacturer, who contracts with firms that specialize in this work. Sponged fabrics, when sold by textile mills, are called "ready for the needle." Woolen and worsted fabrics that come through regular branded resources and are sold at sewing centers and over-the-counter yard goods departments are sponged before being offered for sale. Fabrics that come through jobbers or other secondary sources may not be sponged, however.

FIGURE 10.6
A garment with permanent pleating.

Progressive Shrinkage

Progressive shrinkage occurs each time a fabric is laundered. Unlike relaxation shrinkage, which occurs just once, progressive shrinkage continues and the fabric shrinks a bit more with each laundering. Of the major fibers, only wool (and similar natural-hair fibers) and viscose rayon are subject to progressive shrinking action. It occurs with wool because the wool fiber undergoes felting action while being laundered (see p. 40).

How shrinkage is controlled by the textile finisher, so that the apparel producer receives essentially preshrunk fabric, depends on the fiber content and method of construction of the fabric.

Soil-Release Finishes

Soil-release finishes are chemical finishes that permit relatively easy removal of soils (especially oily soils) with ordinary laundering. These finishes are necessary because hydrophobic fibers and resins have very low water absorbency. The fiber cannot become thoroughly wetted in laundering and thus the soils cannot be readily removed. The problem is most acute with stains of an oily nature because oily substances have an affinity for both the polyester and resin. Substances that have this attraction for oil are called **oleophilic**.

There are several types of soil-release finishes. They all accomplish the result of making the fiber more absorbent (hydrophilic), thus permitting better wettability for improved soil removal.

Most soil-release finishes are applied at the same time that the resins are applied to textiles. Most are durable through 40 to 50 launderings and are routinely applied to fabrics for work clothes and tablecloths. They are also often applied to fabrics for pants and skirts.

Several other benefits arise from the use of soil-release finishes. These include improved antistatic properties, improved fabric drapability, decreased pilling, and somewhat greater comfort in hot weather.

Use of Fluorocarbons

The application of **fluorocarbon** finishes imparts a durable stain repellent and stain (soil) release property. This finish imparts a fabric protector that enables the fabric to repel spills and stains on contact. Its non-stick properties have been widely recognized as a cookware coating Teflon® is a well-known fabric protector (DuPont™).

The stain-repellent finishes apply a coating to the fibers. The fluorocarbon stain-repellent finish penetrates the individual fiber, becoming part of the fiber. The surface property of the fabric is not altered. Liquids can be blotted up, soils wiped off and stains released during laundering.

The fluorocarbon treatment also results in making the fabric water repellent. This finish is being used in a wide range of fabrics and fiber types. Scotchgard™ (3M Corp.) is a widely used fluorocarbon-type durable repellent.

Ultraviolet-Absorbent Finish

It has been well documented that solar **ultraviolet** radiation (UVR) has a detrimental effect on the skin, including sunburn and skin cancer. The awareness of the need for adequate protection is increasing as is the recognition that summer-season clothing often provides poor protection.

The UVR passes through both the fibers and the spaces between the fibers (and yarns). The fabric construction affects the degree of protection. Wool and polyester inherently absorb ultraviolet rays whereas cotton and nylon allow them to pass through. A more compact, thicker, and woven fabric will offer more protection. (Knits usually have more spaces than a comparable woven material.) Also darker fabrics usually protect better than lighter fabrics of the same color (more dyestuff in the fabric).

Ultraviolet-absorbent finishes (also called UV blockers and sun-protective) offer protection since the chemicals used in the finishes applied absorb the UVR. The finish can coat the fabric surface or provide for fiber impregnation, which is more durable. Also, manufactured fibers can be produced with a sunlight resistant property. Another possible alternative is to have an additive incorporated into the washing detergent.

It would be helpful to the consumer if textile products were rated with the effective level of sun protection. However, washing, shrinkage, and wear can alter the rating. A rating system of sunscreen lotion already exists. A lotion with a sun-protection factor (SPF) of 30 blocks better than one with an SPF of 15.

Water Repellents

Water repellents are chemical finishes that resist the penetration of water into or through the fabric, but permit the passage of moisture or air through the fabric. (See Figure 10.7a.) The principle behind this ability is that the yarns, rather than the whole fabric, become coated with the repellent chemical, thus permitting the passage of vapor and air between the interlacings in the fabric. The chemicals used are waxes, emulsions, or other chemicals that allow raindrops and other liquids to remain on the fabric surface in a small bead rather than to spread out and become absorbed. (See Figure 10.8a and b.) The effect is similar to that observed when raindrops fall on a freshly waxed automobile. The same chemicals used for water repellence also function as stain repellents because they cause the liquid stain substances (gravy, fruit juice, coffee, etc.) to remain on the fabric surface and are easily

a

b

FIGURE 10.7
(a) Water repellent and (b) waterproof rainwear.

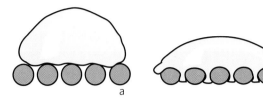

FIGURE 10.8
An enlarged view of a droplet of water on a fabric's surface. In fabric that has been treated with water-repellent finish, (a) the droplet beads up and remains on the surface. In fabric that is untreated (b) the water droplet spreads out and wicks between the yarns to the fabric back.

blotted up. Many different chemicals are used as repellents, and all are not equally effective. Repellents are categorized as nondurable or durable, and are also categorized by their ability to repel oily liquids (e.g., salad oil, gravy) as distinguished from water and water-bearing liquids (e.g., coffee, fruit juice).

Nondurable Repellents

Nondurable repellents are low in cost, easily applied, and in general provide excellent water resistence. However, they are easily removed in laundering or dry cleaning. Nondurable repellents are widely used and provide satisfactory service on tents, tarps, and other products that are not expected to be laundered or dry cleaned. Nondurable repellents do not provide satisfactory resistance to oily liquids.

Durable Repellents

There are several types of **durable water repellents.** Some are durable only to laundering, some only to dry cleaning, and others to both. Rainwear buyers and dealers in these products need to be certain that the types of repellent fabrics offered to them are compatible with the intended method of cleaning.

Additional Facts About Repellent Finishes

The effectiveness of water repellents depends as much on fabric construction as on the **repellent finish** itself. To be effective, repellents must be applied to tightly constructed fabrics. Professional buyers consider fabric construction specifications one of the most important criteria in the selection of rainwear and similar items.

The presence of soil in water repellent-treated fabrics drastically reduces its effectiveness. Similarly, hard creases and wrinkles in fabrics reduce effectiveness in the area of the crease or wrinkle.

Water-repellent garments do not provide protection in long, continual exposure to adverse wet weather. For example, police officers who require long-duration protection must wear coated or rubberized fabric garments for complete waterproofing. These fabrics are completely impermeable and, although they keep the wearer dry, are uncomfortable because they do not permit the body to breathe.

Small, seemingly negligible residues of soap or detergent that may be left in garments after laundering or dry cleaning can ruin the effectiveness of water repellents. Even the most durable of repellents is rendered nearly worthless unless the garment is very thoroughly rinsed to remove all traces of soap or detergent.

An easy examination to determine whether a fabric is water-repellent treated (or to determine whether a treated fabric is effective) is to sprinkle droplets of water on the material surface and wait for several minutes to see if it becomes absorbed. Water-repellent fabrics do not absorb. Rather, droplets form and remain on the surface.

Waterproof-Coated Fabrics

Fabrics can be made completely **waterproof** to provide protection under nearly all conditions of wet weather. A waterproof fabric, unlike a water-repellent fabric, is completely moisture-proofed. To achieve this, the fabric is coated or laminated with a film of natural or synthetic rubber or plastic, such as vinyl or polyurethane.

Even though they afford a greater measure of protection, coated or laminated waterproof fabrics are not necessarily more desirable than water-repellent fabrics. The former are uncomfortable, especially when worn for long periods of time or in active pursuits, such as hiking. Additionally, waterproof fabrics usually possess a rather firm, nondrapable hand, whereas the hand of water-repellent fabrics is not altered as a consequence of the particular finish. (See Figure 10.7b.)

Woven, knit, and nonwoven materials could be coated with a liquid layer of polymer. The resulting properties, in addition to waterproofing, can include stain resistance, dimensional stability, fire retardancy, and improved durability. The end uses include rainwear, a fireman's coat, roofing of air-supported structures, upholstery, luggage, awnings, hot air balloons, window shades, tents, and geotextiles.

A special type of coated material is a poromeric material (see p. 230). This unique material is waterproof yet breathable. Thus, both protection and comfort results.

Nonaqueous Finishing

Foam-chemical finishing of cloth has been successful on many fabrics. This process consists of making a concentrated solution of the finishing chemical using a reduced quantity of water, and the addition of a foaming

chemical. The blend is then run through a foaming machine to obtain the proper foam density and uniformity of bubble size. The same amount of chemical is in the air mixture as would be in a water solution, except that air is the dilutant.

The foam may be applied to the fabric by using various techniques, such as through knife coating, with a kiss roll followed by a doctor blade, using a horizontal padder, and by rotary screen. After application, the foam is collapsed so that the chemical migrates into the fabric and then is dried or cured.

The benefits of finishing using foam include energy conservation because of the smaller heated-water requirements and faster fabric-drying times, as well as a reduction of waste water (and steam). (See Figure 10.9.) Nevertheless, even the reduced waste and processed water needs to be properly disposed of rather than discharged into streams and rivers without treatment.

With **solvent finishing** a solvent is used instead of water to form a solution. A result is decreased energy cost and reduced water pollution. It is less used than foam finishing because of the cost of solvent, the reclaiming process is expensive, health concerns and regulations.

Final Fabric Drying

Textile wet processing, including dyeing, printing, and finally finishing, utilize large quantities of water. Fabrics eventually need to be dried, and the methods for drying large quantities of material, often several thousand yards in a single lot, require specialized processing and machinery. Two widely used methods are (1) dry cans, and (2) tenter frame. The tenter frame, the most widely used, is often called the workhorse machine of textile finishing. Prior to actually drying, fabrics are passed over vacuum cylinders to remove excess water, leaving damp rather than completely wet materials to be dried by drying machines (see Figure 10.10).

Plasma Processing

Plasma is a state of matter distinct from solids, liquids, and gases. (It is sometimes referred to as the fourth state of matter.) It is produced by passing electricity through a gas. The result is a partially ionized gas containing neutral (e.g., free radicals) and changed (e.g., ions and electrons) particles. Plasma is usually generated either in a vacuum or under atmospheric pressure.

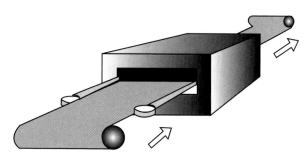

FIGURE 10.10
A tenter frame and a drying oven.

A plasma field can be used in textile finishing to change the surface properties of material passing through it. Fibers can, for example, become more absorbent, have increased dye intake, and possess better adhesive (i.e., bonding) properties. Results include improved colorfastness, easier cleaning, and more uniform color. Also there is less pollution since less energy and chemicals are required during processing as compared to traditional wet finishing.

Plasma processing works best where the ratio of surface area to the amount of fabric is high. For example, fabrics with very fine fibers get better results than fabrics with coarse fibers (more surface area). Deterrents to the use of plasma include capital cost, durability, and production speeds. While plasma applications at present have been limited (mainly in the nonwovens industry), there is a great potential.

Nanotechnology

Nanotechnology is the science and technology of manipulating molecular structures. New and improved fiber/fabric properties are being developed since changes are being made with molecular structures. (See p. 52 and p. 223.) (See Figures 10.11 and 10.12.)

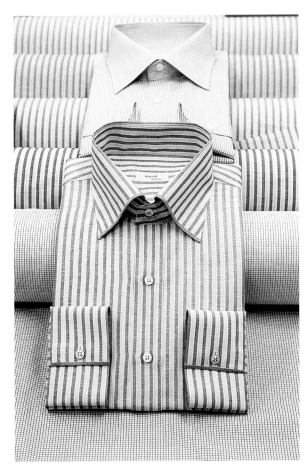

FIGURE 10.12
Wrinkle-free button down shirts.

FIGURE 10.11
Stain-resistant suit using nanotechnology.

Nanofinishes continue to grow in importance. These durable finishes are applied to fabrics as a surface coating of one or more layers of microscopic particles (nanoparticles). Various properties can result from nanocoatings:

► Water and oil repellency as well as stain resistance

► Antistatic and antimicrobial

► Ultraviolet-absorbent

► Better moisture management—wicking (see p. 28)

► Crossover properties with smart fabrics (see p. 225)

► More rapid dyeing, with longer lasting color.

Since the finish is on the molecular level, there is no change in aesthetics (hand, luster, or drape).

Coatings can be deposited in nanolayers to provide more than one additional property to the fabric. Thus, a membrane layer or poromeric material combined with a biologically active layer of enzymes, which can destroy toxins, could result in a waterproof, breathable, antibacterial fabric. This could be desirable for bedding or jackets.

Microencapsulation technology is being used to deliver various consumer benefits. A substance is contained in nanosized capsules which are stored on the fiber structure. As the fabric garment moves and rubs against the skin, capsules break and release the contents. The contents could be a moisturizing agent, which would hydrate the skin. It could be an antibacterial agent, which eliminates odor. It could be a fragrance agent, a medicine to soothe arthritic pain or an insect repellent. Undivided customized reload solutions are being developed. Through the use of an emulsion, foam, or a spray being applied to the fabric or garment, the original microcapsules can be reloaded or new microcapsules can replace the original ones. Thus moisturizing or other property can be permanent. Nanofinishes are applied to fabrics for apparel and upholstery, as well as luggage.

Imperfections of Finishing

The following is a list and description of the most frequently occurring imperfections that may result from finishing processes:

Bias fabric (skew): The filling yarns (or courses) are straight but not at right angles to the warp. This is caused by improper alignment on the tenter frame. The condition is especially serious in plaids, checks, and stripes across the fabric because it prevents proper joining of pattern parts in garment manufacture and also creates problems with the way fabrics hang on the body. The condition is also known as skew. Fabrics with this imperfection are called skewed fabrics or off-grain fabrics. (See Figure 10.13a.)

Bowed fabric: The filling yarns curve in the fabric and do not go straight across. This is caused by improper tenter-frame procedures, sometimes the result of the frame operating at too high a speed. Bowed fabrics are especially serious in fabrics of plaid, check, or stripe design because they prevent proper joining of pattern parts in garment manufacture. (See Figure 10.13b.)

Boardy fabric: Fabric that is too stiff, firm, and nondrapable compared to the standard or referenced sample. This finishing imperfection may result from excessive amounts or improper application of chemical finishing agents.

Limp fabric: A limp fabric is too soft and does not have proper body compared to the standard or referenced sample. This finishing imperfection may result from inadequate amounts or improper application of chemical finishing agents. The condition is sometimes called sleazy finish.

Off-grain fabric: See *bias fabric.*

Tender goods: Weakened fabric that results from excessive or improper application of chemical finishes.

Uneven finish: The fabric does not have the same character or degree of finish throughout.

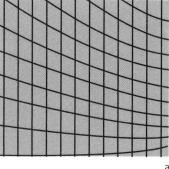
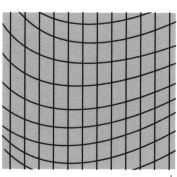

FIGURE 10.13
(a) Skewed fabric and (b) bowed fabric.

a

b

1. List five general reasons why fabrics are finished, and then indicate one finish that would provide each effect. (For example, reason—to provide comfort; finish—napping.)

2. Why is the pretreatment process known as singeing important for fabrics that will be printed?

3. Why is the pretreatment of greige goods essential before dyes, pigments, or finishes are applied?

4. Explain how you can distinguish between an embossed design and a woven design (dobby or jacquard) on a fabric.

5. Explain the difference between a napped fabric and a cut pile fabric. How would you identify one from the other when examining a fabric?

6. State several reasons for a fabric to be calendered.

7. When using fabrics with a plaid or check design, one must be careful to avoid a particular imperfection that may occur in finishing. Name the imperfection, and state how to check for it.

8. Why might you be hesitant about recommending the use of a highly napped wool fabric coat for active winter sportswear, even though the material provides added warmth and a softer hand due to its napped surface.

9. What manufactured fibers can be given a permanent embossed calendering finish? Why?

10. State three methods that can be used to make a fabric fire resistant.

11. How can a finish developed through nanotechnology be considered permanent while resin finishes are considered only durable?

12. State three functional properties that can result from nanocoatings.

13. State two apparel and two non-apparel end uses in which the use of antimicrobial fibers/finishes would offer functional advantages.

CHAPTER ELEVEN

Care and Renovation of Textiles

Objectives

▶ To understand how laundering and dry cleaning processes affect textiles.

▶ To understand the principles of soil removal of the different types of soil by either laundering or dry cleaning.

▶ To be able to classify soiling of textiles into various types.

▶ To be able to relate textile materials to appropriate care requirements.

 All of the fabrics of the Fabric Science Swatch Kit *are applicable to this chapter.*

Key Terms Related to Textiles

additives
bleaches
charged dry cleaning system
chlorine bleach
detergent
dry cleaning
Drycleaning & Laundering
  Institute
enzymes
fabric softners
fluorescent brightners
foam cleaner

fragrance
hydrocarbon cleaner
International Fair Claims
  Guide for Consumer
  Textile Products
laundering
non-chlorine bleach
non-water-soluble soil
perchlorethylene (perc)
powder cleaner
professional wet cleaning
soap curd

soaps
Stoddard solvent
soil redeposition
spotting
starches
surfactants
ultrasonic
water repellent
water softners
water-soluble soil

Knowledge of cleaning processes and the ways in which they affect textile materials is important to an overall understanding of textiles.

U.S. Federal regulations and those of various other nations require the labeling of garments and fabrics with directions for proper care and cleaning. The writing of care labels and the determination of the cause of damages and the necessary adjustment of articles returned to a store or manufacturer are examples of situations in which knowledge of cleaning processes is necessary to a fashion or textile professional.

The two main methods of cleaning textile products are laundering and dry cleaning. Each is one of the largest service industries in the United States. Both are discussed in this chapter.

The change in the business dress code from suits and dresses towards more casual dress resulted in a drop in volume of clothes being dry cleaned from the mid-1990s to the early 2000s. This also resulted in a decrease in dry cleaning plants (stores). Most of those that were able to remain in business upgraded their machinery. Today, the industry is using fifth-generation equipment, with the result being greater efficiency and the usage of less cleaning solvents.

Soil Types

It is important to understand the nature of soil and how to remove the different types. Soil can be divided into two main categories: **water-soluble soils** such as soda and coffee, which can be dissolved and removed by immersion in water, and **non-water-soluble soils,** such as fruit and vegetable staining, which can be removed by the assistance of a detergent or soap and heat. Some non-water-soluble soils such as soot or cinder can be removed by mechanical action such as shaking, or liquid action such as agitation with water, causing the soil to dislodge and float away. Soil such as lint or dust, held to the fabric by electrostatic force, is neutralized when immersed in water and the lint or dust is then removed. Other soil, such as dried soil, can be removed mechanically by brushing. Oily salad dressing, paint, and grease usually require the use of a solvent, such as dry cleaning fluid. Finally, the removal of some soil may require chemical action, such as the elimination of a stain by using bleach. There are also types of soil or combinations of soil that may require several cleaning actions in order to be removed.

Garments cleaned regularly last longer. Accumulations of perspiration, grit, and dust particles can shorten the life of your garment. Delay in cleaning the garment that has been stained can cause the stain to become permanently set.

Laundering

Laundering, the most common method of renovation for washable textile products, uses water combined with cleansers, such as soaps or detergents, and other additives for soil removal. Water is a solvent (natural) since it is a liquid that dissolves other materials (e.g., salt from perspiration). Organic solvents are used in dry cleaning.

The effects of laundering and the degree of cleaning obtainable depend on the cleanser and auxiliary agents used, the water quality, the temperature, the material being cleaned, and the water-to-weight-of-fabric ratio in the machine or laundry tub. Separating of colors to prevent color fading and laundering at optimum temperatures for both cleansing and to prevent shrinkage, dye and fiber damage are important considerations in laundering. Care labels permanently attached to garments (see Chapter 17) should be followed carefully to avoid laundry problems.

The fiber content of the garment being laundered is important. Some hydrophobic fibers (e.g., polyester) are not only water hating but are also oil loving (that is, oleophilic). Therefore, water-borne soil such as coffee, fruit sugar, and chocolate are initially partially repelled by the fiber. This soil can be removed by laundering action when the fiber has become thoroughly wetted. (This requires extra tumbling or soaking due to the low absorbency of the fiber.) The oil-borne soils in hydrophobic fibers, however, are more difficult to remove. Soils such as gravy, mayonnaise, and motor oil are absorbed and held tenaciously by the fiber because of their oleophilic character. Removal by laundering is often ineffective, and dry cleaning must be used. However, soil-release finishes for polyester (see p. 197) assist in removal of oil-borne soils. (It must be noted that most of these finishes become less and less effective with each succeeding wash, and are completely eliminated by the eighth to tenth laundering.)

Hydrophilic fibers (e.g., cotton, rayon, flax) readily absorb all soils—soluble, insoluble, and oily. However, hydrophilic fibers, when wetted, swell in size, allowing higher water penetration and resulting in increased surface area. This facilitates soil removal of all types. In general, cotton launders better and cleans more easily than polyester or nylon. Larger quantities of oil-borne soils, however, must be removed from cotton and other hydrophilic materials with dry cleaning.

Cleansers

Cleansers used in home laundering fall into two categories: soaps and detergents.

Soaps are sodium salts of a fatty acid. They are excellent cleaners in soft water (which has a low concentration of dissolved minerals) but are less effective in hard water (which has a high concentration of dissolved minerals).[1] The minerals in the water combine with the soap to form an insoluble gray curd or scum that is difficult to rinse out. (**Soap curd** is the material that forms as a ring around the bathtub after a bath with soap.) Once the soap has combined with the minerals in the water (e.g., calcium, magnesium), less soap is available for cleansing.

The term **detergent** is usually used to refer to synthetic detergents. They are an organic composition other than soap, produced by chemical synthesis. They dissolve readily and, unlike soaps, do not form a curd in hard water. A greater quantity must be used in hard water, however (as with the use of soap).

Neither soaps nor detergents adversely affect textile fibers. The exception is heavy-duty soaps, which are strongly alkaline and make wool and silk weaker and harsher. However, soaps and detergents may adversely affect finishes and cause certain dyes to run.

Laundry detergents are produced in both liquid and powder form. The formulation, however, varies with the type of detergent and manufacturer.

Soil Removal

Soap and detergent remove soil by first decreasing the surface tension of water so that water wets fabrics faster and is able to penetrate more completely. Soap or detergent molecules then help to dislodge soil from the fabric during the washing action. They also prevent soil in suspension from being redeposited on the fabric as the washing process continues. The soil and the soap or detergent are removed when the fabric is later rinsed. Some soiling creates stains. These are items such as lipstick, crayons, fruit, ink, etc. Special procedures are sometimes needed for their removal. Table 11.1 describes these stain removing procedures.

Cleansers not only remove soil from fabric, but also hold soils in suspension in the wash water and prevent the soil from redepositing on the washload. The major soap or detergent problems in home laundry are caused by either excessive or insufficient use. Using too little cleanser is a major cause of **soil redeposition.**[2] Insufficient quantities of cleansers may satisfactorily remove the soil, but may not be sufficient to keep the soil in suspension. It then becomes redeposited. Excessive amounts of cleansers are difficult to rinse out and remove, and cause harshness in fabric. Oddly, excessive amounts of cleansers also contribute to soil redeposition and graying of fabric because the excess cleansers not completely rinsed out remain in the fabric, and the soil in suspension becomes redeposited. Detergents also possess antiredeposition agents which help to prevent soil redeposition.

With the process of laundering, usually soil is removed more easily if the water temperature is high, but some detergents are specifically formulated to work in cold water. Nevertheless, most effective cleaning is with high water temperature. Also, high water temperature provides a degree of bacterial removal that does not occur in cold water unless accompanied by a chlorine bleach additive.

Additives

Various **additives** can be used to improve the cleaning action of soaps and detergents. They are often added to the wash water, but many are contained in the soap or detergent box or bottle, so separate additives are not required. The soap and detergent boxes or bottles on supermarket shelves usually list these additives as ingredients. A brief description of the most-used additives follows.

Surfactants　**Surfactants** are substances that lower or reduce the surface tension and so allow water to penetrate soil and suspend the soil particles for easy removal. Soaps and synthetic detergents are examples of surfactants.

Bleaches　**Bleaches** do not clean clothing. They only oxidize coloring matter, thus whitening the fabric and removing certain stains. Oxidation also has a weakening effect on textile fibers. Bleaching too frequently or using higher-than-recommended quantities of bleach for a given washload can significantly reduce the wear life of clothing.

---

1. Dissolved minerals, mostly calcium and magnesium salts, are present in water as natural substances. Soft water has very small amounts; hard water, large amounts. Most hard water is from underground sources (wells) where the water has flowed through mineral deposits in the earth. Water softeners, used in many homes and industries, chemically remove the natural mineral salts.

2. Soil redeposition refers to soil that is first removed from a laundered article, but later, in the same wash cycle, is redeposited as a thin soil film on the entire surface of the article. The effect is a dullish gray, sometimes yellowish, appearance of the laundered item.

TABLE 11.1	Stain Removal Guide for Washable Fabrics
Adhesive tape	Rub with ice; scrape with dull knife; sponge with cleaning fluid; wash.
Ballpoint ink	Soak with hairspray; rinse; hand scrub with liquid detergent; rinse well. Can try rubbing alcohol, glycerine, or prewash spray.
Blood	Soak in cool water with enzyme presoak; rub with detergent; rinse. Can try hydrogen peroxide or ammonia solution; wash.
Candle wax, paraffin	Freeze and scrape; place between paper towels or tissues and press with warm iron; place face down on paper towels and sponge with cleaning fluid or rubbing alcohol; wash.
Chewing gum	Harden with ice; scrape with dull knife; can soften with egg white; sponge face down on paper towels with cleaning fluid; wash.
Chocolate, cocoa	Soak in club soda or cool water with enzyme presoak; sponge with cleaning fluid and later with detergent; launder in hot water.
Coffee, tea	Soak with enzyme presoak or oxygen bleach; rub with detergent; wash in hot water.
Cosmetics	Dampen and rub with detergent; rinse; sponge with cleaning fluid; rinse; wash in water as hot as fabric care permits.
Crayon	Scrape (can loosen with cooking oil); spray with prewash or rub with detergent; rinse; sponge with cleaning fluid face down on paper towels; rinse; launder in hot water with bleach.
Deodorants	Scrub with vinegar or alcohol; rinse; rub with liquid detergent; wash hot.
Egg	If dried, scrape with dull knife; soak in cool water with enzyme presoak; rub with detergent; launder in hot water.
Felt-tip pen ink	Rub with strong household wall and counter cleaner; rinse; repeat if needed; launder; this stain may not come out.
Fingernail polish	Sponge white cotton with nail-polish remover and all other fabrics with amyl acetate (banana oil); scrape with dull knife; wash.
Fruits and juices	Soak with enzyme presoak; wash. If stain remains, cover with paste of oxygen bleach and a few drops of ammonia for 15 to 20 minutes. Can also try white vinegar; wash as hot as possible.
Grass	Soak in enzyme presoak; rinse; rub with detergent; hot wash with bleach; if stain remains, sponge with alcohol.
Gravy	Scrape with dull knife; soak in enzyme presoak; treat with detergent paste and later cleaning fluid; hot wash with bleach if safe.
Grease	Scrape off all excess or apply absorbent powder (talcum or cornstarch) and brush off; pretreat with strong detergent; rinse; sponge with cleaning fluid; hot wash with extra detergent; bleach if safe.

(continued on page 209)

All the bleaches used in household laundering are oxidizing agents and fall into two categories: chlorine-bearing type and non-chlorine-bearing type. **Chlorine bleaches** must never be used on spandex or protein fibers because they yellow and weaken spandex and eventually destroy protein fiber materials.

Non-chlorine bleaches, such as hydrogen peroxide and sodium percarbonate, are more costly, slower-acting, and weaker than the chlorine type. They are, however, safe for all fibers and may be used on most fabrics that are colorfast to this weaker bleaching agent and acceptable for laundering. Manufacturers of non-chlorine-type bleaches recommend testing for colorfastness on a hidden spot on the garment before use.

Fluorescent Brighteners A fluorescent object absorbs light of shorter wavelengths, such as ultraviolet rays, and emits it at longer wavelengths in the visible region, such as blue light. The result is a greater amount of light reflection, making a brighter white or brighter colors. Laundry soaps and detergents often use such **fluorescent brighteners** and refer to their result as "whiter than white." These chemicals do not remove soil, but only mask the soil while making yellow or dingy fabrics look white.

Fluorescent brighteners are usually combined as an additive in soap and detergent boxes and bottles. They are usually not added separately in the laundering process. Household incandescent lighting contains no ultraviolet, so fluorescent brighteners have no effect in this

TABLE 11.1	Stain Removal Guide for Washable Fabrics (continued)
Ice cream	Soak in enzyme presoak; rinse; rub with detergent; rinse and let dry; sponge with cleaning fluid if needed; rinse; hot wash with bleach if safe.
Iodine	Treat with ammonia or soak in color remover; wash.
Lipstick	Moisten with glycerine or prewash; wash; bleach if safe.
Margarine	Same as for grease.
Mayonnaise, salad dressing	Rub with detergent; rinse and let dry; sponge with cleaning fluid; rinse; hot wash with bleach if safe.
Mildew	Rub with lemon juice; dry in the sun; rub with detergent; hot wash with bleach; if stain remains, sponge with hydrogen peroxide.
Milk	Soak in enzyme presoak; rinse; rub with detergent; launder.
Mud	Soak in water with dishwashing detergent and 1 Tbsp. vinegar; rinse; sponge with alcohol; rinse; soak in enzyme presoak; wash with bleach if safe.
Mustard	Spray with prewash or rub with bar soap or liquid detergent; rinse; soak in hot water and detergent; launder with bleach if safe.
Oil	Same as for grease.
Paint	Do not let paint dry; sponge oil-based types with turpentine or paint thinner; rub with bar soap; launder. Saturate water-based (latex) paints with water and soap (or detergent) immediately; launder.
Peanut butter	Saturate with mineral oil to dislodge oil particles from fibers; blot; apply cleaning fluid and blot between absorbent mats; rinse and launder.
Perspiration	Soak in salt water, enzyme presoak or rub with baking soda paste; rinse; rub with detergent; can apply ammonia to fresh stain and white vinegar to old stain; rinse and launder.
Scorch	Soak with enzyme presoak or wet with hydrogen peroxide and a drop of ammonia; let stand 30 to 60 minutes; rinse well; wash in hot water; rub with suds; bleach; dry in sunshine; may not come out.
Shoe polish	Scrape off excess; rub with detergent; wash.
Soft drinks	Dampen with cool water and rubbing alcohol or enzyme presoak; launder with bleach if safe; stain may appear later as a yellow area.
Tomato products	Sponge with cold water; rub with detergent; launder in hot water with bleach if safe.
Water ring	Rub with rounded back of silver (not stainless steel) spoon.
Wine	Same as for fruits; sprinkle a red wine spill immediately with salt.

type of lighting. Fluorescent brighteners are also called optical brighteners, optical whiteners, and fluorescent whitening agents.

Before fluorescent brighteners were developed for use in the household, bluing was used to treat white laundry. Bluing is a product that actually is a weak blue dye (colorant). It is added to the rinse cycle to further whiten the laundry. It masks the yellow color by reflecting more blue-white light. Too much bluing, however, can give white articles a blue tinge.

Water Softeners Water hardness is defined as the total concentration of calcium and magnesium minerals dissolved in the water, expressed as calcium carbonate

equivalent, from soft (low amount of minerals) to very hard (very high level of minerals).

A higher degree of hardness adversely affects the sudsing and cleaning action of soaps and detergents (the dissolved minerals combine with the cleanser). Although no special treatment for water is required for detergents unless the water is extremely hard, the effective use of soap requires the water to be soft.

Water-conditioning chemicals called **water softeners** can be added to the laundry when hard water is used. They combine with the minerals that cause the water to be hard. Thus the minerals are removed or bonded to other molecules. When water softener is added to the wash water, it is equally important that it be added to the rinse water to be sure that all the curd formed is removed. Calgon® is a well-known water softener.

Some detergents contain high concentrations of phosphates, which reduce water hardness by attaching themselves to the dissolved calcium and magnesium minerals in the water and keeping these minerals from impeding laundering. Ecological concern about the quality of water has resulted in pressure to stop the usage of phosphate-containing detergents. When high concentrations of phosphate are discharged into the waste system, they may work their way into natural water resources, causing environmental imbalances. Many states have outlawed their use for laundering purposes. Non-phosphate water softeners contain sodium carbonate or other substances.

In areas where hard water is present, many households install water-softening systems directly in the plumbing system. These systems chemically remove the objectionable minerals causing water hardness. Soft water is thus available for kitchen, laundry, and bath, throughout the home, and water-softening laundry additives are unnecessary. Most commercial laundries and textile dyeing and finishing plants have installed water-softening systems.

Fabric Softeners **Fabric softeners** provide a lubricating film on fibers, allowing them to move more readily against each other, making fabrics softer and fluffier and minimizing wrinkles. The lubricating film also absorbs and holds moisture, providing a path for the discharge of the static electricity that forms, reducing static cling as well as lint sticking to materials, especially with manufactured fiber fabrics.

Fabric softeners have a tendency to build up on fabrics in a greasy layer, resulting in less-absorbent fabrics. It is therefore not recommended that fabric softener be used every time a product is laundered. Different forms of fabric softeners can be added to the wash, rinse, or drying cycles.

Starches **Starches** are sizing, which help restore the body of limp fabrics. Aerosol spray starch and vegetable starches must be reapplied after each washing. Resins, an alternative to starches, usually available as spray products, last longer—through at least several launderings. Starches are seldom used today in the wash.

Fragrances **Fragrances** are often added to the cleaner to give the laundered article a "clean" smell and mask any chemical odors. Two examples are Proctor & Gamble's Tide® with Febreze® and The Dial Corporation's Purex® with Renuzit™.

Pretreatment

Some types of stains, such as protein-based stains—for example, body soils, blood, eggs, grass stains, and chocolate—are especially difficult to remove. They may require a special pretreatment using enzymes.

Enzymes are organic substances that break down certain soils to simpler, water-soluble forms that are then more readily removed by soap or detergent. Enzymatic pretreatments need more time to work than most other additives, so a presoak of a half hour or more is recommended. Most enzyme pretreatments attack protein fibers as well as the protein-based stains they are designed to remove (e.g., body soil, blood, eggs, grass stains). Their use should be avoided on wool, silk, and similar fibers.

Dry Cleaning

Dry cleaning is a process in which the articles being cleaned are immersed in an organic solvent cleansing fluid and tumbled in a machine much the same way that clothing in a home laundering machine is tumbled. The process is called dry cleaning because the cleaning liquid is not water based and does not wet the fabric as water does. These solvents evaporate readily and dry fabric at temperatures below body heat. The organic cleansing agent used in dry cleaning is very effective for cleaning soils of an oily nature (gravy, oily perspiration, hair tonics, etc.), but only marginally effective for cleaning water-based soils (salt, sugar, fruit stains, etc.). Moisture contained in clothes to be dry cleaned help water-soluble soil be removed.

In professional dry cleaning, articles are carefully separated by color (dark or light) as well as by delicacy of fabric, and put into separate loads. The temperature of the solvents used in dry cleaning is carefully controlled, barely lukewarm never reaching more than 90°F (≈32°C). The fluids are continuously circulated and filtered to remove fiber particles and other soils.

For both economic and environmental reasons, used dry cleaning solvents are not discarded; instead, they are recycled and reused. Solvents are purified, and accumulated soil is removed either by filtration or distillation. The continual use of dirty solvent will interfere with cleaning. The purification process consists of distillation, in which the solvent is boiled and vaporized. The pure solvent separates from the undesirable ingredients and is then condensed back into liquid and reused. The residue that is left over after the distillation process is picked up by a waste recycling company that extracts any remaining solvent and then incinerates the balance.

After clothes have been immersed in solvent, they need to be dried. The clothes dryer used captures the vapor and condenses it into pure solvent for reuse. The dry cleaning industry is eco-friendly with the use of efficient machines, the recycling of solvent, and the controlled disposal of waste.

After a textile product is cleaned, it often must be ironed, pressed, or steamed using hand irons, presses, or form finishers. This is done to remove wrinkles, sharpen creases or pleats, and smooth seams.

Because the organic solvents used in dry cleaning are nonaqueous, or non-water-bearing, they do not wet the fiber as does water. Therefore, no fiber shrinkage or damage to fibers occurs to fabrics such as rayon, which becomes weaker when wet with aqueous (water) solutions. Further, there is no effect on most dyes or finishes (although some pigments are sensitive to dry cleaning fluids). The dryers used for dry cleaning are low temperature units where drying temperature is usually 100°F (≈38°C).

A better quality cleaning process will occur if solvent detergents are added to the liquid solvent. When this occurs, the system is called a **charged system.** Since some of the detergent is absorbed into the garments, more must be periodically added to the system. (The soil remains in the solvent.) The detergent acts as a conditioning agent, anti-static agent (non-cling, less lint collection, and less pilling), as well as an optical brightener when in the product. The detergent can be automatically added through the machine-injection system or by hand.

Dry Cleaning Solvents

There are various solvents that are used in the dry cleaning industry.

1. **Perchlorethylene** (perc or PCE) is the oldest synthetic solvent used. Introduced in the late 1940s, it became the most used solvent by 1960. It remains #1 today, aided by being nonflammable and giving the best overall result at a reasonable price. The fumes from perc, however, are toxic so caution has to be exercised in its use. There is also concern that this solvent is a carcinogen. Thus there should be reduced exposure and emissions.

2. **Hydrocarbons** are synthetic petroleum solvents and are the second most used. While they are flammable, hydrocarbons have a high flashpoint and so will not burn easily under normal conditions. DF 2000 is a newer hydrocarbon solvent. Controls for the vapors that form are incorporated in the dry cleaning machines, particularly the dry-to-dry systems. Thus, air pollution is minimal.

3. **Stoddard** is a petroleum solvent, which was developed in the 1920s. It is slightly flammable and requires special equipment and handling. It is still used because of its low price, but to a limited extent.

(In many areas it does not meet the fire code, but Stoddard solvent was an improvement compared to gasoline and other highly flammable solvents used prior to its development.)

4. New developments include machines using liquid CO_2 cleaning systems. It is a very eco-friendly system since CO_2 has a negligible effect in the environment. The machines are expensive, however.

An alternative solvent is GreenEarth®, which is silicone-based (sand). It has a high flashpoint and so is not considered a hazardous substance. It also is not an ozone depleter and is considered by the Environmental Protection Agency (EPA) not to be a volatile organic compound (VOC).

Spotting

Garments and other articles stained with substances that are insoluble in dry cleaning solvent (blood, ink, rust spots, etc.) are removed by the dry cleaner in a procedure called **spotting**.

A wide assortment of chemicals and procedures are available for this type of stain removal. A dry cleaning spotter must know the interactions of these chemicals with the various fibers and dyes as well as the nature of the stain. Improper spotting can permanently damage a fabric. Customers who identify stains for the dry cleaner make the cleaning task easier and ultimately improve their satisfaction with the cleaned product.

Water-Repellent Garments

Water-repellent garments need special attention when dry cleaned. As previously noted, detergents are used in dry cleaning baths to help the cleaning process. The use of these detergents presents a special problem for water-repellent rainwear, however. The presence of even minute residues of detergent remaining on a water-repellent fabric after cleaning (or laundering, if the repellent is a launderable type) severely reduces the water-repellent capabilities of a fabric. Many otherwise durable water-repellents are therefore very short-lived because of the great difficulty in removing the last traces of soap or detergent. The remedy is usually found in retreatment of the water-repellent finish. These repellents, applied by the dry cleaner, are usually temporary and are applied in spray methods or by dipping the entire garment into a tank containing the liquid water-repellent.

Cautions in Dry Cleaning

Some apparel and other textile products should never be dry cleaned, or should be thoroughly checked for dry cleanability before being offered for sale as a dry clean-able item. These include the following:

Vinyl plastics and vinyl-coated fabrics: These materials contain plasticizers (softeners) that leach out in the presence of solvents. The result is a hard, brittle (likely to crack when folded) vinyl substance.

Polystyrene plastics: Sometimes used for buckles, buttons, and sequins. This plastic dissolves in dry cleaning solvents.

Dyed leather trim: These should be carefully checked for dry cleaning fastness to color. Leather dyes often run in the presence of dry cleaning solvents.

Pigment-colored fabrics: These should be checked for colorfastness as well as possible shade changes.

Flocked, bonded, laminated, or cemented components (belt backing, for example): These should be checked to ascertain that the cements are not solvent soluble.

Heavy and light fabrics: A garment to be dry cleaned should not be composed of both heavy-weight and light fabrics. An example of this might be a winter-weight wool dress with a lace shoulder bodice. The dry cleaner will either clean the heavier fabric, to the possible detriment of the more frag-ile component, or else provide a cleaning cycle for the more delicate component and not thoroughly remove soil from the heavier portion.

Liquor, coffee, tea, or (most) juices: These liquids possess a substance called tannin, which is invisible until heat is applied, as from pressing. The tannin then becomes permanent and often leaves a stain. Although the dry cleaning process should remove the tannin, it is best to advise the dry cleaner of the stain (even if invisible) so it can definitely be removed in the spotting process.

Home Solvent Cleaning

For people who want to dry clean their garments at home, a consumer kit is available (e.g., Dryel® dry cleaning kit). It is designed for cleaning 'dry clean only' clothes. The kit contains a bottle of stain remover (and absorbent pads), coated fabric bag, and solvent-treated moist cloths. After testing the article for colorfastness, the garments and a moist cloth are placed in the fabric bag. The closed bag is placed in an empty clothes dryer, that is vented to the outside, for 30 minutes at a medium heat setting. The heat activates the solvent in the moist cloth and the

tumbling encourages the cleaning action. The articles need to be promptly hung to minimize wrinkling. The kit works best with simple garments, such as sweaters and slacks, that are only lightly soiled and no special care or processing is required. While commercial dry clean-ing is more effective, some periodic home cleaning will reduce cleaning costs.

Dry Cleaning Versus Laundering

Although water and dry cleaning solvents are both liq-uids, they have different properties. For example, grease and oily stains do not dissolve in water, but do dissolve in solvent. Salt from perspiration does not dissolve in a solvent, but does in water. Thus dry cleaning is best for soil of an oily nature such as gravy stains. Laundering is best for soil such as perspiration stains and odor, and things like mud, grass stains, and nonoily food soils (e.g., ketchup, fruits).

Most textile products can be cleaned by either laun-dering or dry cleaning, but some should be cleaned by using only one method. A wool coat, for example, should not be washed because the wool will felt and shrink excessively in laundering water. A vinyl plastic raincoat should not be dry cleaned because the result will be a stiff, brittle material.

The choice of which cleaning system to use is deter-mined by variables such as the type of dirt, safety of the material, and cost of cleaning.

Professional Wet Cleaning

With concern about the use of organic solvents, such as perc, alternatives to dry cleaning are being developed. It was found that articles which are dry cleaned can be exposed to water, but under very controlled conditions. Thus, the **professional wet-cleaning** process was developed.

The wet-cleaning process uses more controls than a washing procedure. This is now available through tech-nology. Temperature, moisture (water) levels, mechani-cal agitation, soap or detergents, and cleaning additives must be monitored carefully to prevent shrinkage and dye bleeding. Water, heat, steam, and soaps or detergents are used to clean. Tumble-drying and vacuuming are used in the drying process. Pressing is used to restore the appearance of the article.

The process is labor-intensive and more costly than dry cleaning. The machinery in wet cleaning is computer-controlled and significant water and energy is used. There are, however, fewer health problems and less environmental contamination than with the use of dry cleaning solvents. Also, the equipment is less expensive, so less capital is required compared to opening a dry cleaning plant. The cleaning potential is very good.

The alternative to wet cleaning is to hand wash and dry.

Ultrasonic Washing of Textiles

In a fluid medium (e.g., water), agitation generated by high-intensity sound (ultrasonic) is very efficient in dissolving and displacing contaminants (which adhere to the surface of materials (e.g., soil). (**Ultrasonic** sound refers to sound above the human hearing range.) Although this technique has been used in non-textile industrial cleaning applications for many years, it also has strong potential in textile care systems.

The benefits of using ultrasonic sound for washing, as compared to conventional methods, include reduced time of the washing cycle (seconds instead of minutes), less energy needed to wash the same amount of textiles, less water required, and reduced pollution (e.g., less discharge of waste cleaning agents). The degree of cleaning (soil removal) is very good and the process may be more gentle to the product being cleaned than conventional laundering.

An ultrasonic washing machine includes a vibrating plate that produces ultrasonic sound waves through the washing solution. Bubbles are produced, which then collapse generating fluid jets and shock waves. The microagitation, which occurs in the vicinity of each bubble, displaces soil particles bound to the fabric as well as accelerates the dissolving of soluble contaminants. This agitation takes place both on the textile surface and within the fabric structure.

The Branson Ultrasonics Corporation produces tabletop ultrasonic cleaners.

Trade Associations

There are two major trade associations in the laundering and dry cleaning industries. Both associations offer technical and business assistance to their members. Publications, problem-solving laboratory, and professional expertise are available from both associations:

▶ The **Drycleaning & Laundering Institute** (DLI) (formerly International Fabricare Institute) has more

than 13,000 members in 50 countries. Its headquarters is in Silver Springs, Maryland.

▶ The Neighborhood Cleaners Association has a national United States membership. Although smaller in size than the DLI, it is nevertheless a very active organization. Its headquarters is in New York City.

Both organizations undertake research and technical support for new cleaning methods, detergents, and equipment. Each offers courses and seminars in laundry and dry cleaning methods and management. (See Figure 11.1.)

The Soap Detergent Association is the main trade group for the United States cleaning products industry.

Trade Shows

The major United States trade show for the cleaning industry is called the Clean Show. It is biennial and serves people providing commercial laundering and

Clothing Care

Refer to the chart on the proper steps to care for your clothing. The fabric care symbols are inserted in your clothing labels.

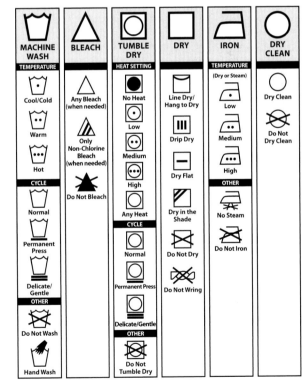

FIGURE 11.1
Federal Trade Commission care symbols for apparel.

dry cleaning, as well as equipment, supplies, and auxiliary products from around the world. Various associations sponsor this show, including DLI.

The Texcare Show sponsored by the Neighborhood Cleaners Association is another well-known show. It is held in the Meadowlands in New Jersey every two years. This show mainly focuses on the dry cleaning and laundering processes.

A major international trade show held outside the United States is the LORSA trade show. Like the Clean Show, it attracts attendees from all over the world. There are also other shows held periodically in Europe and Asia.

Claiming Damages

Articles that become damaged in commercial laundering or dry cleaning often become the subject of debate and argument as to whether the article was faulty or the launderer or dry cleaner caused the damage by using improper procedures. Knowing where the fault lies may become the basis of claims for damages.

The most widely used guide for determining liability or responsibility for damaged articles is the **International Fair Claims Guide for Consumer Textile Products.** This widely used document was drawn up by the International Fabricare Institute (now DLI), with the cooperation of representatives of consumer, retail, and textile manufacturing groups.

This guide includes sections that aid in determining adjustment values as well as clarifying label conditions and terms.

The Environment

The United States government as well as state governments are intensifying their scrutiny of perc solvent. They believe it is a carcinogen and should be removed from use. The Drycleaning and Laundry Institute, after testing, says that this has not been proven and perc (with proper controls) is a safe and effective solvent. Through more efficient machines, there has been an 80 percent reduction in perc emissions in the last decade.

Some governments are still not satisfied. California has approved a phase-out that will result in a complete ban by 2023. New Jersey, Massachusetts, Maine, and Canada are looking to eventually phase out perc dry cleaning.

n-Propyl Bromide (NPB) was introduced in 2005 as a solvent for dry cleaning. It is similar in properties to perc and may become a replacement. It is a crossover solvent from metal degreasing. Costs would rise, however, since perc is cheaper.

Some hotels and lodgings have optional programs to protect the environment through conservation of water and decreased use of detergents. For guests wanting to participate, linens and towels are not changed every day of their stay. (Both, however, are automatically changed after every guest checkout.)

Study Questions

1. Why is it helpful for the consumer to identify stains for the dry cleaner?

2a. Prepare a comparison table that indicates at least six differences in processing between laundering and dry cleaning.

b. Prepare a similar table that indicates at least six differences in the action on textiles and types of soil removal between laundering and dry cleaning.

3. If you were preparing the information for apparel care labels, why would it be important that you do the following:

a. Specify mild soap or detergent for laundering of wool or silk garments?

b. Specify nonchlorine bleach for white wool or silk garments?

c. Check the dry cleanability of plastic buttons for a rayon print dress?

d. Avoid the use of vinyl plastic trim in items that are to be dry cleaned?

e. Check the dry cleanability of the leather trim on a wool sport coat?

4. What faulty dry cleaning practice might you suspect if a pair of wool slacks that had been dry cleaned with no problems on several previous occasions suddenly shrank and became partially felted on the next dry cleaning?

5. Several white 100-percent cotton blouses, and several white pants of 100 percent cotton were all laundered together. They were grayish and dull when removed from a washing machine.

    a. To what probable cause or causes can you attribute this condition?
    b. What step would you take to restore the original whiteness?

6. Explain why some garments are best cleaned by laundering and others are best cleaned by dry cleaning.

7. Can a bleach remove soil? Explain your answer.

8. State three additives found in a laundry detergent that help to improve the cleaning action. Briefly explain their function.

9. Some designers and apparel manufacturers label a garment "Dry Clean Only" because they believe that any garment can be safely dry cleaned. Are they correct?

10. Why is the Environmental Protection Agency concerned about dry cleaners using perchlorethylene?

CHAPTER TWELVE
Unique Fabrications and Innovations

Objectives

▶ To become aware of textile materials that go beyond ordinary performance expectations and fulfill unique functions.

▶ To be able to recognize materials made with these fabrications.

▶ To be able to relate performance properties of these materials with end uses.

 Use fabrics in the Miscellaneous Fabrics section in the Fabric Science Swatch Kit for this chapter.

Key Terms Related to Textiles

breathability
comfort cooling
dead air
electrotextiles
evaporative cooling
fluorescent dyes
geotextiles
moisture transport
nanotechnology
phase change material
push/pull effect

smart fabrics
temperature/humidity
  gradient
thermal insulation
ultrasonic
waterproof
wicking

Plastics:
expanded vinyl
membrane
polyurethane

poromeric
thermoplastic
thermosetting
vinyl film

Leather:
curing
grain
hide
patent leather
skin
split leather

suede leather
tanning
top grain

Fur:
dressing
faux fur
fur hair
Fur Products Labeling
  Act
fur ranching
guard hair
pelt

The strength of the United States textile industry is in the research and development of technology applicable to the marketplace. Efficient mill production alone is no longer sufficient to insure a strong, vibrant business. This chapter discusses various unique fabrication processes and products, both manufactured and natural.

The first section of this chapter focuses on textile materials that are made with special properties. The second section contains three materials that may not be considered "textile materials" (e.g., not composed of fibers and yarns) but are used to make textile end uses (e.g., apparel). They are plastics, leather, and furs.

Fabrics with Special Features

Traditional fabrics have in many cases been found to be unsuitable or marginal for the intended end use. For example, polyester is hydrophobic and so is normally unsuitable for active sportswear garments worn next to the skin. However, by modifying the fiber shape and composition, its wicking ability (ability to transport moisture) is greatly enhanced to move moisture (perspiration) away from the skin. The result is greater comfort for the wearer. (See Chapter 3 for additional discussion of fiber innovations.)

Fabrics with special features can be found in non-consumer products, such as inflated buildings for sports events, hot-gas filters, artificial arteries, uniforms that protect firefighters, heat shields on space shuttles, and car airbags. Inasmuch as this book primarily encompasses consumer textiles, the concentration will be in this area.

Three categories will be examined in this section. They are (1) moisture transport, (2) waterproofing and breathability, and (3) **thermal insulation**. These categories all relate to *moisture management performance.*

Moisture Transport

Moisture transport is the term applied to textiles that have the ability to move moisture away from the skin and through the fabric to the next layer of clothing or to the outside air. In the air, it evaporates, thus cooling the wearer. This group of fabrics, therefore, also provides **comfort cooling.** The key to keeping cool in hot weather is to induce evaporation—the more rapid the evaporation, the more effective the cooling. Cotton, flax, and rayon are absorbent materials, but they hold moisture and do not release it (let it evaporate) as quickly as the moisture-transport products described in this section. Thus they do not create as effective a cooling condition.

Moisture is transported in textiles through capillary action or wicking. In textiles, the spaces between the fibers effectively form tubes, which act as capillaries, and transport the liquid away from the surface. As a rule, the narrower the spaces between the fibers in a fabric, the more effectively they will draw up moisture. For this reason, fabrics with many narrow capillaries, such as microfibers, are ideal for moisture transport. (See Table 12.1.)

There are several methods by which moisture-transport textiles function: fiber innovations, push/pull fabric constructions, and the chemical grafting of hydrophobic fibers.

Fiber Innovations
Hydrophobic manufactured fibers, while having poor absorbency, are capable of **wicking,** or transporting moisture. Many have been modified through polymer modification prior to extrusion from the spinnerette, through fiber shape and size modifications at the spinnerette, or a combination of both (see pp. 20–22). The principal fibers used are polyester, nylon, and olefin.

A widely used trademark in the category of moisture transport is COOLMAX®. It is an INVISTA™ registered trademark for certified performance fabrics, garments, and accessories. The combination of polymer additives and fiber shape is the key to its moisture-transport property. The tetrachannel (four channel) configuration enhances the capillary action movement of moisture along the fibers' outer edges (polyester and nylon). Fabrics (woven and knitted) are categorized for "everyday" (e.g., in the office), for "active" (e.g., working out), or for "extreme" (e.g., mountain climbing).

Moisture transport is also achieved in a modified nylon fiber that is a patented copolymer (two polymers extruded together as one) named Hydrofil®, produced by Honeywell Nylon Inc. (See Figure 12.1.) Hydrofil® is more absorbent than regular untreated nylon, but not so absorbent as to hold the amount of moisture retained by natural hydrophilic fibers. Hydrofil® prevents moisture condensation (which occurs with untreated nylon) and allows fabrics to breathe similarly to a natural fiber. Moisture is wicked throughout the fabric surface, enhancing rapid evaporation. Hydrofil® nylon is used in both woven and knitted fabrics.

Permanent moisture-transport capabilities on fibers such as nylon, polyester, and acrylic have also been achieved by permanently combining hydrophilic molecules to the surface of these hydrophobic fibers. Moisture vapor is transported along the hydrophilic-fiber surface to the next clothing layer or to the outside air, thereby increasing the comfort level over ordinary untreated manufactured fibers. The hydrophilic molecules draw

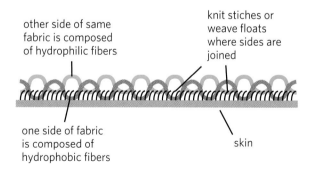

a

b

FIGURE 12.1
Fabrics with special features include (a) athletic top and shorts by Splits 59, and (b) Techfit PowerWeb apparel by Adidas.

moisture away from their neighboring molecules, spreading moisture over a wide surface, thus enhancing the vapor transport and evaporation rate.

Two-Sided Fabric Systems

Various woven and knitted fabrics are made with two distinct sides. Different fibers or yarns may dominate on each side. The result is to remove moisture quickly away from the skin (perspiration), have it transported to the outer surface of the fabric where it will evaporate rapidly (**push/pull effect**) (see Figure 12.2). The skin remains dry and comfortable. The fabrics could be made to be worn against the skin or as layered clothing.

Tactel® Aquator™ is an INVISTA™ trademark for such a two-sided fabric system. The inner layer pulls water away from the skin by a wicking action and transports it to the outer surface area where it rapidly evaporates. The inner layer is made of Tactel® nylon specialty fibers while the outer layer may be composed of other fibers.

Transpor, Inc. has also developed a moisture transport system. The Transpor® material is bilayer. The skin side is the dry layer and the outside is the wicking layer, where evaporation occurs.

Effects of Temperature and Humidity

Moisture-transport fabrics can be very efficient and comfortable or very inefficient and uncomfortable depending on the air temperature and relative humidity during wear.

The ability to transport moisture from the skin side of a fabric to the outside air is dependent on the differences in temperature and humidity between the inside (skin side) and the outside. This difference is technically called the **temperature/humidity gradient**. It causes the effect that results in the moisture vapor moving from the warmer, more humid skin side to the cooler, dryer outside. What happens if the outside temperature and humidity are both high and the skin side is only slightly more hot and humid (as in a summer rainstorm)? Very

PUSH/PULL FABRIC

other side of same fabric is composed of hydrophilic fibers

knit stiches or weave floats where sides are joined

one side of fabric is composed of hydrophobic fibers

skin

FIGURE 12.2
Push/pull fabrics have two sides. The hydrophobic side belongs next to the skin, and the hydrophilic side belongs on the outside. Perspiration is pushed from the hydrophobic side and pulled to the hydrophilic side so that the skin remains dry and comfortable.

TABLE 12.1 Examples of Moisture Transport/Comfort Cooling Textiles			
Type	Brand Name	Fiber	Fabric Types
Fiber configuration	COOLMAX®	Polyester	Knits and wovens
Fiber modification	Hydrofil®	Nylon	Knits and wovens and outer side of push/pull fabrics
Fine-denier polypropylene	(Generic)	Polypropylene	Skin side of push/pull fabrics
Specialty nylon	Tactel® Aquator™	Nylon	Skin side of push/pull fabrics
Chemical grafting	Intera®	Acrylic	Knits and wovens

little or nothing happens. On a hot, humid day, little or no moisture transfer occurs. However, in cooler and dryer weather or in hot but dry weather, the moisture transport fabrics are ideal for keeping people comfortable while hiking, cycling, playing tennis, or performing any activity that causes perspiration to form on the skin.

Cotton Incorporated has developed a moisture management treatment (finish), Wicking Windows™, for 100-percent-cotton fabric. The product greatly increases wicking capabilities. Thus, the skin is drier and there is less fabric cling. It is used in athletic wear.

Waterproof Breathable Fabrics

Protective textile fabrics for keeping dry in the rain and inclement weather cover a wide variety of protective capabilities. These fabrics range from water repellent, which protects only in relatively light showers, to water resistant, which offers greater resistance to water but will eventually leak, to those that are so waterproof that gloves and boots made from these textiles remain leakproof even when completely immersed in water.

Special waterproof fabrics, in addition to protection against wetness, also provide the important element of **breathability** (which is the ability to transport moisture from inside the clothing to the outside, and air from the outside inward through the clothing). Ordinarily water-repellent fabrics, as indicated in Chapter 10, are breathable but leak badly in medium or prolonged rain. Regular coated fabrics (see p. 199) are completely waterproof because they are mostly coated with neoprene rubber, vinyl plastic, or polyurethane. Although very waterproof, they are also completely impermeable, and thus not breathable and quite uncomfortable. By contrast, special waterproof fabrics combine both important attributes for wet-weather protection: resistance to water and breathability for comfort.

Structure

Completely waterproof fabrics that are also breathable use a special **membrane** in a layer construction. The material is also completely windproof.

Fabrics in this category are two-layer or three-layer in structure. The *two-layer* structure consists of an outer-shell fabric laminated to a thin waterproof, breathable membrane (Figure 12.3a). A separate garment liner is required to protect the membrane. *Three-layer* systems are laminates consisting of an outer shell, a waterproof, breathable membrane (middle), and a lining fabric. A separate garment lining is not required (see Figure 12.3b). In general, two-layer types are softer, more flexible, and more breathable than three-layer types, but three-layer fabrics are more durable.

The use of a **waterproof** fabric does not guarantee a completely waterproof garment (Figure 12.4). Leakage through seams, especially in heavy, prolonged exposure severely compromises the waterproof ability of clothing. Making garments completely waterproof requires that all seams be sealed, which is a very labor-intensive and costly process. Nevertheless, the very best (and most costly) waterproof, breathable clothing have all sewn seams sealed with a sealant and waterproof tape. A well-known trade name of waterproof, breathable fabrics is GORE-TEX® (W.L. Gore & Associates, Inc.). Table 12.2 summarizes the differences between water-resistant and waterproof, breathable fabrics.

Effect of Temperature and Humidity

The use of waterproof, breathable fabrics is not of itself a guarantee that a wearer will be comfortable in this clothing. Breathability and comfort in waterproof clothing is largely dependent on the difference between the temperature and humidity inside the clothing and the temperature and humidity outside the clothing. The *temperature/humidity* gradient creates the effect that moves warm, moisture-laden air (inside) to dry, colder air outside. The colder and dryer the outside air, the better the movement of moisture vapor to the outside. This effect is the same as previously discussed with moisture transport fabrics.

Thermal Insulation

Keeping warm, or insulating our bodies in cold weather, involves wearing clothing that slows down or prevents

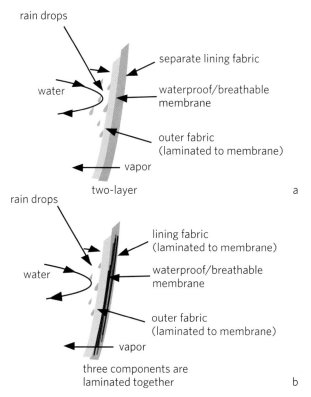

FIGURE 12.3
Membrane-type waterproof, breathable fabrics may be
(a) two-layer or (b) three-layer systems.

FIGURE 12.4
Waterproof fabric made into garments with sealed seams
provide complete downpour protection.

the loss of body heat. Textile fabrics and clothing assemblies, no matter how esoteric or sophisticated, do not of themselves produce warmth. Any parka, for example, whether it keeps us warm or allows us to become cold quickly, depends only on the ability and efficiency of the textile fabrics and components to keep body heat from escaping to outside the garment.

Principles of Fabric/Garment Insulation

Efficient insulation for textiles and clothing in cold weather is dependent on the ability of fabrics and garments to maintain dead air spacing, avoid dampness in the fabric, and to be resilient for the maintenance of thickness. Each of these areas will now be discussed.

Dead Air   Textile materials of and by themselves do not significantly prevent body heat loss. Heat loss is prevented by the entrapment of air within fibers and/or between fibers or yarns. Air is, theoretically, the perfect insulator, as long as it is **dead air** (i.e., not moving). When air moves, as through a garment neck opening or through a sweater from wind, the insulating effect is reduced and there is body heat loss.

TABLE 12.2	Examples of Water Resistant and Waterproof, Breathable Fabrics	
Category	Type	Comments
Water resistant	Fiber/fabric type	Not windproof but most breathable
Waterproof	Coated type	Windproof but not breathable
Waterproof	Membrane type: two-layer or three-layer	Windproof; two-layer more flexible and more breathable than three-layer; three-layer more durable

Wetness If dead air trapped within a textile structure is the nearly perfect insulator, moisture and wetness are the opposite. Water dampness, or moisture, is an excellent conductor of heat, so perspiration trapped within the layers of cold-weather clothing quickly becomes compromised and heat loss increases. Wearing cold-weather clothing is thus a constant battle of sweating and freezing. Sweating when active, as in skiing or hiking, and freezing when the perspiration that clings to your skin introduces dampness to your clothing. Special cold-weather textiles and clothing overcome this problem. Dissipation of perspiration is an important feature that distinguishes *special* cold-weather fabrics and clothing from *ordinary* cold-weather fabrics and clothing.

Resilience The entrapment of dead air requires that an insulating fabric or batting maintain its established thickness. Loss of thickness means loss of entrapped dead air. Thus, materials used in thermal insulation must be resilient and not mat (flatten) or become thin after brief wear. For example, cotton batting, which has the ability to entrap dead air but has low resiliency, is not a good candidate for cold-weather clothing. Polyester batting, which is highly resilient, is an excellent candidate and is widely used as an insulation batting in such articles as ski jackets and sleeping bags.

Special Insulation Materials

Both fabrics and battings have been used in apparel to help insulate the wearer from the cold. A brief discussion of each follows.

Outerwear Fabrics Outerwear insulating fabrics, both knit and woven, achieve superior performance primarily as a result of the fiber's ability to entrap dead air. Comparing two fabrics, for example, the fibers, yarn construction, and finish must be examined since each element can effect each fabric's insulation value. Garment design can also be a factor (no hood allows heat loss through the head).

Thermolite® Base is an INVISTA™ trademark for fabrics made from its hollow-core fibers. This provides greater insulation since air is also entrapped inside the fiber. The larger surface fibers, in addition, allow for faster movement of moisture (perspiration) moving from the skin to the fabric surface where it can evaporate quickly. The result is more comfort (and warmth) since the skin surface is dry.

Polartec® is a well-known trade name used for a line of fabrics produced by Foss Manufacturing Company. Each material is engineered to serve specific functions relating to cold weather activities. The 100-percent-polyester knit fabrics are sold to apparel manufacturers whose products have been approved by Foss Manufacturing Company (licensing).

The Polartec® fabrics designed as the inner layer to be worn next to the skin (e.g., under garments) provide good moisture transport for comfort. A bicomponent construction is used in which there are different yarns on either side of the fabric. The result is moisture being wicked to the outside surface and then rapid evaporation, as it spreads on the surface.

The Polartec® fabrics designed to be used as the middle clothing layer (e.g., sweater or shirt) provide insulation (warmth without weight). The lofted (brushed) surface fibers trap in air and thus better retain body heat. Fabrics of various weights are available to provide a choice of insulation values.

The Polartec® fabrics designed to be used for outer-layer garments (e.g., jackets) provide insulation (lofted-surface fibers), wind resistance (tight construction), and water resistance (durable finish).

A three-layer laminated Polartec® material is available for active sportswear garments (Windbloc-ACT®). The inner-layer fabric provides moisture management. The middle layer is a stretch polyurethane perforated membrane for blocking the wind and enhancing material breathability. The outer layer is a warmth-without-weight insulating fabric with a durable water-repellency finish.

Nautica has a series of outerwear garments that employ innovative features combining form and function relating to climate protection (NX: Nautica Series). Their NX 4000 Series provides a garment that is waterproof, breathable, wind resistant, double and triple layers, and seam sealed. The material uses laminates in its construction.

Aquator™ is a weather-protection fabric system (Invista). The materials are windproof, waterproof, and breathable. Aquator™ material is an adhesive laminate using a membrane, which provides the durable waterproof/windproof protection. The fabrics are usually finished with Teflon® (a fluorochemical fabric treatment) which forms a molecular shield around the fiber so there is no staining (see p. 197). Water-repellency results from a lowering of the fabric surface tension. The membrane also transfers perspiration away from the skin.

Battings Special batting materials are distinguished from ordinary batting in that they possess one or more superior property such as resilience, loft, air entrapment, and moisture transport. The following are two examples of such battings:

▶ Thinsulate™ Insulation: Thinsulate™ Insulation was introduced about 1980 and was the original high-loft, fine denier warmth-without-weight insulation batting. The original product was made from a blend of olefin and polyester fibers. The types of Thinsulate™ Insulation marketed today range from 50 percent olefin and 50 percent polyester, to increasing percentages of polyester. 3M produces this product. The material is used in a variety of end uses, such as general outerwear, skiwear, hunting clothes, footwear, and gloves.

▶ Primaloft® is a batting composed of staple microdenier polyester fibers. Although the polyester fibers are themselves hydrophobic, Primaloft® is additionally treated with a patented hydrophobic finish, which results in almost no moisture regain. The material is used in end uses such as comforters, pillows, pads, gloves, and clothing.

This product was originally developed through a project of the U.S. Army for development of synthetic down insulating batting for soldiers' cold weather uniforms. (Down is the soft underplumage of geese and ducks.) The final development results, which are today's Primaloft®, not only match natural goose down for insulation value but have softness, loft, and resilience closely resembling those of natural down. The properties attained are largely due to the microdenier staple structure, whose denier size is nearly the same as the down fibrils of the natural product. The additional benefit of Primaloft® is the special treatment of the polyester fibers, which ensures that moisture or water does not become entrapped between fibers. Perspiration moisture does not collect within the insulation fiber, but quickly passes through the next clothing layer or evaporates to the air. Primaloft® is, like most polyester battings, hypoallergenic. Thus, persons who are allergic to goose down and feathers will not suffer distress. Albany International Corporation produces this product.

Thermal Comfort

Thermal comfort relates to the interaction of the garment and the body's temperature control. Normally garments can be added if a person becomes cold for additional warmth or removed if the person is getting too warm. The body gives heat from internal metabolic processes (which result when physical activity occurs), from the environment (heated air), and from radiant heat (sunlight). The body loses heat (cooling effect) from sweat evaporation and being surrounded by cooler air and surfaces (which results in convective transport of heated surface air away from the skin). If the body is not properly cooled the internal body temperature can rise, leading to disorientation, serious injury, or death. The fabric being used must be sufficiently permeable for convective heat and moisture (water vapors) transport to occur.

Apparel comfort is an aesthetic opinion. Individual preferences, work activity, temperature, humidity, and expectations are some attributes that impact on comfort. Workers place value in protective apparel (e.g., flame-resistant suit or hazmat outerwear) that is comfortable, protective, and durable. The concept of a material that allows a body-cooling effect through moisture (vapor) transmission, while also preventing contact with harmful liquids or other dangerous items is the challenge of protective apparel. An example of such a concept is the surgical gown where both thermal comfort and protection from bacteria is desired.

The measurement of the insulation value of a fabric is determined by the thermal transmittance test. The results of the test will indicate if the fabric is suitable for the desired result.

Clo Values

Clo is a unit of measurement for expressing the thermal resistance of textile materials. The higher the clo number, the greater the insulation effect. It is analogous to the R-value used in evaluating housing insulation.

One clo is defined as the insulation required to keep a person at rest comfortable in a normal indoor environment (i.e., about 70°F or 20°C, with little air movement). By adding the value of each garment worn, a total clo value can be obtained. For example, a person wearing a summer business suit ensemble (i.e., including undergarments, shirt, socks, and shoes) would be rated as wearing clothing with an effective clo value of about 1.

An active skier should be wearing clothing with an effective clo value of about 2, when the temperature is about 25°F (≈4°C). A sleeping bag to be used in ordinary camping conditions should have about a 4-clo value. Arctic survival wear should be rated about 6 clo, with the sleeping bag rating at least 8 clo. A well-known department store advertised a down- and polyester-filled parka with hood, engineered for warmth, as having a clo factor of 3.69.

Nanotechnology

Nanotechnology is the science and technology of manipulating molecular structures. The ability to create and adjust at the molecular and atomic levels means that new materials, devices, and substances can be created. The term nanotechnology comes from nanometer—a unit of measure one-billionth of a meter in length (the size of a benzene molecule). To be true nanotechnology, materials must behave at the nanoscale in ways not observed at a large scale and those behaviors must enable new applications that would not be possible at a large scale. Materials engineered at the nanoscale are engineered to have a particular property.

Nanotechnology, as it relates to fibers, has already been discussed on page 52. Through this technology, fiber properties have been altered so that, for example, cotton fibers can be made water and stain repellent. Through nanotechnology olefin fibers also can be given suitable dye sites inside the fiber so that they can be dyed using dyes instead of having to use pigments in the extrusion stage. Colored pigment particles can be made nanosize, which makes it easy for them to diffuse into any polymer. (Usually their size is too large to diffuse into some of the fibers.) Various new finishing effects are now available which differ from traditional finishes because chemicals can be attached to fibers and permanently bonded to fabrics at the molecular level. Nanotechnology relating to finishing has been discussed on page 201.

Whereas this technology was initially applied to apparel and home furnishings, it is now moving toward medical, automotive, and industrial applications.

The application of these technologies onto fabrics is able to be performed using existing textile equipment, is value-based, has a reasonable cost, and seems safe for workers, the environment, and the consumer. Nano-Tex™, Inc. was founded in 1998 to develop consumer-focused textile applications using nanotechnology. It was the first company to do so. Nano-Tex™ licenses its innovations to other companies.

Nanotechnology can be used to provide authenticity for branded textile products. Nanoscale fibers can be produced within a matrix of another extruded filament fiber (multicomponent fiber). The specific nanofibers embedded in the nylon, polyester, or polypropylene fiber (for example) can be colored so to produce a design (logo) which appears in the cross-section of the fiber produced. The special nanofibers are the same base polymer as the regular fiber, but may contain different additives. The resulting multicomponent fiber (or yarn) can be incorporated in the fabric, label, or sewing thread providing a covert marking system. Detectors can read the markers or identifiers by scanning, for example, the seam of the textile product. These security fibers and yarns are offered by ARmark™ Authentication Technologies, LLC.

The Institute for Soldier Nanotechnologies (ISN) is a research collaboration between the U.S. Army and Massachusetts Institute of Technology (Cambridge, MA). The ISN focuses on creating an array of innovation in nanoscience and nanotechnology intended to dramatically improve the serviceability and protection of soldiers. One goal is to create a new generation of uniforms for soldiers. Nanotechnology offers engineers the potential to create new material properties as well as the potential for miniaturization, thus reducing the weight a soldier must carry in the field. Designing the soldier system of the future is a formidable task.

There are developing problems with regard to the field of nanotechnology. These are several of them:

► No agreed terminology or definitions for nanotechnologies

► No agreed protocols for toxicity testing of nanoparticles

► Existing test methods may not be suitable for nanoscale devices and dimensions

► No standardized protocols for evaluating the environmental impact of nanoparticles

The National Nanotechnology Initiative (NNI) is an organization of 23 federal agencies which are involved with the field of nanotechnology. Some have research and development budgets. The National Nanotechnology Coordination Office (NNCO) helps coordinate federal efforts in this field. The NNI was established in 2000.

Electrotextiles

The continued development of fabric technology has paved the way for **electrotextile** growth (also referred to as electronic textiles). These are **smart fabrics** that can sense, respond, and adjust to stimuli such as pressure, temperature, or electrical charge. One use for smart fabrics would be the production of thermal products that protect from the cold weather, such as blankets and jackets. Another is a fabric which can have its color changed on demand, for fashion or camouflage. Finally, smart fabrics could be used to monitor heart rates of the wearer.

Fabric structures can provide a network used to contain flexible electronic circuitry, and made to have multiple layers and spaces that accommodate electronic devices. With the use of special yarns able to contain solar cells, batteries, and electronic devices built with submicron thickness, many new features can be provided for use in areas such as comfort, protection, and fashion.

Electroweaving would require modifications of existing machining since the yarns are different from traditional yarns. The production of electrowoven fabrics require short runs and a versatile operation to produce different circuits and to manufacture fabrics with closely monitored specifications and high quality.

The functioning of smart fabrics will be easier to achieve with the use of nanotechnology. Possible examples include fibers that harness the energy of the sun to make an air-conditioned garment (warm or cool wearer), garments that will not get dirty (self-cleaning), as well as garments that can monitor health signs of the wearer, and also carry and deliver medication.

Phase-Change Materials

A **phase-change material** (PCM) is a substance that alternates between being a solid and a liquid. It gives off heat when it changes to a solid state and absorbs heat when it returns to a liquid state. PCMs in the form of a microcapsule can be incorporated within a fiber (e.g., nylon, polyester, and acrylic) or foam, or may be coated onto a fabric.

When used with clothing, body heat is absorbed and stored resulting in a cooling effect, and when later released, the result is a heating effect. Temperature-adaptable fabrics have been used in a variety of products, including outdoor jackets, socks, boots, gloves, mattresses, comforters, and automobile seating.

The applications of phase-change materials are limited since the thermal comfort produced is only temporary. The warming or cooling effect ceases when the PCM completes its phase change since no more heat will be absorbed or given off. Also, if there is no temperature change, the PCM fabric will produce no effect. Thermal effect is maximized when the wearer repeatedly goes back and forth between a cold and warm environment, thus causing phase changes in the microcapsules.

A variety of companies are interested in developing phase-change materials. AcordisGroup has produced acrylic fibers containing PCMs, while Outlast Technologies, Inc. has produced PCM products for apparel and bedding. Freudenberg Nonwovens Group has produced phase-change lining materials (Comfortemp®).

Ultrasonic Sound Technology

The term **ultrasonic** sound refers to sound at high intensity and frequency, normally above the human hearing range. The short wavelengths of these sounds along with the use of special receivers provide useful information about the object. There are a variety of industrial and medical applications for this technology, such as to perform prenatal examination for pregnant women, clean materials, accelerate physical and chemical reactions, and for sensors to detect the edge of a fabric or film so it can be properly guided and positioned as it passes through a processing machine.

The energy from the vibrations producing the ultrasonic sound is also used in textile processing. One of these uses is based on the ability to use ultrasonic energy to induce heat in order to join thermoplastic materials (no thread or adhesive is required). The resulting continuous seam provides a barrier to air, chemicals, and organisms, unlike sewn seams. The pieces are joined by overlapping the material sections and bonding them with the resulting heat. Glue may be used for additional strength. The seam will be slightly thicker than a sewn seam. A tape made of polyurethane could be used to bond the two edges of the fabrics together. The heating machine melts the tape. Sonic bonding is more costly than a sewn seam. Major applications include its use in making disposable diapers, window shades, surgical gowns, filtration products, and quilting effects as seen on bedspreads and mattress pads. Ultrasonic welding technology is also valuable for making composites of fabric, foam, and film. The Branson Ultrasonics Corporation produces an ultrasonic bonding machine—Pinsonic Thermal Joining Machine.

One technique used for ultrasonic bonding passes two materials between a solid metal rotary drum (anvil) and an acoustical device (horn). The horn applies pressure against the thermoplastic material and vibrates when it produces the ultrasonic sound, causing friction against the material. The heat produced softens or melts the material and when the ultrasonic vibrations stop, the molten material solidifies with a thermal bond achieved. A bonding pattern can be achieved by using an engraved drum. A stationary technique could be used so to seal filter bags, for example. The material could be stationary while the horn descends to make contact with the stationary anvil.

The fabrics and fibers best suited to ultrasonic bonding contain at least 65 percent thermoplastic fibers, possess high abrasion resistance, have a uniform thickness, and are able to accept energy at the material interface. Polyester, nylon, and olefin are considered to be good fibers for this technique.

Another major use for ultrasonics is the slitting of thermoplastic fabrics and films. With this technique a smooth, clean, durable edge can be made, with no discoloration or unraveling. There is also no bead or build-up of thickness on the slit edge to add bulk to rolled materials.

Additional uses for ultrasonic sound technology include ultrasonic washing of textiles (see p. 213), quilting (see p. 147), acting as sensors to detect and remove foreign fibers from the fiber mix before yarn or material is made, and improving textile processes (such as dyeing, and bleaching) by the use of the ultrasonic energy to reduce processing time, amount of chemicals required, and amount of energy used.

Industrial Fabrics

The emphasis in the textile industry has traditionally been on apparel and interior fabrics. The industrial fabrics area has been a much smaller segment. It is different from the two major areas, where fashion plays an important role.

Industrial fabrics are engineered to meet special performance requirements. They focus on function rather than aesthetics. Other terms used instead of industrial fabrics are "technical fabrics," "engineered fabrics," "high-performance textiles," and "hi-tech fabrics." There are many applications for these fabrics that enhance our lives and contribute to a productive economy. These include fabrics in the air (airplanes), under the ground (geotextiles), implanted in our bodies (medical uses), reinforcing tires, wrapping wires, filtration units, and for agriculture. The fabric weights range from very heavy to very light. (See Table 12.3.)

Fabrics used in the industrial segment usually fall into one of three categories according to their use:

1. Fabrics that are incorporated directly into a finished product, such as sails, awnings, and soft luggage.

2. Fabrics that are consumed in processes of various kinds, such as filters, buffing wheels, and twine.

3. Fabrics that are combined with other materials, such as hose, rubber footwear, and belting.

The industrial market is composed mainly of organizational customers (e.g., manufacturers, government, and institutional buyers) rather than individual consumers. Unlike the consumer market, the industrial market is often composed of a relatively small number of customers for a particular industrial product.

Many people are unaware of the importance and potential of the industrial fabrics industry. This is partly because industrial fabrics frequently are components of other products (e.g., shoe linings, tires, and fire hoses), and often are not recognized as textiles in the end-use application.

Sales of industrial fabrics are based primarily on specifications and performance tests. Color, printed designs, and other fashion criteria are not usually factors. The fabric selected must meet the needs of the particular industry. Price is often less important than factors such as quality, product uniformity, delivery assuredness, and service.

The growth and development of the industrial fabrics industry follows changes in the United States. For example, canvas was used for sails on sailing ships in the 1700s and 1800s. Canvas also covered the prairie schooners (i.e., covered wagons) as they traveled westward across the country. Fabric covering protected the automobile driver and passenger in the early 1900s (ragtops) and then later as convertible tops. Fabrics covered airplanes initially so they could fly (airplane cloth). Industrial fabrics were also used on space vehicles and in space suits for the astronauts. Fabrics for parachutes were first developed for pilots, but later also used in recreational activity.

Specialty Fibers

Specialty fibers for specific industrial textile applications were once considered a sideline for fiber companies. Their focus was fibers for apparel and the interior. Various "consumer" fibers, however, have been used for industrial end use. For example, the use of olefin continues to grow. It is versatile and inexpensive. Olefin is an excellent fiber when used as a geotextile material, furnishings fabrics for boats, surface covering for outdoor items, and filter materials.

Cordura® nylon (INVISTA™) is a special type of nylon which has very high tenacity and abrasion and tear resistance. It is well established in the luggage, backpack, and outdoor outerwear markets.

Kevlar® and Nomex® aramid fibers (DuPont™) have been used for decades in heat-protective clothing, ballistic protective vests, and tires. These fibers can be blended with other fibers (e.g., rayon/nylon) to make a fire-resistant fabric.

Carbon fibers are used in plastic reinforcements for industrial uses as well as in heat shields of space shuttle wings.

Sulfar is highly resistant to acids and alkalies as well as heat. End uses include hot-gas filtration and electrical insulation.

PBI has excellent heat and chemical resistance. It is suitable for heat-resistant apparel (e.g., fireman turn-out coat), hazmat suits, space suits, and covering for foam cushions for upholstery to prevent ignition and resulting smoke.

It is interesting to note that the success of PBI was the direct result of Celanese Corporation working with leading textile, aircraft, seat, and airline companies to develop fabrics which would meet the Federal Aviation Administration's commercial-aircraft-seat burning standards. It was originally developed in conjunction with the National Aeronautic Space Administration and the U.S. Air Force to protect astronauts after the tragic fire at Cape Canaveral in which three Apollo astronauts were killed.

Protective Garments

People who work in hazardous occupations are given protective clothing to wear. The fabric as well as the garment must be designed to protect against specific hazards. Also, the garment must provide a degree of comfort, or the worker will not be efficient. This includes garment/fabric flexibility, thermal comfort (see p. 223), and design.

Thermal Resistance

Various occupations require work clothing to be worn that must provide thermal resistance. This includes clothing that is flame-resistant as well as resistant to external heat. The worker must be protected from burns that can occur from both factors. Firefighters, racecar drivers, and foundry workers are examples of people who must be protected from this danger.

Resistance to Penetration

Under certain situations, a fabric must be able to resist the penetration of various substances. These include chemicals, biological organisms, and radioactive dust. Composite structures made of nanofibers are an excellent choice for such specialized filtration applications.

People who face chemical exposure include workers who help produce liquid chemicals, agricultural workers who use pesticide applicators, soldiers, police who may be faced with potential exposure, and factory workers who use chemicals to treat products. The protective garments range from inexpensive latex gloves to suits that encapsulate the entire body.

People who are exposed to biological agents such as bacteria and viruses (e.g., medical personnel), must protect themselves from direct exposure to the organisms as well as fluids that can be used to transmit them. In the field of biotechnology live organisms are handled and so the technicians, research personnel, and others must have protection.

Protective clothing once contaminated is usually not reused. Thus, they are usually disposed of with no attempt to clean. These garments are frequently made from nonwoven material. Since a single suit is unable to protect against all possible hazards, companies offer a range of products that meet most of the needs in the marketplace (biological, chemical, and nuclear radiation protection).

Soft body armor, another type of protective garment, is used by military personnel, police, and correctional guards in prisons. Apparel, such as protective vests, protect against gunfire and knife attack. Fibers used in this type of personal protection garment include Kevlar® aramid fiber (DuPont™). The fabrics are also called impact-protection textiles.

Honeywell, Inc. has produced a Spectra® polyethylene fiber that is very strong and tough. It has been incorporated into a composite material made by bonding parallel fiber strands with an advanced resin system. The material forms a basis for insert plates used in bullet-resistant vests, as well as military aircraft and vehicle armor.

Geotextiles

An important usage of nonwoven materials is in the field of **geotextiles**. This term is used for products made of textiles and related structures used in construction and civil engineering applications. The products are produced by assembling fibers into flexible fabric to provide a porous interflow across and within their manufactured plane. The term "geotextile" is still used to describe these products, but a broader category of product is now encompassed by the term "geosynthetics."

In geotextile applications, the nonwoven fabric performs one of the following functions: drainage, filtration, reinforcement, separation, protection, or a moisture barrier (when coated or impregnated). The following are examples in which nonwoven geotextiles are used.

Drainage and Filtration

Water in and around buildings, roadways, and other such structures is a major cause of damage and deterioration. Nonwovens can be used to control this moisture. The material has pores or openings small enough to prevent individual soil particles from passing through the geotextile, but these openings are uniform and numerous enough to allow large quantities of water to pour through. Thus, it can be used to line a drainage system or be placed under a roadway to allow water to pass that otherwise would be retained.

A silt fence made of geotextile is a very effective method to reduce silt loss from water runoff at a job site. (Silt is a fine-grained sandy sediment.) The geotextile acts as a filter, retaining the silt while allowing the water to flow through.

Stabilization/Reinforcement

Nonwovens are also used to stabilize and reinforce roadways, parking lots, and building sites. It accomplishes these functions by keeping the load-bearing soils from the select fill or road-base material. It also reinforces the road base by confining the material and preventing local soil movement.

Erosion Control

Nonwovens are very effective in preventing soil erosion from the flow of rivers or the result of ocean waves. The geotextile acts as a filter, allowing water to pass through both sides, while protecting and holding soil in place. John Boyle & Co., Inc. owns knitting machines capable of producing heavy polyester material as wide as 20 feet. The high strength of this material is used to hold back soil behind retaining walls.

Protection

Geotextiles are being placed under or on top of liners used to contain liquids or solid waste. They provide a cushion for the liner as well as protection from puncture and abrasion. The usage is of particular interest when there is an environmental concern, such as with landfills and waste dumps.

Moisture Barrier

In this application, the nonwoven fabric is positioned just below the surface of a roadway. The fabric has been processed so as to produce an almost impermeable membrane, preventing water from entering the road base. Thus, less roadway maintenance will be required and the roadway will have a greater life expectancy.

Biotechnology

An increasing number of textile products are being developed in the biotechnology field. Knitted, woven, and nonwoven structures have been developed for very specialized products. Applications include tissue engineering and implementation within the body to help it heal where tissue has been damaged or destroyed. Mesh has been developed to support body-wall reconstruction (hernia repairs) and provide flexibility in the face, neck, breast, or abdominal wall beneath the skin surface. Also textile materials have been engineered to provide support for regenerating tendons, ligaments, and other connective tissues until they can return to being fully functional. In addition, stents have been made using high-tech fibers.

Narrow Fabrics

Narrow fabrics have experienced an enormous upswing in usage. These materials are usually no wider than 12 inches (≈30.5 cm). They are mainly produced on so-called narrow-weaving machines or on warp-knitting machines. The looms used are not narrow, but weave many narrow fabrics side-by-side. The fabrics produced include both elastic and nonelastic types. Narrow fabrics include ribbons, safety belts for automobiles, medical bandages, labels, webbing for cargo control, and various tapes (window blind and carpet-edge tapes as well as underwear waistbands).

TABLE 12.3 Industrial Technical Fabrics Market (Illustrates the wide range of uses and products)	
Transportation	Automobiles, buses, trucks, railways, airplanes, ships, and others.
	Airbags, brake liners, convertible tops, filters (air and gas), floor and interior coverings, gaskets, hose reinforcement, insulation (sound and heat), seat belts.
Geotextile and Geomembrane	Liners for waste ponds, soil-erosion control, reinforce roadbeds, filtration (air, water, gas), landfill coverings.
Medical	Bandages, artificial arteries, surgical drapes and gowns, sutures, masks, sheets, hygiene.
Safety	Protection from heat, fire, chemicals, toxic fumes and radiation, safety flags, insulation from cold and sound, work gloves.
Production Facility	Conveyor belting, V-belts, papermaker felts, printer's blankets, abrasive belts, buffing cloths, netting, filters.
Military	Belts, ballistic protection, floatable bridges, parachutes, backpacks.
Construction	Reinforcing building materials, roofing systems, screening, building components, inflatable buildings (warehouse, sports), tarpaulin.
Agriculture	Seed-bed protection, shade material, insect netting, crop covers, green houses, fruit wrappers, weed control, tree wraps.
Recreational	Sails, inflatable rafts, water bags, balloons, tents, banners.
Miscellaneous	Awnings, coffee filters, sacks, animal leashes, casket linings, sandbags, bookbinders.

Reflective Safety Apparel

Reflective garments have been made for many years. Mostly, however, the reflective materials are applied to the fabric surface. The result is usually a less drapable garment and a garment that has a less fashionable design. It is also more difficult to clean. Converting the reflective material into a yarn, however, reduces the aforementioned problems since the yarn is incorporated into the material. It also maintains the safety qualities. Uniforms (public safety professionals), actionwear, and children's wear offer growth for the future. There is also a growing acceptance of ANSI 107, the voluntary standard that provides consistent authoritative guidelines for the selection and use of high-visibility apparel in the United States.

Retroglo® Yarn

The Metlon Corporation has developed a unique yarn that combines nighttime safety with versatility. The yarn reflects the light that shines on its surface, such as car lights, back to the light source (180° reflection). The yarns become a brilliant white to the driver, thus increasing the safety of joggers, bicycle riders, walkers, and highway workers at night. This yarn is marketed under the trademark Retroglo®.

Retroglo® yarns are thin and flat like a metallic yarn. They are made by laminating 3M Scotchlite™ Reflective Film in roll form to a roll of clear polyester film. (The reflective film has 50,000 minute glass beads to the square inch.) The rolls are cut into narrow widths (e.g., $1/32$ of an inch or 0.8 mm) to make the yarn.

Retroglo® yarn can be woven, knit, or braided into fabrics or trim applied to fabrics (or garments). The yarn is a neutral gray color which blends almost unnoticed into fabrics in the daytime. The yarns can be contained throughout a garment (e.g., suit), in only part of a garment (e.g., yoke of a child's sweater), or in appliqués, panels, or trim. Thus, Retroglo® yarns provide nighttime safety without destroying the aesthetic appearance of the fabric.

Fluorescent dyes can be used to increase the wearer's visibility at night. They absorb light in the visible wavelength range and then re-emit it in the ultraviolet range, making the surface appear brighter. The safety feature is not as effective as with the use of reflective beads.

Growth

There is much opportunity for growth in the industrial fabrics of the textile industry. Since there is great diversity of products being produced as previously indicated, the result is great potential usage of special textiles.

There are also increasing government regulations that relate to safety, both in the workplace and outside. Thus protective clothing is being used to an increasing degree. Protection from hazardous waste cleanings, chemical spills, and toxic fumes is essential to human safety.

A growing use for industrial specialty fibers is fiber optics. Fiber optics is that field of physics which deals with the transfer of light from one place to another through long, thin, flexible fibers of glass or plastic. These fibers are called optical fibers. Optical fibers have the ability to transfer light around corners because the sides of the fibers reflect light and keep it inside as the fiber bends and turns. A thin fiber cable can carry more messages with less signal distortion than a heavy copper cable. Optical fibers being relatively immune from static can be useful around power lines. Also, small light sources can be used, which allows light to be focused in very small places. This is very helpful to dentists drilling a tooth or doctors wanting to see an internal part of the body.

Advances in fiber, yarn, fabric, and manufacturing techniques continue to lead to new application opportunities and are helping fabric manufacturers meet the continuously expanding technical objectives and expectations of their customers.

Trade Association

The Industrial Fabrics Association International (IFAI) is an international trade organization representing the technical and industrial fabric manufacturers. IFAI membership also includes related companies, such as fiber producers, weavers, nonwoven producers, finishers, laminators, jobbers, and testing laboratories.

Some of the programs of IFAI include public relations for the industry, sponsorship of production, and technical seminars and the publication of market reports and periodicals. The organization also tracks and influences standards, specifications, and building codes which affect the industrial fabrics industry.

The *Industrial Fabrics Product Review* is the major magazine for the industrial fabrics industry and is published monthly.

Plastic, Leather, and Fur

Many products usually made of fabrics are also made from these three unique materials—plastic, leather, and fur. The first is a man-made product and the last two are animal products. Traditional textile end uses, such as apparel (e.g., coats) and interior products (e.g., upholstery) use these special materials. Each of these products is discussed in the following sections.

Plastic

Plastic is a manufactured material consisting of long chains of molecules called polymers. It is formed in the liquid state and then hardens. Plastics can be shaped into almost any form. The substances from which most plastics are made (called synthetic resins) are derived primarily from petroleum. By using various chemical additives, different types of plastics can be made, each with their own properties. (There are hundreds of different plastics.) Thus, many end uses are possible, such as squeeze bottles, tubing, automobile fenders, and toys, with a variety of shapes, colors, and surface textures. Plastic films can be made in a range of thicknesses and weights, from very thin and light (e.g., sandwich bags) to thick and heavy (e.g., upholstery). The United States is one of the leaders in plastic production.

Manufacturers make plastic products from plastic resins which melt to a liquid when heated. The methods used include *molding* (pressure forces the liquid plastic resin into a mold in which it hardens), *calendering* (produces sheets by having liquid plastic resin pressed between two rollers), *extrusion* (liquid plastic resin is forced through a shaping die (hole), and *foaming* (introduces a gas into the heated plastic resin).

All plastics belong to one of two basic types, based on how they behave when heated:

▶ Thermosetting plastic—can be heated and set only once. They cannot be remelted or reshaped because of the chemical reaction that occurs.

▶ Thermoplastics—can be melted and reformed again and again.

Textile Materials

For plastics to be useful as a fabriclike material, it must be able to be made into thin sheets or a film that can be easily folded and creased without cracking. These plastic films are usually made by extruding a heated liquid solution through flat dies (or holes), which then hardens into a thin sheet, or by calendering (rotating heated rollers which squeeze the solution into sheet form). The film can be made in varying thicknesses, clear or colored, smooth surfaced or with a grain (pattern). It is inexpensive.

The textile industry uses plastics to replace natural fibers, such as cotton, silk, and wool. The plastics used to produce manufactured fibers include nylon, polyester, and acrylic plastics (same names as the fiber produced). They are all thermoplastic. Plastics are also used to create synthetic leathers and furlike material.

Main Types The two main types of plastic used to make film for use in the textile industry (apparel and interior products) are **polyvinyl chloride** (also referred to as PVC or vinyl) and **polyurethane** (also referred to as urethane). Other plastics, such as polyethylene and cellophane, are used to make film for such end uses as photographic film, balloons, shopping bags, and wrapping.

Vinyl film—flexible but with poor drape. Soft in warm weather, but it becomes stiff and brittle when cold. It is cleaned by wiping it with a damp cloth. Do not clean with dry cleaning solvent since vinyl will then become stiff and it will crack when bent. It is waterproof, but since it is nonbreathable, it will be uncomfortable if worn as apparel. The film has excellent stain and soil resistance and is thermoplastic. End uses include shower curtains, tablecloths (may be fabric backed), rainwear, and leatherlike material for upholstery. (Unlike leather it is cold to the touch and not as soft.)

Polyurethane film—remains soft and flexible when both warm and cold. It is washable and dry cleanable, as well as waterproof and nonbreathable. The film has excellent stain and soil resistance and is thermoplastic. A major end use is leatherlike material (more leatherlike than vinyl). A layer of polyurethane foam is used in laminated fabric material, as well as the underlay or backing material for carpeting. It can be applied to various fabrics for use in end uses such as outerwear, tents, sleeping bags, and filters.

These films are often attached to a substrate of a textile fabric, becoming a reinforced or supported film. This adds strength and results in the unlikelihood that the film will crack or tear.

A coated fabric can be made by having a layer of vinyl or polyurethane film applied to a fabric surface. The result would be a protected material (e.g., from water), a more functional fabric (e.g., opaque window covering), or a special surface effect (e.g., leather grain). Polyurethane is better than vinyl for fabrics with elastic properties.

Poromerics Polyurethane film can be used for a poromeric membrane (waterproof, but breathable). It can be processed so micropores are created in the material. The result is a much more comfortable apparel, which is also windproof.

Poromeric materials are those which are waterproof, but can also breathe (allow water-vapor and air to pass). Thus, a more comfortable garment, for example, can be made since perspiration can escape.

A very thin (approximately 0.0005 of an inch or 0.013 millimeter thickness) microporous membrane film is used. This material is usually made of PTFE (polytetrafluorethylene). The film transmits water vapor through tiny pinholes in the material called micropores, but it is waterproof and windproof. The holes are so small that water droplets (rain) do not penetrate. Air and moisture, however, are able to pass through. This is possible because the air- and water-vapor (perspiration) molecules are a fraction of the size of a water molecule. The film is then laminated to an outershell fabric for support and protection. Usually, a lining fabric is also laminated directly to the other side of the membrane for a sandwich effect, with the membrane in the middle (see Figure 12.3). The resulting laminated material is employed in various end uses, such as outerwear and sleeping bags. A well-known trademark for such a laminated material is GORE-TEX®, produced by W.L. Gore Associates.

Another poromeric material being used is suedelike. It is a multicomponent, nonwoven fabric composed of polyester microfibers embedded in a layer of polyurethane foam. The surfaces are brushed to provide a suedelike effect. The result is a durable, soft, leatherlike material which is also machine-washable and dry cleanable. It is made of 60 percent micropolyester fibers and 40 percent polyurethane foam. End uses include apparel and interior furnishings. A well-known trademark for this material is Ultrasuede® by Ultrasuede (America), Inc., Toray Group. Ultraleather® is also a poromeric material. It is 100 percent polyurethane and made with a knit backing of 70 percent rayon and 30 percent nylon. The fabric is embossed and is lightweight, water-repellent, and soft. End uses include apparel and interior furnishings. It is also manufactured by the Toray Group.

Foaming

Foaming is a process to introduce a gas into the heated plastic solution. The gas expands and creates bubbles in the cooling solution. The resulting material is lightweight foam. It can be made in various thicknesses. Depending on the resin chemicals used, the result can be soft and rubbery, such as foams used in furniture, cushions, and pillows, or stiff. Foam is used in laminated fabric material (e.g., bras) as well as the underlay or backing material for carpeting. Polyurethane is most frequently used to create a foam material, but polyethylene can also be used.

Expanded Vinyl Vinyl made with a foaming process is called **expanded vinyl.** The result is a soft, spongy insulating material, but not as abrasion resistant as plain vinyl film. It is also impermeable to air and water. A woven, knit, or nonwoven material is attached to the expanded vinyl foam (backing fabric) to provide durability A surface film could also be applied to make a three-layer composition.

Naugahyde® is a well-known expanded vinyl product made in a three-layer configuration. (It is produced by Uniroyal Engineered Products, LLC.) The colored vinyl surface film is thin and so its leatherlike grain (NaugaLeather®) cannot be obtained from embossing rollers. The pattern is made when heated liquid vinyl is poured onto paper with a grain design. As the film cools and hardens, the surface shape of the paper becomes the surface shape of the plastic film on contact. The paper is reusable. A layer of foam (expanded vinyl) is then adhered to the vinyl film, followed by the addition of the backing fabric. A clear coating is finally applied to the surface for protection. Various other surface effects are also offered. The Advanced Beauty Gard® finish provides an excellent level of disinfectability.

The Environment

How to dispose of plastic waste has become a major environmental concern. Plastic waste contributes to environmental pollution since plastics are not biodegradable by environmental processes. They are disposed of in landfill space. A problem is that the amount of plastic waste is growing, but the amount of landfill space is limited.

Thermoplastic products can be recycled by remelting with virgin material and reforming them into new products. Thermoset plastic products can usually be either ground into fine powders or shredded to be used as insulation for such products as quilted jackets and sleeping bags. While thermoset products cannot be reprocessed, sometimes the chemicals used to make the products can be recovered and reused.

Polyethylene bags returned from dry cleaner customers are being recycled into new bags as well as other products. Some dry cleaners have replaced plastic bags with re-usable nylon bags to cover clean garments. (The bags are first cleaned before reuse.) The bags are returned by customers when they bring in their next order and used again.

Leather

Leather has been used since prehistoric times. It is the skin of an animal, bird, or reptile with the hair or fiber removed. Leather is a fibrous, organic material which has been treated so it will not putrefy (rot). It varies greatly in thickness, surface markings, size, and uniformity. Leather is often a byproduct of a food supply. The United States is one of the world's largest producers of leather, with New York, Massachusetts, California, and Wisconsin as the leading leather-producing states.

The skins of large animals are called **hides** (e.g., cowhide and buffalo hide). Those from smaller animals are called **skins** (e.g., pigskin, snakeskin, calfskin, and

UNIQUE FABRICATIONS AND INNOVATIONS

231

sheepskin). Cattle hides provide the source of most leather. Some of the more expensive skins include ostrich, eel, and alligator. Hides and skins are internationally sourced.

The surface marking is called the **grain.** It can be natural (real grain) or an added pattern by an embossing process (embossed grain). It varies from species to species (e.g., pig and cow), from animal to animal within the same species (e.g., cow to cow), as well as within an individual animal skin (e.g., side and belly). Ostrich has a unique dimpled grain due to sockets from which the feathers were pulled.

Leather products include balls, gloves, saddles, luggage, wallets, coasters, apparel, and furniture. China, Morocco, Cyprus, Argentina, and Italy are some nations that export leather apparel to the United States.

Properties

Leather can be made as flexible as a fabric or as stiff as a wood board. It can be made thin or thick. It can also be finished (e.g., dyed, polished, or embossed). Thus, it is used in many products. Examples are coats, shoes, gloves, industrial drive belts, luggage, handbags, footballs, and upholstery (see Figure 12.5). There has been a large increase in the use of leather for furniture and seats in corporate aircraft. Because of new technologies, leather can be made lighter, enabling garments to be fashioned for year-round-use.

Leather has excellent air- and water-vapor permeability which adds to its comfort, particularly when used for chair or sofa covering. The quality of leather is not uniform throughout the hide or skin as is plastic film. Synthetic or artificial leather (a plastic, leatherlike material) is uniform but does not have natural leather's ability to breathe (allows water vapor to pass, but not water) and thereby remove perspiration.

Polyvinyl chloride (vinyl) plastic with a grain on the surface is the material most frequently used to replace leather. It is very resistant to wear and scratches, but it is cold and not as soft to the touch as leather. Sometimes upholstered furniture is made of a combination of plastic and leather to reduce the cost. The leather covers the areas that come into contact with the individual.

The quality of leather also depends upon the location on the animal's body. The leather made from either side of the backbone, from the rump to the shoulder, provides the finest leather. The shoulders produce the next best quality. The head section produces good leather, but the pieces are small. The belly and legs produces the poorest leather since it is very uneven and tends to stretch.

Thin leather can be made softer than thicker leather, however, it is less durable and less scratch resistant. Thus, sometimes there needs to be a trade-off between softness

FIGURE 12.5
Leather jackets.

and durability when determining which hide or skin to use.

Hides and skins are usually not as large as full-width fabrics and are of limited length. Thus, leather products have to be more carefully designed to maximize the utilization of the size of the piece of leather and minimize the number of seams required to make the article.

Leather garments may shrink as they relax over time. This can be from the leather being stretched during processing (e.g., tanning), or from age and cleaning. It is best to buy a slightly larger size garment.

Manufacturers often use a code to indicate the quality of the leather used. However, there is no overall code uniformity, so comparison of leather products is more difficult.

Split Leather

Thicker hides (from the larger animals) can be cut into thinner layers by a process called **splitting.** The layer showing the grain on one side is called **top grain.** Layers that do not include the grain surface (bottom or flesh layer) are called **split leather** (or **splits**). They are usually either sanded or napped to produce a soft suede effect, or embossed to produce a grain (pattern) on the surface.

Top grain is the best quality leather, since it wears well, and finishes well. The closer the splits are to the flesh of the animal, the poorer the quality since it is less durable (skins are denser on the outside or grain side), less flexible, and not very soft. It is also cheaper. The term **full-grain leather** means that the leather has not been split.

Suede leather is usually made from split leather, most often from cowhide (thick hide). Soft chamois leather, often used as a washing and polishing cloth, is made from split leather, often from sheepskin (see Figure 12.6).

Leather Processing

There are many processes that must be performed before hides and skins become leather. The following is an abbreviated listing:

1. **Curing**—this prevents skins from rotting before being transported to the tannery. Salting and drying are two procedures included in this process.

2. **Fleshing**—the removal of fat and meat on the flesh side of the skin.

3. **Unhairing**—the removal of hair attached to the skin.

4. **Tanning**—its main purpose is to prevent the skin from rotting. It is performed in a tannery where the skins are treated chemically so they will not become hard and crack. Properties of the resulting leather depend upon the method used. Firmness, water repellency, wear resistance, softness, and cost are affected.

The following are the main tanning methods:

▸ Vegetable tanning—this process uses bark, wood, or root extract from certain trees. The leather is firm, very water resistant, and requires a long time period for processing (usually one to three months, but as much as one year for thick skins). Good for shoe soles.

▸ Chrome tannery—this is a mineral tanning process using chrome salts. The leather is less water resistant, more resistant to scratching, more flexible and elastic, and easier to later make soft. Chrome tanning leaves leather with a light blue color and is usually completed in several hours. It is used for upholstery, gloves, luggage, wallets, and shoe uppers.

▸ Oil tanning—this process results in very soft and flexible leather. This method is used to make chamois leather.

FIGURE 12.6
This fashionable light-weight garment is made from split leather.

Often two tanning methods are used for the skin. For example, a skin to be used for shoe soles could be processed using a combination tanning of vegetable and chrome tanning. The result compared to only vegetable tanning would be reduced cost, reduced processing time, increased flexibility, and reduced durability.

5. Splitting—the process by which tanned leather is split into layers (with a splitting machine). This occurs with thicker hides.

6. Coloring—this process includes dyeing and printing. Aniline dye provides the best color properties for leather. If it is **aniline dyed,** the leather usually has also been dyed in a vat and it is completely colored throughout. Thus, if the leather is scratched, it still will exhibit color in the area scratched because

of the complete dye penetration. Printing may be performed to obtain a two-tone surface effect.

7. Finishing—the group of final processes used to provide certain properties. These include glazing (for shine), buffing (for smoothness), embossing (for design), sanding (to even the surface and color), and milling (tumbling in drums to achieve a soft and supple effect). A hard finish can also be achieved (e.g., for leather to be used for a briefcase).

8. Protection—this is a coating substance, such as polyurethane, that can be applied to protect the leather from staining.

Some of the processes are also performed in order to camouflage or correct flaws, scars, and other surface irregularities. These include embossing, sanding, buffing, and dyeing. Tanners sometimes use fillers before dyeing to mask any scar tissue, hair follicles, or other imperfections on the leather. Cleaning may remove some of the fillers and cause the defects to appear.

Various substances are sprayed on the surface of leather during the finishing process (e.g., glazing). The layer applied must not only be firmly attached so as not to peel off, but it must also be pliable, elastic, and have the same degree of stretch as the leather to which it is affixed.

Patent Leather

A special effect on leather can be achieved by applying successive coats of polyurethane or another substance (e.g., a heavy oil varnish) at the end of the finishing process. The resulting high-gloss is durable. The product is called **patent leather.** A similar technique can be performed on vinyl film. The product is called **patent vinyl.**

When shipping patent leather (or vinyl), two sheets are placed face-to-face and then rolled. Thus the shiny surfaces are protected from damage and scratching. The dull backs are exposed to abrasion.

Sports Uses

Leather has been associated with balls used in sports. For example, the Wilson Company has made a cowhide football since 1941. Contrary to popular myth, footballs never have been made from pigskin. In baseball, the Rawlings Company switched from horsehide to cowhide leather coverings for the balls in 1974.

The Spalding Company makes National Basketball Association (NBA) game balls. In 2006 the ball was changed from leather to one made of a synthetic microfiber composite material. The change was made to meet the need for a more consistent ball instead of the unevenness and sometimes lopsidedness of the leather ball. The synthetic material spreads moisture evenly across the ball's surface for quicker evaporation so to give the player better control of the ball. The ball, however, was changed back to being made of leather the same season due to player complaints.

Care

Leather is moisture dependent and needs cleaning, conditioning, and protection to ensure its beauty, durability, and value. Cleaning leather products requires special care, often being done by a specialist. Problems that occur could be a fault in the leather processing (e.g., the use of dyes that are not fast), the manufacturer's use of an improper component (e.g., fusible interlining which shrunk during cleaning), or the dry cleaner not realizing that solvents make leather stiff and so it may crack if bent. (Oils must be replaced for the leather to again be soft and pliable.)

People who are leather cleaners are often skillful in restoring original appearances and color as well as continuing to hide existing defects when a finish is removed in the cleaning process.

Leather coats should be hung on a wide hanger to preserve shape. Also, leather products should not be positioned with a plastic covering which allows moisture to reach it. When wet, leather should be dried slowly (not near a fire) to avoid damage. Surface dirt on grain leather can be removed by using soap (weak solution) and water—not detergent. Shoe polish, as well as leather cleaner, help to preserve the leather by adding wax and oil. There are various such products available to the public. Leather shoes should be stored on shoe trees to help retain their shape and size.

Association

The Leather Industries of America (LIA) located in Washington, DC, represents the interests and concerns of the tanning industry of the United States. LIA provides environmental, technical, educational, statistical, and marketing services to its members. It represents the leather industry to the government. The Leather Research Laboratory, located at the University of Cincinnati, provides services in various areas of leather production, such as performance testing and research. The LIA sponsors a pavilion at the Asia Pacific Leather Fair in Hong Kong.

Fur

Fur products have been used for thousands of years, both for protection against weather and for decorative covering. (See Figure 12.7.) Furs were traded by the Phoenicians and other ancient Mediterranean civilizations. The search for fine skins (including sable) lays behind Russia's push eastwards, in the 17th century, into Siberia and the

FIGURE 12.7
Fur coat by Bibhu Mohapatra.

Pacific regions. The fur trade was also the economic force that drove adventurers to explore North America during the same period.

Fur is the skin of an animal with the fiber or hair attached. The skin is treated so it will not putrefy or rot. Most fur-bearing animals of commercial importance have two sets of hair. One is the *underfibers*, which are short and dense. They keep the animal warm by trapping air and holding it close to the skin like a blanket. They are called **fur hairs** or **duvet.** The other set is longer, tougher, and usually stiffer. They lie over the fur hair and repel water. They are called **guard hairs.** Ponies and colobus monkeys only have guard hair covering.

Furs can vary from one species to another. For example, sable has long, silky (luxurious) hair. Persian lamb has wooly, tightly curled hair. Raccoon has coarse guard hairs. Opossum has short underfur (and regular guard hair). Beaver is prized for both its soft underfur and its guard hairs. Chinchilla has unusual coloring.

Sources

Fur-bearing animals from all over the world are used by the fur industry. The two main sources are animals in the wild (obtained by trapping), and farming (the animals are bred on special farms). Most furs today come from farmed animals.

Trapping   Most trapping of animals is done in their natural surroundings in the winter, when the animal's fur is thickest, longest, and shiny. Animals that are trapped include the beaver, coyote, fox, fisher, lynx, marten, mink, muskrat, opossum, and raccoon. The leading countries that trap popular fur-bearing animals are Canada, Russia, and the United States.

Farming   Farming, or **fur ranching,** began in the late 1800s. Ranch-bred animals are kept in individual cages of a size that will permit them to move about. It is believed that with better care, better furs are produced. Ranchers try to produce animals with new and different colored fur (for a variety of natural colors), larger bodies (fewer animals required to produce a coat), thicker underfur, softer fur, and more guard hairs of even length. The farmed animals include mink, chinchilla, and sable (expensive furs) as well as silver fox and Persian lamb. Mink has been the most popular fur since the 1950s, and it is both trapped and farmed. Major fur-ranching countries include the United States, Canada, Afghanistan, Denmark, Finland, the Netherlands, Poland, Russia, and Sweden.

A small amount of fur comes from animals that are domesticated. They are neither trapped nor farmed. Examples include sheep and lamb.

Quality

Furs vary in color, texture, quality, and cost. Furs of good quality have soft, dense fur fibers and long, luxurious guard hairs. Quality is affected by the age and health of the animal and the season in which it was killed. (Late fall to mid-winter is best since the animal's coat is most dense at this time.)

Product quality decreases when the hair or fibers are falling out, the hair is not fluffy, glossy, or soft, and the skin is no longer soft and pliable.

Furs from these animals usually wear well: beaver, marten, mink, mouton lamb, muskrat, nutria, sable, and seal (Alaska fur).

Faux fur (fake fur) is made from manufactured fibers (including acrylic, modacrylic, and polyester) and is processed to look like fur. It costs less, but it is not as warm as natural fur. Furlike fabrics can be made from pile fabrics, sliver-pile knits, or heavily brushed fabrics (fleece). With printing, a real fur design can be achieved, such as mimicking the fur of a leopard or ocelot (both have spots).

Processing

The complete processing of furs, from pelt removal to finished product (e.g., coat) has not been included in this section. Enough information, however, has been included to provide a general understanding of the transformation that occurs.

Initially, the **pelt** (entire skin of the animal with the hair attached) is removed by the ranchers or trappers. The fat and tissue is removed from the flesh side and then the pelt is dried. Pelts (or peltries) can remain in this dried state for a long time without damage, particularly if kept cool. They may have to be shipped long distances to the buyers, so a nondecaying pelt is essential. After they are sold, the pelts are processed using various techniques. Dressing and dyeing are two important procedures to make the pelts suitable for manufacturing fur products.

Dressing   The **dressing** process keeps the skins from rotting (putrefying) and makes them pliable and soft. Since most of fur-bearing animal skins are thin, this preservation process takes only from a few hours to a few days (after being properly prepared). It is important that the surface hairs not be damaged. The skin section is prepared and tanned. The pelts are then combed and brushed. The cleaning process follows, consisting of putting the furs in moving drums containing treated sawdust in order to polish the hairs and clean.

Dyeing   Dyeing is used to improve the natural color of the leather or to provide a particular fashionable color. By dyeing only the tips of the guard hairs (called *tipping*), pelts can be better matched to make a more uniformly colored and textured product. *Stenciling* can be done to provide a pattern which makes the fur look as though it came from another animal (e.g., a spotted animal, such as leopard). Muskrat fur can be altered to resemble the more expensive seal fur by removing the coarse guard hairs before dyeing.

Other Processes   Some animals, such as beaver, have their guard hair plucked and the underfur sheared to a uniform height (pluck and shear) for a plush effect. Some animals, such as the rabbit and muskrat, have the guard hairs clipped, leaving short guard hairs with fur fibers. Animals can have their fur grooved to create a textured surface effect (e.g., various heights) and a lighter weight coat.

Marketing

Most furs are sold to manufacturers (e.g., coat) and retailers either at public auctions or directly from the trappers or farmers, called *private treaty*. The fur buyers inspect the pelts (the entire skin of the animal with hair attached). Major auction houses are located in the United States (Seattle Fur Exchange), Canada (North American Fur Auction, Toronto, and Fur Council of Canada,

Montreal), and Northern Europe (Copenhagen Fur Center as well as at centers in Helsinki and St. Petersburg). Most sales occur between January and June.

Some fur garments require relatively few pelts (large animals). In contrast, the chinchilla is a very small animal and as such as much as 120 pelts may be required for a full-length coat.

Efforts by animal rights activists have reduced the demand for fur products. Their main argument is that it is immoral to kill animals when other materials can be used to provide warmth. Rebuttals include arguments that governments and the fur industry monitor and mentor the trapping and farming of fur animals, the standards of care at fur farms have to be high to ensure good-quality fur, trapping is an important part of wildlife management, and the fur industry avoids killing endangered species. (The Federal Endangered Species Act of 1970 requires that imported skins must be accompanied by the certification that they were taken legally.)

There are various well-known fur trade associations. The International Fur Trade Federation (IFTF) brings together 36 national fur trade associations and organizations from 30 countries. IFTF seeks to protect the interests of the fur industry and promote innovation, high standards, and a positive image of the fur industry internationally. It is headquartered in London.

The Fur Information Council of America (FICA) is a trade association whose members include fur retailers, wholesalers, fashion designers, and others who are involved with the fur industry. It provides guidance on industry developments, research on market trends, represents the North American fur industry in various capacities, as well as performs fashion promotion of fur products. It is affiliated with other organizations, such as the IFTF.

International trade fairs are held in such cities as Frankfurt, Moscow, Hong Kong, Beijing, Milan, and Montreal.

Care

Fur products must be specially cleaned. Since dry cleaning (with solvents) removes oils that keep the skin and hairs soft and pliable, another method is usually used. Tumbling the fur in a drum containing proper combinations of chemicals and sawdust (various sizes) provides cleaning, softening, and conditioning. Also, since fur has poor abrasion resistance and can mat, this method offers a gentle cleaning process. **Glazing** is performed to bring a shine to the fur.

Fur products should be able to breathe and therefore should not be stored in plastic bags. Also, furs remain in better condition if not stored in humid (hot and damp) places. Cold storage, where temperature and humidity is controlled, is best.

Everyday care should include hanging the fur coat on a wide hanger (to preserve shape) as well as not crowding the coat with many other hanging garments (allows it to breathe and the fur not to be flattened).

Finally, since fur fibers have low abrasive resistance, a minimum of rubbing is desirable. For this reason and the possible flattening effect, sitting on a fur garment for long periods of time should be avoided. Also, fur garments should be shaken and not brushed to prevent the hairs from being damaged.

Climate affects the fur product. In a drier atmosphere, fur hairs have a tendency to dry and break off. Also, leather has a greater tendency to crack. In damp areas fur has a tendency to mat, spoiling its appearance and reducing abrasion resistance since a greater surface area is exposed.

Fur Products Labeling Act

Fur products are regulated by the **Fur Products Labeling Act** of 1952 (amended in 1998). It defines fur as an animal skin with hair, fleece, or fur fibers, either in its raw or processed state that is not to be converted into leather. A fur product is defined as an article of apparel made partly or wholly of fur, except when the fur is of little value or used in relatively small quantities. Thus, a bearskin rug (not apparel) and low-quality sheepskin earmuffs (inexpensive) are not considered fur products.

This Act requires all fur garments to contain a label stating the following:

1. The name in English of the animal that produced the fur.

2. The country of origin of the fur if the fur or garment is imported.

3. Whether the fur color is natural or from dye.

4. If the garment contains fur from paws, bellies, or other scrap parts.

5. If the fur has been previously used.

Before the Fur Products Labeling Act was passed, furs called Hudson Seal, Chinchillette, and Ermaline were sold. The first was muskrat plucked and dyed to resemble seal. The latter two were rabbit fur made to look like chinchilla and ermine. Of course, the implication was that the furs named were more expensive than the inexpensive rabbit fur actually used. These marketing names, as well as others, cannot be used on fur garments.

Study Questions

1. Describe the typical temperature and humidity conditions that allow moisture-transport fabrics to function most effectively.

2. Briefly explain how a material can be constructed so to allow water vapor (moisture) to escape but not to allow rainwater to penetrate.

3. State two advantages and two disadvantages of using "down" in a coat as compared to 100 percent polyester batting for insulation.

4. List five different categories of industrial (technical) textiles and state an end use for each.

5. Why are nonwoven fabrics widely used as protective clothing in medical and other settings?

6. State four end-use examples of nonwoven material being used as a geotextile.

7. State several ways in which the qualifications of buyers of industrial fabrics differ from the buyers of apparel fabrics.

8. State three different types of plastic that are used as a textile material.

9. Why is a poromeric plastic material more desirable than a vinyl material when making a garment?

10. State three textile fibers that are plastic.

11. State an end use where a thick leather is preferable to a thin leather. Also indicate a preference for the reverse.

12. State at least one advantage and one disadvantage of using leather to cover a sofa as compared to vinyl plastic.

13. How can split leather be made to resemble the more expensive top grain leather?

14. Name three animals whose:
    a. Skin is used to make consumer leather products.
    b. Fur is used to make consumer products.

15. State several cautions that should be exercised by the owner of a fur coat with regard to its care.

16. State some advantages and disadvantages of using faux (artificial) fur material to produce a coat as compared to real fur.

17. To obtain maximum warmth, a fur coat should be worn inside-out. This is the opposite way they are usually worn. Explain.

CHAPTER THIRTEEN

Textiles for Interiors

Objectives

▶ To understand the interior furnishings industry and its marketing structure.

▶ To define the terminology used in the interior furnishings industry.

▶ To be knowledgeable of and to be able to evaluate the performance characteristics of the various fabrics used for the major end-use categories in the interior furnishings market.

 Use suitable fabrics from Fabric Science Swatch Kit *for this chapter.*

Key Terms Related to Textiles

Axminster carpet
batting
broadloom
carpet
carpet tile
carpet underlay
casement
ceiling covering
commercial/contract
curtains
cut-and-loop pile
cut-and-sew
cut pile
cut size
decorative fabrics

delamination
domestics
down and feathers
draperies
electronic welding
fiberfill
foam-slab cushioning
ground
home fabrics
home furnishings
home textiles
institutional textiles
interior decorator
interior designer
interior furnishings textiles

knitted carpet
loop pile
manufactured products
modular carpet
needle-punched carpet
pile portion
plush carpet
porosity
railroading
residential
rug
runner
shag
shredded foam particles
soft floor covering

space dyeing
tabletop products
ticking
tuft-bind strength
tufted carpet
up the bolt
upholstery
upholstery fabric
upholstery padding
velvet carpet
wall covering
wall hangings
Wilton carpet
window fabrics
woven carpet

Some textile materials are used in interior environments, such as homes, offices, hospitals, hotels, schools, aircraft, and automobile interiors. These textiles are generally referred to as **interior furnishings textiles,** but may also be called **home furnishings.** The latter term is an old and traditional name, still very widely used, and carried over from the time when most textiles used indoors were meant for home use. Today textiles are used everywhere indoors, and the term interior furnishings textiles is becoming the widely accepted name for this industry. This name is used throughout this chapter.

Many fabrics used for interiors have the same name as fabrics used for apparel. Velvet used for pants and velvet used for an upholstered chair are both velvet. They differ in that upholstery velvet is generally heavier (more ends and picks per inch), probably yarn dyed with better dyes (better penetration and better colorfastness), and may have flame- and stain-resistant finishes. The upholstery velvet costs considerably more than the velvet made for pants. Textiles for interiors often represent substantial financial outlays and are expected to remain serviceable for long periods, often ten years or more. Additionally, because they are used extensively where public safety is important (hotels, aircraft seating, public buildings), they are subject to rigid requirements and extensive testing for fire retardancy, smoke emission, and other safety elements. Most fabrics for interiors are produced and marketed especially for interiors and are not ordinarily adaptable for clothing application. (See Table 13.1.)

Some interior furnishings end uses are very specialized and applicable only to interior environments. Examples of these are floor coverings and fabrics used for upholstery. Other interiors textiles such as towels and bed sheets are less specialized.

The interior furnishings industry is affected by various factors. These include economic trends, trade regulations, government regulations, cost of materials, and fashion.

The NeoCon World's Trade Fair is a major industry event for "commercial interiors and the built environment." Design professionals can view new products, attend seminars, and interact with other attendees.

Interiors Product Classifications

Traditionally, the interior furnishings textile industry is grouped by several product classifications that also relate the marketing and distribution arrangements for the respective products. These classifications are not universal; there is some overlap, and some fabrics may be found in more than one classification. The classifications are discussed in the following sections.

Decorative Fabrics

Decorative fabrics in the context of the interior furnishings industry are textiles that are used for **upholstery, draperies, wall hangings,** and **curtains.** (See Figure 13.1.) The category applies to textile fabrics used in custom furniture, draperies, and fabrics marketed to manufacturers of furniture and draperies. This category does not include the manufactured (cut-and-sew) products described later in this chapter. Decorative fabrics are produced and marketed in several ways:

Large producing mills: These mills sell to manufacturers of large-scale mass-market furniture. These are generally medium- to low-priced fabrics.

Smaller mills: These mills produce exclusive designs and small production runs that sell to smaller and higher-priced furniture manufacturers, and to decorators and designers for use in custom products. These mills often sell through their own showrooms, located in principal cities and often centrally located buildings designated as D&D (design and decoration) buildings.

Converters: Converters function in the traditional converter role (i.e., purchasing greige goods and converting these to finished fabric). Converters sell to the broad range of the interiors market, including furniture manufacturers, decorators and designers, and jobbers.

Jobbers: Jobbers sell to decorators and designers as well as to smaller furniture manufacturers and custom shops for reupholstery and draperies. Jobbers may buy regular and current lines from mills and converters, and out-of-style or unpopular designs at off prices.

Soft Floor Coverings

Soft floor coverings are textile products used as flooring material; the term *soft* is used to distinguish them from floor covering of tiles, linoleum, marble, and similar area floor covering. They include carpets and rugs, and the underlay material that acts as their cushioning base. Area rugs are also included in this grouping.

Rug and carpet are not interchangeable terms. **Rugs** are usually color patterned and of a given size to cover a large part of a floor, and **area rugs** are smaller and cover

TABLE 13.1	Widely Used Interiors Fabrics			
Fabric Name	Upholstery	Drapery	Other	(Examples)
Antique satin	x	x	x	bedspread, wall covering
Bengaline	x	x		
Brocade	x	x	x	bedspread
Brocatelle	x	x	x	
Burlap		x	x	wall covering
Calico			x	curtain
Canvas		x	x	wall covering
Casement (malimo and raschel)		x	x	curtain
Chenille			x	bedspread
Chintz	x	x		
Corduroy		x	x	bedspread
Crash			x	towels
Cretonne	x	x	x	bedspread
Damask	x	x	x	tablecloth
Dimity			x	curtain
Dotted Swiss			x	curtain
Frieze	x			
Gingham			x	curtain
Homespun		x	x	wall hanging
Hopsacking (printed)			x	wall hanging
Marquisette			x	curtain
Matelassé	x		x	bedspread
Monk's cloth		x	x	wall covering
Muslin			x	sheet
Ninon			x	curtain
Nottingham lace		x	x	tabletop
Ottoman	x			
Percale			x	sheet
Sailcloth		x	x	wall covering
Sateen	x	x	x	bedspread
Taffeta		x	x	bedspread
Tapestry		x	x	wall hanging
Terry			x	towels
Velour (heavy)	x		x	bedspread
Velvet (heavy)	x	x	x	wall covering
Voile			x	curtain

FIGURE 13.1
Textiles are extensively used in interior décor. Notice the variety of fabrics in the room.

a small portion of a floor. **Carpets** cover the entire floor of a room from wall to wall.

Carpet and rug manufacturing machinery (tufting machines and carpet looms) are special types of equipment not adaptable to other types of textiles. Carpets and rugs are produced by mills whose only products are soft floor coverings. Branded lines and strong consumer name acceptance are an important part of the marketing strategies of these companies. Bigelow and Mohawk are examples of names consumers identify with television and magazine advertising. Carpet mills sell their products to department stores and retail specialty carpet shops, who in turn sell to consumers.

The American Floorcovering Alliance (AFA) strives to provide members with a competitive advantage by promoting the industry's products and services and educating members and others through seminars, press releases, and trade shows (e.g., Floor Tech Expo). Membership is open to any company in the floorcovering industry or in a floorcovering-related industry.

Manufactured Products

Manufactured products are traditionally called **domestics,** and are also known by the more current and widely accepted terms, **home textiles** and **home fabrics.**

This category encompasses a vast array of textile products that have been fabricated into interior end-use products (as distinct from custom fabricating or custom sewing). These end-use products are classified into several subcategories:

Window and wall coverings: Ready-made draperies and curtains, as well as ready-made slipcovers.

Bedroom: Blankets, comforters, bedspreads, sheets, pillowcases, shams, dust ruffles, duvets, and some curtains.

Bath: Towels, shower curtains, bath rugs, and bath mats.

Kitchen and tabletop: Towels, pot holders, tablecloths, napkins, placemats, and runners.

Decorative pillows and throws: Furniture and daytime bed decoration.

Manufactured items may be produced directly by weaving mills and sold as finished items, including towels, sheets, pillowcases, blankets, and other items that require only minimal (usually hemmed edges) sewing operation. These items are often referred to as **cut-and-sew** products (Figure 13.2a and b).

Ready-made curtains, draperies, comforters, and articles that require more extensive sewing are produced by companies that purchase fabric and undertake large-scale cut-and-sew operations to produce finished articles.

Manufactured interior items are sold by their various producers directly to the retail industry (department and specialty shops, discount stores, etc.) and to wholesale jobbers, who in turn sell to small independent retailers.

The manufactured interiors market is a strongly fashion-oriented part of the interior furnishings industry, second only to apparel in terms of color and design-change frequency. The fact that the industry designates itself as the "home fashion" industry reflects that theme. Heavy emphasis on brand-name product identity (e.g., Springmaid®, Wamsutta®, Fieldcrest®), and famous-name fashion designers (e.g., Ralph Lauren, Calvin Klein, Tommy Hilfiger) underscore this fashion emphasis.

Residential and Commercial Interiors

The interior furnishings textile industry divides into two main classifications: residential and commercial. Most textile and carpet mills and dealers engage their business with one or the other. An exceptional few deal in both areas.

Residential, as its name indicates, applies to the area of home decor and the textile products used therein. This

a   b

FIGURE 13.2
Various cut-and sew products in (a) a bathroom and (b) a bedroom.

could include houses, apartments, mobile homes, and other private residences. The textile emphasis is on aesthetics. Function and performance of fabrics are important considerations, but often may be compromised, or trade-offs may be made to favor desired aesthetics.

Household textiles used in residential interiors include bedding, toweling, and tabletop accessories such as napkins, tablecloths, and runners. These products, when used in hospitals or care-type facilities, are referred to as **institutional textiles.** The performance standard and safety codes to which these products must conform may be different than when used for household products.

Commercial, also referred to as **contract,** applies to the broad range of textile uses in office buildings, hotels, bank lobbies, airport decor, religious buildings, stores, restaurants, and so on. End-use categories include upholstery, drapery, carpets, and wall applications. Here the emphasis is on function and performance. Aesthetics, of course, are also important, but long use life, long-term appearance, frequency and ease of cleaning, and conformance to local building- and fire-safety codes and smoke-emission regulations are requirements that usually take priority over aesthetic considerations. Textiles for commercial interiors are designed and constructed for longer service and stricter conformance to specifications and standards than residential textiles and carpets. As may be expected, commercial fabrics and carpets are more expensive than residential.

Commercial installations are often large and costly projects involving formal and quite lengthy contracts

(hence the term *contract* as a synonym for commercial). Fabrics and carpets are now also designated as residential, or as commercial or contract. Some fabrics meet the criteria for both areas.

The Association for Contract Textiles (ACT) is a trade association that promotes contract fabrics for its members. These include textile manufacturers and wholesalers as well as furniture manufacturers and suppliers. In addition, ACT has formulated a series of symbols which, when placed on contract fabrics, provide assurance that they meet suggested industry standards of performance (see Table 13.2). ACT has its headquarters in Fort Worth, Texas.

Interior Decorators and Interior Designers

Design professionals in the interiors field practice as interior decorators and/or interior designers. As a general rule, **interior decorators** practice primarily in residential markets and address issues that are mainly aesthetic, involving function and performance to a lesser degree. **Interior designers,** on the other hand, practice in contract or commercial interiors (e.g., hospitals, restaurants, commercial offices). Their work goes considerably beyond aesthetic issues. Performance (long-term appearance, ease of cleaning, etc.) and public safety (fire resistance, smoke emissions, etc.) are more critical

TABLE 13.2	The Association for Contract Textiles Performance Guidelines
Symbol	Property
(flame symbol)	Fire Retardency
(droplet symbol)	Colorfastness to Wet and Dry Crocking
(starburst symbol)	Colorfastness to Light
(star symbol)	Physical Properties
A a	Abrasion Resistance

These symbols, when used with contract fabrics, denote compliance with ACT-recommended standards of performance.

to interior designers and may sometimes need to take precedence over aesthetics. Building codes, fire-safety regulations, acoustics, textile-related noise transfer and abatement, and insulation considerations are among the many things interior designers need to know. They must be sufficiently knowledgeable and prepared to specify the technical requirements of fabrics they select. Interior designers often work directly with or serve on the staffs of architects or building contractors.

Interior decorators who deal primarily with residential (single-family homes, rental apartments, condominiums, etc.) are usually involved in much smaller projects and involve less formal and more intimate client relationships than commercial projects. Commercial interiors usually involve much larger projects and are of longer duration. In addition, they often involve corporate clients, larger fees, and the extensive preparation of drawings. The client relationship is more formal and less personal. The agreement for design services to be provided is usually in the form of a formal contract. By contrast, the agreement for services relative to a residential project might well be a simple letter of agreement or even a mutual verbal agreement.

There is a strong professional movement for licensing qualified professional interior designers. Various states, including Alabama, Connecticut, Louisiana, and New York, have passed title acts, which regulate the use of a professional title (e.g., certified interior designer). Foundation for Interior Design Education and Research (FIDER) accreditation is becoming desirable for interior design programs in schools and universities. The test to determine competencies in textiles and other areas is

given by the National Council for Interior Design Qualification (NCIDQ).

Many professionals in the field function as both decorators and designers and undertake both residential and commercial projects.

Flammability

Flammability testing is conducted to help determine how a product will react when exposed to an ignition source. It is important that interior designers and manufacturers, as well as others who are involved with home furnishings fabrics, be familiar with the various flammability codes and performance standards in their product area.

There are several flammability tests used for live-in occupancies. These include homes (residential) and nonresidential places, such as hospitals, prisons, hotels, and restaurants. Different tests apply to different end uses. Thus, the tests for carpets, upholstery, and drapes are each different. Some of these tests are briefly discussed in various sections of this chapter. Also see Chapter 17.

Flammability factors to be determined include the following:

▸ If a material is flammable and, if so, simply burns with applied heat or if it supports combustion (adds fuel to the fire)

▸ The degree of flammability (how fast fire spreads across it)

▸ How much smoke and toxic gas the material produces when ignited

Many organizations are involved with flammability testing and performance for interior products, including agencies of the United States government, states and cities, as well as industry groups. Additional information about flammability tests can be obtained from the National Institute of Standards and Technology (NIST), National Fire Protection Association (NFPA), American Society for Testing and Materials (ASTM), and Upholstered Furniture Action Council (UFAC).

Upholstery

Upholstery fabrics are often subjected to greater in-use stress than most other textiles (Figure 13.3). Fabrics for upholstery are stretched tautly over furniture frames and cushions (rather than draped and hung) before they are put to use. Although the fabric is in this rigid, strained condition, the consumer expects, rightly, that the fabric will not fade or stretch out of shape, will be comfortable,

FIGURE 13.3
Upholstery fabric must not only be appealing but also resist the effects of wear.

will wear well, and will clean easily for years. These fabrics receive rigorous use, which may include day-in, day-out seating for several hours each day.

Upholstery fabrics are marketed as either residential or contract. Contract upholstery fabrics usually have higher performance standards than residential upholstery fabrics because they usually receive greater usage. They are especially designed and constructed with tighter weaves, higher abrasion resistance, and better flame resistance than most residential fabrics. Industry standards and guidelines have been established through the joint cooperation of furniture manufacturers and textile mills. (The Joint Industry Fabrics Standards and Guidelines Committee, High Point, North Carolina, was established for this purpose.)

Upholstery fabrics need to possess the following properties:

▶ They should have high abrasion resistance and high tensile strength. Variables that determine these properties include fiber content, yarn type (novelty and other nonsmooth yarns wear poorly), yarn twist (high twist increases wear resistance), yarns per inch, finish, and fabric weight.

▶ The hand must be pleasing because it is touched as it is sat upon. Harsh or very slippery hand is usually undesirable.

▶ Fabric type is an important factor and should be consistent with end use. For example, woven fabric provides more stability than knit fabric, and novelty-yarn fabric does not last as long because it has low abrasion resistance.

▶ Colorfastness to crocking, frosting, light, and environmental pollutants are vitally important for upholstery fabrics.

▶ High resistance to seam slipping and yarn distortion are needed.

▶ The fabric must not pill or shed.

▶ Stain- and soil-repellent fluorocarbon finishes such as Scotchgard™ are very desirable finishes for upholstery fabrics. Crypton® is another finish for upholstery fabrics that provides stain and soil repellency as well as being antimicrobial.

▶ Flame-resistant finish is highly desirable for residential, and almost always required in contract upholstery.

▶ Fabrics, particularly stripe and plaid designs, must be true on grain and not exhibit bow or skew.

▶ **Porosity**, the measure of a fabric's capacity to transmit air or moisture, relates directly to seating comfort. The longer the occupant is in contact with the material, the greater the importance of this property. Porosity depends on factors such as fiber content (absorbent fibers transmit moisture better), fabric construction (open construction allows easier

TABLE 13.3 Examples of Standard Performance Specifications for Woven Upholstery Fabrics

Test	Test Methods	Standards or Guidelines
Abrasion resistance	ASTM D4157 (Wyzenbeek Tester)	Medium duty: 9,000 cycles minimum (furniture used one or two hours daily)
Breaking strength	ASTM D5034 (Grab method)	Warp-wise or filling-wise: 50 lb. Minimum
Breaking elongation	ASTM D5034	Warp-wise or filling-wise: 5% maximum 1% minimum
Dimensional change	ASTM D3597	Warp-wise or filling-wise: from washing 5% shrinkage, maximum 2% gain, maximum
Tear strength	ASTM D2262 (Elmendorf Tearing Tester)	Warp-wise or filling-wise: 6 lb. minimum
Colorfastness tests:		
to burnt gas fumes (gas fading)	AATCC 23	Shade 4 minimum after two cycles
to crocking	AATCC 8	Dry: shade 4 minimum Wet: shade 3 minimum
to light	AATCC 16 (Xenon arc lamp)	Shade 4 minimum after 40 hours
to ozone	AATC 129	Shade 4 minimum after one cycle
to water	AATCC 107	Color change: shade 3 minimum Staining: shade 4 minimum

Note: See Chapter 14 for discussion of the test methods and guidelines.

TABLE 13.4 Upholstery Fabrics In-Use Application Terms

In-Use Household Application	Description	Example
Light duty	Upholstered furniture is used mainly for decorative chair used only several times a month.	A decorative rather than functional purposes.
Moderate duty	Upholstered furniture is used infrequently.	A couch in a formal living room used only once or twice a week.
Medium duty	Upholstered furniture is used occasionally.	A reading chair used for one or two hours daily.
Heavy duty	Upholstered furniture is used constantly for several hours or more daily.	A sofa used to watch TV every evening.

Note: No household furniture fabrics are designed or intended for abusive applications.
Source: Joint Industry Fabric Standards Committee, *Woven and Knit Upholstery Fabric Standards.*

passage of air and moisture), finish applied (glazing blocks fabric's air passages), and density of the cushioning material (denser material reduces porosity). Fabrics that contain air spaces—such as provided by thick, bulky yarns—and fabrics with irregular surfaces are good airflow conductors.

Frequently the same fabric is used for both draperies and upholstery. For this reason, many fabric mills produce fabrics that are suitable for both end uses and are specified and pretested for both uses. Where the fabric mill or converter has not indicated such mutual end use, decorators and consumers must be alert for, and give careful attention to, fabric-performance properties and specifications to ensure that both end-use criteria are satisfied. (See Tables 13.3 and 13.4.)

Upholstery Fabric on Furniture

The placement of the pattern and the direction of the fabric are important considerations for upholstery fabric. (See Figure 13.4.) Sometimes it is desirable to position the same design or motif in the center of each back pillow or cushion. It is important that patterns with repeats should match on furniture, from cushions to the sofa, for example. With patterns that appear to have no repeat, there is no specified position for the pattern. The warp of the fabric is the strongest and should be placed so that the greatest strain is on the warp. This is usually in the vertical position on furniture.

Some materials are nondirectional, meaning that they can be positioned either horizontally or vertically in the same piece of furniture. An example is a balanced plain-weave fabric of a solid color. The other extreme is a one-way-patterned fabric, such as one showing an animal in motion, in which design placement is crucial to customer satisfaction.

Many upholstery-fabric design features require special attention. These include the following:

Stripes: Stripes can be run in either direction. A satin stripe, however, usually is placed vertically to obtain the maximum luster of the stripe. This direction also increases the wear life of the fabric. Care must be taken with stripes to be sure they match from one side of the piece of furniture to the other

(e.g., across several cushions), or from the top of the back pillows down to the front of the seat cushion.

Pile: Cut-pile fabrics, such as velvet and corduroy, as well as fabrics with cords, usually run with the pile or ribbed direction down the back of the piece of furniture and toward the front of the seat cushion. This provides the best wear and comfort.

Railroading: The directional feature of the fabric pattern and repeat determines whether a fabric should be cut up the bolt or be railroaded. (See Figure 13.5a and b.) **Up the bolt** refers to placing the fabric so that the warp is from top to bottom of a chair or sofa (e.g., vertically up a chair back). (See Figure 13.6.) When a fabric is **to railroad,** it is at 90° from the up-the-bolt direction. Thus a fabric with a warp stripe would run vertically from top to bottom of a chair in up the bolt. If the same fabric were placed to railroad, the stripe would be horizontal, going from left to right on the chair.

Dyed fabrics without print or other design effect can be placed in either direction. A pattern or particular design dictates whether a fabric can be placed in railroad configuration. For example, a fabric with a pattern of growing flowers could not be cut to railroad since the flowers would appear to be growing sideways and not upward. Also, usually pile fabrics are not railroaded if the same fabric is used elsewhere in the room (e.g., drapes) since the pattern directions probably would be different. The advantage of railroading a fabric is maximum fabric utilization. For

  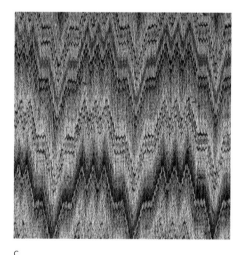

a   b   c

FIGURE 13.4
Classic upholstery fabrics designs: (a) a medallion design with the medallion symmetrical in four parts; (b) a traditional goose-eye design, a dobby weave; and (c) a traditional flame-stitch design.

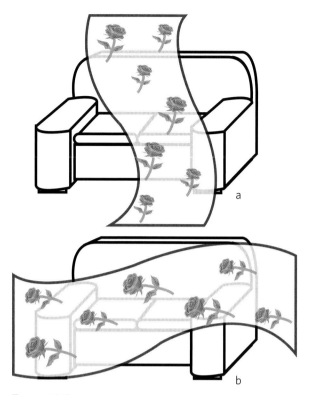

FIGURE 13.5
Upholstery fabrics may be positioned as (a) up the bolt to (b) railroad.

example, a 72-inch-long (183 cm) sofa back can be covered with a 45-inch-wide (114 cm) fabric, with a savings of fabric quantity. Also there will not be any seams showing on the furniture back. Up-the-bolt direction places the fabric in a stronger position on the piece of furniture.

Defects: Fabric defects such as small yarn slubs, broken ends, occasional knits, slight dye streaks, and so on are to some degree normally expected in window and apparel fabrics. Such defects, when relatively few, become hidden in folds or are not readily observed when fabrics drape and hang as window fabrics or, in the case of apparel fabrics, on the body. Upholstery fabrics are held snugly and tightly without folds or drapes (except in chair or sofa skirts), and defects tend to stand out boldly and create an unsightly appearance. Moreover, some defects, such as slub yarns or yarn knots, may seriously affect fabric wear due to the added abrasion to which the defect may be subjected. Careful inspection of the fabric is necessary before it can be committed for use in upholstered furniture. In many instances, careful cutting of fabric during the manufacture of

furniture can place the defect in chair backs, sides, skirts, or other hidden parts. On upholstered pieces already made, careful inspection should be made for fabric defects and dye streaks (in both daylight and artificial light) before acceptance.

Curves and corners: The places in furniture where fabric is weakest are the curves and corners. Fabric is stretched tightly around these areas to avoid puckers and bumps and to ensure a smooth fit, but these areas are subject to maximum abrasion. This abrasion is most severe with pile fabrics. In examining fabric, the ground weave of a pile fabric should not show through the pile when the fabric is stretched over a closed fist, or at curves and corners of a finished piece.

Many upholstery fabrics, particularly materials of low construction, or low-twist yarns, may have latex backing sprayed on the fabric back to add strength and yarn stability to the fabric. When these fabrics are stretched around curves and corners, the latex backing sometimes shows through on the fabric face. The same examinations described previously for pile fabrics should be given to latex-backed goods. Because the latex backing is usually a different color than the fabric, if the backing shows through the fabric, its use should be avoided.

Flame Resistance of Upholstered Fabrics

Flame resistance of upholstered fabrics is voluntarily regulated by a furniture industry group, the Upholstered Furniture Action Council (UFAC).[1] The council, located in High Point, North Carolina, was created to form an industry-wide joint effort to maintain fire retardancy in upholstery. (The designed flammability standard uses a cigarette as the ignition source in the test procedure.) Members of UFAC consist of furniture, textile, and fiber producers. Furniture that meets UFAC standards for flame resistance has a UFAC hangtag that certifies compliance to UFAC's standards. Consumers should look for UFAC certification on ready-made furniture and seek UFAC certification of fabrics for custom upholstery. Upholstery fabrics used in automobiles and aircraft are treated to comply with flame-resistant regulations established by the U.S. Department of Transportation. Upholstered furniture may also have a barrier fabric between the upholstery

---

1. Flame resistance means that a fabric will be slow burning, not that it will be fireproof. There are no fireproof fabrics for upholstery. Flame-resistance-treated fabrics make it possible for persons to exit burning premises before being overcome by fire.

FIGURE 13.6
The fabric on this seating is cut "up the bolt."

FIGURE **13.6**
The fabric on this seating is cut "up the bolt."

and the filling (like an underliner). Barriers are films that release chemical flame retardants on heating (upon burning of upholstery fabric), preventing or inhibiting burning of upholstery filling materials and further slowing the burning of the cover upholstery fabric.

Avora® FR is the trademark for licensed fabrics containing 100 percent inherent FR polyester fiber from INVISTA™. The flame resistance of this material is permanent and does not wash out or wear out. The fabric is used in hospitality and contract furnishing applications. Avora® FR fabrics must be certified by INVISTA™ to exhibit the tradename.

Filling and Padding of Upholstered Furniture

Several types of material are used as filling and **upholstery padding** of upholstered furniture.

Polyester **batting** is produced from bulked crimped filaments that have been resin-treated to reduce fiber slippage. The best quality of filling is made from two layers of batting, the top layer of fine low-denier fibers, the lower layer of coarser higher-denier fibers. The top layer is flexible and soft. The bottom layer offers firm support and compression resistance. Polyester batting provides excellent resilience.

Foam-slab cushioning is made from polyurethane foam, produced to the desired cushion thickness and cut to size to accommodate the particular cushion. Foam-slab cushioning is produced in a variety of densities to provide a wide range of comfort levels, from very soft to very firm. Excellent resilience over a long life is an outstanding property of polyurethane foam. Foam slabs and polyester batting are sometimes combined. Low-denier polyester batting is used on the cushion top and bottom, with a dense polyurethane-foam center. The top and bottom provide softness, and the center provides firmness and compression resistance. (See Figure 13.7a and b.)

Shredded foam particles, often made from scrap and overruns of slab productions, are low-cost cushioning materials. The shredded material is usually stuffed into an inner fabric bag before being stuffed into cushioning. Shredded foam particles clump and shift under extended use and should therefore be avoided in most interior applications.

Down and feathers are the softest and most costly of all cushioning materials.[2] Resilience of the material, although excellent, is very slow; a down cushion may take several days to recover from being compressed. Hand fluffing of cushions is usually done to restore them to proper

---

2. Down is the soft, protective, fine, furlike growth surrounding the skin layers of ducks and geese. Feathers are the coarser hairlike quilled coverings. Best grades of down have a high percentage of down a lower percentage of feathers. Lower grades contain more feathers than down.

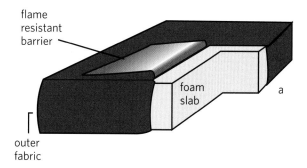

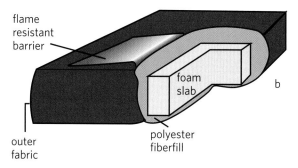

FIGURE 13.7
(a) Upholstered furniture foam slab construction and
(b) foam slab cushion with inner cover of polyester fiberfill.

TABLE 13.5	Upholstery cleaning codes
W	Use water-based upholstery cleaner only.
S	Use solvent-based upholstery cleaner only.
WS	Can use either water- or solvent-based upholstery cleaner.
X	Do not clean with either water- or solvent-based upholstery cleaner; use vacuuming or light brushing only.

The Environment

The Polyurethane Foam Association (PFA) has a platform on sustainability. The principles of this trade association regarding green issues include reduction of solid waste, encouragement of product sustainability, support of energy-saving technologies, and improvement of product safety. The flexible-polyurethane-foam industry has been recovering and recycling scrap produced in the production and fabrication process for many years. More recently foam-recovery programs have expanded to include post-consumer foam.

Flexible Foam Products, Inc., has developed Bio-Flex™ Hybrid Foam. It is made with bio-based polyols, which provide a "smaller environmental footprint." The resource is a replenishable product (soybeans) and not oil. The foam is used in furniture and bedding.

Carpet

Carpet is a heavy fabric used for soft floor covering. Once considered a luxury, it is taking the place of traditional flooring materials such as vinyl, linoleum, and wood. It is being used in almost every type of room or area, and can be found in hotels, theaters, stores, restaurants, schools, offices, hospitals, and trains, as well as in the home. Carpet provides better sound absorbency and thermal insulation properties than other floor surfacing materials.

Generally speaking, if the floor covering is securely fastened to the floor it is referred to as a carpet, while a loosely laid material is called a rug. Carpeting is sold by the yard. Rugs are available in various sizes, shapes, designs, and textures. The edges are usually bound. The term **broadloom** is frequently used to identify roll goods that are more than 54 inches (137 centimeters) wide. The term does not describe the method of construction. **Wall-to-wall** carpet indicates that the entire floor space, from baseboard to baseboard, is covered. Thus, there are no loose edges to cause tripping and no material shifting, but it is difficult to remove for relocation and the repair

dimensions. Another disadvantage is a possible allergic reaction to down and feathers. In actual function, down is less desirable than polyester batting or foam slabs since it has reduced resilience and possible allergic reaction. Nevertheless, it continues to be popular in higher-priced items, probably because of its prestigious image.

Care and Maintenance of Upholstery Fabrics

The best routine maintenance for upholstery fabrics is frequent and thorough vacuuming. The same airborne dust that settles on wood furniture also settles on upholstered pieces and should be removed by vacuuming with the same regularity with which dust is removed from wood pieces. Dust particles not removed become embedded, making later removal difficult, and reducing fabric wear life.

When cleaning of upholstery fabric becomes necessary, cleaning agents and methods that have become standardized in the industry may be used. The cleaning agents and instructions are designated by codes, which are also available to the consumer. A good general rule when spills occur is to blot immediately with an absorbent towel; never rub a spot. (See Table 13.5.)

FIGURE 13.8
This unique design results in a contract carpet that combines function with aesthetics.

of large damaged areas. A **runner** is a long, narrow piece of carpeting installed on stairs or in hallways. They are usually 27 inches (68.5 centimeters) wide and cut to any length. The raw edge sides are usually finished by binding with tape or serging (machine overcasting). The cut ends are either fringed or serged.

Modular carpet, also called **carpet tile,** is precisely cut, usually 18–36 inch square, carpet material. Modular carpets range from very low cost to high-cost custom designs. They are most widely used in contract applications. Ease of installation and the ability to replace small sections rather than a whole installation, as in a very-high-traffic store entrance, are advantages of modular carpet. Also modular units can be removed to allow access to cabling and electrical connections. Disadvantages include high initial cost and the risk that edges can curl with low-quality tiles.

Carpet used in homes for personal use is referred to as residential carpet. All other carpet, such as the type found in hotels/motels, business offices, shopping centers, and other public spaces are usually referred to as contract or commercial carpet. The contract-carpet segment of the floor-covering industry accounts for about 40 percent of all U.S. carpet. Contract carpet is different from carpet for residential use because of its wear demands, the size of area covered, and safety factors. (See Figure 13.8.)

Carpet is manufactured by carpet mills and sold to retailers or dealers both from an open or running line as well as from a customized, exclusive, or confined line. The open line is the group of carpet types, designs, and colors generally available for the duration of a season and sold to any customer. The customized line consists of carpet types, designs, and colors usually produced for only one customer. A much larger minimum order must be placed with the carpet mill for a customized line than for an open line.

Although wool now only accounts for less than 1 percent of the carpet fiber market (its high cost has caused it to lose popularity), it is still the standard other fibers try to emulate. In 1950, 85 percent of the fibers used for the carpet face (i.e., the part of the carpet you see) were wool. Today, however, almost all carpet-face yarns (pile yarns) are composed of manufactured fibers. Nylon now accounts for about 75 percent of the fibers used. Olefin (polypropylene) and polyester account for most of the balance, with acrylic and wool each accounting for about 1 percent.

Major U.S. carpet mills include Beaulieu Group of America, Shaw Industries, Inc. (which is the world's largest carpet manufacturer), and Mohawk Industries, Inc. (which includes the Bigelow and Karastan brand names).

The trade association that represents the U.S. carpet and rug manufacturing industry is The Carpet and Rug Institute, which is located in Dalton, Georgia. Georgia provides about two-thirds of all carpets and rugs produced in the United States.

Table 13.6 indicates various factors that should be considered when evaluating carpet quality.

How Carpets Are Made

Carpet consists of the **pile portion,** which contains the yarns observed when carpet is on the floor, and the **ground** or **back,** which is the portion that holds the pile yarn.

Various methods are used to make carpet material. Tufting, weaving, and needle punching are the most commonly used methods. Each type of construction is not necessarily a determinant of quality. To be desirable, the carpet must meet specific needs, such as performance, price, and style, in a wide range of qualities. The factors of quality include such variables as fiber content, surface-pile density and height, method of construction, and type of backing.

Tufted Carpet

Until 1950, most carpet was woven. Then tufting started to grow rapidly. Today about 97 percent of all carpets are tufted. Tufting is an economical method of producing carpet and is more than 20 times faster than weaving. (See p. 150 for additional discussion of tufting.)

TABLE 13.6 Factors to Consider When Evaluating Carpet Quality

Durability Factors	Appearance Retention Factors	Nonappearance Factors
Fiber content	Abrasion resistance	Heat resistance
Yarn type	Cleanability	Sound absorption
Pile density	Color retention	Static control
Pile height	Dimensional stability	Thermal insulation
Pile weight	Pilling propensity	
Tuft bind strength	Resiliency	
	Soil and stain resistance	
	Tuft bind strength	

Tufted carpets usually have two fabric backings. The primary backing is the material to which the face yarns are anchored. The secondary backing is bonded to the primary backing after the carpet is made. The secondary backing provides added strength, dimensional stability, and body. It is unnecessary to use a secondary backing with woven carpets. A tufted carpet can usually be recognized by its secondary backing. It is important that there be a strong bond between the primary and secondary backings to prevent separation or **delamination.** The result could be surface bubbling, seam stress, or carpet movement.

The face yarns are secured to the primary backing, usually by applying a coating of latex to the back surface or by fuse bonding. Latex also provides the adhesive for the secondary backing. Fuse bonding uses no adhesive and fuses the face yarns, primary backing, and secondary backing (all thermoplastic) together using heat.

If the face yarns are not secured to the backing, a run (where a row of tufts are pulled out) can occur down the entire length of the carpet, leaving an unpleasant-looking space called a runner. (This cannot occur with woven carpets because of the different method of construction.) The force required to pull the loop or tuft from the carpet is called the **tuft-bind strength.** Figure 13.9 shows the construction of a typical tufted carpet.

The secondary backing also could be made of a material that is not a fabric. Sponge rubber or foam material could be used, which would give a more cushioned effect and a nonslip surface. Such a rubberized backing could also be bonded to a woven carpet, thus acting as an underpadding or cushion.

Olefin (polypropylene) fiber is the main fiber used for the backing fabrics, both primary and secondary. It is strong and nonabsorbent. Spills and moisture on olefin do not result in rot, mildew, or shrinkage problems.

Compared to the other methods of carpet construction, tufting is faster and less expensive, and it uses less-skilled workers. Fancy jacquard designs cannot be made with tufting, so the method has design limitations. The durability of tufted materials is mainly dependent on fiber content, yarn type, closeness of the surface loops or tufts, and tuft bind strength.

Woven Carpet

Only about 2 percent of all U.S. carpet production is woven. Nevertheless, it still is considered important in certain segments of the industry. **Woven carpets** are made on three types of looms. Each results in a different type of carpet: velvet, Wilton, or Axminster carpet. (See Figure 13.10.)

Velvet Carpet **Velvet carpet** is the least expensive woven carpet to produce. More than half of the woven carpet sold in the United States is velvet.

The pile surface is created by having horizontally inserted wires raise some of the warp yarns (i.e., pile yarns) into the loop. The wire is withdrawn after each

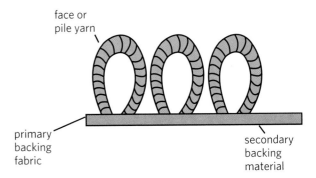

FIGURE 13.9
Tufted carpet construction.

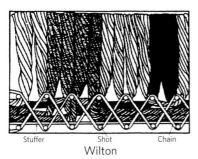

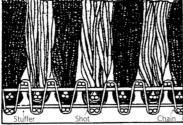

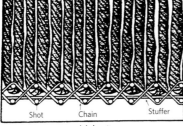

FIGURE 13.10
A construction of the major types of woven carpeting. In Wilton carpets, unlike velvet and Axminster carpets, colored warp pile yarns remain within the carpet until that color is needed for the formation of the design on the surface.

horizontal row of loops is made. If the loops are to be cut, a cutting section at the end of the wire cuts the loop. The height of the wire determines the height of the loop (and pile). Textural effects can be achieved by using different wire heights to form high and low loops and also by alternating cut pile with uncut loops.

The velvet-carpet construction results in most of the pile yarn being on the surface, so this construction makes for a durable carpet surface. The color designs are limited because of the lack of design versatility of the loom used (i.e., it has no jacquard mechanism). Patterns with very sharp details (or outlines) cannot be produced.

Wilton Carpet **Wilton carpet** is made on a loom similar to that which makes velvet carpet, except that it has a jacquard attachment so that woven patterns can be formed on the surface. The jacquard system selects the appropriate pile for the carpet face, which is lifted to the carpet surface to loop over inserted horizontal wires. The other colored pile yarns remain buried in the carpet, giving added strength, resiliency, and body. Thus, there may be several colored pile yarns beneath the face for each one showing on the surface.

Although there is almost unlimited woven design capability, there is a limited color availability within the pattern because of the limited number of pile yarns that can be used. (Too many pile yarns make the carpet very bulky and excessively expensive.) A multilevel surface composed of uncut and/or cut pile is available with Wilton carpets.

A special feature of Wilton carpet designs is that they are sharp and clear. The details and outline are more precise than those of the Axminster or velvet types. The slowness of production and the amount of yarn required, much of which is not on the face, makes Wilton carpet construction the most expensive.

Axminster Carpet **Axminster carpet** has each loop or tuft of face yarn inserted from a different spool of yarn, making the number of colors available for the design as well as the design capability almost unlimited. This carpet imitates handmade rug weaves. The strands of yarns are usually cut, forming a level cut-pile surface. Intricate designs at reasonable prices are available, provided that enough yardage of the same design is being made.

Because of the type of construction used to make Axminster carpets, there are no yarns buried or concealed. Thus, there is much surface pile from the yarns used to make the carpet. The backing is heavily ribbed, resulting from the use of double filling yarns laid in the carpet. Therefore, Axminster carpet can only be rolled lengthwise (i.e., bending the warp yarns). Most Axminster carpet is now produced abroad.

Woven Versus Tufted Carpet

Even though most of the carpet sold today is of the tufted-construction type, some buyers still prefer the more expensive woven type because of the cleaner lines in the patterns (see Figure 13.11), no problem with backing delaminating (woven carpets do not have a secondary backing), no possibility of yarn runners, better stability, and tradition.

If carpet is made properly and is correct for a particular use, it will perform well regardless of the construction used. For areas of very heavy traffic, woven carpet is usually more durable because it has better stability and no problem with face yarns possibly coming out of the carpet. The width of both types has been standardized at 12 or 15 feet (3.7 or 4.6 meters) for broadloom carpet.

FIGURE 13.11
A machine-made rug with an intricate hand-hooked carpet design.

Other Methods of Manufacturing Carpets

There are also other methods of making carpet material. Needle punching and knitting are two of these.

Needle-Punched Carpet

A small amount of carpet is made by one of the methods used to make nonwoven fabrics: needle punching (see p. 142). The resulting material resembles felt.

The durability of **needle-punched carpet** is determined by the density of the material as well as the fiber content, which is usually either nylon or olefin. A scrim-like fabric, if desired, can be placed under the web of fibers as it is being fed to the needles so that it will become embedded in the needle-punched carpet. The result is a stronger and more stable material. A coating of weather-resistant latex or similar material is usually applied to the back. Foam rubber is sometimes coated to the back to form a cushion backing and provide a slip-resistant surface on the back.

The needle-punching method results in the least expensive carpeting because it is produced at a very high rate with little labor involved and requires no primary backing, as does tufting. The carpet produced, however, is usually dull, flat, and feltlike.

The primary end use for needle-punched carpeting is for indoor/outdoor carpet, which is usually used on patios, boats, and kitchen floors.

Knitted Carpet

Carpet can also be produced by knitting. **Knitted carpet** is usually raschel warp knit, which provides more stability than weft knitting. The carpet produced is usually plush (high pile), with various densities, textures, and patterns. Although knitted carpets offer a more economical construction method in terms of volume of yarn used, its structure usually will not provide a high wear-resistant surface. A coating of latex and secondary backing material is applied to the back to provide dimensional stability.

Types of Carpet Pile

Although most carpets are made with a loop-pile surface, a multitude of surface effects still can be used. Some of these are discussed in the following sections.

Loop Pile

A loop-pile surface is a surface covered with yarns in the form of loops. Woven terry cloth and knit-terry fabrics both have this surface. When all the loops are the same height, the **loop pile** is referred to as a level type. A smooth surface is produced, which is suitable for heavily

FIGURE 13.12
Loop-pile construction. Pile density can vary from high (left) to low density (right).

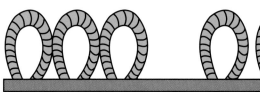

high density   low density

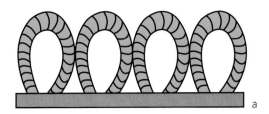

FIGURE 13.13
(a) Level loop pile and (b) multilevel loop.

used areas; it is long-wearing because the abrading force is absorbed by the entire surface. (See Figure 13.12.)

With multilevel-loop pile, loops are made at different heights to create a pattern or textured surface. This type is also called high-low or hi-low. It is less durable than the level type because the higher loops take a disproportionate share of the wear. However, it has better soil-hiding characteristics. (See Figure 13.13a and b.)

Cut Pile

During carpet construction, the pile loops are frequently cut, leaving two individual tufts of yarn, producing

cut-pile carpet. The cutting is done either with a blade or by a shearing process. (Shearing results in a more level surface.) Yarns cut at different levels result in a sculptured look, which makes it seem as if the design has been carved into the carpet surface. (See Figure 13.14.)

If the carpet has a dense, level surface with deeper-than-normal cut pile, it is frequently referred to as **plush carpet.** Plush carpet usually has single yarns instead of plied yarns, for a softer effect. It tends to show footsteps because the surface yarns, having little twist, possess a minimum degree of resiliency. They can also inhibit the movement of furniture with casters.

A cut-pile surface compared to a loop-pile surface appears darker since less light is reflected off the yarn ends. A cut-pile surface also has a softer effect and is less abrasion resistant since there is less surface to absorb the abrading force.

Three classic cut-pile surfaces are velvet, saxony, and frieze as shown in Figure 13.15a–c:

Velvet: The surface yarns in velvet carpets have very little twist. The ends tend to blend together to give a smooth, soft surface.

Saxony: The surface yarns in saxony carpets have more twist than those of velvet carpet, but not a very large amount. Usually the yarns are plied and the surface is level.

Frieze: The surface yarns in frieze carpets have very high twist, giving a random, pebbly, snarled effect. The high-twist yarns result in a longer-wearing carpet and also help avoid footmarks and shading.

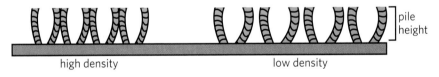

high density   low density

FIGURE 13.14
Cut-pile construction. Pile density may vary from high (left) to low (right).

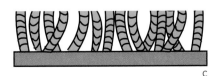

FIGURE 13.15
Pile configurations for (a) velvet, (b) saxony, and (c) frieze.

Cut-and-Loop Pile

Cut-and-loop pile is made with a combination of both loop and cut yarns and can be either level or multi-level (i.e., high-low) type. It is also called a **random shear.** As a result, a multitude of surface effects can be achieved that could not be obtained with any other method. The loop areas appear lighter because more light is reflected off the yarns forming the top of the loops than the yarn ends forming the cut surface. (See Figures 13.16 and 13.17.) Sometimes the three-dimensional appearance is referred to as a **sculptured** surface.

Shag

Shag carpet has long-pile yarns (usually at least 1 to 2 inches). Because of the length of the pile yarns, they flop or lie down and do not stand erect. The result is a soft, informal effect. The density of the pile yarns in this type of carpet can be reduced and the carpet could still appear as a compact material even though it is not. (The bent yarns lying on the surface give the appearance of a greater density than actually exists.) The pile may be cut or uncut. This type of carpet is more difficult to clean because of the type of surface. (See Figure 13.18.)

Carpet Construction Terms

The construction of carpet affects its suitability for particular end uses. Some of the most important construction terms for both woven and tufted carpeting are the following:

Pile height: The height of the loop or tuft expressed to the thousandths of an inch, in decimal form (e.g., 0.187 inches). The measurement is from where the yarn emerges from the backing structures to its extremity. With woven carpets, it is also called wire height or size because the loops are made by passing the yarn over a metal wire.

Pile thickness: The thickness of the carpet pile under standard pressure, as applied by a thickness gauge. Pile thickness can differ substantially from pile height because of the weight of the pressure plate on the pile. It is indicated in thousandths of an inch (decimal form).

Face or pile weight: The amount of yarn used in the pile of the carpet (above the backing), indicated in ounces per square yard.

Total weight: The weight of the entire carpet, including face weight, adhesive backing (e.g., latex), if used, and backing material(s). It is indicated in ounces per square yard.

FIGURE 13.16
Level cut-and-loop construction.

FIGURE 13.17
Multi-level cut-and-loop construction.

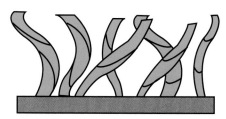

FIGURE 13.18
Shag pile configuration.

The following construction terms are used only with tufted carpet:

Gauge: The distance between two needle points across the width of a tufting machine, expressed in fractions of an inch ($\frac{5}{64}$ inch is a very high or fine gauge, and a very coarse gauge would be $\frac{5}{16}$ inch). The higher the gauge, the greater the number of loops or tufts per inch in the carpet width.

Needles per inch: The number of needles per inch across the width of a tufting machine. A $\frac{1}{4}$-inch gauge would be produced by a tufting machine with four needles per inch.

Stitches per inch: The number of stitches per inch lengthwise. Five stitches per inch would be a low number of stitches, and twelve per inch would be a high number.

Loops or tufts per square inch: This is determined by multiplying the needle per inch by the stitches per inch. For example, a looped tufted carpet made with 8 needles per inch ($\frac{1}{8}$-inch gauge) and 7 stitches per inch would have 56 loops per square ($8 \times 7 = 56$). This characteristic is also referred to as **pile density** or **tuft density.**

Average Density: The term used to indicate the compactness of the carpet surface. The average density range for residential carpeting is about 2000–6500. The formula is the following:

$$\text{Average Density} = \frac{(36) \ (\text{average pile weight-oz./sq. yd.})}{(\text{average pile thickness-inches})}$$

The following construction terms are used only with woven carpet:

Pitch: The number of ends of yarns per 27 inches of loom width. This term is the equivalent of needles per inch in a tufted carpet multiplied by 27. A 270-pitch carpet would have 10 ends of yarns per inch. In metric measurement, pitch is designated as ends per 10 cm of width.

Rows per inch: The number of loops per inch lengthwise. This term is the equivalent of stitches per inch in a tufted carpet.

Loops or tufts per square inch: This is determined by dividing the pitch by 27 (to obtain a per-inch basis) and multiplying by the rows per inch. Twenty loops or tufts per square inch would make an open construction, and 140 loops or tufts per square inch would make a tightly constructed carpet. For example, a woven carpet made with 243 pitch and 10 rows per inch would have 90 loops per square inch ($243/27 = 9$ ends per inch; $9 \times 10 = 90$ loops per square inch). This characteristic is also referred to as pile density or tuft density. Metric measurements are frequently used in expressing carpet construction terms and in carpet specifications. A metric-to-English system (inch, yards, pounds, etc.) conversion table should be referred to for these conversions.

Note that gauge, needles per inch, pitch, stitches per inch, rows per inch, and loops (tufts) per inch refer to the machine settings and may result in different carpet construction than theoretically calculated. For example, the tufted carpet produced with the machine settings given in the previous example may not actually have exactly 56 loops per square inch because the carpet may have shrunk or grown after being made.

Fibers, Yarns, Dyeing, Printing, and Finishing for Carpets

When carpeting is evaluated, the entire structure must first be examined. The different variables are the same as for any textile material—fiber, yarn, construction, coloration, and finish. These different areas will now be briefly discussed, except for construction that has already been examined.

Fibers

The following fibers are used for carpet manufacture:

Acrylic: Wool-like appearance. Less abrasion resistant and less resilient than other manufactured fibers. Best used in loop-pile constructions in low-traffic areas.

Nylon: Outstanding abrasion resistance and resiliency. Most-used carpet fiber. Many property improvements (e.g., soil resistance, antimicrobial, and reduced static buildup). Anso® nylon (Honeywell) and Tactesse® BCF nylon (INVISTA™) are two well-known brand names.

Olefin (polypropylene): Mostly used in tufted loop-pile and needle-punched constructions. Less resilient than nylon but still good. Usually solution dyed, so spectrum of colors is limited. Hydrophobic, thus, is resistant to waterborne stains. Mostly used in low-cost carpets.

Polyester: Softer to the touch, but less durable than nylon. Best suited for low-traffic areas where color and style are the main criteria.

Wool: Presents a beautiful appearance. Natural luster and hand. Less abrasion resistant than nylon or polyester. Resilient and more expensive than manufactured fibers. Naturally fire resistant.

Many of the manufactured fibers used in carpet are modified to enhance their performance. Moreover, most of the modifications become part of the fiber structure and are permanent for the life of the carpet. Modified carpet fibers are used extensively in contract carpet and to a lesser extent in residential because of their higher cost.

Manufactured-fiber producers devote substantial research and development resources and very heavy cash outlays to the development and testing of modified and improved fiber. To achieve optimum performance benefits from these fiber improvements, it is imperative that the carpet construction (e.g., pile density, height) also be adequate for the particular fiber and carpet end use. Fiber producers and carpet mill manufacturers have joined programs whereby the fiber producer licenses use of a particular modified fiber brand name on condition that the carpets be made in accordance with predetermined acceptable standards. When these conditions are met, the fiber producer, not the carpet manufacturer, accepts responsibility for the way a carpet performs. The fiber producer guarantees the product and pledges replacement in the event of failure. This permits a consumer to buy carpet from a little small-town carpet shop and have a large corporation stand behind it.

The following are two warranties provided by fiber producers:

- Stainmaster® (INVISTA™): Provides resistance to matting, staining, soiling, and static shock.

- Scotchgard™ (3M™): Provides resistance to staining and soiling.

Carpet manufacturers also provide limited warranties. These include resistance to stains, soil, color change from sunlight, static shock, abrasion, and appearance change.

Yarns

Both filament and spun yarns in approximately equal quantities are used in carpet manufacture. Both are heavy denier, in the range of 1,200 to 5,000 denier. Manufactured fiber for carpet yarns are always textured to eliminate high luster and to add bulk and loft. (See p. 71.) Filament yarns used for carpeting are frequently called BCF yarns, which stands for **bulked continuous filament.** The chief advantage of filaments is that they are less likely than spun yarns to pill (because there are no fiber ends). Most spun yarns are singles, but ply yarns are also used, especially for better-quality carpets.

Heat-setting of yarns after twisting and prior to tufting is extremely important because this establishes and sets the yarn, thus preventing later untwisting and premature pile crushing during use.

Dyeing

Tufted carpets of solid color are usually piece dyed, frequently on large continuous dyeing ranges. Batch dyeing using large jet-dyeing machines (see p. 161) is also employed. The first backing of latex is applied to the carpet greige goods prior to dyeing.

Yarn dyeing of carpet yarns is done when multicolor yarn effects are needed.

Solution-dyed nylon yarns are available for certain types of higher-priced contract carpet. These are the most permanent colorations (see p. 164), but color choices are limited to a few selections.

Printing

Both rotary and flatbed printing are performed on carpets. Jet printing, in which the carpet passes under small jets, each of which sprays a particular color, is a newer method. The Millitron® printer, developed by Milliken & Company, uses small jets that squirt a specific amount of aqueous dye solution according to a computer program, enabling it to produce prints with fine line detail. The machine can also change from printing one design to another without stopping. This allows the printing of particular designs in relatively small quantities and the ability to change to a new design without interrupting production.

Space Dyeing

A popular effect is obtained by a coloration technique called **space dyeing** (Space Dye® is a registered trademark of Fred Whitaker Company), in which the yarn achieves two or more colors along its length (for example, a segment of red followed by a segment of blue followed by a segment of green, continuously repeated along the length of the yarn). A multicolored speckled effect is obtained in the carpet surface. One method used to obtain this effect is called knit-deknit. As the name indicates, the yarn is initially knit (into a jersey fabric). The fabric is then printed, usually with a diagonally striped pattern of different colors. Afterward, the material is deknit, or unraveled. The yarn is used as the pile or surface yarns of the carpet. This method, although seeming to be an expensive method, is really not. Another method is to print directly on the yarns.

Finishing

Finishing in the classical sense—i.e., the application of mechanical or chemical processes after dyeing or printing—is usually not used in carpet production. Improvements in carpet that make the product more suitable for intended end uses are achieved through fiber modifications and are thus permanently engineered into the carpet structure. This includes resistance to soiling, staining, and static shock as well as antimicrobial and odor protection.

Carpet Underlay

A **carpet underlay,** or cushion, is a padding material placed between the carpet and the floor. It can be separate from the carpet or it can be bonded to the carpet back. Underlays are available in various weights, thicknesses, and densities. The types of underlays now being used include the following:

Felt: Feltlike or weblike material usually made from animal hair and/or jute fibers. Can be needle-punched. Lowest in cost of all underlay products. Tends to disintegrate over time. Not recommended for heavy-traffic areas.

Synthetic fiber: Fibers such as polyester are bonded into a cushioning material. Many varieties are available with a wide range of softness and compressibility.

Foam: Usually flat with less resistance to compression effects of furniture and heavy traffic. Provides firm, uniform support. Frequently attached to the carpet as a backing. Rubber or urethane types are available.

Sponge rubber: Usually has a waffle or ripple pattern. Filled with air cells like foam type, but has thicker cell walls and is heavier. Soft and highly compressible, usually favored for residential use. Heavy commercial use results in breakdown of cell structure, and it is therefore not recommended for heavy-traffic contract application.

Carpet underlay frequently does not receive the attention it deserves. Among the many advantages of using an underlay are the following:

▶ Extended wear life of the carpet. Padding increases the resiliency of the carpet by causing the surface yarns to regain their upright position more quickly. With a more erect pile, it is easier to remove abrading dirt particles, and the carpet better resists wear.

▶ More luxurious and comfortable feel to the floor, including a bouncy effect. Inexpensive thin carpets can feel more elegant with an underlay.

▶ Increased effectiveness of vacuum cleaning by forming air pockets below the carpet, which, when pulled through the carpet, help remove dirt and dust.

▶ Increased acoustical control achieved because the underlay absorbs unwanted airborne sounds.

▶ Improved thermal characteristics that help to control heat and cold. Underlays improve the insulation of a room.

▶ Improved evenness of floor. The underlay helps to make the floor look smooth and level.

▶ Additional stability of the carpet. Underlay makes it difficult for the carpet to shift and possibly wrinkle.

The proper underlay material to be used depends on the area requirements. Thick, low-density (i.e., soft) types give a more cushion-like effect for walking, but carpet that is too soft makes walking more fatiguing. When wearing high-heeled shoes, walking on soft carpet is also more difficult. Firm, thin, flat sponge rubber is good for heavy-traffic residential areas. Thick padding absorbs more noise than thin padding. Jute padding is not desirable if moisture tends to accumulate on the floor; a mildew problem may develop. Frequently, the cost is the final determinant of which padding type to use.

In most large commercial projects carpet is glued directly to the floor, without an underlay. This results in longer wear. When low-pile carpet is used, the direct-glued installation is best for people in wheelchairs and on crutches. Safety in stores and institutions is an important factor.

Carpet Flammability

Large carpets and rugs sold in the United States must meet the Federal Flammability Standard 16 CFR 1630 (Methenamine Tablet Test ASTM D 2859). Small carpets and rugs must meet Federal Flammability Standard 16 CFR 1631. In addition, many regulatory agencies require the Flooring Radiant Panel Test (ASTM E 162 and NFPA 253-National Fire Protection Association) for commercial applications in nonsprinkler environments. This test measures the ability of the carpet to withstand high-heat exposure while burning, without further spreading the flame. Less resistance means that the flame will spread a longer distance on the carpet before the flame self-extinguishes. Flame-resistant finishes are not usually used for carpeting. Additional areas of carpet flammability that should also be examined include smoke generation (ASTM E662 and NFPA 258), toxic gases produced, and padding (carpet underlay) contribution to flammability problems.

Traffic Classifications

Carpeting for commercial and industrial installations is usually classified by the level of traffic the carpet is capable of withstanding. The classifications frequently are Class I (light traffic, such as in an executive office or boardroom), Class II (medium traffic, such as in a locker room or lounge), and Class III (heavy traffic, such as in a cafeteria or retail store aisle). (See Table 13.7.)

Carpet for residential installation sold in retail stores is now also classified by the level of foot traffic the carpet is capable of withstanding. A Performance Appearance Rating (PAR) numbering system of 1–5 is one method used. A higher PAR number means less carpet appearance change from the original appearance after the wear test. Thus, a carpet with a PAR-1.5 would be suitable for light traffic (e.g., a guest room). A PAR-3.0 rating would be suitable for carpeting in a living room or study (i.e., normal traffic), and a PAR-4.0 rating would be necessary for carpeting in a very active area, such as a family room or often-used stairs.

TABLE 13.7 Carpet Traffic Ratings	
Traffic Ratings	**Examples**
Class I (Light traffic)	Apartment
	Room of worship
	Executive office
	Hotel-motel room
Class II (Medium traffic)	Recreational boat
	Locker room
	Lounge
	Library
	School classroom
	Office clerical area
Class III (Heavy traffic)	Cafeteria
	Bank teller window
	Convention center lobby
	Retail store aisle
	Theater
	Airport

The Carpet and Rug Institute has developed a change-in-appearance scale to assist specifiers in selecting commercial carpets with acceptable appearance-retention performance in a specified end-use application. The Carpet Appearance Retention Ratings (ARR) identify change in appearance on a 1–5 numbered scale: 5 represents no change in appearance after a specified abrasion test and 1 represents a very severe change. Thus, a carpet with a higher ARR, such as 4.0, will retain its original appearance longer in various traffic conditions than a carpet with a lower ARR, such as 2.5.

In addition to using these ratings, construction details are often provided with the carpet sample, including yarn twist, density of the face of the carpet, and face weight. The higher these numbers, the more wear-resistant the carpet.

Another problem beside the quantity of walk-ons (i.e., degree of traffic) the carpet will receive concerns the nature of the walking area. This includes a straight area (i.e., corridor), a turning area, and a stair area. Turning and stair areas receive much more abrasive wear than straight areas with the same number of walk-ons.

Carpet Soiling

The degree of carpet soiling and its appearance are affected by many factors. Fiber shape and surface will affect soil and stain appearance in carpeting. Soil settles in fiber recesses as well as in between the yarns.

Fibers with crimp, non-round cross section and twist will scatter light and so tend to mask carpet soiling. Fibers with irregular cross section retain soil but will not show soil as readily as those made from round cross-section fibers. Thus, they will not look as dirty when the same amount of soil is present.

Fibers with a smooth surface and a comparatively large diameter, made into smooth yarns and relatively compact fabrics, tend to resist soiling because they do not provide as many places for soil to become lodged in the fabric structure. Loosely twisted yarns that are somewhat coarse are readily penetrated by soil as are yarns composed of short-staple fibers. The latter may be somewhat difficult to clean, for the soil may be lodged tightly in the yarns and resist efforts at removal.

Fabrics of an open structure tend to permit penetration of soil more easily.

Carpet Maintenance

To help carpeting retain its appearance, periodic cleaning should be performed. The result is that the wear life can be extended as well as the need for premature replacement. Also, soiled carpeting gives the appearance of being worn when it actually may not be.

The frequency of cleaning depends upon the amount of traffic in the carpet area as well as the amount of dirt deposited. The longer the dirt remains, the harder it is to remove as it burrows further down into the carpet.

Pretesting stain and carpet cleaners is important since it minimizes the possibility that they will cause color change, leave a sticky residue, damage the fibers, or cause color bleeding. The testing procedure can be performed in an inconspicuous area of the carpet.

An important action to prevent staining is the prompt removal of solid and liquid substances that are spilled or deposited on the carpet. Prompt vacuuming of solids or the blotting of liquids with absorbent, white tissues or towels may be all that is necessary. Additional procedures may be required if this is not successful (see Table 13.8).

Methods of Cleaning

There are various methods available to remove the soil or dust from carpeting. Each method has its advantages and disadvantages. The following are various methods of carpet cleaning:

Carpet Sweeping Method—Carpet sweepers pick up crumbs, lint, some dust, and other dirt from the surface. However, they do not remove the embedded soil and, therefore, are suitable mainly for daily light cleaning.

Table 13.8 Removal of Spots and Stains from Nylon Fibers

Stain/Procedure		Stain/Procedure		Procedure A	Procedure E	Procedure I
Asphalt	A	Lard	A	Apply solvent	Detergent	Denatured
Beer	E	Linseed Oil	A	*POGR	Blot	alcohol
Berries	E	Machine Oil	A	Blot	Ammonia	Blot
Blood	B	Mascara	A	Apply solvent	Blot	Repeat, if
Butter	A	Mayonnaise	B	Detergent	Acetic acid	necessary
Candle Wax	G	Mercurochrome	E	Blot	Blot	Note: pretest
Candy (Sugar)	D	Merthiolate	E	Ammonia	Detergent	as for other
Carbon Black	A	Milk	B	Blot	Blot	solutions
Catsup	B	Mimeo Correction Fluid	C	Detergent	Water	
Charcoal	A	Mixed Drinks	E	Blot	Blot	
Cheese	B	Model Cement	L	Water		
Chewing Gum	G	Mustard	E	Blot		
Chocolate	B	Nail Polish	L			
Coffee	E	Paint—Latex	A	**Procedure B**	**Procedure F**	**Procedure J**
Cooking Oil	A	Paint—Oil	A	Detergent	Detergent	Detergent
Crayon	A	Rubber Cement	A	Enzyme	Blot	Blot
Crème de Menthe	F	Rust	D	digestor	Acetic Acid	Vinegar
Dye—Blue, Black, Green	F	Shellac	I	Soak	Blot	Blot
Dye—Red	E	Shoe Polish	A	Ammonia	Ammonia	Ammonia
Earth	B	Shortening	A	Blot	Blot	Blot
Egg	B	Soft Drinks	E	Detergent	Water	Detergent
Excrement	B	Soy Sauce	B	Blot	Blot	Blot
Fish Slime	B	Starch	B	Water		Water
Foundation Makeup	A	Tar	A	Blot		Blot
Fruit Juice	E	Tea	E			
Furniture Polish	A	Tooth Paste	B	**Procedure C**	**Procedure G**	**Procedure K**
Furniture Polish with Stain	H	Typewriter Ribbon	A	Apply solvent	Freeze with	Blot
Gravy	A	Urine—Dry	J	*POGR	ice cube	Water
Hair Oil	A	Urine—Fresh	K	Blot	Shatter w/	Blot
Hair Spray	A	Varnish	C	Apply Solvent	blunt object	Ammonia
Hand Lotion	A	Vaseline	A	Blot	Vacuum out	Blot
Ice Cream	B	Wax—Paste	A	Detergent	chips	Detergent
Ink—Ball Pen	A	White Glue	B	Blot	Apply solvent	Blot
Ink—Fountain Pen	F	Wine	E	Water	Wait several	Water
Ink—India	A			Blot	minutes	Blot
Ink—Marking Pen	A				Blot	
Ink—Mimeo	A				Repeat, if	
Lacquer	C				necessary	
				Procedure D	**Procedure H**	**Procedure L**
				Detergent	Apply solvent	Polish
				Blot	Wait several	remover
				Acetic acid	minutes	(non-oily)
				Blot	Blot	Blot
				Rust remover	Detergent	Repeat
				Blot	Blot	
				Detergent	Water	
				Blot	Blot	
				Water		
				Blot		

*Paint, Oil, and Grease Remover. Courtesy of Allied Fiber.

Vacuum Method—Vacuum cleaners remove dirt by both a sucking action and a mechanical beating action (i.e., brushing). Whereas most of the dirt is removed by this dry mechanical action, soil held to the fibers by grease or other substances must be removed by other means. Vacuuming will remove short lengths of loose fibers, which initially accumulate from cut-pile surfaces (shedding).

Shampoo Method—This method uses a shampoo cleaning solution mixed with water that is forced into the carpet usually by a brushing motion. The greasy dirt is emulsified and loosened. A thorough vacuuming follows, which sucks the liquid as well as the dry matter from the carpet. Any residue left will accelerate resoiling since new dirt will adhere. Caution must be used not to overwet the carpet, causing the backing to become wet and shrink. Also, this method requires a long drying time and pile distortion may result since brushes are used. (Brushing should be done in one direction only in order to minimize the distortion.) If drying is not complete, microbe-related problems can result (e.g., growth of mildew as well as odor).

Foam Method—This method uses a foam rather than a water solution for cleaning. Foam can be sprayed by hand (from an aerosol can) or applied by machine on the carpet surface and worked into the carpet using either handheld sponges or mechanically driven brushes. The dried foam and soil are then usually removed by vacuuming. This method is not effective on heavily soiled carpeting since there is no liquid flow to force out the deeply embedded dirt. If the foam solution is not completely removed, soil redeposition will be accelerated.

Hot-Water Extraction—This method utilizes a shampoo or detergent solution with hot water sprayed under pressure into the carpet. A powerful vacuum system quickly removes soil and water. The carpet-cleaning machine usually performs both the spraying and prompt extraction processes. Since no brushes are used, there is a minimum of pile distortion. Also, this method cleans very effectively. However, shrinkage can occur if too much water penetrates to the back and the drying period is long. Stains must be removed before the cleaning so that the hot water will not set them. Also, the cleaning solution must be completely removed to prevent rapid resoiling. This method is sometimes referred to as **steam extraction** even though no steam is used.

Dry Powder Method—This method uses a dry soil-absorbent powder saturated with cleaning fluid and solvent which is sprinkled on the carpet surface. The powder is brushed into the carpet either by hand or machine and then removed by vacuuming. This method is simple and inexpensive, with no pile distortion. It is not suitable for heavily soiled carpets and is usually used as a supplemental method.

Other Methods—Sometimes an appearance problem can be eliminated by scissors or a knife, such as by cutting surface pills, snags, and protruding ends. An area of carpeting crushed by the weight of furniture can often be restored by using steam from a hand iron held about four inches above.

The Environment

Carpets contain many different chemicals. These involve flame retardants, stain guards, water repellants, antimicrobial property, and fiber treatments. The Carpet and Rug Institute (CRI), a trade association of carpet manufacturers, established a volatile organic compound (VOC) emissions program in response to health issues associated with carpets. The Green Label Plus designation indicates that the carpet meets established CRI air quality standard for VOC emission.

Low-VOC-emitting materials have become more important for household items as homes have become more energy efficient through improved insulation and reduction of fresh air ventilation.

Shaw Industries has a carpet-to-carpet recycling program, which turns post-consumer nylon carpeting into new Anso® nylon carpet.

Window Fabrics

Curtains and draperies constitute a major application of textiles for the interiors industry. Curtains are relatively sheer and lightweight and are hung without linings. Draperies are heavy, often opaque, and usually have a lining. They are often patterned and sometimes used with sheer curtains. A **casement** is a medium-weight window covering with a degree of transparency (but less than that of a curtain). The textile industry often refers to curtain, drapery, and casement fabrics collectively as **window fabrics.**

Window fabrics are used for a variety of purposes. The following is a partial list:

▶ Provide privacy

▶ Eliminate or reduce glare from sunlight

- ▶ Hide an undesirable outside view

- ▶ Provide aesthetic effect

- ▶ Provide insulation (thermal, acoustic, and from the sun's rays)

- ▶ Provide camouflage (over a radiator, beam, cracks, etc.)

The more open the fabric construction, the greater the visibility of the outside view, the light penetration, and the ventilation; however, such open construction also provides less privacy and less insulation. Casement fabrics offer a combination of privacy and light/view control.

Almost all fibers, yarn types, and fabric constructions may be used in window fabrics. The selection of particular fiber, yarn, fabric construction, and dye and finish are important factors in providing optimum service due to the unusual conditions of their use. For example, window fabrics are exposed for many months, sometimes years, to sunlight, pollution gases, stresses of heavy panels sagging under their own weight, and other environmental and physical stresses.

Window-treatment fabrics are most often covered by the codes developed by cities, such as New York and Boston, as well as states, such as California and Massachusetts.

How Fiber Properties Affect Window Fabrics

All textile fibers are subject to degradation and decay from prolonged, continual exposure to ultraviolet rays (sunlight), but some fibers are more seriously affected than others. Fiber degradation takes place slowly over time. The rate and extent of fiber damage is influenced by such variables as the fiber composition, length of exposure, intensity of sunlight, and atmospheric conditions. Because window fabrics are subject to very minimal stress such as abrasion and bending during use, the degradation is often not evident until the fabric is laundered or dry-cleaned. Eventually tears in the fabric may occur from these processes.

Table 13.9 indicates the relative resistance of various textile fibers to ultraviolet degradation. The data in this table indicates that fabrics of nylon, wool, and silk are considered poor choices for window fabrics. Lining fabrics for draperies of acrylic, polyester, or cotton tend to slow down ultraviolet degradation and are almost a necessity for draperies made of nylon, wool, or silk.

Fabrics often change dimensions due to alterations in humidity. Material made from hydrophilic fibers will create more of a problem. An increase in humidity results in fiber swelling and shortening, producing fabric shrinkage. When the humidity drops, fiber swelling is reduced or disappears and the fibers extend, producing fabric growth. The alternating condition of shortening and lengthening is referred to as a "yo-yo" effect. It can occur several times in one day. This effect will not occur with hydrophobic fibers, such as glass and most synthetic fibers.

How Yarn and Fabric Construction Affect Window Fabrics

The yarn and fabric constructions used for window fabrics are as varied as textiles themselves. Practically all yarn types and weave types are used in window fabrics to appeal to a variety of tastes and styles. No one yarn type or weave type is functionally superior to another. Sheer woven fabrics and woven window fabrics with open-weave construction for maximum light and ventilation should ideally be made in leno weaves to minimize yarn slippage and fabric distortion. Knit fabrics used for window fabrics are of warp knit; both tricot and raschel are used. Weft knit fabrics are not used because they eventually sag and stretch out of shape from their own weight and interlooped construction arrangement.

Fabrics with heavier yarns possess greater resistance to sunlight degradation since there are more fibers (i.e., mass). Loosely woven fabrics and heavy fabrics will sag more than tightly woven fabrics and light fabrics.

TABLE 13.9 Fiber Resistance to Ultraviolet Degradation	
Fiber	Ranking
Glass*	Highest resistance to ultraviolet degradation
Acrylic	Highest resistance to ultraviolet degradation
Polyester	Highest resistance to ultraviolet degradation
Linen	Good resistance
Cotton	Good resistance
Rayon	Good resistance
Acetate	Good resistance
Olefin	Good resistance
Nylon	Poor resistance
Wool	Poor resistance
Silk	Lowest resistance to ultraviolet degradation

*Glass fabrics are difficult to handle and launder. Glass fibers splinter off the fabric and become embedded in fingers that touch them. Also, glass fabrics should not be laundered with other fabrics.

How Dyes and Prints Affect Window Fabrics

When fabrics are dyed or printed for window fabrics, the dyes or pigments should be especially selected to provide the required lightfastness. Fabrics that have been dyed or printed for apparel use do not usually meet these standards and are almost always subject to premature color fading when used as window fabrics.

Fabrics made from acetate fiber present a special problem for window fabric use. Acetate must be solution dyed or pigment dyed to be used as window fabric due to the propensity of this fiber to gas fade when dyed with the disperse dyes required for this fiber. (See p. 157.)

Fabric Finishing for Window Fabrics

Many of the finishes described in Chapter 10 are appropriate for window fabrics. Flame resistants (see p. 195), soil and stain resistants (see p. 197), mildew resistants (see p. 192), and water repellents (see p. 198) are especially useful finishes. In addition, several important precautions need to be observed in finishing processes to ensure resultant problem-free window fabrics:

Bowed and skewed fabric: Most drapery and curtain fabrics are made from two or more panels that are seamed, selvage-to-selvage, along the fabric length. Any patterns, plaids, or stripes must be matched at these seams so that the entire window treatment appears as one continuous pattern sweep. Seam matching cannot be done if the fabric has been skewed in finishing (see p. 202). The problem is most severe in filling stripe fabrics. (See Figure 13.19a and b.)

Relaxation shrinkage: Fabric that has not been subjected to complete relaxation-shrinkage finishing or not completely heat-set in finishing tends to relax and gradually shrinks over time while hanging. The shrinkage effect is magnified because of the often large lengths of fabric in window fabrics. For example, floor-length drapery (approximately 7 feet or 2 meters) that is said to have a low 2 percent shrinkage, shrinks more than 1½ inches (3.8 cm), which is substantial.

Flame resistance: Drapery fabrics (including cubicle curtains and window treatments) sold in the United States must pass the NFPA 701 Small Scale Test. The flame resistance is assessed using the Vertical Flammability Test Cabinet.

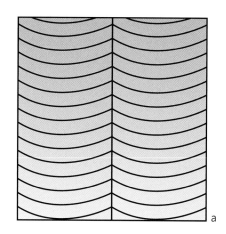

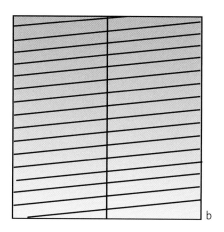

FIGURE 13.19
Fabrics for curtains and draperies must be true on grain, and not (a) exhibit bow or (b) skew.

There are also several fabric coatings used for window fabrics that improve its function:

Foam acrylic: Acrylic (air cellular) foam provides increased insulation for drapery fabrics. The insulation coating is usually white to maximize heat reflectivity in summer. As an additional advantage, the excellent sunlight resistance of the acrylic coating acts as a barrier to reduce ultraviolet decay of the main drapery fabric.

Vinyl: Black and other dark colors are used to produce a completely opaque window covering for room darkening or total blackout.

Metallic: These coatings are usually finely powdered aluminum particles suspended in resin binders. The silverlike coating acts as a heat- (sunlight) reflective surface and is beneficial as summer insulation. Metallic coatings are semi-opaque and can be used for partial room darkening.

Drapery-Lining Material

Drapery fabrics can be self-lined, with either a coating or a film sheeting. These are permanently attached to the back of the drapery fabric. Other types of linings are usually fabrics, which are separately hung panels installed behind the drapery.

Drapery-lining materials reduce the adverse effect of radiant energy (sunlight) on the fibers and colorant used on the drapery material. The linings also provide functional benefits such as noise reduction, greater insulation, or reduced light penetration, and a more pleasing appearance to outside viewers.

Wall and Ceiling Coverings

Fabrics placed on walls and ceilings can be both visually interesting and functional. Large pieces are called **wall coverings** and **ceiling coverings.** Such fabrics reduce noise in a room by absorption. They can also be used to cover damages in the wall. They experience few stresses, little abrasion, and no repeated flexing as with draperies. Thus, the focus of the fabric designer can be on aesthetics and not performance, and many types of fabrics of complex novelty yarns, surface effects, and even three-dimensional fabric can be used for wall coverings. Most textile wall and ceiling coverings are applied the same way as wallpaper. The fabrics are backed with paper or spunbonded nonwoven (see p. 142).

Heavy wall-covering fabrics may be tacked or nailed to a wall. Frequently used wall-covering materials include macramé and tapestry. (Macramé hangings are produced by knotting and twisting textile yarn, cord, and rope.) Carpeting may also be put on walls.

Smaller pieces of textiles, called wall hangings, can also be placed on the walls. These are hung primarily for aesthetic appeal, similar to paintings.

Flame-resistant and stain- and soil-resistant finishes are important finishes for wall and ceiling coverings. Many local building codes and some entire states require flame-resistance properties in textiles that are used as wall and ceiling coverings. (NFPA 255).

Care and maintenance of wall and ceiling coverings is best done by frequent brushing and/or vacuuming, as well as cleaning when necessary.

Manufactured Products

Manufactured products for interiors include products that are not upholstery, window and wall coverings, or soft floor coverings. The areas of both bath and bedding products are briefly discussed in the following sections. It should be noted that the word *linens* is often used as an overall designation for bedding, towels, tablecloths, napkins, and other products of this type since they were originally made from flax (linen) fibers.

Bath Products

Textile bath products include towels, bath mats, bath rugs, shower curtains, and bathroom ensembles. (See Figure 13.20.)

Towels

The two most common toweling fabrics used are terry cloth (noncut loops) and velour (cut loops). The factors of quality for these products include density of the

FIGURE 13.20
A bathroom that shows coordination of design.

pile (more compact increases wear resistance); height of the pile (higher is more absorbent); yarn strength; yarn twist (more twist increases durability, but reduces absorption and softness); selvage (should be firm and even); and hems (if turned under, they should be sewn with short, regular stitches). Toweling usually needs to have its edges finished (hemmed) since the material ends are usually cut. Sometimes, however, they are left with a yarn fringe.

Flat or nonterry toweling is also produced. Two such woven fabrics are **crash** and **huck.** A small amount of terry-type fabric is made by the stitch-bonding process (Malipol®)—see page 147.

Most towels are made with 100 percent cotton. Some towels, however, are made with the ground weave of a blend of polyester and cotton. This does not affect absorbency. Velour towels are not as absorbent as uncut-pile towels but are often chosen for aesthetic purposes.

Towels are available in different sizes and types. They include bath towels, hand towels, kitchen towels, and beach towels as well as washcloths and bath sheets. Beach towels usually do not last as long as bathroom towels because of the greater exposure to sunlight, chlorine, water, sand, and dirt.

Bath Rugs and Mats

Bath rugs are small, decorative soft flooring, light in weight so that they can be conveniently lifted and laundered. Bath mats are similar but smaller than bath rugs and are meant to be kept in front of a tub, shower, or vanity to serve as an insulator, and a slip-resistant and absorbent surface. Bath mats are functional and more absorbent, whereas bath rugs are decorative, and not meant to be absorbent.

Bath rugs usually have tufted or pile-knit constructions. Tufted fabric pile yarns in bath rugs are much less dense than in carpet, but are much longer, usually ranging from ½ inch to 3 inches (13 to 76 millimeters). They are usually cut from larger roll goods and then finished by hemming or with a separate fabric binding. These bath products are finished with a slip-resistant backing that also serves a secondary purpose of stabilizing the fabric structure. The backing finish is usually a latex compound that is brushed or sprayed directly on the fabric back.

Bath mats are usually made from uncut-warp-pile weaves woven in widths of 16 to 28 inches (41 to 71 cm) and include jacquards, florals, and other designs. Better qualities are woven to exact widths and have selvage edges. Lesser qualities are cut from wider widths and have sewn fabric binding edges. Bath mats should possess maximum absorbency, so 100-percent-cotton products are most desirable.

Bath rugs and bath mats are subject to flammability regulations of the U.S. government. The applicable standard is 16 CFR 1631: Standard for the Surface Flammability of Small Carpets and Rugs. Products that do not meet the standard may nevertheless be sold. They must, however, have a permanently attached label that reads as follows: "Fails U.S. Consumer Products Safety Commission Standard 16 CFR 1631; should not be used near sources of ignition." Needless to say, consumers and decorators should seek to avoid products that do not meet the flammability standard.

Shower Curtains

Shower curtains are made from sheet-plastic products or from textiles (usually woven). Almost any fiber, yarn, and fabric construction, except excessively stiff constructions, may be used for shower curtains. The inside of a fabric shower curtain may be coated to protect it from water and soap residue. Plastic film sheetings used for shower curtains differ in thickness (gauge), level of transparency, color, and styling (e.g., print).

A secondary unattached lining curtain of plastic or water-repellent fabric is often used to protect decorative fabrics or those that have not been water-repellent treated. Most commercially available ready-made fabric shower curtains are manufactured with water-repellent finishes.

Bedding Products

Textile bedding products are also called domestics. This category includes sheets and pillow covers (cases), blankets (and covers), and mattresses (including pads and covers), as well as bedspreads, comforters, quilts, shams, dust ruffles, and duvets. (See Figure 13.21.)

Sheets and Pillowcases

Sheets and pillowcases are usually either 100 percent cotton or a blend of polyester and cotton. A cotton article provides more comfort, but a blend lasts longer and does not have to be ironed.

The two most common sheet and pillowcase fabrics are muslin and percale. The better-quality fabric is percale, which is made of combed yarns and usually has between 170 and 220 yarns per square inch. This is referred to as "thread count." Thus, a 200-thread percale sheet has 200 yarns per square inch.

Muslin sheeting fabric is made of carded yarn and usually has a thread count of between 110 and 140. Both muslin and percale fabrics are usually made with an approximately equal number of warp yarns and filling yarns per inch.

FIGURE 13.21
Fabrics can be used to bring springtime into the bedroom.

Sateen sheets and pillowcases are the most costly of these products. They are made with very fine-combed pima or Egyptian cotton yarns and a satin weave. (Muslin and percale fabrics are made with a plain weave.) The thread count is usually between about 300 and 650, but 1000-thread products are available. The result is a shiny, silky, very smooth sheet and pillowcase.

In an attempt to charge higher prices, some manufacturers have counted the 2-ply yarn in the fabric as being two yarns and not one for the thread count. Thus, a sheet 160 × 140 in construction made with 2-ply yarns is really a 300-thread count and not a 600-thread count, according to accepted industry practices.

Some sheets are made with filament satin weave (called satin sheets) that provide a luxurious sleeping surface. Other sheets, such as flannel sheets, are napped (brushed) to provide greater softness and warmth.

Fabrics used for bed linens should be colorfast to washing and frosting (loss of color from rubbing). Some bold pigment prints look very attractive but are not very colorfast. Sheeting fabric should also possess good dimensional stability and have no more than 2 percent shrinkage.

Blankets

Most blankets are woven, but other production methods that can provide comparable insulation at lower cost are becoming increasingly popular. These are as follows:

Tufted blankets: Tufting (see p. 150) processes, when used for blanket production, include napping on both face and back. The face side usually has a high, luxurious napped surface, the back a lower surface. Unfortunately, the pile becomes matted and unsightly after only minimal use. Tufted blankets are therefore not recommended for extended use.

Knitted blankets: Knitted blankets are raschel knits, popularly known as thermal blankets. They are characterized by their almost three-dimensional surface. This fabric surface has small high and low areas much like a waffle, and these fabrics are called waffle knit. Raschel knit thermal blankets provide remarkably good insulation for their light weight, primarily due to their surface-effect knit structure.

Needle-punched nonwoven blankets: Needle-punched nonwovens (see p. 142) are also used as low-cost but effective insulation blankets. These nonwovens are finished by napping. They are widely used in hotels, motels, and hospitals, and their relatively low cost allows for economical replacement.

Flocked blankets: Flocked blankets are produced by flocking (see p. 180) nylon fibers into thin-slab polyurethane foam sheeting. Flocking is done to both sides of the slab. When proper adhesives are used, the flocked blanket has excellent machine launderability. These blankets are very heavy and soft, and they have excellent insulation properties.

Bedspreads, Quilts, and Comforters

A bedspread may be defined as an outer bed covering, placed over blankets and sheets for appearance and warmth. Bedspreads may be made from any fiber, yarn, and fabric construction, with attention given to the various physical properties of textile materials and dyes and finishes mentioned in earlier chapters. Excessively stiff fabrics should be avoided in bedspreads, however, because they do not drape well over a bed.

Quilts and comforters are also bed covers, but are designed to be insulators and to provide warmth. Quilts and comforters are both composed of two layers of fabric with an insulation substance between them (e.g., fiberfill). The three layers are stitched together in patterns to prevent shifting of the insulation. The bonded area is a very small portion of the total surface area so that loft is not sacrificed. The distinction in definitions between quilts and comforters tends to overlap. Quilts, however, always have a decorative top fabric, while the top fabric of comforters may be decorative, undyed, or solid color. Also, comforters tend to be thicker and provide more insulation than quilts.

The stitching of components and insulation in quilts and comforters is done by sewing (using quilting machines that produce sewn seams) or by electronic welding. **Electronic-welding** quilting machines apply heat, which softens thermoplastic fibers and welds the components in appropriate patterns. At least 50-percent-thermoplastic-fiber content must be present in each of the components (top, insulation, and bottom) to accomplish electronic welding. Sewn stitching is superior to electronic welding. Electronic welding tends to separate and open more easily than sewn seams.

Quilting can also be accomplished using ultra-high frequency sound (above detection by the human ear). Parts are joined and held under pressure and then subjected to ultrasonic vibrations. The resulting heat causes thermoplastic fibers to melt and fuse. Layers of material can then be joined. The Pinsonic® Thermal Joining Machine uses this technique (Branson Ultrasonics Corporation). It is used on some mattress pads and less expensive bedspreads. One problem is that the outer material may tear at the seams. (See page 225 for additional information about Ultrasonic Technology).

The insulation component of quilts and comforters may consist of polyester fiberfill, polyurethane batting, or down. Polyester **fiberfill** is the most widely used product and provides excellent resilience combined with light weight in thick layers (better insulation). Polyester fiberfill is relatively low in cost.

Polyester batting is used where relatively thin layers of insulation are required (as in a summer quilt). This product is low in cost, has good resilience, and is lightweight.

Down insulation is a luxury product, highest in cost of all quilt and comforter combinations. It is the lightest in weight per unit volume and is the most resilient. To prevent the very fine down fibers from coming through the top or bottom layers, products insulated with down require very tightly woven top and bottom layers with a calendered finish to close up weave interlacings. Alternatively, a separate inner lining that is tightly woven and calendered may be used.

Pillows

Pillows are classified into two separate categories: bed pillows (for sleep) and decorative pillows (for removable chair covers or as a daytime bed decoration). Decorative pillows are also known as throw pillows. Decorative pillows are produced in a wide variety of sizes and shapes (e.g., square, rectangle, round, cylindrical). Bed pillows are rectangular and sized to fit the bed in which they will be used.

Decorative and bed pillows may be filled with the same materials (e.g., polyester fiberfill, down, polyurethane foam). Polyester fiberfill and polyurethane foam (both of which are thermoplastic) are usually preformed to the pillow shape and size by heat-setting techniques as part of the pillow manufacturing process.

All bed pillows (as well as mattresses) have a fabric covering known as **ticking,** encasing the filling material. When a pillow is intended to be washed, the ticking should be a washable fabric. Down-filled pillows, as previously indicated, require closely woven fabric and calendered finish. Commonly used fabrics include muslin, percale, twill-weave ticking, cotton damask, and spunbonded-olefin fabric.

Mattresses

Beds usually have two basic units, a mattress and a mattress foundation (e.g., box-spring unit). To protect and prolong mattress usage, covers and pads are often used. Cotton and noncellulose manufactured fibers dominate the fiber usage for the mattress market.

Mattresses are usually made in two basic constructions, with inner springs or foam core. The foam-core mattress has a slab of rubber or urethane foam. The level of support varies with the foam density.

Ticking has become a generic term for fabric used to cover the exterior of mattresses, box springs, and pillows. Elaborately patterned fabrics such as damask are replacing the traditional twill-weave ticking fabric with its blue and black lengthwise stripes.

Mattress covers may completely encase the mattress or only cover the exposed surfaces (top and sides). Mattress pads act as a cushion while they also protect the mattress. Most pads have a batting of polyester between two fabrics and cover the sleeping surface. Mattress covers and pads may be treated with antimicrobial finishing chemicals, especially if used in health-care facilities and hospitals.

The applicable federal flammability standard for mattresses is 16CFR Part 1633. Effective July 1, 2007, this standard is used to minimize/delay flashover (when a fire becomes so hot that it begins to feed off the oxygen in the room and grows exponentially). The total heat (energy) release of the mattress when exposed to open flame must be below a specified level during the test.

The International Sleep Products Association (ISPA) represents the sleep products industry. Members include manufacturers of mattresses and bedding components, as well as machinery and service suppliers. ISPA provides a wide range of legislative, informational, and educational services.

Textile Tabletop Products

Textile **tabletop products** are items that adorn dining tables and include tablecloths, napkins, placemats, dresser scarves, and doilies. Most of these products are made from textiles in a wide assortment of fibers, yarn types, and constructions. Plastic-sheeting products are also used, but to a relatively minor extent.

The fibers used in tabletop products are predominantly cotton, rayon, and polyester. Flax (linen) is used to a lesser degree, primarily in higher-priced and luxury fabrics.

Fabric constructions for tabletop products are woven or lace. (See Figure 13.22.) The lace is usually machine-made Nottingham lace or raschel lace.

Jacquard-woven fabrics in damask construction are used in formal tablecloth and napkin sets. These fabrics have a satin-weave background or a satin-weave design and plain or twill-weave background. Woven floats on damask fabrics may range from 4 to 18. The higher floats offer better light reflection and provide more lustrous highlights in the fabric. Long floats, however, are more exposed to surface friction and snagging, and the use life of these fabrics (over many launderings and pressings) is lower than those of less lustrous fabrics with shorter floats. Utility damask tablecloths have a design or background of five-harness satin weave with a float of four. These fabrics, due to their weave-float arrangement, need to be tightly woven. Yarns should not shift or move easily within the fabric. Loose weaves allow yarn to slip and cause premature wearing out in the float area.

Dyeing and finishing of tabletop products play a very important role in their quality and potential use life. These products are subject to frequent food soiling and staining, and due to their size and bulk almost always require machine laundering. The following quality aspects of dyeing and finishing should be observed:

▶ Resin finishes of moderate add-on should be used for cotton, rayon, and linen products to overcome the poor resiliency of the fiber and to make pressing easier.

▶ Polyester and polyester blends should be heat-set and finished as precured durable-press (no iron) items.

FIGURE 13.22
This tablecloth brings elegance and grace to the dining area.

▶ Soil-release finishes, particularly for any product containing polyester, should be applied to these fabrics. The application of Teflon® fabric protector usually results in liquid stains wiping off easily.

▶ These products often require bleaching to remove certain fruit and/or wine stains. Wherever possible, therefore, the dyes should be fast to bleaching agents, e.g., vat dyes for cotton (see p. 157).

The two terms, napery and linens, should be distinguished. **Napery** is a general term for tablecloths and napkins. Although it is no longer widely used in commercial activities, it is used in various standards and labeling rules. **Linens** is a general term for tablecloths and napkins, but also for sheets, towels, and other related products formerly composed of flax fibers (linen). Although the use of flax fiber in these products has greatly declined, the term linen is still used as the name of the storage area (e.g., linen closet).

Labeling laws relating to tabletop products require conformance to the Textile Fiber Products Identification Act. In addition, conformance to a U.S. regulation known as the Labeling as to Size of Tablecloths and Related Products Law is required. This law requires disclosure on a label or other conspicuous location of the **cut size** of the product being sold, which means the size dimensions (measured in inches) of the product after all hemming and trimming has been done.

Hospitality Industry

The facilities that welcome guests and travelers constitute the hospitality industry. This includes hotels, restaurants, bars, casinos, sports arenas, and spas. The textile products include towels, sheets, carpets, furniture, upholstery, tablecloths, and wipes. For textiles there must be a balance between appearance and performance. The appearance may be long lasting, bright, festive colors, or a particular design/logo. The performance aspect may be cleanability and durability.

Study Questions

1. Why is it important to examine colored textiles for interiors in the setting in which they will be used?

2a. Explain the differences between fabrics used for apparel and fabrics for interior use.

 b. What problems may be encountered in using apparel fabrics for interiors?

3. Why are tightly twisted, plain, ply yarns preferable to loosely twisted, novelty yarns for upholstery fabrics?

4. Briefly discuss how fabric shrinkage and fabric growth affect the appearance of an upholstered chair.

5. State three factors relating to carpet construction that will affect carpet durability.

6. Briefly explain the importance of the placement direction of fabric with floral design for a sofa (with regard to being cut to railroad or up the bolt).

7. Indicate several ways in which the surface texture of a carpet can be changed.

8. State one advantage and one disadvantage of each of the following cleaning methods on a high pile, heavily used carpet:

 a. Vacuum method
 b. Shampoo method
 c. Foam method

9. State five external factors that will affect the durability of a specific carpet. (Do not include construction.)

10. Numerous differences exist within the categories of carpet padding or cushioning. Name five.

11. Compare the following two carpets in appearance and performance. Assume that all other factors not indicated below are the same for both materials (e.g., same fiber content).

Carpet	Manufacture	Style	Pile Yarn Weight (oz./sq.yd.)	Gauge or Pitch	Stitches/In. (or Rows/In.)	Pile Height (In.)
A	Woven	Level Loop	43.5	216	9.0	.225
B	Tufted	Cut Pile	36.0	5/32	9.2	.280

12. State the differences in fabric construction that you would expect between a summer and winter blanket.

13. Why is it important that patterned fabrics used for draperies be finished on grain, without bow and skew?

14. Name four different functional finishes that may be applied to drapery fabrics, and state the benefits gained from each.

15. Explain the roles of fabric yarn size and yarns per inch (compactness) of a fabric for a window treatment when determining the amount of brightness in a room.

16. Explain the dominance of cotton in the toweling market.

17. What differences would you expect between a towel used in an inexpensive motel and a towel used in an expensive hotel?

18. Why are 600-thread sheets made with a satin weave and not a plain weave?

19. Name several surface textures and colorations that help to camouflage soil or stains on a textile product.

20. Compare the positive and negative properties of down, wool, and polyester for use as filling materials for outdoor and indoor products.

CHAPTER FOURTEEN

Determining Fabric Quality

Objectives

▶ To be familiar with the tests and procedures for evaluating textile quality.

▶ To understand the role of fabric standards and specifications in domestic and international textile trade.

▶ To understand how fabric end-use suitability is determined.

▶ To understand how basic fabric components affect product quality.

▶ To be able to present and analyze textile data.

Key Terms Related to Textiles

abrasion resistance
air permeability
American Association of Textile
   Chemists and Colorists
American National Standards Institute
American Society for Testing
   and Materials
appearance tests
breaking strength
bursting strength
colorfastness to burnt gas fumes
colorfastness to crocking
colorfastness to dry cleaning
colorfastness to frosting
colorfastness to light
colorfastness to laundering
conditioning room
crocking
dimensional change

durable press
elastic fabric
elastomeric fiber
fabric count
fabric length
fabric thickness
fabric weight
fabric width
fabric-performance testing
flammability
frosting
functional tests
growth
International Organization for
   Standardization
linear yards per pound
metamerism
National Fire Protection Association
ounces per linear yard

ounces per square yard
pick glass
pick needle
pilling propensity
shrinkage
soil-release finish
specification
standard test method
standards of performance
stiffness
stitches per inch
surface-friction tests
tearing strength
thermal insulation
wavelength
wrinkle resistance
yarn distortion
yarns per inch
yield

This chapter will focus on the product performance aspect of fabric quality. By examining its fabrication (construction) and knowing its properties through testing, it is possible to determine if the material is suitable for the intended end use. If it is not, then the fabric would have to be modified or a different end use would have to be selected. The basic knowledge of textiles covered in the preceding chapters will help the reader understand the different factors that influence product quality.

In the global network constituting the modern textile products industries, it is not unusual for a design to be created in the United States, in cities such as New York or Los Angeles, and the end product, including fabrics, to be produced in another, far-away part of the world. These products, once in production, may never be actually seen or even physically touched by the designer, any interim customers, or the ultimate retailer until their final arrival on a retail sales floor. How can all the parties in this chain of production/distribution ascertain that the quality that is being delivered is what was ordered and bought? How, for example, does JCPenney know that the dresses they ordered from a New York dress company that had fabrics and garments bought and made in China is getting the same merchandise originally sampled? The answer lies in an internationally agreed-upon system of measuring and communicating practically every aspect of fabric properties and characteristics.

Many of these properties are determined through precise laboratory analysis. Others are relatively simple, and because they do not require special laboratory facilities, are often referred to as "table-top tests." This chapter addresses both types of tests, laboratory based and table top, and explains how, through proper testing procedure, fabric quality can be determined and maintained.

Basic Fabric Measurements

All textile fabrics can be described by their basic structure, various segments of which are discussed elsewhere in this book. They include yarn twist, yarns (or stitches) per inch or per centimeter, fabric thickness, fabric weight, and the weave or knit. These fundamental components form the core of fabric specifications. Determining them is not always done in certified laboratories. Often they are done locally "in house," sometimes by buyers and marketing persons. For this reason, detailed descriptions for these tests are given in the following sections.

How to Use the Pick Glass and Pick Needle

The pick glass and pick needle have become universal in their applications in the field of textiles and clothing. Designers, technicians, students, and teachers have all found them to be important tools for better and clearer examination of fabrics. Yarn types, fabric weaves, knit stitches, and cloth defects can all be more easily identified through the proper use of these items. The pick glass and pick needle are particularly useful in determining the yarns per inch in woven fabrics or the stitches per inch in knit fabrics.

The **pick glass** is composed of a frame, a magnifying lens, and a measured opening in the base opposite the lens. When the pick glass is properly opened, the measuring lines on the base are visible when looking through the lenses. The measured opening may vary from a square ¼ inch (.64 centimeter) on each side to a square of 3 inches (7.62 centimeters) or more. The most common pick glass has a 1-inch (2.54 centimeters) square opening.

The fabric to be examined should be set on a smooth, flat, well-lit surface. The opened pick glass is placed on the material, and the individual looks through the glass to view the cloth.

The **pick needle** consists of a needle section with a holder. It can be used in conjunction with the pick glass for tasks such as pointing while counting yarns per inch in a fabric. The pick needle can also be used independently, as when trying to open a yarn to see whether the dye has penetrated into the yarn sufficiently.

Determining Yarn-Twist Direction

As was previously explained on page 66, there are two designations for the direction of yarn twist: S-twist and Z-twist.

The direction of yarn twist can be determined from the direction in which one turns the yarn to untwist it. In using this method, hold in a vertical position one end of the yarn with the fingers of one hand and untwist the other end of the yarn with the fingers of the other hand. During the untwisting, the yarn should be slackened to help the fibers separate. If the upper end of the yarn is held with fingers of the left hand and the other end is untwisted with the fingers of the right hand, a Z-twist yarn untwists by turning clockwise. If the yarn untwists turning counterclockwise with the fingers of the right hand, it is an S-twist (see Figure 4.5).

If the twist direction is difficult to determine because there is very little twist in the yarn, attach a paper clip

FABRIC SCIENCE

274

to one end of the yarn while holding it by the other end. The clip will begin a definite rotation, indicating the twist direction in the yarn. Before untwisting the yarn, it is helpful to scrape it lightly between the fingernails to remove any chemical finish.

Fabric Count

Fabric count is the number of ends (lengthwise yarns) or picks (widthwise yarns) per inch for woven fabrics, or the number of wales or courses per inch for knit fabrics. Measurement is made with the fabric in a flat and relaxed condition. Variations in fabric count occur because of the weaving or knitting process and finishing processes. Usually, the higher the fabric count, the better the quality and the higher the cost of the fabric. It is frequently easy to lower the cost of a fabric by reducing the fabric count and adding a finish to make up for the weight loss. This reduces the fabric strength, however. For this reason, the piece-goods buyer should be aware of any variations in fabric construction from one shipment of the same fabric to another.

Determining Yarns per Inch[1]

The **yarns per inch** often varies in different parts of the same fabric. Because of this, if a full-width piece of cloth is available, the warp count should be taken at several places along the width and the filling count taken at several places along the length of the fabric.

Fabric count usually is an average of tests in the length and width directions and is reported to the nearest whole number (e.g., 82 × 68, which is expressed as "82 by 68.") The first number is the ends per inch, and the second is the picks per inch.

If the fabric is not of uniform construction (e.g., seersucker or satin stripe), the following formulas can be used:

$$\frac{\text{Ends per repeat}}{\text{Inches per repeat}} = \text{Average ends per inch}$$

$$\frac{\text{Picks per repeat}}{\text{Inches per repeat}} = \text{Average picks per inch}$$

Counts of full-width pieces of fabric should not be made close to the selvage because the yarns may be packed closer together near the edges of the cloth (not a representative area). For the same reason, yarns per inch should not be counted near the end of the fabric. If only a small swatch is available, the yarn counting should be done in the middle (a more representative area) and not at the edge.

A two-ply yarn is counted as one yarn. In a simple leno weave that has warp yarns crossing each other in pairs, the crossing yarns are not counted as a ply yarn, but each pair is counted as two yarns.

The following sections describe three methods used in determining yarns per inch.

Method 1: Counting Individual Yarns   Look through the pick glass and determine whether the counting can be done more easily on the face or on the back of the fabric. It is often easier to see one set of yarns on the back and the other set on the face. If the fabric is dark, place it against something light, and vice versa, for a better view of the yarns.

Line up the left edge of the opening in the base of the pick glass with the first yarn to be counted. Use a pick needle to point to the yarns as you count them from one edge to the opposite edge in the base. If 40 yarns are counted with a 1-inch glass, the yarns per inch is 40. If, however, 40 yarns are counted with a ½-inch glass or are counted for only ½ inch, the yarns per inch would be 40 times 2, or 80. It is best to count a full 1 inch because if a mistake is made in counting over a smaller area, or if the counting is done in a nonrepresentative area, the size of the error will increase over calculating the number of yarns in 1 inch. For example, if 47 yarns are counted in ½ inch and the true figure is 49 (error of 2 yarns), then the yarns per inch will be calculated as 94 instead of the true figure, 98 (error is increased to 4 yarns).

Method 2: Counting Groups of Yarns   In counting yarns per inch in a fabric having a check pattern, such as a gingham, groups of yarn instead of individual yarns can be counted. If every colored stripe has 8 yarns and every white stripe has 8 yarns, the number of complete stripes in the inch is counted and then multiplied by 8. The yarns in the incomplete stripe at the end are then added. Thus, if in 1 inch there are 12 stripes and 6 yarns of an incomplete stripe, the total is 12 times 8, plus 6, or 102 per inch.

Finding the yarns per inch can also be done by counting weave repeats instead of individual yarns. The yarns are counted in groups, with the group depending on the weave used.

With some fabrics, counting by weave repeats is the only possible way of determining the yarns per inch.

---

1. Although the English term "yarns per inch" is used in this chapter, the metric term "yarns per centimeter" could easily be substituted.

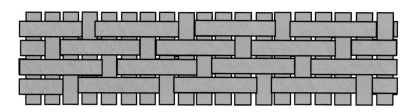

FIGURE 14.1
In this example, every fifth warp yarn passes over the same filling yarn. Thus yarns per inch can be determined by counting groups of yarns.

Closely woven fabrics with fine filament yarns are an example. The loosely twisted filaments spread, making it impossible to count the yarns because one cannot tell where a yarn begins or ends. If a fabric is made with floats (where one warp yarn floats over two or more filling yarns, or vice versa) and the yarns are crowded together, they will slide under one another and not be seen on that side of the fabric.

A good example is counting the warp yarns in a closely woven satin fabric. It is easier to count the warp on the back of this fabric. As seen in Figure 14.1, warp yarns pass over the filling yarns at definite intervals. On close examination, it is seen that every fifth warp yarn passes over the same filling yarn. (This can be seen by looking at the top filling yarn in the figure.) Because the weave is a five-shaft satin weave, it repeats on every fifth warp. Thus, if in 1 inch there are 40 repeats plus 3 remaining yarns, the yarns per inch is 40 times 5, plus 3, or 203.

Method 3: Using Line Gratings   Another method that can be used for counting yarns per inch is with line gratings. The **gratings** are specially prepared plastic plates measuring about 3 inches by 4 inches that are placed on the fabric. The number of fabric yarns per inch is then read off the scale on the grating. The gratings are composed of ruled, accurately spaced sets of lines. When a grating is placed on a piece of fabric, a moiré pattern of light and dark bands appears because of the partial coincidence of the lines on the grating and the yarns of the fabric.

The grating is placed on the fabric with the longest edge parallel to the yarns to be counted. The grating is then adjusted until a cross appears. The number of yarns per inch is indicated where the arms of the cross cut the scale. (See Figure 14.2.)

The range of each grating is limited to about 40 yarns per inch. To count any number between 10 and 200 yarns per inch, a set of about 10 different gratings is required. (There is an overlapping of one grating with the next in the set.)

The gratings can only be used if the yarns in a fabric are clearly visible. The yarns per inch of a high-count satin, where some of the yarns have slid under others, for example, cannot be accurately counted with this device.

Determining Stitches per Inch[2]
The **stitches per inch** in different parts of the same fabric often vary. Because of this, if a full-width piece of cloth is available, the wales per inch should be taken at several places along the width and the courses per inch taken at several places along the length of the fabric.

Fabric count usually is an average of tests in the length and width directions and is reported to the nearest whole number (e.g., 26 × 32). Counts of full-width pieces of fabric should not be measured near any edges or ends because the area may not be representative of the fabric.

The main method used in determining stitches per inch is to count the individual stitches per inch. The procedure would be the same as that outlined on page 275, Counting Individual Yarns.

Dimensional Properties of Fabric

The dimension and construction properties of textile fabrics are important for the control of quality as well as for end-use determination. They are often of special importance when materials are bought and sold. Most fabrics are made in a range of width, constructions, and weights rather than with any one set of specifications. The following sections describe some of the most important physical properties.

Length
Fabric length is the distance from one end of the material to the other. Measurement is made parallel to the edge of the fabric with the fabric flat (having no wrinkles or folds) and under no tension. The length is expressed in yards or meters and is usually measured either with a yardstick or a measuring machine. The measurement can be either near the edge or at the middle of the fabric and is usually indicated to the nearest 1/8 yard (e.g., 102 3/8 yards), or 1/10 meter (e.g., 96.3 meters).

_____

2. Although the English term "stitches per inch" is used in this section, the metric term "stitches per centimeter" could easily be substituted.

Width

Fabric width is the distance from one edge to the other. Measurement is made perpendicular to the fabric edge (selvage), usually including the selvage area, with the fabric flat (having no wrinkles or folds) and under no tension. The width is expressed in inches or centimeters and is usually an average number of measurements taken at evenly spaced intervals along the fabric piece. Fabric width is usually expressed either as a whole number (e.g., 45 inches or 58 inches) or as a range (e.g., $^{44}/_{45}$ inches), depending on how well the fabric shrinkage in finishing can be controlled. Often a specific fabric width is required, such as 114 centimeters, because of the size of the garment parts or the width of the cutting tables. The range of width for most woven fabrics is about 45 inches to 100 inches (e.g., 114 centimeters to 254 centimeters). Some fabrics are less (e.g., silk brocade could be 27 inches) and some are more (e.g., sheeting fabric could be 144 inches). The range for knit fabrics is 36 inches to over 200 inches (for tricot), or 91 cm to over 508 centimeters.

The width of a tubular knit fabric not cut open is twice the distance of the fabric laid flat on a table (i.e., the diameter).

The width variations of finished fabrics exist because of different sizes of looms and knitting machines and because different amounts of shrinkage occur when the greige goods are being finished.

Thickness

Fabric thickness is the distance between the upper and lower surfaces of the material. It is measured using a thickness tester. (See Figure 14.3.) Warmth and bulk properties depend on the fabric thickness-to-weight ratio. Materials for blankets, pile fabrics, felt, and carpets are some items that would normally be measured for thickness.

Fabric thickness can also be used as a performance indication of abrasion resistance or shrinkage tests by measuring fabric thickness before and after the abrasion test. Thickness is also important in determining settings to be used on sewing machines and calculating the number of fabric layers (plies) that can be cut at one time by the garment manufacturer.

Fabric thickness is usually measured in $^{1}/_{1000}$ inch, or in $^{1}/_{100}$ millimeter, and is usually an average of several tests taken at random over the fabric.

Weight of Fabric

Fabric weight is the mass per unit area. It is a factor of quality when two fabrics of the same type are being compared. For example, a heavier terry cloth is considered to be of better quality than a lighter one. Fabric weight is also important in order to determine whether the cloth is suitable for a specific end use. Fabrics are sometimes

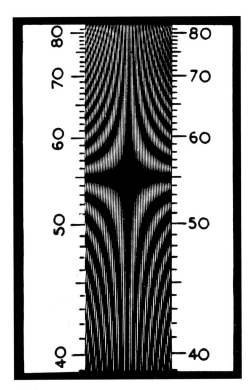

FIGURE 14.2
Taper line gratings used to determine fabric yarns per inch.

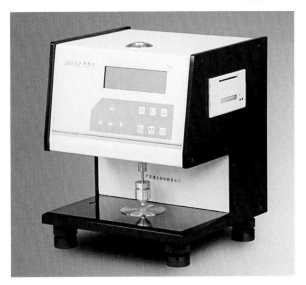

FIGURE 14.3
A thickness tester measures the thickness of materials.

sold with the fabric weight indicated as one of the fabric specifications, which is why people involved in textile transactions or desiring a better understanding of fabric quality must be familiar with the fabric-weight system.

Usually, fabric weights vary because of differences in the number of yarns per inch as well as in yarn size. Fabric weight is an expression of several measurements taken at random over the fabric and averaged. The wide range of fabric weights and types has developed because textile mills and manufacturers have tried to obtain the best balance between the factors of cost and end-use performance. (See Table 14.1.)

Expressing Weights of Fabric

The weight of fabric can be expressed in the following ways:

▶ **Ounces per square yard** is the weight of a piece of fabric 36 inches by 36 inches. The metric measurement is grams per square meter.

▶ **Ounces per linear yard** is the weight of a piece of fabric 36 inches long and as wide as the entire fabric. The metric measurement is grams per linear meter in a specified centimeter width.

▶ **Linear yards per pound** is the number of yards of the cloth equal to 1 pound in a specified width. The metric measurement is linear meters per kilogram in a specified centimeter width. Figure 14.4 shows how a fabric's weight can be determined directly without calculations.

In expressing weights by the first two methods, the lighter the fabric, the lower the number of ounces or grams, and vice versa. In the third method, the lighter the fabric, the higher the yards per pound or meters per kilogram and vice versa. Gauze cloth used as bandages, for example, may be as light as 23 yards per pound or 46 meters per kilogram. Canvas used as truck covers may be as heavy as 1 yard per pound or about 2 meters per kilogram.

FIGURE 14.4
A yield scale indicates fabric weight (ounces per yard) directly by weighing a specific size sample.

Ounces per square yard and ounces per linear yard are technically expressed to the nearest $1/10$ ounce, although half numbers and ranges are also used. Some examples are 5.3-, 6-, $8^1/_2$-, and 10- to 11-ounce fabric. Linear yards per pound, however, are expressed to the nearest $1/100$ yard (e.g., 1.78 fabric is expressed as a "one seventy-eight weight" fabric and means that there are 1.78 yards in one pound of this fabric). Unless the fabric width is known, the ounces-per-linear-yard and linear-yards-per-pound figures have little value.

The method of expression used depends on the fabric type and the segment of the industry making or using the fabric. For example, in the woven-goods industry, ounces per linear yard is usually used for woolen or worsted suiting fabrics, and linear yards per pound is usually used for cotton and cotton-blend dress material. The weight of industrial type fabrics is frequently expressed as ounces per square yard.

In the knitting industry, fabric weights are most frequently expressed on the basis of the number of linear

Type	Ounces per Square Yard (grams per square meter)	Examples of End Uses
Very lightweight	Less than 1 (less than 25)	Curtains, sheer blouse, gauze, mosquito netting
Lightweight[a]	2–4 (50–95)	Lining, summer dress, shirt or blouse, summer pajamas
Medium weight[b]	5–7 (120–170)	Summer suit, slacks, tablecloth, lightweight jacket
Heavyweight	9–11 (215–260)	Lightweight coat, winter suit, working clothes, toweling
Very heavyweight	Over 14 (over 350)	Winter coat, heavy sweater, heavy canvas

TABLE 14.1 Range of Fabric Weights

a. Fabrics in this approximate weight range, used for shirts, blouses, etc., are frequently called top-weight fabrics.
b. Fabrics in this approximate weight range, used for slacks, shorts, etc., are frequently called bottom-weight fabrics.

yards per pound. (This is called **yield** in the knitting industry.) A specification for knits might thus require a yield of 2.5 linear yards per pound based on a 45-inch width (e.g., 5.0 linear meters per kilogram).

Converting from One System to Another

Quite often fabrics are specified in one manner, but must be compared to a fabric whose weight is designated differently. For example, two seemingly similar fabrics may be shown to a buyer. One is a 45-inch wide fabric and is presented as 6 ounces per square yard. The other fabric, also 45 inches wide, is presented as 7 ounces per linear yard. Which fabric is heavier? To make this determination, it is necessary to convert from one system to another. The formulas and examples that follow illustrate how this may be done.

English System   The following formulas should be used when converting from one English system to another:

1. Ounces per square yard to ounces per linear yard

$$= \frac{\text{Ounces/linear yard fabric width} \times \text{ounces/square yard}}{36}$$

2. Ounces per square yard to linear yards per pound

$$\text{Linear yards/pound} = \frac{36 \times 16}{\text{width} \times \text{ounces/square yard}}$$

3. Ounces per linear yard to ounces per square yard

$$\text{Ounces/square yard} = \frac{36 \times \text{ounces/linear yard}}{\text{width}}$$

4. Ounces per linear yard to linear yards per pound

$$\text{Linear yards/pound} = \frac{16}{\text{ounces/linear yard}}$$

5. Linear yards per pound to ounces per linear yard

$$\text{Ounces/linear yard} = \frac{16}{\text{linear yards/pound}}$$

6. Linear yards per pound to ounces per square yard

$$\text{Ounces / square yard} = \frac{36 \times 16}{\text{width} \times \text{linear yards/pound}}$$

The following are examples of the English system:

▶ Express the weight of a 6 ounces-per-linear-yard print cloth fabric that is 60 inches wide in linear yards per pound.

Using formula 4, the answer is 2.67 linear yards per pound:

$$\text{Linear yards/pound} = \frac{16}{6} = 2.67$$

Note that the linear yards per pound is expressed to two decimal places.

▶ Which of the following fabrics is heavier?

Poplin: 6 ounces per square yard, 45 inches wide

Gabardine: 8 ounces per linear yard, 54 inches wide

When comparing fabric weights, it is best if both fabrics are expressed in ounces per square yard. Thus, equal amounts of fabric are being compared (i.e., 1 square yard) and a direct comparison can be made. The fabric width must be considered if either of the other weight systems is used. You cannot compare directly the weights of two fabrics of different width because the fabric amounts are different (e.g., 7 ounces/linear yard–48 inches compared to 8.5 ounces/linear yard-60 inches).

Using formula 3, the gabardine fabric weighs 5.3 ounces per square yard.

$$\text{Ounces/square yard} = \frac{36 \times 8}{54} = 5.3$$

Thus the poplin fabric is heavier.

Metric System   Imported fabrics, especially those from European countries, often have weights expressed in the metric system. These fabrics may be sold on the basis of grams per square meter, grams per meter in a specified centimeter width, and meters per kilogram in a specified centimeter width. When these fabrics are sold in the U.S. market, or when U.S. fabrics are sold in the export markets, it often becomes necessary to convert from the metric system to the English system (e.g., yards, ounces, pounds) and vice versa. Table 14.2 should be used to execute these conversions.

The following are examples of the metric system:

▶ Express an imported fabric whose weight is 250 grams per square meter in ounces per square yard.

Step 1: Convert grams to ounces (see Table 14.2):

250 grams × 0.0353 = 8.821 ounces

Step 2: Convert square meters to square yards (see Table 14.2):

1 square meter × 1.196 = 1.196 square yards.

The fabric weighs 8.821 ounces per 1.196 square yards.

TABLE 14.2	Metric-English Conversions			
English to Metric			**Metric to English**	
To Convert	*Multiply by*		*To Convert*	*Multiply by*
Inches to millimeters	25.40		Millimeters to inches	0.03937
Inches to centimeters	2.540		Centimeters to inches	0.3937
Feet to centimeters	30.48		Centimeters to feet	0.03281
Feet to meters	0.3048		Meters to feet	3.281
Yards to meters	0.9144		Meters to yards	1.094
Sq. yards to sq. meters	0.8361		Sq. meters to sq. yards	1.196
Ounces to grams	28.3495		Grams to ounces	0.0353
Pounds to grams	453.5924		Grams to pounds	0.00221
Pounds to kilograms	0.4536		Kilograms to pounds	2.205

Step 3: Calculate ounces per square yard:

$$\frac{8.821}{1.196} = 7.38 \text{ ounces per square yard}$$

▶ Express an American-made cotton broadcloth whose weight is 3.52 yards per pound, 45 inches wide, in meters per kilogram. Also state fabric width in metric.

Step 1: Convert yards to meters:

3.52 yards × 0.9144 = 3.22 meters

Step 2: Convert pounds to kilograms:

1 pound × 0.4536 = 0.4536 kilogram

The fabric weighs 3.22 meters per 0.4536 kilogram.

Step 3: Calculate meters per kilogram:

$$\frac{3.22}{0.4536} = 7.10 \text{ meters per kilogram}$$

Step 4: Convert a 45-inch width to a centimeter width:

45 inches × 2.54 = 114.3 centimeters

Thus the fabric is 7.10 grams per kilogram and 114.3 centimeters wide.

Weave Layout

Graph paper is used to show the weave, or the order in which the yarns interlace in a fabric. The completed designs show the interlacings from the face side of the cloth. Graph paper is used by textile designers to portray their designs. It is also used by textile technicians to analyze fabric weaves. Fabric-weave analysis is done with the face side whenever possible.

Each vertical row of squares represents a warp yarn and each horizontal row of squares represents a filling yarn. A warp yarn crossing over a filling is usually shown by marking in the square. A blank square is used to show the filling yarn passing over the warp.

The vertical and horizontal rows of squares are the same size. A weave on graph paper only shows the order in which the yarns interlace. Two fabrics with the same weave are shown by the same diagram, even though in one the yarns may be much farther apart. The weave diagram does not show the relative number of yarns per inch between warp and filling, nor does it indicate the yarn size and type.

To illustrate the fabric weave on graph paper, every interlacing in one repeat must be examined to determine whether the warp or the filling is the surface yarn. Although most weaves are analyzed from the face side, in some fabrics, the interlacings can be seen more clearly on the back of the cloth. In such cases, the analysis can be made from the back, but the finished design must show the interlacings as they appear in the face. A warp passing over a filling on the back would be a filling passing over the warp on the face.

The diagram on the top in Figure 14.5 shows the interlacing yarns of a satin weave. The interlacings are numbered from 1 to 25. In the middle, a graph is shown with the squares numbered to correspond with the interlacings in the satin weave. A filled-in square is used to show an interlacing in which the warp yarn passes over the filling yarn (raiser) and a blank square is used for an interlacing in which the filling yarn passes over the warp yarn (sinker). Beginning in the upper-right corner, the first warp yarn crosses under two filling yarns, over one

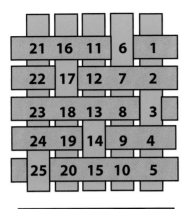

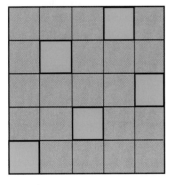

FIGURE 14.5
A weave representation on graph paper.

filling yarn, and then under two filling yarns. Square 1 is blank because the filling yarn is over the warp yarn. Square 2 is blank for the same reason. Square 3 is filled because the warp yarn is over, and squares 4 and 5 are blank because the filling is over for those interlacings. Squares 6, 14, 17, and 25 are filled because the warp yarn passes over the filling yarn for those interlacings.

The diagram on the bottom in Figure 14.5 shows the weave on graph paper.

Analyzing the Weave

In analyzing a fabric, an examination is made of the interlacing arrangement of the yarns. This arrangement is set down on graph paper, as explained previously, on

p. 280. In analyzing the weave, proceed as described in this section.

Hold the samples with the face side up and warp yarns vertical. Make a fringe on the top and right edges of the sample. Each fringe should be at least ½ inch long. With a pick needle or a pin, move the first warp yarn into the fringe on the right edge. Use a pick glass or magnifying lens to see the interlacing of the warp yarn with the filling yarns, starting from the first filling yarn across the top. (See Figure 14.6a and b.) According to the interlacing, fill in each succeeding square, from the top down, in the first vertical row of squares on the right edge of the graph. Use a filled-in square to show a raiser (warp over) and a blank square to show a sinker (filling over). Continue down for as many filling yarns as are necessary for two repeats of the weave vertically. (The extra repeat is used to check the accuracy of the work.)

Remove the first warp yarn and move the second warp yarn into the fringe. In the same way, record the interlacing of the second warp yarn in the vertical row of squares to the left of that used for the first warp yarn; continue for the same number of squares as used for the first warp yarn.

Proceed the same way with the other warp yarns in the weave until two repeats have been completed horizontally and vertically. One repeat is complete horizontally when a warp yarn is reached that weaves the same as the first warp yarn. Two repeats are complete when another warp yarn is reached that also weaves like the first. This last warp yarn, however, is not included in the two repeats.

Usually it is easier to follow the interlacing of a warp yarn in a fringe of the filling because the filling yarns are farther apart. However, occasionally it is easier to work with filling in a fringe of the warp. In this case, the design would be made a horizontal row at a time. If the interlacings are studied from right to left, the squares of the graph must be filled in that order.

The weave in a fabric may be analyzed starting at any one of the four corners and working horizontally or vertically, but all interlacings must be recorded on the graph in the same relative positions as they are in the fabric.

Analyzing the Color Effect

Analyzing a fabric for color effect is similar to analyzing a fabric for weave effect. The procedure is outlined in the following paragraphs.

Have the sample with the face side up and warp yarns vertical. Fringe the top edge and the right edge of the swatch, leaving a complete stripe of one color across the top and a complete stripe of a different color along

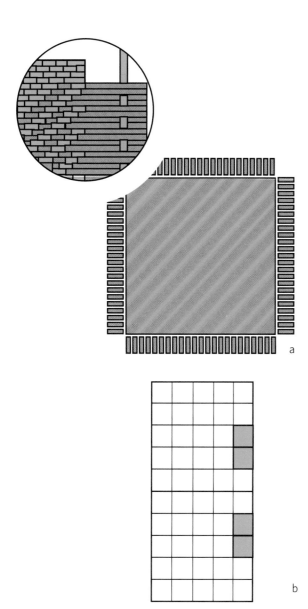

FIGURE 14.6
The separated warp yarn in the fringe shown (a) in the insert is (b) represented on graph paper.

Fabric performance testing, as indicated earlier, involves formalized, exacting procedures and requires trained technical personnel and laboratory facilities for their undertaking. However, the procedures and the meanings of results of these tests can and should be understood by all textile professionals, both technical and nontechnical. This is particularly important today because textile product testing continues to expand and companies realize that quality standards and performance indicators are necessary to sustain competitiveness and ensure market access. Fabric test procedures and the interpretation of test results are therefore included in this section. See Figure 14.7 for a view of an area of a textile testing laboratory.

There are also other reasons for textile testing besides quality control. These include development of new fabrics, analysis of the cause of cloth problems (e.g., fabric defects and poor colorfastness of dye), determination of the acceptable consumer performance level (to prevent product failure or customer returns), and adherence to government regulations.

After the fabric tests are performed, the results must be studied in order to determine whether the fabric should be used for the intended end use. Is the fabric strong enough to be made into men's trousers? Will the swimwear fabric fade too quickly from repeated exposure to the sun? Is the shrinkage of the shirting fabric considered excessive? The answers to these questions (and many others) determine the suitability of the fabric for the desired use. The importance of a test must also be decided. For example, the fact that a 100-percent-wool-coating fabric fades very quickly when washed should not be considered important because the coat will undoubtedly be dry cleaned and not laundered. If, however, the fabric is considered to be very weak for this purpose, then the fabric should be rejected for this end use because strength is an extremely important property for coats.

Textile Standards and Specifications

It is important that the textile tests used be standardized. The same test method used for determining a particular property of a fabric, such as breaking strength, should be followed by everyone in the textile-testing field. If different procedures or testing apparatus are used, the results will vary. Thus a **standard test method** specifies the procedure and conditions of the test as well as the apparatus for determining the characteristics or property of a product.

the right edge. Move the first warp yarn into the fringe on the right edge and follow the same procedure used for picking out a weave (see p. 281). Instead of using filled-in squares for a warp yarn interlacing over, and blank squares for filling yarns over, fill each square with the color of the warp yarn or filling yarn passing over. Use vertical strokes of color if the yarn passing over is warp, and horizontal strokes of color if the yarn passing over is filling. This makes it easier to check the accuracy of the work. It is best to make at least two vertical and two horizontal repeats of the pattern.

FIGURE 14.7
A section of a textile testing laboratory.

There are also **standards of performance,** which prescribe a required level of performance of materials, and provide an efficient means of judging product acceptability for a particular use. For example, a fabric must have a colorfastness-to-washing rating of at least a Grade 4 (very good resistance to color change) to be acceptable to a fabric buyer for a blouse manufacturer. Many up-scale, higher-price-level producers establish higher performance standards than the industry standards, whereas some producers in very competitive low-priced markets establish lower standards of performance, thus reducing their cost (as well as the quality of their fabrics).

A fabric **specification** is a part of the legal purchasing document. It states or specifies the performance levels of the fabric being bought. Some contracts include performance specifications for many properties of the fabric, whereas others contain only a few. Some purchase orders merely indicate the mill fabric name or number designation (and color) and no performance specifications. In this last situation the buyer relies on the mill integrity that the fabric is suitable for the end purpose intended. Some standards of performance are not optimal or voluntary but are mandatory, as in the case of flammability standards for consumer products (see p. 334).

Test methods are developed by research groups through extensive investigations and interlaboratory comparisons. Simplicity, reproducibility, applicability, cost of performing the test, and the time required to perform the test are all important considerations in each test-method development.

Test Methods—Organizations

Two technical and scientific organizations are the leaders in publishing methods for testing textile materials in the United States. Both organizations are composed of many technical committees whose members include a wide cross section of the textile industry. The recommended test methods of both organizations have generally been accepted and are used by the textile industry. The test methods are also used by government agencies.

The first organization is the **American Society for Testing and Materials International** (ASTM International). Organized in 1898, it has grown to be the world's largest nongovernmental standards-writing organization. Its procedures, used throughout the world, focus on the physical characteristics of a wide range of materials, such as steel, rubber, adhesives, plastics, and concrete. The organization publishes an *Annual Book of ASTM Standards* containing more than 70 volumes, 2 of which are devoted entirely to textiles (volumes 7.01 and 7.02). Breaking strength, abrasion, fabric thickness, and resistance to pilling are examples of the types of tests that this ASTM book contains. There are more than 130 ASTM technical committees covering diverse industry areas.

The second organization is the **American Association of Textile Chemists and Colorists** (AATCC). Founded in 1921, it focuses on the dyeing and finishing aspects of textiles. Its memberships include representatives from over 60 countries. Colorfastness to sunlight, shrinkage, water resistance, wrinkle recovery, and soil release are examples of the types of tests developed. The organization publishes an annual *AATCC Technical Manual* containing testing procedures. The Society of Dyers and Colourists (SDC) in the United Kingdom has long been a sister organization of AATCC in spreading the knowledge of textile coloration around the world.

Throughout this chapter and for the various tests discussed, reference is made to particular ASTM and AATCC test methods.

The U.S. government also publishes a book containing methods for testing textile materials, *Federal Test Method Standard No. 191*; it is used for testing fabrics for government purchase. Many of the test procedures contained in the *Annual Book of ASTM Standards* and the *AATCC Technical Manual* are also in the *Federal Test Method Standard No. 191*.

Two other U.S. scientific associations are involved in establishing testing standards relating to textiles as well as other products:

▶ The **National Fire Protection Association (NFPA)** develops test methods and performance specifications relating to fire.

▶ The **American National Standards Institute (ANSI)** is the major coordinating organization for the U.S. voluntary national standards system. It collects and publishes test methods and standards for industry groups and the United States government. ANSI headquarters are located in Washington, DC, but it also has an office in New York City.

With world trade growing rapidly, the formation of international standards is of great importance. The need is being fulfilled by the **International Organization for Standardization (ISO),** which is a specialized international agency for testing standardization. Founded in 1947, ISO's objective is to develop international standards to facilitate international exchange of goods and services. About 150 countries participate in ISO through their national standardization organizations. ISO is based in Geneva, Switzerland.

A "member body" of the ISO is the national organization most representative of standardization in its country. The United States is represented through ANSI. Europe is represented by the Committee for European Normalization (CEN). CEN (Comité Europeén de Normalisation) was established for the benefit of trade within Europe. The membership of CEN consists of the countries of the European Union (EU) and countries participating in the European Free Trade Agreement. Japan formulates standards through the Japanese Industrial Standards Committee (JISC), whereas Great Britain uses the British Standards Institute (BSI) to develop standards. The results of ISO's technical work are published as international standards.

The evolution of the global marketplace and the emergence of global companies have changed the face of international standardization. The time when U.S. standards were the de facto standard for the world has passed. The members of the World Trade Organization (WTO) are bound by the rules in the WTO's agreement on Technical Barriers to Trade (TBT). The central obligation is that of nondiscrimination. This means, as an example, Germany cannot treat imports from France better regarding acceptance of standards than Germany treats imports from the United States.

Textile Testing Laboratories

Many mills, manufacturers, and retail companies have their own textile testing laboratories. There are also independent testing laboratories. These companies—which are located worldwide, in every important textile center—will perform standard tests on textile samples submitted and send the results to the company or individual requesting the information. The charge for this service varies, depending on the type of test performed. The following are several of the independent textile testing organizations within the United States:

▶ Albany International Research Company, Mansfield, MA

▶ Applied Textiles Lab Services, Byron Center, MI

▶ DSET Laboratories, New River, AZ

▶ Govmark Organization, Inc., Farmingdale, NY

▶ Inter-City Testing and Consulting Corporation, Sacramento, CA

▶ International Textile Center, Lubbock, TX

▶ MTL-Acts Testing Labs, Inc., Buffalo, NY; Chicago, IL; Minneapolis, MN

▶ Q-Lab Weathering Research Service, Homestead, FL; Buckeye, AZ

▶ SGS U.S. Testing Company, Inc., Fairfield, NJ; Los Angeles, CA; Tulsa, OK

▶ Stork Twin City Testing Corporation, St. Paul, MN

▶ South Florida Test Service, Miami, FL

▶ Trace Laboratories, Denver, CO

▶ Vartest Laboratories, Inc., New York, NY

There are also many textile testing laboratories located outside the United States. The following are some of these:

- Cesmec Ltd., Santiago, Chile

- Gearing Scientific Ltd., Ashwell, Herts, United Kingdom

- Intertek Testing Services HK Ltd., Hong Kong

- Laboratoire National d'Essais (LNE), Paris, France

- Merchandise Testing Labs, Manila, Philippines

- MTL-Acts Testing Labs Ltd. (a Bureau Veritas Company), Tokyo, Japan; Seoul, Korea; Lille, France

- SGS Ltd., Bombay (Mumbai) and Madras (Chennai), India; Singapore; and Beijing, China

- STR Testing and Inspection A.G., Steinach, Switzerland

- Textile Technology Centre, St. Hyacinthe, Canada

The American Society for Testing and Materials International (ASTM International) publishes an International Directory of Testing Laboratories in which the focus is on textile products.

Relationship Between Laboratory Tests and Usage

The challenge in textile testing is to develop test procedures that not only correlate with consumer usage, but also allow tests to be performed on a volume basis and at reasonable costs.

There is frequently a problem of directly correlating the laboratory tests with the actual fabric end use, especially in the area of apparel. There are many reasons for this: different people wear out their garments at different rates; fabrics being worn are usually subjected to repeated stresses of low magnitude, whereas the laboratory tests are accelerated because of time limitations, using test stresses of high magnitude; and fabrics for apparel usage are subjected to various combinations of wear forces at the same time, which cannot be easily and economically duplicated in the laboratory (e.g., a simultaneous combination of rubbing, bending, and twisting).

Correlation between laboratory tests and both interior furnishings and industrial end uses are much less difficult because there are fewer variables.

Types of Test Methods

Although textile testing is broad in scope, encompassing many textile properties, most of the tests performed on textiles can be grouped into the following major categories:

- **Physical tests:** These tests are physical or mechanical in nature. Examples include breaking strength, abrasion resistance, and pilling propensity.

- **Tests to determine colorfastness properties:** These tests are used to determine the resistance of dyed or printed fabrics to color change under various conditions. These include colorfastness to sunlight, washing, and crocking (rubbing off of color).

- **Chemical tests:** In these tests, chemicals are used as part of the test procedure. Examples include fiber identification using the solubility method, determination of antibacterial activity in fabrics, and determination of the presence of mercerization in cotton fabrics.

- **Optical tests:** In these tests a microscope or another magnifying device is used. Examples include grading of wool fibers, fiber identification, and inspection of textile defects.

Textile tests can also be grouped according to their relationship to general fabric characteristics, such as aesthetics, care, comfort, durability, environment, and safety. In this chapter, a variety of the most frequently used textile tests is included. They are grouped according to type of test: strength, surface friction, appearance, functional, and colorfastness (see Table 14.3).

Conditioning Test Specimens

Physical properties of textiles are often affected by the amount of moisture in the air. For example, cotton fabric is stronger when wet, but rayon becomes weaker. Thus, for most physical tests, the fabric (or yarn) should be conditioned first so that reproducible test results on textile products can be achieved.

The procedure is as follows: The test specimens are placed in an oven and brought to a low moisture content. They are then placed into the **conditioning room** or chamber, which is set for a temperature of 70°F (21°C) and a relative humidity of 65 percent. The samples are left in the conditioning room or drawer to absorb moisture. When moisture equilibrium is reached (weight increase stops), the samples are considered conditioned. The testing should take place in this atmosphere.

TABLE 14.3   Common Textile Tests

Strength Tests	Definition of Tests	Important for
Breaking strength	Force required to break a fabric when it is under tension (being pulled)	Wovens
Tearing strength	Force required to continue a tear or rip already started in a fabric	Wovens
Bursting strength	Amount of pressure required to rupture a fabric	Knits, felts, nonwovens, laces, and others
Surface-Friction Tests	**Definition of Tests**	**Important for**
Abrasion resistance	Resistance to the wearing away of any part of a material when rubbed against another material	Most end uses
Yarn distortion	Change in symmetrical fabric surface appearance by the sliding or shifting of yarns following the application of rubbing action or force	Fabrics with low yarns per inch
Appearance Tests	**Definition of Tests**	**Important for**
Pilling propensity	Formation of pills on the surface of a fabric	Hydrophobic fibers and fabrics with fuzzy surfaces
Soil release	Textile finish that assists in the release of soil and oily stains during home laundering	Oleophilic and hydrophobic fiber (polyester)
Stiffness	Resistance to bending	Drape
Wrinkle resistance	Ability to recover from folding or bending	Smoothness and crease retention
Functional Tests	**Definition of Tests**	**Important for**
Air permeability	Rate of airflow through a material under differential pressure between two fabric surfaces	Curtains, parachutes, insulation, and others
Dimensional change	Increase (growth) or decrease (shrinkage) in the length or width of a fabric	Apparel fit, interior appearance, and others
Durable press	Finish that results in a garment being highly resistant to fabric wrinkles and seam-puckering creases and pleats	Garment appearance as well as maintaining sharp
Flame resistance	Ability to resist burning	Safety
Stretch in elastic fabrics	Stretch and recovery properties of fabrics containing elastomeric fibers (e.g., spandex)	Comfort
Colorfastness Tests to	**Ability to Resist Color Change from**	**Important for**
Burnt gas fumes	Pollution gases	Use in large cities and near factories
Crocking	Resist transference of color by rubbing from one colored textile material to another	Linings, upholstery, colored sheets, and others
Dry cleaning	Dry cleaning process	Dry cleanable articles
Frosting	Localized flat abrasive action	Rear pocket of trousers and others
Light	Sunlight	Outdoor articles, curtains, and draperies
Laundering	Washing (or laundering) process	Washable articles

Variations in temperature and humidity may also have a significant effect on color. The fabric dyed in Brazil in December may appear a different shade when examined by the buyer in New York (winter vs. summer environment). It is best to condition samples before color is examined or measured by both the dye plant and the textile buyer. A conditioning cabinet can be used if a conditioning room is not available.

For additional information about conditioning test specimens, refer to ASTM Test Method D1776.

Fabric Strength Tests

Various fabric strengths can be measured. These include breaking, tearing, and bursting. A strong fabric with good abrasion resistance usually results in a long-lasting material.

Breaking Strength

Breaking strength is the force required to break a fabric when it is under tension (being pulled). Breaking elongation is the increase in length that has occurred when the fabric breaks. These tests are usually performed simultaneously because both results can be obtained from the chart used with the test. Wear life of a fabric correlates to both properties and not to strength alone. With all other factors equal, a fabric with lower breaking strength and higher elongation may remain wearable for as long a period as a stronger fabric with lower elongation. The extra elongation enables fabrics to better withstand the forces of normal wear.

These tests are used mainly for woven fabric because the tests are unidirectional and this material has unidirectional yarns. Tests are done both lengthwise and widthwise. Knitted fabrics are not usually tested in this manner because as the loops elongate, failure would probably occur at the sections where the loops are joined as a result of a shearing force and not a breaking force. Knit fabrics also tend to curl at the edges when elongated, thus preventing good reproducibility of the test results.

Other materials, such as felt, nonwovens, lace, and netting, are also usually not tested for breaking strength because their weakest point may not be in the direction the breaking force is being applied. These materials are usually tested for bursting strength, which gives a more meaningful result. (See p. 288.)

The factors that produce a strong fabric include fiber content, yarn size and type, weave, and yarns per inch. Thus a 100-percent-nylon material with heavier yarns, plain weave, and relatively high yarns per inch would be inherently strong.

Breaking strength is important for various end uses such as automotive safety belts, parachute harnesses, and pants (when bending). Breaking strength can also be used to test the effects of destructive forces on a woven fabric, including sunlight, abrasion, laundering, and some finishing processes such as napping, embossing, and those using resin chemicals on cotton fabrics.

The breaking strength is expressed in pounds and the elongation is expressed as a percentage. In both cases, a number of warp (lengthwise) tests and filling (widthwise) tests are performed. An average is then calculated for both the warp test and the filling test. Neither the thickness nor the weight of the fabric is considered in these tests.

The devices most used for this test are the **Constant-Rate-of-Traverse (CRT)** type tester and the **Constant-Rate-of-Extension (CRE)** type tester (See Figure 14.8.). The Constant-Rate-of-Load (CRL) is another type of tester. For additional information about breaking-strength tests, refer to ASTM Test Methods D5034 and D5035.

Tearing Strength

Tearing strength is the force required to continue a tear or rip already started in a fabric. The tearing-strength test is used mainly to test woven fabrics, but is also used on nonwoven materials. (See p. 140.) The test is unidirectional, with the tests made both for the lengthwise and the widthwise directions. Tearing strength is not related to the force required to start the tear and is usually of a low magnitude.

If the yarns shift easily in a woven fabric, then the tearing force does not break successive individual yarns, but rather breaks groups of yarns that have shifted together. As a result, the tearing strength indicated is greater than if the yarns do not shift easily. This is why a plain-weave fabric usually has a lower tearing strength than a comparable twill-weave fabric.

It is possible for a woven fabric that has a high breaking strength to have a relatively low tearing strength. A cotton fabric with thin yarns but a large number of yarns per inch is an example.

Tearing strength is expressed either in pounds or grams. The averages of the lengthwise and widthwise tests are each given as the result. The most used devices for this test are the **Elmendorf Tear tester** (Figure 14.9) and the CRE tester (for the tongue method).

For additional information about tearing-strength tests, refer to ASTM Test Methods D1424, D2261, and D5587 for testing woven fabrics and D5733, D5734, and D5735 for testing nonwoven materials.

FIGURE 14.8
With a Constant-Rate-of-Extension type tester, the test specimen is held at each end by a clamp. The pulling clamp applies an increasing stress on the material unit it breaks. This electromechanical strength testing instrument also functions with a computer.

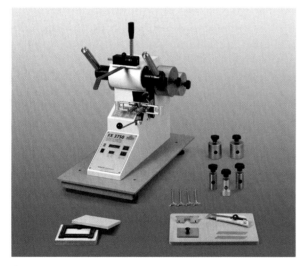

FIGURE 14.9
With an Elmendorf (Falling-Pendulum) Tearing tester, the stationary clamp holds half the specimen. The other clamp, holding the other half of the specimen, is attached to the pendulum. When the pendulum swings (i.e., falls), the fabric tears.

Bursting Strength

Bursting strength is the amount of pressure required to rupture a fabric. The force is applied at right angles to the plane of the fabric. Either a rubber diaphragm is expanded by liquid pressure until it pushes its way through the fabric clamped over it, or a steel ball is pushed through the fabric. All yarns or areas are tested simultaneously for the weakest point because the testing force is applied radially and not in one direction, as in breaking- or tearing-strength tests. Fabrics tested in this manner are either those that do not have yarns or those in which the yarns are not in any given direction (e.g., knits, felt, nonwoven, lace, netting). Elongation, however, cannot be determined with these procedures.

Bursting strength is expressed in pounds and is an average of the tests. The devices used for this test are the **Mullen® tester** for the diaphragm-bursting strength method (Figure 14.10), and a breaking-strength tester with a ball-bursting attachment for fabrics that exhibit a high degree of ultimate elongation.

For additional information about bursting-strength tests, refer to ASTM Test Methods D3786, D3787, and D6797.

Surface-Friction Tests

Surface-friction tests are performed by rubbing action. The two tests that are discussed here are abrasion resistance and yarn distortion. Some colorfastness tests, such as those for crocking and frosting, could also be included, but they are discussed in the colorfastness section, where they more properly belong.

Abrasion Resistance

Abrasion resistance is the resistance to the wearing away of any part of a material when it is rubbed against another material. The various conditions of use of the end product create a problem in trying to correlate the results of an abrasion-resistance test with the actual wear in the intended end use. Some of the variables that must be considered are type of abradant, amount of pressure between fabric and abradant, position of fabric while being abraded (e.g., flat, curved, or folded, as at the edge of a shirt collar), frequency and time duration of each abrading sequence, and tension exerted on the fabric while it is being abraded.

The factors that produce an abrasion-resistant fabric include smooth surface, tightly twisted yarns if spun, heavier yarns, and higher yarns per inch.

Both widthwise and lengthwise directions are tested, if possible, with the final result an average number of cycles, or "rubs," before the test is terminated. Three popular criteria used to determine when the end of the

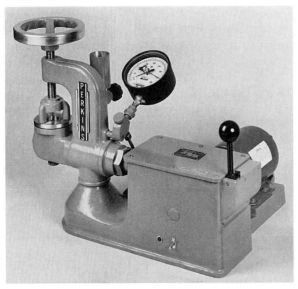

FIGURE 14.10
With Mullen Burst tester, fluid forces a heavy rubber diaphragm to expand through the lower plate opening and exerts a constantly increasing pressure against the unsupported area of the sample until the sample bursts.

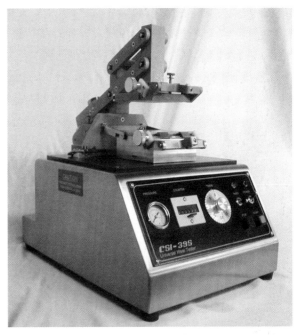

FIGURE 14.11
With a Stoll Flex tester, the material is passed around a bar (dull blade) to determine the resistance of fabrics to flexing and abrasion.

test has been reached are the completion of a specified number of cycles on the testing machine (the fabric appearance, strength, weight loss, thickness, etc., is then checked); visual assessment (e.g., first sign of wear or a yarn breaking); and specimen breaking or being completely rubbed away.

Various testing devices can be used. Each one uses a different abrader and different abrading action. The most appropriate test is determined by the degree of correlation with the end product. The following are five examples of different types of abrasion testers. The **Flexing and Abrasion tester** uses a flexing abrasion action in which the specimen is rubbed back and forth over a thin metal bar or blade so that it is doubling back and also rubbing against itself when not in contact with the blade. The **Stoll Flex tester** shown in Figure 14.11 is one type of this tester. The **Taber Abraser** uses a flat abrasion action in which the fabric specimen is placed on a rotating platform and, as it turns, is rubbed by two abrasive wheels. (See Figure 14.12.) The **Martindale Abrasion tester** also uses a flat abrasion action, but the specimen is rubbed against an abrading fabric. The rubbing motion begins as a straight line which gradually widens into an ellipse and then narrows until it again becomes a straight line in the opposite direction. The cycle repeats. The **Wyzenbeek tester** uses a curved abrasion action in which the curved specimen is rubbed

FIGURE 14.12
A Taber Abraser provides an accelerated flat wear test. The specimen is mounted on a rotating turntable and subjected to the wearing action of two abrasive wheels applied at a specific pressure.

over a curved abrasive screen. This method is used to test upholstery fabrics.

For additional information about surface-friction tests, refer to ASTM Test Methods D3884, D3885, D3886, D4157, D4158, and D4966, and AATCC Test Method 93.

Yarn Distortion

Yarn distortion is a condition in which the symmetrical fabric-surface appearance is changed by the sliding or shifting of yarns following the application of rubbing action or force. (See Figures 14.13 and 14.14a and b.)

One of the basic reasons for yarn shifting is that the number of yarns per inch in the fabric is low. Thus, the yarns can move from side to side. A good example is the ease with which yarns can shift in cheesecloth because the yarns are woven so far apart.

Another factor contributing to yarn distortion is the type of yarn. Filament yarns are smoother and more even than spun yarns, so filament yarns slip more than spun yarns. Nylon yarns shift more than wool yarns because the nylon fiber has a smooth, rod-like shape, whereas wool has a rough, irregular surface.

The weave also should be considered. Plain weave, which has many interlacings, holds the yarns in place better than satin weave, which has a minimum of interlacings. The leno weave is especially suited to reduce yarn distortion in open-structure fabrics such as marquisette. (The leno weave holds the filling yarns in place, but the warp yarns can still shift.)

The finish affects yarn movement, too. Resin finishes applied to cotton fabric bind the yarns so that they tend not to slip. Glazed finishes act the same way. The

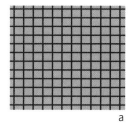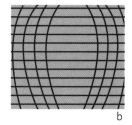
a   b

FIGURE 14.14
Yarn distortion in a fabric. A comparison of (a) undistorted and (b) distorted fabric.

felting of wool fabrics causes the fibers and yarns to come together so that there is no yarn distortion. The mercerized finish of combed-cotton yarns tends to increase yarn shifting as the yarns become smoother and more even.

Fabrics in which yarn distortion is a problem may also experience a problem with yarns slipping in the seam area. As a result, an area of distortion may be created adjacent to the seam. Sometimes, the seam may actually open without any yarns breaking and with the sewing thread still intact. Because seam slippage is virtually impossible to repair, fabrics that slip under stress should be avoided for apparel and upholstery purposes.

The device most used for the yarn-distortion test is the **Fabric-Shift Tester.** For additional information about this test, refer to ASTM Test Method D1336.

Appearance Tests

Appearance tests are tests for determining how fabrics will look after being used. Often a textile product is discarded not because of excessive wear or use but because of an undesirable appearance. Other tests besides pilling propensity, soil release, stiffness, and wrinkle resistance could be included in this section. Examples include colorfastness, dimensional change, and durable press. It was decided to place these in the colorfastness and functional tests sections.

Pilling Propensity

Pilling is the formation of small balls of fibers called pills on the surface of a fabric. **Pilling propensity** is the tendency of pills to form on a surface. (See p. 27 for a discussion of pilling.) Pills occur only when there is rubbing or an abrasive action on the surface of the fabric. Otherwise, the fibers are unable to become tangled and form a pill. This action occurs during normal wear and also while clothes are in a dryer.

Evaluation of pilling propensity should be made, taking into account the size, number, and visibility of the pills as well as the type and degree of other surface change (e.g., amount of fuzz and color change). The final

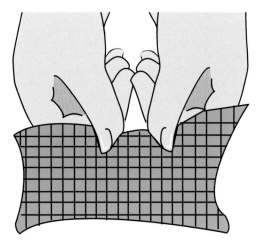

FIGURE 14.13
Holding fabric for a yarn distortion test.

evaluation is largely subjective because it ultimately must be decided whether the effects of the pilling will cause great customer dissatisfaction or only slight annoyance. To compound the problem, garments that are actually worn show a wider pilling-resistance range than the same fabrics subjected to controlled test conditions because actual wear varies with different individuals.

After the test, each of the specimens is first evaluated for pilling, usually on a pilling scale of 1 to 5 (Class 1: very severe pilling; Class 5: no pilling). Then surface appearance is evaluated for both color change and fuzz (untangled fiber ends projecting from a fabric surface). An average of ratings is usually taken to reach a result.

The devices most used for this test are the **Random-Tumble Pilling tester**, the **Brush-Pilling tester**, and the **Martindale tester**. (See Figures 14.15 and 14.16.)

For additional information about pilling propensity tests, refer to ASTM Test Methods D3511, D3512, D3514, and D4970.

Soil Release

A serious cleaning problem exists with fabrics that are oleophilic (have an affinity for oily substances) and hydrophobic (have low water absorbency). They cannot become thoroughly wet during laundering; therefore, soil—especially oil stains—cannot be removed readily. An example of this fabric type is 100-percent-polyester fabric.

Fabric finishes have been developed to assist in the release of soil and oily stains during home laundering. These **soil-release finishes** (see p. 197) make the fibers more absorbent, which allows the fabric to be cleaned more easily.

With the increased absorbency, other fabric properties also improve. These include less tendency to cling (reduced static), increased softness, improved comfort in hot weather (perspiration transported away from the body), and reduced soil redeposition while washing.

Soil-release finishes are usually not applied to fabrics with water-repellency finishes because they reduce the effectiveness of the repellency. Also, they are not normally used with printed fabrics; the colorant may be released (i.e., eliminated) if it has been lightly applied.

The soil-release test involves staining the fabric with the type of oily stains that can be found in wearing apparel and then washing the soiled article in an automatic home washing machine. These specimens are rated by reference to stain-release replicas (photographs). Class 1 represents the poorest stain removal; Class 5, the best.

For additional information about these soil-release tests, refer to AATCC Test Method 130.

Stiffness

Stiffness is resistance to bending. The draping qualities of fabrics are related to fabric stiffness. A highly drapable fabric is one that can be arranged in folds when

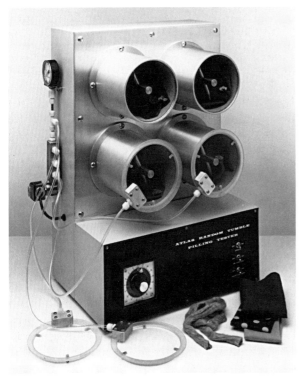

FIGURE 14.15
With a Random-Tumble Pilling tester, propeller-like blades rotate at a high speed, causing the specimens to rub against the liner inside the cylinders. Both regular pills and lint pills (from cotton fibers added to the cylinder) can result.

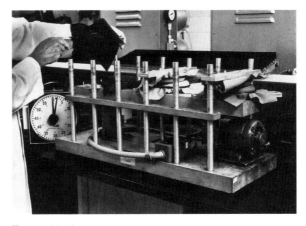

FIGURE 14.16
With a Brush-Pilling tester, the fabric is first rubbed by a brush and then with another sample of the same fabric in order to determine the pilling tendency of the material.

hung. A fabric may drape poorly but be desirable for a certain garment because it has some stiffness (e.g., suiting fabric). For a different use, such as a negligee, a fabric with excellent drape would be desired.

Fabric stiffness is affected by several factors: fiber content—a dress of 100 percent acetate has better drapability than one made of 100 percent polyester; yarn twist—highly twisted spun yarns usually reduce the draping qualities of fabrics; yarn size—fine filament yarns are more pliable than thick-filament yarns, which are stiffer; fabric thickness—a coating on women's winter suiting is quite stiff compared to that of a blouse; and finish—fabric finishes often reduce the drapability, especially the resin finishes used on cotton cloth.

One indication of a fabric's drapability is how it bends under its own weight when pushed over a horizontal edge. Another is to measure the fabric's resistance force to bending. One method would be to determine the maximum force required to push a flat folded swatch of fabric through an orifice in a platform.

An average of the lengthwise tests and of the widthwise tests are each given as the result (see Figure 14.17). The devices used for this test are the **Circular-Bend Stiffness tester** and the **Cantilever-Bending tester.**

For additional information about stiffness tests, refer to ASTM Test Methods D1388, D4032, and D5732.

Wrinkle Resistance

Wrinkle resistance is the property that enables a fabric to recover from being folded and from forming undesirable wrinkles. The wrinkle recovery of fabrics depends on various factors, as follows:

▶ Fiber content is very important (some fibers, such as wool and polyester, have an inherent resiliency).

▶ More twisted yarns reduce the tendency of fabrics to wrinkle because there is little fiber displacement.

▶ A closely woven fabric (many yarns per square inch) shows wrinkles more than one that is loosely woven because there is less yarn mobility to relieve the strain.

▶ Thick fabrics do not wrinkle as much as thinner ones because there is more mass to absorb the strain.

▶ A plain-weave fabric (many interlacings) wrinkles more than a 4 × 4 basket weave (few interlacings) because there is less yarn mobility to relieve the strain.

▶ Color on a fabric, such as a print, often makes wrinkles less noticeable.

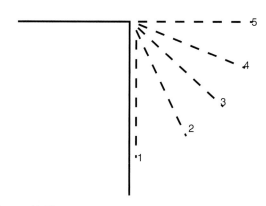

FIGURE 14.17
Fabric stiffness ratings. Note that the higher the rating number, the stiffer the fabric.

▶ Finishes also can be used to improve the resiliency of the fabric, especially materials containing cellulose fibers such as cotton, flax, lyocell, and rayon.

▶ Rough surface fabrics are less likely to show wrinkles than fabrics with smooth surfaces.

A fabric that has good wrinkle resistance also resists a crease being pressed into it. Therefore, a sharp crease usually cannot be pressed into a pair of woolen trousers, but can be pressed into a garment made of cotton that has poor wrinkle resistance. Through use of the heat-setting process, articles made with thermoplastic fibers can have sharp and permanent creases even though they may be highly resilient.

Two methods can be used to test the wrinkle recovery of the fabric. One test measures the angle at which the fabric remains bent after being creased and compressed (Recovery-Angle Method) and the other checks the appearance of the fabric after induced wrinkling, using Three-Dimensional Wrinkle-Recovery Replicas (Appearance Method). (See Figure 14.18.)

For additional information about wrinkle-resistance tests, refer to AATCC Test Methods 66 and 128.

Functional Tests

Functional tests are tests for special-purpose properties. The tests that are included in this section are for air permeability, dimensional change, appearance change, flammability, and stretch. Examples of other tests that are in this category are for water resistance, antiseptic, and antistatic.

Air Permeability

No one structural property dominates or controls **air permeability.** Rather, it is the interaction of

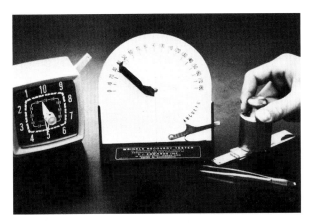

FIGURE 14.18
A Wrinkle-Recovery tester measures the angle of the fold placed in the specimen after a specified recovery period. The greater the fabric's wrinkle recovery, the larger the (inside) angle of the fold. On the right, the specimen is being creased under a weight.

variables, such as fiber crimp, yarn size and twist, fabric yarns per inch or stitches per inch, finish, and fabric thickness. With some products, such as curtains, high air flow is desired, whereas with other products, such as cold-weather clothing, low air permeability is wanted. The device used to measure air permeability is the **Air-Permeability tester.** Air permeability is expressed as cubic feet of air per minute per square foot of fabric at a stated pressure differential between two surfaces of the fabric. For additional information about air-permeability tests, refer to ASTM D737.

Dimensional Change

An increase or decrease in the length or width of a fabric is called a **dimensional change.** A decrease in size is referred to as shrinkage and an increase as growth. Dimensional changes are usually expressed as a percentage of the original size of the item.

Shrinkage Usually all the **shrinkage** that will occur in a garment does not take place during the first washing or dry cleaning. Although most shrinkage does take place at this time, additional shrinkage usually occurs during the next several cleanings.

Less than 1 percent shrinkage has virtually no effect on the size or fit of a garment. Most finished fabrics are sold with a 2 to 3 percent residual (i.e., remaining) shrinkage, the effects of which an individual will feel. Five percent shrinkage makes most garments unwearable. For example, after a 1 percent shrinkage, a man's size 15 collar would measure 14.85 inches and would still be very close to the original size. Thus, a 1 percent

shrinkage only slightly affects the comfort of the collar. A 2.5 percent shrinkage reduces the man's collar size .37 inches, making it almost a 14½-inch size. This results in some discomfort, but the garment is still wearable. After 5 percent shrinkage, a size 15 collar measures .75 inches less, or 14¼ inches, which makes it unwearable if a size 15 is needed. A 5 percent shrinkage also means that a dress has shrunk about half a size.

Some textile articles, such as sweaters, are dried under tension to stretch them back to their original size. Many garments have been restored almost to their original size in this way even though there was an initially high percentage of shrinkage from the washing process.

Various factors, such as water, heat, and agitation, cause a fabric or garment to shrink. When testing fabric for shrinkage, the test should reflect how the ultimate garment will be cleaned. For example, a woolen suiting fabric should be tested for shrinkage from steam pressing, whereas a white cotton fabric to be used for children's pajamas should be tested in hot water.

The factor that reduces the amount of shrinkage is compactness. Fabrics that have higher-twist yarns and high yarns per inch shrink less than fabrics that do not have these constructions.

Additional discussion of the topic of shrinkage can be found on p. 195.

Growth **Growth** results when a fabric is elongated and then does not completely return to its original dimension within a certain time period after being released. Growth causes problems because it results in ill-fitting garments. A pair of pantyhose that remains baggy at the knee after being worn by a seated person is an example of the adverse effect of growth. The fact that the fabric will eventually recover does not alleviate the problem because the individual must continue to wear the unsightly garment. Quality stretch garments recover quickly and completely.

Calculations Relating to Dimensional Change Two marks can be placed a certain distance apart on the fabric to determine shrinkage and growth. Frequently an original distance of 10 inches is used because it is long enough for the desired accuracy and it is a mathematically convenient number. Also, calculations are usually easier if fractional measurements are first changed to decimals.

Shrinkage Calculations The distance at the start between the two marks in the warp direction of a fabric is exactly 10 inches (or 25 centimeters). After washing, drying, and pressing, the distance between the marks is

$9^{13}/_{16}$ inches. What is the percentage of warp shrinkage of the given fabric?

The following are the needed formulas:

$$\text{Percentage shrinkage} = \frac{\text{Original length} - \text{final length}}{\text{Original length}} \times 100$$

$$\text{Percentage shrinkage} = \frac{10 - 9.81}{10} \times 100 = 1.9\%$$

Growth Calculations   Fabrics and yarns usually grow from being stretched and then relaxed, not from being cleaned. Thus, the growth test is performed with the specimen either repeatedly stretched and relaxed or with the specimen stretched for a period of time, released, and then allowed to recover for a specified time. The difference between the original length and the final length is the amount of growth.

Assume that the test specimen is 50 centimeters long. After it has been stretched for the test period and allowed to recover, the specimen measures 53 centimeters. What is the percentage growth of the textile material?

The following are the needed formulas:

$$\text{Percentage growth} = \frac{\text{Final length} - \text{original length}}{\text{Original length}} \times 100$$

$$\text{Percentage growth} = \frac{53 - 50}{50} \times 100 = 6\%$$

For additional information about shrinkage tests, refer to AATCC Test Methods 96, 99, 135, and 150.

Appearance Change

Some fabrics are specially treated so to maintain certain appearance properties after being laundered and dried. Durable-press fabrics/garments would be an example. These properties include the following:

▶   Smooth fabric appearance: The fabric should be highly wrinkle resistant so that the garment may be worn after being washed and dried without need of ironing. Objectionable wrinkles should not occur while the garment is being worn.

▶   Flat seams: The garment seams should not pucker from either cleaning or wearing. They should remain smooth in appearance.

▶   Crease retention: The fabric creases or pleats should remain sharp and not become less defined after being washed or worn.

Durable-press garments are not the same as wash-and-wear articles. The latter claims only wrinkle

FIGURE 14.19
A textile technician preparing durable press slacks to be rated.

resistance and does not normally retain creases or pleats, nor does it necessarily have flat seams. Frequently, special washing and drying instructions are attached to wash-and-wear garments. This is not required for durable-press items.

Each property is rated on a scale of 1 to 5, Class 1 being the worst rating, Class 5 being the best. Test garments, after they have been subjected to laundering and drying procedures, are compared to photographic or 3D-replica rating charts, which show what the garment should look like in order to be evaluated with a particular rating. For example, to determine the seam-smoothness rating of permanent-press trousers, the test garment is compared to a chart that shows photographs of five seams with varying degrees of pucker. The first seam is very smooth (Class 5 rating), the second is a little less smooth (Class 4 rating), and the last one is greatly puckered (Class 1 rating). Usually, an average rating is given as the result. (See Figure 14.19.)

A discussion of the durable-press finish can be found on page 193.

For additional information about durable-press tests, refer to AATCC Test Methods 88B, 88C, and 124.

Flammability

Persons who work with textiles need to be knowledgeable about a fabric's ability to burn (fabric **flammability**) to be sure that their product will conform with the various federal standards (see p. 334). Perhaps more important, no one wants to knowingly offer for sale fabrics or clothing items that may contribute to a wearer's personal injury in a fire.

For a fabric to be properly evaluated, a multitude of characteristics should be measured:

▶ Ignition properties: Time and temperature required before fabric begins to burn.

▶ Burning rate: Speed of flame.

▶ Burning properties: Self-supporting, self-extinguishing, afterglow.

▶ Ease of extinguishing.

▶ By-products: Molten fiber, dripping, smoke intensity, fume toxicity.

▶ Extent of damage: Surface flash only, substrate not affected, entire fabric damaged.

▶ Rate of heat transfer: Speed at which heat moves through or along a fabric.

Fabric Characteristics Affecting Flammability Various fabric characteristics affect the degree of flammability of a fabric. These are as follows:

▶ **Fibers:** The fiber from which a fabric is made is the most important single factor determining fabric flammability. Some fibers, such as cotton, rayon, and acetate, ignite and burn readily. Some, such as saran, vinyon, and modacrylic, do not ignite readily, but burn once ignited. Others, such as wool, do not ignite readily, and once burning, self-extinguish when the ignition source is removed. Finally, some fibers, such as glass and asbestos, are noncombustible. The burning characteristics of the natural and manufactured fibers can be found on page 30.

Various manufactured fibers have been developed in which the difficult-to-ignite, self-extinguishing characteristic has been engineered into the fiber formulation. The flame-retarding modifier is part of the polymer; therefore, no topical fire-retardant chemical after-treatment is required.

▶ **Yarns:** Fabrics with loosely twisted, soft yarns tend to ignite more readily and burn more rapidly than fabrics with high-twist yarns.

▶ **Fabric construction:** Fabrics of open, loose construction ignite more readily and burn more rapidly than fabrics that are densely woven or knitted. In addition, fabrics with a pile surface ignite more readily and burn more rapidly than flat fabrics. Fabric weight also affects the rate of burning; a heavier fabric is less flammable than a light one.

▶ **Finish:** Chemical finishes, including some resins, can have an important adverse effect on the flammability of fabrics. Fabrics of glass fiber, for example, which are ordinarily nonflammable, when treated with certain finishes and resinous materials, ignite, and the finish substance burns on the surface. Similarly, fabrics of silk fiber are ordinarily difficult to ignite and are self-extinguishing. When treated with certain finishes, however, they burn to an extent sufficient to be considered unlawful under the federal flammable fabric regulations. Some mechanical finishes also affect fabric flammability. One example is napping, which increases surface flammability.

▶ **Garment:** Tests on sewn garments reveal that sewing threads carry a flame (i.e., burn), causing ignition and burning in otherwise fire-retardant fabrics. Trim can obviously have an even more pronounced effect if, for example, the trim material burns, but the basic fabric by itself does not. Tailored, fitted garments are less flammable than those that are loose and flowing.

▶ **Method of laundering:** Use of phosphate detergents, strong chemicals, fabric softeners, chlorine bleach on cotton fabrics, and soap may render a flame-retardant finish ineffective after a number of washings. (See p. 195.) This can be of particular concern for children's pajamas.

Flammability Categories Fabrics can be categorized as to their degree of flammability. The following are examples:

Flammable: Easy to set on fire. Ordinary untreated fabrics made of generic fibers such as cotton, rayon, acetate, nylon, and polyester are in this category.

Flame resistant: Resists flames better than ordinary fabrics. More difficult to ignite and burns more slowly than flammable category. Materials made of wool and silk are in this category.

Fire retardant: Resists flames much better than fabrics in the flame-resistant category. Fabrics made of modacrylic, saran, and aramid fibers are in this category. Also, fiber variants (flame-retardant chemicals added), such as for polyester, nylon, and rayon, as well as fabrics treated with a fire-retardant finish, are in this category.

Flameproof: Does not burn. Fabrics made of glass, PBI, and asbestos are in this category.

Other aspects of the topic of flammability appear in other sections of this book. The Flammable Fabric Act is discussed on page 334. Flammability as a fiber-performance property is discussed on page 26. Flame-retardant finishes are discussed on page 195.

For additional information about flammability tests, refer to ASTM Test Method D1230.

Stretch in Elastic Fabrics

An **elastic fabric** is one that contains an **elastomeric fiber** and that stretches under tension and returns immediately and forcibly to approximately its original dimensions. The fabric may be a woven, knitted, or other type of textile material.

Three properties in an elastic fabric should be examined: the amount of stretch a given length of fabric possesses under various loads (percentage of stretch); the force or pounds it takes to stretch the fabric a certain elongation (power); and the degree of return after being stretched (recovery). In all these cases, the degree of each property varies as the fabric is repeatedly stretched. It is also important to know to what extent the properties change. Usually an average for each property is given as the result.

The device often used if a woven-elastic fabric is to be tested by repeated cycling (stretch and relax) is the Constant-Rate-of-Extension type tester. Stretchable fabrics also can be tested by using a stretch-and-hold method before relaxation.

For additional information about stretch tests, refer to ASTM Test Methods D2594, D3107, D4964, and D6614.

Thermal Insulation

Various tests have been developed to assess the thermal-insulation value of a fabric. Two such tests are the Thermal-Transmittance Test and Thermography Test.

Thermal-Transmittance Test The thermal-transmittance test covers the determination of the overall thermal-transmission due to the combined action of conduction, convection, and radiation for textile materials. It measures the time rate of heat transfer from a heated, horizontal, metal plate up through a layer of the test material to a relatively calm, cool atmosphere. The result of the test will indicate if the fabric is suitable for the desired use in fabricating cold-weather protective clothing.

Since electricity is used to provide heat, the insulating value of the fabric is determined by the amount of electricity used in the test. The better the insulating value of the fabric, the less electrical energy is required to maintain a specific temperature of the heated metal plate.

The device used for this test is the Thermal-Conductivity Tester. For additional information about thermal transmittance refer to ASTM Test Methods D 1518 and D 7024.

Thermography Test Thermography is a temperature-measuring technique using the infrared radiation emitted from objects to determine their temperature. The radiation is received by a scanner, which transfers it onto a monitor, such as a television screen. An image is produced on the monitor, revealing differences in the invisible infrared heat being radiated from the object. Thus, the relative heat loss from a clothed individual can be observed. The infrared radiation received by the scanner can be electronically transferred to film, thus making a *thermograph*. Thermography was introduced in the mid-1960s to satisfy an increased demand for the quantification of thermal loss. Lighter-patterned areas represent lost body heat through clothing. The solid-dark areas indicate that little or no body heat is being lost through clothing.

Thermographs are normally produced in color. A color-temperature scale is used to visually depict relative insulation values. White indicates the most heat loss, with red, yellow, green, blue, magenta, and black forming the descending color-temperature scale. Each color indicates a different degree of heat loss.

The scanning device and monitor are portable, which makes the use of the device more flexible. Thus, the testing of winter clothing can be conducted either in an environmental chamber or under actual wearing conditions.

Understanding Color

A color can be described as having three dimensions—**hue**, **value**, and **chroma**. Simply defined, hue is the color name (e.g., blue), value is the degree of lightness or darkness (shade), and chroma is the intensity or saturation of pure color.

When light strikes the surface of a textile material, some of the light is reflected to the eye where it is absorbed by the retina. The light, which is a form of electromagnetic energy, is then converted into electrochemical energy, which the optic nerve transmits to the brain. In this manner we see light.

Light travels in waves (not in a straight line). When the wavelength is between about 380 and 760 nanometers (nm), light is visible to humans. (1 nanometer equals one-billionth of a meter or the size of a benzene molecule.)

The color seen depends primarily on the wavelength of light received by the eye. For example, if the wavelength of light received is about 460 nanometers, then the brain interprets this light as a blue color. Thus, color is a visual sensation and since it is the mind that perceives color, it is a subjective observation. The color seen can vary from one individual to another because of the influence of psychological, physical, and physiological factors. If more than one wavelength of light is reflected, then more than one color is being transmitted to the observer.

Surfaces are colored because they reflect light discriminately (i.e., selectively). The color of an object is seen as a result of the object's selective absorption of light rays. Thus, if an object is pure blue, this means that its physical and chemical composition causes it to absorb all wavelengths of light except those of blue light, which are reflected back. The same occurs with other pure colors, but a different light wavelength is reflected.

In those colors that are not pure (i.e., containing a blend of colors) two or more colors are being transmitted back to the observer. For example, a fabric seen as turquoise is reflecting blue and green colors while absorbing the others. If the object is pure white, this means that the full visible spectrum of light is being reflected back in approximately equal quantities. If it is pure black, then all colors in the spectrum are being absorbed by the object.

The color of an object that a person sees depends on a variety of factors, including the colorant used, light source, individual aptitude, material surface and translucency, angle of illumination, and size of the object being viewed. Thus, if the color of a fabric (or any material) is to be measured or observed, all factors affecting the color seen should be the same for each viewing. This condition should exist for evaluating color by machine (instrument) or by eyesight. This condition is very important for color matching and determining color change in colorfastness tests. (See Metamerism, p. 158.)

For additional information about the proper measurements of color of specimens by instrumental means, see AATCC Evaluation Procedure 6.

Color Specifications

All fabric specifications include a color-specification clause to properly describe the color or colors being ordered. There are several ways in which this is accomplished:

▶ An actual swatch of the color is included as an integral part of the purchasing order, along with all the other fabric specifications.

▶ A digital or graphic representation of the color is provided as part of the fabric specification. The color representation is derived from a spectrophotometer/

computer analysis of an original sample, as described in Chapter 8 (see p. 158).

▶ A Pantone® reference number is specified as a color requirement. The Pantone® number is a six-digit number, with each number designating differences in hue, lightness, and saturation of all colors in the color spectrum. Each Pantone® number is also available as a color chip or swatch.

It is the responsibility of the seller to match the color specified. When a color swatch or Pantone® number is the color specification, the seller provides a piece of the dyed fabric to be delivered. Where the seller may be half a world away, sending physical samples may be too time-consuming and uncertain in time-sensitive fashion markets. In global trading where digital or graphic color representations are specified, the seller furnishes by fax a digital or graphic read-out of the dyed fabric to be delivered.

Colorfastness Tests

Textile materials change color because of the influence of various conditions. Environmental factors, such as sunlight and pollution gases, and wear factors, such as abrasion, cause alteration in colors. Perspiration, as well as laundering and dry cleaning, also cause color changes in fabrics. In addition, color may change during a finishing process when exposed to high temperature, as happens with durable press. Some materials change color greatly while they are being used. Others change very little or not at all. The ability to evaluate a fabric requires knowledge of the factors that cause these color changes and how the changes are rated or reported.

A material that experiences little color alteration when exposed to a fading force is said to have good colorfastness. For example, a fabric that has excellent resistance to color change from washing is said to possess good colorfastness to washing. If the color does not hold, then the fabric has poor colorfastness to washing.

Colorfastness is generally more of a problem with deep colors, bright colors, and red because any color change in these is more obvious than with pastel or lighter shades. Because lighter shades frequently are not tested on a specific fabric, it is possible that one particular color will have good colorfastness when another color does not.

After each of the colorfastness tests has been completed, a comparison is made between the color or shade of the tested sample and that of the original fabric. (Colorfastness to crocking is the exception. See p. 298.)

The specimens are usually evaluated on a 1 through 5 scale, where Grade 1 means a very great shade change and Grade 5 means no shade change. An average of the ratings is taken as the result. Colorfastness to light (sunlight) is sometimes rated on an L1 through L9 scale, with L1 being the worst rating and L9 the best. Textile buyers and other people involved with fabrics are familiar with this rating system.

A test for possible staining is important because garments are often in contact with each other, especially while being worn or cleaned. The migration of color from one garment to another can result in the stained article becoming unwearable. The staining effect can be determined at the same time the colorfastness test is performed by attaching a white fabric swatch to the test specimen at the beginning of the test and evaluating the swatch after the colorfastness test has been completed (Grade 1: heavy staining; Grade 5: negligible or no staining).

It is possible for a material to change color from the colorfastness test and not exhibit any staining. It is also possible for the test specimen to stain and not seem to change color. Finally, some specimens both change color and exhibit staining from the test.

When a sample is examined under sunlight and then under a fluorescent light, the color seen is not necessarily the same (this is called **metamerism;** see p. 158). Therefore, the source of light is a factor that must be considered in the assessment of the colorfastness tests. To eliminate the source of light as an error factor, it is suggested that evaluation be made in a color-viewing booth using different lights.

Colorfastness to Burnt Gas Fumes (Gas Fading)

One cause of color change in textile materials is the atmosphere. The air we breathe contains various gaseous impurities, among which are small quantities of nitrous oxide, derived from the combustion of illuminating or heating gases. Therefore, textiles must be tested for their **colorfastness to burnt gas fumes.**

Of the various textile fibers presently used, the most susceptible to these gases is acetate. There is usually no difficulty with fabrics containing other fibers. The problem lies with the disperse dyes that are used on acetate. These dyes, of themselves, are not affected by the gases, but when in combination with acetate, severe color changes can occur. The major problem color is blue, which begins to turn purple after being exposed to the nitrous oxide. Frequently, the shoulders of a blue acetate dress begin to turn purple if left in a closet for an extended period of time. Inhibitors can be used in

FIGURE 14.20
An atmospheric fume chamber determines the colorfastness of materials when exposed to burnt gas fumes (atmospheric oxides of nitrogen derived from the combustion of illuminating or heating gas). The source of burnt gas fumes is a Bunsen burner placed at the bottom of the instrument.

the finishing process to reduce the amount of fading, but these are not permanent and are usually removed with the first cleaning. They are also often removed by rubbing. Solution dyeing (see p. 164) eliminates the problem, but it is an expensive method of dyeing.

Colorfastness-to-burnt-gases tests are usually performed in an exposure chamber. (See Figure 14.20.) For additional information about these tests refer to AATCC Test Method 23.

Colorfastness to Crocking

Crocking is the transference of color by rubbing from one colored textile material to another. The scope of the **colorfastness-to-crocking** test does not include how well a textile material withstands rubbing action before physical signs of wear or a color change begin to appear. These are examined in an abrasion test or a colorfastness-to-frosting test.

Dark shades are more likely to crock than light shades. There is more dye in and on dark-shaded fabric; therefore, more dye can be rubbed off. Printed fabrics often crock more easily than dyed fabrics because most of the dye of the former is on the surface and not inside the fabric, as with dyed fabric. Wet fabric crocks more easily than dry because the moisture present assists in removing dye. Colorfastness to crocking is especially important for fabrics used for apparel and upholstery.

Washing or dry cleaning may affect the result of the test. The test can be performed before, after, or both before and after such treatment. Upon completion of the test, the white testing cloth that has been rubbed on the specimen is examined to determine whether any color has been transferred from the surface of the colored material. By matching the depth of the color now on the white testing cloth to a chart (Color Transference Scale), a rating is determined (Class 1: large amount of crocking; Class 5: negligible or no crocking).

The device used for this test is a **Crockmeter**. (See Figure 14.21.) For additional information about the colorfastness to crocking test, refer to AATCC Test Method 8.

Colorfastness to Dry Cleaning

Many individuals believe that although the color of a textile material may change because of laundering, there is no need to worry about color change from dry cleaning. This is a popular misconception; the solvents used in the dry cleaning process can change the color shade.

The **colorfastness to dry cleaning** test gives an indication of what will happen to the color of textile materials after repeated commercial dry cleanings. Perchlorethylene is used in the test since it is the most widely used dry cleaning solvent.

The most used device for this test is the **Launder-Ometer**®. (See Figure 14.22.) Dry cleaning solvent instead of water is used as the liquid in the containers.

For additional information about the colorfastness to dry cleaning test, refer to AATCC Test Method 132.

Colorfastness to Frosting

Frosting is a localized color change produced by a relatively severe, localized flat abrasive action, such as that produced on the back pocket of a pair of trousers where a wallet is carried.

Various types of fabrics are particularly affected by frosting. Fabrics that have poor dye penetration fade quickly from abrasion as the surface-dyed fibers wear away, leaving an area of very little color. Blended fabrics where each fiber is a different color (cross-dye) can change shade if each fiber has a great difference in abrasion resistance. For example, in a blend of white polyester and black cotton, which forms a dark gray fabric, the black cotton fibers abrade much more quickly than the white polyester fibers. The fabric then develops a light gray or whitish area. Union-dyed fabrics can also be a problem for the same reason.

FIGURE 14.22
A Launder-Ometer® determines a material's colorfastness to washing and staining as well as to dry cleaning. The specimens are placed in containers in which there is either water or dry cleaning solvent. The containers rotate inside the Launder-Ometer®, agitating the specimens.

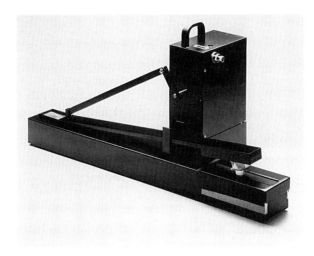

FIGURE 14.21
With a Crockmeter, the arm is rotated back and forth causing the white crock test cloth to rub against the specimen. The cloth is removed and evaluated.

The device used most for **colorfastness-to-frosting** tests is a **surface abrader** with a frosting unit. The rubbing action is multidirectional. For additional information about colorfastness-to-frosting tests, refer to AATCC Test Methods 119 and 120.

Colorfastness to Light

Dyed fabrics that are exposed to sunlight in time fade or change color. (The property is called **colorfastness to light,** not colorfastness to sunlight.) Originally, to test this property, fabrics were exposed to sunlight for a certain period of time, and then evaluated. As this was very time-consuming, accelerated methods, using light sources that duplicate the fading action of the sun, have been developed.

Many apparel fabrics are tested for periods of up to 40 hours. Pajama fabric is usually tested for only 10 hours because fabric for this end use requires little resistance to sunlight. Material to be used for a man's suit is usually tested for 40 hours because this fabric will have to resist the fading effect of the sun to a great degree. Similarly, drapery fabric is usually tested for 80 hours, and canopy fabric for 160 hours.

When evaluated, the number of hours that the specimens are in the testing machine should be indicated (e.g., Class 4–40 hours means that the specimen was rated Class 4: little color change, after being tested for 40 hours).

The device most often used for this test is the Weather-Ometer®.

For additional information about colorfastness-to-light tests, refer to AATCC Test Method 16.

Colorfastness to Laundering

There are a number of variations used in the tests for **colorfastness to laundering** because there are differences in the washing procedures for different fibers and even in the washing procedures for the same fiber. For example, wool fabrics cannot be washed like cottons (that is, with considerable mechanical action in hot, soapy solutions). Some cottons are given a mild wash at a relatively low temperature for a short period of time, whereas others are washed at a much higher temperature for longer periods of time.

The important elements to be considered in a washing test are the following:

▶ The washing temperature used has a very great affect on colors. Often the dye is loosened from the fabric by the action of hot solutions.

▶ Time is also important. For example, articles from which the dye runs should be washed without long periods of soaking because the dye will continue to run. Washing should be done quickly because the longer the washing time, the greater the amount of color running out.

▶ The additions to the bath (besides detergent or soap) also affect the test results. Some wash tests are made with the addition of sodium carbonate and/or bleach. The alkaline, sodium carbonate, intensifies the washing action, making it more severe on the color. Bleach should not be used in washing 100-percent-colored articles. Sometimes, however, it is used on fabrics that have both white and colored areas, as a white towel with a colored border, or a white shirt with a colored stripe. Dye used on such materials, however, should be fast to bleaching. For this reason, bleach is added to the washing solution for some washing tests. Any test should include whatever action or chemical the article encounters in actual use.

▶ In the same way, mechanical action to which fabrics are subjected during laundering must be included in the washing test.

▶ The proportion of liquid to the amount of material washed is also important in laundering. If the volume of liquid is too high, the materials just float around without the squeezing and twisting action that comes from tumbling in a smaller volume of wash solution.

A test for staining should also be performed with the colorfastness-to-laundering test.

The device used for these tests is the Launder-Ometer®. (See Figure 14.22.) For additional information about colorfastness-to-laundering tests, refer to AATCC Test Method, 61 and 190.

Outdoor Testing

Many products are used outdoors exclusively (or almost). These include automobiles, outdoor furniture, awnings, sails, camping equipment, and boat tops. Thus testing for color change or physical damage from weather (and sunlight) in the outdoors under actual conditions may provide more accurate results than using a testing instrument with an accelerated procedure. The drawback to outdoor testing is the length of time necessary to get results.

Outdoor textiles are also subject to ultraviolet exposure from the sun. High levels of UV radiation along with high temperatures and moisture are the main source of color change and physical damage. Radiation from sunlight in the 380–760 nm wavelength range produces visible light (and colors). Ultraviolet light is produced in the 250–400 nm range.

Ultraviolet radiation is classified into three categories: UV-A rays (315–400 nm) which, while are not very intense over the short time, penetrate deeper into human skin over time and are primarily responsible for the long-term effects of aging of the skin. UV-B rays (280–315 nm) penetrate only the top layers of skin, but are more intense in the short term; these rays are responsible for sunburn and skin cancer. UV-C rays (180–280 nm) have lethal effects on humans, but are absorbed by the earth's ozone layer.

Suntan lotions and some garments offer UV-protection. Suntan lotions use an SPF (sun protection factor) system for rating the protection provided by sunscreens. Garments are rated using a UPF (ultraviolet protection factor) system. A ultraviolet protection factor (UPF) of 15 is the minimum suggested protection. A UPF rating of 30 is considered very good protection. Often a balance needs to be struck relating to garments between UV protection and other attributes, such as fabric breathability and comfort in activewear.

For additional information refer to AATCC Test Method 183 and ASTM D 6603.

Performance Standards and Their Application

After a fabric has been tested, the results must be evaluated to determine whether the material is satisfactory for the specific use desired. The *Annual Book of ASTM Standards,* Volumes 7.01 and 7.02, Textiles, contains performance specifications for textile fabrics based on end use. The end uses include girls', women's, boys', and men's garments, and household textiles. The book is intended as a guide to aid the manufacturer, the consumer, and the general public. It is not used as a binding

FIGURE 14.23
The sport of rock climbing can be most enjoyable, but without proper textile standards and specifications, these climbers' lives would be in jeopardy.

industry standard. Some companies use higher standards, whereas others use lower ones. The standards establish a suggested minimum quality level below which textile products should not fall (see Figure 14.23).

Table 14.4 shows various standard performance specifications for fabrics and selected end uses. By comparing fabric test results with minimum fabric performance levels for a particular end use, it can be determined whether the particular fabric should be used for a specific end use.

TABLE 14.4 American Society for Testing and Materials (ASTM) Standard Performance Specifications for Fabrics and Selected End Uses

End Use	Minimum Breaking Or Bursting strength (lbs.)	Minimum (Tongue) Tearing Strength (lbs.)	Maximum Dimensional Change (5 washes)	Light Minimum Appearance Rating (DP)	Minimum Colorfastness Rating (Shade) Laundering Shade Change	Laundering Staining	Dry Cleaning Shade Change	Dry Cleaning Staining
Women's and Girls'								
Woven blouse or dress	25	1.5	3.0%	4–20 hrs.	4	3	4	3.5
Knit corset	50	—	5.0%	4–10 hrs.	4	3	—	—
Woven dress coat	25W, 20F	3.0	2.0%	4–20 hrs.	4	3	4	—
Woven sportswear	35W, 30F	2.0	3.0%	4–20 hrs.	4	3	4	3.5
Knitted sportswear	50	—	3.5%	4–40 hrs.	4	3	4	3.5
Knitted gloves	75	—	5.0%	4–20 hrs.	4	3	4	—
Woven robe	20	1.5	2.5%	4–10 hrs.	4	3	4	3.5
Men's and Boys'								
Woven handkerchief	18	1.0	5.0%	4–20 hrs.	4	3	—	3.5
Woven overalls	70	3.0	2.5%	4–20 hrs.	4	3	4	3.5
Woven pajamas	25	1.5	3.0%	4–20 hrs.	4	3	—	3.0
Knitted dress shirt	50	—	3.0%	4–20 hrs.	4	3	4	3.5
Woven sport shirt	25	1.5	2.0%	4–40 hrs.	4	3	4	3.5
Woven sport slacks	40	2.5	3.0%	4–40 hrs.	4	3	4	3.5
Home Furnishings								
Woven drapery	20	1.5	3.0%	4–60 hrs.	4	3	4	3.5
Woven bed sheet	50	1.5	2.0%	4–20 hrs.	4	3	—	3.0
Woven slipcover	50	3.0	2.5%	4–40 hrs.	4	3	4	3.5
Woven tablecloth	30	2.0	5.0%	4–20 hrs.	4	3	—	3.5
Woven towel (terry)	50W, 40F	—	10%W, 4%F	4–20 hrs.	4	3	—	—
Woven umbrella	30D, 20W	5.0	3.0%	4–20 hrs.	—	—	—	—

Note differences in some warp and filling directions.

Study Questions

Questions Relating to Structural Analysis of Fabrics

1. Select a textile product. By touch and observation alone describe the fabric as completely as possible. Include its hand, aesthetics, weight, structure, color/design, and any other characteristics.

2. State three reasons why a fabric would be analyzed.

3. The following is a description of a fabric. Identify each item of its construction:

   65% polyester and 35% cotton

   40/1 × 30/1

   100 × 80

   58

   2.71

4. State two reasons why fabric thickness is measured.

5. Mill A is selling a fabric that is 59 inches wide and weighs 14.8 ounces per linear yard. Mill B is selling a similar fabric that is 52 inches wide and weighs 1.19 linear yards per pound. Which fabric is heavier on an ounces-per-square-yard basis?

6. Complete the following metric-to-English conversions:

   a. An imported fabric is being sold in the United States as 6 meters per kilogram, 120 centimeters wide. Express this fabric in yards per pound, in the proper inch width.

   b. A U.S. export broker is presenting a 22-ounce-per-square-yard fabric, 54 inches wide, to an Italian fabric house. Express the fabric weight in grams per linear meter.

7. List five reasons why one woven fabric could be heavier than another. Do the same for two knit fabrics.

8. Which units of measure should always be used in comparing fabric weights of varying fabric widths? Why?

9. What physical aspects can be engineered into a fabric to reduce flammability?

10. When analyzing the weave of a fabric, why is it desirable to indicate at least two vertical and two horizontal repeats of the pattern?

Questions Relating to Fabric Performance Testing

1. Briefly explain why it is important that nontechnical people such as retail buyers, designers, and marketing individuals be able to understand testing reports from textile-testing laboratories.

2. Give an example of the concept of offsetting a deficiency of one aspect of the fabric structure (e.g., fiber content) by utilization of another (e.g., finishing).

3. Why is wear testing the best test to identify the consumer satisfaction of a garment? State any disadvantages.

4. Measurement of the abrasion resistance of a fabric is complex because it is affected by many factors. Explain.

5. State three factors that result in one fabric having greater air permeability than another.

6. Why does cotton terry cloth burn so easily?

7. A specimen measuring 15 inches in length shrinks to 14 inches after being washed and dried. What is the percentage of shrinkage? (Calculate to the nearest 0.1 percent.)

8. How can a fabric such as gauze, which possesses a relatively low breaking strength, also possess a high tearing strength?

9. Briefly explain why two individuals who are evaluating the color of a fabric can disagree on its color and the amount of fading in a colorfastness test.

10. State four factors that influence the color an observer sees.

11. Weathering is the adverse response of a material or product to the climate. What climate factors should be examined to determine the effect of climate on an exposed article?

12. When the quality of a fabric is unacceptable, a variety of problems can arise. State two reasons why textile testing is important to each of the following companies (do not repeat reasons):

   a. Textile
   b. Garment
   c. Retail store

13. Choose a textile end use. List four fabric performance characteristics which the buyer would want to examine.

14. How can domestic purchasers of textiles made offshore be sure that quality is being maintained before the textile products are shipped to the purchaser?

CHAPTER FIFTEEN

Textiles and the Environment

Objectives

▶ To understand that textiles and textile products have an effect on the environment.

▶ To be aware of the efforts of the textile industry to be environmentally responsible.

▶ To realize that there is a global responsibility to provide for a safe and healthy environment.

Key Terms Related to Textiles

biodegradable
conservation
contaminated
eco-fashion
ecology
energy saving
Environmental Protection Agency
environmentally friendly

Foxfibre®
green product
hazardous waste
landfill
nonhazardous
Occupational Safety and Health
  Administration
organic cotton

pollution
post-consumer
recycling
renewable
resource conservation
sustainability
toxic
transition cotton

The twentieth century has been an awesome period in human history. Most modern technology has been developed during this time period. Cars, jets, computers, manufactured fibers, the artificial heart, television, and cell phones have benefited mankind. It has been the golden age of science and technology.

This age, like the industrial revolution period that preceded it, had minimal ecological concern. It was assumed that the planet could absorb an infinite amount of toxins. The air, water, and soil were used as disposal dumps, adversely affecting the biodiversity of nature and its resiliency and cleansing ability.

More recently, however, the environmental impact of consumer products has gone from being a fringe issue supported mainly by activist groups to a mainstream concern. Many leaders in corporate America have embraced the movement to improve the environmental profile of their products. The leaders of giant companies such as Procter & Gamble, Wal-Mart Stores (see Figure 15.1), and General Electric as well as leaders of many small companies now realize that **environmentally friendly** products sell—and consumers and the investment community look favorably upon firms that are perceived as being a "friend to the environment."

Substances that are detrimental to the environment have an effect on animal, plant, and human life. The air, land, and/or water can be **contaminated**. Many factors must be considered when an industry is developing programs that will reduce unfavorable effects on the environment. Cost, material availability, customer usage and care, health and safety concerns, public image, and government regulations are some of these factors.

Sometimes choices are not as obvious as they seem. For example, a cotton fabric may be chosen over a similar polyester fabric because of biodegradability. Yet, if the polyester fibers used are made of recycled soda bottles and the cotton fibers used come from an agricultural area in which pesticides and much irrigation (water) are required, perhaps the polyester fabric should be favored even though it is made from a limited resource (petroleum). Another example is rayon. This fiber is processed from a naturally occurring and renewable material—trees, which are **biodegradable**. While this fiber is an environmentally friendly product, it is not completely eco-friendly because the use of acid is required in its production, which could escape into the air or surface water. Also, when mixed with **landfill** materials, the fibers may not degrade quickly. In addition, the harvesting of trees to provide wood pulp may be criticized if overharvesting occurs (e.g., land clearing).

Various factors have caused a change in how people view the environment. Globalization has connected

FIGURE 15.1
Solar panels at Wal-Mart in McKinney, Texas.

the entire world and so allows opportunities for major changes. Consumer input has greatly increased through purchasing decisions that affect the planning of what products are being produced. Also a greater social awareness has occurred about the need to protect the environment. In addition, fashion now includes the use of materials for textile products that previously would not be acceptable (e.g., recycled). (See Figure 15.2.) Finally, through technology previously unacceptable, consumer products now often can be made acceptable.

Green Product Characteristics

Consumer pressure to make environmentally friendly products has had an impact on the textile and other industries. The color green has become a symbol for product characteristics that relate favorably to the environment. Green living, green design, green-friendly material, and **green product** are some terms frequently used. (See Figure 15.3.)

FIGURE 15.2
A creation made with bamboo and scraps of recycled batik cloth by Indonesian designer Mardiana Ika during Eco Chic Fashion in Jakarta, Indonesia. It is the first in a series of fashion shows to raise environmental awareness throughout Asia.

FIGURE 15.3
The green product "I'm not a plastic bag."

All aspects of the product should be examined when evaluating its green characteristics. This includes production, shipping, use, care, and disposal. When the terms "going green," "eco-friendly," or other similar phrases are used, it connotes that the product or process has been evaluated with regard to environmental safeguards, **conservation** of energy, and waste minimization. Since few products completely satisfy all criteria, the greater the satisfaction the greener it is said to be.

Often the term **sustainability** is used when there is a reference to green products. It indicates an approach to environmental stewardship that looks at the full environmental impact of the systems and processes over the lifetime of a product. Various criteria are discussed in the following section.

Renewable

Renewable refers to material that comes from a resource that is easy to replace or replenish. Plants (trees), animals (sheep), and recycled materials are some examples. Even though there is still a large quantity of oil in the ground, petroleum cannot be considered a renewable material source. Eventually this resource will be depleted. This will affect the production of synthetic fibers (e.g., polyester), some dyes and finishes, and well as other products. (See Figure 15.4.)

Resource Conservation

Resource conservation refers to products that are made using less natural resources and, thus, support the environment. Also, waste is minimized in production and waste disposal is controlled.

Recycling materials, products, and waste enable manufacturers to use less resources, as well as reduce pollution. This is further discussed on page 308. Conservation of water is also an important consideration. With less water being used by industry, there is less chance of pollution from chemical discharge and less risk of damaging the environment.

FIGURE 15.4
Lundström's recycled polyester two-layer coat.

Energy Saving

Energy saving refers to products that are made using a reduced amount of energy. More efficient machines and a reduced number of processes required will decrease energy usage. Also, products requiring less energy when used are desirable. An example is the fluorescent light bulb that uses less energy (electricity) to create an equal amount of light, and lasts longer (Figure 15.5).

The source of energy used in production should be considered. A renewable fuel is preferred. Thus, using sunlight (solar panels) as the energy source makes for a greener product than using oil (e.g., thermal tanks for hot water). The burning of fossil fuel at power plants can contribute to smog (fine airborne particles), acid rain, and global warming. Thus, the less fuel used, the less air pollution generated.

The method of transportation of the fuel to the production facility as well as how far it was moved is another consideration. The product is less green if much non-renewable fuel was used in the transportation process. Thus, a pipeline to move oil would be preferable to using trucks (if feasible).

Nonhazardous

Nonhazardous refers to materials that do not adversely affect the health or safety of an individual or the environment.

Some insecticides (used in cotton fields), volatile substances used in some cleaning solvents (produce gases), and some finishes (chemicals) are not completely safe. Also, carcinogens are sometimes generated during the manufacture of products. For example, during the manufacture of plastic film containing polyvinyl chloride, dioxin (a carcinogen) is generated. In these situations there should be controls and safeguards to ensure the safety of the workers or end users. These include protective masks and clothing, air-quality controls, and programs for safe disposal of waste.

Sometimes a toxic material is used because it performs much better, is much cheaper, and/or is more available than the alternatives. There is an obligation by industry to continue research to develop a suitable, safe alternative.

Recycling

Recycling refers to products that when they are used and considered waste, are used again to make similar or different materials or products. The feasibility of converting recovered materials into new products as well as the resulting product quality and potential liability (e.g., cost) must be determined at an early stage of a developing recycling program.

Organic substances biodegrade when they are broken down by microorganisms into their constituent parts and recycled by nature. Substances break down much faster with the aid of oxygen as it helps separate the molecules. Most landfills are compacted so tightly that biodegradation takes place very slowly because there is very little oxygen and few microorganisms. Products that are photodegradable (will biodegrade when exposed to sunlight) may not degrade quickly if buried deep in a landfill. Some landfills are now being designed to promote

FIGURE 15.5
Compact fluorescent lightbulbs (CFL).

biodegradability through the injection of water, oxygen, or microbes.

The term *recycling* came into common usage with the counter culture of the late 1960s. Because solid-waste disposal in local landfills was inexpensive and convenient, there was little economic incentive for communities to support recycling programs. Only products with resale value, such as glass bottles, aluminum cans, and newspapers, were involved with recycling programs. These efforts were modest at best. In the late 1980s there was a renewal of environmental awareness as landfill costs dramatically increased. Also the availability of landfill sites decreased while the volume of solid waste continued to increase. As national news media brought increased attention to the situation, recycling legislation was introduced. The result was that billions of dollars were spent on mandated environmental protection measures. Today, many of these materials are recycled within a company or sold for reuse.

The waste of one company can become the raw material of another. The textile industry's recycled products include fibers, yarns, fabrics, garments, carpets, and used chemicals. The result of recycling includes less landfill deposit, reduction in material usage, an improved environment, and possible cost reduction. (See Figure 15.6.)

Figure 15.6
A center for clothing and shoes is an important part of recycling.

The market acceptance of recycled textile products includes the willingness of manufacturers to participate in research, development, and production of these products into new textile products. There must also be increased retailer and consumer awareness of and demand for recycled products. Textile recycling may result in increased cost, reduced product quality, and a reduction in desired aesthetics. In this case more research must be performed. Consumer education must include the realization that some cheaper foreign goods were produced in countries that have few, if any, regulations pertaining to the environment.

As technologies improve, waste disposal becomes more expensive, consumer demand for recycled materials increases, and legislative initiatives and mandates continue, the amount of recycled textiles and other materials will rise. As an illustration, apparel companies offered recycled-polyester products in the early 1990s without success. The material was stiff and too expensive. A better product and growing ecological concern around the world have made recycled-polyester textile items more desirable and undetectable by the consumer unless labeled.

Cost Consideration

Cost is always a consideration when evaluating a product. But the cost should not be evaluated in terms of dollars alone. The green rating should also be considered.

The conversion of making the change to producing an eco-friendly product can be expensive. New production equipment, the purchase of recycling equipment, and new disposal techniques are several areas in which a company must invest. However, substantial savings can often be achieved with a proper program.

Hopefully, more companies will exhibit a policy of social responsibility. They must be willing to reduce profits to address "the larger picture." The long-term effect of environmental damage should not be traded for the short-term goal of increased profitability.

Eco-Friendly Textiles

The textile industry used to be a significant polluter of the environment. Large quantities of contaminated water were discharged into rivers and lakes. The contaminants included chemicals used in processing, dyes, cleansing agents, materials from natural fibers (e.g., lanolin from wool), as well as compounds used to make manufactured fibers. Some of the substances were **toxic**. Air **pollution** resulted from the discharge of exhaust fumes and airborne fibers. Noise pollution affecting the workers was obvious in weaving rooms and yarn spinning rooms.

The textile industry has changed and has become more eco-friendly through its efforts and programs to reduce and control pollutants, reduce energy consumption, and monitor **hazardous waste** disposal. These are discussed in the following sections.

Fibers

There has been renewed interest in using plant fibers with previously little appeal for textile products. These include hemp, ramie, and bamboo (bast fibers). Fiber performance properties, cost, and availability are reasons for their limited usage, particularly in apparel. However, the increased desire by the consumers for eco-fabrics has caused the textile industry to reexamine the potential use of these fibers. (See Figure 15.7.)

FIGURE 15.7
Symphony Fabrics Corporation's bamboo and cotton thermal; Ecotex's organic cotton swiss dot; Jasco Eco's organic wool interlock; Invista's seersucker-type flat knit with Xtra Life Lycra and wool; Be Mode Textile Company's Tencel and linen; Epic Textiles Incorporated's reversible organic cotton; and Farbetex SA's interlock organic cotton.

Some cotton growers now provide manufacturers and consumers with more information about the environmental conditions under which cotton is grown. Organic cotton and transition cotton are two special categories that are used.

Organic and Transition Cotton

For **organic cotton**, the government must certify that organic farming practices have been used for at least three years. Also, no synthetic commercial pesticides, herbicides, or fertilizers that are a threat to health or the environment can be used. If cotton is marketed in the United States as organic, regardless of the country of origin, it still must meet the same strict U.S. standards as if it was produced here in the United States. These organic standards were implemented in October 2002, and only a USDA-certifying agent can verify that the cotton—wherever it was produced—meets the U.S. standards. **Transition cotton** is cotton produced on land that has been organically farmed for less than three years.

Organic and transition cotton are much more expensive than conventional cotton. Lower yield per acre, more expensive processing costs, and a segregated supply chain are several reasons for this occurrence. Also, chemicals that qualify for processing organic cotton are limited. Thus, it may be difficult for some manufacturers and retailers to offer clothing that is completely organic.

About 25 countries grow organic cotton. Turkey, India, China, Syria, and Peru are among the largest producers. (See Figure 15.8.) Most organic cotton in the United States is grown in Texas. The total organic cotton supply is very small, less than one percent of global cotton production.

Labels on textile products usually do not indicate the source of the fiber used (country) or the conditions under which it is grown. (See Figure 15.9.) The customer does not know (using cotton as an example) if there is a water conservation policy in effect, if there are harmful environmental and human effects from using the pesticides, or if there are any human rights abuses (e.g., use of inappropriate child labor). Thus, while the cotton fiber may be considered eco-friendly because it is replenishable and biodegradable, it may not be considered a green fiber because of the way it was produced.

Physically, organically grown, and conventionally grown cotton fibers are identical. There is no performance difference or difference in strength. Because there is no direct test of the fiber that can prove if it is organic, the onus is on the source to provide correct certification to prove the cotton's authenticity. Thus, there must be care in choosing a supply-chain partner.

FIGURE 15.8
Organic cotton farms, like this one in India, have sprung up around the world to meet the increasing demand for environmentally friendly apparel.

The Better Cotton Initiative (BCI) promotes environmentally, socially, and economically sustainable cotton cultivation around the world. Clothing manufacturers and stores are members as well as cotton growers.

The other common natural organic fiber is wool. Organic wool is classified when farmers follow organic livestock production standards. The sheep receive organic feed, no synthetic hormones, cannot be dipped in toxic insecticides to control external parasites (e.g., ticks), and have access to outdoors with living conditions appropriate to their species. The Organic Trade Association (OTA) has developed the standards that apply to the processing of organic wool. New Mexico is the leading producer of certified organic wool in North America.

FIGURE 15.9
An eco-friendly, certified organic cotton clothing tag.

There has been an effort to reduce the quantity of chemicals used to produce manufactured fibers. A sizable amount is now recycled. For example, the solvent used to produce lyocell is recovered, purified, and reused.

Yarns and Fabrics

There are many adverse conditions that occur when yarns and fabrics are produced that are not eco-friendly. Various actions have been taken to reduce these effects on workers and the environment. (See Figure 15.10.)

In the production of cotton yarns and fabrics, for example, large amounts of fiber, lint, dust, trash (debris from plants), and other contaminants become airborne. Air filtration and vacuum heads on and around machines are used to remove these airborne contaminants. The waste can be used for such items as nonwoven materials, mattress fillers, and filters.

In yarn and fabric production (especially in the weaving rooms where shuttle looms are still used) there is a high level of noise. Safety regulations in some countries now require workers in some areas to wear acoustical protection to prevent permanent hearing loss.

Other areas that could be examined are energy consumption, production comparison, and recycling. Energy consumption varies with different yarn-making processes. For example, open-end and rotor spinning require more energy than ring spinning. If you compare the knitting process to weaving, knitting uses fewer chemicals, there is less lint in the air, noise levels are lower, and it uses less energy. An example of recycling done with the

FIGURE 15.10
India's first organic cotton clothes-making factory in Umbergaon. Purecotz has manufactured organic cotton since 1998, and has more recently instituted Fair-Trade policies to ensure good working conditions for all company employees.

yarn production process is the warp sizing (used with warp yarns) being recovered after processing and reused.

In the production of spunlace nonwovens, foam binders are being used. The result is that less water is needed (replaced by air) and so there are reduced energy costs for drying. Spunbond nonwoven products are becoming more environmentally friendly by using renewable resources, recycled polymers, and lower-weight fabrics that reduce the usage of resources.

Dyeing and Printing

The dyeing and printing processes have an additional component relating to an adverse impact on the environment. In addition to chemicals (e.g., acids, metals, and salts), there are also dyes and pigments contained in the discharge water. Dyes and pigments can create problems with the photosynthesis of marine plant life.

Color is used in response to consumer demand. Fewer dyed and printed fabrics can be produced, but even white fabrics create problems with the use of bleaches. Naturally colored cottons and wools can be encouraged, but at present a full color range is not provided, and the colors are low in intensity. Consistency and availability are issues, and they are expensive. Also few natural dyes (e.g., indigo) are used commercially. (See Figure 15.11.)

Newer sulfur dyes use less salt, pigment inks use less metal content, and chromium-free dyestuff is being developed. Also, better quality control results in less redying of fabrics that were incorrectly dyed, and, thus, less usage of the chemicals required to remove the colorant. Textile dye baths are being reused, which reduces the need for additional chemicals and dyes.

A reduction of water usage has occurred with the use of jet-dyeing machines. Using other carriers instead of water is another possibility to reduce water pollution. Liquid carbon dioxide, for example, decreases energy use, treatment of waste, amount of water used, and quantity of chemicals required. This substance can also be recycled.

Machinery manufacturers are trying to increase output with lower amounts of energy, water, and dyestuff, while also trying to improve the end product. For example, using ultraviolet light for curing pigment-based printing inks during the drying stage reduces energy requirements.

Cotton that is naturally colored is eco-friendly. Thus, the dyeing process can be eliminated. Long-staple "color grown" cotton has been cultivated since the 1990s and is mainly due to the efforts of Sally Fox. Her patented cotton **Foxfibre**® is mostly grown organically and is used in clothing, bedding, and furniture.

Finishing

The finishing processes add favorable characteristics to textiles, but they also can damage the environment. Large amounts of water and chemicals are used as well as large amounts of energy.

The industry has developed many programs to become a greener industry. Newer finishes requiring less water (e.g., foam finishes) are being developed. More efficient methods of water extraction prior to drying are being used. Better heat recovery methods to minimize energy usage are also being researched. Biodegradable finishes are more in use.

FIGURE 15.11
A worker hangs up cloths to dry at Dali Bandhnu workshop in China. Bandhnu, also known as plangi or dyed colorful cloth, is produced from pure white cotton cloth or white cotton-hemp cloth with indigo as the dyeing material.

Reduced usage of dangerous finishing chemicals is becoming more common. An example is formaldehyde, which is a carcinogen and used in some durable-press treatments, dyeing/printing processes, and leather finishing. Upon becoming a gas and being released into the air, a hazardous condition can occur (air pollution). Formaldehyde-free binders, thickeners, and other auxiliaries used in pigment printing and resin finishing are being developed.

Restrictions on waste discharge are increasing. On-site treatment plants allow factories to reclaim and reuse chemicals as well as remove contaminants, such as metals and some compounds, before discharging the waste.

Increased computer monitoring of dyeing, printing, and finishing processes increases efficiency. This not only reduces fabric defects and seconds, but also results in less energy, chemical, and material usage.

New concepts and processes in continuous bleaching have reduced processing time, energy consumption, water consumption, and chemical impact of conventional bleaching, while yielding comparable results. There can also be a reduction in the number of steps required, so there is a reduction in opportunities for errors.

Milliken & Company, as part of their environmentally sustainable practices, assesses the amount of carbon in their carbon dioxide and other major greenhouse gas emissions caused by direct energy use and electricity. The company also does analysis of emissions caused indirectly from its activities and its supply chain.

Care of Products

Many state and local governments are supporting the concept of greener cleaning, requiring safer cleaning products. They encourage the use of cleaning products that meet EcoLogo and Green Seal safety standards (see p. 318). A brief discussion of activities in the dry cleaning and laundering industries follows.

Dry Cleaning

Dry cleaners were recycling before the term became popular. Dirty solvent was purified on the premises using a distillation process. Also solvent was recaptured from garments during the drying processes and condensed back into clean solvent for reuse.

The newer dry cleaning solvents have replaced the earlier benzene, gasoline, and other highly flammable chemicals. Today's most-used solvent is perc, but its fumes are toxic and this solvent is suspected to be carcinogenic. Regulations restrict its use and disposal. Fluorocarbon cleaners, such as Valclene®, have been phased out because there was concern about the environmental impact (ozone layer). Hydrocarbon solvents, such as DF

2000, are available as replacements. Green-system solvents include liquid carbon dioxide and GreenEarth®, which is a silicone-based cleaning solvent introduced in the late 1990s.

Dry cleaners have also reduced the loss of solvents by evaporation (air pollution) by using more efficient equipment. Dry-to-dry type machines result in both the cleaning and drying process occurring in the same machines. Thus, loss of solvent to the air is minimal.

Laundering

Detergent manufacturers have changed their formulation to reduce the environmental impact. Laundry detergents no longer contain phosphates (banned in 1990) because of ecological concern about water quality and environmental imbalance. Biodegradable surfactants are being used in detergents. (A surfactant is a chemical that lifts dirt and helps cleaners do a better job of stain removal.) Enzymes are being developed to enable detergents to use less surfactants and other chemicals. Also, there is an increase in the level of naturally based surfactants, using alcohols from natural oils to reduce the level of petrochemically based surfactants.

In 2005, Procter & Gamble Company began to sell an effective cold-water detergent—Tide Coldwater (Figure 15.12). Other companies followed. Cold-water detergents reduce energy bills by not having to use heated wash water. The laundry products industry has also developed more concentrated liquids and powders. The result is less energy being required for each cleaning and also a smaller consumer product package. Thus, there is

FIGURE 15.12
Cold-water detergents help to save energy.

energy savings and reduced waste. The plastic or paper packaging material used is recyclable. Attempts to sell concentrated cleaners, however, have lead some consumers to think they are getting less for their money.

Wal-Mart has announced it would work with suppliers to substitute "chemicals of concern," relating to health and the environment.

Another environmental concern is the use of NPE, an acronym for the family of chemical compounds known as nonylphenol ethoxylates. NPE is used in household detergents and industrial cleaning agents as a surfactant. They are excellent soil removers and have a low cost, but may be associated with an elevated risk of cancer as well as being harmful to the environment. Europe effectively banned NPEs in the 1990s for all down-the-drain applications. No legal prohibitions exist at present in the United States, but the Environmental Protection Agency's Design for the Environment program recognizes companies that voluntarily phase out the manufacture and use of NPEs. The result is that no major U.S. brand of laundry detergent contains NPEs. Producers of NPE are developing replacements (green chemistry).

Washers and dryers have also been improved. They now use less water and less energy. Microwave dryers result in a decrease in energy required in the drying process.

Various substances are not broken down by septic systems (septic tank) before they are released into the ground. Because as much as 25 percent of the residents in the United States use septic tanks or cesspools as their primary method of water-waste removal, it is important to know what these systems remove or do not remove. Many washing detergents are not harmful to septic tanks and are biodegradable.

Recycling Programs

More cast-offs than ever are being recycled in many industries. Some products are labeled "100% recyclable" and can be returned to the manufacturer. Recycled products include apparel, batteries, cell phones, printer cartridges, iPods, and plastic bottles. There is, however, still a negative image by some people that recycling is not necessary and manufacturers do not want it.

Fashion contributes to an overabundance of used products because there is rapid and continual change of style. This occurs in both the apparel and home furnishings industries. While some textile products are recycled and reused, much is disposed of as landfill waste.

Various company recycling programs exist in the textile/textile products industries. Shaw Industries, Inc., has adopted an environmental policy in which carpet products are broken down and reused again. Mohawk

Industries (Bigelow brand) has a program in which plastic soft drink containers made with PET (polyethylene terephthalate) resins are ground into fine chips, cleaned, melted, and then extruded into fibers and spun into carpet yarns. (See Figure 15.13.) Collins & Aikman Floorcoverings produces Powerband® RS commercial carpet tiles with ER3 vinyl backing made from **post-consumer** and post-industrial waste. EarthGuard™ is the trademark of Earthguard, Inc., its erosion-control product that includes recycled carpet fibers.

Polartec™ Recycled is a tradename for garments made by Polartec, LLC, using recycled polyester fibers. DyerSport E.C.O.™ is a trade name of Dyersburg Corporation for its double-sided brush fleece made of recycled fibers. Levi Strauss has a denim fabric recycling program. The reused fibers make yarn, paper, and other products. Ecofi™ is a recycling program by Foss Manufacturing Company, Inc., for its polyester fiber. Recycled bottles (PET) and 100-percent-polyester fabrics are melted to a liquid state and reextruded as a new polyester fiber. This company uses recycled polyester fibers (Ecofi™) for industry filters to be used in factories, hospitals, and other places. DuPont™ uses recycled olefin in its Tyvek® Protective Wear Performance Materials. It is made of 25 percent post-consumer recycled polyethylene.

Patagonia®. (outdoor apparel manufacturer) has expanded its Common Threads Recycling Program. It now includes Polartec-branded garments made by Patagonia apparel. The articles are returned by mail or at any Patagonia retail store to be recycled into polyester fiber. (See Figure 15.14.)

In 2006 Toray Industries, Inc., introduced a collection of recycled nylon 6 fibers and fabrics—Recyclon®. Also Unifi, Inc., sells a 100-percent-recycled-polyester

Figure 15.13
Flattened polyethylene terephthalate bottles (PET bottles) at Tokyo PET Bottle Recycle Co.

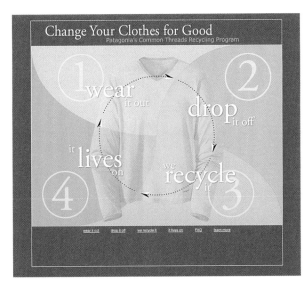

FIGURE 15.14
Patagonia's Common Threads Recycling Program.

Repreve® yarn made from post-industrial fiber waste and post-consumer plastics.

The Carpet America Recovery Effort (CARE) is an industry/government effort to increase the amount of recycling and reuse of post-consumer carpet. Commercial contractors in particular can contact the CARE organization to see where they can send carpets to be recycled (carpet reclaimers).

Dry cleaners have started plastic bag recycling programs. Polyethylene bags that are returned by customers are collected by a recycler, reprocessed, and turned into new bags as well as other products. The paperboard box containing laundry detergents is often made using recycled paper (at least 35 percent post-consumer).

Recycling has been done in the wool industry for centuries. Woolen fabrics (used and not used) have been shredded back into a fibrous state by a garnetting process and made into other wool products. (See Wool Products Labeling Act, p. 334). The main reason for the early recycling of wool fiber probably is the fiber's high cost. Thus, it was profitable to reclaim the wool.

Eco-Fashion

The eco-fabric thrust has been identified as an area where consumers are prepared to seek out and pay for fabrics that have a "green" element. This is similar to the organic food sector, which began slowly but is now having a real effect on purchasing decisions. Although the percent of the marketplace is small, the eco-friendly apparel market is definitely growing.

FIGURE 15.15
The Battallion's bamboo jersey dress.

Newer firms are motivated by concern for **ecology** and human well-being, and established firms have begun to become more aware of the value of producing environmentally friendly fabrics. The use of hemp, organic cotton, bamboo, and other fibers helps to make sustainable materials. (See Figures 15.15 and 15.16.)

A difficult part of designing sustainability is the sourcing of green fabrics and materials. Choice is limited in terms of color and print, often because mills and suppliers have high minimums for customizing fabrics. As consumer demand grows for sustainability-produced clothing, the range of stock fabrics and colors will be broadened.

People who buy an **eco-fashion** item may do so because of the design and not the sustainability aspect. The majority of shoppers are still influenced by color, style, and price. Thus, garments must still be attractive to the buyer. The eco-friendly aspect alone may not be enough to sell the product. It is usually better to combine

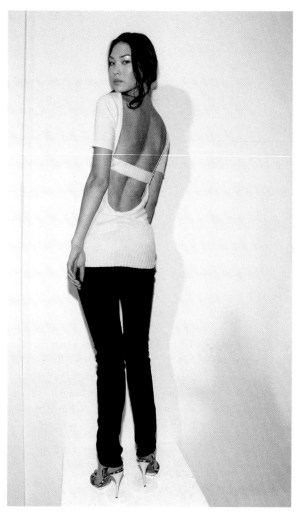

FIGURE 15.16
Avita's design made from bamboo and recycled cashmere fabrics.

a

b

FIGURE 15.17
Eco-friendly collections by (a) Maggie Norris and (b) Eco Ferragamo.

this aspect with other garment/fabric attributes. (See Figure 15.17a and b.)

Companies that have eco-friendly lines of merchandise include the "Levi's Eco" jeans made with organic cotton (Levi Strauss), men's organic T-shirts from the Gap, and American Apparel's Sustainability Edition organic line. Nordstrom department store in 2007 created two women's brands that are based on sustainable fabrics: the athletic line Zella and the sportswear brand Stem. Wal-Mart and Nike have moved toward increased use of organic cotton in their 100-percent-cotton products.

Sustainable fashion can be best realized when people, production processes, and the environment are interconnected. Independent transactions at each level should be replaced by a coordinated supply chain—fiber

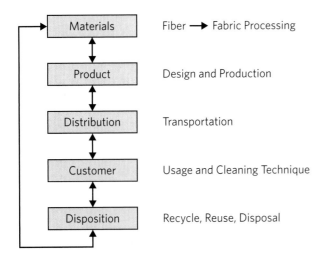

Materials	Fiber → Fabric Processing
Product	Design and Production
Distribution	Transportation
Customer	Usage and Cleaning Technique
Disposition	Recycle, Reuse, Disposal

FIGURE 15.18
Sustainable fashion flow chart.

producer to retailer. Information and responsibility occur "downstream" (toward the customer) and "upstream" (back toward the raw materials resources). Through technology and planning a sustainable fashion system can be developed, which includes environmentally sensitive procedures at each phase. (See Figure 15.18.) Social entrepreneurship enables both design and merchandising personnel to develop products together, in consultation with textile technology expertise.

Product Visibility

When a product is labeled as either "green" or "environmentally friendly," consumers may consider this to be too vague to be meaningful. The phrase is then viewed as a general claim, with no government or official definition. It implies that the product or packaging has some environmental benefit, or causes little or no harm to the environment. There is a need for organizations to independently certify this claim. Also there is a need for industry terms, standards, and certifications.

Using a cotton garment as an example, information about the cotton farmer and chemicals used in growing the cotton, chemical additives during product production, transportation information, and quality standards would be useful to the consumer.

Wal-Mart, the world's largest retailer, is implementing an eco-scorecard system for its suppliers. Details such as the amount of fuel used to manufacture fabrics, impact of dyes used, amount of greenhouse-gas emissions, and waste-water treatment and cleaning requirements (e.g., machine wash) are examples of what would

be examined for textile/apparel articles. The company will help its suppliers become more successful in meeting the required standards for sustainable products.

Nike also has an eco-index for new products. Using factors such as waste production, PVC usage, and organic cotton content, the index rates footwear on a gold-silver-bronze scale and mandates that all footwear receive a gold-level rating by 2011.

There is an additional challenge relating to product information. If there is a problem (e.g., fiber is not organic cotton as indicated on the label or eco-friendly chemicals were not used), who is responsible and what is the penalty? The supply chain includes the manufacturer, the importer, the brand company, and the retailer.

Organizations

There are various organizations that help and encourage environmental controls and safeguards that are not in the product-supply chain.

The Council for Textile Recycling diverts post-consumer textile products waste from landfills to other outlets. These include exports, making rags, and making recycled products. A recognized certification organization that verifies environmental claims is the Scientific Certification Systems (SCS). It also provides an environmental profile of products.

Green Seal is an independent, non-profit organization that strives to achieve a healthier and cleaner environment by identifying and promoting products and services that deliver eco-friendly cleaning products for homes and businesses. The products that pass the safety standards become Green Seal certified (Figure 15.19).

There are also various international efforts to protect the environment. The International Organization for

FIGURE 15.19
Green Seal approval logo.

Standardization (ISO) coordinates many groups world-wide with regard to setting standards for the testing of goods to facilitate international trade (see p. 284). Their ISO 14000 environmental-management program enables a company to form a plan to analyze and control all steps in their manufacturing process in order to provide for environmental protection. Industrial companies, both textile and nontextile, use ISO 14000 certification to show their commitment to reducing environmental hazards.

The International Oeko-Tex® Association provides global information on textile products, including those which are environmentally friendly and do not contain unsafe substances. The Association grant certificates to manufacturers whose products satisfy Oeko-Tex® standards regarding harmful substances.

Organic Standards

To reduce confusion about which standards are being applied for organic cotton products (differences from country to country), various countries are adopting a Global Organic Textile Standard (GOTS). The first certificates for GOTS were issued at the end of 2006. The standard works on strict minimum criteria for fabric standards and social criteria. All aspects of processing, dyeing, and finishing are addressed.

After a natural fiber leaves the farm, organic certification ends. Just because the fiber is grown organically doesn't mean the final textile product is environmentally friendly, whether that product is a T-shirt or a skein of knitting yarn. Some organic products are sometimes compromised at a country's border (i.e., point of entry through customs) by being fumigated. Certifying environmentally friendly finished textile products is what GOTS has been formed to accomplish.

The main international fiber and sustainable-textile standards organization is the International Federation of Organic Agricultural Movements (IFOAM). The U.S. Organic Trade Association (OTA) is the main organization in this country. The U.S. Department of Agriculture (USDA) also has a national organic program (NOP). Other countries have their own associations. Most legitimate organic-standards associations are accredited through IFOAM. A fiber needs to meet the regulations of the importing country to be labeled organic, no matter where it is grown.

As certification organizations grow in number and consumers are able to get more information that substantiates claims, environmentally friendly products will become a stronger consumer niche. Also as standards and practices develop for "green" products, companies will find their levels of participation.

Government Regulations

Two federal government agencies were formed to protect the environment and the workers:

▶ The **Environmental Protection Agency** (EPA), which regulates water, air, and noise pollution as well as waste disposal.

▶ The **Occupational Safety and Health Administration** (OSHA) which develops standards for safety of workers as well as creating educational training programs for workers.

The EPA has passed various laws and regulations relating to the environment. These are some that impact on the textile industry.

▶ The Clean Air Act of 1970 was designed to improve air quality. This can be obtained by limiting airborne items from production (e.g., lint) or coal-burning facilities (e.g., fly ash) and chemical by-products from burning fuels (fume emissions). Sulfur dioxide (acid rain), carbon dioxide (global warming), and nitrous oxides (smog) are major by-products of combustion.

▶ The Clean Water Act of 1972 was passed to reduce the contamination of water, both on the surface and in the ground. Improved wastewater treatments have been beneficial.

▶ The Resource Conservation and Recovery Act of 1976 regulates solid- and hazardous-waste disposal. This applies to the product lifecycle, from production to final disposition.

▶ The Federal Insecticide, Fungicide, and Rodenticide Act (FIFRA) applies to products that incorporate antibacterial or antimicrobial agents. Some textile products have these agents in fiber additives or finishes. The primary focus of the FIFRA is to provide federal control of pesticide distribution, sale, and use. Although it was enacted in 2007, the Act was previously titled The Federal Environmental Pesticide Control Act of 1947 (amended in 1972). Labeling is required, providing content and safety precautions.

▶ The Pollution Prevention Act of 1990 is designed to minimize waste, improve treatment of toxic chemicals, and encourage recycling programs.

The Consumer Product Safety Commission (CPSC) is a subdivision of the Federal Trade Commission (FTC). It is responsible for the enforcement of various safety standards, such as requirements relating to flammability of

TABLE 15.1 SUSTAINABILITY CRITERIA	
Production	Non-Production
Renewable material	Distribution—transportation
Resource conservation	Usage—cleaning
Energy savings	Disposal—recycling, reuse
Nonhazardous material usage	
Minimum waste	

textiles. In addition, states have departments which are focused on environmental problems.

Not all countries have the same concern for the environment as does the United States. Many have placed economic growth and technical advancement ahead of concern for the environment. These governments have focused more on export orientation. Today, many of these countries have linked pollution management and eco-friendly policies with their economic goals, understanding that both can be accomplished.

Study Questions

1. Do all products labeled "green" or "eco-friendly" possess the same qualifications? Explain.

2. Name three pollution problems that can occur during textile production.

3. Define the term "organic cotton."

4. While cotton and wool are natural fibers and considered by many to be eco-friendly, their environmental impact is not always favorable when being grown. Briefly discuss this statement.

5. Explain the following statement: "The process leaves a very small environmental footprint."

6. List several ways you can reuse textile products at home.

7. State three industry recycling programs for textile products.

8. Briefly explain how recycling can be beneficial to (a) the consumer, (b) the manufacturer, and (c) the environment.

9. Do you anticipate a large growth in the field of eco-fashion? Why?

10. List at least three federal laws that relate to the protection of the environment and workers.

CHAPTER SIXTEEN

Guide to Fabric Selection

Objectives

▶ To understand that fabric performance properties result from each component's relationship and effect on all other components.

▶ To understand that the performance expectations of fabrics differ with each end use of that fabric.

Key Terms Related to Textiles

abrasion resistance
air permeability
cover
drapability
dye penetration

environment
fabric imperfections
fiber content
performance expectations
porosity

seam slippage
tearing strength
wrinkling
yarn properties

In the previous chapters, each component link in the textile chain (fibers, yarns, fabric constructions, dyeing, etc.) was discussed and explored separately. Each chapter dealt with the way these components may affect the appearance and performance properties of the final finished textile fabric. When these various components come together as a finalized textile, however, each component tends to affect the others, usually reinforcing each, but sometimes with an adverse effect. Selecting a textile fabric that is best suited for a particular use involves knowledge of each of the components and an understanding of textile properties in finished fabric.

The tabletop and observational/visual examinations for fabric selections in this chapter are intended as a general guide, or as a screening tool. In many instances of fabric selections, especially where large mass-production quantities are involved, more formal testing using laboratory procedures, as indicated in Chapter 14 need to be applied.

Examining for Aesthetics

Examinations and selections of fabric for particular uses are usually initially made on the basis of appearance. Color, luster, touch, and drape must first be correct and appealing for the product before any further considerations can be made. After accepting these first criteria of taste and fashion, the choices for selection then become a matter based on the performance properties of the fabric. This can be accomplished by applying the guidelines in this chapter. These guidelines can be equally useful to a fashion designer creating a line, a store buyer or merchandiser placing purchase orders, an interior designer decorating a home, or a consumer shopping for a new outfit.

Examination of the fabric for defects is also important. Many of these are easily seen. The following are examples of **fabric imperfections:**

Missing yarn: Occurs in the fabric.

Very nonuniform yarn: Thick area on the fabric.

Bowing or skewing: Stripe is not straight across the fabric and does not meet properly at the seams.

Misweave or misknit: Error in the design.

Nonuniformity of color: Shading or color streaking occurring on the fabric.

Off-register: The parts of a printed pattern do not fit properly.

Uneven finish: Fabric does not have the same degree of finish throughout.

Examining for Suitability

The important guideline determining the suitability of a fabric for a particular use is how it must perform. Obviously, fabric for a formal gown worn on infrequent occasions will have different performance expectations than a fabric for blouse and skirt separates that are worn frequently and are laundered or dry cleaned often. Likewise, the fabric for a man's shirt that will be laundered at home and worn again with little or no ironing will need to have different expectations than the fabric for a man's shirt that will be professionally laundered and delivered back to a customer ready to wear again in a pressed condition. After determining the fabric's ultimate use and **performance expectations,** certain definitive knowledge-based judgments can be applied. (See Figure 16.1.)

Examining for Durability and Serviceability

How durable do textile products need to be? Most fabrics in clothing are not worn to a point where a garment is discarded because it has worn out. Several seasons of wear is the usual expectation. Clothes are discarded because they are no longer in style or because the consumer wants something new. What is expected, however, is that the textile product will remain in reasonably good appearance and not show undue signs of wear or fading, shrinking, or stretching out of shape during its expected use life. The most durable product and the choice of fabric that goes into such a product are not necessarily the most optimum choice. Again, it is important to clearly define how and where a fabric will be used. (See Figure 16.2.)

Many textile products, however, require maximum durability (i.e., high strength, high abrasion resistance, excellent color retention, and high seam strength). These products are items subject to high stress during wear and, in many instances, are purely utilitarian rather than fashion or style related. Such items include most utility work and uniform clothes, active sportswear, camping gear, children's play wear, and many home fashion fabrics whose expected use life may be as much as ten or more years.

Applying Fabric Selection Guidelines

A fabric should be examined based on its properties to determine its suitability for its particular end use. Various guidelines should be applied to selecting the appropriate fabric; these are examined in the following sections.

a

b

c

FIGURE 16.1
Fabrics are evaluated based on their condition of use. For example, it should have (a) great durability, (b) sunlight exposure with little abrasion, and (c) strength and weather resistance.

Figure 16.2
Textile materials are sometimes selected primarily for appearance and not for performance properties. This gown is elegant but would not be considered durable.

Fiber Content

Initially, look at the label or examine the fabric to determine the exact **fiber content.**

The main key to optimum fabric selection lies in a thorough understanding of fiber properties. Fiber, the initial building block, governs the physical and chemical properties of the ultimate fabric. Properties can be modified as, for example, crease-resistant finishes for cotton, but a fiber that is completely unsuitable for a particular use will nevertheless fail either initially or during use. Fiber properties are covered in Chapter 2, and all these properties should be considered in fabric selection decisions. Fabrics of acetate, for example, may be strongly considered when silkiness and excellent drapability are needed, but would be undesirable where high strength and abrasion resistance are required.

When considering fiber properties, blends or mixtures (and their performance) as well as 100 percent one-fiber content should be taken into account. Also, many fiber modifications of manufactured fibers are produced and may offer improved fabric performance for certain uses. Finally, some natural fiber fabrics are made from premium grades of fiber, such as Pima cotton and Merino wool. Premium fibers may be desirable if the end use of the fabric warrants the additional cost.

Yarn Properties

In addition to the properties inherent in the fiber, the type of yarn made from these fibers has considerable effect on the aesthetics and performance of a fabric. Appearance differences between spun and filament yarns are obvious, but the following additional **yarn properties** need to be examined as part of fabric selection decisions.

Woolen and Worsted/Carded and Combed

Woolen yarns are coarser and fuzzier than worsted-wool yarns, which are smoother and more uniform. (See p. 68.) Carded yarns are coarser and less uniform than combed cotton, a more uniform yarn with greater strength and luster. (See p. 67.) You can often differentiate between carded- and combed-cotton yarns in blouse-weight fabrics by holding the fabric up to a light and noticing the degree of yarn uniformity.

Again, the end use for this fabric needs to be considered in making an optimum selection. Combed yarns and/or worsted yarns, seemingly better and more costly, are not an optimum choice if, for example, a homespun, country look is the design under consideration.

Abrasion Resistance

Yarns that are not uniform in thickness either because of poor spinning quality or by design, as in novelty yarns, have lower **abrasion resistance** than uniform yarns. Active sportswear, children's play wear, upholstery, and fabrics used for seating require good to excellent resistance to abrasion. Yarns in the fabric should be looked at very carefully to judge the uniformity of yarn thickness. Using a pick glass or holding fabric up to a light can help in this examination.

Pilling Propensity

Yarn configuration bears importantly on the pilling propensity of those fibers that are subject to pilling. Yarns that show high amounts of fiber protruding from the yarn are more likely to pill. Thus, low-twist (soft-twist) yarns and yarns that have been napped in fabric finishing are candidates for pilling, whereas filament and highly twisted (hard-twist) yarns are less likely to create a pilling problem.

Strength and Softness

Yarn strength and yarn softness in spun yarns are closely related and are primarily governed by the amount of twist in the yarn. Low-twist yarns are more flexible and drapable and are usually satisfactory for casual and leisure wear, or window fabrics. By contrast, fabrics with high-twist yarns should be selected for higher-strength fabric uses, such as active sportswear, children's wear, and upholstery. The high-twist yarns tend to be less flexible and less drapable, however.

Filament yarns are stronger than spun yarns of the same thickness and fiber content, but flexibility and drapability are dependent on the denier size of individual filaments making up the yarn. (See p. 65.) Filament yarns of high-tenacity fibers are proper and logical selections for end uses in which light weight and high strength are desired. Parachutes and ski wear are two such examples.

Fabric Properties

The fabric structure and the properties created by this structure also need to be considered in the fabric-selection process. This should also be done with the realization that there is an interrelationship with the fiber and yarn properties.

Woven-Fabric Structure

Ends and picks per inch are a definite indicator of fabric quality. In most end uses, higher ends and picks per inch are preferable to a lower count for end uses where durability is important. Children's wear, active sportswear, and similar applications are examples. Some applications require the lightest possible fabric consistent with the desired serviceability. Lightweight summer shirts and blouses are examples. Yarn and seam slippage as well as fabric strength are often of particular concern in lightweight fabrics. Attention to these items, as indicated in the following sections, is advised.

Knitted-Fabric Structure

One of knitted fabrics' most important properties is the ability of these materials to mold easily to body shapes and thus contribute to wearer comfort. The ability to recover from stretching and molding and to retain shape is equally important, however. No one wants a sweater that becomes so baggy at the elbows that it is unsightly. In screening fabric for possible selection, a useful rule-of-thumb test is to stretch a sample of fabric (or garment part) in your hand. It should offer reasonable resistance to stretching. Fabrics that stretch too easily have a tendency to remain stretched and have poor recovery, which is an undesirable property.

Fabric Strength

Two major types of fabric strength are tensile, or breaking, strength and tearing strength. Of the two, **tearing strength** usually has more direct relationship to fabric performance than breaking strength. In general, tearing strength tends to be lowered if the yarns in a fabric cannot easily move or shift during the process of tearing. Any fabric with a coating has a reduced tearing strength because its yarns cannot move or shift. Plain-weave fabrics of high-twist and tightly woven yarns may tear more easily than twill or satin weaves because the yarns in the plain weave are more tightly locked in and cannot shift or move as easily as the higher-float twill or satin. Knit fabrics in which the yarns are interlooped are rather free to move or shift easily, so knit fabrics do not generally tear.

A simple screening test to assess fabric tearing strength consists of making a scissor cut in a fabric, and then tearing by hand to determine the resistance to tearing. Fabrics for children's wear, hiking and camping clothing, work clothes, and uniform clothing are examples of applications in which high tearing strength is needed.

Yarn and Seam Slippage

Slippage of filament yarns in woven fabrics occurs because of the smoothness and low friction of the filaments. Conversely, the propensity toward yarn and/or **seam slippage** is reduced if the yarn friction is increased. Plain-weave fabrics, which have maximum interlacing, are less likely to slip than satin-weave fabrics, which have long floats. For these same reasons, tightly woven fabrics are less likely to slip than loosely woven fabrics, and filament-yarn fabrics with a napped finish are not likely to slip at all. A useful and simple test for yarn slippage is to examine a fabric swatch and note the relative ease or difficulty of removing both warp and filling yarns from a cut edge of fabric. Yarns should offer some resistance to separation from the fabric.

Other Fabric Properties

Many properties of textiles that become part of selection determinations can be made by effective informal examinations. This can be done on a sample garment or a piece of the fabric as well as by a consumer on a finished garment on a store rack. Some of these are described in the following paragraphs.

Air Permeability **Air permeability** relates to breathability, or the amount of air passing through a fabric. Fabrics used for summer clothing or in warm temperatures should have high air permeability, allowing fabric to breathe and have a cooling effect. Fabrics used in clothing for outdoor wear, especially in windy conditions, should have very low permeability. Coated fabrics that have zero permeability are usually undesirable in clothing because they do not allow fabric to breathe and are

uncomfortable. However, for certain functional purposes such as heavy-duty rainwear for police, crossing guards, fire fighters, and so on, nonpermeability is necessary to attain the protection needed.

You can judge the air permeability of a fabric by holding it tightly against your mouth and exhaling. (See Figure 16.3.) Overcoat fabrics that may look thick and warm, but that you can too easily breathe through, are not good candidates for cold weather outdoor use.

Cover Cover relates to the degree of opaqueness in a fabric. A fabric with low or poor cover is somewhat translucent. A dark blouse tucked into a white skirt would show through if the skirt fabric had poor or low cover. You can check fabric cover by placing a darker colored fabric behind the lighter colored fabric being considered for selection. If the fabric cover is adequate, the darker fabric will not show through. (See Figure 16.4.)

Drapability The **drapability** of a fabric relates to the manner in which a fabric folds when in a garment. A fabric that drapes well will form soft, natural folds in a flared skirt, for example. A fabric with low or poor drape will tend to form fewer folds in the same flared skirt. You can check for fabric drape by gathering the fabric width between your hands and, while closing your hands together, observe the flowing of the folds that are formed.

Wrinkling A **wrinkling** test provides an indication of how well a fabric resists wrinkling as well as how rapidly it might recover from wrinkles.

Take a fabric or garment part in hand. Grab a tight fistful of the fabric, holding it for about 20 seconds, then release. Is the fabric badly wrinkled, or barely so? Now smooth the fabric out for about 40 seconds. Are the wrinkles disappearing, or do they remain essentially badly wrinkled? Any fabric that is going to be used in a garment worn for long periods (e.g., clothes worn in the office, where much sitting is done) should perform well in this test.

Dye and Print Properties

Colorfastness, for the most part, cannot be assessed by visual examinations. Colorfastness to light, laundering, perspiration, and so on can only be determined by

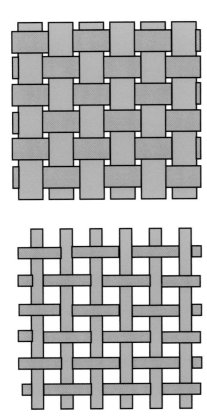

FIGURE 16.4
The fabric with thicker yarn and same cloth count possesses better cover.

subjecting fabric to conditions that simulate actual conditions, or to laboratory tests, as described in Chapter 14. Several important color-related assessments can, however, be made by visual examination and can be a useful guide in fabric selection for specific end uses.

Colorfastness to Crocking

Colorfastness to crocking (see p. 298) can be assessed by simply rubbing a white cloth briskly on the fabric being tested. The fabric should be tested in both dry and dampened conditions. No color, or at worst only the slightest trace of color, should transfer to the white cloth if the intended use of the fabric is such that it will rub against other fabrics or the wearer's skin while worn.

Dyes and Pigments

Pigments, particularly in dark shades, generally have poor colorfastness to repeated machine laundering as well as to crocking. They also tend to make fabrics stiffer than they would otherwise be if the same color were applied with dyes. Although dyes generally are more desirable than pigments (depending on their particular fastness properties), a pigment fabric may nevertheless

provide satisfactory serviceability, particularly if in light to medium shades and if the item is not subjected to severe laundering.

Dye Penetration

Heavy fabrics of high-twist yarns that are also densely woven are likely to have poor **dye penetration** if they have been piece dyed. (See p. 160.) Fabrics with poor dye penetration should be avoided in end uses that will be subjected to frequent laundering and/or abrasion. Upholstery fabrics and children's play clothes are typical end uses in which fabrics with good dye penetration are required. Check for dye penetration by removing several yarns from a fabric and then untwisting the yarns so that the center fibers can be observed. Good dye penetration is evident if the color is equally distributed throughout the yarn in the surface fibers as well as the center fibers. Also, observe the interlacings of warp and filling yarns. If the fabric possesses good dye penetration, the color throughout the yarns removed from the fabric should be uniform, and not lighter or undyed where yarn interlacings occurred.

Printed Fabrics

Caution needs to be exercised in the selection of fabrics that involve printed designs. In some prints, color is merely on the fabric surface and has not penetrated through the fabric back. In other prints, usually with lightweight fabrics, the color strikes through and the design thoroughly penetrates the fabric. Printed fabrics that exhibit color on the surface only are not serviceable in items such as shirts, children's wear, or other items that are subject to frequent wear and laundering. In the latter items, the fabric surface will develop a faded or frosted appearance in a relatively brief use period. This condition does not present a problem on fabrics that are subject to ordinary wear, such as fashion blouses and dresses that are dry cleaned or laundered in a gentle cycle or by hand.

Finish Properties

Various finishing procedures, described in the following sections, can affect fabrics in ways that need to be considered in fabric selection decisions.

Resin Finishes

Resin finishes, including durable press, reduce both strength and abrasion resistance of fabrics. Chintz fabric, which is usually resin treated and calendered, possesses tearing strength that is usually too low to be considered for apparel use. Doing a simple tearing strength test (as described previously in this chapter) should be a routine procedure for resin-treated fabrics.

Napped Finish

Fabrics with a napped finish, particularly outerwear fabrics of wool that have a napped surface, are often not serviceable except in garments that are worn only occasionally. An everyday winter overcoat, for example, will begin to appear threadbare (especially at sleeve bottoms and buttonholes), usually before the end of one season's use, because the nap has greatly reduced the abrasion resistance of the fabric. The effect on cotton flannel or napped tricot fabric, frequently used in nightwear, is not as severe and is not usually a problem, primarily because the visual effect of the nap abrasion is not as unsightly as that of outerwear.

Carpet Floor Coverings

Carpet floor coverings involve their own unique sets of performance criteria based primarily on the fact that carpets are made and used differently than most other textiles.

A consumer should examine several factors:

Fabric content: Nylon, polyester, and olefin provide very good abrasion resistance.

Pile density: The more compact the pile, the better the carpet appearance and durability. Bending the carpet allows the viewer to see the density of the pile. (See Figure 16.5.)

Pile height: A lower pile height results in a longer-lasting carpet, whereas a higher pile results in a softer effect.

Finishes: Stain-repellent and antistatic properties are desirable and should be requested.

There is more information available to the consumer regarding carpets than probably any other textile product. Check the labels on the carpet samples in the store. Information that can be determined include fiber content, carpet traffic ratings, finishes, construction, and warranties provided. Thus, a comparison among carpets can be made.

The Environment

Many consumers have developed a relationship between products sold and the environment. Designers and merchandisers are being encouraged to make and sell eco-friendly textile products.

At the present time, however, there is often a trade-off between quality, cost fashion, and the effect on the environment. A "green" fabric may not be fashionably

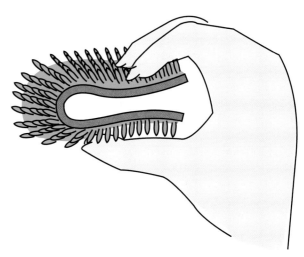

FIGURE 16.5
Folding small carpet swatches back onto themselves can provide a good basis for judging and comparing differences in pile density and height.

designed and is more costly. Thus the consumer may have to choose between environmental correctness and, for example, wearing a garment whose fabric is not completely satisfying.

Another situation is where two competing textile products are both not eco-friendly. An example is diapers. Disposable diapers significantly add to landfills and also must be disposed of properly because of possible fecal contamination of groundwater. Reusable cloth diapers must be cleaned and use significant amounts of water and laundry detergents. Hopefully a more eco-friendly product will be developed soon.

Fabric Selection

Fabric selection is based on information obtained. It could be based on limited information using simple tests and little technical input or it can be the result of industry-approved testing procedures and extensive technical knowledge gained about textile fabric composition.

Sometimes it is not realized how important a property is for the end use. An example is the property **porosity**, which is the measure of a fabric's capacity to transmit air or moisture. Whereas it can be readily realized the importance of comfort this property would be for apparel in contact with the body (e.g., underwear), it may not be so readily apparent that it also is important to upholstery material. The longer an occupant is in contact with the material, the greater the importance of this property to seating comfort. (Try sitting for a long period of time on a plastic-covered chair or sofa.)

It is important to be aware of changes and new developments within the textile industry. They impact on fabric selection and product availability. New technology (see Chapter 12) results in the creation of textile products with special value-added properties previously unavailable. Expanding global trade has forced companies to study resources and marketplaces outside the United States as well as international trade agreements and regulations (see Chapter 17). Also newer social issues such as the **environment** (see Chapter 15) and fair trade (see Chapter 1) must be considered when selecting fabrics.

A concept developing in the textile and apparel industries is to include input from vendors in the supply chain in the decision making process (e.g., fiber producers, mills and chemical companies). This results in a proactive program of fabric development and selection (i.e., total supply chain integration).

Thus, there are many factors that must be examined to determine which fabric should be selected. Fabric construction, properties, performance, and market suitability are some of these. There will always be a need for individuals who possess the technical and market knowledge to determine the suitability of a fabric for a particular end use.

CHAPTER SEVENTEEN

Textile Laws, Regulations, and Trade Agreements

Objectives

▸ To know the specifics of the federal laws relating to fibers, textiles, and textile products.

▸ To understand the rationale of these laws.

▸ To be able to interpret labels on textile products correctly.

▸ To understand the impact of international regulations on the textile industry.

Key Terms Related to Textiles

Care Labeling Rule
care labeling symbols
Consumer Product Safety
    Commission (CPSC)
country of origin
Federal Trade Commission (FTC)
Flammable Fabrics Act

garnetting
generic name
new wool
percentage of fiber
quotas
recycled wool
subsidies

tariff
Textile Fiber Products
    Identification Act (TFPIA)
torch fabrics
trade agreements
virgin wool
Wool Products Labeling Act

The production of fiber through the manufacturing of consumer end products in the textile industry is complex, with the content of the material often determining end use. Because of this complexity and the need to provide standardized information to end users, governments have adopted rules and regulations which require manufacturers to provide certain standardized information about their product. This chapter will address the major laws affecting textiles manufactured or sold in the United States and highlight the importance of understanding that as textiles are a global industry, international rules and regulations have a major impact.

The United States federal government has established various laws and regulations relating specifically to the selling of textile fibers, materials, and products within the United States. The laws are intended to provide standards for content, consistency, quality, and performance. These laws and regulations are in effect whether a product is wholly or partially produced in the United States and/or produced entirely outside the United States but sold in the United States. Four main laws are the Textile Fiber Products Identification Act, the Wool Products Labeling Act, the Flammable Fabrics Act, and the Care Labeling Rule. Each is discussed in the sections that follow.

FIGURE 17.1
Labels showing fiber content and other information.

Textile Fiber Products Identification Act

The **Textile Fiber Products Identification Act (TFPIA)** states that specific information relating to the fiber content of textile products must be contained on labels conspicuously attached and securely affixed to the item at the time of sale and delivery to the ultimate consumer (see Figure 17.1). It applies to apparel and household textiles (e.g., carpets, draperies, bedding). Certain consumer articles are exempted, including belts, lawn chairs, book cloth, and backpacks. Certain provisions of this act also extend to advertisements in newspapers and magazines.

The following are the most important items that must appear on the labels:

▶ The **generic names** of the fibers present in the fabric. (See p. 42 for a list of manufactured fiber names.) Fiber trade names can be included, if desired. If the hair or fiber of a fur-bearing animal is present, it is included in the fiber-content designation.

▶ The **percentage of fiber** content by weight, listed vertically and in descending order of predominance by weight. If there is less than 5 percent of a fiber present, it is designated as "other fiber," unless it has a definite functional significance (e.g., 4 percent spandex for elasticity). If there are two or more fibers, each of which is less than 5 percent, with no definite functional significance, then their presence is indicated as "other fibers" (e.g., 4 percent flax and 2 percent silk is indicated as 6 percent other fibers).

Where textile fiber products contain fabric ornamentation not exceeding 5 percent of the total fiber weight of the product, the label could be as follows:

60% cotton

38% polyester

2% spandex for elasticity

Exclusive of ornamentation

In disclosing the required fiber content information as to floor coverings, the disclosure shall be made in a segregated manner. This is indicated in the following example for a tufted carpet:

Pile 100% nylon

Backing 100% olefin

▶ Disclosure of the **country of origin.** The country where the textile product is "processed and manufactured" (i.e., the country where the product is principally made) must be disclosed, even if it is made in the United States. The importer or person/firm first introducing the product in interstate commerce is responsible for the proper labeling of imported textile products. For products made in the United States, the manufacturer is responsible.

Textile products made wholly or partly in the United States are divided into three categories:

- When the product is entirely made in the United States, using domestically manufactured materials (including yarn and fabric), the term "Made in the U.S.A." or its equivalent is used.

- When the product is made in the United States but is composed of imported materials, the label must disclose this fact (e.g., "Made in U.S.A. of imported fabric" or "Knitted in the U.S.A. of imported yarns"). The specific foreign country need not be named.

- When the product is partially made in the United States and partially manufactured in a foreign country, the label must show the manufacturing process performed in the relevant countries. Some examples are "Imported fabric, finished in U.S.A.", "Sewn in U.S.A. of imported components" (the specific name of the foreign country need not be stated), and "Assembled in Colombia of U.S. components".

In determining the country of origin, each manufacturer need only go back one manufacturing step. Thus a yarn manufacturer would look to the sources of the fiber, and a fabric manufacturer would look to the source of the yarn. The four manufacturing categories addressed by the rules are the making of fiber, yarn, fabric, and textile products. Items excluded from this requirement, such as trim, thread, and linings used for structural purpose, do not require indication of origin.

In order to change the country of origin of merchandise produced in one country and sent to a second country for processing, the merchandise must be subsequently transformed in the second country into a new and different article of commerce by a substantial manufacturing or processing operation. Apparel sewn and assembled into finished apparel in one country from parts cut in another country shall be considered the product of the country where the sewing and assembling is done. However, in the case of knitwear in which parts are knit to shape in one country and assembled into finished garments in a second country, the country that produces the parts shall be considered the country of origin.

▶ The manufacturer's name or a registered identification number assigned by the **Federal Trade Commission (FTC)** instead of the company's name (e.g., RN [registered number] 99). If consumers or others want to know the identity of the manufacturer, the FTC will furnish this information if given the RN number.

The following are three examples of proper textile product labels:

Jones Textile Company	RN199	RN198
55% wool	60% lyocell	90% combed cotton
45% Dacron® polyester	37% silk	10% nylon
Made in U.S.A.	3% other fiber	Made in Italy
	Made in Korea	

▶ When the textile fabrics in a garment are composed of two or more components (e.g., lining and outer shell), the required information about fiber content is usually separated in the label to show the composition of each component. Labeling in this manner is mandatory in cases where such information is necessary to avoid deception.

The following are examples of proper labels for this situation:

Diane's Jacket Company	RN 197	RN 172
Body all wool	60% cotton	Filling:
Lining all acetate	40% rayon	100% polyester
Sleeves all leather	Lining:	Covering:
Made in Sri Lanka	55% nylon	50% polyester
	45% polyester	50% cotton
	Made in China	Made in U.S.A. (This label would be for a comforter)

As a general rule, textile garments with a neck must have the country-of-origin information on a label affixed to the inside center of the neck, between the shoulder seams. If the main brand label is already affixed to this spot, the country-of-origin label may be placed next to or under the other label. All other textile products should have the label attached so that it may be readily seen by the purchaser when the product is offered and displayed for sale.

If each unit or part of the product is of the same fiber content and origin, and the units are sold as a pair (e.g. a suit), only one of the units needs to carry the required information. Otherwise each item must have its own attached label. For textile products contained in a package, the label must be affixed to both the product and the package unless the label can be read through the package. Hosiery is an exception; only the package need carry the label for this product.

Wool Products Labeling Act

The main purpose of the **Wool Products Labeling Act** is to protect manufacturers and consumers from the unrevealed presence of wool-fiber substitutes in manufactured wool products. The act has been amended several times and is enforced by the Federal Trade Commission.

Unless a wool product is exempt, a label or tag containing the percentage of fiber content by weight and the wool-fiber category must be securely attached to wool products. Note that the term *wool* usually means fiber from the fleece of sheep or lambs. Hair of the angora goat (mohair), cashmere goat (cashmere), and alpaca, camel, llama, or vicuna is designated as either wool or by the name of the specialty fiber (e.g., camel hair).

Some textile-fiber products are shredded back into a fibrous state by a process called **garnetting.** Wool is a fiber that can be recycled, which resulted in the act specifying that wool fibers be placed in one of the following categories:

Wool: Fiber that has never been reclaimed from any woven or felted-wool product. Included in the category are:

- ▶ Fibers that have never been previously manufactured or used, which may also be called **new wool** or **virgin wool.**

- ▶ Waste fibers from such processes as carding, combing, and spinning that were recovered and processed again, but never previously used.

- ▶ Fibers reclaimed from unused products not woven or felted, such as unused spun yarns or knitted products.

Recycled Wool: Recycled wool includes wool fabrics containing wool fibers that previously had been made into wool products and then reduced to their fiber state through the garnetting process.

Most sections of the TFPIA require conformity in the labeling of wool products. The registered identification numbers issued under the Wool Products Labeling Act have a WPL prefix (e.g., WPL 97).

The following are examples of proper wool product labels:

Smith Manufacturing Co.	WPL 137	Made for F.B.C. Inc..
50% wool	All wool except 5%	50% alpaca
25% recycled wool	nylon reinforcement	35% camel hair
25% unknown	added to toe and heel	15% angora rabbit
Reclaimed fibers	Made in New Zealand	
Made in Australia	Made in China	

A wool product made of 100 percent virgin wool does not necessarily mean that it is stronger or has a softer hand than a comparable product of 100 percent recycled wool. Because there are various quality grades of each, a good quality recycled wool fabric might actually be more desirable than a poor quality virgin wool fabric (see p. 39).

Cashmere is an expensive fiber and has become a status symbol along with pashmina. This has created significant demand for the product and has led to mislabeling problems. According to the Cashmere & Camel Hair Manufacturers Institute, pashmina is an ambiguous marketing name for the wool of the cashmere goat. The Federal Trade Commission has indicated that any item sold under the term pashmina must be labeled under the rules of the Wool Labeling Act. Thus, luxury items that are identified as pashmina must include the fiber name wool or cashmere as part of the permanent label.

Flammable Fabrics Act

Each year thousands of people suffer injuries from burns associated with flammable fabrics. Many of these injuries are fatal; others result in long periods of hospitalization and repeated reconstructive surgery. When ignited, most textile fabrics burn. Some, however, given the right combination of fiber content, yarn twist, weave, and finish, burn so rapidly as to constitute a severe hazard. Fabrics of this type are called **torch fabrics** because the wearer could be engulfed in flames in a matter of seconds if the garment were to catch fire. These dangers and potential dangers resulted in the enactment of the **Flammable Fabrics Act.** This federal regulation is administered by the **Consumer Product Safety Commission (CPSC).** The agency was given powers to accomplish two basic functions: to create and enforce safety standards and other rules designed to eliminate or reduce product hazards, and to gather and disseminate information relating to product hazards and injuries caused by them. The CPSC has responsibility for both textile and nontextile products.

The Flammable Fabrics Act requires a formal certification known as a guarantee. This guarantee verifies that a fabric has met the minimum requirements under the appropriate federal code. The guarantee must be based on reasonable and representative tests. A retailer can request a guarantee from the manufacturer who may request it from the fabric producer. Thus, each company on the distribution chain does not have to test to be sure that the textile product meets the minimum safety standard. Reliance can be placed on the earlier guarantee.

Flammability Standards

The following standards are in effect to provide the public with a greater degree of safety from flame hazards. These standards are cited in various parts of Title 16 of the Code of Federal Regulations (16 CFR) and are designated by the following numbers to indicate product category:

16 CFR 1610: The general flammability standard for wearing apparel. It applies to most articles of clothing. Uses the 45-degree angle test in which the specimen is placed at a 45-degree angle to the ignition source and touched by a flame. Ease of ignition and time of flame spread are the properties measured.

16 CFR 1611: This standard prescribes a test to ensure that vinyl plastic film intended for wearing apparel has met a minimum standard for flammability.

16 CFR 1615: The children's sleepwear standard. Applies to children's sleepwear sizes 0-6X. Uses the vertical test, in which the specimen is hung vertically and then exposed to a flame. The char length is the property measured. Both fabric and seam are tested as well as the results after 50 washings and dryings of the specimens.

16 CFR 1616: The children's sleepwear standard. Applies to sleepwear sizes 7-14. Uses the same test as described for 16 CFR 1615.

16 CFR 1630: The carpet standard. Applies to large carpets and rugs in which one dimension is greater than 6 feet and the surface area is greater than 24 square feet. Uses the pill test, in which a pill on the specimen is ignited by a simulated lit cigarette to test the burning properties of the carpet. The area of flame spread is the property measured.

16 CFR 1631: The carpet standard. Applies to small carpets and rugs in which no dimension is greater than 6 feet and the surface area is not greater than 24 square feet. Uses the pill test (described for DOC FF 1-70). The area of flame spread is the property measured.

Small carpets and rugs that do not meet the flammability standard may be sold if labeled as follows: "FLAMMABLE (FAILS U.S. DEPARTMENT OF COMMERCE STANDARD FF2-70): SHOULD NOT BE USED NEAR SOURCES OF IGNITION."

16 CFR 1633 replaces old 16 CFR 1632: This standard is for determining the flammability of mattresses, mattress sets, and futons when exposed to a lit cigarette or a small open flame.

Proposed:

16 CFR 1634 (new) replaces old 16 CFR 1633: This is a proposed flammability standard for residential upholstery. It contains a cigarette smoldering test for the upholstery but does not have a provision for an open flame test nor for the other components of the furniture.

Interior textiles used in airplanes and motor vehicles are regulated by the Federal Aviation Administration (FAA) as well as the Department of Transportation (DOT).

Other organizations involved with textile flammability test methods include the National Fire Protection Association (NFPA), City of New York, City of Boston, State of California, and the Underwriters Laboratory Inc. (UL).

Care Labeling of Textile Wearing Apparel

The Federal Trade Regulation Rule Relating to the Care Labeling of Textile Wearing Apparel, generally called the **Care Labeling Rule,** requires that care labels be affixed to most textile apparel used to cover or protect the body and also be included with most piece goods sold to consumers for home sewing into apparel. This rule applies to both domestic and imported goods, and is administered by the Federal Trade Commission. The effect of this rule is to protect the consumer from economic loss because of lack of awareness on how to safely clean the product. Care labeling of furniture upholstery, carpets, rugs, draperies/curtains, and industrial textile products is not required.

The care label must be provided by the manufacturer or the importer. It must contain regular care instructions for the ordinary use of the product. The label must be attached in such a manner that it will not become separated from the product and will remain legible during the useful life of the product. It must also be seen or easily found by consumers at the point of sale. Care information must also appear clearly and conspicuously on the end of each roll or bolt of cloth sold at retail for home sewing (over-the-counter piece goods).

The amendment to the rule, besides spelling out what care instructions are required, also includes a glossary of labeling terms to use with those instructions. In addition, a reasonable basis for the appropriateness of the particular care instruction used is required.

Exemptions

Some of the products exempt from the Care Labeling Rule include the following:

1. Items not used to cover or protect the body, such as belts, neckties, suspenders, and handkerchiefs.

2. Apparel whose appearance or usefulness would be harmed by a permanently attached label. (The Federal Trade Commission must be petitioned for this exemption.)

3. Products sold to institutional buyers for commercial use, such as uniforms provided for hospital employees.

4. Shoes, gloves, and hats.

5. Nonwoven, one-time-use garments.

6. Manufacturer's fabric remnants of less than 10 yards (9.14 meters) in length when the fiber content is unknown and cannot be easily determined.

7. Trim up to 5 inches (12.7 cm.) wide.

8. Products that can be cleaned safely under the harshest procedures, for both washing and dry-cleaning (e.g., hot water, hot-drying setting, hot-ironing setting, all commercially available bleaches, and dry-cleaning solvents).

Care Labeling Contents

The amendment to the Care Labeling Rule requires that only one care method need be included on the label. Thus a care label need only provide washing instructions, dry-cleaning instructions, or a statement that the product cannot be cleaned successfully (see Figure 17.2). If a product can be either washed or dry-cleaned, the label is only required to list one of these methods. Both, however, could be included if desired.

Because only one method of cleaning need be indicated, any safety problems with the other method (not stated on the label) need not be disclosed, nor the warning indicated on the label.

The following sections discuss care labeling in more detail.

Dry Cleanable Product

Dry cleaning refers to a process that removes soil from a product in a machine using common organic solvent (e.g., petroleum, perchlorethylene, fluorocarbon)

located in a commercial establishment. A label may say "Dry-clean" if the garment can be dry-cleaned by any commercial method using any of the available dry-cleaning solvents. If any part of the dry-cleaning process will harm the product, a warning must be given. For example, if steam should not be used, the label must include "No steam." The term "Professionally dry-clean" is used when the dry-cleaning process must be modified to ensure optimum results. (Thus the label for the preceding example should state "Professionally dry-clean, no steam".)

Washable Product

Four specific areas of activity must be included when labeling a washable textile product. These are washing, bleaching, drying, and ironing:

Washing: The care label must indicate whether the product should be washed by hand or machine as well as the water temperature setting if regular use of hot water will be harmful to the product.

FIGURE 17.2
Care labels.

Bleaching: The care label need not mention bleach if all commercially available bleaches can be used on a regular basis. If, for example, a chlorine bleach would be harmful to the product but a nonchlorine bleach would not, then the label must state "Only nonchlorine bleach, when needed." If all commercially available bleaches would harm the product when used on a regular basis, "No bleach" would be used.

Drying: The care label must indicate a safe method of drying. If machine drying is called for, then the drying temperature setting must be stated if regular use of a high temperature will harm the product.

Ironing: The care label must indicate ironing information if ironing will be needed on a regular basis. If required, then a safe temperature setting must be stated if regular use of a hot iron will be harmful to the product.

The care label must also contain a warning against a regular procedure that will harm the labeled product or another product being cleaned with it. For example, if the article is not colorfast, the label must state "Wash separately" or "Wash with like colors."

It should also be noted that on labels silence has meaning. For example, if there are no bleaching instructions, then the product is to be considered safe from all bleaches.

If the product cannot be cleaned by any available cleaning method without being harmed, the label must state that. For example, the label might say, "Do not wash," "Do not dry clean," or "Cannot be successfully cleaned."

Warnings are not necessary for any procedure that is an alternative to the procedure prescribed on the label. For example, if an instruction states "Dry flat," it is not necessary to give the warning "Do not tumble dry."

Failure to produce reliable care instructions and warnings for the useful life of an article, as required, constitutes a violation of the Federal Trade Commission Act and could subject the violator to enforcement action and penalties of up to $10,000 per offense.

Basis for Care Information

A manufacturer or importer must establish a reasonable basis for care information by possessing, prior to sale, reliable evidence to this effect. Approved methods include testing of the product, relying on warranties provided by the suppliers, and using current technical literature, past experience, and industry expertise.

Glossary of Standard Terms

The Care Labeling Rule also provides a glossary of standard terms so that the meaning of terms used on the care labels is standardized for all users. For example, "hot water" means a water temperature up to 150°F (66°C), and "steam only" means steam without contact pressure. The use of the glossary should help to reduce confusion about the meaning of words used on care labels.

Care Labeling Symbols

The Federal Trade Commission permits clothing manufacturers to use specific symbols to indicate appropriate care instructions for garments. The **care labeling symbols,** developed by the American Society for Testing and Materials (ASTM), are intended to coordinate domestic care instructions with those of Canada and Mexico (see p. 213).

Because the ASTM care symbols are so comprehensive, they were adopted over the International Organization for Standardization (ISO) symbols used by European countries (ISO 3758). The ASTM and ISO symbols are very similar but not identical. The number of countries where retailers sell their own goods has become very large—over 100. Due to multiple languages, care labels are the easiest way to have a multilingual label. Harmonization of care label symbols has not yet happened on a global basis.

Responsibility of Industry and Care Labeling

The Federal Trade Commission has left to the industry the accuracy of the care labeling instructions. It is unusual to place such a high degree of responsibility on those being regulated. The manufacturer, by attaching the care label, is indicating that the care instructions are correct and, when followed, will not substantially affect the use of the item. Apparel manufacturers and fabric mills, therefore, must pretest and evaluate their products to determine the proper care procedures.

International Textile Regulations and Trade Agreements

Textile raw materials and manufactured goods have been traded among nations for centuries. Beginning in the 1970s there was considerable movement among producers, manufacturers, and retailers to seek out international sources to lower their costs and develop new markets. Today there are over 100 countries engaged in the textile industry as growers, suppliers, manufacturers, or designers. While each country has its own regulations, there is a significant need to coordinate and standardize how textiles and related materials are identified. In addition to content, there are a wide variety of rules and regulations regarding the import and export of textiles that govern the location and nature of how the textiles are manufactured or where the product is constructed.

Countries try to limit the quantity of products imported from other countries, or they encourage their own domestic industries through protective means such as quotas and tariffs. In addition, the governments of some countries offer subsidies or tax incentives to aid domestic industry. Using **quotas,** a country like the United States has tried to prevent the oversupply (by limiting it) of its markets with goods (e.g., textile products) produced in foreign countries where wages and costs are much lower. Another method to inhibit import of goods is by a **tariff** (or duty) which is a tax imposed by the government for products being imported from another country. Finally, **subsidies,** which are payments by governments to help an industry or product manufacturer defray the cost of production, are used to make the product more competitive by lowering its cost to the importer and the consumer.

The following section provides an overview of the major international trade agreements affecting the industry.

International Regulations

Although it is beyond the scope of this text to provide a survey of the international textile regulations affecting the industry, it is important to be aware that each country involved in the production of textiles or manufactured goods will have its own rules and regulations covering the import, export, and production of textiles. These regulations are enacted to provide quality standards, protect the integrity of local products, and often to limit imports into a particular country. With the tremendous growth in international trade in the past 25 years there has been a strong movement for countries to adopt global standards for textiles products. Because of the size and importance of the United States market to foreign producers, the standards set by the United States Government are often the standards utilized internationally. Various industry trade associations have also worked to promote global standards and encourage governments to adopt them to insure that standards of content, performance, and product integrity are maintained.

The movement toward globalization of the textile trade and regulations has also changed the focus of regulations from individual countries to large geographically concentrated trading blocs. These groups of countries unite to form free trade associations among their members and adopt common standards for the import, export, production, and manufacture of textile products and raw materials.

Trade Agreements

The textile industry is very large and global. It is governed by many laws, regulations, and international treaties. As previously stated, there are over 100 nations that sell fabrics and/or sewn products to the United States.

Governments have formed international trade structures (i.e., organizations), agreements, and laws for greater access and flow of goods. They are going beyond the traditional international trade concept (i.e., trade between nations) toward globalization, which affects partnerships between business, government, and people. The European Union (EU), the Central American Free Trade Agreement (CAFTA), and trade associations amongst nations of the Asian bloc are examples of this trend.

Various international agreements and U.S. legislative regulations encourage imports and generally enhance global trade in textiles. Important among these are the following:

▸ **The General Agreement on Tariffs and Trade (GATT):** GATT was an international agreement that set the rules on world trade of all commodities and products, including textiles. More than 100 countries, including the United States, were members. In accordance with GATT agreements, quotas on textiles and sewn products were gradually reduced and were eliminated on December 31, 2004. GATT was replaced by the World Trade Organization (WTO).

▸ **World Trade Organization (WTO):** WTO is the international body that replaced GATT and now sets the rules on world trade. The range of topics the WTO considers includes antidumping and subsidies, investments, competition policy, trade facilitation, transparency in government procurement, intellectual property, and tariff reduction as well as other issues. About 175 countries are involved.

- **The North American Free Trade Agreement (NAFTA):** NAFTA is a **trade agreement** of the United States, Canada, and Mexico that permits the generally free trade and movement of goods (not restricted by tariffs or quota) among the three nations. This was the second free trade agreement for the United States, implemented in 1994.

- **The United States - Israel Free Trade Agreement (FTA):** This FTA eliminates all duties and restrictions on trade and was consented to in 1985. This was the first free trade agreement set forth by the United States.

- **The United States - Jordan Free Trade Agreement (FTA):** This FTA eliminates duties and barriers for goods and services originating in almost all areas of industrial products and agricultural products within 10 years of signing. This is the third free trade agreement for the United States, implemented in 2001.

- **The Caribbean Basin Trade Partnership Act (CBTPA):** CBTPA allows a company to have domestic textiles cut into garment parts, sewn offshore, and then reimported to the United States with minimal duty.

- **The Andean Trade Preference Act (ATPA):** ATPA provides duty-free advantages for specific textile and apparel produced in Colombia, Bolivia, Ecuador, and Peru.

- **The Central American Free Trade Agreement (CAFTA-DR):** CAFTA-DR provides duty-free advantages for specific textile and apparel produced in El Salvador, Guatemala, Honduras, Nicaragua.

- **The African Growth and Opportunity Act (AGOA):** AGOA allows for the importation of knitted-apparel products with little or no duty providing the yarn or fabric comes from the United States or Africa.

- **Free Trade of the Americas (FTAA):** FTAA is the effort to unite 34 countries in the Americas into the largest free trade collaboration containing about 800 million people forming a $13 trillion market.

- **Mercosur:** Regional trading bloc of a group of South American nations with the United States (Brazil, Venezuela, Columbia, etc.).

Laws governing textiles are numerous and complex. The Committee for the Implementation of Textile Agreements (CITA) oversees matters concerning textile trade as they relate to regulations and control within the United States. CITA was established by the President in 1972 and consists of representatives from the Departments of Commerce, State, Labor, and Treasury among others. The Commerce Department's Office of Textiles and Apparel (OTEXA) provides technical support, analysis, and statistics to aide CITA as it monitors all agreements. Both are a good source of information on the current status of textile regulations and the pending developments affecting the industry. In addition to CITA and OTEXA, the following Web sites may be accessed for more information on textile regulations:

Federal Trade Commission
www.ftc.gov

Consumer Products Safety Commission
www.cpsc.gov

Study Questions

1. Here are four labels. Correct those labels that are incorrect according to the TFPIA:

   Made in U.S.A.
   74% Antron acrylic
   20% Tussah silk
   6% ramie
   RN 95

   Smith Bedspread Company
   56% viscose
   40% durable acetate
   4% nylon

   35% cotton
   65% Fortrel
   Imported from Taiwan
   by Lee Shirt Company

   55% polyester
   45% recycled wool
   RN 75
   Made in Europe

2. Why should store buyers be alert to garments suitable for children's sleepwear but labeled "play wear"?

3. Can an apparel manufacturer of a washable/drycleanable item provide only drycleaning instructions and not also indicate that the garment could be laundered if the consumer so desired? Explain.

4. Prepare a label for the following garment in accordance with the TFPIA, based on the information provided: socks imported from Hong Kong that contain 99 percent cotton and 1 percent nylon, which is in the heel for reinforcement. The registration number is 84.

5. Why are descriptive terms, such as combed cotton or solution-dyed acetate, permitted on labels, but terms such as silky polyester and durable cotton are not? Explain.

6. Indicate how a label should read on a blouse made in the United States of fabric imported from Malaysia.

7. Indicate which of the following textile products would not be covered by the TFPIA:

   a. Lawn chairs   e. Mops
   b. Dog coats   f. Sleeping bags
   c. Awnings   g. Patio umbrellas
   d. Belts   h. Backpacks

8. How is the TFPIA helpful to the

   a. consumer?
   b. dry-cleaner?

9. Brushed rayon skirts made of a lightweight chiffon can no longer be marketed. Why?

Textile Trade and Professional Associations

American Apparel & Footwear Association
www.apparelandfootwear.org

American Association of Textile Chemists and Colorists
www.aatcc.org

American Fiber Manufacturers Association
www.fibersource.com

American Flock Association
www.flocking.org

American National Standards Institute
www.ansi.org

American Society for Quality
www.asq.org

American Society of Interior Designers
www.asid.org

American Society for Testing and Materials
www.astm.org

Association of the Nonwoven Fabrics Industry
www.nonwovens-industry.com

Carpet and Rug Institute
www.carpet-rug.org

Cotton Incorporated
www.cottoninc.com

Fashion Group International
www.fgi.org

Industrial Fabrics Association International
www.ifai.com

Drycleaning & Laundry Institute
www.ifi.org

International Furnishings and Design Association
www.ifda.com

International Textile and Apparel Association
www.itaaonline.org

Leather Industries of America
www.leatherusa.com

Masters of Linen
www.mastersoflinen.com

Mohair Council of America
www.mohairusa.com

National Association of Decorative Fabrics Distributors
www.nadfd.com

National Cotton Council of America
www.cotton.org

National Fire Protection Association
www.nfpa.org

National Home Furnishings Association
www.nhfa.org

National Textile Association
www.nationaltextile.org

Neighborhood Cleaners Association
www.nca-i.com

Society of Plastics Industry
www.plasticsindustry.org

Surface Design Association
www.surfacedesign.org

Textile Clothing Technology Corporation
www.tc2.com

The Color Association
www.colorassociation.com

The National Retail Federation
www.nrf.com

The Soap and Detergent Association
www.sdahq.org

The Woolmark Company
www.woolmark.com

Textile Care Allied Trades Association
www.tcata.org

Textile Institute
www.textileinstitute.org

Upholstered Furniture Action Council
www.ufac.org

Bibliography

TRADE DIRECTORIES

Trade directories provide company names, addresses, and products-produced information. Directories are useful in locating sources of material and supplies as well as providing leads for marketing and job searching.

AATCC Review
American Association of Textile Chemists and Colorists
P.O. Box 12215
Research Triangle Park, North Carolina 27709
Annual buyer's guide in July issue each year. Directory for sources of dyes, pigments, chemicals, machinery, and supplies for textile wet processing.

Davison's Textile Blue Book
Davison Publishing Company
3452 Lake Lynda Drive, Suite 363
Orlando, Florida 32817
Directory of U.S. textile mills (woven, knitted, and nonwoven), yarn spinners and dealers, dyers, printers, finishers, and suppliers of chemicals and services used in the textile industry.

Industrial Fabric Products Review Buyer's Guide
Industrial Fabrics Association International
1801 County Road W.
Roseville, Minnesota 55113
References fabrics, films, chemicals, supplies, and services used by manufacturers of industrial fabrics products (awnings, tents, luggage, truck covers, etc.).

Interior Design Buyers Guide
Reed Business Information
360 Park Avenue South
New York, New York 10010
Annual buyer's guide in January issue each year. Product, service, and company listings of all materials used in the interiors industry, including fabrics and carpets.

Nonwovens Industry
Rodman Publications, Inc.
70 Hilltop Road
Ramsey, New Jersey 07446
Annual buyer's guide in July issue each year. Directory of producers, converters, and machinery manufacturers of nonwoven textiles.

Textile World
Billian Publishing, Inc.
2100 Powers Ferry Road
Atlanta, Georgia 30339
Annual buyer's guide in July issue each year. Directory of suppliers of products used in the manufacture of textiles.

TEXTILES PERIODICALS

AATCC Review
American Association of Textile Chemists and Colorists
P.O. Box 12215
Research Triangle Park, North Carolina 27709
Published monthly. Deals primarily with the chemistry of textiles and color. Very technically oriented.

American Drycleaner
360 North Michigan Avenue
Chicago, Illinois 60601
Published monthly. Covers all areas of interest to cleaners, including management and sales.

Arpel
Ars Arpel Group srl
Via Ippolito Nievo, 33
Milan, MI 20145, Italy
Published semi-annually. Contains articles and photos of international fashions on fur and leather garments.

Draperies & Window Coverings
Clark Publishing Company, Inc.

666 Dundee Road
Northbrook, Illinois 60062
Published monthly. A magazine for the U.S. window covering professional.

Fabricare
Drycleaning & Laundry Institute
14700 Sweitzer Lane
Laurel, Maryland 20707
Published monthly. Provides news and information that apply to the dry-cleaning and laundering industries.

Fiber Organon
Fiber Economics Bureau, Inc.
1530 Wilson Boulevard
Arlington, Virginia 22209
Published monthly. Provides market data for both the natural and manufactured fiber industries.

Floor Covering Weekly
Hearst Business Publishing Company
645 Stewart Avenue
Garden City, New York 11530
Published weekly. A business newspaper of the floor covering industry.

Furniture Today
Reed Business Information
7025 Albert Pick Road
Greensboro, North Carolina 27409
Published weekly. A business newspaper of the furniture industry.

HFN (Home Furnishing News)
333 Seventh Avenue
New York, New York 10001
Published weekly. A newspaper of home products retailing.

Home Textiles Today
Reed Business Information
360 Park Avenue South
New York, New York 10010
Published 26 times annually. Covers marketing, merchandising, and retailing of home textiles products.

Industrial Fabrics Products Review
Industrial Fabrics Association International
1801 Country Road W
Roseville, Minnesota 55113
Published monthly. Features product and industry news as well as other information relating to industrial fabric and product manufacturers.

Interior Design
Reed Business Information
360 Park Avenue South
New York, New York 10010
Published monthly. For the professional interior designer. Provides information on trends and new products.

Journal of Home Economics
American Home Economics Association
2010 Massachusetts Avenue, NW
Washington, DC 20036
Published monthly. Includes articles in the field of textiles and clothing that are primarily consumer oriented. Official organ of the American Home Economics Association.

JTN (Japan Textile News)
Osaka Senken Ltd.
3-4-9 Bingo Machi, Chuo-ku
Osaka-shi, 541-0051, Japan
Published monthly. An international textiles magazine.

Nonwovens Industry
Rodman Publications Inc.
70 Hilltop Road
Ramsey, New Jersey 07446
Published monthly. Features articles on manufacturing processes, distribution, and use applications of nonwoven textile products.

Sew News
PRIMEDIA Enthusiast Group
741 Corporate Circle
Golden, Colorado 80401
Published monthly. A magazine for people who sew. Focuses on fashion fabrics and home sewing.

Southern Textile News
Mullen Publications, Inc.
P.O. Box 5885
Columbus, Georgia 31906
Published bi-weekly. Covers matters of interest to textile manufacturers, with emphasis on the southern United States.

Textiles
Textile Institute
St. James Building, Oxford Street
M1 6FQ Manchester, United Kingdom
Published quarterly. An international textiles magazine.

Textile World
Billian Publishing, Inc.
2100 Powers Ferry
Atlanta, Georgia 30339
Published monthly. Covers technical developments in the textile industry.

WWD (Women's Wear Daily)
Fairchild Publications, Inc.
750 Third Avenue
New York, New York 10017
Published daily. Covers news of the fashion industry, trends, designers, and events in the social world.

BOOKS

Fibers and Yarns

Carty, P. *Fibre Properties*. Newcastle upon Tyne, England: Pentaxion Ltd., 1996.

Greaves, P. H. *Microscopy of Textile Fibres*. Oxford, England: BIOS Scientific in association with the Royal Microscopical Society, 1995.

Hamby, D. S. *The American Cotton Handbook*, Third ed. New York: John Wiley & Sons, Inc., 1965.

Lewin, M. and J. Preston, eds. *Handbook of Fiber Science and Technology: Volume III: High Technology Fibers, Parts A–D.* New York: Marcel Decker, Inc., 1985 (Part A), 1989 (Part B), 1993 (Part C), 1996 (Part D).

Lord, P. R. *Handbook of Yarn Production: Technology, Science and Economics*. Boca Raton, Florida: CRC Press, 2003.

Morton, W. E. and J. W. S. Hearle. *Physical Properties of Textile Fibres*, Third ed. Manchester, England: Textile Institute of Great Britain. Dist.: State Mutual Book and Periodical Service, Ltd., 1993.

Warner, S. B. *Fiber Science*. Upper Saddle River, New Jersey: Prentice-Hall, Inc., 1995.

World Dictionary of Manufactured Fiber Producers. Arlington, Virginia: Fiber Economics Bureau, annual.

Fabric Construction

McGehee, L. *Creating Texture with Textiles*. Iola, Wisconsin: Krause Publications, 1998.

Oelsner, G. H. *A Handbook of Weaves*. New York: Dover Publications, 1952.

Knitting

Gartshore, L. *The Machine Knitter's Dictionary*. New York: St. Martin's Press, 1983.

Spencer, D. J. *Knitting Technology*, Third ed. Boca Raton, Florida: CRC Press, 2001.

Wilkens, C. *Warp Knit Fabric Construction: From Stitch Formation to Stitch Construction*. Bridgehampton, New York: Textile Institute of Great Britain. Dist.: State Mutual Book and Periodical Service, Ltd., 1995.

Dyeing, Printing, and Finishing

American Association of Textile Chemists and Colorists. *Basics of Dyeing and Finishing*. Research Triangle Park, North Carolina: Author, 1991.

Aspland, J. R. *Textile Dyeing and Coloration*, Research Triangle Park, North Carolina: American Association of Textile Chemists and Colorists, 1997.

Broadbent, A. *Basic Principles of Textile Coloration*, Bradford, England: Society of Dyers and Colourists, 2001.

Flick, E. W. *Textile Finishing Chemicals: An Industrial Guide*. Park Ridge, New Jersey: Noyes Publications, Inc., 1990.

Fresener, S. and P. Fresener. *How to Print T-Shirts for Fun and Profit*. Tempe, Arizona: U.S. Screen Printing Institute, 2003.

Heywood, D. *Textile Finishing*. Bradford, England: Society of Dyers and Colourists, 2003.

Johnson, A., ed. *The Theory of Coloration of Textiles*, Second ed., Bridgehampton, New York: Textile Institute of Great Britain. Dist.: State Mutual Book and Periodical Service, Ltd., 1989.

Joyce, C. *Textile Design: The Complete Guide to Printed Textiles for Apparel and Home Furnishing*, Lakewood, New Jersey: Watson-Guptill Publications, Inc., 1997.

Liles, J. N. *The Art and Craft of Natural Dyeing*. Knoxville, Tennessee: The University of Tennessee Press, 1990.

Perkins, W. S. *Textile Coloration and Finishing*, Durham, North Carolina: Carolina Academic Press, 1996.

Rivlin, J. *The Dyeing of Textile Fibers: Theory and Practice*. Philadelphia: Philadelphia College of Textiles and Science, 1993.

Trotman, E. R. *Dyeing and Chemical Technology of Textile Fibers*, Seventh ed. Forrestburgh, New York: Lubrecht & Cramer, 1991.

Wells, K. *Fabric Dyeing and Printing*. Loveland, Colorado: Interweave Press, Inc., 1997.

Textile Marketing

Allen, P. *The Market for Home Textiles*. New York: Find-SVP Publishing Company, Inc., 1989.

Berkstresser, G. *Textile Marketing Management*. Park Ridge, New Jersey: Noyes Publications, Inc., 1984.

Cohen, A. C. *Marketing Textiles: From Fiber to Retailer*. New York: Fairchild Publications, Inc., 1989.

Dickerson, K. G. *Textiles and Apparel in the Global Economy*, Third ed. Upper Saddle River, New Jersey: Prentice-Hall, 1999.

Woodruff, J. L. and J. M. McDonald. *Handbook of Textile Marketing*. New York: Fairchild Publications, Inc., 1982.

Textile Testing

Aft, L. *Fundamentals of Industrial Quality Control*, Second ed. Milwaukee, Wisconsin: ASQC Quality Press, 1992.

American Association of Textile Chemists and Colorists. *AATCC Technical Manual*. Research Triangle Park, North Carolina: Author, annual.

American Society for Testing and Materials. *Annual Book of ASTM Standards (Section: Textiles)*. Philadelphia: Author, annual.

Besterfield, D. H. *Quality Control*, Fourth ed. Englewood Cliffs, New Jersey: Prentice-Hall, 1994.

Birren, F. *Light, Color and Environment*. New York: Van Nostrand Reinhold, 1982.

Collier, B. J. and H. Epps. *Textile Testing and Analysis*. Upper Saddle River, New Jersey: Prentice-Hall, 1999.

General Services Administration. *Federal Test Method Standard. No. 191. Textile Test Method*. Washington, DC: Author, 1978.

Kadolph, S. J. *Quality Assurance for Textiles and Apparel*. Second ed. New York: Fairchild Publications, Inc., 2007.

Kawabata, S. *The Standardization and Analysis of Hand Evaluation*. Osaka, Japan: The Textile Machinery Society of Japan, 1980.

Mehta, P. V. *An Introduction to Quality Control for the Apparel Industry*. Milwaukee, Wisconsin: Marcel Dekker (ASQC Quality Press), 1992.

Merkel, R. S. *Textile Product Serviceability by Specification*. New York: Macmillan Publishing Co., 1991.

Saville, B. P. *Physical Testing of Textiles.* Harrison, New York: Woodhead Publishing, Great Britain. Dist.: American Education Systems, 1999.

Interior Furnishing Textiles

Carpet and Rug Institute. *Carpet Specifiers Handbook.* Dalton, Georgia: Author, 1989.

Geddes-Brown, L. *Home Furnishings with Fabrics.* New York: Ryland Peters & Small, Inc., 2001.

Jackman, D. and M. Dixon. *The Guide to Textiles for Interior Beginners,* Second ed. Winnipeg, Canada: Penguin Publishing Ltd., 1990.

Lederer, D. P. *The Perfectionist's How To Drapery Books,* 3 Volumes. Asheville, North Carolina: Lederer Enterprises, Inc., 1992.

Watkins, C. *Book of Soft Furnishings.* Sausalito, California: Parkwest Publications, Inc., 1991.

Yaeger, J. *Textiles for Residential and Commercial Interiors,* Second ed. New York: Fairchild Publications, Inc. 2000.

Industrial and Nonwoven Fabrics

Adanur, S., ed. *Wellington Sears Handbook of Industrial Textiles.* Boca Raton, Florida: CRC Press, 1995.

American Chemical Society. *High-Tech Fibrous Materials: Composites, Biomedical Material, Protective Clothing, and Geotextiles.* Washington, DC: Author, 1991.

Association of the Nonwoven Fabrics Industry. *Nonwoven Handbook.* Cary, North Carolina: Author, 1999.

Jirsàk, O. and L. C. Wadsworth. *Nonwoven Textiles.* Durham, North Carolina: Carolina Academic Press, 1999.

General Texts

Blackmon, A. G. *Manual of Standard Fabric Defects in the Textile Industry.* Graniteville, South Carolina: Graniteville Co., 1975.

Blewett, M. H. *The Last Generation: Work and Life in the Textile Mills of Lowell, Massachusetts, 1910–1960.* Amherst, Massachusetts: University of Massachusetts Press, 1990.

Collier, B., M. Bide and P. Tortora. *Understanding Textiles,* Seventh ed. Upper Saddle River, New Jersey: Prentice-Hall, Inc., 2009.

Conway, G. L. *Garment & Textile Dictionary.* Albany, New York: Delmar Publishing, Inc., 1997.

Earnshaw, P. *A Dictionary of Lace.* New York: State Mutual Book and Periodical Service, Ltd., 1988.

Glock, R. E. and G. I. Kunz. *Apparel Manufacturing: Sewn Products Analysis.* Third ed. Upper Saddle River, New Jersey: Prentice-Hall, 2000.

Gray, S. *CAD-CAM in Clothing and Textiles.* Brookfield, Vermont: Ashgate Publishing Company, 1998.

Greaves, P. and P. Daniels, eds. *Identification of Textile Materials,* Eighth ed. Bridgehampton, New York: Textile Institute of Great Britain. Dist.: State Mutual Book and Periodical Service, Ltd., 1996.

Hethorn, J. and C. Ulasewicz. *Sustainable Fashion: Why Now?.* New York: Fairchild Books, 2008.

Humphries, M. *Fabric Reference,* Fourth ed. Upper Saddle River, New Jersey: Prentice-Hall, Inc., 2009.

Jayaraman, S. *Computer Science & Textile Science.* (Textile Progress Set. Vol. 27, No. 2.) Bridgehampton, New York: Textile Institute of Great Britain. Dist.: State Mutual Book and Periodical Service, Ltd., 1996.

Jerde, J. *Encyclopedia of Textiles.* New York: Facts on File, Inc., 1992.

Kadolf, S. *Textiles,* Tenth ed. Upper Saddle River, New Jersey: Prentice-Hall, 2007.

KoSa. *Man-Made Fiber and Textile Dictionary,* Seventh ed. Charlotte, North Carolina: Kosa, 1999.

Kunz, G. and M. Garher. *Going Global: The Textile and Apparel Industry.* New York: Fairchild Publications, Inc., 2007

Ozbalkan, N. *Textile Dictionary In Four Languages (Turkish, English, French, German).* Kinderhook, New York: IBD Ltd., Inc., n.d.

Slater, K. *Comfort Properties of Textiles.* New York: State Mutual Book and Periodical Service, 1989.

Slater, K. *Environmental Impact of Textiles: Production, Processes, and Protection.* Boca Raton, Florida: CRC Press, 2003.

Textile Institute (UK) Staff. *Textile Terms and Definitions.* New York: State Mutual Book and Periodical Service, 1991.

Tortora, P. and R. Merkel. *Fairchild's Textile Dictionary.* Seventh ed. New York: Fairchild Publications, Inc., 1996.

Wilson, J. *Handbook of Textile Design: Principles, Processes, and Practice.* Boca Raton, Florida: CRC Press, 2002.

Worth Street Textile Market Rules. Washington, DC: American Textile Manufacturers Institute Inc., 1986.

Zeldis, L. *Spanish-English–English-Spanish Dictionary of Fashion, Garment and Industrial Textiles.* Kinderhook, New York: IBD Ltd., Inc., 1988.

Credits

New illustrations by Tori Bukowski

Ch. 1

1.0	Courtesy of Fairchild Publications, Inc.
1.2	Courtesy of Fairchild Publications, Inc.
1.3	David McNew/Getty Images
1.4a	Courtesy of Fairchild Publications, Inc.
1.4b	Courtesy of Fairchild Publications, Inc.
1.5	Courtesy of Fairchild Publications, Inc.
1.6	Construction Photography/Corbis

Ch. 2

2.0	Courtesy of Fairchild Publications, Inc.
2.6	Courtesy of Invista

Ch. 3

3.0	Courtesy of Fairchild Publications, Inc.
3.1	iStock Photo
3.2	Courtesy of Fairchild Publications, Inc.
3.3	iStock Photo
3.4	iStock Photo
3.5	Courtesy of Woolmark
3.6	Courtesy of Invista
3.7	Courtesy of Fairchild Publications, Inc.
3.8	Courtesy of Fairchild Publications, Inc.
3.9	Courtesy of Fairchild Publications, Inc.
3.11	Courtesy of Nanotex
3.12	Courtesy of Fairchild Publications, Inc.
3.13	G.K.& Vikki Hart/Getty Images

Ch. 4

4.0	Courtesy of Fairchild Publications, Inc.
4.2	Courtesy of Fairchild Publications, Inc.
4.8	China Photos/Getty Images
4.11	Courtesy of Fairchild Publications, Inc.
4.13	AP Photo/Stuart Ramson

Ch. 5

5.0	Courtesy of Fairchild Publications, Inc.
5.1a	Courtesy of Fairchild Publications, Inc.
5.1b	Courtesy of Fairchild Publications, Inc.
5.6	Courtesy of Macy's, Inc.
5.19	Courtesy of Fairchild Publications, Inc.
5.21	Veer
5.22	V&A Images/Alamy
5.24	Courtesy of Fairchild Publications, Inc.
5.25	Courtesy of Fairchild Publications, Inc.

Ch. 6

6.0	Courtesy of Fairchild Publications, Inc.
6.1	Courtesy of Stoll
6.3	David Copeman/Alamy
6.6	M. Angelo/CORBIS
6.18	Courtesy of Fairchild Publications, Inc.
6.22	Courtesy of Fairchild Publications, Inc.
6.23	Courtesy of Fairchild Publications, Inc.
6.24	Courtesy of Fairchild Publications, Inc.
6.25	Courtesy of Fairchild Publications, Inc.
6.26	Benoit Decout 2008/Redux
6.31	Courtesy of Fairchild Publications, Inc.
6.33	Courtesy of Fairchild Publications, Inc.
6.34	Courtesy of Fairchild Publications, Inc.
6.35	Courtesy of Fairchild Publications, Inc.
6.37	Courtesy of Macys, Inc.

Ch. 7

7.0	Courtesy of Fairchild Publications, Inc.
7.1	Max Power/Corbis
7.2	Richard Broadwell/Alamy
7.6	Courtesy of Fairchild Publications, Inc.
7.7	Courtesy of Fairchild Publications, Inc.
7.8	Courtesy of Fairchild Publications, Inc.
7.9	Courtesy of Fairchild Publications, Inc.

Ch. 8

8.0	Courtesy of Fairchild Publications, Inc.
8.1	Courtesy of Fairchild Publications, Inc.
8.2	Courtesy of Fairchild Publications, Inc.
8.4	Lucy Nicholson/Reuters

Ch. 9

9.0	Courtesy of Fairchild Publications, Inc.
9.1	Ciaran Griffin/Getty Images
9.2a	William Taufic/Corbis
9.2b	Ariel Skelley/Veer
9.4	Cara Howe © 2009 Condé Nast Publications
9.7	Reuters/Ina Fassbender

Ch. 10

10.0	Courtesy of Fairchild Publications, Inc.
10.4	Courtesy of Fairchild Publications, Inc.
10.5a	FRANCK CAMHI/Alamy
10.5b	FRANCK CAMHI/Alamy
10.5c	FRANCK CAMHI/Alamy
10.6	Courtesy of Fairchild Publications, Inc.
10.7	Courtesy of Fairchild Publications, Inc.
10.9	Horizon International Images Limited / Alamy
10.12	Courtesy of Fairchild Publications, Inc.

Ch. 11

11.0	Courtesy of Fairchild Publications, Inc.

Ch. 12

12.0	Courtesy of Fairchild Publications, Inc.
12.1	Courtesy of Fairchild Publications, Inc.
12.4	Blue Jean Images/Getty Images
12.5	Courtesy of Fairchild Publications, Inc.
12.6	Courtesy of Fairchild Publications, Inc.
12.7	Courtesy of Fairchild Publications, Inc.

Ch. 13

13.0	Michael Robinson/Beateworks/Corbis
13.1	Courtesy of Mitchell Gold & Bob Williams
13.2a	Veer
13.2b	Andrew Twort/Alamy
13.3	Erik Snyder/Getty Images
13.4a	Ruge,K./Veer
13.4c	Angelo Hornak/Alamy
13.6	Winfried Heinze/Redcover.com
13.8	Adrian Wilson/Beateworks/Corbis
13.11	iStock Photo
13.20	Henry Wilson/Redcover
13.21	Courtesy of Sferra Brothers
13.22	Chloe Brown/Redcover
13.25	Dan Duchars/Redcover.com

Ch. 14

14.0	Courtesy of Fairchild Publications, Inc.
14.7	AP Photo/Ed Betz
14.9	Courtesy of Advanced Testing Instruments Corporation
14.23	Veer

Ch. 15

15.0	Randy Brooke/WireImage/Getty Images
15.1	Costea Photography Inc.
15.2	AP Photo/Achmad Ibrahim
15.3	Gareth Cattermole/Getty Images
15.4	Courtesy of Fairchild Publications, Inc.
15.6	StockImages/Alamy
15.7	Courtesy of Fairchild Publications, Inc.
15.8	Simon Isabelle/SIPA/AP Images
15.9	Alex Hinds/Alamy
15.10	Simon Isabelle/SIPA/AP Images
15.11	Reuters/Nir Elias
15.13	Katsumi Kasahara/AP Images
15.14	Courtesy of Patagonia
15.15	Courtesy of Fairchild Publications, Inc.
15.16	Getty Images for Avita
15.17	Courtesy of Fairchild Publications, Inc.
15.19	Courtesy of Green Seal™

Ch. 16

16.0	Courtesy of Fairchild Publications, Inc.
16.1a	Norbert Schäfer/Masterfile
16.1b	Rob Atkins/Getty Images
16.1c	Digital Vision/Getty Images
16.2	Courtesy of Fairchild Publications, Inc.
16.3	Andrew Hetherington/Redux

Ch. 17

17.0	Courtesy of Fairchild Publications, Inc.
17.1	Jerry Arcieri/Corbis
17.2	WireImageStock/WireImageStock/Masterfile

Index

barré, 134
basket weave, 92–93
bast fibers, 41
bath products, 242, 265–266
bath rugs, 266
batiste, 104
batting, 147, 222–223, 249, 268
beam dyeing, 162, 164
Beaulieu Group of America, 251
bedding products, 242, 266–269
bedford cord, 104
bedspreads, 267–268
bengaline, 104
Better Cotton Initiative (BCI), 311
bias bindings, 84
bias fabric, 202
bicomponent fibers, 58–59
biological agents, 227
biotechnology, 228
birdseye fabric, 134
blankets, 267
bleach, 31, 187, 207–208, 337
blended yarns, 70–71
blocks, 170
blotch prints, 180
boardy fabric, 134, 202
boil-off, 186–187
bonded fabrics, 145–146
bonded finish of threads, 79, 80
bottom of fabric, 89
bouclé yarns, 75
bowed fabric, 134, 202, 264
breaking strength, 287
breathability, 220–221
Britain, Fair Trade in, 14
broadcloth, 104
broadloom, 250
brocade, 104
brocatelle, 104
broken filaments, 134
broken-twill weaves, 95
brokers as fabric source, 8
brushed tricot, 130
Brush-Pilling Tester, 281, 291
buckram, 104
bulked continuous filament, 258
bulk fiber shape, 21, 22
bulk-textured yarns, 72
burlap, 104
burning test, 28, 29–31
burn-out prints, 181
burnt gas fumes, colorfastness to, 298
bursting strength, fabric, 288, 289
butcher cloth, 104
buyers' responsibilities, 10–12

cable-stitch fabrics, 115, 135
calendering, 188–190
Calgon, 210
calico, 104
cambric, 104
camel hair, 40, 42

Cantilever-Bending Tester, 292
canvas, 104, 226
carbon fibers, 58, 226
carbonizing, 187
carcinogens, 308
carded-web nonwovens, 142
carded yarns, 67, 324; ring spinning of, 69–70; in woolens, 68
cardigan fabrics, 135
careers in textile industry, 14–15
Care Labeling Rule, 335–337; symbols of, 337
care of textiles: carpet and, 260–262; fur and, 236; leather and, 234; See also cleansers and cleaning
Caribbean Basin Trade Partnership Act (CBTPA) (2000), 339
Carpet America Recovery Effort (CARE), 315
Carpet and Rug Institute, 251, 260, 262
Carpet Appearance Retention Ratings (ARR), 260
carpets, 242, 250–262, 327; environmental issues and, 262; flammability of, 259; pile types of, 254–256; process of making, 251–258; quality of, 252; recycling of, 315, 319–320; soiling of, 260; in tiles, 319; tiles of, 251, 314; tufted, 251–252; underlay of, 258–259; wool, 251; woven, 252–253
casement cloth, 104, 262–264
cashgora fiber, 40
cashmere fiber, 30, 40, 42, 334
cationic dyes, 157
cavalry twill, 104
Celanese Corporation, 226–227
cellulase, 192
cellulosic fibers, 24, 30, 43
cements, 212
Central American Free Trade Agreement (CAFTA), 338, 339
certification, organic, 310–315, 318
certification marks, 43–44
challis, 104
chambray, 104
chantilly lace, 149
charged systems, 211
cheesecloth, 104
chemicals: exposure to, 227; finishing and, 313; recycling of, 13; tests of textiles with, 31–32, 285
chenille yarns, 75–76
cheviot, 105
chevron weaves, 95
chiffon, 105
chino, 105
chintz, 105
chlorine bleach, 31, 208
chroma, fabric color, 296
chrome dyes, 159
Circular-Bend Stiffness Tester, 292
circular knitting, 114
ciré calendering, 189
claiming damages, 214
Clean Air Act (1970), 318
cleansers and cleaning, 206–214; additives and, 207–210; Care Labeling Rule and, 335–337; claiming damages and, 214; dry cleaning and, 210–212; environmental concerns of, 214, 313–314; industry trade shows and, 213–214; soil types and, 206; trade associations of, 213; ultrasonic washing and, 213; wet-cleaning and, 212–213; See also dry cleaning

pile construction, 98–99, 247
pile height, 256
pile knits, 124, 136
pile portion, 251
pile thickness, 256
pile weaves, 97–99
pile weight, 256
pilling, 290–291, 324; of fibers, 27; of yarns, 70
pillowcases, 266–267
pillows, 242, 268
Pima cotton, American, 36–37
Pinsonic Thermal Joining Machine, 225, 268
piqué, 107
PLA fiber, 30, 47
plain weave, 91–92
plasma processing, 200–201
plastic, 229–231; thermoplastic fibers and, 24, 71, 230; thermoplasticity and, 27–28
plating, 124
plissé, 107, 191
plush carpet, 255
plush fabrics, put-up of, 7
ply, 68–69; yarn count and, 78, 79
pointelle, 136
Polartec®, 222, 314
pollution, 13, 308; lyocell and, 45; *See also* environmental issues
Pollution Prevention Act (1990), 319
polyacide fiber, 30, 47
polyester fiber, 47–48; burning characteristics of, 30; carpet and, 257; chemical solubility of, 32; degradation of, 263; environmental issues and, 306; image of, 23; properties of, 43, 51; in sewing threads, 79; yarns blending and, 70
polyethylene fiber, 46, 314
polypropylene fiber, 46; *See also* olefin fiber
polystyrene plastics, 212
polyurethane, 230
polyvinyl chloride (PVC), 230
pongee, 107
Ponte di Roma, 136
poor boy, 136
poplin, 107
poromeric materials, 230–231
porosity, 245–247
postcuring, 194
pound goods, 7
power net, 136
power-stretch fabrics, 72, 74
precuring, 194
press-offs, 134
pretreatment process, 186–187, 210
Primaloft®, 223
print paste, 171
prints and printing, 7, 170–180; automatic-screen, 171, 172, 178; basic types of, 177, 178–179; carpet and, 258; color features of, 176–177; domestic, 9; environmental concerns of, 176, 312; imperfections and, 181; industry advancements in, 175–176; methods of, 171–175, 178; properties of, 326; special types of, 180–181; window fabrics and, 264
private labels, 12

processing fur, 236
Procter & Gamble, 306, 313
product visibility, 322
progressive, 197
projectile looms, 86
protection with geotextiles, 228
protective garments, 227
protein fiber, 24, 30
purl-knit fabrics, 120, 122–123, 136
purl stitches, 118
push/pull effect, 219, 221
put-up, 7

quality of fur, 235
quilted materials, 147
quilts, 267–268
quviut fiber, 41

railroading, 247–248
ramie fiber, 30, 41, 310
ramie yarns, 77
Random-Tumble Pilling Tester, 291
rapier looms, 86–87
raschel fabrics, 130–131, 136
raschel lace, 148
Rawlings, 234
rayon fiber: burning characteristics of, 30; chemical solubility of, 32; cuprammonium, 48; degradation of, 263; environmental issues and, 306; fiber surface of, 22; HWM, 49; as hydrophilic, 25; in sewing threads, 79; viscose, 43, 48–49, 51
reactive dyes, 159
recovery, 26, 72
recycling, 13, 308–309, 314–315
Recyclon, 314–315
reeds, 85
reembroidered lace, 150
reflective safety apparel, 229
relaxation shrinkage, 195, 196, 264
remnants, fabric, 7
renewable materials, 307
repp, 107
residential furnishings, 242–243
residential upholstery, 245
resiliency, 27, 222
resin add-on, 188
resin finishes, 327
resins, 187–188
resin treatments, 194, 196
resistance to penetration, 227
resist prints, 177, 179
resource conservation, 307
Resource Conservation and Recovery Act (1976), 319
retail stores, 9
Retroglo® yarn, 229
reverse engineering, 24
ribbon-hole lace, 150
rib gaiting, 120
rib-knit fabrics, 120, 121–122, 136
right-hand twill, 93, 94
ring spinning, 69–70
roller printing, 173–174, 178

rotary-screen printing, 171, 172–173, 178
roving, 69
rubber fiber, 26, 57
rugs, 240, 242, 250
rugs, bath, 266
run (woolen yarn count system), 77
runners, 251
runs, 134

safety standards, 313
sailcloth, 107
Salon International de l'Habillement Masculin (SEHM), 14
samples, 10
saran fiber, 30, 32, 57
sateen fabrics, 96, 107
satin fabrics, 89, 96, 104, 107
satin tricot, 130
satin weaves, 95–96
Saxony carpet, 255
Schiffli embroidery, 150
Schiffli lace, 149, 151
Schiffli machines, 150–151
Schreiner calendering, 190
Scientific Certification Systems (SCS), 317
Scotchgard™, 245, 258
scouring, 186–187
screen printing, 171
scrim, 107
Sea Island cotton, 36
Seal of Cotton®, 37
seamless knitting, 127–128
seams: appearance of, 80–81; breaking strength of, 80; slippage of, 325; stress of, 66
Sears, 12
seed yarns, 75
seersucker, 108, 191
selling seasons, 12
selvages, 84, 87–88
serge, 68, 107
sericin, 38
sericulture, 38
serviceability, 322
set-textured yarns, 72
sewing threads, 78–81
sewn stitching, 268
shade, depth of, 157
shade bar, 166
shag carpet, 256
shag pile configuration, 256
shaker, 136
shantung, 107
sharkskin, 108
Shaw Industries, Inc., 251, 262, 314
shearing, 191
sheath-and-core: blending of yarns, 70–71; fibers, 59
sheds, 85
sheep breeds, 39
sheets, 266–267
shorts, fabric, 7
shower curtains, 266
shrinkage, 195–197, 264, 293

shuttleless looms, 86
shuttles, 86
side-by-side: blending of yarns, 70–71; fibers, 59
silk, tussah, 23, 38
silk fiber, 10, 38–39; burning characteristics of, 30; chemical solubility of, 32; degradation of, 263; diameters of, 42; dupion, 38; fiber length of, 21; filament yarns from, 64; image of, 23; international trade in, 4; properties of, 36, 51; yarns and, 77–78
silkworms, 20; cultivation of, 38
simple calendering, 188
simplex fabrics, 131
singeing, 187
singles equivalent, 78, 79
single yarns, 68–69
sisal fiber, 41
skein dyeing, 160
skewing, 135, 202
skin comfort, absorbency and, 25
skins, 231–232
sliver, 67, 69; of wool, 68
sliver knits, 124
slub yarns, 75
smoothness of yarn, 65–66
social responsibility, 309
softener finishes, 191
soft finish of threads, 79, 80
softness, 324
soft-twist, 66; See also twist
soil-release finishes, 197, 291
soil removal, 207
soil types, 206
solution-dyeing, 157, 166
solvent finishing, 200
solvents, 167, 313
solvent scouring, 187
sorting of wool, 39
SOYSILK®, 56
space dyeing, 258
Spalding Company, 234
spandex fiber, 49–50; in bare elastic yarns, 74; burning characteristics of, 30; chemical solubility of, 32; in core-spun yarns, 74; as elastomeric fiber, 26; properties of, 51
specialty fibers, 226–227
specifications, fabric, 283
specific gravity, 27
Spectra® polyethylene fiber, 227
spectrophotometer, 160
spinnerettes, 20
spinning, 21; invention of, 64; ring spinning, 69–70
spiral yarns, 75
sponge rubber, 259
sports, 234
spotting, dry-cleaning and, 211
spring beard needles, 115, 116, 117
Springs Global, 8
Springs Industries, 7
spunlaced nonwovens, 142
spunlaid systems, 141
spun threads, 79

woolen fabrics, 68
woolen yarns, 68, 324; blending of, 70; count system of, 77; yarn count standards and, 77–78
wool fiber, 6, 39–40; burning characteristics of, 30; carpet and, 257; chemical solubility of, 32; comparison with cotton, 37; cover of, 26; crimp of, 22; degradation of, 263; diameter of, 42; length of, 21; as natural bicomponent fiber, 59; organic, 311; properties of, 36, 51; shape of, 22; surface of, 22
wool industry, 320
Woolmark®, 40
Wool Products Labeling Act (1939), 334
workers, health of, 13
World Fair Trade Day, 14
World Trade Organization (WTO), 338
World War II, international trade and, 4
Worsted Count System (wc or New), 77
worsted fabrics, 68
worsted yarns, 68; count system of, 77; yarn count standards and, 77–78
woven carpet, 257
woven fabrics, 84–108, 324; basic weaves of, 91–96; carpet and, 252–253; computers and, 101; cost of, 102; designs in, 99–101; features of, 87–90; special weaves of, 96–99; types of, 103–108
woven-goods industry, 12

woven-pile fabrics, 97–99
wrinkle-free fabrics, 194
wrinkle recovery, 27, 292; absorbency and, 25
wrinkle resistance, 193–194, 292
wrinkling, 326
Wyzenbeek Tester, 289–290

yak fiber, 41, 42
yarn count system, 77–78, 79
yarn guide bars, 128–129
yarn numbering systems, 76–78
yarns, 6, 20, 64; air jet, 69; blended, 70–71; carpet and, 258; chenille, 75–76; cotton, 67, 70, 77–78; dyeing of, 162, 167; eco-friendly, 311–312; linen, 67–68, 77–78; novelty, 75; open end, 69; pilling of, 70; ply, 68–69, 79; properties of, 65–66, 324; recycling of, 13; ring spun, 69; roto-spun, 69–70; sizes of, 77; slippage and, 325; spun silk, 38; stretch, 72, 74; tow *vs.* line, 67–68; twist of, 274–275; window fabrics and, 263; yarn distortion and, 290; *See also* filament yarns; spun yarns
yarns per inch, 66, 89–90, 96, 275–276
yield, 278–279

"Zero Twist" cotton, 67
Z-twist, 67, 69